PATERNOSTER BIBLICAL AND

C000295660

Baptism and the Baptists

Theology and Practice in Twentieth-Century Britain

PATERNOSTER BIBLICAL AND THEOLOGICAL MONOGRAPHS

A full listing of all titles in this series
appears at the close of this book.

COMMENDATIONS

'Dr Cross here presents an authoritative, comprehensive and well-contexted analysis of British Baptist attitudes to the theology and practice of baptism in the last century, which will be of equal value to Baptists and those of other traditions. The strength of the work is in the range of the documentary sources consulted which embrace not only weighty theological treatises but more transient documents such as debates within the pages of the *Baptist Times*, pamphlets, and study material written by local pastors. These are used to articulate a theological position which could have easily been confined to academic writings. Dr Cross is not frightened of essaying judgments and analysis which some may judge lead him to unexpected and even provacative conclusions, which may lead some to have to rethink their own positions.'

John H.Y. Briggs
Pro-Vice-Chancellor and Principal,
University of Birmingham, Westhill,
Birmingham.

'Anthony Cross has written a timely and necessary book. Baptism is back on the scholars' agenda and this work will be of interest to more than the Baptist community. The scholarship is thorough. The whole work will be an important resource for historians and theologians together. It has profound ecumenical and pastoral challenges for all the churches.'

Brian Haymes
Principal,
Bristol Baptist College.

'Anthony Cross's book is an engaging and detailed study of an important period in Baptist theological thought. I have thoroughly enjoyed reading it, and have learned both much about the large sweep of the history of this period and many interesting details related to the individuals involved. I recommend this book highly.'

Stanley E. Porter
Professor of Theology,
Centre for Advanced Theological Research,
University of Surrey Roehampton, London.

'Dr Cross has produced a major contribution to the period and topic he investigates in this book. Its clarity, careful assessment of complex issues, and originality are a model of how an historian should approach the subject.'

Arthur Gibson
Literary Executor,
Trinity College,
Cambridge.

PATERNOSTER BIBLICAL AND THEOLOGICAL MONOGRAPHS

Baptism and the Baptists

Theology and Practice in Twentieth-Century Britain

Anthony R. Cross

Foreword by George R. Beasley-Murray

paternoster
press

First published 2000 by Paternoster Press

Paternoster Press is an imprint of Paternoster Publishing
P.O. Box 300, Carlisle, Cumbria, CA3 0QS, U.K.
and P.O. Box 1047, Waynesboro, GA 30830–2047, U.S.A

03 02 01 00   7 6 5 4 3 2 1

British Library Cataloguing in Publication Data
A catalogue record for this book is available from the British Library

ISBN 0–85364–959–6

Printed and bound in Great Britain
for Paternoster Publishing
by Nottingham Alpha Graphics

To my parents
Fred and Dorothy Cross
With love and thanks

Contents

FOREWORD

The subject of this book is more than ordinarily important. It is a veritable mine-field in which casualties have been numerous through the generations. British Baptists are a phenomenon of the seventeenth century onwards and have taken their place in the mainline churches of modern times, including the ecumenical move-ment of which they have been founder members. Baptists have had a notorious reputation through their rejection of infant baptism, which for most of the churches' history has been acknowledged as the door into the church. Baptists have insisted that, according to the New Testament, baptism has been rightly applied only to people who turn to God in repentance and faith. The difference on this matter between Baptists and Paedobaptists has been highlighted through the modern ecumenical movement, Baptists having often been viewed as intransigent in this matter. In *Baptism and the Baptists*, Anthony R. Cross examines the theological reasons behind Baptists' understandings of baptism. An introductory survey of Baptist views in the nineteenth century opens his review of twentieth-century developments, which he divides into three periods: 1900–1937, 1938–1966, and 1967–1999.

Dr Cross has accomplished a notable task in this book. He has worked carefully through an immense amount of primary and secondary material. While his primary purpose is that of reporting and evaluating, he has brought to light in a masterly way issues and their importance for the whole Christian church. This work will be illuminating for all who read it.

George R. Beasley-Murray
Hove
October 1999

Acknowledgments

There are many people I would like to thank for their help in the research for this book. Professor John H.Y. Briggs, Pro-Vice-Chancellor and Principal of the University of Birmingham, Westhill, the late Rev. Dr W.M.S. West, former Principal of Bristol Baptist College, and his successors, Rev. Dr John Morgan-Wynne and Rev. Dr Brian Haymes. Especial thanks are due to Professor Stanley E. Porter of the Centre for Advanced Theological Research, University of Surrey Roehampton for his friendship, help and encouragment in so many ways, the late Rev. Dr George R. Beasley-Murray, Rev. R.E.O. White and Dr Daniel Falk of Oregon State University. Also for the friendship and support of Craig and Natasha Brown, and my colleagues at the Centre for Advanced Theological Research, University of Surrey Roehampton, Matt Brook O'Donnell and Wendy Porter for their invaluable help with the technical side of this project. To Rev. Dr Paul Fiddes, Principal of Regent's Park College, Oxford, Rev. David Harper and Rev. Dr Roger Hayden. I am grateful for many who have always taken such an interest in me and my research at my home church, New Road Baptist Church, Bromsgrove, especially my pastors there, the late Rev. D. Keith Blades and Roger Harber. I am also deeply grateful to my aunt, Mercedes Carvel, for all her help. Thanks are also due to the many scholars, ministers, authors and churches, of many different Christian traditions, who have kindly and generously supplied me with so much material and support.

I am grateful to those who helped me financially: my parents, Rev. Frank Fitzsimmonds and the Particular Baptist Fund, and Rev. Dr Bill Hancock and the Baptist Union Scholarship Committee.

The research was greatly aided by the use of a number of libraries and their staff: Cambridge University Library; Tyndale Library, Tyndale House, Cambridge; Stella Read and Mary Barker, Librarians of the Bristol Baptist College; Baptist House, Didcot; Susan Mills, Librarian and Archivist of the Angus Library, Regent's Park College, Oxford; Dr Williams's Library, London; and Bristol University Library.

Thanks too to Jeremy Mudditt and Paternoster Publishing for their taking on board and publishing this book.

To my brothers and especially my parents, Fred and Dorothy Cross, for their constant love, support, friendship, patience and Christ-likeness. And to my precious daughters, Laura and Katja, and above all, my beloved wife, companion and best friend, Jackie, without whom I could not have done it. With love and thanks always.

Abbreviations

ABQ	*American Baptist Quarterly*
ACCR	Advisory Committee for Church Relations
ACTS L&P 9&10 Geo5 1919	*The Local and Private Acts Passed in the Ninth and Tenth Years of the Reign of His Majesty King George the Fifth; Being the First Session of the Thirty-First Parliament of the United Kingdom of Great Britain and Ireland with an Index* (1919)
AUSS	*Andrews University Seminary Studies*
B&FBS	British and Foreign Bible Society
BCC	The British Council of Churches
BCH	*The Baptist Church Hymnal* (1900)
BCHR	*Baptist Church Hymnal (Revised)* (1933)
BEM	*Baptism, Eucharist and Ministry* (F&O Paper No.111, Geneva, 1982)
BH	*The Baptist Handbook*
BHB	*The Baptist Hymn Book* (1962)
BHH	*Baptist History and Heritage*
BM	*Baptist Magazine*
BMJ	*Baptist Ministers' Journal*
BMS	The Baptist Missionary Society
BPW	*Baptist Praise and Worship* (Oxford, 1991)
BST	Bible Speaks Today
BQ	*The Baptist Quarterly*
BQSup	*Baptist Quarterly Supplement*
BRF	Baptist Revival Fellowship
BRG	Baptist Renewal Group
BT	*The Baptist Times*
BT&F	*The Baptist Times and Freeman*
BU	The Baptist Union
BUD	*Baptist Union Directory*
BUGB	The Baptist Union of Great Britain
BUGB&I	The Baptist Union of Great Britain and Ireland
BUild	Baptist Union Initiative with people with Learning Disabilities
BWA	Baptist World Alliance
BWC	Baptist World Congress
CCBI	The Council of Churches for Britain and Ireland
CCC	Churches' Council for Covenanting in England
CCLEPE	Consultative Committee for Local Ecumenical Projects in England
CEC	Conference of European Churches
CTE	Churches Together in England
CTP	Christian Training Programme
CTS	College Theological Society (American)
CU	The Congregational Union
CUC	Churches Unity Commission
EMBA	East Midland Baptist Association

ExpTim	*The Expository Times*
EvQ	*The Evangelical Quarterly*
Frat.	*The Fraternal*
FBCC	Fellowship of Baptist Churches for Covenanting
FCC	Free Church Council
FCEFC	Federal Council of the Evangelical Free Churches
FCFC	Free Church Frederal Council
F.I.E.C.	Fellowship of Independent Evangelical Churches
FoR	The Friends of Reunion
FUE	Faith and Unity Executive
F&O	Faith and Order
GBM	*General Baptist Magazine*
GBMW	Grove Booklet on Ministry and Worship
HUCA	*Hebrew Union College Annual*
ICP	Inter-Church Process
IJT	*Indian Journal of Theology*
JLG	Joint Liturgical Group
JPTSup	*Journal of Pentecostal Theology Supplement*
JSNT	*Journal for the Study of the New Testament*
JSNTSup	*Journal for the Study of the New Testament Supplement*
JTS	*Journal of Theological Studies*
LBA	London Baptist Association
LBC	London Bible College
LEP	Local Ecumenical Project/Partnership
NABPR	National Association of Baptist Professors of Religion (American)
NCBC	New Century Bible Commentary
NCEFC	National Council of the Evangelical Free Churches
NFCC	National Free Church Council
NIDNTT	C. Brown (ed.), *New International Dictionary of New Testament Theology* (3 vols.; Exeter, 1975)
NIV	New International Version (Hodder & Stoughton, 1986)
PBTM	Paternoster Biblical and Theological Monographs
PEQ	*Palestine Exploration Quarterly*
ResQ	*Restoration Quarterly*
RevExp	*Review and Expositor*
RTR	*Reformed Theological Review*
SBT	Studies in Biblical Theology
SBET	*Scottish Bulletin of Evangelical Theology*
SCM	Student Christian Movement
SJT	*Scottish Journal of Theology*
SL	*Studia Liturgica*
TBHS	*Transactions of the Baptist Historical Society*
TCDTBW	Theological Consultation on Doing Theology in a Baptist Way
TNTC	Tyndale New Testament Commentary
TrinJ	*Trinity Journal*
TST	Toronto Studies in Theology
TynBul	*Tyndale Bulletin*

URC	United Reformed Church
Voyage	*Voyage: Bulletin of the British Council of Churches*
WBC	Word Biblical Commentary
WBT	Word Biblical Themes
WCC	World Council of Churches
WORGLEP	The Baptist Union's Working Group on Local Ecumenical Projects
YBA	Yorkshire Baptist Association

Local Ecumenical Project/Partnership Classifications

Up to 1994

LC	Local Covenant
B	Shared Building
C	Shared Congregational Life
M	Shared Ministry

From 1994

1	Congregations in covenant
2	Single congregation partnership
3	Shared building partnership
4	Chaplaincy partnership
5	Mission partnership
6	Education partnership

Introduction

Christian baptism has been one of the most contentious doctrines and practices the church has ever had. This perhaps has never been more so than in the twentieth century, when it has been one of the key issues facing the denominations involved in the burgeoning ecumenical movement. The most distinctive characteristic of the Baptists is their restriction of baptism to that of believers by immersion, a practice which sets them apart from the other major, historic denominations. This study sets out a history of the beliefs and practices of Baptists on the Christian rite of initiation.

In a similar study, the historian David Bebbington has cogently and convincingly argued that Evangelicalism is not and never has been a single homogenous whole,[1] and has explored 'the ways in which Evangelical religion has been moulded by its environment.'[2] The relevance of this analogy with Evangelicalism and Baptists lies in two observations: both movements incorporate diversity within unity, and the Baptists are arguably the most evangelical of all the mainline denominations, therefore it is likely that they too have been affected by these same influences. This view has been expressed with regard to Baptists in the nineteenth century, whose baptismal and eucharistic theology were clearly influenced by Tractarianism and individualism.[3] I will test the theory that the Baptist doctrine and practice of baptism in the twentieth century is contextual (something that has only rarely been admitted by Baptists),[4] and that as contexts have changed so too have Baptist

---

1   D.W. Bebbington, *Evangelicalism in Modern Britain: A History from the 1720s to the 1980s* (1989), 2-17, shows that it is a grouping comprised of various theological positions and practices unified by a four-fold emphasis on conversionism, activism, biblicism and crucicentrism.

2   Bebbington, *Evangelicalism*, ix. He concludes that Evangelicalism has been 'Moulded and remoulded by its environment...', p.276. He further remarks that 'Nothing could be further from the truth than the common image of Evangelicalism being ever the same', p.271. Bebbington has demonstrated that it has developed by its interaction with and response to three major cultural movements: Enlightenment rationalism, Romanticism and Modernism, see *Evangelicalism, passim*, and in this is followed by D. Tidball, *Who Are The Evangelicals? Tracing the Roots of Today's Movements* (1994), *passim*.

3   E.g. J.H.Y. Briggs, *The English Baptists of the Nineteenth Century* (Didcot, 1994), 43-69; and M.J. Walker, *Baptists at the Table: The Theology of the Lord's Supper amongst English Baptists in the Nineteenth Century* (Didcot, 1992), 84-120.

baptismal beliefs and practices. I will, therefore, seek to identify and examine what these influences have been and accordingly will examine how the doctrine and practice of baptism has developed.

It has increasingly been recognized that the distinctive feature which sets apart the present Christian century from all previous ones is its ecumenical nature.[5] In light of this, I intend to help Baptists understand the breadth, depth and variety of their own beliefs and practices of baptism, and also to help their ecumenical partners better to understand Baptist convictions, beliefs and practices.

From the outset it is important that terms are clearly defined. 'British Baptists' here refers to those Baptist churches in membership with the Baptist Union of Great Britain (throughout abbreviated to BU), the ministers serving those churches and those in membership with them. The unqualified use of 'Baptist' at any point signifies a 'British Baptist' so defined, any other type of Baptist being specifically identified as such, for example, Strict Baptist. In its unqualified form, 'baptism' refers to believer's baptism, and, when referring to another form, for example, infant baptism, this will always be stated.

The year 1900 is a most appropriate starting date for the present study because the dawn of a new century was looked forward to by the denomination with a general mood of 'confidence and expectation.'[6] In the words of Ernest Payne, 1900 witnessed a 'new century, a new leader,[7]

---

4   This was recognized at the F&O Louisville Consultation in 1979, see W.M.S. West, 'Towards a Consensus on Baptism? Louisville 1979', BQ 28.5 (January, 1980), 225-32, and J.F.V. Nicholson, 'Baptism in Context: Further Reflections on Louisville 1979', BQ 28.6 (April, 1980), 275-79.

5   H. Davies, *Worship and Theology in England: V. The Ecumenical Century 1900–1965* (Oxford, 1965), 5, explained the reason for his subtitle as being 'to emphasize the fact that for Christian life in England as elsewhere this marks the decisive difference between the *competitive* character of nineteenth and the *cooperative* character of twentieth century Christianity.' Also, S. Neill, 'Towards Christian Unity', in S. Neill (ed.), *Twentieth Century Christianity: A Survey of modern religious trends by leading churchmen* (1961), 340, and it is illustrated throughout A. Hastings, *A History of English Christianity 1920–1990* (3rd edn, 1991).

6   E.A. Payne, *The Baptist Union: A Short History* (1959), 169.

7   Though J.H. Shakespeare requested that no biography be written, there are a number of sources for his life, work and significance to both Baptists and to the twentieth-century ecumenical movement: 'John Howard Shakespeare: The Story of His Life', *Supplement of the BT* March 15, 1928, i-iv; R.W. Thomson, *Heroes of the Baptist Church* (1937), 120-35; G. Shakespeare, *Let Candles Be Brought In: The Memoirs of the Rt. Hon. Sir Geoffrey Shakespeare Bt* (1949), 335-47; E.A. Payne, 'John Howard Shakespeare (1857–1928)', in A.S. Clement (ed.), *Baptists Who Made History: A Book about Baptists written by Baptists* (1955), 126-36; M.E. Aubrey, 'John Howard Shakespeare, 1857–1928', *BQ* 17.3 (July, 1957), 99-108; R. Hayden, 'Still at the Crossroads? Revd. J.H. Shakespeare and Ecumenism', in K.W. Clements (ed.), *Baptists*

a new paper,[8] new resources[9] and with these a revised constitution,[10] a new hymnbook,[11] new departments and new responsibilities',[12] to which can be added the last significant rise in membership in 1905.[13] The century is then divided into three sub-sections: 1900–1937, 1938–1966 and 1967–1999. The theological debate throughout the first period was conducted largely around the twin poles of the mode and subjects of baptism, with only the beginnings of the realization that it was the theology of baptism which would provide the most profitable way forward in the discussion of the baptismal issue from both the Baptists' and also Paedobaptists' point of view.[14] The beginning of the second period coincides with the seminal work by the Swiss theologian, Emil Brunner, which was quickly followed by the better known work by Karl

in the Twentieth Century (1983), 31-54; K. Hipper, *Rev. J.H. Shakespeare MA, 1857–1928* (n.d.); M. Townsend, 'John Howard Shakespeare: Prophet of Ecumenism', *BQ* 37.6 (April, 1998), 298-312; P. Shepherd, 'John Howard Shakespeare and the English Baptists, 1898–1924' (Durham University PhD, 1999).

8   In October 1898 the previously privately owned *Freeman* (f.1855) was combined with *The Baptist Times*. In 1910, the BU acquired *The Baptist* (f.1872) which was amalgamated with *The Baptist Times and Freeman*, see Payne, *The Baptist Union*, 160, and 'The Editorial Succession', *BT* February 28, 1991, 2. From September 10, 1925 the paper became known simply as *The Baptist Times*.

9   In 1899 the Twentieth Century Fund was launched, aiming to raise £250,000 for church extension, stipend maintenance, various educational and propaganda purposes, scholarships and a new denominational headquarters, a figure achieved within three years, see Payne, *The Baptist Union*, 157-59; and J.H. Shakespeare, *The Story of the Baptist Union Twentieth Century Fund, with the Financial Report* (1904). In April 1903 the Baptist Church House was opened in Southampton Row, see E.A. Payne, *The Baptist Union and Its Headquarters* (1953), 5-6.

10   In 1904 the BU revised its constitution and adopted the threefold Declaration of Principle which has, with a number of amendments, formed the basis of the BU ever since. See D.C. Sparkes, *The Constitutions of the Baptist Union of Great Britain* (Didcot, 1996), 19-55, and R.L. Kidd (ed.), *Something to Declare: A Study of the Declaration of Principle* (Oxford, 1996), 20-25.

11   *The Baptist Church Hymnal* (1900). See R.W. Thomson, *The Psalms and Hymns Trust: A Short History of the Trust and the Work of Publishing Baptist Hymn Books* (1960), 15-19.

12   Payne, *The Baptist Union*, 160.

13   Payne, *The Baptist Union*, 169, reported that in the early years of Shakespeare's secretaryship, which began in 1898, denominational statistics rose steadily, to the point in 1905 when an increase of nearly 32,000 was recorded, a growth attributed to the previous year's Welsh Revival. See also P. Shepherd, 'Denominational Renewal: A Study in English Baptist Church Life and Growth 1901–1906', *BQ* 37.7 (July, 1998), 336-50.

14   This was also recognized in the review of Baptist baptismal theology by the Presbyterian J.M. Ross, 'The Theology of Baptism in Baptist History', *BQ* 15.3 (July, 1953), 100-12.

Barth, and together these works set the theological agenda as far as baptism was concerned for the next three decades.[15] Baptists were late to join this debate, which they did so predominantly from the mid–1950s to the mid–1960s, the latter providing the close of the second period, which was also marked by the publication of two important books by George Beasley-Murray and Alec Gilmore. The third period, examines the developments which have taken place since 1967 up to the close of the century, which has witnessed unprecedented developments within the domestic ecumenical scene. While there is the inevitable arbitrariness with these divisions, with many issues spanning more than one period, they provide a convenient framework for this study.

There are, broadly speaking, two general approaches to writing history—the chronological and the thematic. The chronological is suited to reflect developments in thought and practice and to show the pioneer thinkers and innovators on whose work others have built. The thematic is suited to the examination of doctrines and the relationships between them, for baptism is not simply a practised rite but a doctrine built on and related to other doctrines, and Baptists believe that their practice grows out of their beliefs.[16] The approach, therefore, which has been adopted here has been to try to mix these two methods, discussing the various themes within an overall chronological framework, thereby seeking to reflect accurately the developments in both the theology and practice of baptism, recognizing that this has led to some repetition, though an attempt has been made to minimize this.

The sources available for this study have been many and various, but the attempt has been made to examine not just the work of Baptist scholars but, as far as it is possible, the views of grass-roots Baptists.[17] However, there have been only several Baptists who have sought to

---

15   D.M. Thompson, 'Baptism, Church and Society in Britain Since 1800' (unpublished Hulsean lectures, 1983–84), 86-87, comments that, 'By the 1950s...baptism in particular and sacramental theology in general had become an ecumenical concern. They were no longer the property of any one school of thought in the Church. Most fascinating of all, the concern over baptism owed next to nothing to the discussion of the subject among the defenders of believer's baptism.' Thompson, p.87, remarks that the work of the Congregationalist, P.T. Forsyth, *Lectures on the Church and the Sacraments* (1917), had foreshadowed this development.

16   This is reflected in the first Declaration of Principle: 'That our Lord and Saviour Jesus Christ..., is the sole and absolute authority in all matters pertaining to *faith and practice*, as revealed in the Holy Scriptures...', italics added, see *BUD* 1996–97, 7.

17   In the footnotes, the convention followed is to identify, as far as it has been possible, laymen and laywomen as such by prefixing their names with Mr, Mrs or Miss. When female writers are noted and there is no indication of their marital status, their first names have been used. Writers with no title prefixed, or the title Dr, can be taken to be ministers, though several professional scholars, historians and theologians are exceptions to this rule, the majority of whom will be known to readers.

present a systematic discussion of the theology of baptism (principally H.W. Robinson, N. Clark, G.R. Beasley-Murray and R.E.O. White), therefore the present study has had to glean the theology of baptism from more fragmentary sources and many different writers.

CHAPTER 1

The Theology and Practice of Baptism Among British Baptists in the Nineteenth Century

David Thompson has noted that 'One of the most striking differences in the life of the British Churches between the last quarter of the eighteenth century...and the last quarter of the twentieth..., must surely be the changed attitude to the sacraments.' A sacramental revival has taken place within the Church of England, Church of Scotland and in some parts of Nonconformity within the modern period.[1] From the fifth century to the Reformation, infant baptism was virtually the sole form of baptism known in the church,[2] a position challenged by the radical wing of the Reformation, when first Anabaptist groups,[3] then a century later the General and Particular Baptists and the Society of Friends rejected the practice, though for different reasons. Thompson commented that 'their rejection of infant baptism was quite rightly seen as only one aspect of a more broadly based radical religious position; and the touchstone for developments in sacramental theology in the Reformation was the Lord's Supper.' By the early eighteenth century, however, this radical upsurge had become a spent force; Baptists and Quakers had become more defensive and introspective, threats to religious orthodoxy coming from within in the form of unitarianism and socinianism, and in deism and scepticism from without. The Evangelical Revival, however, changed this, old issues re-emerging and new ones appearing. Its emphasis on personal religious experience

---

1   Thompson, 'Baptism', 1. See also his 'The Theology of Adult Initiation in the Nineteenth and Twentieth Centuries', in D.A. Withey (ed.), *Adult Initiation* (Alcuin/ GROW Liturgical Study 10/Grove Liturgical Study 58; Nottingham, 1989), 6-23.

2   Though the first undisputed reference to infant baptism is to be found in North Africa at the beginning of the third century in the writings of Tertullian, who disapproved of the practice, *De baptismo* 18, it was not until the fifth century that it gained the ascendancy over believer's baptism. See P. Bradshaw, *Early Christian Worship: A basic introduction to ideas and practice* (1996), 31-36.

3   See W.M.S. West, 'The Anabaptists and the Rise of the Baptist Movement', in A. Gilmore (ed.), *Christian Baptism: A Fresh Attempt to Understand the Rite in terms of Scripture, History, and Theology* (1959), 223-72.

brought out the tension between individual and social religion, placing the debate between infant and believer's baptism in a new light. The emphasis on the Bible brought a new interest in biblical patterns for church life and a re-examination of the biblical evidence for infant baptism. The contrast drawn between vital and formal religion brought a new questioning of sacramental theology. All these issues crystallized around the emphasis on conversion. If conversion was necessary to the Christian life, what was the significance and meaning of baptism? Did baptism, particularly the baptism of infants, effect anything?[4]

Thompson has convincingly argued that from 1800 to 1830 three sets of issues concerning baptism came to dominate, the Evangelical Revival having significantly affected the way in which they were expressed and discussed. First was the issue of the proper subjects of baptism which was most keenly debated in Scotland. Second was the terms of communion— whether communion was only for those baptized as believers or whether baptism was necessary for communion, or, by extension, for membership. Third was the matter of baptismal regeneration, which preoccupied mainly the Church of England.[5]

For roughly the first half of the century the baptismal debate focused primarily on the mode of baptism[6] and more specifically on the meaning of the Greek verbs βάπτω and βαπτίζω, leading Jim Perkin to the hyperbolic statement that, 'No other single word had so much written about it in the last century as this one.'[7] As the baptismal controversy

---

4   Thompson, 'Baptism', 3. For a brief survey of Baptists and baptism, see D.M. Himbury, 'Baptismal Controversies, 1640–1900', in Gilmore (ed.), *Christian Baptism*, 273-305.

5   Thompson, 'Baptism', 4. He discusses each of these issues on pp.5-10, 10-12 and 12-17 respectively. Briggs, *English Baptists*, 43, agrees with this classification of the issues, and discusses them on pp.43-44, 44-45 and 45-50 respectively. J.R.C. Perkin, 'Baptism in Non-Conformist Theology, 1820–1920, with special reference to the Baptists' (Oxford University DPhil, 1955), 6, similarly identified this period, but especially 1820–30, as marked by an increased interest in baptism. That baptism was, at this time, a significant and widespread issue 'lies in the fact that books, pamphlets and tracts are being written on baptism in the early nineteenth century, whereas thirty years before they were not. But publication was a response to the fact that the issues were being debated among Christians; and some indication of this is seen in the growth of the Baptists during the period, and also in the divisions that produced new Baptist congregations.' Thompson, 'Baptism', 4.

6   Examples of Baptist works are J. Bowes, *Scriptural Reasons for giving up the Sprinkling of Infants* (1839); F.W. Gotch, *A Critical Examination of the Rendering of the Word Βαπτίζω* (1841); A. Carson, *The Mode and Subjects of Christian Baptism* (1841); T.B. Crowest, *Sprinkling the Great Error of the Professing Church of Christ* (1845).

7   Perkin, 'Baptism', 25. An example of the controversy over the mode is the dispute between the BMS and the British and Foreign Bible Society in the 1830s over the translation of βαπτίζω. Baptists felt it should be translated 'to dip or immerse' and not be

wore on, the tendency was to give more importance to the subjects of
baptism and on the conception of the church which underlies it.[8]
More than anything else, it was the concept of the church made up of
believers which determined the Baptist attitude to infant baptism. In fact,
the nineteenth century proves that the 'distinguishing feature of Baptists
is not their doctrine of baptism, but their doctrine of the Church.'[9]
Though this was seldom made explicit in the period from 1820–1920,
the whole controversy cannot be understood unless it is realized that it
was this difference in ecclesiology which caused the clash.[10]

Perkin contended that the decade ending 1864 saw little of the
controversy, especially when compared to 1830–40. Questions other than
the philological ones had taken on a new importance and in general the
books written became shorter and kinder in tone.[11] By 1870 it had
become clear that the question of baptism had entered a new stage in its
history, a stage which was the prelude to the twentieth-century debate.
The latter part of the nineteenth century saw the virtual passing away of
the pamphleteer, the writer of theological doggerel and the preacher of
unkindly, eclectic sermons.

> Men were trying to use the Bible as a basis and guide for their theology, not a
> hunting ground for proof-texts; sermons took on a new note of practical
> application of the gospel and denominational rivalry began to change into
> toleration. In the womb of the nineteenth century the twentieth was already being
> formed.[12]

---

simply transliterated 'to baptize'. This led to the withdrawal of Baptist support for the
B&FBS and the establishment of their own (Baptist) Bible Translation Society (f.1840).
See Briggs, *English Baptists*, 56-59; Payne, *The Baptist Union*, 80-81.

8   So Perkin, 'Baptism', 211, 217-18.

9   Perkin, 'Baptism', 10-11. This is true even if it is acknowledged that Baptist
ecclesiology was not all it should have been. See Briggs' discussion of 'John Clifford's
Diminished Ecclesiology', *English Baptists*, 22-27, which is set within a larger discussion of the nineteenth-century Baptist theology of the church, pp. 15-30.

10   Perkin, 'Baptism', 11. The implications of the primacy of ecclesiology for
baptismal theology can best be shown in recognition of the fact that Baptists maintain
that baptism is solely for *believers*, those already converted. This is why Baptists used to
be called Antipaedobaptists.

11   Perkin, 'Baptism', 335-36. In 1864 C.H. Spurgeon launched his vitriolic attack
on evangelical Anglicans through his famous sermon condemning baptismal
regeneration, on which see M. Nicholls, *C.H. Spurgeon: The Pastor Evangelist* (Didcot,
1992), 122-29; Briggs, *English Baptists*, 48-50.

12   Perkin, 'Baptism', 337.

Thompson agrees that baptism receded from the forefront of theological debate from the early 1860s, offering four reasons for this.[13] First, the Gorham judgment of 1850 resulted in a stalemate as far as baptismal doctrine in the Anglican communion was concerned, though it had established the legitimacy of an Evangelical reading of the *Book of Common Prayer*.[14] Second, controversy over the eucharist became more widespread in the 1850s with the development of the ritualist movement.[15] Third, the transformation of Calvinist Dissent into an evangelical theology attached relatively little importance to the sacraments. The 1860 Norwich Chapel Case effectively settled the Baptist communion controversy which had flared up in the second decade of the century around the two figures of Robert Hall of Leicester and Joseph Kinghorn of Norwich.[16] From this time, the practice of open communion began to spread, to the point that, by mid-century, it had become the norm among Baptists.[17] Fourth, the development of biblical criticism and historical scholarship began to undermine the simpler defences of

---

13   Thompson, 'Baptism', 72. See Walker's discussion of C.H. Spurgeon's and John Clifford's theologies of communion, *Baptists at the Table*, 164-96, both preachers having more to say on communion than baptism. According to Nicholls, *Spurgeon*, 158, the 1899 index to the *Metropolitan Tabernacle Pulpit* lists only 4 sermons by Spurgeon on baptism.

14   On the Gorham case, see Thompson, 'Baptism', 30-33.

15   Thompson, 'Baptism', 72, commented that, 'In so far as the baptismal controversy in the first half of the century had been one between catholic and Calvinist sacramental theology, this division received much sharper focus in the second half of the century over Holy Communion. Antipathy to the Mass, transubstantiation, the real presence etc., was more easily mobilised than suspicion of baptismal regeneration.'

16   The most recent discussions of this controversy are to be found in Walker, *Baptists at the Table*, 32-83, and Briggs, *English Baptists*, 61-68. Briggs, p.65, writes: 'The close communionists defended a higher view of the sacraments than that to which Hall by default was driven. As relations across denominational boundaries opened up, so the pressures for open communion—and later open membership—developed. In such a context it was all too easy for the low view of the sacraments Hall had come to support to become widely pervasive, especially as it accorded with evangelical antipathy to a revived catholicism, which made Baptists far too negative and reactive in their thinking about the sacraments, now more frequently referred to as ordinances, although all too often conceived in such minimalist terms as even Zwingli would not own.'

17   Thompson, 'Baptism', 68. Many of the churches which retained closed communion formed the Strict and Particular Baptist churches. However, the Baptist Evangelical Society was formed in order to defend strict-communionist principles, whose work was not seen as antagonistic to that of the BU. See G.R. Breed, *The Baptist Evangelical Society—an early Victorian Episode* (Dunstable, 1987), who is careful to distinguish between 'strict' and 'strict communion'.

existing baptismal practice, forcing a reassessment of the basis of baptismal theology within the churches.[18]

Baptist antipathy to the theory of baptismal regeneration was a major factor in the 'down grading' of baptismal theology. 'The vehemence of the rejection of baptismal regeneration, particularly by Baptists, led to the reduction of the rite to a mere sign in many quarters.'[19] But other factors were also involved. In his detailed study of the Baptist theology of the Lord's Supper, Michael Walker has shown that the majority of Baptists were influenced in their eucharistic theology by both Zwinglianism and Calvinism, while others had inherited more from the radical Anabaptists with their separation of spirit and matter and their suspicion of anything approximating to ritualism.[20] These influences equally affected Baptist baptismal theology, as none of these 'controlling' influences predisposed Baptists to think 'sacramentally' about baptism. The Catholic Revival of the 1830s–40s received a very negative reaction from Baptists, so much so that anything which could be construed as in any way 'Catholic' was vehemently repudiated. For instance, Charles Williams of Accrington stated, 'Baptists do not regard either baptism or the Lord's Supper as a sacrament in the ecclesiastical sense of the word... To them the ordinance is neither the cause nor the medium of grace.'[21]

While some Baptists allowed their Zwinglianism to lead them into an extreme subjectivism, others were discontent with the memorialist position imposed by the denominational norm.[22] Contrary to the prevailing closed-communion stance of the majority of the denomination, Robert Hall contended that Paedobaptists should be welcomed to the Lord's Table, rejecting bare memorialism in favour of the Supper as a participation in the sacrifice offered by Christ.[23] Careful to ensure that his views were incapable of being interpreted as speaking of the presence of Christ in the eucharist, Hall maintained that it was the Holy Spirit's presence in communion who raised the believer into Christ's presence where they could feed upon him by sharing in his risen and glorified life, enabling him to speak of a 'spiritual participation' in the body and

---

18   Thompson, 'Baptism', 72, believes that in the long term this was the most significant development.

19   Perkin, 'Baptism', 160-61.

20   Walker, *Baptists at the Table*, 3.

21   C. Williams, *The Principles and Practices of the Baptists* (1879), 23. One of the weaknesses of Perkin's work is the scant attention he pays to the Oxford Movement, while it is one of Walker's strengths.

22   Walker, *Baptists at the Table*, 8-9.

23   R. Hall, *On Terms of Communion*, in O. Gregory (ed.), *The Entire Works of the Rev. Robert Hall, A.M., with A brief Memoir of his Life, and a Critical Estimate of his Character and Writings* (1831), II, 63-64, where Hall referred to holy communion as a 'federal rite'.

blood of Christ.[24] Walker pointed out the irony that Hall's belief in the value of the Lord's Supper eventually led others to value both it and baptism less highly than he did. Hall argued that a rite which had such implications for the Christian life should not be kept from fellow Christians on the grounds of baptismal 'irregularity', believing that admission to the Lord's table was more important than whether the communicant was a Baptist or Paedobaptist. This eventually led him to relegate baptism to the status of merely the 'ceremonial', a view which later Baptists also assigned to the Lord's Supper.[25]

Both Perkin and Walker stand within the Baptist tradition which has sought to re-establish the sacramental nature of baptism, and both highlight those nineteenth-century Baptists who recognized in baptism the nature of a sacrament. Perkin, for example, comments that, 'A large part of the dearth of sacramental theology among Baptists must be laid at the door of the Victorians. On the other hand, there was throughout the whole period a "minority movement" within the Baptist denomination which stood for a sacramental view over against the *nuda signa* doctrine of its contemporaries.'[26] For most nineteenth-century Baptists, baptism was a sign that indicated something previously done through faith at conversion. Its necessity lay in it being an imitation of Jesus' example, not because it did anything for the candidate. Even Nonconformist Paedobaptists tended to regard baptism merely as a sign rather than a sacrament, though, for a minority of Baptists only a sacramental interpretation of baptism could adequately accord with New Testament teaching.[27]

Many of these sacramentalists were those who became Baptists later on in their lives. The best known of these was the former Anglican, Baptist Noel, who commented on Acts 2:38: 'Since, then, baptism is thus necessary to remission of sins, and is so closely connected with it... [r]epentance and baptism are declared in the text to secure the gift of the

---

24   Hall, *On Terms of Communion*, 64.

25   Walker, *Baptists at the Table*, 9-10.

26   Perkin, 'Baptism', 11. Cf. p.244, 'It must be regarded that the majority of Baptists did not regard baptism as a sacrament at all; at best it was a sign of something already accomplished.'

27   Three writers have recently shown that there have been forms of baptismal sacramentalism in Baptist thought from the seventeenth century onwards, and that it is, therefore, erroneous to suppose that baptismal sacramentalism is an innovation of recent times. See S.K. Fowler, 'Baptism as a Sacrament in 20th-Century British Baptist Theology' (Toronto University DTh, 1998), 7-175; P.E. Thompson, 'A New Question in Baptist History: Seeking a Catholic Spirit Among Early Baptists', *Pro Ecclesia* 8.1 (Winter, 1999), 51-72, and 'Practicing the Freedom of God: Formation in Early Baptist Life' (CTS/NABPR paper; 1999); A.R. Cross, 'Dispelling the Myth of English Baptist Baptismal Sacramentalism' (TCDTBW; 1999; forthcoming in *BQ*).

Holy Ghost.'[28] A number of 'life-long' Baptists also used sacramental language of baptism. William Hawkins interpreted baptism as a Roman soldier's *sacramentum*, 'a sovereign oath...to our Sovereign Prince, in which we swear allegiance to him...', a use which was followed by the anonymous author of six articles in the *Baptist Magazine* in 1857.[29]

The sacramental interpretation was attacked, especially by advocates of personal religion. Isaiah Birt, recently retired from a Birmingham pastorate, understood baptism in terms of a personal contract between God and the individual, 'that baptism was not instituted either to be a substitute for any graces, or to convey any blessing', and 'If religion be personal, all religious acts and ordinances must be so.'[30] Charles Williams declared that 'blessing was not present in the baptism, it was not communicated by the baptism. Those baptismal waters were not either the cause or the means, though they may have been the occasion of these blessings.'[31] John Howard Hinton, Joint Secretary of the BU from 1841–66, affirmed 'in the most unqualified terms, that baptism is not a means of conferring any spiritual blessings whatever', later adding, 'Baptism...cannot be any part of the terms on which spiritual blessings are enjoyed.'[32] Believing that he was speaking for all Nonconformists, John Clifford wrote:

> The 'Sacraments' of themselves do not bring the soul into living union with the Saviour. They cannot. They are of the earth, earthy. They reveal truth of such peerless worth, that they are its supreme symbols... But the 'real presence' of the

---

28   B.W. Noel, *Essay on Christian Baptism* (1849), 99. Cf. the former Independent Isaac Orchard's sermon, *Christian Baptism* (1829), 11, 'Baptism is an appointed means for obtaining a greater outpouring of the Holy Spirit', cited by Perkin, 'Baptism', 197. On Noel, see Perkin, 'Baptism', 322-34; Briggs, *English Baptists*, 46-47, 49-50, 54, and *passim*; and D.W. Bebbington, 'The Life of Baptist Noel: Its Setting and Significance', *BQ* 24.8 (October, 1972), 389-411.

29   W. Hawkins of Portsea, *A Sermon on Baptism* (1827), 22, cited by Briggs, *English Baptists*, 51-52; and, e.g., Anonymous, 'Sacramental Meditations', *BM* 49 (January, 1857), 22-23.

30   I. Birt, *Personal Religion Vindicated in Relation to Christian Baptism* (1833), 25 and 27. On Birt's individualistic understanding of faith and baptism, see Briggs, *English Baptists*, 53, see also p.44.

31   C. Williams in H. Pitman, *A Discussion of Infant Baptism* (1858), being the report by Pitman, reporter for the *Manchester Courier*, of a public debate between Williams and Rev. Dr Joseph Baylee, Principal of St. Aidan's College, Birkenhead, on three consecutive evenings in September 1858. See Perkin, 'Baptism', 254-55; Briggs, *English Baptists*, 50.

32   J.H. Hinton, 'The Ultimatum', in *The Theological Works of the Rev. John Howard Hinton, M.A.. Volume V. Lectures* (1865), 465-79, quotations from pp.466 and 472.

Christ is the Divine answer to the penitence, trust and worship of the humble and devout soul.[33]

Earlier he had said: 'Broadly speaking, we hold that Baptism and the Lord's Supper are not "Sacraments" in the ecclesiastical sense, i.e. they are not mysteries or miracles, not causes of grace, not in themselves vehicles of grace.'[34] Of this, Walker remarked that 'His description of them as "of the earth, earthy", coupled with his passionate claim that religion was essentially inward and individualist, and his unwise polarisation of matter and spirit, placed him at the extreme wing of the radical anabaptist position.' In this, Clifford's 'reduction of the sacraments to mere symbols placed him in a position no different from many of his fellow Baptists.'[35]

This individualistic understanding of baptism was often linked to an unecclesial view of the rite. Clifford was the best known advocate of this position, which was worked out in practice by the few churches which practised open membership.[36] According to Clifford, baptism was

---

33   J. Clifford, *The Ordinances of Jesus and the Sacraments of the Church* (1888), 19, cited by Walker, *Baptists at the Table*, 188.

34   Clifford, *Ordinances of Jesus*, 4, cited by Walker, *Baptists at the Table*, 188. In a number of places, Briggs discusses the widespread view which saw baptism as an individual rite: e.g., J.A. of Perth, *New Baptist Miscellany*, October 1830, 415-16, 'baptism is simply a personal obligation, over which [churches] ought to have no control'; Dr Richard Glover, 'The Baptist Church', in *Our Churches and why we belong to them* (1898), 86, '[baptism is] an individual rite, in which each simply confesses his submission to the Lord'; in Briggs, *English Baptists*, 102 and 28 respectively.

35   Walker, *Baptists at the Table*, 188. For a detailed discussion of Clifford's theology of, specifically, the Lord's Supper, but, by extension, baptism as well, see pp.182-92. A concomitant of this impoverished theology of baptism was a discomfort with the relationship of the Holy Spirit to the rite. Perkin, 'Baptism', 13-14, observed that Baptists 'did not feel happy about the doctrine of the Holy Spirit, whether in conjunction with baptism or not. This constitutes a serious lacuna in the theology of the period.' As a reason for this he suggested that at this time 'Baptist theology...was essentially empirical and practical rather than theoretical. Obedience, faith, the church, dying, rising—all these were concrete ideas, readily interpreted and understood. But the gift of the Spirit belongs to a realm of experience and theology only spoken of by the very learned and the very ignorant', p.261. In this he is followed by Himbury, 'Baptismal Controversies', 274. Briggs, *English Baptists*, 54-55, however, has noted that this inhibition did not extend to Baptist hymn-writers—e.g. Maria Saffery, ''Tis the great Father we adore' (1818), which includes verse 4, 'Blest Spirit! with intense desire,/ Solicitous we bow;/ Baptize us in renewing fire,/And ratify the vow', in *Psalms and Hymns* (1858), no. 707; and B.W. Noel, 'Lord, Thou has promised to baptize' (1853), *Psalms and Hymns* no. 713.

36   The best known open membership Particular Baptist churches at this time were Bloomsbury, Regent's Park, Hampstead, Clapton and Camden Road, all in London, Broadmead and Tyndale in Bristol, St. Mary's, Norwich, all the Birmingham churches

associated with a person's spiritual welfare, but was never described as a condition of admission to the church. 'Uniformly and exclusively it is prescribed as a solemn transaction between the soul and the Saviour—nowhere as a portion of church government, or as indispensable in order to entrance upon a church state.' Extending this line of argument to the issue of church relations, Clifford believed that when baptism was viewed in this way and when Congregational churches accepted people into membership by profession of faith, then the argument for union between the two denominations was compelling.[37] In his discussion of the Baptist understanding of faith, baptism and the church, John Briggs writes, 'All too many Baptist apologists were at once too protestant, too rational, too didactic and too individualistic. Sacraments smacked of magic; by contrast, post-Enlightenment Baptists saw believer's baptism as the mental response to the revelation of truth, undertaken with free volition by rational men and women.'[38]

There were, then, three distinct phases of the baptismal debate in the nineteenth century running from approximately 1800 to 1840, 1840 to 1864, and from 1864 to the twentieth century, and four major factors have been identified as having influenced Baptist baptismal theology in the nineteenth century. The first factor was individualism. Walker writes:

> The nineteenth century was the century of the individual and the voluntary society and some Baptists in the early years of the century saw themselves as pioneers breaking away from the old ways. Impatience with forms and ceremonies and emphasis on the inner and spiritual forces at work in the life of the individual were to be the hallmark of a new breed of Christian men, a breed that was to find its most eloquent spokesman amongst the Baptists in John Clifford. The church too, believed that it was discovering a new freedom, liberated from the restraints of the

---

except the New Connexion church, and all but one of the new churches founded by the LBA. See Briggs, *English Baptists*, 137, citing J. Clifford in the *GBM* February 1883, 53-54.

37   Clifford in *GBM* December 1877, 448-49, April 1881, 122, and March 1883, 89, cited by Briggs, *English Baptists*, 135-36. Clifford was followed by W.L. Jones of Spalding in his General Baptist Association Letter for 1882, but was opposed by Joseph Fletcher, see Briggs, pp.136-37. On the possibility of union with Congregational churches, see Briggs, pp.121-22, and also p.176 where he quotes Clifford, *GBM* March 1887, 103: 'Will it be long before Baptists and Independents are able to unite in the New Testament principle that "the obligation to be baptized springs out of the relationship of the soul to the Saviour, and not from the relationship of the believer to the church", and that therefore "the whole question of baptism must be left to the individual conscience"', quoting from the Constitution of his Westbourne Park church which is printed in Sir James Marchant, *Dr. John Clifford, C.H.: Life, Letters and Reminiscences* (1924), 45-46.

38   Briggs, *English Baptists*, 52.

past, the concern for right order and what was viewed as the theological bickering that went with it.[39]

Walker immediately proceeded to identify the second factor. 'This process could only have greatly accelerated with the coming of the catholic revival',[40] at the centre of which was the doctrine of baptismal generation.[41] Third, there was the impact of increased population mobility which caused Baptists, among others, to think carefully as to who they could share fellowship with.[42]

Fourth, there were the beginnings of movement towards ecumenism. Walker called this 'the age of initiative', when 'Christians were not so much drawn together as thrown together' in, for instance, missionary endeavour and philanthropic work. 'For Baptists, these changes called for a reappraisal of their doctrinal position', for their ecclesiology 'drew a clear line of demarcation between the church and a world in whose life and welfare they were increasingly engaged. Their doctrine of baptism, especially when accompanied by the corollary of closed communion, separated them from Christians with whom they increasingly worked in common cause.' The communion controversy, then, can be understood in terms of the way Baptists responded to a situation vastly different from

---

39   Walker, *Baptists at the Table*, 130-31.

40   Walker, *Baptists at the Table*, 131.

41   Almost all English Nonconformity rejected the doctrine of baptismal regeneration, which has been described as 'the very foundation of the Oxford Tracts', see the *Christian Observer* 36, 1837, 179, in its comments on a letter by J.H. Newman in defence of the Tracts for the Times in March 1837. R.W. Church, *The Oxford Movement: Twelve Years, 1833–1845* (3rd edn, 1892), 136, likened Pusey's Tracts on Baptism of 1835 (numbers 67 to 69 which contained the main tractarian teaching on baptism) to 'the advance battery of heavy artillery on a field where the battle has hitherto been carried on by skirmishing and musketry'; both cited by Thompson, 'Baptism', 18: see the whole of his discussion, pp.18-35. Briggs, *English Baptists*, 45-53, 223-27, discusses the whole issue of baptismal regeneration and the threat of tractarianism as they affected Baptist thought, as has Walker, *Baptists at the Table*, 84-120. Broader studies of anti-Catholicism are to be found in P. Toon, *Evangelical Theology 1833–1856: A Response to Tractarianism* (1979), and J. Wolffe, *The Protestant Crusade in Great Britain, 1829–1860* (Oxford, 1991).

42   Differences over the terms of communion led many churches which wished to remain closed in membership and communion to form the Strict Baptists, now Grace Baptists, on which see Payne, *The Baptist Union* 40-41, 86-87. Hall's rejection of closed communion has been examined in detail by Walker, who has drawn attention to the three major areas which influenced his theology of communion, *Baptists at the Table*, 45: 'The first is his basic conviction that it is a sign of the church's unity. The second is his argument that faith takes precedence over "ceremonial". Thirdly, Hall deals with the way in which the church is historically conditioned, thus making it impossible in any dispute to return to an original and pristine state in which the world of the New Testament is reproduced in later centuries.' See Walker's wider discussion of Hall, pp.45-65.

the seventeenth and eighteenth century.[43] John Briggs offers the following summary:

> The history of Baptists in the nineteenth century is very largely a reactive and responsive one: consciously to the Catholic Revival, which must be held partly responsible for the development of low views of churchmanship, ministry and the sacraments; and unconsciously to the many secular pressures which also shaped the pattern of church life... Baptists particularly faced difficulties as Christians became more tolerant of one another, because their restrictive baptismal practice, that is their distinction in confining baptism to believers only, necessarily challenged any easy accommodation even to other recognizably evangelical groupings; the consequences of that are to be seen in the debates about open communion and open membership, and the long-running dispute with the Bible Society on the legitimacy of translating βαπτιζω by words signifying immersion.[44]

By the close of the nineteenth century, then, baptism was, with a few exceptions, described as an ordinance, the subjective, personal testimony of a believer's faith in Christ and not an objective means of conveying the grace of God and the benefits of redemption through Christ to those who believe. More recently, Stan Fowler has offered the following six refinements to the previously mentioned factors which effected this shift, though he avoids the danger of seeing these as all the factors involved. First, was the neglect of discussion of the meaning of baptism due to Baptists' controversy with Paedobaptists and preoccupation with the subjects and mode of baptism. In all this, sacramentalism came to be identified with infant baptism and rejected with it. Second, emphasizing the confessional aspect of baptism focused Baptists on what precedes baptism. Third, a sacramental understanding was perceived to be a threat to the doctrine of justification by faith alone. Fourth, the influence of eighteenth-century Hyper Calvinism on Particular Baptists had led to the undermining of the human side of faith. Fifth, the Evangelical Revival, which originated within the Church of England, seemed to have demonstrated that God's saving work was not tied to baptism and seemed to confirm the point already made on justification *sola fide*. Sixth, most

---

43   Walker, *Baptists at the Table*, 42-43. See W.R. Ward, 'The Baptists and the Transformation of the Church, 1780–1830', *BQ* 25.4 (October, 1973), 168-69. The attitude of Baptists towards unity received considerable impetus internally in the process which led to the formation of the BU in 1812–13, on which see Payne, *The Baptist Union*, 28-42, and externally when, e.g., the Evangelical Alliance was formed in 1846, see Payne, *The Baptist Union, passim*, and through participation in the many philanthropic societies, on which see Bebbington, *Evangelicalism, passim*; K. Heasman, *Evangelicals in Action: An Appraisal of their Social Work* (1962); and the various essays in J. Wolffe (ed.), *Evangelical Faith and Public Zeal: Evangelicals and Society in Britain 1780–1980* (1995), *passim*.
44   Briggs, *English Baptists*, 11-12.

Baptist works on baptism were attempts to correct the errors of Paedobaptists who seemed to overemphasize the efficacy of baptism to the point of its operation *ex opere operato* and, in the process, went to the opposite extreme. Baptists were clearer on what baptism was not, than on what it was.[45] This all said, however, there were a not insignificant number of Baptists who advocated baptismal sacramentalism and who paved the way for twentieth-century developments.

---

45   Fowler, 'Baptism as a Sacrament', 91-93.

CHAPTER 2

Common Ground

Introduction

While the present study will quickly reveal that there is no *one* Baptist theology of baptism, there is, nevertheless, a common core on which Baptists are almost unanimously agreed or over which there is little contention. This chapter outlines these areas of the theology of baptism on which Baptists have spoken with a common voice, though recognizing that there have been, from time to time, exceptions, which will be discussed throughout the rest of the study. Three main divisions will be examined here: the mode, the subjects and the theology of baptism.

The Mode of Baptism

On the issue of the mode of baptism modern Baptists have been all but unanimous: baptism is by immersion and its basis in scripture is enshrined in the second Declaration of Principle of the Baptist Union: 'That Christian Baptism is the immersion in water into the Name of the Father, the Son, and the Holy Ghost, of those who have professed repentance towards God and faith in our Lord Jesus Christ who "died for our sins according to the Scriptures; was buried, and rose again the third day."'[1] This understanding of immersion has been substantiated by scholarly research.[2] Though the original mode adopted by the earliest Baptists was affusion and it is unclear precisely when immersion was adopted, by 1642 it was being advocated by the General Baptists.[3] While

---

1   This second principle has remained unchanged through the four revisions of the Declaration of Principle, the last one being in 1938, and it has been supported most recently by the four English Baptist College Principals in their study of the Declaration, see Kidd (ed.), *Something to Declare*, 20-24. See also Sparkes, *Constitutions*.

2   The most important recent Baptist discussion of βαπτίζω, its cognates and related Greek words is G.R. Beasley-Murray, 'Baptism, Wash', in C. Brown (ed.), *NIDNTT I:A–F* (Exeter, 1975), 143-54 (which is followed by R.T. Beckwith, 'Infant Baptism: Its Background and Theology', 154-61).

comparatively few Baptist authors have acknowledged this historical fact,[4] much Baptist writing has given the impression that Baptists have always practised immersion and, for the overwhelming majority of Baptists, it is true to say that the only legitimate form of baptism is immersion.[5]
A further reason for the retention of immersion is the belief that it is important that a symbol be appropriate to that which it symbolizes. A.C. Underwood wrote, 'The mode...is not so important as the question as to the person..., but it *is* important.' He believed immersion to be much more impressive and memorable than sprinkling and a much better symbol, representing complete surrender to Christ, burial with Him, death to sin and resurrection to newness of life. Further, in a sacrament, it is most important that the symbolic actions should be appropriate 'if they are to mediate God's help and grace to men in response to their faith and love.' A properly chosen religious symbol, then, will feed and nourish faith as well as express it.[6] Berkeley Collins, however, went further, when he maintained that 'the distinction between a symbol and the thing symbolized scarcely existed in ancient times. The "symbol" itself was believed to be an effective agent.'[7]

---

3   See B.R. White, *The English Baptists of the Seventeenth Century* (Didcot, 2nd edn, 1996), 29, where he cites Edward Barber, *A small Treatise of Baptisme or Dipping* (1642), 11-12, in which baptism is assumed to be by immersion and not any other mode. However, it is possible that there is an earlier reference to the practice of immersion, though the reference is inconclusive, see W.T. Whitley, 'Baptized—Dipped for Dead, 1560 Text, 1614 Comment, 1640 Practice', *BQ* 11.4-7 (January-December, 1943), 175-77.

4   Among those who have are H.W. Robinson, *Baptist Principles* (3rd edn, 1938), 16 [unless otherwise stated all quotations are from the 1960 reprint of the 3rd edn]; 'The Baptist Doctrine of the Church', *BQ* 12.12 (October, 1948), 445; W.M.S. West, *Baptist Principles* (3rd edn, 1975), 26 (unless otherwise stated, all quotations are from this 3rd edn).

5   E.g. 'H', 'Some Thoughts on Baptism', *BT&F* June 15, 1900, 480; A. Phillips of Leamington Spa, *What Baptists Stand For; and Gleanings in the Field of Baptist History* (1903), 39-40. This has often been combined with an appeal to the archaeological evidence, e.g. by F.F. Whitby, *Baptist Principles from a Layman's point of view* (n.d., [1908]), 53.

6   A.C. Underwood, 'Why Be Baptised? An Imaginary Conversation', *BT* September 1, 1938, 675. Cf. C.H. Watkin, 'The Meaning of Baptism', *BT&F* January 10, 1913, 19, 'The primary or external meaning of the ordinance must correspond to the spiritual meaning. A symbol can only have the symbolism for which it is fitted. But further, both must correspond to the state of mind and heart which has been reached by the candidates for baptism'; and R.E.O. White, *The Biblical Doctrine of Initiation* (1960), 311, 'The first requirement of any symbol, one would suppose, is that it should symbolise.'

7   B.G. Collins of Bluntisham, 'The Sacrament of Baptism in the New Testament', *ExpTim* 27.1 (October, 1915), 38.

Charles Brown developed the symbolic significance of baptism when he referred to it as an enacted word, a dramatic symbol. In this ordinance the doctrine of regeneration was taught: the meaning of baptism being the death of the old life and the beginning of the new.[8] Baptists have always been a confessional rather than credal people, and this understanding of baptism as an enacted word developed, chiefly through the many and influential writings of Wheeler Robinson. For example:

> Its symbolic significance, *i.e.*, the spiritual death to self, union with Christ, and resurrection of the believer was emphasized by Paul: it expressed in vivid manner the very heart of Christian experience, as he conceived it. It is an action that speaks louder than words; by its unspoken eloquence, it commits those who are baptized to the most essential things. Yet it leaves each generation free to interpret the fundamental truths in its own way.[9]

Drawing chiefly upon Romans 6:1-11, but also Colossians 2:12, Baptists have identified immersion as symbolic of, first, the death, burial and resurrection of Christ, and the believer's participation with him through faith,[10] the baptistry being understood as a watery grave;[11] second, repentance;[12] third, a washing or cleansing from sin, implying a new moral life for the believer;[13] and fourth, of the baptism of the Holy Spirit.[14]

The dominant image of immersion is of the death, burial and resurrection of Christ and the believer's own death, burial and resurrection with Christ by faith.[15] Contrary to the many critics of the Baptist position, this is not to elevate the believer's response of faith over the prevenient grace of God, the subjective over the objective, for without the objective reality of Christ, his death and resurrection, there can be no

---

8   C. Brown, 'The Old and the New', *BT&F* January 5, 1906, 3.

9   Robinson, *Baptist Principles*, 27-28.

10   W.T. Whitley, *Church, Ministry and Sacraments* (1903), 161-64.

11   N.H. Marshall of Heath Street, Hampstead, *Conversion or the New Birth* (1909), 62-63, explained that water baptism told of a grave in which the past was left behind, from which the person rises to newness of life.

12   Whitby, *Baptist Principles*, 60.

13   P. Beasley-Murray, *Radical Believers: The Baptist way of being the church* (Didcot, 1992), 13.

14   *Reply of the Churches in Membership with the Baptist Union to the 'Appeal to all Christian People' issued by the Lambeth Conference of 1920*, in J.H. Rushbrooke (ed.), *The Faith of the Baptists* (n.d., [1926]), 88.

15   E.g. A.W. Argyle, 'The New Testament Doctrine of the Resurrection of Our Lord Jesus Christ', *ExpTim* 61.6 (March, 1950), 188, 'the victory must be appropriated by faith; that is, by self-surrender to, and self-identification with, the Lord Jesus Christ, expressed and symbolized in baptism.'

salvation, therefore, among other things, no baptism. W.Y. Fullerton stated:

> We are baptized to proclaim that God intervenes in the affairs of men: to set forth the fact of history that Christ died for us and rose again; to assure ourselves that if the God who created us came once in the flesh to our rescue, bearing our sin and reinforcing our humanity, we may expect to receive His grace again and again. Baptism proclaims this fact in symbol. It tells us that God is no passive spectator of the human drama.[16]

In baptism the believer acts out the gospel experiences of Jesus Christ, linked by faith with Christ, thus signifying salvation from sin and the promise of new life.[17]

Immersion, therefore, is understood to represent and symbolize the religious significance and values of baptism in a way that affusion or sprinkling cannot. The BU's *Report of the Special Committee* (1937), representing the major views within the denomination, unanimously declared, 'We are all agreed that baptism is incumbent upon every believer and that the proper mode of baptism is immersion and that no other mode so plainly proclaims the full message of the Gospel of the grace of God.'[18]

---

16 W.Y. Fullerton, 'The Meaning of Baptism', *BT* August 16, 1928, 592. See also H.H. Rowley, 'The Christian Sacraments', in H.H. Rowley, *The Unity of the Bible* (1953), 172-73, 'Baptism is a symbol, and it is the constant teaching of the whole Bible that the symbol has no meaning without that which it symbolizes. As a mere external act it is as dead as the sacrifices which the prophets condemned... The religious ritual that is valid...is that which is charged with meaning in the moment of its performance... The robbing of baptism of its Biblical significance leads to the creation of something else to take its place, something which is not called baptism, but to which the real meaning of New Testament baptism has to be transferred. The symbol is of less importance than that which it symbolizes. It is of importance that Baptists no less than others should remember this. What matters most is not that a man has been voluntarily immersed, any more than that he has been baptized in infancy, but that he had truly died with Christ and been raised again to newness of life in Him... The symbol is worthless without that which it symbolizes. It must be the organ of the soul's approach in faith and surrender to God before it can become the organ of God's approach in power to him.'

17 West, *Baptist Principles*, 27. See also 'The Baptist Doctrine of the Church', 445.

18 *Report of the Special Committee Appointed by the Council on the Question of Union between Baptists, Congregationalists and Presbyterians* (n.d., [1937]), 7. See also A.C. Underwood, 'Conversion and Baptism', in Rushbrooke (ed.), *Faith of the Baptists*, 32, 'the New Testament mode of administering baptism by immersion helps to make it a means of grace as nothing else can, for immersion gives us in perfect symbolism the core of the evangelical faith—death unto sin and resurrection to a new life in Christ.'

The Subjects of Baptism

On the matter of who should be baptized Baptists speak with one voice: baptism is for believers only.[19] For Baptists, baptism is the logical consequence of their belief in the believers' church: 'Because we hold the Church to be a community of Christian believers, the ordinance of baptism is adminstered among us to those only who make a personal confession of repentance and faith.'[20] Henry Cook similarly expressed this priority of ecclesiology, explaining 'that here our name does us a real injustice' for it suggests that 'our main contention in this matter is the ordinance, whereas in fact our chief point of concern is the nature of the Church. Our fundamental position is that the ordinances of the Church are intended only for members of the Church.'[21]

As the New Testament rite is for believers only,[22] personal repentance towards God and faith in Christ are the prerequisites for baptism.[23] For these reasons Baptists have always been both quick and adamant in distinguishing *adult* from *believers'* baptism.[24] Alfred Phillips wrote, 'for

---

19   Baptists have variously written and spoken about 'believer's baptism' and 'believers' baptism'. By these phrases they have meant the same thing, though obviously one is singular the other plural. This study has generally followed the form of expression used by the writer under discussion at any particular moment. However, several writers have been conscious of the difference. H. Cook, *Why Baptize Believers Only?* (1952), 5, maintained that, 'For them [Baptists] baptism is believer's baptism and the word is believer's, not believers'. There is no such thing as baptism in the mass. Baptism is an individual thing, and it rests on personal acceptance of the gospel. Baptism comes after and not before the declaration of allegiance to Christ, and as such it is a *sacramentum*, literally the oath of allegiance...' R.L. Child, *A Conversation About Baptism* (1963), 31, included as a footnote (n.2), 'Some writers use the form "believer's baptism"; others prefer "believers' baptism". It seems simplest to omit the apostrophe altogether, as is done in other cases of a similar kind. (E.g. "Trades Council", "Commons debate".)' This procedure can be seen in the title of the volume F.C. Bryan (ed.), *Concerning Believers Baptism* (1943).

20   E.g. *Reply*, 88.

21   H. Cook, *The Why of Our Faith* (1924), 81.

22   G.R. Beasley-Murray, *Baptism in the New Testament* (1962), 274, 'It goes without saying that this theology of faith and baptism, which is found throughout the New Testament, has been constructed by the Apostolic writers on the presupposition that baptism is administered to converts.' Similarly, R.E.O. White, *Invitation to Baptism: A Manual for Inquirers* (1962), 12, 'It must be remembered throughout our studies that what is here said about baptism is true only of the baptism of those who know Christ, believe in Him, accept Him as their Saviour and their Lord, and are resolved to follow Him throughout their lives.'

23   R.L. Child, 'The Ministry and the Sacraments', *BQ* 9.3 (July, 1938), 136.

24   J.E. Roberts, *Christian Baptism, Its Significance and Its Subjects* (n.d., [1905]), 34; and 'Do We Teach Adult Baptism?', *BT* March 10, 1916, 157; H. Townsend,

while we refuse to baptise any who cannot believe, yet we are always willing to baptise those disciples, be they old or young, who are prepared to make a profession of faith in Jesus Christ.'[25] Robinson argued that of the subjects and the mode, it is the former which is the more important, and the very fact that Baptists baptize believers and not adults has a 'very important bearing on the constitution of the Church into which such believers enter by their faith.'[26] What distinguishes the Baptists from Paedobaptists is not the amount of water used in baptism but the subjects of the rite, and they are convinced that this position is no trivial matter, but a question of principle.[27]

There are a number of consequences which derive from the baptism of believers.

Baptists and Infant Baptism

The belief that believers are the rightful subjects of baptism has led Baptists to reject infant baptism, and in this they have adopted broadly two lines of argument—the historical and the biblical-theological—though more often than not a combination of the two has been used.

'The Free Churches and Ourselves', *Frat.* 58 (September, 1945), 4; Child, *Conversation*, 31-32; P. Beasley-Murray, *Radical Believers*, 9.

25 Phillips, *What Baptists Stand For*, 38. Robinson, *Baptist Principles*, 12, wrote, '*The baptism of the New Testament is the immersion of intelligent persons, as the expressive accompaniment of their entrance into a new life of moral and spiritual relationship to God in Christ*', italics his.

26 H.W. Robinson, *The Life and Faith of the Baptists* (1927), 80. Cf. E.C. Pike, *Some Unique Aspects of the Baptist Position* (n.d., [1901]), 54-55, for the similar view that infant baptism made the distinction between 'a converted church and an unconverted world' difficult. Likewise, the *Reply*, 88, stated, 'In our judgment the baptism of infants incapable of offering a personal confession of faith subverts the conception of the Church as the fellowship of believers.'

27 So W.H. Rowling of Hamsterley, 'The Paedobaptist Position in Relation to Baptist Principles and Practices', *BT&F* March 8, 1901. This is also reflected by the 5 books written by Baptists with *Baptist Principles* in the title—C. Williams, F.F. Whitby, W.T. Whitley, H.W. Robinson and W.M.S. West, see bibliography for dates and details. A. Gilmore, *Baptism and Christian Unity* (1966), 63-64, rightly notes that Anglicanism, too, believes in adult baptism, but it is for those who have not been infant baptized, and he believes that this needs to be distinguished from the Baptist practice of believers' baptism, and he proceeds: 'what we...really mean to express by believers' baptism is not the baptism of believers but the making of believers by baptism. Baptism is not to be regarded as an appendage to a man's becoming a disciple; it is rather a focal point of the initiation experience, which finds its culmination in communion and admission to membership.' However, he notes that Baptists have tended to make baptism an appendage, separating faith and baptism, spirit and water, in Christian initiation.

The most detailed historical repudiation of infant baptism by a Baptist was made by T. Vincent Tymms, former Principal of Rawdon College, who located the beginning of the practice and doctrine chiefly in the middle of the third century, but that it did not come to prominence until after Augustine in the fifth century,[28] a chronology which has been followed, with only minor variations, by most Baptists.[29]

As scripture contains no specific reference to infant baptism the strongest arguments against it, according to Baptists, are biblical. As the 1937 *Report* succinctly declared:

> Our conviction is that so far as the New Testament is made our authority for faith and practice, Baptists in their practice of Believers' Baptism have firm ground on which to stand and that Paedobaptists must go outside its words to discover any basis for their doctrine. We know that to multitudes of our fellow Christians the practice of Infant Baptism stands for a great deal which is precious to them, but we believe that it means something different from the New Testament rite and that we are in line with the New Testament. The baptism of believers as opposed to the baptism of children is thus justified, as we believe, by the evidence of the New Testament and the practice of the rite in the primitive Church, and to most Baptists that will appear to be a sufficient answer to any critic.[30]

Underwood stated that it was of the utmost importance to make plain the precise grounds of the Baptist refusal to baptize infants and offered five reasons: there is no trace of it in the New Testament; it perpetuates the outworn dogma that infants dying unbaptized are in peril of the guilt

---

28   T.V. Tymms, *The Evolution of Infant Baptism and Related Ideas* (n.d., [1912]), 220, 306-07.

29   See, e.g., H.G. Wood, '"BAPTISM" (Later Christian)', in J. Hastings (ed.), *Encyclopaedia of Religion and Ethics II* (Edinburgh, 1909), 395; W.T. Whitley, *The Witness of History to Baptist Principles* (2nd edn, 1914), 83-88; Robinson, *Baptist Principles*, 31-40; A.W. Argyle, 'Baptism in the Early Christian Centuries', in Gilmore (ed.), *Christian Baptism*, 192-218; Beasley-Murray, *Baptism in the New Testament*, 306.

30   *Report of the Special Committee*, 12-13. Similarly, K.W. Clements, 'A Baptist View', in R.E. Davies (ed.), *The Truth in Tradition: A Free Church Symposium* (1992), 6, 'Their rejection of infant baptism in favour of believers' baptism is based on their reading of the New Testament. In rejecting infant baptism they reject one of the most venerable and universal traditions of Christianity, and thereby they invest even more in the authority of scipture, as against tradition, than do others of the Protestant and Free Church family.' It is of the utmost importance to note this place scripture has for Baptist faith and practice. The first Declaration of Principle states, 'That our Lord and Saviour Jesus Christ, God manifest in the flesh, is the sole and absolute authority in all matters pertaining to faith and practice, *as revealed in the Holy Scriptures*, and that each Church has liberty, under the guidance of the Holy Spirit, to interpret and administer His Laws', *BUD* 1996-97, 7, italics added. See, among the vast literature on this, Robinson, *Baptist Principles*, 22-24; H. Cook, *What Baptists Stand For* (5th edn, 1964), 17-31; West, *Baptist Principles*, 5-11; Kidd (ed.), *Something to Declare*, 28-36.

involved in original sin; it fosters the notion that a sacrament could have meaning and effect apart from the faith of the recipient; it obscures the fact that salvation is by faith alone; and obscures the doctrine of the church as a converted membership.[31] J.E. Roberts rejected infant baptism by reference to the significance of baptism. He brushed aside arguments that infant baptism emphasizes the prevenient grace of God, by arguing that this was not the truth baptism was designed to set forth.[32] Rather, baptism was ordained for the admission of the baptized into the visible church, that it is a seal of regeneration, of remission of sins and for the baptized to give themself to God in newness of life, and this is the believer's dedication of themself, not something done for them.[33] Whether, then, by detailed exegesis of the biblical texts[34] or by a more dialogical and interactive approach with specific paedobaptist texts and/or authors,[35] or with paedobaptist literature in general,[36] Baptists have effectively accused Paedobaptists of faulty exegesis and erroneous theology.[37] Leonard Champion, for instance, declared that Baptists retain believer's baptism 'primarily and because it expresses the nature of divine grace and human faith, and we believe these are distorted in infant baptism; we are confirmed in this view by the testimony of Scripture to the place of believer's baptism in the life of the apostolic church.'[38]

---

31   A.C. Underwood, 'Views of Modern Churches (g) Baptists (2)', in R. Dunkerley (ed.), *The Ministry and the Sacraments* (1937), 224-25.

32   J.E. Roberts, '"Thoughts on Infant Baptism"', *The Expositor*, 8th Series, Vol. 13 (1917), 29.

33   Roberts, 'Thoughts', 443.

34   The most comprehensive and important of which are Gilmore (ed.), *Christian Baptism*; White, *Biblical Doctrine of Initiation*; and Beasley-Murray, *Baptism in the New Testament*.

35   E.g. J. Brown of Hove, *Baptism: True or False* (1905); B.I. Greenwood of Shoreham, *Two Letters on Infant Baptism* (1920); P.W. Evans, 'Can Infant Baptism Be Justified?', *EvQ* 15 (1943), 292-97 (a reply to D.M. Baillie, 'The Justification of Infant Baptism', *EvQ* 15 (1943), 21-32); E.A. Payne, 'Professor T.W. Manson on Baptism', *SJT* 3 (March, 1950), 50-56 (see Manson's 'Baptism in the Church', *SJT* 2.4 (December, 1949), 391-403); A. Morgan Derham of Rickmansworth, 'But Why Baptise Believers?', *The English Churchman and St. James's Chronicle* June 5, 1959, 4 (a reply to D. Winter, 'But Why Baptise Babies?', *The English Churchman and St. James's Chronicle* May 22, 1959, 4); G.R. Beasley-Murray, 'The Case Against Infant Baptism', *Christianity Today* 9.1 (October 9, 1964), 11-14 (see G.W. Bromiley, 'The Case for Infant Baptism', 7-11, in the same edition).

36   See Roberts' *Christian Baptism*, and the collaborative Baptist–Churches of Christ *Infant Baptism To-day*, by P.W. Evans, H. Townsend and W. Robinson (1948).

37   For a combination of these arguments see the *Report of the Special Committee*, 8-13, 25-29.

38   L.G. Champion, 'The Baptist Doctrine of the Church in Relation to Scripture, Tradition and the Holy Spirit', *Foundations* 2.1 (January, 1959), 32.

Such has led many Baptists to view infant baptism as no baptism at all. James Mountain went so far as to declare that infant baptism was borrowed from paganism,[39] Child spoke of 'Our repugnance to Infant Baptism',[40] White described it as the major soteriological heresy because of its contradiction of the whole New Testament emphasis on repentance, hearing the gospel and faith as the prerequisite to salvation,[41] while others simply underlined that it was not apostolic practice.[42] In recent years, however, a more conciliatory and even open attitude has become more in evidence among more ecumenically-minded Baptists.[43]

The most celebrated rejection of infant baptism is that of George Beasley-Murray in 1962. After an eighty page discussion of the subject he concluded, 'It seems that a small amount of water is bestowed on a small infant with a very small result. And this, it is alleged, is *baptism!* Can it be wondered at that Baptists should be strengthened in their determination to strive for the retention of the fullness of baptism, ordained of the Lord and continued in the Apostolic Communities, and that they should continue to lift up their voices among the Churches to plead for a return to this baptism?'[44]

Baptist Anti-Sacerdotalism

Baptists have always had a strong antipathy towards sacerdotalism and this has led them to reject what they associated with it, sometimes referred to as sacramentalism, at other times to sacramentarianism,[45] but whichever of the two words is used the focus of attack is always the same.[46] When

---

39   J. Mountain, *My Baptism and What Led To It* (n.d., [1904]), 59.

40   Child, 'The Ministry and the Sacraments', 136.

41   R.E.O. White, 'New Baptismal Questions—II', *BT* August 24, 1961, 2.

42   E.g. Whitley, *Witness of History*, 87.

43   See chs. 8 and 9.

44   Beasley-Murray, *Baptism in the New Testament*, see 306-86, quote from pp.385-86.

45   Sacerdotalism is here understood as the priestly control of religion, an understanding associated by Baptists with the Catholic and Anglican traditions and which Baptists reject in favour of the doctrine of the priesthood of all believers. Sacramentalism/sacramentarianism is an understanding of religion as focused in sacramental acts which only the priests can perform, therefore precluding lay administration of the sacraments.

46   E.g. J.D. Freeman, 'The Lambeth Appeal', *Frat.* os 13.5 (March, 1922), 6, who drew attention to the 1920 Lambeth Appeal's 'manifest sacramentalism' and its 'undisguised sympathy with sacerdotalism'. Whitley, *Church, Ministry and Sacraments*, 244, discussed Heb. 8:3 and declared that 'Sacerdotalism and sacramentalism are twin errors.' Belief in one entails belief in the other—to destroy one means the other will be destroyed. On p.271 he contended that sacerdotalists appended the Bible to tradition. See also pp.276-81 and his *Witness of History*, 35-55, and *Missionary Achievement* (1908),

Baptists have contended for the non-sacramental character of the ordinances they have been arguing against any magical or superstitious interpretations of either baptism or the Lord's Supper. R.C. Lemin dismissed the sacramentarian teaching that a Christian was made in and by the sacraments, advocating in its place the Protestant belief that sacraments are a means of grace not a regenerating agency.[47] The rite of infant baptism lends itself to a mechanical and quasi-magical conception of faith and grace which Baptists have found repugnant to the gospel on the grounds that it perverts the evangelical message. Believer's baptism, on the other hand, stresses and preserves the personal meaning of both faith and grace.[48] D.R. Griffiths appealed to the Spirit's activity as the safeguard against any notions of magic in baptism: 'The persistent stress on the activity of the Holy Spirit...[is the] feature of the sacramental teaching in general which safeguards it from the materialistic and the magical.'[49]

The doctrine of infant baptism has been closely linked with the origin and growth of the sacerdotal system.[50] At the turn of the century Newton Marshall declared, 'We Baptists...may rejoice that we are free from all reproach in reference to the present revival of sacerdotalism', and alerted the denomination to the encroachment of sacerdotalism within the Anglican and Free Churches.[51] Any hints that baptism acts *ex opere*

---

cited by I. Sellars, 'W.T. Whitley: A Commemorative Essay', *BQ* 37.4 (October, 1997), 169 and n.40. However, in order to rediscover a truly biblical sacramentalism, H.W. Robinson argued that Baptists were anti-sacramentarian, and that 'sacrament' in the sense of the 'oath of allegiance' was acceptable to Baptists, *Baptist Principles*, 26 and 29n.

47   R.C. Lemin of Moseley, Birmingham, 'Protestantism and the Interpretation of the Sacraments', *Supplement to BT&F* October 10, 1913, III.

48   R.L. Child, 'The Baptist Contribution to the One Church', *BQ* 8.2 (April, 1936), 84-85. H.W. Robinson, 'Hebrew Sacrifice and Prophetic Symbolism', *JTS* 43 (January-April, 1942), 137-38, proposed that Rom. 6:3-5 could legitimately be regarded as a form of symbolic magic were it not for the fact that baptism was the act of a believer.

49   D.R. Griffiths, 'The Fourth Gospel and 1 John', in Gilmore (ed.), *Christian Baptism*, 170. Beasley-Murray, *Baptism in the New Testament*, 264-65, refers to Paul's teaching in 1 Cor. 10:1-5 as giving a clear warning against any magical-sacramental view of the sacraments.

50   Pike, *Some Unique Aspects*, 44. See also Tymms' *The Evolution of Infant Baptism*.

51   N.H. Marshall, 'Priestcraft and Baptism', *BT&F* November 14, 1902, 844. Its presence among the Church of England and Free Churches led Mountain, *My Baptism*, 2, to exclaim that the 'perversion of baptism...by sacerdotalists and ritualists is causing many evangelical Christians to depreciate these sacred ordinances, and, in some cases, even to reject them altogether.'

operato or as 'magic' have been strongly denounced[52] and sacerdotalism disclaimed as 'Papistical error'.[53]

It should be noted, however, that as the century has progressed Baptists
have tended to drop such intemperate tones, choosing instead to refer to
the faith of the believer as the guarantee against such superstitious
connotations. Child noted that in the New Testament baptism was the
outward sign of the candidate's own faith and this was the 'effective
safeguard against that tendency to superstition which clings persistently
about the rite of baptism.'[54]

Baptists and Baptismal Regeneration

As with the rejection of sacerdotalism, Baptist antipathy to baptismal
regeneration, though always present, was a particular feature of the first
half of the century. Baptists have always staunchly opposed this
doctrine,[55] maintaining that salvation is by grace through faith, not by a
rite of any kind. Regeneration, they believe, is the work of the Holy Spirit
and that baptism is the outward sign of this,[56] and that Paedobaptists have
confused the two.[57]

---

52   E.g. J. Clifford, 'The Baptist World Alliance: Its Origin and Character, Meaning
and Work', in *The Baptist World Alliance, Second Congress, Philadelphia, June 19-25,
1911* (Philadelphia, 1911), 64, 'We have to lift up our voice against the capital error of
Christendom, that source of immeasurable damage to the gospel and to souls, the magical
interpretation of baptism and the Lord's Supper, the treatment of the baptism of the babe
as obedience to the will of the Lord, as expressed in the New Testament and as a way of
salvation. We must stand aloof from it. We can have no part or lot in it. In a word, we
must be in a position to give a full, clear, unconfused witness to the cardinal principles of
our faith and life.'

53   Phillips, *What Baptists Stand For*, 29, adding that the Church of England was
'doing with eagerness the work of Rome.'

54   R.L. Child, 'The Practice of the Apostolic Church' in Bryan (ed.), *Concerning
Believers Baptism*, 17-18.

55   A.C. Underwood, 'Baptism and Regeneration', *BT* March 1, 1928, 144.

56   Robinson, *Baptist Principles*, 24, 'the Spirit is the agent in that regeneration
which is the Godward side of conversion...'. Marshall, *Conversion*, 82, stated that
according to 'New Testament usage Conversion and Regeneration are but two aspects of
the one experience—two ways of looking at one set of facts.' See also pp.80-107.
Underwood agreed with Marshall, see A.C. Underwood, *Conversion: Christian and Non-
Christian: A Comparative and Psychological Study* (1925), 112-13, who argued that
believers are not baptized in order to be regenerated, for their conversion is their
regeneration. Rather, they are baptized in order to be admitted into the rights and
privileges of God's society; their religious experience is deepened and heightened when
they undergo the rite in the proper frame of heart and mind.

57   E.g. Whitby, *Baptist Principles*, 136-37, also p.30. Several others sketched the
rise of the doctrine of baptismal regeneration and stated their belief that infant baptism

Wheeler Robinson contrasted the regeneration by the Holy Spirit with the theory of baptismal regeneration:

> There are two distinct ways of representing the operation of the Spirit of God in regard to baptism. We may think of the external act, and the material means, as the prescribed channel of the work of the Spirit, and then the result is what is commonly known as sacramentarianism. Or we may think of the internal conditions, the personal faith and conversion emphasized in Believer's Baptism, and see in them the true realm of the Spirit's activity... In fact, when we speak of Believer's Baptism, we mean that baptism in the Spirit of God, of which water baptism is the expression.[58]

The depth of Baptist feeling on this subject can be illustrated by the language used to denounce it: Phillips declared that 'Against baptismal regeneration we show the necessity for the new birth'; J.D. Freeman repudiated it as 'subversive of the truth of the Gospel'; and Underwood described it as 'a doctrine abhorred by all true Baptists.'[59] To correct it, J.H. Rushbrooke contended that when the Baptist doctrine of baptism is fully upheld—setting forth the supremacy of faith, its nature and implications, involving an immediate relationship with God in Christ—it cuts at the root of any magical view of the ordinance. 'Baptismal regeneration is to us a doctrine as perilous as it is unscriptural. The paradox of our denominational life is that by means of a rite we offer decisive testimony against ritualism.'[60]

The Theology of Baptism

Ecclesiology and Baptism

Wheeler Robinson declared:

> The Baptist stands or falls by his conception of what the Church is; his plea for believer's baptism becomes a mere archaeological idiosyncrasy, if it be not the expression of the fundamental constitution of the Church. We become members of the living body of Christ by being consciously and voluntarily baptized in the

---

was actually the logical result of it. See Tymms, *Evolution of Infant Baptism*, 17; Wood, 'BAPTISM', 395-97.

58   Robinson, *Baptist Principles*, 24-25. Marshall, *Conversion*, 61-62, believed that advocates of baptismal regeneration had confused 'the symbol with the reality, the material testimony with the spiritual experience'. See also H.J. Wicks, 'Baptismal Regeneration', *BQ* 5.1 (January, 1930), 20-22.

59   Phillips, *What Baptists Stand For*, 31; Freeman, 'Lambeth Appeal', 7; Underwood, 'What Mean Ye By This Service?', in Bryan (ed.), *Concerning Believers Baptism*, 62.

60   Rushbrooke, 'Protestant of the Protestants', in Rushbrooke (ed.), *Faith of the Baptists*, 80-81.

Spirit of Christ—a baptism witnessed by the evidence of moral purpose and character as the fruit of the Spirit.[61]

Because believer's baptism emphasizes the necessity of conversion and forms a direct link between the spiritual authority of the New Testament and the Lord it reveals,[62] it carries with it the unmistakable definition of the church, for which it is the door. Henry Cook wrote, 'It is from this point that our Baptist emphasis takes its rise, not from Baptism. Our whole contention is that Baptism is misunderstood and its meaning completely perverted when the nature of the Church is obscured or ignored; and, on the other hand, only when the nature of the Church is emphasised and understood does Baptism get its rightful place.'[63] Believer's baptism, then, provides a constant and much-needed testimony to the spiritual basis of the church, which is neither a social nor a political but a religious community,[64] grounded in a spiritual relationship with Christ and answerable finally only to him.[65]

Baptism as a Profession of Faith

As the only legitimate recipients of baptism are believers, Baptists have always stressed baptism as a profession of faith. For this reason, Robinson argued that 'to equate the practice with the principle would be to stultify the principle itself, which emphasizes the *inner essential of faith*, and declares that without it all external ceremonies are valueless.'[66] George Beasley-Murray expressed the connection carefully: 'the faith that responds to the good news turns to the risen Lord and reaches its climax in baptism.'[67] The understanding of baptism as a profession of faith has

---

6 1   Robinson, *Life and Faith*, 84.

6 2   Robinson, *Baptist Principles*, 17-24.

6 3   Cook, *Why of Our Faith*, 82-83, see also p.92.

64   D. Tidball, 'Social Setting of Missionary Churches', in G.F. Hawthorne, R.P. Martin and D.G. Reid (eds.), *Dictionary of Paul and His Letters* (Leicester, 1993), 885, 'Baptism is a ritual which symolizes and effects a dramatic break with the candidates' former way of life and their incorporation into the church.'

65   So Child, 'The Baptist Contribution', 85. In this Baptists are being true to their origins as inheritors of a separatist ecclesiology which they had gained from the Puritan conception of the church, though they developed it further than either the Puritans or Separatists. So Robinson, *Life and Faith*, 83, for whom believer's baptism was 'the only type of baptism which is properly consistent with the logic of "Separatism" and the whole conception of a separated Church of believers.' Similarly, Underwood, 'Conversion and Baptism', 26.

66   Robinson, *Baptist Principles*, 15, italics added. See also p.27 where he said that 'form can have no spiritual value apart from the attitude of the baptised to it.'

67   G.R. Beasley-Murray, 'Faith in the New Testament: A Baptist Perspective', *ABQ* 1.2 (December, 1982), 140.

been the most widely and firmly held Baptist view of baptism, a fact borne out by the sheer volume of references made to this in the literature.

The issue that separates Baptists from Paedobaptists is precisely this: the nature of the faith required in and for baptism. For the former it is the faith of the individual, for the latter the vicarious faith of the church or godparents suffices. Both parties have had to tackle for themselves the nature of the relation between faith and baptism, but Baptists have repudiated the notion of vicarious faith for salvation.[68] Baptists refer to baptism in a variety of ways, each of which expresses essentially the same truth that baptism is the believer's 'profession of faith'[69] and this language clearly reveals the Baptist understanding and emphasis on the necessity of conversion.[70]

Though Baptists in the seventeenth century declared their beliefs and principles in confessions of faith, over time they became wary of and reluctant to produce formal confessions.[71] Though new Associations/ Connexions in the late eighteenth and early nineteenth centuries were not against producing such articles, they were more covenantal. In the twentieth century there has been a significant move within the denomination to see baptism not only as an 'acted parable', but as an 'acted creed'. Though the origin of these phrases is unknown, the first mention seems to be a statement by Wheeler Robinson in 1904,[72] later popularized in his *Baptist Principles*: 'baptism by immersion takes the place

---

68   Whitley, *Church, Ministry and Sacraments*, 35-36 and 91-92.

69   'Baptist Doctrine of the Church', 446. This is expressed by a series of virtually synonymous expressions, including 'profession of discipleship', see C. Williams, *The Principles and Practices of the Baptists* (2nd edn, 1903), 20; 'profession of personal repentance and personal faith', see H. Cook, *The Theology of Evangelism* (1951), 111; 'confession of faith', see Rushbrooke, 'Protestant of the Protestants', 8; or the 'witness' to their faith, see Whitby, *Baptist Principles*, 48, 72, 97; their 'expression' of faith, see Marshall, *Conversion*, 64-65; a 'profession of loyalty to Christ', see H.W. Robinson, 'The Faith of the Baptists', *ExpTim* 28 (1927), 455; and a 'public' profession or confession of faith, see E.A. Payne and S.F. Winward, *Orders and Prayers for Church Worship: A Manual for Ministers* (1960), 132.

70   So 'Our Denominational Witness', *BT* January 25, 1940, 54, 'The Baptists have from the first stood for the fact of Spiritual regeneration, through faith in the Lord Jesus Christ. For this reason they have emphasised believers' baptism as a personal confession of an experience of conversion...'

71   See W.J. McGlothlin, *Baptist Confessions of Faith* (1910), and W.L. Lumpkin, *Baptist Confessions of Faith* (Valley Forge, 2nd edn, 1969).

72   H.W. Robinson, 'The Confessional Value of Baptism', *BT&F* February 12, 1904, 121. It would appear that he came to this position through his study of the Hebrew concept of 'prophetic symbolism', as reflected in his later article 'Prophetic Symbolism', in D.C. Simpson (ed.), *Old Testament Essays* (1927), 14-16, and his book *The Christian Experience of the Holy Spirit* (1928), 192-95.

amongst Baptists of a formal creed.'[73] He understood both sacraments as acted parables of the Lord's death, burial and resurrection, 'the cardinal verities of evangelical faith and the historical basis of Christianity.'[74] It was by these expressive acts that the believer identifies themself with Christ, professing the simplest form of confession of faith, 'Jesus is Lord' (Romans 10:9, cf. 1 Corinthians 12:3), this later being expanded into the trinitarian baptismal formula of Matthew 28:19.[75] One of those who followed this lead, Gilbert Laws, declared, 'When a man goes down into the solemn waters to be buried with Christ by baptism, and thence is raised in the power of a new life, *what a tremendous creed he has professed!*'[76] Another, Irene Morris, announced, '[Baptism] is an acted parable, and preaches truths hard to express in words'.[77]

Baptism and Death, Burial and Resurrection

More important than symbolizing the repentance and faith of the believer, baptism even more fundamentally symbolizes the prevenient grace of God in the death, burial and resurrection of Christ. Though logically and theologically this symbolism of grace precedes its symbolism of faith, Baptists have rarely expressed matters in this way, and the profession of faith in the death, burial and resurrection of Christ would be a more accurate description of the way the majority of Baptists have spoken of baptism.

---

73   This was first printed in C.E. Shipley (ed.), *The Baptists of Yorkshire: Being the Centenary Memorial Volume of the Yorkshire Baptist Association* (1912), 20, and *Baptist Principles*, 28.

74   Robinson, *Life and Faith*, 90, cf. also on the Lord's Supper pp.116-17.

75   Robinson, *Life and Faith*, 90.

76   G. Laws, 'Vital Forces of the Baptist Movement', in Rushbrooke (ed.), *Faith of the Baptists*, 14, italics added. Robinson, 'The Place of Baptism', 216, expressed this more fully: 'We, less than any other part of the Christian Church, are dependent on creeds, because we have maintained that personal profession of faith in baptism from which these creeds themselves have sprung. Because of that personal profession of loyalty, made in baptism itself more clearly and forcibly by us than any other part of the Church, we can afford to make less of any form of words, however true. One of the great reasons for maintaining the method of immersion is its symbolic expression of the historical truths on which our faith rests—the death and resurrection of our Lord Jesus Christ—and of that personal union with Him which true faith implies. That is our creed, expressed in a manner far better than mere words.'

77   I. Morris of Queen's Road, Coventry, *Thoughts on Church Membership* (1919), 22. Among others, this idea is to be found in 'The Baptist Doctrine of the Church', 445; and West, *Baptist Principles*, 31.

The most important baptismal text to Baptists is Romans 6:1-11, and what Paul says there he succinctly reiterates in Colossians 2:12.[78] The relationship between the believer in baptism and these events, however, has been differently interpreted by Baptists. Some have been content merely to state that baptism witnesses to Jesus' death, burial and resurrection, and signifies the believer's death to sin and resurrection to a new life,[79] but others have developed this theology further, believing that, by faith, the believer actually participates in these events.[80] These issues were summarized by Donald Guthrie:

> It is in the passage in Romans 6:1-4 that the apostle sets out most fully his thoughts about baptism. It is essentially connected with death and resurrection, and not with cleansing. Baptism signifies burial with Christ in his death (Rom. 6:4). But baptism also means new life: a sharing of Christ's risen life. It exhibits the transition which has occurred from death to life. Paul goes on to expound the significance of the change, particularly in relation to the death of the old self. He clearly saw the theological meaning in the baptismal act. But the crucial question arises over the time when the radical change occurred. Did it happen at baptism? Or did it happen before baptism, in which case the ordinance has the function of a public demonstration of what had already happened? The issue has been hotly debated.[81]

While Guthrie primarily had in view the academic/theological debate over baptism, his comments also reflect the divided state over the baptized believer and their relation to and participation in the death, burial and resurrection of Christ. The assessment of which position is the more representative position among Baptists is difficult to make, though it is

---

78   Beasley-Murray, *Baptism in the New Testament*, 152, stated, 'Col 2.11ff provides a significant exposition of the theology we [believe] to lie at the back of Romans 6.' Beasley-Murray provided a detailed discussion of Col. 2 in his 'The Second Chapter of Colossians', *RevExp* 70 (1973), 469-79.

79   See, e.g., West, *Baptist Principles*, 27, who noted that repentance and faith were linked with baptism, and this fact demanded for its symbolism 'the immersion of the believer, signifying the dying with Christ, i.e. the identification with the Cross of Christ, and the coming up out of the water, signifying the rising with Christ, i.e. the identification with the resurrection of Christ. In baptism, therefore, the believer acts out the Gospel experiences of Jesus Christ, linked by faith with Christ, and thus signifying salvation from sin and the promise of new life.' See also W.W. Sidey's hymn (1856–1909), *BCH* 502 vv1 and 2: 'Buried with Christ! Our glad hearts say,/Come see the place where once He lay/Risen with Him! Allured by Love,/Henceforth we seek the things above.'

80   E.g. H.W. Robinson, *The Christian Doctrine of Man* (Edinburgh, 2nd edn, 1913), 124-25, commented that the Romans passage implied not merely a symbolic but a realistic union with Christ; Beasley-Murray, *Baptism in the New Testament*, 126-46; White, *Biblical Doctrine*, 215-16.

81   D. Guthrie, *New Testament Theology* (Leicester, 1981), 756.

probably the least developed, as less sophistication is often the mark of a popular and widespread belief.[82] Despite their differences, Baptists have agreed that however else they appropriate the benefits of or participate in the death, burial and resurrection of Christ, faith is required from the believer,[83] a fact made explicit in Colossians 2:12 and Galatians 3:26-27, on which Beasley-Murray commented that, as in the one so in the other 'faith is integrated into the baptismal event. *In baptism* the baptized is raised *through faith.*'[84]

Baptism and Union with Christ

The same Romans 6 passage says (v.5) that if the believer is 'united with [Christ]...in his death, we will certainly...be united with him in his resurrection' (NIV), a union which is clearly relational, entered into through faith and baptism.[85] 'For Paul', Robinson argued, baptism 'meant an experimental union with Christ in His redeeming acts, deeper in meaning than words can express...' Citing Romans 6:4, he pressed, 'If it is asked just what the outer act of baptism contributed to these inner experiences of forgiveness, regeneration, faith and fellowship with Christ, we must reply that *the New Testament never considers them apart* in this detached manner. The baptism of which it speaks is no formal act, but a genuine experience; on the other hand, the New Testament knows nothing of unbaptized believers.'[86]

---

82   This conclusion, it is believed, is borne out by the rest of the present study. The evidence assessed throughout this book suggests that grass-roots Baptists (the majority within the denomination) have little interest in or knowledge of the more technical, theological discussions of baptism, and that the latter have not made great inroads into the Baptist constituency at either the level of theology or practice.

83   E.g. J.B. Middlebrook, 'The Command of Christ', in A.T. Ohrn (ed.), *Golden Jubilee Congress (Ninth World Congress), London, England, 16th–22nd July, 1955* (1955), 253; Payne and Winward, *Orders and Prayers*, 131, 'In baptism we are united with Christ through faith, dying with him unto sin and rising with him unto newness of life'; White, *Invitation to Baptism*, 44-50.

84   Beasley-Murray, *Baptism in the New Testament*, 154, italics his. See also his 'Baptism' and 'Dying and Rising with Christ', in Hawthorne, Martin and Reid (eds.), *Dictionary of Paul*, 60-65 and 218-22, and, in the same volume, L.J. Kreitzer, 'Resurrection', 805-12.

85   S.F. Winward, *The New Testament Teaching on Baptism: In the form of Daily Bible Readings for the Instruction of Candidates for Baptism* (1952), 46-47. So too A.B. Crabtree, *The Restored Relationship: A Study in Justification and Reconciliation* (1963), 65.

86   Robinson, *Baptist Principles*, 14-15. That the New Testament 'knows nothing of unbaptized believers' is a key, though seldom expressed, tenet of Baptist belief. The relational aspect of this union was underscored by J. Lewis, 'Baptised into Jesus Christ', *Frat.* os 19.3 (December, 1927),16, 'the form expresses most appropriately, not a formal

Aware of the separation between conversion and baptism which had taken place in so much Baptist baptismal practice, Underwood believed that at their conversion believers' experience of union with Christ began, but at their baptism that experience was so deepened and enhanced that, with Paul, they could say that baptism united them to Christ and enabled them to 'put on Christ'. Baptism increased joy, enhanced faith, stimulated courage, deepened the sense of sins forgiven, and quickened the sense of union with and responsibility to the Lord Jesus Christ. However, an infant who was baptized was deprived of these sacramental experiences 'which have always accompanied the baptism of believers in Christ.'[87]

Child developed this union beyond the individual when he observed that 'St. Paul speaks of baptism as uniting believers directly with Jesus Christ. They are baptized into Jesus Christ and buried with Him.' He continued: 'the Christian life is essentially a spiritual union of the believer with Jesus Christ' and spoke of baptism as 'first of all an act of uniting the believer with Christ.' Only then was baptism incorporation 'by faith into a spiritual society, the Church, of which Jesus Christ is the Head, and His followers are the living members', which meant that 'the inward and the outward are integrally related, and spiritual union with Christ is perfected through the growing fellowship of His people with one another in mutual love, and through the service which they unitedly render to their one Lord.'[88] This union with the church is often described in terms of initiation or incorporation into Christ, hence its proper place at the beginning of the Christian life.[89]

Baptism: Not Essential for Salvation

Baptists have spoken with one voice when they contend that baptism is not essential for salvation. This has, however, always proved difficult for them, for they have tried to walk the tightrope between rejecting it as

---

but a personal and individual union with a person, a union which in the very nature of the case, requires intelligent faith and entire surrender...' See also, e.g. *Report of the Special Committee*, 5-6.

87   Underwood, 'Views of Modern Churches', 228.

88   R.L. Child, 'The Significance of Baptism to St. Paul. Union with Christ in Baptism', in Bryan (ed.), *Concerning Believers Baptism*, 23-25.

89   Whitby, *Baptist Principles*, 45. See also Whitley, *Church, Ministry and Sacraments*, 193; Underwood, *Conversion*, 36 and 112, and his, 'Conversion and Baptism', 35; Robinson, 'The Place of Baptism in Baptist Churches of To-day', *BQ* 1.5 (January, 1923), 209. Elsewhere, Robinson, *Life and Faith*, 79, remarked that believer's baptism seemed to have been an invariable accompaniment, if not definite sign, of entry into the Christian community. This is clearly the logic of closed membership churches.

essential to salvation while maintaining that it is important for discipleship. The 'Preface' of *Concerning Believers Baptism* stated,

> We do not want to magnify the importance of baptism or to give it a position not warranted by New Testament teaching and practice. We do not put it on a level with saving faith or hold that it is necessary for salvation. *But, on the other hand*, we do find that there are a surprising number of references to baptism in the New Testament. It was, as far as the records show, an observance to which a believer invariably submitted when he confessed his faith and was received into the Church.[90]

White wrote, 'To say that in the kerygma baptism was essential to salvation would be to go beyond the evidence, yet baptism is neither optional nor unimportant. It is the one form of response specified in the kerygma...'[91] Faith, not baptism, is what is essential for salvation.[92]

Baptism and Morality

Wheeler Robinson wrote: 'When [Jesus] came forward, He was first baptized with John's baptism, and proclaimed John's message, as though to remind us that, whatever else Christian baptism may mean, it means something profoundly moral.'[93] Underwood adopted the phrase 'ethical sacramentalism', by which he meant that grace is conferred in the sacraments but that it is ineffective apart from the faith of the recipient.[94] One of George Beasley-Murray's conclusions is that 'Our consideration of the New Testament evidence has frequently led us to the recognition that baptism in the Apostolic Church is a moral-religious act.'[95] At an

---

90   'Preface', in Bryan (ed.), *Concerning Believers Baptism*, 6, italics added. See also W.G. Channon, *Much Water and Believers Only* (1950), 45-46; G.E. Shackleton, 'Conversion and Discipleship: 13—The Place of Baptism', *BT* May 17, 1962, 11; S.I. Buse, 'Baptism in the Acts of the Apostles', in Gilmore (ed.), *Christian Baptism*, 116, and, in the same volume, also R.E.O. White, 'Baptism in the Synoptic Gospels', 98; and A.W. Argyle, 'The Early Christian Centuries', 214.

91   White, *Biblical Doctrine of Initiation*, 139.

92   C.J. Pike, *Under Christ's Control: Studies in Discipleship and Church Membership* (1950), 12-13.

93   Robinson, *Baptist Principles*, 13. On pp.13-15, Robinson progressed from baptism as a moral act to a connection with it implying a cleansing from sin, this being the first of four things New Testament baptism means: cleansing from sin; association with the gift of the Spirit; its administration to believers; and experimental union with Christ. Child, 'The Significance of Baptism to St. Paul', 25-26, believed that rightly understood baptism 'is ethical, through and through.'

94   Underwood, 'Baptism and Regeneration', *BT* March 1, 1928, 144, and also 'Views of Modern Churches', 225.

95   Beasley-Murray, *Baptism in the New Testament*, 284. See also the similar conclusion of White, *Biblical Doctrine of Initiation*, 271. White's views were further

early date the baptismal confession of the kerygma was supplemented by an acceptance of certain basic ethical obligations and that the use of the aorist tense in Romans 6:17 supported the view that baptism provided the occasion for the receiving of such teaching.[96] 'From whatever angle we view it, baptism signifies the end of the life that cannot please God and the beginning of a life in Him and for His glory. In baptism we *put on* Christ; the baptismal life *is* Christ; in so far as it is truly lived it will be Christ-like', concluding that, 'In his baptism, thus, the Christian's participation in the redemption of Christ becomes the means of deliverance, the pattern of living, the fount of renewal, and the anticipation of glory.'[97] Again Romans 6[98] is a key passage for Baptists, Beasley-Murray noting that Paul's exposition of baptism here is incidental to the process of his argument which is ethical.[99] Child put it succinctly: 'This is a moral act, or it is nothing',[100] and such a position led Robinson to the view that the first and foremost contribution Baptists could make to the church catholic, like that of the Hebrew prophets, was the essential and primary place of the moral within the religious. 'The moral change wrought within conversion, the personal repentance and faith which are the religious features of that conversion, the open confession which commits the life to a new purpose—these great truths

---

expounded in his 2 volume study of ethics, *The Changing Continuity of Christian Ethics Volume 1: Biblical Ethics* (Exeter, 1979), and *The Changing Continuity of Christian Ethics Volume 2: The Insights of History* (Exeter, 1981), and also in his earlier *Into the Same Image* (1957), 31-51.

96   Beasley-Murray, *Baptism in the New Testament*, 285, this conclusion, he believed, was probably supported by 1 Tim. 6:12-14 and 1 Peter.

97   Beasley-Murray, *Baptism in the New Testament*, 286-87, italics his, and 290 respectively. In *Baptism Today and Tomorrow* (1966), Beasley-Murray, developed this position, pp.70-79. See also R.E.O. White, *Meet St Paul* (Cambridge, 1989), 104-05.

98   Other passages which are frequently appealed to are discussed by Beasley-Murray, *Baptism in the New Testament*, 284-90.

99   Beasley-Murray, 'Baptism in the Epistles of Paul', in Gilmore (ed.), *Christian Baptism*, 132-33. See also his 'Baptism in the New Testament', *Foundations* 3 (January 1960), 25-27. Discussing 1 Peter, S.I. Buse, 'Other New Testament Writings', in Gilmore (ed.), *Christian Baptism*, 181, rejected the notion that 1 Peter suggested the possibility of infant baptism as the preacher appealed to the experience through which they were passing and urged them to keep in mind the ethical consequences of the step they were taking, the whole epistle assuming mature believers. See also p.176. Many Baptists believe that baptism forms the foundation for Paul's moral exhortations, e.g. Robinson, 'The Place of Baptism', 215; Whitley, *Church, Ministry and Sacraments*, 161-64; L.G. Champion, *The Church of the New Testament* (1951), 73; Guthrie, *New Testament Theology*, 647 and 718.

100   Child, 'The Baptist Contribution', 85.

are admirably and forcibly expressed in believer's baptism by immersion, and expressed as no other Church expresses them.'[101]

Baptism as an Act of Obedience

The least sophisticated understanding of baptism is arguably the most widespread among grass-roots Baptists[102] even though in the extant writings it has not held a prominent place.[103] It is connected to the definition of 'ordinance' as that which was prescribed by Christ in command and example.

The understanding of baptism as an act of obedience, implicit in all Baptist thought, is substantiated by the Baptist appeal to the continuing validity of the New Testament rite which is based on the centrality of the Bible for faith and practice. That Jesus himself submitted to baptism is reason enough for the believer to follow him through the baptismal waters,[104] but that the Lord enjoined it upon the church in, for example,

---

101 Robinson, *Life and Faith*, 175.

102 Robinson, *Life and Faith*, 94, commented that this was the motive which in practice appealed most powerfully to many Baptists, 'viz., the desire to obey the direct command of Christ (Matt. xxviii.19) and to imitate His own acceptance of baptism at the hands of John (Mark i.9, 10).' He continued by explaining why he himself paid more attention to other themes of the doctrine of baptism: 'I do not doubt (whatever be the date of Matt. xxviii.19) that our Lord instituted the baptism of believers, but I believe it is in accordance with His spirit to emphasize the intrinsic meaning of the rite, rather than its extrinsic aspect, as an act of formal obedience.' 'Why Should I Be Baptized?', *BT&F* April 24, 1925, 279, expressed it succinctly: 'The all-sufficient reason is, Jesus commanded it.' *The Report of the Special Committee*, 5, in one of its moments of consensus, began its overview of the practice of baptism in the New Testament with the recognition of baptism as 'an act of loyalty to the will of Christ and as a following of His example [which] brings the believer into more conscious and more direct relation with Him, such loyalty consisting of obedience to what is regarded as a command of Christ or as the Will of Christ revealed to the Church.' See also, H. Tydeman Chilvers, 'Preachers of the Day. My Witness. A Sermon by Rev. H. Tydeman Chilvers', *BT* May 28, 1936, 419; Underwood, 'Conversion and Baptism', 34; Wicks, 'Baptismal Regeneration', 21; H.D. Brown, 'Why I Am A Baptist', *BT* January 1, 1931, 6; R.C. Ford, *Twenty-Five Years of Baptist Life in Yorkshire, 1912–1937* (1937), 31; and see the correspondence in 1949 which clearly highlighted this: 'Northern Baptist', 'Believer's Baptism as Obedience', *BT* February 24, 1949, 6: Joan Armitage, 'Why I am a Baptist', *BT* March 3, 1949, 2; W.L.R. of Barry, 'Believer's Baptism as Obedience', *BT* April 21, 1949, 8; and W. Powell, 'Baptists and Baptism', *BT* November 3, 1949, 6.

103 It is often true that that which is widely believed is often assumed and seldom set down in writing precisely because it is so broadly accepted that it is beyond contest. Popular Baptist tradition, though frequently theologically unsophisticated, has always been tenacious.

104 Mountain, *My Baptism*, 33, who said that for Jesus' followers his baptism was an example for them to imitate.

the Great Commission is all the more reason,[105] as is Paul's implicit assumption that all Christians had been baptized (1 Corinthians 12:13) and Peter's injunction on the day of Pentecost that his hearers should 'Repent and be baptized' (Acts 2:38).[106] Even if baptism were the least of Christ's commands,[107] baptism is an obligation on every believer.[108]

Mountain, though himself christened in infancy and a Christian long before becoming a Baptist, took this a step further, declaring that baptism is still obligatory even if the believer was converted many years earlier, long since having received the Holy Spirit,[109] and though such references to this effect are few, there is no doubt that it is widely held and practised by most Baptists. This explains why the majority of Baptists have always been prepared to baptize those from paedobaptist communions who have sought baptism as believers yet who have wished to remain within their own churches and why they baptize their own members even though their baptism has been separated from their conversion sometimes by many years.

Because baptism is an act of obedience, it is also an act of consecration,[110] and has also been described as a badge or mark of Christian discipleship.[111] According to Child, the second great contribution of Baptists to the one church is 'a particular conception of Christian Discipleship and Church Membership which is expressed and fostered by a special Rite, namely, that of Believers' Baptism.' It is not a rite but the 'outlook and temper' which is fostered by that rite which Baptists add to the church. The truths expressed in believers' baptism are three: the personal meaning of faith and grace; the moral change which takes place in conversion; and the spiritual nature of the church.[112] From a pastoral

---

105 P. Beasley-Murray, *Radical Believers*, 9-10, 'The first and ultimately the most powerful reason for baptism is found in the Great Commission... Jesus here issues a command, whose validity does not expire until "the very end of the age". Baptism is therefore no optional extra, but an observance ordained by Christ for all who would be his disciples.'

106 See P. Beasley-Murray, *Radical Believers*, 10-11.

107 Williams, *Principles and Practices*, 13-14.

108 Mountain, *My Baptism*, 27. A.H. Stockwell, *Baptism: Who? How? Why?* (n.d., [1908]), 12, stressed that baptism was essential in order to complete discipleship, for those who loved their Lord obeyed his command to be baptized.

109 Mountain, *My Baptism*, 181. This has most recently been argued by P. Beasley-Murray, 'Baptism for the Initiated', in S.E. Porter and A.R. Cross (eds.), *Baptism, the New Testament and the Church: Historical and Contemporary Studies in Honour of R.E.O. White* (JSNTSup, 171; Sheffield, 1999), 466-75.

110 Morris, *Thoughts on Church Membership*, 23; *Report of the Special Committee*, 5.

111 Pike, *Under Christ's Control*, 11, and Channon, *Much Water*, 77, respectively.

112 Child, 'The Baptist Contribution', 84. That baptism is viewed as a necessary part of discipleship was similarly reflected in G. Laws' tract, *What is Baptism?* (n.d.), 7:

point of view, Child spoke of baptism's design by God 'to evoke and nurture...discipleship',[113] and M.E. Aubrey remarked that nothing else could so impress on young hearts the privilege and meaning of discipleship.[114]

Baptism as Gospel Proclamation

To the majority of Baptists there is little doubt that baptism is ideally a part of evangelistic preaching as well as part of the instruction of the household of faith. Howard Jones appealed to Philip's baptizing of the Ethiopian Eunuch: 'Doubtless, Philip had woven into his discourse our Lord's parting command to His disciples to go "teach all nations, baptising them..."'[115] From his examination of primitive Christian preaching, White concluded that in the presentation of the gospel by the first evangelists 'baptism was *preached*—was part of the message to be presented, expounded, understood and obeyed, in closest accord with the commission to the church by the ascending Lord.'[116] This led to the logical conclusion that baptism therefore has a rightful and necessary place in evangelism.[117]

'If you have experienced the change of heart which scripture calls a new birth, baptism is for you. It should have been the next step. Do not any longer delay. Arise and be baptised.' Pike, *Under Christ's Control*, 11, lamented, 'We would that in these days people thought of baptism as the badge of discipleship rather than as a badge of the Baptist Denomination.'

113 Child, *Conversation*, 72.

114 M.E. Aubrey, 'From the Secretary's Chair. The Forward Movement, Sunday Schools and Baptism', *BT* February 17, 1938, 122.

115 G.H. Jones of Derby, 'International Lesson Notes. Lesson for March 16th: The Ethiopian converted.—Acts viii.26-40', *BT&F* February 28, 1902, 171.

116 White, *Biblical Doctrine of Initiation*, 139. Later he argued that the church's conviction that her baptism possessed the authority of Christ was expressed, in part, by its place in the kerygma, pp.270-71. On p.271 White also noted that the cross made possible the symbolism 'of burial and rising again, so making baptism an appropriate expression of the kerygma's story.' See also N. Clark, 'The Theology of Baptism', in Gilmore (ed.), *Christian Baptism*, 306; S.F. Winward, 'The Church in the New Testament', in A. Gilmore (ed.), *The Pattern of the Church: A Baptist View* (1963), 68.

117 F.G. Hastings of Derby, 'Evangelisation and the Ministry of the Word', *BT* February 16, 1939, 130. A variation of this point can be seen in those who advocate the baptismal service as an evangelistic opportunity and vehicle, e.g., R.W.A. Mitchell of Gateshead , 'The Evangelistic Use of the Baptismal Service', *BT* December 16, 1943, 6; F.C. Bryan, 'Preparation, Administration and Visitation', in Bryan (ed.), *Concerning Believers Baptism*, 74; H.C.C. McCullough of Clacton-on-Sea, 'Baptism and Evangelism', *BT* March 1, 1945, 6; W.W. Bottoms, *Meet the Family* (1947), 20; P. Beasley-Murray, *Faith and Festivity: A Guide for Today's Worship Leaders* (Eastbourne, 1991), 105.

As a symbol of great spiritual truths,[118] baptismal services are frequently occasions and means of proclaiming the gospel. 'Every time a Baptist Church holds a baptismal service, it is saying in plain words: "We believe in the necessity of conversion, and this rite is the symbol of that experience."'[119] Robinson believed that both the Lord's Supper and baptism, in their different ways, have an evangelistic function as they preach the cardinal facts on which an evangelical faith rests, namely, the death and the resurrection of Jesus Christ. 'More impressively than by any verbal recital of a creed, the historical basis of every Christian creed is constantly brought before a Baptist Church.'[120]

Underwood noted that 'baptism is in itself a magnificent proclamation of the gospel', and he illustrated this with the recognition that conversions often occur during baptismal services.[121] Certainly, many ministers and churches have made baptismal services into evangelistic services. Rushbrooke asked, 'Is there anything in all the world to compare with our Christian baptism as a means of setting forth the supremacy of faith, its nature and its implications?'[122] Finally, the principle which believer's baptism expresses, Robinson asserted, pledged Baptists to evangelism both at home and abroad.[123]

---

118 Phillips, *What Baptists Stand For*, 41.

119 F.T. Lord, 'The Value of Baptist Witness To-day', *BQ* 1.2 (April, 1922), 53.

120 Robinson, *Life and Faith*, 92-93, and 116. Laws, 'Vital Forces', 15, asserted that around the ordinances, 'you can teach all the gospel, and, except you do violence to them, you cannot teach from them anything else. Baptism and the Lord's Supper...will go on proclaiming the atonement, the new birth, and power through the risen Lord, even if the pulpit be hesitant or dubious.'

121 Underwood, 'Conversion and Baptism', 34.

122 Rushbrooke, 'Protestant of the Protestants', 80. He added, p.82, 'Baptists see in the ordinance a divinely appointed means of ensuring the simplicity and purity of the Gospel. We exist for nothing else than the propagation and defence of the Gospel; in the fulfilment of that purpose, as God gives us light and guidance, we find the final, the only, and the sufficient justification of our existence as Christian churches.'

123 H.W. Robinson and J.H. Rushbrooke, *Baptists in Britain* (1937), 30.

CHAPTER 3

Ecumenical Developments 1900–1937

Introduction

The nineteenth century witnessed an increasing number of co-operative ventures between the denominations. These movements were many and various, both missionary and philanthropic, and led to a greater closeness and understanding, particularly between the Free Churches, but also with the state church,[1] which inevitably led to prejudices being dismantled and the cross-fertilization of ideas, including the increasing willingness of some among the Free Churches to recognize the sacramental character of baptism.[2] The most significant of these for Baptists was the integration in 1891 of the Particular and General Baptists in a series of geographical associations within the fellowship of the BU, though it must be acknowledged that this was still effectively a union within a denomination: that is, two Baptist traditions.[3]

The Early Days of the Free Church Movement

The developments of the nineteenth century culminated in the holding of the first Free Church Congress in November 1892[4] and the establishment of the National Council of the Evangelical Free Churches (NCEFC) at the 1896 congress. Within this movement there were a great many Baptists, often holding and playing key roles: among them John Clifford and F.B.

---

1   E.g. Bebbington, *Evangelicalism, passim*; D.L. Edwards, *Christian England* (revised and combined edn, 1989), III, *passim*; Heasman, *Evangelicals, passim*; E.K.H. Jordan, *Free Church Unity: History of the Free Church Council Movement 1896–1941* (1956), 15-16, 22-25, 55-56.

2   Perkin, 'Baptism', 335-426; and for the broader context, Thompson, 'Baptism'.

3   See J.H.Y. Briggs, 'Evangelical Ecumenism: The Amalgamation of General and Particular Baptists in 1891', Part I, *BQ* 34.3, (July, 1991), 99-115; Part II, *BQ* 34.4 (October, 1991), 160-79, and also his *English Baptists*, 96-157.

4   D.W. Bebbington, *The Nonconformist Conscience: Chapel and Politics 1870–1914* (1982), 64, noted that 30 of the 375 attenders identified themselves as Baptists.

Meyer from London, Richard Glover of Bristol, C.F. Aked of Liverpool, Alexander MacLaren of Manchester and J.G. Greenhough of Leicester.[5] However, the most significant step for Baptists was the appointment of John Howard Shakepeare to the secretaryship of the Union, for the decisions he took and the influence he had paved the way for all subsequent developments, though at the time of his appointment it is unlikely that Baptists had any idea of the depth of his 'ecumenical' convictions and the path on which he would lead them. His only pastorate, St. Mary's, Norwich, was of a church which had originated as a seventeenth-century mixed Independent congregation,[6] which had been greatly influenced in the early nineteenth century by the ardent strict communionist who nevertheless possessed a 'catholic spirit',[7] Joseph Kinghorn, and which had gone through a deeply painful split over strict communion in the mid-nineteenth century.[8] It was into this situation, with all the hurts still fresh in the people's memories, that Shakespeare had come in 1883. Of Shakespeare, one writer paid tribute that, 'The vision of a reunion of Protestant Christendom was no sudden inspiration of the moment. It had been in his thoughts all through his ministerial life.'[9] The history, then, of St. Mary's considerably influenced the young minister, reinforcing what appears to have been an already existing conviction.[10]

---

5   See Bebbington, *Nonconformist Conscience*, 61-83; Jordan, *Free Church Unity*, 17-76; Payne, *The Baptist Union* (1959), 151-52; A.R. Cross, 'Service to the Ecumenical Movement: The Contribution of British Baptists', *BQ* 38.3 (July, 1999), 108-09.

6   See C.B. Jewson, 'St. Mary's, Norwich, II', *BQ* 10.3, (July, 1940), 175-77.

7   This is how Kinghorn was described by C.B. Jewson, 'St. Mary's, Norwich, V', *BQ* 10.6 (April, 1941), 346, who also described him, p.341, as 'A rigid and uncompromising Baptist, he was a saint of the Church Universal. Inevitably the grace of his personality over-flowed the bounds of his denomination', for he helped and worked with non-Baptists. Kinghorn, minister from 1789–1832, was an ardent strict communionist, and is best known for his twelve year communion controversy with Robert Hall.

8   Despite the respect in which Kinghorn, and all that he had stood for, was held by the church, both of his successors, William Brock and George Gould, were open communionists. This led not only to years of internal friction but also to the infamous court case between 1858–60, which caused a split in the church. In fact it was the presence of a number of non-Baptists regularly in the congregation which led Brock finally to break from the restriction of the pledge he had made on his arrival at St. Mary's not to preach against strict communion. For details, see Walker, *Baptists at the Table*, 36-40.

9   'John Howard Shakespeare. The Story of His Life', *Supplement to the BT* March 15, 1928, iii. Hastings, *History of English Christianity*, 98, described Shakespeare as 'the most deeply and consistently ecumenical of all the Church leaders of the time.'

10   Aubrey, 'John Howard Shakespeare', 100, reported Shakespeare's involvement in the organization of a united Free Church mission early on in his pastorate in Norwich

More than any other leader the Baptists had known, Shakespeare opposed the old form of independency, becoming increasingly convinced that the Free Church organizations were too individualistic.[11] At the 1910 meeting of the National Free Church Council (NFCC), he pleaded with 'impassioned eloquence' for a United Free Church of England,[12] setting in motion events which culminated in 1919 with the establishment of the Federal Council of the Evangelical Free Churches (FCEFC). The International Missionary Conference held in Edinburgh the same year injected added impetus to this movement, not least through its report, 'Co-operation and the Promotion of Unity'.[13] Free Church Inquiry committees, set up in 1913, carried out detailed investigations into the issue of unity, but nearly petered out because of the war,[14] when, in 1916, Shakespeare addressed the NFCC in Bradford.[15] His proposals met with hopeful signs and provided the needed stimulus to rejuvenate the movement.[16] Thousands of copies of the address were circulated by the Free Church Council (FCC), while Shakespeare and other unity advocates began tours of the country to rally support.[17] The final proposals submitted by the ecumenical conferences in 1917 to the denominations stated that no attempt was being made to interfere with the autonomy of each federating body, being designed, not for absorption or amalgamation, but to make possible concerted action and economy of resources wherever possible.[18]

The BU was the first denomination to consider the proposals at its Assembly in April 1918.[19] Prior to this, a committee had been convened under Shakespeare's chairmanship whose purpose was to bring three resolutions before the Assembly, the third of which stated: 'With regard

---

under the lead of the Wesleyan Hugh Price Hughes. See also Shepherd, 'Shakespeare', 45-46.

11   J.C. Carlile, *My Life's Little Day* (1935), 158-59.

12   Jordan, *Free Church Unity*, 127. See also Shepherd, 'Shakespeare', 131-33.

13   See J.W. Grant, *Free Churchmanship in England 1870–1940: With special reference to Congregationalism* (n.d. [1955]), 261-62. For the text see W.H.T. Gardiner, *Edinburgh 1910* (1910).

14   Jordan, *Free Church Unity*, 128.

15   For the text see 'The Free Churches at the Cross-Roads', *BT&F* March 10, 1916, 150-52, and the *Free Church Year Book* (1916), 9-24.

16   At the Council meeting, F.B. Meyer proposed that the necessary steps should be taken to bring Shakespeare's principles and proposals before the representative bodies of the Evangelical Free Churches of England, see 'National Free Church Council. The Bradford Meetings', *BT&F*, March 10, 1916, 155.

17   Jordan, *Free Church Unity*, 130-33.

18   Jordan, *Free Church Unity*, 133.

19   The text of the report can be found in Shakespeare's *The Churches at the Cross-Roads: A Study in Church Unity* (1918), 214-20; also in Payne, *The Baptist Union*, 275-78.

to membership and communion, it is understood that the Federation will not infringe the convictions or practices of any of the Churches of the Baptist Union.'[20] Shakespeare presented the report of the representatives of the Evangelical Free Churches of England, with the assurance that it was federation, not organic union, that was being sought. Acknowledging that they were the first denomination to consider the report, he urged, 'It is unthinkable that Baptists should wreck the movement or even look upon it with distrust and hesitation.'[21] After quoshing an amendment from a small group of conservative dissenters who wished the matter to be referred back to the local churches and associations, the original motion was carried with only a small minority in opposition.[22]

While many were prepared to go along with Shakespeare and the plans for closer Free Church unity, the movement was not without those who were cautious of it, and those who openly and vigorously opposed it. In an interview in 1901, John Clifford had drawn a distinction between Union churches of Baptists and Congregationalists and the creation of a United Congregational Church, declaring that of the latter Baptists were

---

20 'The Closer Co-operation of the Free Churches', *BT&F* March 8, 1918, 148-49. The committee also included F.G. Benskin from Bristol, W.E. Blomfield, Principal of Rawdon College and also the minister at Harrogate from 1917–19, Dr Charles Brown of Ferme Park, Dr John Clifford, W.Y. Fullerton, Home Secretary of the BMS (on whom see his autobiographical *At the Sixtieth Milestone: Incidents of the Journey* (n.d.)), Dr G.P. Gould, Principal of Regent's Park College, London, J.G. Greenhough, Mr Herbert Marnham, a London stockbroker and Treasurer of the BU 1900–35, Dr F.B. Meyer of Christ Church, Westminster Bridge, Thomas Phillips of Bloomsbury, J.E. Roberts of Manchester and Mr H.G. Wood.

21 'The Union Sessions', *BT&F*, May 3, 1918, 277.

22 The motion was proposed by Marnham, seconded by Fullerton, having received support from Charles Brown, another leader in the Free Church Movement and whole-hearted supporter of Shakespeare and the cause of a United Free Church. See 'The Closer Co-operation of the Free Churches', *BT&F* April 26, 1918, 253-54; Jordan, *Free Church Unity*, 133-34; D.W. Bebbington, 'Baptists and Fundamentalism in Inter-War Britain', in K. Robbins (ed.), *Protestant Evangelicalism: Britain, Ireland, Germany and America, c.1750–c1950*, Festschrift W.R. Ward (Oxford, 1990), 300. On Brown's ecumenical involvement, see H. Cook, *Charles Brown* (1939), 83-85. Brown is another Baptist whose attitude towards reunion was and has often been misrepresented and misunderstood. Cook, p.84, writes, 'The devotion of Dr. Brown to the cause of Re-union has sometimes been misunderstood. On the one hand he has at times been accused by enthusiastic Baptists of a readiness to compromise their fundamental position by his willingness to concede liberty in a reunited Church to those who do not accept the doctrine of Believer's Baptism and Believer's Baptism only; while on the other hand he has been accused by some advocates of Reunion as being unwilling, for the sake of the ultimate cause, to give up some Free Church "prejudices". Probably anyone who endeavours to mediate between divided camps must always run the risk of being misunderstood by both.'

interested but cautious observers.[23] There had been discussion of Baptists and Congregationalists uniting since the 1880s, and indeed suggestions much earlier, and Clifford noted that there were increasing numbers from both denominations going to each others' churches, thus evincing a growing mutual respect for one another's baptism.[24] The 1901 autumn Baptist Assembly had discussed the reunion issue at length,[25] and Clifford's address identified some of the issues which would have to be examined. For him, the Baptist interpretation of baptism was a witness to the truth, and reunion could not involve the compromise of truth. He also stated that the unity of the church was found in the common Christ, not in the sacraments.[26] At the 1916 Assembly, J.E. Roberts expressed his position as the mind of the denomination: 'I believe I interpret the Baptist conscience... Many of us are prepared to go all the way open to us, short of compromising principle.' Under no circumstances could the admission be made that infant baptism was the New Testament baptism. A United Free Church was possible *only* by federation, after all, the Baptist denomination itself was already a federation of different churches of different patterns, as illustrated by the existence of churches practising closed communion and membership, open communion and closed membership, open communion and membership, Union churches, Scottish churches and Free churches.[27] Anything other than union by federation was to Roberts, and undoubtedly the majority of Baptists, unacceptable.

Apprehensions about where it was all going were further fuelled by the publication of Shakespeare's *The Churches at the Cross-Roads* in 1918.[28] While primarily an exposition of the 'federal' conception of

---

23   'Interview with Dr. Clifford. The United Congregational Church', *BT&F* June 21, 1901, 415. Similar caution was being voiced in 1936 by C.E. Wilson, *The Baptist Missionary Society: How It Works and Why* (n.d., [1931]), 36.

24   'Interview with Dr. Clifford', 415. This is perhaps one of the earliest references to the effect of increasing population mobility.

25   See the whole of the *Supplement to the BT&F* October 18, 1901.

26   J. Clifford, 'The Place of Baptists in the Progress of Christianity', *Supplement to the BT&F* October 18, 1901, v-ix. Others who opposed the compromise of principle included the Welsh Baptist, G. Hay Morgan, *Supplement to the BT&F*, April 27, 1900, vii (Morgan was a barrister who had also been the minister of Woodberry Down church, London, but was the newly elected MP for Truro in 1906: on his political career, see Payne, *The Baptist Union*, 173; S. Koss, *Nonconformity in Modern British Politics* (1975), 95, 111 and 116; and Bebbington, *Nonconformist Conscience*, 139-40); and the anonymous 'Surreyside', 'Baptist Principles and the Free Church Council', *BT&F* February 15, 1901, 113.

27   J.E. Roberts, 'Christian Unity—Our Relation to Other Churches', *Supplement to the BT&F* May 12, 1916, II-IV, quotations from III.

28   *Cross-Roads* and the reception it received is discussed by Shepherd, 'Shakespeare', 195-200; and Townsend, 'Shakespeare', 302-04.

unity it went further by envisaging a United Church of England. Shakespeare believed that the three main contentions of the Free Churches was that the church comprises those who are born again, that it is a spiritual fellowship, and that the church's authority is vested under Christ in the people of God. While these formed the common ground of the Free Churches, he contended that each could be given a different emphasis, or be expressed in different forms of polity, or the common truth might be witnessed to by a different form of baptism.[29] He believed that Free Church differences were like the natural differences of members of the same family, that the process of time had softened them and that the denominations were drawing together in both doctrine and practice.[30] 'The ground of the separation is that the conscience of the adherent does not permit him to be a member of a Church which does not avow a certain tenet, or maintain a certain order, or observe a certain rite.'[31] Later he announced: 'In my judgment we have reached the stage when the gains [of Separation] do not outweigh the loss...'[32]

Though an ardent Baptist,[33] Shakespeare's passionate conviction was that the only way forward was by means of a United Church. To this end he drew a clear distinction between unity and uniformity,[34] because uniformity could only be found in something dead, whereas church unity 'is the unity of a living body.'[35] The way to accomplish such unity, he was convinced, was through federation so 'that religion itself may be saved', though he recognized that 'nothing is more difficult than to translate visions into actualities.'[36]

This very maxim had been only too true for Shakespeare himself. In the meetings held to discuss the unity question between 1916 and the publication of his book two years later, he and his fellow advocates of corporate union had been unable to convince others, so they had had to content themselves with the idea of federation. Shakespeare accepted federation somewhat reluctantly, but it was at least a step in the right direction. At their meeting held at Mansfield College, Oxford, he and his colleagues had discovered that 'the desires of no one representative

---

29 Shakespeare, *Cross-Roads*, 55-56.
30 Shakespeare, *Cross-Roads*, 56-57.
31 Shakespeare, *Cross-Roads*, 61.
32 Shakespeare, *Cross-Roads*, 72.
33 Shakespeare, *Cross-Roads*, 82. He claimed, p.82, 'No-one could ever regard me as an indifferent Baptist.'
34 Shakespeare, *Cross-Roads*, 110-11, though in order to demonstrate his point he had to indulge in no small amount of special pleading. One such example is when he stated that 'The Catholic Church has in all ages recognized diversities of faith, rites, ceremonies and operations', p.111.
35 Shakespeare, *Cross-Roads*, 111 and 115
36 Shakespeare, *Cross-Roads*, 117.

group could be exactly and entirely satisfied.' The different groups were not prepared to sacrifice principles, yet they had agreed that there had to be give and take.[37] Shakespeare himself stated that federation would not require any such shredding of principle but that the participating denominations would have to limit the freedom of their actions.[38]

Much of the rest of Shakespeare's book explored how federation could take place. Of two American plans, 'the Maine Plan' found favour with him. Here, a church in membership with one denomination would be open and free from all sectional restrictions.[39] Though he denied it, the only way such a plan could succeed would be if baptism was relegated to a secondary position, and along with it the other distinctives which set apart the different Free Churches, though these were, in actual fact, the very reasons for their separation from each other in the first place. Further, he seemed unaware that the majority of Baptists were not prepared to concede as much as he was, hence the opposition which he felt so deeply and personally. His preparedness to come under episcopacy and submit to episcopal re-ordination might have seemed to him to be small matters, but, along with baptism and other Baptist and Free Church principles which would have to go, they were nothing of the sort.[40] In this, Shakespeare seriously misjudged the temper and convictions of the denomination as a whole.

The importance of this book cannot easily be overstated. It rings with a kind of idealistic naivete, for it never truly got to grips with the real areas of contention. Baptism was one but by no means the only such issue.[41] Shakespeare's practical and theological goal was unity, all else was pragmatically subsumed to the cause and relegated in importance in order that a united church might be born.[42] He did not enter into the debate of the legitimacy of infant baptism, aware that he could not afford to do so because of the convictions of both Paedobaptists and Baptists.

---

37 Shakespeare, *Cross-Roads*, 118-21.

38 Shakespeare, *Cross-Roads*, 123-24.

39 Shakespeare, *Cross-Roads*, 135.

40 Cf. Shakespeare's comment, *Cross-Roads*, 82: 'A yet more serious consequence of the existing divisions is that they tend to belittle the big things of religion and to magnify the small things. In other words, they afford a most striking instance of the tragedy of the misplaced emphasis.' To Shakespeare, church unity was unquestionably of primary significance, while episcopacy and episcopal re-ordination, and presumably baptism, were by comparison secondary.

41 Shepherd, 'Shakespeare', 304, comes to a similar conclusion: 'He seemed to believe that a combination of exhortation and action would cause the underlying tensions over such things as church government, the ministry and baptism to disappear.'

42 Shakespeare's theological pragmatism is highlighted by Shepherd, 'Shakespeare', 13, 80, 96 and 156.

To have entered into detailed discussion of the divisive subjects would have been contrary to the stated irenic nature and tone of the book.[43]

The book is the seminal ecumenical call this century and the man arguably the leading ecumenist of the first quarter of the twentieth century. Unfortunately, the importance of Shakespeare within both Free Church union and Free Church–Anglican discussions has seldom been adequately acknowledged.[44] Adrian Hastings has described *The Churches at the Cross-Roads* as 'in principle one of the most important books of twentieth-century English Christianity *because it sets out so clearly the logic of the forthcoming ecumenical movement.*'[45] All in all he was a man ahead of his time. He occupied a pivotal position and his eloquent appeals began a movement which has gathered pace throughout the century.

Henry Wheeler Robinson was the first of three key figures who spearheaded opposition to Shakespeare: the other two were Dr T.R. Glover, the Cambridge Classicist, and Dr John Clifford. From 1895 to 1900, with a break for study on the continent, Wheeler Robinson's College days brought him into constant contact with those of other traditions which clearly had a deep and lasting effect on his attitudes towards other traditions,[46] and during his early ministry he was also

---

43   Shakespeare, *Cross-Roads*, 181.

44   Shepherd, 'Shakespeare', 238, agrees, and provides a detailed discussion of his involvement in the unity movement, pp.167-242. E.g. G.K.A. Bell, *Randall Davidson: Archbishop of Canterbury* (2 vols; Oxford, 1935), contains no reference to Shakespeare with regard to reunion or the Lambeth Appeal. Also silent on Shakespeare's involvement is R.E. Davies, *Methodism* (1963), while R.T. Jones in *Congregationalism in England, 1662–1962* (1962), 363-64, devotes only half a page to him, and H.R.T. Brandreth, 'Approaches of the Churches Towards Each Other in the Nineteenth Century', in R. Rouse and S.C. Neill (eds.), *A History of the Ecumenical Movement 1517–1948* (Geneva, 3rd edn, 1986), 268, simply refers to him as 'one of the most notable Baptists ecumenists of his day', this being the only reference to him in the entire volume. Little better are Grant, *Free Churchmanship in England*, 263-65, 315; H. Townsend, *The Claims of the Free Churches* (1949), 312-13; though his importance is recognized by Jordan, *Free Church Unity*, 127-35 and *passim*.

45   Hastings, *History of English Christianity*, 98, italics added. There is a lot to be said for Shepherd's point, 'Shakespeare', 319, when he dissents from Hastings' assessment of *Cross-Roads*, arguing, rather, that 'it sets out Shakespeare's passion for unity, which had little to do with logic. That passion was Shakespeare's greatest contribution to the ecumenical debates of the twentieth century.'

46   Robinson read theology at Mansfield College, Oxford, the Congregational College, during which time he also attended lectures in the hall of Balliol College, where over three hundred ministers from many denominations would gather. See E.A. Payne, *Henry Wheeler Robinson: Scholar, Teacher, Principal: A Memoir* (1946), 31-37, and E. Kaye, *Mansfield College Oxford: Its Origin, History, and Significance* (Oxford, 1996), 117-18, 179-80 and 196. The influence of such 'ecumenical' gatherings, with all their

involved in Free Church work.[47] Robinson, then, was no narrow denominationalist. Favourably disposed towards issues of Christian unity, he
played a leading role on the committee which prepared a reply for the
BU Council to certain pamphlets on unity,[48] and his review of
Shakespeare's *The Churches at the Cross-Roads* concluded: 'This is a
book to make its readers say, "I must be in that, too."'[49] But in time, like
many others, he became sceptical of the possibility of organic union as
advocated by Shakespeare. Like many, he did not believe that
ecclesiastical compromises or manoeuverings were the way forward,
rather he believed in the need for clearer thinking and greater charity.[50]

The 'Declaratory Statement' which formed the doctrinal basis of the
FCEFC was adopted at the meeting of the Council of the Evangelical Free
Churches of England on March 26, 1917, and it was this report which
went before and was approved by the BU Assembly in April 1918.[51] It
affirmed the autonomy of the federating churches with regard to faith
and practice and, of the two sacraments (it also used the language of
'ordinances', employing the words synonymously), stated that they were
'signs and seals of His Gospel', that they 'confirm the promises and gifts
of salvation', and 'when rightly used by believers with faith and prayer,

---

opportunities for discussion and debate and an increased appreciation of the differences
between the denominations, can only be inferred, but, appear to have been considerable.
This conclusion is supported by the fact that in later life Robinson was closely associated
with the Quakers and had a keen interest in, e.g., the writings of J.H. Newman, see Payne,
Henry Wheeler Robinson, 59-60. In the same volume, cf. also Robinson's 'Lectures. I.
John Henry Newman', 110-31. On Robinson generally, see 'Celebration of the
Centenary of the birth of Henry Wheeler Robinson, Ninth Principal of Regent's Park
College, 7th February, 1872', *BQ* 24.6 (April, 1972), and R. Mason, 'H. Wheeler
Robinson Revisited', *BQ* 37.5 (January, 1998), 213-26.

47   During the winter of 1916–17 he lectured on the Christian experience of the
Holy Spirit and other devotional themes to Free Church ministers throughout the North of
England, Payne, *Henry Wheeler Robinson*, 62-63.

48   *Report of the Baptist Union Council* (1937), Appendix IV, cited by Payne,
Henry Wheeler Robinson, 91 and n1.

49   H.W. Robinson, 'Churches at Crossroads', *BT&F* November 8, 1918, 663. See
also Payne, *Henry Wheeler Robinson*, 92. Both the first and second editions of
Shakespeare's book were positively reviewed in the *BT&F*, by Robinson just mentioned,
and M.E. Aubrey, April 23, 1920, 270. In his review of the second edition, Aubrey noted
the growing impatience of the younger generation with the old divisions. Shakespeare's
book was also defended by J.E. Roberts, 'The President on Christian Unity', *BT&F*
January 17, 1919, 30, against an adverse review in *The British Weekly* of January 9,
1919.

50   Payne, *Henry Wheeler Robinson*, 92.

51   See the 'Declaratory Statement of Common Faith and Practice' reproduced in
Payne, *The Baptist Union*, 275-78.

are, through the operation of the Holy Spirit, true means of grace.'[52] The careful wording of the statement made it acceptable to all the Free Churches, but it did not clarify the issue of the subjects or mode of baptism.

Though primarily commending Free Church federation, Shakespeare was also advocating union with the Church of England. This the denominational mainstream was not prepared to tolerate. He clearly alienated himself from the fundamentalists who formed the Baptist Bible Union to oppose any such moves.[53] Despite the assurances of the Committee who brought the resolution to the 1918 Assembly that no sacrifice of principle was involved, there were many, less extreme than the Bible Unionists, who followed Clifford and J.E. Roberts, expressing their complete opposition to any surrender of principle, and specifically believer's baptism.[54]

At the Baptist Assembly on April 29, T.R. Glover led the denominational opposition to Shakespeare in carrying a resolution which indicated that the price of conceding to episcopacy was too high to pay.[55] This, together with Robinson's reserve concerning organic union, represented the feeling of the mainstream of the denomination.

While the issue of baptism did not figure prominently in these early days of the Free Church movement, it undoubtedly lay beneath the surface, and the developments which were to take place later, in which baptism came to play an increasingly significant role as far as the Baptists were concerned, cannot be understood without a grasp of this important

---

52 See Payne, *The Baptist Union*, 276-77.

53 Bebbington, 'Baptists and Fundamentalism', 300. Among their ranks was James Mountain, a convert to the Baptist position from the Countess of Huntingdon Connexion. See Mountain, *My Baptism*. In the preface to the book, F.B. Meyer stated that the tone of the book displayed Christian charity 'without a word of unkind reflection on those who differ from him' (n.p.). However, Mountain was not so pacific or conciliatory on other matters. For his later vitriolic attacks on the likes of F.C. Spurr and T.R. Glover on the issue of biblical criticism, see Bebbington, 'Baptists and Fundamentalism', 316-18. Mountain's vitriol against those he deemed to be theologically liberal stands in stark contrast to the irenic and pastoral tone of his earlier autobiographical book on baptism.

54 Eg. D.J. Hiley of West Norwood, 'Baptist Witness and the Problems of To-day', *BT&F* May 7, 1920, 305-07; F.T. Bloice-Smith of Sutton-in-Craven, 'Some of the Real Problems of Reunion', *BT&F* February 4, 1921, 72; J.H. French of Banbury, 'The Baptist Witness and Reunion', *BT&F* January 6, 1922, 5-6; F.C. Spurr of Handsworth, Birmingham, 'A Baptist Apologetic for To-day', *BT* September 5, 1925, 639, according to whom the spirit of compromise which accompanied the reunion movement had led to the abandonment of anything like specific Baptist testimony in order to avoid division, and that this was, e.g., seen in Union churches. Mutual toleration regarding baptism 'does not help the specific Baptist witness.'

55 H.G. Wood, *Terrot Reaveley Glover: A Biography* (Cambridge, 1953), 153.

early debate. The establishment of the Free Church movement was, therefore, a necessary first step in the ecumenical process, for, without it, the Church of England would have been unlikely to hold conversations with the separate Free Church denominations.

The *Lambeth Appeal*

The distrust of Baptists in particular, and Free Churchmen in general, was sufficiently softened by the conciliatory tone of the 1920 *Appeal to all Christian People*[56] for a series of conversations to take place over a four-year period between representatives of the Free Churches and the Church of England.[57] The *Appeal* called all the churches to 'unite in a new and great endeavour to recover and to manifest to the world the unity of the Body of Christ for which He prayed',[58] its proposals for reunion being based upon the 1888 Lambeth Quadrilateral[59]—acceptance of the scriptures, the creeds, the sacraments, and a ministry authorized by the historic episcopate.[60]

Though Baptists were involved in the formal conversations there still remained the sceptical majority. In a sermon, Charles Brown rejoiced that the *Lambeth Appeal* recognized for the first time the validity of Baptist baptism and their membership of the one church of Christ, yet he did not consider a great and organic union either possible or a great advantage to the Kingdom of the Lord.[61]

It was T.R. Glover who spoke for the denomination as a whole.[62] His jealous defence of the Baptist and Independent position in relation to the

---

56   Jones, *Congregationalism*, 364. The Appeal was warmly welcomed by Baptists, see 'The Lambeth Conference and Reunion', and 'The Prospect of a United Church', *BT&F* August 20, 1920, 545-46 and 547 respectively

57   Jordan, *Free Church Unity*, 168-75.

58   The text was published in the *BT&F* August 13, 1920, 539, under the title 'Reunion of Christendom', and can also be found in G.K.A. Bell, *Documents on Christian Unity, 1920–4* (1924), 1-5, quotation from p.5.

59   For the text see Shakespeare, *Cross-Roads*, 213.

60   See the discussion of the FCEFC's initial response, *The Free Churches and the Lambeth Appeal* (1921), in Shepherd, 'Shakespeare', 220-21, and also the whole of his section on the *Appeal*, pp.209-37.

61   C. Brown, 'The Appeal of the Lambeth Conference', *BT&F* August 27, 1920, 566-67. Three years later, W.E. Blomfield announced that as a result of the joint conversations a few Evangelical/Broad Church Anglican leaders, with some reservations, were prepared to admit that Free Church ministries were real ministries of Christ's Word and sacraments in the universal church, 'Reunion', *BT&F* September 28, 1923, 679.

62   Glover was a Fellow of St. John's College, Cambridge, and Public Orator in the University. Wood, *Terrot Reaveley Glover*, 9, noted that Glover's 'fundamental Christian convictions were nurtured in the setting of orthodox Dissent, marked by an emphasis on

reunion proposals won him the support of the majority in the denomination, and Shakespeare was identified with the policies of which Glover was most distrustful.[63] Glover defined his position in *The Free Churches and Re-Union*, in the 'Preface' of which John Clifford endorsed the contents of the book as not only the author's views but also 'the convictions and experiences of Baptists everywhere.'[64]

Due to his opposition to Shakespeare, Glover is often thought to have been totally opposed to any form of reunion, but this is untrue. Glover, and a great many other Baptists, opposed the compromise of principles and believed that the discussions of their day were forcing theology to be set to one side. Glover maintained that the belief that religion was better off without theology had led to an increasing vagueness, that charity covered a good deal of absence of mind, and conviction and principle had come to be identified with bigotry.[65] For him, the quest for 'truth' was safer and surer when the great authorities disagreed and, therefore, were compelled by that very fact to re-examine their evidence and add to it.[66] 'The problem with re-union will not be helped forward by quick talk and impulsive resolutions, whether of individuals or of assemblies.'[67] Glover, then, was not against reunion proposals per se, but against any compromise of the truth and he believed that the Free Church theory of the church, the ministry and the sacraments more closely approximated to the truth than did the Anglican. If this were so, the Free Churches were not at liberty to give them up, for such would be 'deliberate falsehood'.[68] There is little doubt that this is a barely veiled reference to

---

individual responsibility characteristic of the Baptists. Glover grew up a convinced Dissenter and a Baptist.'

63   Wood, *Terrot Reaveley Glover*, 152.

64   T.R. Glover, *The Free Churches and Re-Union* (Cambridge, 1921), Preface, n.p.. Glover's title deliberately mimicked A.J. Carlyle, S.H. Clark, J.S. Lidgett and J.H. Shakespeare (eds.), *Towards Reunion: being contributions to mutual understanding by Church of England and Free Church writers* (1919), discussed by Shepherd, 'Shakespeare', 206. Glover's position in *Free Churches and Re-Union* and his opposition to the Lambeth Appeal are also discussed by Shepherd, pp. 224-29.

65   Glover, *Free Churches and Re-Union*, 4-5.

66   Glover, *Free Churches and Re-Union*, 21.

67   Glover, *Free Churches and Re-Union*, 49. Outlining the story of the Arian controversy, pp.49-51, how the inclusive creed suggested by Eusebius of Caesarea was set on one side for Athanasius' creed which excluded the Arians, he commented, p.51, that 'The whole story is a warning to go to work slowly upon any eirenicon till we are clear what fundamental principles are involved. The fatigue of the war, the emotionalism that it induced, the general decline of interest in religious truth, even the practical man's restless wish to "get things done", may conspire with higher motives to produce a desire to settle the matter, to achieve re-union, and to be done with it. But Truth is not served by decisions reached in fatigue.'

68   Glover, *Free Churches and Re-Union*, 58.

Shakespeare's willingness to submit to episcopacy and episcopal re-ordination. Equally, there can be little doubt that the doctrine of baptism, among others, was also implied in what Glover said.

Glover was not at all convinced that the quest for truth would be aided by such moves as were being proposed. There were two ways to proceed: by pooling of differences and letting questions drop, or by courteous and Christian determination to be loyal to truth as God had revealed it until he should give clearer light and surer guidance. What the Free Churches had received from their forefathers was not to be surrendered even for Christian charity.[69]

On Jesus' prayer for unity in John 17, Glover, after raising the question of its authenticity, commented: 'We are not yet clear that Jesus did wish to see his Church one organization.' Earlier he had written on the same passage: 'that they all may be one', is a 'notorious passage', often interpreted in an 'unhistorical way', and is the favourite text of a certain type of mind. 'Jesus read human nature far more shrewdly. Men do not quickly harmonize where they are divided on vital issues. It is the false religions that have based faith on tradition, and found truth in compromise, and have therefore most logically been ready to tolerate other religions of the same type.'[70]

This is where interpreters of Glover's position often finish, but he continued: 'This is not to give a negative reply to an overture; even if it were, it might not be wrong, or even discourteous. It is quite plain that any ultimate reunion is still a long way off.'[71] In favour of pulpit exchanges, sharing work and missions, he by no means ruled out working with Anglicans, and contended that the churches should 'do everything we possibly can in the direction of common work.' 'What God may have in store for us half a century hence is not our most immediate duty... What He does then is His affair. What does He want us to do now?'[72] Thus Keith Clements overstated the case when he wrote: 'In part, Glover owed his post-war popularity among Baptists to his opposition to *any form of reunion* of the Churches in response to the *Lambeth Appeal*, and along the lines being advocated by J.H. Shakespeare...'[73] It is true that Glover opposed the form of reunion being tabled by Shakespeare and

---

69   Glover, *Free Churches and Re-Union*, 53. He further believed that if the Free Churches were more loyal to Christ, more brotherly, more intelligent and intelligible, they might bring those who held differing views of the church nearer to the Free Church position, for to bring a man clearer light was more like Christian charity than to let him hold an erroneous view.

70   Glover, *Free Churches and Re-Union*, 53 and 12-13.

71   Glover, *Free Churches and Re-Union*, 54.

72   Glover, *Free Churches and Re-Union*, 54-55.

73   K.W. Clements, *Lovers of Discord: Twentieth-Century Theological Controversies in England* (1988), 119, italics added.

the *Lambeth Appeal*, but he did not oppose reunion as such. Like Wheeler Robinson, Glover was not in any way narrow-minded and his work in the University of Cambridge brought him into contact with many of other denominations.[74] *Pace* Clements, Glover's main objection was not on the grounds of religious freedom, though this was a secondary reason,[75] but on the compromising of truth.[76]

Glover's position has been analysed at length precisely because he spoke on behalf of so many in the denomination, but John Clifford similarly showed a disdain for compromise. In a letter to W.E. Blomfield, he expressed his opinion that there was a real and an unreal unity. For him 'material and mechanical unity' was not enough, the real unity was unity 'of soul and spirit and does not depend on the identity of ideas as to forms and policies.'[77] Clifford was forthrightly opposed to Romish principles and practices, whether in Roman or Anglican Churches. As far as he was concerned the *Lambeth Appeal*'s references to baptism were vague generalities, and any concessions towards the like would jeopardize English Baptists' relations with, for example, American Baptists.[78] He was anti-sacerdotalist, stating in another letter to Blomfield, that the upholders of an episcopalian type of Christianity stood for 'a materialistic and mechanical interpretation of the grace of God; and that is, and has always been, a menace to the Religion of the New Testament.'[79]

Clifford's ecumenical ambitions were reflected in the constitution of his Westbourne Park church, formulated by Clifford himself in the 1870s when the church moved there from Praed Street. Though a convinced Baptist, he led the church to be 'open to all who are members of "His Body"—i.e., to all who confess Christ, strive to learn and obey His law, not only in their individual life, but in and by association for mutual help, common worship, and beneficent work.' The second article stated that while the church taught and practised believer's baptism each applicant

---

74   For a time he wavered on the edge of joining the Society of Friends and frequently worshipped at Emmanuel Congregational Church, P.T. Forsyth's charge in Cambridge, see Wood, *Terrot Reaveley Glover*, 81-83 and 18-19 respectively. It was their rejection of baptism which prevented Glover from becoming a Quaker, see Cook, *What Baptists Stand For*, 133-34.

75   Clements, *Lovers of Discord*, 118, citing Glover, *Free Churches and Re-Union*, 13-14.

76   A similar position to that taken by Glover on reunion issues was adopted by H.H. Rowley during and in part as a response to the Anglican–Free Church discussions prompted by the Lambeth Appeal, see *Aspects of Reunion* (1923). An overview is provided by J.F.V. Nicholson, 'H.H. Rowley on "Aspects of Reunion"', *BQ* 38.4 (October, 1999), 196-99.

77   Marchant, *Dr. John Clifford*, 260-61.

78   See Marchant's notes to Clifford's letter to Rev. Dr W.E. Blomfield, June 10, 1922, *Dr. John Clifford*, 262.

79   Marchant, *Dr. John Clifford*, 263, letter dated October 7, 1920.

for membership was expected to make their own decision before God.[80] By this, Clifford sought to maintain the tension between the Baptist doctrine of baptism and the liberty of conviction and conscience of the individual which he prized so highly.[81] He realized and advocated the New Testament mandate for believer's baptism, but recognized and made allowance for the divergence of belief and practice which had grown up in history. It was his ability to maintain this tension without loss of principle which enabled him to be both an ardent denominationalist and also Free Church leader.[82]

Clifford had little time for or interest in interdenominational conferences on union, recognizing that the will to unite was weak and, to his mind, the Anglican attitude towards Baptists and the Free Churches was condescending. He, like Glover, despised the kind of union which could only be secured by the absence or sacrifice of personal convictions. 'He gave some the impression that he was intolerant on the subject of "Christian unity". But those who knew him best knew that this was not the real explanation of his attitude...'[83] He claimed a kinship as a Christian with all other Christians, but with other Free Churches, despite their differences, he believed there was an inner spiritual affinity which warranted an outward expression of unity,[84] hence his involvement with the FCC.

At the Baptist Assembly in April 1921, a resolution was passed endorsing the report of the Joint Committee of the FCEFC and the NCEFC,[85] and requested that the BU Council continue its work with a view to a better understanding between the Free Churches and the removal of such obstacles as still remained.[86] The Joint Committee report was never intended to be a reply to the *Appeal*, that was for the individual Free Churches to do, rather it was meant to elucidate the Free Church

---

80   Marchant, *Dr. John Clifford*, 45. On the Westbourne Park church, see H.E. Bonsall and E.H. Robertson, *The Dream of an Ideal City: Westbourne Park 1877–1977* (1978), and on baptism in the church and Clifford's views, see pp.11, 83-84.

81   See G.W. Byrt, *John Clifford: A Fighting Free Churchman* (1947), 98-100.

82   For a useful summary of his Free Church involvement from the movements' inception in the 1890s, see Byrt, *John Clifford*, 113-21.

83   Byrt, *John Clifford*, 113.

84   Byrt, *John Clifford*, 116-17.

85   It was entitled 'The Free Churches and the Lambeth Appeal', see Bell, *Documents on Christian Unity, 1920–4*, 120-41. See also 'The Free Churches and the Lambeth Appeal—Being the report of a Committee Appointed by the Federal Council of the Evangelical Free Churches and National Free Church Council', *BT&F* March 25, 1921, 180-82.

86   Bell, *Documents on Christian Unity, 1920–4*, 104.

position.[87] At the same time, it showed Free Church readiness to respond to the idea underlying the *Appeal*, 'the idea of fellowship'.[88]

It soon became apparent that most Baptists were not in sympathy with Shakespeare's views and the reunion movement. However, a considerable debate did result from his advocacy. In 1921 two prize essays based on Shakespeare's book were published in *The Baptist Times and Freeman*. J. Ivory Cripps admitted, 'We have not succeeded in converting the paedo-Baptist bodies to our view; they have hitherto ignored our witness. But I believe the whole situation would alter if the rite we stand for could be removed from the denominational atmosphere and be allowed to make its own unanswerable appeal to the membership of a United Church of England. Those who contend that this would destroy our witness seem to me to trust the power of truth too little.'[89] A.J. Burgoyne drew attention to the existence of Union churches which were sometimes fitted with both a baptistry and a font, and were presided over sometimes by Baptists, sometimes by Congregationalists: 'The only inference that can be drawn is the complete possibility of a Federated Church. Desirability is another matter and must, we suppose, always remain a question of opinion.'[90] Later that year and the following year there were two lengthy correspondences discussing the pros and cons of reunion, but neither of them referred explicitly to baptism.[91]

---

87   Bell, *Documents on Christian Unity, 1920–4*, 129. See also p.122. The Assembly discussed the document before its official publication, on April 27, while, according to Bell, *Documents on Christian Unity, 1920–4*, 120, the report was not issued till May 22.

88   Bell, *Documents on Christian Unity, 1920–4*, 125.

89   J. Ivory Cripps of Hagley Road, Birmingham, 'On "Christian Unity". With Special Reference to Dr. Shakespeare's Book', *BT&F* January 14, 1921, 22-23, quote from p.23.

90   A.J. Burgoyne of Gloucester, 'Christian Unity. With Special Reference to "The Churches at the Crossroads"', *BT&F* January 28, 1921, 54-55, quote from p.54.

91   The first series was triggered by the publication of a lecture by M.E. Aubrey, 'Reunion from the Point of View of the Baptist Church', *BT&F* April 15 and 22, 1921, 230-31 and 246. The ensuing letters were all headed 'Baptists and Reunion', see L.H. Foulds of Trinity College, Cambridge, *BT&F* May 20, 310; Aubrey, *BT&F* May 27, 328; Foulds, *BT&F* June 3, 344; Aubrey, *BT&F* June 10, 359. See W.M.S. West, 'The Reverend Secretary Aubrey: Part III', *BQ* 34.7 (July, 1992), 324-25, on the original lecture by Aubrey at Cambridge. The following year, the debate continued, though again, the baptismal issue lay implicit within the general discussion, the exception being J.H. French, 'The Baptist Witness and Reunion', *BT&F* January 6, 1922, 5-6. See, W.T. Whitley, 'The Right Approach to Unity', *BT&F* February 17, 1922, 100; F.C. Spurr, 'The Trusteeship of the Free Churches and Reunion', *BT&F* May 12, 1922, 301-02; 'Church Unity. Conferences Between Representatives of the Church of England and Federal Council of the Free Churches', *BT&F* June 2, 1922, 351-52; three articles entitled 'The Lambeth Report on Christian Unity', H. Townsend, *BT&F* June 23, 1922, 402, and W.E.

In an address delivered at Bristol Cathedral, Shakespeare[92] set out the Baptist contribution towards a United Church and spent considerable time enunciating the Baptist understanding of baptism. The Baptist communion, he declared, is constituted 'on a certain view of baptism and the implications to which it leads. In our view Christian baptism should be by immersion. This is entirely secondary to us and is only valid because it is related to our doctrine of conversion and is a symbol of burial with Christ and the rising with Him to newness of life. But the real issue is as to the subject, not the mode.' Baptism is in the name of the Trinity, on a personal profession of repentance and faith, and though sometimes called adult baptism, this he repudiated as an entire mistake. 'We baptize children if it is their desire and if they understand what it is to follow Christ', and he cited the example of Alexander MacLaren, baptized at the age of eleven, and declared that the corresponding Anglican service was confirmation. Though infants were not baptized, Baptists believed that through the merits of Christ, they were born into a state of grace and into a redeemed world, that the Lord loved them and called and saved them, but that baptism was not connected with this initial stage.

Shakespeare denied that Baptists were the ritualists of the Free Churches, rather, he explained, the reason for their emphasis on baptism was that 'we are opposed to everything in religion that is magical. We do not like a religion that is by proxy instead of being based on a personal and intelligent act. A saving change is to us always a moral and spiritual change', and this change is an act of God. He then expounded Baptist ecclesiology: 'Our doctrine of baptism is related to our doctrine of the Church.' Since baptism was administered only to those professing personal faith in Christ, and was the symbol of admission to the visible church, the church on earth was a community of regenerate persons. Though many Baptists were less ready than Shakespeare to see confirmation as the equivalent of baptism and perhaps to demote the mode to secondary importance, in all other respects Shakespeare clearly presented the common Baptist understanding of baptism.[93] It was

---

Blomfield and J. Leslie Chown, *BT&F* June 6, 1922, 418. See also the lengthy correspondence under the title 'The Problem of Reunion', *BT&F* June 30, 1922, 421; July 7, 434; July 14, 452; July 21, 470; July 28, 485; August 4, 503.

92   J.H. Shakespeare, 'Baptists and Reunion', *BT&F* December 22, 1922, 836-37, citations from p.836. The following two paragraphs are based on this address.

93   Shakespeare also published a tract called *Christian Baptism* (n.d.), however, a copy of this has not been traced. Due to his responsibilities within the BU and Free Church movement, Shakespeare wrote relatively little, though his concern for them both was reflected in his first book *Baptist and Congregational Pioneers* (1906), which only dealt with baptism in a descriptive historical way. In it he defined 'Baptist pioneers' as 'English Separatists, Congregational in Church polity and anti-paedobaptist in practice, who gave rise to indigenous Churches in this country, and with whom the English

possibly this fact, which confused many Baptists: how their General Secretary could be both a traditional Baptist in so many ways and yet such an advocate for reunion. They could not understand how a United Church could come into existence without the loss of essential Baptist principles.[94]

Under the sub-heading 'The Splendid Dream', J.D. Freeman reiterated that the avowed objective of the *Appeal* was nothing less than the organic reunion of all Christendom.[95] Acknowledging that the war had had a considerable effect upon the churches, 'disposing us towards this new comradeship', he cautioned that it would be possible to draw wrong inferences from the abnormal state of affairs created by the war.[96] Shakespeare had argued that the war was but another sign for the necessity of a United Church,[97] but now Freeman added his voice to Glover's. He denied that the soldier fighting in the war would have ever 'asked for any sacrifice of principle',[98] and identified two formidable barriers to the path of reunion. The first was the 'manifest sacramentalism' and 'undisguised sympathy with sacerdotalism' of the *Appeal* in every reference to the 'ordinances' of baptism and the Lord's Supper; the second was the familiar Anglican claim for the necessity of the episcopate.[99] Such teaching had been largely responsible for driving Baptists from the Church of England in the first place, therefore 'the prospect of becoming re-identified with it seems scarcely likely to woo us

---

Baptists of to-day are in historical, theological, and spiritual succession', pp.16-17. In this way he underlined that the Baptist's doctrine of baptism proceed from their prior understanding of the nature of the church.

94   In 1923 both J.C. Carlile and Shakespeare contributed to J. Marchant (ed.), *The Coming Renaissance* (1923): Carlile, 'Realities of To-day', 54-68; Shakespeare, 'The Great Need', 79-92. In 'The Great Need', 80, Shakespeare referred to the *Lambeth Appeal* as a 'remarkable advance', stating that, 'All those who believe in our Lord Jesus Christ and have been baptised into the name of the Holy Trinity are sharing with us in the universal Church of Christ which is His Body.' This is almost a direct quotation from the opening of the *Appeal*.

95   J.D. Freeman, the Canadian born minister of Belvoir Street, Leicester, 'The Lambeth Appeal', 3-10. On Dr Freeman, see S. Mitchell, *Not Disobedient... A History of United Baptist Church, Leicester including Harvey Lane 1760–1845, Belvoir Street 1845–1940 and Charles Street 1831–1940* (Leicester, 1984), 156-61; *BT&F* March 20, 1925, 189 and *BT* April 28, 1927, 294.

96   Freeman, 'The Lambeth Appeal', 4.

97   Hayden, 'Still at the Crossroads?', 31, 'the event which convinced him...was the trauma of the First World War.'

98   Freeman, 'The Lambeth Appeal', 4. See also p.5.

99   Freeman, 'The Lambeth Appeal', 8.

back.'[100] Quoting the opening words of the *Appeal*,[101] Freeman proceeded to clarify the Baptist view of who were incorporated into this Body: 'The Baptism which incorporates souls into that Body of Christ, is not (in our convention) a baptism of water, but a baptism of the Spirit.'[102] Moreover, the *Appeal*'s formula raised the old question of the subjects of baptism. Freeman asserted that Baptists held infant baptism to be 'no real Christian baptism at all', therefore those who were issuing the *Appeal* were 'men who are themselves unbaptised' according to the 'profound conviction of some nine millions of evangelicals known as Baptists and Disciples.' 'Are they hereby called upon to admit a thing to be what they believe it is not? Does not that involve some juggling with conscience?' he questioned before repudiating the doctrine of baptismal regeneration.[103]

Addressing the Third Baptist World Congress (BWC) in Uppsala Cathedral in July 1923, Shakespeare accidentally knocked the great Bible off the lectern while ascending into the pulpit, an accident which visibly shook him and which he took to be a sign from God that his ministry was effectively at its close. His address on 'No man having put his hand to the plough...' (Luke 9:62) was a plea for both unity and international peace. Over the preceeding five years he noted there had been increasing numbers of inter-denominational co-operative ventures, which, he believed, were contributing towards the glorious vision of Paul's Ephesian letter—a clear reference to ch. 4:5, 'One Lord, one faith, one baptism', though it was never clear what Shakespeare would say on 'one baptism' in his proposed United Church.[104]

Despite Shakespeare's prominence in the BWA, the Stockholm Congress endorsed a message on its behalf to Christians worldwide which was largely the work of the Southern Baptist, E.Y. Mullins.[105] It stressed the importance of world Baptist unity[106] and rejected any notion of Christian unity not based on 'the operation of the Holy Spirit arising

---

100 Freeman, 'The Lambeth Appeal', 6.

101 'We acknowledge all those who believe in our Lord Jesus Christ, and have been baptised into the name of the Holy Trinity, as sharing with us membership in the universal Church of Christ, which is His Body.'

102 Freeman, 'The Lambeth Appeal', 6-7.

103 Freeman, 'The Lambeth Appeal', 7.

104 See J.H. Shakespeare, 'Peace and Unity', in W.T. Whitley (ed), *Third Baptist Congress—Stockholm, July 21–27* (1923), 35, the whole address is recorded on pp.31-36.

105 Shepherd, 'Shakespeare', 279-80. On Mullins and his prior work on this issue, see H.L. McBeth, *The Baptist Heritage: Four Centuries of Baptist Witness* (Nashville, 1987), 677.

106 'A Message of the Baptist World Alliance to the Baptist Brotherhood, to Other Christian Brethren, and to the World', in Whitley (ed.), *Third Baptist Congress*, 223.

from a common faith in Christ', and which wielded power over the individual conscience or maintained a sacerdotal understanding of ministry.[107] It asserted the doctrine of the church comprised of believers only, regeneration being the condition of membership, and the autonomy of the local church. On this basis, baptism is the immersion of the believer on profession of their faith, employing the word ordinance while denying that Baptists were ceremonialists or sacramentalists, and rejecting infant baptism as 'utterly irreconcilable with the ideal of a spiritual Christianity.'[108]

No direct response from Shakespeare exists and Peter Shepherd is right in seeing the 'Message' as undermining Shakespeare's stance on Christian unity. Shepherd notes that it effectively put an end to the Lambeth talks, coinciding with a leaked Anglican memorandum which insisted on the necessity of episcopal ordination if Free Church ministries were not to be regarded as 'irregular or defective'.[109] Although American in origin, the 'Message' was received with acclamation, and was undoubtedly accepted by most English Baptists, including W.Y. Fullerton.[110]

In the years that followed the *Lambeth Appeal* and the subsequent conversations, hopes that the matter would proceed speedily quickly receded. For Anglicans, intercommunion could only be attained by the settlement of outstanding differences in procedure and church life, but for the Free Churches intercommunion was intimately connected to mutual recognition, and they also believed that theological differences were being superficially dealt with.[111] To the related theological and practical difficulties was added the fact that in 1921 the Church of England had begun conversations with the Roman Catholic Church at Malines which continued up to 1925.[112] These alienated the Free Churches, including Shakespeare, who felt that too much had been conceded to the Roman position and as a result he withdrew from the

---

107 'A Message of the Baptist World Alliance', 224.

108 'A Message of the Baptist World Alliance', 224-25.

109 See Shepherd, 'Shakespeare', 280-81, who, p.280, comments that the title of the 'Message' in its use of 'to Other Christian Brethren' effectively answered the *Lambeth Appeal's* 'to all Christian People'. See pp.232-33 on the memorandum.

110 W.Y. Fullerton, 'The Stockholm Congress and Exhibition', *BQ* 1.3 (July, 1923), 291, see Shepherd, 'Shakespeare', 281. Shepherd, pp.282-87, then discusses the resulting domestic debate over the desirability of continuing reunion discussions and the ongoing opposition to Shakespeare which eventually led to his resignation in 1924.

111 Grant, *Free Churchmanship in England*, 318. See also Bell, *Documents on Christian Unity, 1920–4*, 130 and 126-27.

112 See Hastings, *History of English Christianity*, 208-12; Carlile, *My Life's Little Day*, 180-81.

reunion movement,[113] and the discussions with the Church of England, which had begun in 1921, came to an end in 1925.

To mark the end of the five years of discussions arising from the *Lambeth Appeal*, Carlile, editor of the *Baptist Times*, invited Blomfield to write an article on what he believed were the Baptist objections to reunion.[114] Acknowledging the admirable spirit of the *Appeal*, Blomfield however declared that 'it offered no basis for Reunion. It passed from the true assertion that God wills fellowship to the different and very questionable assertion that He wills organic reunion.' The *Appeal* had called for the acceptance of the Nicene Creed as the substance of the faith and the Apostles' Creed as the baptismal confession. Blomfield asked: 'with all due respect to these creeds... "Is there one Baptist minister who would demand such a confession of all candidates for baptism?" If so, would his Church endorse such a demand? I feel sure Baptists would repudiate it.' Citing the *Appeal*'s proposal of 'Acceptance of the Sacraments of Baptism and Holy Communion', he commented that such looked hopeful until probed: 'What is Baptism? Who are its proper subjects? What does it effect? Does it regenerate?' and then concluded that, 'Vague formulas are of no value for a united Church.' After discussing other proposals from the *Appeal* he added a personal note: 'The Resolutions convinced me that nothing could come of the Lambeth proposals', a view undoubtedly held by the majority of Baptists. His closing remark is telling: 'For ourselves let us go on with our own work and bear our own witness. And whilst we proclaim the truth as God has shewn it us, let us cherish an ardent affection for all who love our common Lord.'

The BU's response was released to the press a month before the 1926 May Assembly in Leeds and received extensive and appreciative coverage.[115] Despite poor attendance at the Assembly, the meetings were of the utmost importance. The president that year was J.H. Rushbrooke, but the speakers had been invited to speak on Baptist belief and polity by the new Secretary of the Union, M.E. Aubrey, and they all linked their

---

113 Shakespeare wrote to Carlile urging that a statement be prepared to which he would put his signature withdrawing from attempts at Free Church–Anglican reunion, Carlile, *My Life's Little Day,* 181.

114 W.E. Blomfield, 'Church Reunion. Impasse', *BT* October 22, 1925, 747-48.

115 See 'Baptists and Reunion', *BT* April 22, 1926, 306. The details of the *Reply* were reported sometimes in full (*The Times*) and sometimes in extenso (*The Manchester Guardian*) thereby disseminating the contents to the Baptist community and other denominations, a stroke of good fortune because the opening of the Assembly coincided with the beginning of the General Strike so many delegates did not attend, and many who did returned home immediately. See Payne, *The Baptist Union,* 196.

messages with the Baptist *Reply* to the *Lambeth Appeal*,[116] which was unanimously accepted by the Assembly. The *Reply* declared the Baptist belief that the 'Catholic Church' was the 'holy Society of believers', and that personal faith was necessary for membership of this church.[117] It then dealt at length with the question of baptism and the Lord's Supper, both of which, as dominical institutions, were 'means of grace to all who receive them in faith.' Because the Baptist understanding of the church was a 'community of Christian believers' the ordinance of baptism was administered only to those who made a personal confession of repentance and faith and the mode was immersion, symbolic of the inner baptism of the Holy Spirit. Infant baptism, however, subverted the conception of the church as a fellowship of believers. No rite was needed to bring children into relation with God, though the widespread practice of Infant Dedication among Baptists emphasized the duties, privileges and responsibilities of parents, as the church offered prayers for children and parents.[118] On Christian unity, the *Reply* stated that 'Further progress...can be secured, we are convinced, only by unreserved mutual recognition', and expressed a readiness to join with the Church of England in 'exploring the possibility of a federation of equal and autonomous Churches in which the several parts of the Church of Christ would co-operate in bringing before men the will and claims of our Lord.'[119]

Though there was no attempt to impose uniformity in the approach of each speaker at the Assembly, there was nevertheless an impressive convergence in outlook, stating clearly what can be taken as widely representative of Baptist views on the subjects discussed, and this is nowhere clearer than when the speakers overlapped on the question of baptism and related themes. Three of the five addresses were of particular relevance to the baptismal issue.

Gilbert Laws believed that Baptists could not live as Baptists without believer's baptism. 'This point is so obvious that I surely need not labour it. If we cease to teach and practise the baptism of believers as part of the whole counsel of God in the gospel, it is pretty evident that we shall come

---

116 The addresses were published in Rushbrooke (ed.), *Faith of the Baptists*, and included in full the text of the *Reply*, pp.85-91. The *Reply* was also published in the *BT&F* April 15, 1926, 284. All the messages, with the exception of Gilbert Laws', were published in the *BT&F* May 20, 1926, 344-346, and 349-50. The *Reply* itself had been carefully drawn up by a small committee, under the chairmanship of Dr Rushbrooke and had been convened by Dr F.T. Lord, who moved from Acton to Coventry that year. See Payne, *The Baptist Union*, 197.

117 *Reply*, 86-87.

118 *Reply*, 88.

119 *Reply*, 90-91.

to an end as Baptists.'[120] It was more than a mere external rite, but as part of the gospel, with the Lord's Supper, it was a proclamation of that gospel, symbolical of the burial and resurrection of the believer with Christ (an enacted creed),[121] and it showed a Baptist what their character should be: an utterly consecrated person.[122]

A.C. Underwood asserted that baptism arose from Baptist ecclesiology, being the rite of entry into the church of Christ. The proper subjects of baptism were, therefore, believers, and the proper mode immersion.[123] As Clifford had before him, he denied that Baptists were ritualists. Only when baptism was administered to believers by immersion was it able to retain its full value as a sacrament and run no risk of degenerating into a charm. Only so could it be a means of grace to all who submitted to it in faith.[124] Infant baptism lost all this. As far as the infant was concerned paedobaptism was either a piece of white magic or a meaningless ceremony.[125] He continued:

> This, then, is our position, and this is our message to the modern world. We are not organised as a separate denomination merely to secure the administration of a rite in a particular way. It is not a question of much water or little. We are organised to secure for baptism its full New Testament significance as a means of grace to the regenerate man and to bar out effectively all magical ideas. And we claim that we are the only people who can secure both ends. Congregationalists and other Evangelicals can bar out magic by reducing baptism to a mere ceremony, but then they lose baptism as a means of grace. And further, we claim that the New Testament mode of administering baptism by immersion helps to make it a means of grace as nothing else can, for immersion gives us in perfect symbolism the core of the evangelical faith—death unto sin and resurrection to a new life in Christ.[126]

It will be immediately clear just how significant these words were for the issue of reunion. Underwood then proceeded to call Baptist ministers to 'preach up' baptism along these lines—as a means of grace to all who receive it in faith.[127] He concluded:

> In a word, we can meet all attacks and commend our practice to our age by a return to the full New Testament doctrine of baptism. We have always stressed the New

---

120 G. Laws of West Croyden, 'Vital Forces of the Baptist Movement', in Rushbrooke (ed.), *Faith of the Baptists*, 13.

121 Laws, 'Vital Forces', 14-15.

122 Laws, 'Vital Forces', 19-20.

123 A.C. Underwood, a tutor at Rawdon and soon to become its President, 'Conversion and Baptism', 26.

124 Underwood, 'Conversion and Baptism', 27-29.

125 Underwood, 'Conversion and Baptism', 31.

126 Underwood, 'Conversion and Baptism', 32.

127 Underwood, 'Conversion and Baptism', 33.

Testament mode and the New Testament subjects. Now let us also stress the New Testament doctrine of baptism as a great spiritual experience. Let us preach baptism not only as an act of obedience, not only as a public avowal of faith in Christ, not only as a ceremony of reception into the church, not only as a symbol of the experience of conversion, but also as a means of grace—as a religious experience of the first rank for all those, and only those, who come to it with the receptiveness of faith.[128]

In his presidential address, Dr Rushbrooke, Secretary of the BWA, noting the developments towards unity, again called for there to be no 'sacrifice of principles'. For him, 'central, vital, creative Christian truth demands embodiment; and our denomination exists, and so far as we are able to see will persist, as the answer to that demand.' As far as Baptists are concerned, he claimed, the unifying Christian principle is *sola fide*.[129] 'We are constrained to believe—or we should not be Baptists—that the Evangelical experience of faith has its implications and applications revealed to us by the Spirit of Christ; and therefore that our churches stand for religious values which cannot be surrendered.'[130]

Everything said, he believed, had a bearing on baptism. 'Is there anything in all the world to compare with our Christian baptism as a means of setting forth the supremacy of faith, its nature and implications? Faith involves an immediate personal relation with God in Christ; the requirement of personal confession leaves that fact clear and unmistakable.'[131] Any magical view of the ordinance was excised and baptismal regeneration was a doctrine as perilous as it was unscriptural.[132]

The paradox of our denominational life is that by means of a rite we offer decisive testimony against ritualism. In its very form the ordinance expresses the believer's

---

128 Underwood, 'Conversion and Baptism', 35.

129 Rushbrooke, 'Protestant of the Protestants: The Baptist Churches, Their Progress and Their Spiritual Principle', in Rushbrooke (ed.), *Faith of the Baptists*, 70. There are three biographies of Rushbrooke: M.E. Aubrey, 'J.H. Rushbrooke', *BQ* 15.8 (October, 1954), 369-77; E.A. Payne, *James Henry Rushbrooke 1870–1947: A Baptist Greatheart* (1954), and B. Green, *Tomorrow's Man: A Biography of James Henry Rushbrooke* (Didcot, 1997). Green, *Tomorrow's Man*, 187-203, examines Rushbrooke's involvement and views on the ecumenical developments and the place of baptism within them, which he sums up in his first sub-heading, p.187, 'Committed But Questioning'. Aubrey, 'Rushbrooke', 370, noted Rushbrooke's change in attitude towards ecumenicsm when he became Secretary of the BWA. Green, *Tomorrow's Man*, 199-201, identifies this change to have arisen in 1938–39 when discussing the proposals for the WCC with the Southern Baptist, Dr. W.O. Carver, and these feelings were heightened by seeing how Romanian Baptists were being persecuted by the Romanian Orthodox Church, who were recognized by the WCC.

130 Rushbrooke, 'Protestant of the Protestants', 71.

131 Rushbrooke, 'Protestant of the Protestants', 80.

132 Rushbrooke, 'Protestant of the Protestants', 80-81.

reverence for the sole authority of Christ. The symbolism of immersion guards and proclaims great Evangelical truths and experiences: the saving significance of the death, burial, and resurrection of the Lord Jesus, the new life which is the common life of members of the Body of Christ. *Ex opere operato* nothing is effected; but we know in our own lives that to follow Christ in obedience and faith is to find in His ordinance a means of grace. Therefore we assert in action louder than words that self-dedication is an indispensible element.

To regard an infant as baptized was to divest the ordinance of its meaning and to deprive the child of the right and privilege which they alone could have: to make their own confession and as a believer receive baptism in the Lord's way.[133]

The reason why Baptists stood apart from other evangelical Christians with unwavering resolve, Rushbrooke explained, was to express and guard the conception of the church as the fellowship of Christian people. 'Rightly understood, we cannot make too much of Baptism... Baptists see in the ordinance a divinely appointed means of ensuring the simplicity and purity of the Gospel. We exist for nothing else than the propagation and defence of the Gospel; in the fulfilment of that purpose, as God gives us light and guidance, we find the final, the only, and the sufficient justification of our existence as Christian churches.'[134]

The majority of Baptists could heartily consent to the views expressed from the Leeds Assembly platform and in the *Reply*, even if many of the subtleties and intricacies of argumentation would not have been often repeated. It can be little doubted, though, that the addresses[135] represented accurately the mood if not the opinions of the majority of Baptists regarding reunion. Discussions could continue, as they did, but there was considerable reserve and a determination not to surrender any principles. Together, the addresses and *Reply* registered the Baptist reactions to the conversations which had gone on since 1920. The *Reply* concluded that 'union of such a kind as the Bishops have contemplated is not possible for us.' Further progress 'in the direction' of Christian unity could only be secured by 'unreserved mutual recognition', and the invitation was made 'to join with the Church of England in exploring the possibility of a federation of equal and autonomous Churches in which the several parts of the Church of Christ would co-operate in bringing before men the will and claims of our Lord.'[136]

---

133 Rushbrooke, 'Protestant of the Protestants', 81.
134 Rushbrooke, 'Protestant of the Protestants', 82.
135 Which also included contributions by W.W.B. Emery of Cotham Grove, Bristol, 'The Fellowship and the Table of the Lord', 36-45, and J.O. Hagger of Cambuslang, 'Discipleship and its Implications', 46-59, in Rushbrooke (ed.), *Faith of the Baptists*.
136 *Reply*, 90-91.

The importance of the 1926 *Reply* and Assembly addresses lies in the fact that this was the first time in the thirty years since the founding of the official Free Church movement that the Baptist position on the church, baptism and communion had been clearly and systematically (though briefly) set out. Prior to this, baptism had been subordinated to the broader discussion of the pros and cons of union/reunion and whether or not such could occur without the compromise of Baptist principles, among which baptism was included.

Baptists and the Churches of Christ

In March 1931 two churches previously affiliated to the Churches of Christ, Twynholm and its branch church in Boston Road, were received into the BU. The leading figure in the Twynholm church was Robert Wilson Black, a man of considerable personal means and with great leadership qualities. In 1927 the members of the church had begun to be concerned over the practice of closed communion. Though the church remained closed in membership, in June that year it withdrew from fellowship with the London Association of the Churches of Christ. In the monthly magazine of the church, the *Joyful Tidings* (June 1928), the minister, W. Mander, wrote an article on 'Movements Toward Christian Union', drawing attention to church unions in Scotland, Canada and the three Methodist denominations in Britain. Mander acknowledged the widespread movement which such unions bore witness to and observed that the Churches of Christ were themselves not unaffected by this popular tendency. He then asked: 'Are Churches of Christ to continue in isolation while there are many other Christian people who practise immersion with divergent emphasis, and among whom it might be possible for members of Churches of Christ to maintain their weekly communion and distinctive witness?' There were those, many young members, yearning for such enrichment and broadening of their vision which such sympathetic fellowship with other baptized Christians would bring. 'Ought not the next movement towards Christian Union in this land to be to enhance the churches which practise believers' baptism?'[137]

The Annual Conference of the Churches of Christ discussed the possibility of such a movement, but while favourable views were expressed towards initiating closer union with baptized believers of other denominations, the majority, including J.W. Black, Robert's brother, voted to maintain the isolation of the Churches of Christ. This decision led the Twynholm quarterly church meeting on October 2, 1929, to

---

137 H. Townsend, *Robert Wilson Black* (1954), 70.

withdraw altogether from the Churches of Christ.[138] This set in motion the series of approaches which finally led to the church joining the BU, the principle architect of which was R.W. Black.

Henry Townsend, Black's biographer, recorded that from 1931 'when Mr. Black was received into membership of the Baptist Union, he soon became one of its most outstanding leaders.' Within his new sphere of service, Black vigorously affirmed that repentance, faith in Christ as Saviour and Lord, believer's baptism and remission of sins were essentials of New Testament ecclesiology.[139] From this basis he argued that 'unity by the sacrifice of principle would be a grave disaster.' From the denomination's Declaration of Principle, he spoke on behalf of the Baptist majority when he affirmed that, 'They are not Baptists by choice but by conviction, and to recognise infant baptism in any form would, they believe, be in entire opposition to New Testament teaching and practice.'[140]

Baptist, Congregational and Presbyterian Reunion Discussions

Declarations from the Lambeth Conference in August 1930 proved disappointing as far as the Free Churches and their ministers were concerned, yet this did not prevent further conversations taking place. The following March, the Archbishop of Canterbury, Dr C.G. Lang, formally invited the Federal Council to resume conversations, and in September eighteen representatives were put forward, among them M.E. Aubrey,[141] Gilbert Laws and Hugh Martin, three men of considerably differing views on the ecumenical question. Aubrey, as Secretary of the BU and a participant in both the Free Church and Faith and Order (F&O) movements, was a cautious and diplomatic figure. Laws needed to be persuaded that reunion was possible without the surrender of principles. However, Hugh Martin, from 1929 the editor of the SCM Press and Joint Honorary Secretary of the 'Friends of Reunion' (FoR) from its foundation in 1933, ardently believed and advocated a reunion which would be attainable without the loss of any distinctive principle.[142] These

---

138 Townsend, *Robert Wilson Black* , 70-71. See also D.M. Thompson, *Let Sects and Parties Fall: A Short History of the Association of Churches of Christ in Great Britain and Ireland* (Birmingham, 1980), 138-41.

139 Townsend, *Robert Wilson Black*, 72.

140 R.W. Black, 'Baptists and Christian Unity', *BT* Sept 6, 1934, 628.

141 A detailed study of Dr. Aubrey has been made by W.M.S. West, 'The Young Mr. Aubrey', *BQ* 33.8 (October, 1990), 351-63; 'The Reverend Secretary Aubrey. Part I', *BQ* 34.5 (January, 1992), 199-223; 'Part II', *BQ* 34.6 (April, 1992), 263-81; 'Part III', *BQ* 34.7 (July, 1992), 320-36.

142 On Hugh Martin see A.R. Cross, 'Revd. Dr. Hugh Martin: Publisher and Writer, Part 1', *BQ* 37.1 (January, 1997), 33-49; 'Revd. Dr. Hugh Martin: Ecumenist, Part 2', *BQ*

renewed conversations rambled on throughout the 1930s, until 1938 when an *Outline of a Reunion Scheme* and other documents were published.[143]

The renewed round of conferences sparked off other studies into the reunion question. Seymour J. Price discussed in particular the Free Church doctrine of the priesthood of all believers from the lay perspective, drawing out the obvious gulf which this revealed as existing between the Free Churches and such a Church as the Anglican communion and the implications of this for the sacraments. Of the Free Church context he noted that 'A layman can be appointed minister in sole charge of a Church, and exercise all the functions of a minister, including "administration of the sacraments of Baptism and Holy Communion..."'[144] His conclusion was inevitable: 'It is obvious, when account is taken, not only of the Churches which took part in the Lambeth Joint Conferences, but also of the Roman and Eastern Churches, that Church Union in the sense of one organised visible Church is not within the realm of practical religious politics.'[145] Further, he ruled out the notion that Christian Unity could be achieved on the basis of the minimum formula, believing that the cause of Christian unity could not be helped by avoiding issues which sooner or later would have to be faced. 'So the Christian Unity that is much to be desired must take up into itself all the rich diversity of the varying streams of Christian experience.' Price called for an end to the discussion of 'abstruse and hairsplitting points of Faith and Order' and instead suggested that such conferences should seek fuller spiritual co-operation.[146]

An anonymous writer denied that John 17:21 spoke of unity in terms of one organisation and, taking their stand from the 1926 *Reply*, advocated the concept of federation. The gains of federation would be twofold: 'frank mutual recognition' and 'the wise utilisation of all Christian forces for evangelisation.' Of the former they wrote: 'Federation implies the full recognition of every member of every federating body as a member of the Universal Church of Christ, so that he is welcome at every act of worship in every section...' And then, significantly, they declared that it would not be 'for the Baptist to feel that a man merely christened in infancy has never even been baptised; in each case the man stands or falls to his Master, and the judgement of his own

37.2 (April, 1997), 71-86; 'Revd. Dr. Hugh Martin: Ecumenical Controversialist and Writer, Part 3', *BQ* 37.3 (July, 1997), 131-46, and T. Tatlow, 'Foreword', in R.G. Smith (ed.), *The Enduring Gospel* (1950), 9-18.

143 See Jordan, *Free Church Unity*, 175-79; Payne, *The Baptist Union*, 198-99.

144 S.J. Price, a prominent Baptist layman, 'Laymen and Reunion', *BQ* 5 (July, 1931), 291-92.

145 Price, 'Laymen and Reunion', 299.

146 Price, 'Laymen and Reunion', 300.

body upholds his own convictions. Full mutual recognition is a first condition, and a first gain.'[147]

In the early 1930s Baptists increasingly began to discuss and debate more openly the pros and cons of the reunion/union issue, and this was nowhere more clearly reflected than in the pages of *The Baptist Times*. One such article was entitled 'Is Union of Baptists, Congregationalists and Presbyterians Desirable and Practicable?' to which the answer 'Yes!' was given by E.W. Burt, 'No!' by H.C. Wagnell.[148]

Burt claimed that it was union not uniformity which was under discussion, recognizing that no one of the three bodies could claim a monopoly of the truth. However, he did admit to two principal difficulties: differences in church government and order, and differences over the subjects and mode of baptism. Concerning the latter, he believed that when several considerations were borne in mind union would become possible, because all three denominations rejected baptismal regeneration, affirmed that the baptism of the Spirit was of infinitely more importance than any outward ceremony, each requiring a confession of faith before admittance into full membership, and there was the fact that many Baptist churches held dedication services. In such a union, he said, 'we could well leave the choice of the particular mode of baptism to the individual candidate, provided that a confession of faith were required before admission to fellowship.' He proceeded, 'Indeed, we already have more union than is commonly supposed, for members of the three bodies freely partake of the Lord's Supper in one another's Churches, and membership is mixed and no incongruity is experienced.'

In response to the issue of the desirability of union, Wagnell answered '"Yes" most cordially, given that we could have union without compromising conscience or conviction.' But he did not believe that it was practicable, for 'it would fetter our special witness, and therefore the answer for us is in the negative.' The chief barrier to such a union was baptism and its implications, 'especially the latter'. Baptists believe that they hold and administer baptism as divinely intended and certainly as taught and practised by the church for the first two centuries, therefore, they could neither relinquish nor modify their witness to it as a price of union. 'Nor, what is equally important, can we countenance its perversion by what is misnamed infant baptism. Loyalty to Christ forbids that.' Believing that baptism did not have to be a condition for church

---

147 Anonymous, 'Church Union by Federation', *BQ* 5, (April, 1931), 246.

148 E.W. Burt and H.C. Wagnell, 'Is Union of Baptists, Congregationalists and Presbyterians Desirable and Practicable?', *BT* March 8, 1934, 165. E.W. Burt is not to be confused with G.W. Byrt, one of John Clifford's biographers. Cf. the earlier letters from Mr Richard Jewson of Norwich for such a union, Mr J.H. Stanley of Walthamstow and Mr H.B. Stote from Tenby against, and Mr F.W. Bond, a 'young' Baptist from Liverpool, who was cautiously in favour, all in 'Open Forum', *BT* October 20, 1932, 720.

membership, Wagnell, however, rejected the idea that infant baptism could be accepted as either an alternative or substitute for New Testament baptism. Baptism 'by its very genius and intention' was for none other than those possessing conscious faith in Christ. Responding to the question why Baptists made an ordinance a barrier to a union so ardently desired and in many respects mutually advantageous, he made a number of points. Accepting the authority of Christ and scripture precluded any steps which would invalidate baptism or impair its significance. It was not the ordinance but the implications of the ordinance which justified Baptists' separate existence, the significance of baptism lying in its symbolism as the gospel in a 'figure', thereby conserving and safeguarding the truth of the gospel. Conversely, the introduction and practice of infant baptism neutralized the power of the gospel ministry, and tacitly implied a difference between the sprinkled and unsprinkled child. The cause of division, he maintained, was not of the Baptists' making, for the introduction of a practice unknown in the early church had accomplished that. Baptists, he believed, had the proud distinction of being free from every shred of ritualism which derived its supposed efficacy from priestism or mere tradition.

In November 1932, C.T. Le Quesne presented a memorandum to the BU Council from the committee which had been appointed to discuss the question of Baptist–Congregational co-operation.[149] The only point, he reported, over which any discussion of doctrine would need to take place would be baptism and this would need a more precise definition from both denominations on the meaning, mode and obligation of the sacrament. Then he added, somewhat prophetically: 'It is clear that considerable controversy may or will be aroused in the attempt to arrive at such a definition.' The outcome of the ensuing discussion was that it was agreed that a Special Committee, under Le Quesne's chairmanship, should be set up to consider the broader matter of union between Baptists, Congregationalists and Presbyterians. A second factor leading to its formation was the publication of the pamphlet entitled *A Plea for Unity*, issued in April that year, which advocated an inquiry into the possibilities of such a union between the three denominations, and which had been signed by prominent members from each tradition.[150] Under

---

149 Mr C.T. Le Quesne, K.C., 'Church Union', *BT* November 24, 1932, 816. On Le Quesne see Payne, *The Baptist Union, passim*. It is interesting to note that the question of Baptist–Congregational union had been mooted as far back as November 4, 1887, see *BT* December 7, 1933, 842, and also in 1892, see *BM* November 1892, 505, cited by Briggs, 'Evangelical Ecumenism. Part II', 177 and n.61.

150 Nineteen Baptists signed the Plea: Charles Brown, F.C. Bryan of the Downs Chapel, Clapton, F. Buffard, who moved from Hampstead to Yeovil in 1932, A.J. Burgoyne of Hutton and Shenfield Union Church, H.J. Flowers, who moved to Pantygwdyr from Chorleywood in 1932, E.W. Gibbons of Wealdstone, E.E. Hayward of

Le Quesne's chairmanship the Special Committee was to focus its attention almost exclusively on the issue of baptism, and even the most cursory survey of the letters and articles on the subject reveals that it was this baptismal question, above all else, which was the real matter of contention in a way that it had not been during the second decade of the century when, though discussed, it had not played such a central role.

By this time Dr Hugh Martin had become the leading Baptist advocate of the ecumenical movement,[151] and though there were those who joined with him, to the majority of Baptists his position was greeted with the same kind of scepticism as Shakespeare before him. Addressing the Federal Council on 'The Unity of the Free Churches', a message later issued in pamphlet form, Martin set out his position: 'There are...serious difficulties...in relation to the ordinance of baptism. I speak as a Baptist. I believe in the Baptist doctrine and practice, which I hold to be the New Testament doctrine and practice. I believe that here Baptists have a valuable contribution to bring to a United Church. But our fundamental witness, as I understand it, is to a belief in the spiritual character of the Church which is now shared, whatever may have been the case in the past, by those divided from us as to the administration of the ordinance.'[152] E.K.H. Jordan referred to this as Martin's 'brilliant address', arguing that it injected a 'vigorous "shot in the arm"' into Charles Brown's committee which was exploring the possibility of Free Church union, and this was followed by the establishment of a theological commission which was to study the issues involved.[153]

Goudhurst, Mr Arthur Itter, Mr Richard Jewson, Ruffell Laslett of Watford, F.T. Lord of Bloomsbury, Mr Herbert Marnham, A.J. Nixon of Clapham, T. Powell of Lambeth, F.C. Spurr, H.H. Sutton of Hammersmith, F.J. Walkey, General Superintendent of the Central Area, Mr H. Ernest Wood and Hugh Martin. See H. Martin, 'Baptists, Congregationalists and Presbyterians', *BT* April 21, 1932, 268. Seven of these served on the Special Committee set up to discuss this issue in November, 1932: Brown, Bryan, Itter, Jewson, Lord, Martin and Spurr. A copy of this *Plea* has not been found.

151 On Martin's introduction to the ecumenical movement and his replacing Shakespeare as the foremost Baptist figure, see Cross, 'Hugh Martin: Ecumenist', 71-73. Martin took whatever opportunity he had to further its cause, writing many letters to the *BT*, e.g., Martin, 'Christian Unity', *BT* November 10, 1932, 776, and his 'Baptists and Christian Unity', *BT* August 30, 1934, 612; preached on the matter whenever invited, see, e.g., *BT* November 10, 1932, 776, an advert for a meeting on November 13, when Martin would speak on 'Christian Unity'; and participating in many different committees discussing the matter, including the BU's Special Committee and the FoR. See also Jordan, *Free Church Unity*, 176-78.

152 'The Unity of the Free Churches', *BT* December 22, 1932, 913, reports the contents of Martin's speech. It was published by the SCM Press under the title *The Unity of the Free Churches* (1932).

153 Though the commission periodically reported back and still existed at the commencement of the War, little progress was made, and the matter was eclipsed by the

However, it was the printing of Martin's September address to the Federal Council that sparked off a considerable debate conducted through the pages of *The Baptist Times*. Careful to distinguish between unity and uniformity, he argued that unity of spirit and unity of organization went together and he believed that there were deeper reasons for unity other than those of economics or sharing resources: 'One Lord, one Faith, should mean one Body of Christ', but significantly, though citing Ephesians 4:5, he omitted 'one baptism'. He continued: 'Our denominationalism is outworn and could be ended to-morrow without any sacrifice of principle and with infinite gains for the spiritual enrichment of all of us and for the more effective service of the Kingdom of God.' For him, the onus lay with those who maintained the necessity of continued separation in circumstances vastly different from those in which they had arisen. Some of the difficulties he termed 'evidences of old Adam still alive in us', but the real difficulties were not insurmountable given the will to unity and some hard thinking. With regard to church government, Presbyterians, who had already begun to move away from extreme independency, had much they could teach both Baptists and Congregationalists, but he admitted that there were greater difficulties about baptism, and he then proceeded with what appears to be a reiteration of his apologetic for his reunion stance.[154] 'I speak as a Baptist. I believe the Baptist teaching and practice to be the teaching and practice of the New Testament. Baptists have a great contribution to bring here to a United Church. But our fundamental witness is to the spiritual character of the Church, a belief now shared by those divided from us by the form of the ordinance. In part, too, our denominations have been emphasising complementary truths. Our differences are not adequate grounds for separation. Let us beware of a new Ritualism. In Christ Jesus neither believer's immersion availeth anything nor infant sprinkling, but faith that worketh by love.' As Shakespeare believed before him, 'The real issues today are not denominational and are too big for denominationalism to meet', and Martin pleaded that the time had come to seriously investigate the case for a United Free Church, advocating the establishment of National Commissions set up by the denominations which would study the situation and face the difficulties.[155]

---

proposals which eventually bore fruit in September 1940 when the Free Church Federal Council (FCFC) was born out of the amalgamation of the NCEFC and the FCEFC. See Jordan, *Free Church Unity*, 216.

154 Cf. his comments referred to above in his speech, 'The Unity of the Free Churches', reported in *BT* December 22, 1932, 913.

155 H. Martin, 'Free Church Unity', *BT* September 22, 1932, 653. On Martin's Baptist convictions, which were frequently questioned, see Cross, 'Hugh Martin. Part 3', 139-43.

Martin gained enthusiastic support the following week from Charles Brown who considered it a mistake to refuse to explore the ways and means of achieving closer unity and co-operation, specifically between Baptists, Congregationalists and Presbyterians,[156] and from Herbert Marnham, who agreed that, in general terms, there were truths which Baptists held dear and which they had to maintain, but these should not prevent organic union with the other branches of Christ's church. However, H.L. Taylor and Gilbert Laws voiced their opposition to the views of Martin, Brown and Hayward. Taylor 'queried' these writers' confident assertions that there was a widespread and earnest desire for Free Church unity among younger Baptists, and was concerned that the Baptist witness could well be lost in a United Free Church. He asked Martin, as a member of a Free Church,[157] how many had been baptized on confession of faith in that church during the past ten years. Laws asked the three unity advocates what they were prepared to do with essential Baptist principles in order to unite Baptists with other Christian bodies. These distinctive beliefs were a credible profession of conversion as the prerequisite to church membership; that baptism was for believers only; that a local assembly of believers was a complete church, with full authority to exercise discipline and appoint the ministry; and that every believer was a true priest unto God. On the second Baptists were at odds with Congregationalists; on the second and third with Presbyterians; and on all four with Anglicans. Laws therefore concluded: 'Brethren who ceaselessly urge the subject of union upon us must have some answer to these questions in their mind, and I would respectfully invite them to say what the answer is.'[158]

The following week Charles Brown replied, expressing his grief at the attitude of Laws and Taylor, responding point by point to the issues raised. On Laws' second point, he declared his belief that many Congregationalists would, for the sake of unity, be prepared to substitute a dedication service for infant sprinkling and to provide the means for believer's baptism, then added, 'at any rate, it could be discussed.' He then asked whether Laws and Taylor were really suggesting that baptism was the sole reason for the Baptists' separation from other churches and whether, if they were to start *de novo*, they would form a separate

---

156 C. Brown, followed by E.E. Hayward, *BT* September 29, 1932, 664.

157 Martin was for many years in membership with the Hampstead Garden Suburb Free Church, see Cross, 'Hugh Martin: Part 1', 40.

158 See H. Marnham, H.L. Taylor of Easton, Gordano, near Bristol, and G. Laws of St. Mary's, Norwich, 'Christian Unity', *BT* October 6, 1932, 680. Laws' letter formed the basis of the address he delivered to the fifth BWC two years later, on which see below. Laws became one of the leading opponents of the union movement, even though, like Martin, he sat on the Union's Special Committee and had many letters on the subject published in the *BT*.

denomination on that matter alone. 'I am a convinced Baptist', he declared, 'but the term very inadequately describes me, and, if I may say so, my denomination. I hope I am a great deal more than that. Christ sent me not to baptise but to preach the Gospel. I am persuaded that many people make far more of baptism than our Lord makes of it.'[159]

Ruffell Laslett replied a fortnight later, drawing attention to the Congregationalists' and Presbyterians' demand for a credible profession of faith as the prerequisite for membership, a point, in actual fact, which Laws had acknowledged. 'And though they do not practise our form of baptism, yet the fact that many of our Churches do not make it essential for Church membership but freely admit both Congregationalists and Presbyterians to full membership of the Church, would seem to suggest that further union between us is not quite so difficult as Mr. Laws seems to suggest. Or would he have us return to the old complete Independency, and to close communion, and as it would appear, to the only logical conclusion to that—close membership? For surely those who have a right to the Lord's Table have also a right to His Church?'[160]

In spite of the opposition, Martin continued his work and drew positively from his experiences of Union Churches—Martin had declared, 'I believe that we could now (in the light of experience) formulate principles for the conduct of a Union Church in respect of the teaching and practice of baptism, which would meet any just Baptist complaints.'[161] However, in keeping with his position as General Secretary, Aubrey trod a more cautious and diplomatical path, writing, 'I do not see that at the present time our Churches need concern themselves with particular schemes, which may very well be left at this stage to the Baptist Union Council, on which every point of view is well represented.'[162]

---

159 C. Brown, *BT* October 13, 1932, 700.

160 G.H. Ruffell Laslett, *BT* October 27, 1932, 740. F.J.H. Humphrey of Ealing, *BT* November 3, 1932, 756, expressed his agreement with Laws' statement on beliefs as being important and his questions pertinent, but remarked that their delivery seemed 'more like a pistol than an olive branch.'

161 H. Martin, 'Christian Unity', *BT* November 10, 1932, 776. Under the same heading, A.J. Nixon drew attention to the Baptists 'of the dispersion', those already in membership with a Congregational or Presbyterian church, and used their existence in support of the cause of Christian union.

162 M.E. Aubrey, 'Union', *BT* November 10, 1932, 775. Aubrey went on to clarify his own position: 'My official view, as Secretary, is simply this. Union might mean a disuniting of our denomination as it at present stands. Taking a long view of the welfare of the Church of Christ, even so it might be worth while, though disunion for the sake of union seems strange... I believe every good Baptist will welcome unity if it can be shown to be possible without sacrifice of any principle which we regard as essential to the presentation of the Gospel of Christ in its fulness.' Cf. Peter Aubrey's comment that his

In 1934, Laws delivered a paper to the Berlin BWC on 'Baptists and Christian Unity: What is Possible', in which, after briefly sketching the developments of the previous two decades, focused on the four distinctive Baptist principles: conversion, believer's baptism, the completeness of the local church and the priesthood of all believers. In the light of these, he discussed the relationship between Baptists and Congregationalists, then with Presbyterians and Methodists, and finally with Episcopalians in the light of these principles. In each case it was the baptismal issue which separated Baptists from the other denominations (in the case of Episcopalians it was all four principles). He concluded that there would be no way that union could take place without some recognition of infant baptism. As he had already stated that Baptists were antipaedobaptist, such a union could not, therefore, be done without inconsistency. He argued that 'the Baptist contribution to Christian unity must, for the present, be a domestic effort.' Baptists needed to seek unity within their own tradition, for they had not yet, he believed, 'worked out fully the meaning of an Association, or a Union. Only when this has been done in all countries shall we pass on to work out the meaning of our world fellowship as it is represented in this Alliance.'[163] The address was reproduced in the *Baptist Times* several weeks later[164] and elicited appreciative and whole-hearted support from R.W. Black, but a dismayed response from Hugh Martin, who once again claimed that union could be attained without the sacrifice of principle and that there were weightier matters facing the church than views about baptism.[165] In turn, Martin's letter elicited a response from J.H. Stanley, who recorded with surprise Martin's statement that there was 'a danger in some sections of our denomination of making too much of baptism', reiterating that it was 'the one fundamental principle for which we stand, and is quite

father's main preoccupation was all too often that of a gracious peacemaker, reported by West, 'Aubrey: Part I', 199.

163 G. Laws, 'Baptists and Christian Unity: What is Possible?', in J.H. Rushbrooke (ed.), *Fifth Baptist World Congress, Berlin, August 4–10* (1934), 172-74, quotations from p.173. The call for Baptists to unite among themselves was not a new one. Laws had expressed it as early as 1921, see 'One People In All The World. A Plea For Baptist Unity', *BT* May 13, 1921, 294, and was followed by Anon., 'Baptist Unity', *BT* September 5, 1924, 584; J.H. Rushbrooke, 'Baptist Unity', *BT* October 3, 1924, 651; A. Graham-Barton, 'Shall the Baptist Churches Become One Organic Whole?', *BT* November 23, 1933, 796. See further the letters by W.N. Town and H.C. Woolley, *BT* November 3, 1932, 756; Anon., 'Church Re-Union', *BT* September 14, 1933, 618; G. Cowling, *BT* December 7, 1933, 842; and 'Re-Union At Home', probably by J.C. Carlile, *BT* July 26, 1934, 530, which raised the question, 'Do we really want to unite? If the desire is in our hearts, why not begin with those who are our kith and kin?'

164 G. Laws, 'Baptists and Christian Unity', *BT* August 23, 1934, 601.

165 R.W. Black, 'Baptists and Christian Unity', *BT* September 6, 1934, 628; H. Martin, 'Baptists and Christian Unity', *BT* August 30, 1934, 612.

scriptural...whereas infant *baptism*...is not scriptural, and the New Testament never sanctions it, therefore it becomes a barrier to any denomination not following out this command.'[166]

Throughout this extended debate baptism was repeatedly identified as the principal barrier to any form of reunion or union. This fact was reiterated time and again[167] along with its concomitant that there should be absolutely no surrender of principle.[168] Throughout, the *Baptist Times* provided an excellent forum for much of the debate and this was in no small measure due to J.C. Carlile's editorship, combined with his interest and involvement in the movement.[169] The *Baptist Times* further aided the discussion by giving well-known Free Church Paedobaptists opportunity to express their views and the views of their own communions, thereby further stimulating thought and increasing awareness of the paedobaptist positions.[170]

In 1934 Martin edited *Towards Reunion*, published by SCM, in which members of the FoR sketched the positions of their respective denominations.[171] Martin's belief was that the first step on the road to reunion was for the churches to understand what each other stood for. He

---

166 Mr J.H. Stanley, 'Baptists and Christian Unity', *BT* September 27, 1934, 680. Stanley had already attacked Martin and any other Baptist, Congregational and Presbyterian union, in 'Christian Unity', *BT* October 20, 1932, 720.

167 E.g. 'Re-Union and Baptism', *BT* November 17, 1927, 823; B.I. Greenwood, 'Baptism', *BT* August 2, 1934, 548; H. Townsend, 'The Free Churches and Baptism', *BT* September 13, 1934, 649; 'Christian Union', *BT* August 7, 1937, 522.

168 E.g. J.C. Carlile, 'Union of the Free Churches', *BT* September 24, 1931, 664; M.E. Aubrey, 'Union', *BT* November 10, 1932, 775; Mrs B.M. Carter, *BT* August 2, 1934, 548; J. Brooks, 'Baptism', BT September 6, 1934, 628; M. Evans, 'Our Baptist Testimony', *BT* July 25, 1935, 552.

169 See Carlile, *My Life's Little Day*, 171-86.

170 See W. Mander, 'Churches of Christ and Baptists: Is A Closer Co-operation Desirable?', *BT* July 25, 1929, 562 and *BT* August 1, 1929, 575; Dr S.M. Berry, 'Union of Baptist and Congregational Churches', *BT* November 3, 1932, 760; Prof. P.C. Simpson, 'Baptism in the Presbyterian Church', *BT* June 14, 1934, 435; Dr J.D. Jones, 'A Congregationalist's Views About Baptism', *BT* July 19, 1934, 521; Dr J.S. Lidgett, 'Holy Baptism: The Doctrine of Methodism', *BT* August 2, 1934, 553. See also the Congregationalist Principal A.E. Garvie, 'The Nature of the Church', *BT* September 23, 1937, 713; Dr H.G. Wood, a former Baptist, 'The Nature of the Church and the Problem of Re-Union. A Quaker View', *BT* November 11, 1937, 852. Also C.R. Smith, 'Methodism and Baptism', *BQ* 7.3, (July, 1934), 97-105.

171 On the FoR, its origins in 1933, its purpose and threefold basis, see H. Martin, 'The Road to Unity', in H. Martin (ed.), *Towards Reunion: What the Churches Stand For*(1934), 22; and Cross, 'Hugh Martin: Part 2', 79-80. The second part of its basis of faith was 'Acceptance of the Sacraments of Baptism and of the Holy Communion as of divine appointment, and as expressing for all the corporate life of the whole Fellowship in and with Christ.'

introduced the whole collection of essays by opining that unity should be through mutual comprehension not compromise.[172] Realistic about the contentious issues which divided, he observed that within each tradition diversity already co-existed within denominational unity. He admitted that, 'Of course there are differences of belief and practice amongst us— some of them pretty fundamental. But if complete uniformity is required before we can have organizational unity, then our present denominations must be broken up.'[173] 'The Baptists' was written by F.T. Lord, who began by drawing attention to the common religious heritage held by the Free Churches, Anglicans and Society of Friends. Only then did he identify the peculiar Baptist contribution, which he identified not in worship or church order, but in the Baptist conception of churchmanship, 'for it is from this that the Baptist conception of ministry and sacraments follows', and Baptists based this on the Bible. From scripture, then, Baptists adopted certain definite principles: the essential requisite in Christian discipleship is faith in Christ; the church is a fellowship of the regenerate; and admission to the New Testament church is by immersion administered to those capable of making full surrender to Christ.[174] He maintained that Baptists guarded against externalism by insisting on the change of heart, the reality of conversion and the reality of Christ in personal experience. To be effective, then, a sacrament had to fulfill certain spiritual conditions, therefore Baptists insisted that the proper subjects were believers rather than infants, focusing on the spiritual condition of the candidate. The mode of immersion was retained on account of its New Testament precedent and symbolism. Restricting baptism to those who could make full individual and personal surrender to Christ emphasized the individuality and reality of conversion. The weakness of this position, Lord admitted, was that it appeared to ignore the responsibility of the church towards children. For this reason modern Baptists had developed dedication services, in which the responsibility of the church and parents for the welfare of the child was highlighted.[175] Moreover, it could be added that Baptists were second to none in their concern for the nurture of young people, primarily but not exclusively through the Sunday School movement. After discussing the issue of episcopacy and rejecting the idea of a state-church, where the latter was subject to the former, and declaring the Baptist denial of baptismal regeneration, Lord explained that in so doing Baptists believed they were helping to preserve that quality of religious experience which is the basis

---

172 Martin, 'Road to Unity', 9.

173 Martin, 'Road to Unity', 11.

174 F.T. Lord, 'The Baptists', in Martin (ed.), *Towards Reunion*, 25-28.

175 Lord, 'The Baptists', 29-31. Here he referred to the dedication service contained in M.E. Aubrey's *A Minister's Manual* (n.d., [1927]).

of true churchmanship.[176] But he did not ignore the diversities which existed among Baptists, as reflected by closed and open membership churches.[177]

From its inception to 1943, the FoR sought unsuccessfully to organize a second series of Church of England–Free Church conversations. During this time, Martin published the booklet *Are We Uniting?* for the FoR and published by SCM. In it he lamented the hardening attitude towards Christian unity in England and the tendency to beat the denominational drum.[178] He set about arguing that reunion would come about based on a common faith, being a unity of comprehension not compromise, and one which would preserve the elements of value in the episcopal, presbyteral and congregational forms of government, noting how both the Baptists and Congregationalists had moved towards a more connexional system. This, he believed, would result in a Free Church[179]— free, that is, from state control. However, there were considerable obstacles. As Baptists stood for loyal obedience to the New Testament conceptions of the church and baptism, the recognition of infant baptism would be to encourage a dangerous superstition. In the resulting hesitation, both Baptists and Anglo-Catholics believed that to enter a church in which other conceptions than their own were also permissable would be to jeopardize the truth.[180] The Second F&O Conference in Edinburgh the following year, Martin believed, would aid the development of reunion, but he sought to reassure his readers that the F&O movement existed to promote study and not to propogate plans for reunion.[181]

Arguably the most important Baptist document in this period was the *Report of the Special Committee* which had been appointed in 1932 under C.T. Le Quesne's chairmanship to consider the question of union between Baptists, Congregationalists and Presbyterians.[182] The first ten

---

176 Lord, 'The Baptists', 31-33.

177 Lord, 'The Baptists', 34. He concluded his article, p.36, by referring with implicit approval to a comment from the then Bishop of Gloucester, Dr A.C. Headlam, to the effect that nothing was to be gained by either undue haste or the ignoring of real principles, as, for the general witness of the church, every section of the church had to make its own valid contribution.

178 Martin, *Are We Uniting? Prospects of Reunion in England* (1936), 3.

179 Martin, *Are We Uniting?*, 8-11.

180 Martin, *Are We Uniting?*, 12-15.

181 Martin, *Are We Uniting?*, 15-16.

182 Details of the Special Committee are set out in the *Report of the Special Committee*, 3. Over the five years of the committee's deliberations 35 people in all had been involved, see p.3, and the report's importance comes from the fact that the committee was truly representative of all the views on baptism, communion and membership within the denomination, as it was comprised of representatives from each of the three groups within the BU: those who favoured open membership and open

sections dealt with the preliminaries of the basic Baptist position on various issues.[183] Section XI attempted to forecast what would happen to the doctrine of baptism if such a union were to take place, concluding that membership would have to be by profession of faith, thus permitting the possibility of 're-baptism' if the applicant was persuaded that this was right, and that a great deal would depend on the minister. Two conditions under which the Baptist understanding of the rite would suffer were then identified: if the church did not remain alive to the issue, and if, in order to avoid controversy, a candidate was not required to decide for themself by weighing the arguments of both believer's and infant baptism. Further, the actual administration of the ordinance would raise problems. Could a convinced Baptist minister baptize infants? If they did, they would be administering a rite which they did not believe to be the true Christian one. Rebaptism would also become an issue, a practice rejected by all branches of the church. The report could not agree to the possibility of the mutual recognition of baptism as advocated by P.T. Forsyth,[184] in which infant and adult baptism existed side by side. However, they saw no difficulty in the co-existence in one and the same church of two doctrines of believer's baptism, when the rite was understood as a symbol of confession and when it was recognized as an appointed vehicle of grace to the believer.

Section XII examined again the practice of infant baptism and then set over against the arguments propounded in its defence the doctrine of believer's baptism, emphasizing baptism and the Lord's Supper as not merely symbolic but vehicles of grace. The final paragraph of the section drew attention to the corresponding clash between two conceptions of the

---

communion, closed membership and open communion, and closed membership and closed communion. For the purpose of convenience, and because the *Report* is set out in 21 sections, headed by Roman numerals, all references to it here will be set out in the main text and will refer to the relevant section.

183 This comprised over half the document. The first 5 sections discussed questions of introduction, specifically the New Testament foundation and practice of baptism, based on the authority of Christ himself, and this practice was then supported by an argument from Christian experience (sections I and II). III dealt with the mode, its symbolism and obligation on every believer, and drew attention to the fact that immersion was continued in England until the sixteenth century. IV examined the subjects of baptism, demonstrating that it was on this matter more than on the mode which separated Baptists from the Paedobaptist communions, while V discussed why Baptists rejected infant baptism. Sections VI and VII introduced the three Baptist groups and surveyed the differences between them and their attitudes towards reunion and related issues. Then, sections VIII to X presented the views of the different groups themselves.

184 P.T. Forsyth, *Lectures on the Church and the Sacraments* (1917), 206 and 211.

visible church: one as the society of baptized persons, the other as a society of baptized believers.[185]

XVIII began, 'We are all agreed that, if this question of union...were forced to an issue in England now, it would split our denomination.' Rushbrooke had reported on the exclusion of Chinese Baptists from the BWA because of their fusion with paedobaptist churches to form the Church of Christ in China and drew from this the conclusion that any such union would endanger the world-wide unity of Baptists as expressed in the BWA.[186]

Section XXI summed up the position of the committee by issuing a challenge to the Baptist constituency:

> In conclusion, we wish to repeat that we as Baptists shall not be able to take our due and helpful share in the movement towards some visible realization of the essential unity of the Churches of Christ amongst mankind and, further, shall not be able to justify our Baptist tradition to thoughtful and inquiring minds, unless we give more attention in our Churches and in our homes to the question of baptism. It has been somewhat neglected amongst us in these later years. Until we have considered it more fully, we are not ready to come to a decision on the issue of union with any other Christian Church. Believer's Baptism, whether it be called an ordinance or a sacrament, is a matter of the most serious import, since it is based upon the authority of our Lord Himself and has contributed, as we are convinced, to the welfare of the Christian community and the maintenance of Christian doctrine.

---

185 XIII-XVII dealt with questions of church organization and church unity, and the practical differences over the administration of communion, the question of overlapping or redundancy of churches, colleges, church distribution and Union churches.

186 XIX acknowledged that any such union as was being considered would cause legal problems not just for the BU but for the other denominations as well. One of the most serious of which would be the actual method of effecting such a union. Whatever the case among the two other denominations, the BU Council could not bind the separate churches of its membership, as the assent of each of them would have to be secured before it entered such a scheme of union. XX discussed the difference between Baptist unity and, e.g., that obtaining among Anglicans and Catholics, both of which were united under their conception of episcopacy. Though Baptists had some conception of unity extending beyond the local church which bound them together as Baptists, this, the report ventured to say, was not enough, and suggested that to this should be added 'the conception of the universal Church, of which they are members together with all who love our Lord Jesus Christ in sincerity and truth. If such a conception is missing, some part of the New Testament conception of the Church is missing... We must not omit this conception from our thinking if we are to arrive at an adequate and comprehensive answer to this question, whether we ought or ought not to maintain our separate existence as a Church.' It is significant to note the untypical use of 'Church' at this point—more natural and consistent with Baptist beliefs would have been 'denomination' or 'fellowship of churches.'

Finally, the report reiterated that a right decision could not be reached unless Baptists sought and practised fellowship with other Christians, praying that the Holy Spirit would quicken, deepen and refine the apprehension of spiritual values and truths. 'Let us pray, therefore, that He will revive and illuminate us and inspire us with a right disposition to discern and to do the Will of God in this and in all other things.'

Once the last of the denominations' official commissions had reported, the Free Church Unity Group condensed the results of their own four years of work, which had continued behind the scenes, and produced *A Plan for Unity*,[187] to further the closer study of the difficulties and promote that process of mutual understanding and growing together which would have to precede any formal act of union.[188] The *Plan* outlined proposals for the formation of a United Free Church, which included a statement of faith, proposals of membership, discussion of the sacraments which permitted both believer's and infant baptism, the ministry, the ministry of the laity which recommended that the church be organized locally in districts and Presbyteries (the equivalent of Associations as understood by Baptists) and should have a General Assembly as the supreme body of the Church.[189]

The 1937 Special Committee *Report* was reviewed and discussed over the ensuing months, and this included a discussion on Church Union between Dr Percy Evans of Spurgeon's College and Hugh Martin sponsored by the Baptist Universities Society. After Evans had outlined the past and present issues and course of events, Martin explained that the *Plan for Unity* had been tentatively put forward by a group of Baptists,

---

187 Details are from *A Plan for Unity between Baptists, Congregationalists and Presbyterians in England* (n.d., [1937]), 3.

188 Of the 19 signatories to the *Plan* nine were Baptists: Martin, A.J. Burgoyne, George Evans, E.E. Hayward, Norman Hyde, Ruffell Laslett, R.S. McHardy, E. Murray Page and A.J. Nixon, and these were supported by a group of 34, including 11 Baptists, who wished to express their general approval of the proposals and their sympathy with their aims. This figure presumes that George Evans was one of the two Baptist ministers of that name at this time—the more likely being the minister of the Downs Chapel, Clapton, the other a Welsh minister in Monmouth. The signatures implied general approval and not necessarily agreement with every clause. The Baptist 'sympathizers' were F.C. Bryan, F. Buffard, Herbert Chown, J. Ivory Cripps, F.J.H. Humphrey, J.B. Middlebrook and R.W. Thomson (if this is the same person who is 'mispelled in the *Plan* as R.W. Thompson). See *Plan for Unity*, 4-5.

189 *Plan for Unity*, 5-16. The Group finally suggested that careful consideration should be given to five interim measures, p.16: that churches might be described as 'Evangelical Free Church of England: Baptist' or 'Congregational'; the churches might have a common hymn book; co-operate in ministerial training by the institution of united colleges with provision for denominational instruction; the setting up of united committees for church extension, ministerial training, evangelism, and moral and social problems; and an officially representative triennial Assembly.

Congregationalists and Presbyterians and that whatever decision the churches came to, one of the burning issues of the day was unity. According to the *Plan*, the visible and orderly expression of membership in a United Free Church would be through baptism in the name of the Trinity, due instruction and training in the Christian faith and life, and the giving of the right hand of fellowship. 'We cannot rest until we have found a way to closer union of the Church of Christ. Divisions have outworn their usefulness and are hindrances to the cause of Christ in the world, and barriers in Christian and non-Christian lands.' He did not wish to dispense with Baptist fundamentals (the gathered church, priesthood of all believers, freedom from state control and believer's baptism), but 'baptism is the only point upon which we feel a real difficulty, and many of us need a greater sense of proportion to prevent our erecting an ordinance, however sacred, into a prominence which is non-Christian.' Baptists, he believed, ought to hesitate in condemning an age-long custom such as infant baptism which had been and continued to be a means of grace to many Christians, 'and we need not give up our own idea of baptism so long as we agree about fundamental ideas. What is needed is a unity of comprehension.'[190]

In November, the BU Council received the report and thanked all those who had contributed to it. Addressing the Council, R.W. Black[191] said that he believed that what was taking place was giving a wrong impression to Congregationalists and that instead of promoting union such discussions were in fact causing disunion and discord, that Baptist work was being handicapped and that to a great majority such union meant disloyalty to Christ. Along with a vote of thanks to the committee, he proposed that, at that time, organic union was not practicable, but that Baptists would gladly associate themselves with every attempt to co-operate with other churches in every effort to extend the Kingdom of God.[192] The resolution was passed, and there can be little doubt that it represented fairly the position of the denomination as a whole. Though the possibility of union disappeared for the time being, the whole process which had begun with Shakespeare's advocacy of a United Church of England had brought the English Baptists well into the ecumenical arena and the whole matter to the attention of the denomination as a whole. But it is

---

190 Edna F. Ball, 'Baptist Universities' Society. Discussion on Church Union', *BT* October 28, 1937, 817. See also the discussions in 'Baptists and Re-Union', *BT* April 8, 1937, 261-62; J.C. Carlile, 'Baptists and Church Union', *BT* April 15, 1937, 289.

191 It is interesting to note the difference of position Black adopted in reunion schemes. He was later to be the chief, though unsuccessful, pioneer of union between Baptists and the Churches of Christ who were believer's baptists, while he opposed the possible union with the paedobaptist Congregationalists and Presbyterians.

192 See 'Church Union. Baptist Union Council Reports', *BT* November 25, 1937, 890 and 898, quote p.898.

true to say that by 1937, in the words of R.L. Child, 'the prospect of a re-united Christendom...[was] exceedingly remote.'[193]

Faith and Order

The World Missionary Conference in Edinburgh, 1910, is recognized as the starting-point of the ecumenical movement. Under the inspiration of Charles H. Brent the F&O movement was formed at a meeting in Geneva in 1920, though its planning took a decade, and its realization a further seven years.[194] Between 1910 and 1920, J.H. Shakespeare was involved in various correspondence and meetings with a view to a F&O conference in London, probably in 1917, but the war prevented this, and by the time it was held in 1927, Shakespeare's health had failed him and he had retired.[195]

Official BU interest ended a few months after Shakespeare's resignation as General Secretary when it dissolved its F&O Committee,[196] though J.E. Roberts sought to revive it in when he called for Baptist involvement in F&O. He had represented the BU in Geneva in 1920, and in an article he served notice of the second World Conference which was planned to meet in Washington DC in May 1925. Though he saw reunion as far off, he believed that it would be much nearer were people to really want it.[197]

However, one result of the 1926 Assembly was the BU's decision not to send any official delegates to the F&O's inaugural conference held in Lausanne in August 1927. Two English Baptists, however, funded themselves to attend the Conference: the historian, Dr W.T. Whitley[198] and Dr J.E. Roberts himself. A copy of the 1926 BU *Reply to the Lambeth*

---

193 R.L. Child, 'The Baptist Contribution to the One Church', *BQ* 8.2 (April, 1936), 81. He continued: 'if and when a United Church comes into being, it will not be by the disappearance of everything distinctive in its separated members, but rather by the gathering-up and incorporation in a new form of what is truly vital and worthy in the various denominations.'

194 See T. Tatlow, 'The World Conference on Faith and Order', in Rouse and Neill (eds.), *History of the Ecumenical Movement*, 403-41.

195 On Shakespeare's involvement, see West, 'Aubrey: Part III', 320-21; Townsend, 'Shakespeare', 299-302, 306 (on Life and Work) and 310; Shepherd, 'Shakespeare', 170-72, 202-04. Shakespeare was supported by both F.B. Meyer and G.P. Gould, see Shepherd, 'Shakespeare', 202 and 223 respectively.

196 Shepherd, 'Shakespeare', 317, citing the BU Minute Book, July 7, 1924.

197 J.E. Roberts, 'World Conference on Faith and Order', *Frat.* os 14, (April, 1923), 4-6, though he did not deal with the issue of baptism.

198 On Whitley, see S.J. Price, 'William Thomas Whitley', *BQ* 12.10-11 (April-July, 1948), 357-63; I. Sellars, 'W.T. Whitley: A Commemorative Essay', *BQ* 37.4 (October, 1997), 159-73; R. Otzen, *Whitley: The Baptist College of Victoria 1891–1991* (South Yarra, Victoria, 1991), 20-23.

Appeal was sent, but as the Union was not officially represented it could not and was not accepted as a conference document.[199]

Two months after the conference, Whitley reported back to the denomination in an article which also dealt with the third BWC in Stockholm, 1923. He outlined in particular what had come out of Lausanne. The Roman Catholics, like the English Baptists, had not officially attended, indicating that union on the grand scale was impossible. He quoted with approval the Orthodox conviction that in matters of faith and conscience there was no room for compromise, and then quoted the message which had come from the Stockholm Congress:

> We rejoice that the spiritual unity of all believers is a blessed reality, not dependent upon organisation or ceremonies... Baptists cannot consent to any form of union which impairs the rights of the individual believer. We cannot unite with others in any centralized ecclesiastical organization wielding power over the individual conscience. We cannot accept the sacerdotal conception of the ministry which involves the priesthood of a class with special powers for transmitting grace. We cannot accept the conception of ordination made valid through a historic succession in the ministry... Christian unity, therefore, can only come through obedience to the will of Christ as revealed in the New Testament, which Baptists must ever take as their sole, sufficient, certain and authoritative guide... Primarily, their duty is to make known the will of Christ and secure the willing submission of men to Him, as set forth in the gospel of the grace of God.[200]

As a result of his attendance, Whitley became closely involved in the joint studies which were initiated at Lausanne, while Roberts accepted membership on the Continuation Committee, a place which M.E. Aubrey filled on Roberts' death in 1929.[201]

The reunion issue was by now well established and began to take a much more central place in the denomination's life. With the newly formed Life and Work and F&O movements (1920 and 1927 respectively), and with several inter-church conversations already completed (Anglican–Free Church, and Anglican–Roman Catholic at Malines) the atmosphere was such that it was no longer possible to hide away from the challenge facing the various denominations. The late 1920s provided the seedbed for a vast volume of discussion among

---

199 For further details see W.M.S. West's 'Baptists in Faith and Order: A Study in Baptist Convergence', in Clements (ed), *Baptists in the Twentieth Century*, 56-57. For Baptist interest and involvement in the international ecumenical movement, see the whole of West's 'Baptists in Faith and Order'; E.A. Payne's 'Baptists and the Ecumenical Movement', in E. A. Payne, *Free Churchmen, Unrepentant and Repentant and Other Papers* (1965), 123-29; and Cross, 'Service to the Ecumenical Movement', 112-15.

200 W.T. Whitley, 'Lausanne and Stockholm', *BQ* 3, (October, 1927), 339.

201 West, 'Baptists in Faith and Order', 58. For further details of Aubrey's growing involvement in F&O, see West, 'Aubrey: Part III', 327-34.

Baptists on the related issues of the ecumenical movement, with the baptismal question increasingly coming to the fore, for on no other doctrine were Baptists so clearly at odds with other communions.

Whitley reported back to the denomination on the proceedings at Lambeth in 1930 and, at the same time, on the meeting that same month of the Continuation Committee at Mürren. Concerning the former, Whitley commented that the BU had officially replied to official overtures, requesting that attention should be paid to the basis of church membership and the place of faith, and further asked that the method of federation be explored. 'Neither question', Whitley declared, 'has been touched.'[202] In contrast to the Lambeth Conference's generally discouraging tone, the Mürren conference, so Whitley remarked, was prepared to consider the possibilities of federation,[203] a fact that could not but endear the nascent F&O movement to Baptists.

As the domestic, internal debate gathered pace during the early 1930s, the international ecumenical movement was beginning to have a greater effect on Baptist thought. The F&O Continuation Committee produced six 'Reports' which were submitted to the various denominational organizations for consideration and response. The BU's response was made in 1930.[204] Responding to *Report 1. The Call to Unity*, the BU argued that the Baptists' sense of the spiritual unity of the church was expressed among themselves by the BWA, but then stated, 'We are ready to explore ways to fellowship with other Christians who differ in matters of faith and order.'[205] To *Report VI. The Sacraments*, the reply spoke of the Baptist preference for the word 'ordinance' but expressed the willingness to give careful thought to such a matter, and insisted on the faith of the recipient as a pre-condition for the effectiveness of the sacraments.[206] To the slightly later *Report VII. The Unity of Christendom and the relation thereto of Existing Churches*, it was agreed that each communion should seek to know and understand the faith and order of others and recommended as appropriate summaries of the Baptist position the BWA's 1923 message to *Other Christian Brethren*, the 1926 *Reply to the Lambeth Appeal* and, for more comprehensive studies, Wheeler Robinson's *Baptist Principles* (1925) and *The Life and the Faith of the Baptists* (1927). The report of the 'Malines Conversations', however, drew the frank response that so long as the Roman Church maintained its present government and claims Baptists could not

202 W.T. Whitley, 'Lambeth and Mürren', *BQ* 5 (October, 1930), 146.

203 Whitley, 'Lambeth and Mürren', 149.

204 'The Baptist Union of Great Britain and Ireland', in L. Hodgson (ed), *Convictions: A Selection from the Responses of the Churches to the Report of the World Conference on Faith and Order, held at Lausanne in 1927* (1934), 61-64.

205 'The Baptist Union', in *Convictions*, 62.

206 'The Baptist Union', in *Convictions*, 63.

contemplate any union. As to the nature of unity, the BU's reply closed expressing a 'desire for fuller co-operation along social, evangelistic and other lines' on mission fields and alongside other churches and welcomed 'every effort toward common worship and the promotion of friendships which stretch across the lines of division as means by which knowledge and fellowship may be enlarged.'[207]

In 1931, Whitley published a report on the Life and Work and F&O congresses held in the 1920s, and was specifically concerned with the reports from the Continuation Committee. On the sacraments, he reported the conclusion that their benefits could only be appropriated by faith, in which case, he asked, what was the good of infant baptism? He then fired his broadside: 'There are questions about Order, to which we may return again, but there is one very practical issue that needs attention by Baptists. Whether at Lausanne, at Majola, at Mürren, at High Leigh, Baptists have hardly been represented. This is not fair to ourselves, to other Christians, to the special truths we uphold.'[208] Though J.E. Roberts had sat on the Continuation Committee till the time of his death, when he was replaced by Aubrey, Whitley doubted whether there had been three Baptists at any one meeting. The result of this, he claimed, had been greatly to mislead other communions as to the relative importance of the Baptists and inevitably meant that the Baptist testimony had hardly been heard and was not read. He ended observing that the purpose of the Lausanne Conference and its Continuation Committees was to inform the other traditions of the Baptist beliefs and *vice versa*.[209]

The Continuation Committee appointed three theological commissions to prepare reports for the second World Conference to be held in Edinburgh in 1937.[210] The most important of the three reports appeared in May 1937, included two Baptist contributions, the second of which was written by A.C. Underwood, who began his paper by acknowledging that many Baptists would regard the earlier one by I.G. Matthews as expounding the American view of the ministry and sacraments, but added that 'there is an increasing number of Baptists in both England and America who could not give their assent to Professor Matthews' virtual

---

207 'The Baptist Union', in *Convictions*, 64.

208 W.T. Whitley, 'Faith and Order', *BQ* 5.8 (October, 1932), 360.

209 Whitley, 'Faith and Order', 360-61. Whitley also edited the F&O report *The Doctrine of Grace: A Report and Papers of a Theological Committee of the Faith and Order Movement* (1932). Sellars, 'W.T. Whitley', 159-60 and 171, used this volume to show how Whitley's position changed from the anti-sacramentalism of his earlier *Witness of History* and *Church, Ministry and Sacraments*, both of which reflect the bitterness he felt towards the Establishment who had thwarted his attempts to enter the teaching profession, feelings which later changed, enabling him to participate in the early F&O Conferences.

210 Tatlow, 'World Conference on Faith and Order', 430-31.

reduction of the Sacraments to *nuda signa*.' Underwood's intention, then, was to present this alternative point of view.[211] This he did by drawing attention to the fact that historically Baptists had stood for two things: the proper subjects of baptism—believers, and the proper mode—immersion. Of these the proper subjects was the more important. Therefore, Baptists were not separated from the rest of Christendom simply in order to secure the administration of baptism in a certain manner, immersion as over sprinkling. 'They are not ritualists; they are not Baptists because they baptise by immersion.'[212] He adduced five reasons for the Baptist rejection of infant baptism: there is no trace of it in the New Testament; it perpetuates the theological dogma that infants dying unbaptized are in peril on account of the guilt involved in original sin; it fosters the notion that a sacrament can have meaning and effect apart from the faith of the recipient; it obscures the fact that salvation is by faith alone; and it distorts the doctrine of the church as composed of a converted membership.[213] 'Baptists stand for a *via media*, rejecting, on the one hand, all *ex opere operato* theories of the Sacraments and, on the other hand, all theories which reduce them to *nuda signa*.' They thereby reject baptismal regeneration and also the notion that baptism is nothing more than a dedication service. Baptism is a means of grace, 'a definite religious experience, a genuine Sacrament, but only to those who submit to it in penitence and faith. They claim they are the only Christian body which has preserved the full sacramental value of Christian baptism... Baptists are sacramentalists though they reject sacerdotalism. They believe that the Sacraments are efficacious symbols which mediate the grace of God. They are confident that in the Sacraments God imparts Himself to the believing soul. But their sacramentalism is ethical through and through.' In contradistinction to Bishop Charles Gore, Underwood claimed that this ethical sacramentalism should be applied equally to baptism and not restricted to the Lord's Supper, and quoted Wheeler Robinson in support. 'This is the pith and core of their distinctive witness in regard to baptism. They maintain that it is only when baptism is confined to believers that it can be saved from degenerating into either a charm or a piece of mere symbolism.'[214]

On the mode, Underwood explained that Baptists retained immersion for four reasons: it is the New Testament mode; it has a psychological value for both the recipient and for the observer it is much more

---

211 A.C. Underwood, 'Views of Modern Churches (g) Baptist (2)', in R. Dunkerley (ed.), *The Ministry and the Sacraments* (1937), 223. The first Baptist article was prepared by the American, I.G. Matthews of Crozer Seminary.

212 Underwood, 'Views of Modern Churches', 223-24.

213 Underwood, 'Views of Modern Churches', 224-25.

214 Underwood, 'Views of Modern Churches', 225-26, citing C. Gore, *The Holy Spirit and the Church* (1924), 298, 26, and Robinson, *Life and Faith*, 83.

impressive [than sprinkling]; it has sacramental value, being a better symbol than sprinkling to the truth of complete surrender to Christ, death to sin, burial with Christ and resurrection to new life in him, it being important that symbolic acts should be appropriate; and it has confessional value as a dramatic and effective substitute for a verbal confession of faith. As such it was a pictorial creed.[215]

In contrast to Lausanne, the second F&O Conference held in Edinburgh, 1937,[216] was well attended by an official delegation of British Baptists, Aubrey, Rushbrooke, Laws, Martin and Le Quesne.[217] Aubrey was chairman of Section IV, 'The Church's Unity in Life and Worship', which produced a report strongly favouring the formation of the WCC.[218] Both Martin's popular account and the official report were published by the SCM Press, which published many of the volumes for F&O at this time under Martin's able leadership.[219]

---

215 Underwood, 'Views of Modern Churches', 228-29.

216 In preparation, commissions had been appointed and reports published on the four subjects on which the conference concerned itself: Grace; the Word of God; Ministry and the Sacraments; and the Church's Unity in Life and Worship. The aim was not to reach completely agreed statements, even though this meant that the only way to do this was to include side by side irreconcilable views. A single hostile vote was enough to secure the incorporation of a statement expressing the view held by the dissentient. See H. Martin, *Edinburgh, 1937: The Story of the Second World Conference on Faith and Order* (1937), 21 and 32-33.

217 Payne, *Baptist Union*, 200, omits Martin's presence in the BU's delegation, but this is corrected by G. Laws, 'The Edinburgh Conference. What Was the Good of It', *BQ* 9.1 (January, 1938), 21. Laws was correct, for the official report lists Martin as a 'Delegate. Baptist Union of Great Britain and Ireland', L. Hodgson (ed.), *The Second World Conference on Faith and Order held at Edinburgh, August 3-18, 1937* (1938), 297. Martin was also one of those appointed by the Conference to be on the Continuation Committee, at which point he is again identified with the BUGB&I, and therefore was an official BU delegate, see Hodgson, *Second World Conference*, 371

218 West, 'Aubrey: Part III', 331 and n.45 on p.335. West included the name of Dr John MacBeath among the BU delegates, but omitted Rushbrooke. McBeath, however, was a delegate for the BU of Scotland according to Hodgson (ed.), *Second World Conference*, 297. MacBeath served on Section 2 'The Church of Christ and the Word of God', Laws and Le Quesne on Section 3 'The Church of Christ: Ministry and Sacraments', while Martin served with Aubrey on Section 4, see Hodgson, *Second World Conference*, 307. West makes only one other reference to Martin (see below), so little further light is shed on any friendship he and Aubrey may have had as they worked together as colleagues denominationally and ecumenically.

219 Martin, *Edinburgh, 1937*. Of the Conference Martin, pp.17-18, wrote, 'Yet we were there not only to reaffirm the value of our own traditions. We were there also to reach forward to a full understanding of the Gospel which as yet none of us in our separation possessed... We hoped to gain some new insight which we might carry back to the Churches which had sent us.' The second, official volume was that by Hodgson (ed.), *Second World Conference*. The importance of the SCM within the early ecumenical

It was not until the following January that details began to filter into the denomination's consciousness when reports from Aubrey and Laws were published, both of them concluding that at the present time reunion discussions were at an impasse.[220] Initially, both Martin and Aubrey represented the BU on the Continuation Committee which was to meet for the first time after the war in 1947 in Clarens, but when neither felt able to continue active membership, Ernest Payne was sent as a proxy.[221]

It had quickly become evident that the twin stumbling blocks for Baptist involvement in any United Church or reunion/union scheme were the baptismal issue and episcopacy. Addressing the Northern Convocation at York, Aubrey admitted, with reference to the conversations which had begun in 1932, that Baptists could not see how they could enter into organic union with Congregationalists and Presbyterians, adding, 'though in real Christian unity we are constantly working together.'[222] Laws' report provided a detailed account of the proceedings of the conference, paying particular attention to Section III which dealt with 'The Ministry and the Sacraments'.[223] Here the differences which divided Baptists from other traditions became very apparent, nevertheless, Laws felt that some progress had been made. He reported that on baptism it stated: 'The re-united Church will observe the rule that all members of the visible Church are admitted by baptism; which is a gift of God's redeeming love to the Church; and administered in the name of the [Trinity], is a sign and seal of Christian discipleship in obedience to the Lord's command.' To this the Baptist delegates, Martin

---

movement, and particularly Martin's involvement, is a constant theme in Cross' studies of Martin, but see particularly 'Hugh Martin: Part 1', 34-38. Also on the role the SCM, see J.H.Y. Briggs, 'Baptists and Higher Education in England', in W.H. Brackney and R.J. Burke (eds.), *Faith, Life and Witness: The Papers of the Study and Research Division of the Baptist World Alliance—1986–1990* (Birmingham, Alabama, 1990), 110; Hastings, *History of English Christianity*, 86-91, and *passim*, and T. Tatlow, *The Story of the Student Christian Movement of Great Britain and Ireland* (1933), *passim*. Baptists involved in the SCM at this time included W.E. Blomfield, T.R. Glover, H.L. Hemmens, Hugh Martin, F.B. Meyer, T.H. Robinson, H.G. Wood, Martyn Trafford and H.W. Robinson, see Tatlow, *Story of the Student Christian Movement, passim*.

220 M.E. Aubrey, 'What Edinburgh Meant to Me', *BT* January 20, 1938, 42-44; G. Laws, 'The Edinburgh Conference: What Was the Good of it?', *BQ* 9.1 (January, 1938), 21-29. E.A. Payne, 'Baptism in Recent Discussion', in Gilmore (ed.), *Christian Baptism*, 16, noted that at Edinburgh it proved possible to make more elaborate statements regarding the sacraments than had any previous conference.

221 W.M.S. West, *To Be A Pilgrim: a memoir of Ernest A. Payne* (Guildford, 1983), 67. Possible reasons for Martin's dropping out of F&O are discussed by Cross, 'Hugh Martin: Part 2', 81.

222 Aubrey, 'What Edinburgh Meant to Me', *BT* January 20, 1938, 43. On Aubrey's address to the Convocation of York, see West, 'Aubrey: Part III', 331-32.

223 See also Martin, *Edinburgh 1937*, 57-71.

among them, had secured a note stating that the just quoted statement could be accepted by them only if understood to apply to believer's baptism. In so doing they effectively conceded the important point that baptism marks entry into the church. They also drew attention to a principle enunciated in one of the preliminary documents which recognized that the 'necessary condition of receiving the grace of a sacrament is the faith of the recipient.'[224] The note also expressed the Baptist belief that children belonged to God and that no rite was needed to assure for them his grace.[225] Discussing the report's section on admission to holy communion, Laws reported that some delegates had been unable to understand how Baptists were able to accept the non-baptized into membership, which had led to the gibe, 'Baptists are people who are so strong on baptism that they dispense with it!'[226] Laws' overall conclusion, however, was negative: 'The conceptions of church, ministry and sacrament are so different that it is hard to see how any union can ever be looked for while opinion remains as it is.' The difficulties, therefore, facing Baptists were enormous. Laws wrote:

> On the question of baptism our position is so distinct, and to many so unacceptable, that I see no way of overcoming the difficulty short of equating believer's baptism with infant baptism. This would seem to me to make infant baptism the standard and believer's baptism a sort of tolerated exception. It is not likely that more than a very few Baptists would ever think of consenting to such an equation. It is a very painful thing to have to say to those who set store by infant baptism that we regard it as a perversion of an ordinance of Christ, a substitution of man's devising for a positive institution of the Lord. Yet nothing less than this is the true Baptist position, and as one holds it I see no way, except at the cost of truth, of organic union with other Churches.[227]

Union Churches

The influence of the ecumenical movement can be seen clearly in Baptist life in the growth in the numbers of Union churches.

---

224 *The Report of the Commission*, 27, cited by Laws, 'The Edinburgh Conference', 24.

225 This was also reported by Martin, *Edinburgh 1937*, 58-62. It is important to note that this principle was claimed for children but not for others. This perhaps marks the beginning (or at least an early stage of) the growing awareness among Baptists which recognized that the 'church' includes others than just believers, namely children of Christian parents, children brought to church and also adults attending church. This recognition became explicit in the 1966 report *The Child and the Church*, published by a special study group set up by the BU Council in 1963.

226 Laws, 'The Edinburgh Conference', 25.

227 Laws, 'The Edinburgh Conference', 29.

The consolidation of the Free Church movement from the mid-1890s onwards provided an atmosphere conducive to the formation of Union churches. Usually this happened either between two struggling Free Church causes coming together[228] or in new church planting enterprises.[229] Though the title of 'Union Church' appears to have come into being around the beginning of the twentieth century,[230] their pre-history can be traced at least to the end of the eighteenth century and possibly earlier.

In 1797 the Bedfordshire Union of Christians had been formed. It had grown out of the Evangelical Revival and the resultant deepening of spiritual life, and there can be little doubt that it drew on the legacy left in Bedfordshire and the surrounding counties by John Bunyan and the mixed-communion church which he had led.[231] From such beginnings the conviction had grown that people could be one in spiritual sentiment while various in their ecclesiastical forms. Some of the same men who formed the London Missionary Society in 1795, emulating the Baptist Missionary Society, joined together and founded the Bedfordshire Union.[232] Even though it was a Union of churches from two different denominations and not a 'mixed church', the Bedfordshire Union can justifiably be seen as the precursor of those churches which have become formally known as 'Union churches' by demonstrating that Baptists and Congregationalists could exist together in fellowship and mutual respect for each others' churchmanship, as well as in mission.

The exact date of the first 'Union Church' is unclear. Two comments by Payne suggest they are a twentieth-century phenomenon,[233] and he

---

228 E.g. Wellington Union Free Church, formed in 1920, by the union of Wellington Baptist Church (f.1807) and Wellington Congregational Church (f.c.1820s), both of which were in interregnums by 1916 with little prospect of calling ministers. They had initially come together in 1919. The Union Church moved into the Congregational building which was fitted with a baptistry in 1924, the Baptist building being sold in 1929. See H. Foreman, *The Story of Union Free Church: Old Dissent in Wellington, Shropshire, 1700–1920* (Wellington, 1986), ch. 3, n.p..

229 E.g. the Hampstead Garden Suburb Free Church, see Green, *Tomorrow's Man*, 47-49.

230 As is reflected in a comment by Payne, *The Baptist Union*, 11, 'Early in the twentieth century a few "Union churches" were formed in new areas and these were affiliated to both Unions.'

231 On the mixed communion churches, see Payne, 'Baptist–Congregational Relationships', in Payne, *Free Churchmen, Unrepentant and Repentant*, 96-97.

232 J. Brown and D. Prothero, *The History of the Bedfordshire Union of Christians* (1946), 13-15. See the earlier volume by J. Brown, *Centenary Celebration of the Bedfordshire Union of Christians: The Story of a Hundred Years* (1896). From 1904 it was known as the Bedfordshire Union of Baptist and Congregational Churches.

233 Payne, 'Baptist–Congregational Relationships', 98, also p.8, and see also his comment in *The Baptist Union*, 11, noted above.

cited Letchworth (1905), Amersham-on-the-Hill (1908), Hampstead Garden Suburb (1910) and Hutton and Shenfield (1913) in support of this, but he then proceeded to include Colwyn Bay (1890) and Loughton (1817).[234] Further, a comment from T.V. Tymms a year before the formation of the Letchworth church claimed, 'There are a few "Union Churches"',[235] while the celebration of the jubilee of Union Church, Stretford, was reported in 1915, putting its foundation in 1865,[236] and Union Church, Heathfield in Sussex had been formed in December 1899.[237]

Whatever the date of the first Union Church, a contributory factor to their formation and increasing number was the movement among Baptists advocating and practising open communion and the growing number of open membership churches, a trend which had accelerated by the beginning of the twentieth century.[238] All this reveals that Baptists were increasingly prepared to recognize the churchmanship of other traditions and acknowledge the reality and validity of their faith irrespective of the form of baptism they had received. In 1905, for instance, just outside Bristol, Pill Congregational Church (f. 1787) and Pill Baptist Church (f. 1815) came together to form Pill Union Church. The Congregational Church had been having financial difficulties and problems over the land their church was built on which was owned by the Great Western Railway.

---

234 Payne, 'Baptist–Congregational Relationships', 99. Payne's dating, however, of Loughton is only part of the story. The chapel was originally a Particular Baptist cause established in 1813, though it was not until 1817 that it was formally constituted a church. From the beginning it practised open communion, though from 1822 it was agreed to accept paedobaptists into membership, and it was at this point that the use of 'Union' church was adopted to distinguish it from the Methodists. However, it was not for another 50 years that the church endeavoured to affiliate to the CU as well as the BU, though this, and later attempts in the 1930s to affiliate with the CU, were precluded by the Trust Deeds. However, the church has been called and acted as a Union Church since its beginning. See V. Lewis, *Loughton Union Church, 1813–1973* (Loughton, 1974), 5, 19-20, 26-27 and 44 which includes a copy of the statement placed in the vestibule in 1943, 'Loughton Union Church', which states 'The founders who were Baptists, set no narrow denominational limits to its membership, welcoming other "Protestant Dissenters" into full membership. The Church was known for many years as the Loughton Baptist Chapel, and is still legally Baptist, but the name was later changed to the present one...'

235 T.V. Tymms, 'Independents or Congregationalists', in C.S. Carter and G.E.A. Weeks (eds.), *The Protestant Dictionary* (1933), the first edition of 1904 which was edited by C.H.H. Wright and C. Neil was the volume in which Tymms' article was first published.

236 See 'Union Church Stretford', *BT&F* June 13, 1919, 365.

237 J. Weller, *One Church, One Faith, One Lord: A Short History of Union Church, Heathfield* (Heathfield, 1979), 3-4.

238 B.R. White, 'Open and Closed Membership Among English and Welsh Baptists', *BQ* 24.7 (July, 1972), 334.

Added to this, it would appear that the church was in decline, as the decision to unite with the Baptists was passed unanimously by only nine members.[239] The original intention was that the new Union Church would move to a new site, but until it did so worship would take place in the Baptist chapel. So long as this state of affairs continued it was agreed that the minister should be a Baptist,[240] but as the move was never effected the ministers have always been Baptists. Due to this situation, subsequent practice has meant that whenever an infant baptism was required an outside minister was called in.[241] It was common practice, however, in other Union churches to alternate the ministers between the two denominations.

In the summer of 1910, J.H. Rushbrooke was invited to the pastorate of the Free Church in the Hampstead Garden Suburb, a new development which had allocated space for two churches, one Anglican, the other Free Church. The establishing of the latter owed much to the joint backing of the BU and CU. Though the opening of the church did not take place until October 1911, Rushbrooke accepted the unanimous invitation extended to him in September 1910.[242] Then, in 1911, a joint committee of Baptists and Congregationalists met in order to discuss how they could try to avoid or reduce 'overlapping' in their church planting practices, and it became clear that many had come to favour the idea of Union churches for new areas such as the Garden Suburbs of Hampstead and Letchworth.[243] This whole movement was aided by the 1919 Act of Parliament which permitted the sharing of church premises between different denominations and which placed such a union on a legal basis.[244]

Within the West Country at least three churches benefited directly from the 1919 Act: Pill, already mentioned, Totnes, and Wells. In the latter case, the Congregational (f.1750) and Baptist (f.1815) churches were enabled to unite. The Act allowed the trustees of the chapels to permit the two buildings to be used 'as places for the public exercise of religious worship for and by a church consisting of Baptists and Congre-

---

239 G.S. Hart, *The Story of Pill Union Church* (Bristol, 1987), 4-5.

240 Hart, *The Story of Pill*, 14.

241 Communicated to the writer by Mr G. Hart, a former church secretary, in a letter dated September 8, 1990.

242 Payne, *James Henry Rushbrooke*, 22-25; Green, *Tomorrow's Man*, 47-55. The Hampstead Graden Suburb Free Church included both a baptistry and font as both forms of baptism were recognized and practised, practised infant dedication and open membership, and the Trust Deed, drawn up by the LBA, allowed the church to formulate its own constitition, see Green, *Tomorrow's Man*, 51-53.

243 Payne, *The Baptist Union*, 185.

244 See the forward to Hart, *The Story of Pill*, by Roger Hayden, n.p..

gationalists...and so that adult or infant baptism shall be administered as desired.'[245] On the question of membership the constitution reads:

2. ..The Church will recognize and permit both believer's and infant baptism.

3. ..In the case of persons desiring to join the church by confession of faith in baptism, or by profession of faith without baptism, the Church meeting at which they are nominated shall appoint two members of the Church to visit them.[246]

In 1925, F.C. Spurr claimed that the growth of the Free Church unity movement had in many cases weakened the bonds of denominational loyalty, specifically, that the creation of Union churches had brought together in a common spiritual fellowship persons formerly separated from each other. 'The Baptists in these Churches have not always felt it wise or desirable to insist upon their distinctive doctrines. They have preferred to share a common life with their brethren in Christ rather than cause division by introducing controversy. And so the tendency has been to drop anything like specific Baptist testimony.' Later Spurr reiterated his point: 'Upon some undoubtedly the larger "reunion" movement has had a great effect. Many have openly said that if reunion is to come there must be mutual toleration regarding Baptism. This spirit of compromise does not help the specific Baptist witness.'[247] But Spurr's position was refuted by Hugh Martin, who, seven years later, said that he believed it was then possible, in the light of experience, to formulate principles for the teaching and practice of baptism in a Union church which would meet any just Baptist complaints,[248] though he did not state what such principles would be.

The 1937 Special Committee *Report* defined a 'Union Church' as 'one in which both forms of baptism (i.e., of believers and of infants) may be practised, in which the membership is open, i.e., is not confined to believers who have been baptized by immersion on profession of faith, and in which the ministry is not confined to believers who have been baptized by immersion on profession of faith', and then identified that there were, by that time, about sixty five such Union churches in England, but none were known to exist in either Wales or Scotland.[249] The

---

245 [Ch lxxxiii] Wells Particular Baptists and [9&10 Geo.5.] Congregational Chapels Charities Scheme Confirmation Act, ACTS L&P 9 & 10, Geo.5, 51-100, 1919, 4.

246 Quoted in a letter from the then minister of Wells United Church, Malcolm Smalley, dated May 13, 1992.

247 F.C. Spurr, 'A Baptist Apologetic for To-day. The Present Situation', *B T* September 10, 1925, 639.

248 H. Martin, 'Christian Unity', *BT* November 10, 1932, 776.

249 *Report of the Special Committee*, 14.

difference between a Union church and an open membership church was that in the latter the minister had to be a Baptist and that the only form of baptism administered was by immersion on profession of faith.[250] The anomaly that this situation led to was that some Baptist churches admitted into membership those who had never been baptized at all and, the *Report* observed, this would lead to yet another difficulty as regards any unity of organization between open membership Baptists and other Christians, including Presbyterians and Congregationalists, neither of whom were prepared to admit non-baptized persons into membership.[251] Needless to say, Union churches and open membership churches also provided difficulties to closer unity with closed membership and closed communion Baptist churches.

A later section from the *Report* also had a bearing upon Union churches (and much later on LEPs), though it explicitly dealt with what would happen to the doctrine of baptism in a United Free Church. The *Report* frankly admitted that the Committee had had diffculty in forecasting what would be likely to happen, but it set out what it perceived to be the likely difficulties. The church would have to admit into membership any applicant who demonstrated that they had reached their decision after honest and mature deliberation, whether infant-baptized, believer-baptized or infant-baptized and seeking-to-be-baptized on profession of faith. Much would undoubtedly depend on the minister who, if a convinced Baptist, would find difficulty administering a rite which they did not believe to be the true rite of Christian baptism, thus presenting an administrative problem to the new church. It was further felt that the Baptist point of view would be liable to suffer were the question to cease to be a live issue or were it to be dropped from discussion for the sake of peace. Rebaptism would also become an issue simply because of the problem of maintaining side by side two forms of baptism which were mutually exclusive, and rebaptism as such was a practice rejected by all the Free Churches. The suggestion that it would be plausible for there to be the mutual recognition of the two forms of baptism the Committee strongly repudiated.[252] The very idea of any compromise or abandonment of principle, as has already been shown, was anathema to the majority of the denomination at this time.

---

250 *Report of the Special Committee*, 14-15.

251 *Report of the Special Committee*, 16. However, this last assertion is not strictly true, though widely held. E.g., in his book *Baptists, Congregationalists and Presbyterians* (1933), 24, the Principal of the Yorkshire United Independent College, E.J. Price, admitted 'Congregationalists do not, in general, insist upon Baptism as essential for Church-membership, though many do.'

252 *Report of the Special Committee*, 23-25.

The Influence of Ecumenism

As the ecumenical movement gained momentum and as Baptist involvement within it became both official and more pronounced, this new 'ecumenical' spirit began to permeate slowly more and more the life of the denomination. Various external factors undoubtedly aided this whole process. Advances in transport led to greater population mobility, aiding the dissemination of ideas by personal contact, and church leaders and the advocates of union, such as Shakespeare and Martin, used this skilfully. At the same time came the more rapid transmission of ideas through the denominational and inter-denominational papers, the most important of which for Baptists was the *Baptist Times*. These media were further enhanced through more widespread education, enabling more people to read, and, with the growing standards of living, Christian publishing was able to expand (for example, the SCM Press), resulting in more people being able to buy the literature available, whether tracts, sermons, pamphlets, books or journals.

Further, there can be little doubt that even at an unconscious level members of the different Christian traditions were more readily predisposed to the cross-fertilization of ideas. The co-operative and often philanthropic and missionary societies that had so marked the nineteenth century meant that members of different denominations had become used to working side by side, so a greater understanding of one another's views naturally resulted. The Free Church movement from the 1890s onwards brought Baptists and Paedobaptists closely together, leading to each regularly recognizing each other's churchmanship. As such contacts became more frequent so too they became more widely accepted. Even though Shakespeare's proposals met with staunch opposition, nevertheless, he brought the whole ecumenical issue squarely into the fore of the denomination's life and thought and paved the way for all subsequent developments.

In all this, baptism simmered just below the surface until the mid-1920s when it burst to the surface of ecumenical debate. However, the theology of baptism was of growing concern throughout this period, clearly affected by, but not always consciously so, the ecumenical developments taking place. It is to the theology of baptism we now turn.

CHAPTER 4

The Theology of Baptism

In chapter 2 only those aspects of the doctrine of baptism that were un-contentious were discussed. But it must be noted that usually the absence of reference to them would not imply that the writer was antagonistic towards such views, simply that they had no recourse to discuss them. Attention, therefore, must now turn to four areas over which there was no kind of consensus and considerable debate, disagreement and, perhaps even at the popular level which has not extended into the extant literature, dissension.

Baptism: Ordinance or Sacrament?

In discussions of Baptist theology one of several possible classifications draws the distinction between evangelicals and sacramentalists, the view on baptism being the determinative factor.[1] Though this has been a popular, tenacious and even widespread opinion, it will quickly become clear that it is far too simplistic a dividing line. At the popular level of grass-roots Baptist belief a division did exist between those who used the term 'ordinance' and those who adopted the word 'sacrament'. This was clearly reflected in Henry Cook's *What Baptists Stand For*,[2] but in the period 1900–1937 this distinction cannot be as clearly discerned as many would suspect. In fact, it would be true to say that within this period there was no great controversy within the denomination over which word should be used. It will be shown that more often than not authors meant the same thing by either word.[3]

---

1   E.g. McBeth, *Baptist Heritage*, 511.
2   H. Cook, *What Baptists Stand For* (1947), 69-74.
3   The interchangeability of 'sacrament' and 'ordinance' was not something new to the twentieth century, but is also evident in Baptist thought from the seventeenth to the nineteenth century, see Fowler, 'Baptism', 7-93; Thompson, 'A New Question', 66-68 and 'Practicing the Freedom of God', 8-13; Cross, 'Dispelling the Myth'.

'Ordinance' or 'Sacrament'?

It would be true to say that the preferred word used of baptism by Baptists in the nineteenth century was 'ordinance', but this must not be taken to imply that Baptists did not use the term 'sacrament'. Both J.R.C. Perkin's thesis on baptism[4] and Michael Walker's on the Lord's Supper seek to demonstrate that 'sacrament' was a term used by Baptists in this period, and that this, though a minority point of view, was in fact larger than is often portrayed.[5] Examination of the literature of the early years of the twentieth-century reveals that those who advocated the use of 'sacrament' as a valid description of baptism steadily increased in number and did indeed form a considerable body within the denomination.

Within the extant literary sources for this period the exclusive use of one of these terms is found to be roughly equal,[6] but it would still be true

---

4   Caution must be adopted when using Perkin's dissertation, for by the very nature of his doctorate ('Baptism in Nonconformist Theology, 1820–1920, with special reference to the Baptists'), he was only able to use a narrow selection of Baptist writings. He is undoubtedly correct, though, in highlighting the central role played by H.W. Robinson for the Baptists and P.T. Forsyth for the Congregationalists as the most important Nonconformist writers involved in what he calls 'The Birth of the Modern Controversy', see p.427. He further noted that both men were of catholic views and meticulous scholarship, neither of whom, though, were unreservedly accepted by his denomination during his lifetime. Perkin also saw that Robinson spent most of his time, not on the mode and subjects of baptism, which had preoccupied so much of nineteenth-century Baptist theology, but on the meaning of baptism. And though many of his views had been expressed before, he added some new and startling points (Perkin, p.437) and it was the combination of old with new which made Robinson the most important Baptist writer on baptism for the first half of the twentieth century.

5   Perkin, 'Baptism in Nonconformist Theology', 10; Walker, *Baptists at the Table*, 8-17.

6   'Ordinance' was used in the title to the baptism section in the *BCH*, nos.481-497; Williams, *Principles and Practices*, 11, 13; Phillips, *What Baptists Stand For*, 14; J.W. Ewing, *Talks on Free Church Principles* (1905), 69; F.B. Meyer, 'Baptised into Christ's Death', *BH* 1907, 262; Marshall, *Conversion*, 58-59, and 'Baptists' in *The Encyclopaedia Britannica III* (Cambridge, 11th edn, 1910), 370; J.R. Wood and S. Chick, *A Manual of the Order and Administration of a Baptist Church* ([1910], 2nd edn, n.d.), 10, 24; Freeman, 'The Lambeth Appeal', 6-8; in Rushbrooke (ed.), *Faith of the Baptists*, see Laws, 'Vital Forces', p.14, Hagger, 'Discipleship and Its Implications', p.57, and the *Reply*, p.88.

'Sacrament' was used by Mountain, *My Baptism*, 135; Clifford, 'The Baptist World Alliance', 62; Morris, *Thoughts*, 23-24; Glover, *Free Churches and Re-Union*, 31, 43-44; Robinson, *Baptist Principles*, 29n, and *Christian Experience of the Holy Spirit*, 184-98; Lord, 'Value of Baptist Witness To-Day', 55; in Rushbrooke (ed.), *Faith of the Baptists*, Underwood, 'Conversion and Baptism', p.29, and Emery, 'Fellowship and the Table of to say that 'ordinance' was the more widely known and preferred word and, because of this, it was often assumed rather than stated. This is borne out by those authors who wished to reinstate and emphasize the 'sacramental' aspect of baptism, believing this correction to be much needed within the theology of the denomination. There were also a not inconsiderable number who were quite content to use the terms interchangeably.[7]

Definitions

Only two explicit definitions of 'ordinance' were offered: one positive, the other negative. Henry Cook defined it as 'something commanded, something that has authority behind it, and Baptism and the Lord's Supper, we believe, have come down to us from the Christ Himself.'[8] This definition, which is itself pretty meagre, was implicitly accepted by all Baptists. A.S. Langley, however, defined 'ordinance' by what it was not. They were not sacraments because they did not 'convey saving grace', rather, they were 'symbols observed, and preserved by the churches' and of value 'to those who observe them only as their meaning is discerned.'[9]

As the ordinances were commandments of Christ they were thereby incumbent upon every believer. Obedience to the divine statute was important, but the majority of Baptist writers wished to safeguard against this being the only understanding of the rite. Ordinance, in this respect, thus stood for something ordained by Christ and to be obeyed by the disciple.[10] But even the sacramentalists would have accepted this as far as

---

the Lord', p.36; H.J. Flowers, 'The Holy Spirit', *BQ* 3.4 (October, 1926), 158, and 'The Unity of the Church', *BQ* 3.8 (October, 1927), 350; Whitley, 'Lausanne and Stockholm', 338, and 'Faith and Order', 360; Price, 'Laymen and Reunion', 295-96; H. Cook, 'The Covenant', *BT* October 3, 1935, 716-17.

7   For the use of 'ordinance' and 'sacrament' respectively, see Whitby, *Baptist Principles*, 33; Tymms, *Evolution of Infant Baptism*, 440 and 340; Whitley, *Witness of History*, 19 and 88; H. Cook, *The Why of Our Faith* (1924), 81 and 61; A.J.D. Farrer, 'The Present Position of Church and Dissent', *BQ* 2.5 (January, 1925), 206 and 205; Robinson, *Life and Faith*, 116 and 177, where he used the word 'sacramentalism' instead of his usual 'sacrament'; W.U. Torrance, 'The Sacraments and Authority', *Frat.* 13 (January, 1934), 10; *Report*, 3; G. Laws, *What is Baptism?* (n.d.), 7 and 11. That this was so can be further illustrated by the addresses of Underwood (p.29) and Emery (p.36) which used 'sacrament' and Hagger (p.57) who used 'ordinance' at the 1926 Assembly without any difference in meaning.

8   H. Cook, *The Call of the Church* (n.d., [1930]), 57-58.

9   A.S. Langley, *The Faith and Heritage and Mission of the Baptists* (1931), 8.

10   It is surprising that the view that baptism was an act of commemoration was only used once, particularly considering its use in memorial services and its use in church services, most notably at communion. See Whitley, *Church, Ministry and Sacraments*,

it went, but their position was distinguished in that they sought to develop their understanding of baptism much further.

The definition of 'sacrament' was not quite so simple, as it meant different things to different writers. Part of their understanding of baptism Baptists derived from the Latin *sacramentum* (though this was undoubtedly an unconscious thing for many, especially the large majority for whom anything approximating to Catholicism was anathema). This was evidenced in the belief in baptism as a pledge or act of allegiance,[11] or simply an oath.[12] It was spoken of as an avowal of allegiance to the Saviour,[13] a pledge that one's heart was changed and publicly and formally consecrated to God's service[14] and an expression of the loyalty of the soul to Christ.[15] It was not without significance that this terminology was strongly ethical, once again demonstrating the interrelation between the rite itself, the subjects and the meaning/implications for the baptized. This language was also similar in meaning to that used when baptism was spoken of as an act of dedication on the part of the believer to their Lord.[16] Whitley made this explicit, that *sacramentum* had seriously changed its meaning. For Livy it was an oath of fidelity taken by soldiers. Pliny used it of the oaths of Christians, a view developed by Tertullian to mean a legal action or formula. This usage dropped out and a new technical meaning developed. With Augustine the theory that sacraments conveyed grace became standard throughout the West.[17]

In the main it would be true to say that this definition of 'sacrament' found its way into the Baptist understanding of the rite often without it consciously being understood or used as its definition. When Baptists did define what they meant they usually used it in the sense of 'an outward and visible sign of an inward, spiritual grace', a definition which they inherited through the Catechism of the Prayer Book and beyond that to

---

162, who observed that baptism commemorated Christ's death and resurrection, as the believer turned away in horror from sin and in love to Jesus.

11   Ford, *Twenty-Five Years*, 31.

12   Morris, *Thoughts*, 23.

13   Mountain, *My Baptism*, 97; Whitley, *Church, Ministry and Sacraments*, 71-72; and Whitby, *Baptist Principles*, 32.

14   Whitley, *Church, Ministry and Sacraments*, 182; Whitby, *Baptist Principles*, 48 and 63; H.W. Robinson, 'The Faith of the Baptists', *ExpTim* 28 (1927), 454.

15   C.T. Bateman, *John Clifford: Free Church Leader and Preacher* (1902), 133; Robinson, *Life and Faith*, 116.

16   E.g. Clifford in Marchant, *Dr. John Clifford*, 264. Rushbrooke, 'Protestant of the Protestants', 81, spoke of an act of self-dedication.

17   Whitley, *Witness of History*, 68-70. See also Wood, '"BAPTISM"', 390-406, for the development of this view.

Calvin.[18] Believing Titus 3:5 to be the latest and presumably most developed passage indicating Paul's doctrine of baptism and regeneration, Whitley described the rite as an institution to which, in its early stage of development, the Lord had yielded obedience, but into which he breathed fuller meaning. He enjoined his disciples to administer it to converts, mentioning it in their preaching and ordering it. 'It was the outward acknowledgement of the inward change of heart, the token of a breach with the past, and an enrolment into a new community, a symbol of regeneration by the Holy Spirit from the death-in-life of former existence.'[19] That this was by no means a new way for Baptists to speak of baptism is reflected by Alfred Phillips who preferred the word ordinance,[20] but nevertheless, when examining Romans 6:3, noted, 'We often say "Baptism is an outward and visible sign of an inward and spiritual grace". So it is.'[21] J.E. Roberts explained that 'The essence of the sacramental principle is that ideas are brought home to men's minds by outward forms. Therefore the valuable element in a sacrament is its meaning.'[22]

Baptists, then, had a clear understanding of both the terms 'ordinance' and 'sacrament'. The majority were content with maintaining simply the former, though some were openly antagonistic towards any 'sacramental' connotations. Opposition to the sacramental understanding of the rite revolved around the mistrust of the term's mechanical and semi-magical overtones and its use by Catholics. Without these Baptists would have been happy to accept and use the word, though the preference was undoubtedly for ordinance.[23] Henry Cook made this clear in 1930[24] and then again 1947, in what has often been taken to be the definitive expression of the Baptist position.[25]

18   For its use by Calvin, see A.E. McGrath, *Reformation Thought: An Introduction* (Oxford, 2nd edn, 1993), 182. The phrase goes back to Augustine.

19   Whitley, *Church, Ministry and Sacraments*, 234. Later, p.160, he remarked, 'The outward sign apart from the inward reality was valueless, and [Paul] plainly added that the inward reality apart from that outward sign was invaluable.'

20   Phillips, *What Baptists Stand For*, 22, 38.

21   Phillips, *What Baptists Stand For*, 40. Others who explicitly used this defintion were Mountain, *My Baptism*, 31; Whitby, *Baptist Principles*, 61; Clifford, 'The Baptist World Alliance', 55; Tymms, *Evolution of Infant Baptism*, 340; Morris, *Thoughts*, 23; Underwood, *Conversion*, 110.

22   Roberts, *Christian Baptism*, 3-4.

23   'Baptist Union of Great Britain and Ireland', in Hodgson (ed), *Convictions*, 63. See also G. Laws, 'Denominational Self-consciousness. The Crying Need of the Baptists Today', *BT&F* July 20, 1923, 518.

24   Cook, *Call of the Church*, 57-61.

25   Cf. the comment by Ted Hale of the Abbey Centre, Northampton, 'Declaration of Principle', *BT* August 29, 1996, 7, who referred to *What Baptists Stand For?* as 'a basic primer' on Baptist principles. However, the difficulty of maintaining a consistent

Baptism as a Means Of Grace

In a note on the term 'Sacrament', Wheeler Robinson referred to the meaning of *sacramentum* as an oath of allegiance in the way Whitley and others had done before him, then continued: 'The term "sacrament" is, indeed, often used to imply what Baptists would regard as a mechanical or material conveyance of grace; but this misuse of a useful term ought no more to discredit it than the misuse of the term "baptism" by non-Baptists make us give up that term.'[26] This led him to reject what he termed 'sacramentarianism', though he accepted and used the term 'sacramentalism'.[27] Others spoke of 'anti-sacerdotalism',[28] while Whitley and Freeman objected to both 'sacerdotalism' and 'sacramentalism'.[29] Whatever word they used, it is true to say that the various authors were repudiating the same concept, though most avoided such terms precisely because of their connotations.

The dislike of what Charles Williams called this 'ecclesiastical' sense of 'sacrament', however, led him and a large number of Baptists to reject the notion that baptism was in any way a 'medium of grace'.[30] This widespread rejection was one of the reasons which drove some of the most notable Baptist scholars to argue for the reintroduction of this aspect of the New Testament doctrine into Baptist theology.

Wheeler Robinson contended: 'The Bible itself is no more than a collection of ancient documents till it becomes...a sacrament, that is, something which is a means by which the divine Spirit becomes active in the heart of reader or hearer.'[31] This was most forcefully and eloquently

---

position on this can be seen in a front page article in the *BT* in 1935, when Cook used 'sacrament' solely in the sense of the solemn pledge, H. Cook, 'The Covenant', *BT* October 3, 1935, 709-10.

26   Robinson, *Baptist Principles*, 29n.

27   Robinson, *Life and Faith*, 177. See also his 'The Faith of the Baptists', 455.

28   Whitley, *Church, Ministry and Sacraments*, 271-81; Phillips, *What Baptists Stand For*, 40.

29   Whitley, *Church, Ministry and Sacraments*, 244. On p.271 he stated that sacerdotalists appended the Bible to tradition; Freeman, 'Lambeth Appeal', 6-8. T.R. Glover, *Paul of Tarsus* (1927), 163, rejected the idea that Paul was a 'sacramentalist'.

30   Williams, *Principles and Practices*, 23. He later equated 'sacrament' with 'saving efficacy', that is, baptismal regeneration, pp.67-68.

31   Robinson, *Christian Experience of the Holy Spirit*, 190. See also ch.7 'The Spirit and the Scriptures', 160-83. Robinson also explores 'sacramental mediation' in his *Redemption and Revelation in the Actuality of History* (1942), xxxii and 103-06. Robinson's theology of baptism cannot adequately be discussed without reference to the centrality of his 'sacramental' understanding of the rite. It is precisely for this reason that D.A. Garrett's contribution on 'H. Wheeler Robinson' to the Southern Baptist published, T. George and D.S. Dockery (eds.), *Baptist Theologians* (Nashville, 1990), 402, is to be criticized. Though Garrett's discussion of baptism is brief, the omission of even the word

argued by Robinson in all his writings on baptism, and recognition of this is essential to an understanding of his theology of baptism and the Spirit. With an implicit reference to Baptist antagonism towards the Oxford Movement, Robinson stated that the reaction to a false doctrine of divine grace in baptism had made Baptists suspicious of the genuine sacramentalism of the New Testament. The emphasis had been so much on saying '*believer's* baptism' that they had failed, or at least were then failing, to say with anything like equal emphasis 'believer's *baptism*', meaning the entrance of believers into a life of supernatural powers.[32] He argued for the connection of water-baptism with the Spirit in exactly the sense in which Baptists argued for its connection with personal faith. 'If the New Testament teaches the latter, it assuredly also teaches the former, and Baptists are really committed to both.' It was personal faith which was the realm of the Spirit's activity, so too the confession of that faith in believer's baptism brought a new opportunity for divine grace, because it was an act of personal faith.[33]

In this understanding of baptism as a means of grace Robinson was not alone. Henry Cook affirmed that the two great ordinances, rightly administered, became 'true means of grace to the believer who receives them, but only to the believer.' Their value lay in the believer's perception of the truths they were meant to suggest, and where these truths were either hidden or not perceived, the purpose of the ordinances was frustrated, losing their true significance thereby becoming something they were never meant to be.[34] H.J. Flowers stated that baptism was neither magical nor a mere rite, but a means of grace, having re-creative power, marking the moment when the Spirit is imparted to the believer, uniting them with the church.[35] '*Ex opere operato*', Rushbrooke insisted,

---

'sacrament' perhaps reflects more Southern Baptist aversion to the term than the desire to fairly represent and assess Robinson's baptismal theology.

32   Robinson, *Life and Faith*, 177-78.

33   Robinson, *Life and Faith*, 178. Robinson's understanding of baptism as a means of grace relied on his further development of the relationship of the Holy Spirit to baptism, on which see the section below.

34   Cook, *Why of Our Faith*, 86. He reiterated the same point in his *Call of the Church*, 65, where he explained that the ordinances, 'speak of the deepest things in our faith, and, because they so speak, they are a true means of grace; not that they give grace in the sacramental sense, but they speak of grace; they reveal the love of God, and so they stimulate and quicken the faith of every believer.' It would not be untrue to Cook to take this final statement as a reference also to the edification a witness to baptism would receive. See on this L.H. Marshall, 'Baptists and Church Membership', *BT* October 31, 1924, 712, who wrote that, apart from its rich symbolism, the great value of baptism lay in its ability to cause 'a youth' (and presumably any non-Christian witness) to think more seriously about church membership and Christian discipleship.

35   Flowers, 'The Unity of the Church', 350.

'nothing is effected; but we know in our own lives that to follow Christ in obedience and faith is to find in His ordinance a means of grace.'[36]

What necessitated this re-emphasis of baptism was the trend within the denomination to degrade baptism into a mere sign and symbol. This resulted in those who sought to restore the sacramental element to the doctrine and practice of baptism being tarred with the label 'ritualists'. Recognizing this, Underwood declared, 'But the New Testament is not Zwinglian in its interpretation of the sacraments. In it baptism is every bit as much a means of grace as is the Lord's Supper. Indeed, it is more so... I do not see how anyone who puts off his theological spectacles and reads the New Testament with open eyes can doubt that the New Testament converts underwent at the time of their baptism a definite religious experience.' In baptism, converts make their surrender to Christ more complete, their consecration more absolute, receiving a further endowment of the Spirit and further power to walk in newness of life, and their experience of union with Christ is deepened and enhanced. Underwood, and those in agreement with him, could maintain this position without danger of any mechanical or superstitious overtones by their insistence that baptism is a means of grace *only* to those who believe.[37] Underwood, however, did not stop here, but proceeded to call on ministers to 'preach up' baptism as a means of grace to all who would receive it in faith.[38] Answering the enquiry as to why someone should submit to the rite, he stressed that Baptists had to show that baptism justified itself in Christian experience as a means of grace and that it has great spiritual value only when confined to believers and is by immersion.[39] Gilbert Laws stated that We may therefore expect to receive an increased measure of spiritual life and power from the Holy Ghost

---

36   Rushbrooke, 'Protestant of the Protestants', 81.

37   Underwood, 'Baptism and Conversion', 29-30.

38   Underwood, 'Baptism and Conversion', 33. Throughout the first four decades of the present century there was a widely held conviction that baptism was not taught, preached or practised as it should be. See C.W. Adams, 'The Need for Revival and How We May Get It', *BT&F* January 3, 1908, 3-4; J.E. Compton, *The Place of the Sacraments in the Baptist Church* (1910), 11-12; 'A Grateful Deacon', 'Open Baptistries', *BT* September 13, 1928, 663; C.F. Perry, 'Christian Baptism and the Campaign' (reference to the Discipleship Campaign), *BT* August 31, 1933, 586; D.J. Sheppard of Wellingborough, 'Watery Undenominationalism', *BT* March 19, 1936, 218; A.J. Klaiber, 'The Monthly Grumble. "Watery Undenominationalism"', *BT* February 27, 1936, 163; A.W. Gummer Butt, '"Prove Me Now". Great Forward Movement. The Vision and the Method', *BT* April 16, 1936, 293; Ford, *Twenty-Five Years*, 44; 'Baptists and Re-Union', *BT* April 8, 1937, 262, being a review of the *Report of the Special Committee* (1937); H.H. Briggs of Nelson, Lancashire, 'The Ordinances', *BT* September 23, 1937, 716.

39   Underwood, 'Baptism and Conversion', 35.

when we pass through the waters. According to our faith so will it be unto us.'[40]

Most significantly of all for dissemination of this 'sacramental' doctrine of baptism was its adoption in two important official Baptist declarations: the 1926 *Reply to the Lambeth Appeal* and the 1937 Special Committee *Report*. The *Reply* reported that 'Christian Baptism and the Communion of the Lord's Supper are duly received by us not only as rites instituted and hallowed by our Lord Himself, but as a means of grace to all who receive them in faith.'[41] The *Report* developed the understanding of baptism and the Lord's Supper as symbols, declaring that they were 'appointed instruments and vehicles of grace for those who come to them with a right disposition, and that they (in the words of Calvin) "hold forth and offer Christ to us and in Him the treasures of heavenly grace". Such a view emphasizes an essential element of a sacrament...that it is primarily the Word and Act of God, conveying the grace of God to men.' The Committee then disclaimed any suggestion that such a sacramental view should limit the bestowal of grace to the sacraments or that any priestly mediation was necessary for its proper celebration. Thus, baptism was more than a mere symbol and more than a confession of faith. 'This view treats baptism as a vehicle for the conveyance of grace, but it does not involve the assertion that baptism is an essential condition of regeneration or of salvation and it implies the necessity of a moral response on the part of the baptized person.'[42] The necessity of faith for a true sacramentalism was underscored by Underwood when he wrote, 'The baptism of believers is...a means of grace, a definite religious experience, a genuine Sacrament, but only to those who submit to it in penitence and faith. They claim to be the only Christian body which has preserved the full sacramental value of Christian baptism.'[43]

Such expressions of Baptist sacramentalism did not go unchallenged. Clearly the tendency to stress the faith of the believer was a concern to

---

40   Laws, *What is Baptism?*, 12-14, quotation from pp.13-14. W.Y. Fullerton's tract, *Baptism*, (n.d.), 14, simply observed, 'We apprehend this baptism as a true means of grace.' See also W. Powell, *Christian Baptism as Understood by the Baptists* (n.d.), 12, 'We Baptists do not say that we are better Christians than those belonging to other branches of the Church, but we do say that we have used a means of grace that they have not used.' In this connection, Powell noted that baptism symbolized 'the spiritual fact of belief in Christ.' As a symbol of this, then, 'it strengthens that fact', p.9.

41   *Reply*, 88.

42   *Report of the Special Committee*, 28-29. A footnote after the Calvin quote made reference back to the 1926 *Reply* just quoted. The importance of the *Report* is all the more evident once it is remembered that the Committee was composed of representatives from the different traditions existing within the BU.

43   Underwood, 'Views of Modern Churches', 225.

many, especially those on the more Calvinist wing of the denomination. In an article on 'What Happens at Baptism?', R. Birch Hoyle stressed that 'It is important that we Baptists insist on the point that the baptiser is not so prominent at baptism as is the Divine work then wrought in creating faith and imparting grace.' Later he warned that while Baptists insisted upon conscious faith on the part of the recipient of baptism, 'we must be on guard against the over-emphasis of the human factor of belief at the expense of the Divine Worker.' It was, however, Hoyle's final sentence which incited Alexander Graham-Barton. Hoyle wrote, 'And as Baptists we should emphasise, not the amount of water and immersion therein, but "baptism into the Holy Ghost".'[44] Hoyle had discussed the work of the Methodist C. Ryder Smith, the Anglo-Catholic N.P. Williams, and Karl Barth and Martin Luther. Of all these, Graham-Barton boldly stated, they had 'not a vestige of scriptural authority to justify their assertions that "baptism is a means of grace imparted in the rite" or that "it regenerates the soul" or that it has anything to do "with sacramental self-knowledge", or that "the end of baptism works for forgiveness of sins", or that "its purpose is to save men".'[45]

T.R. Glover attributed the rise of the 'sacraments', not to Jesus, but to the influx of hellenistic 'converts [who] came and brought with them the thoughts and instincts of countless generations, who had never conceived of a religion without rites and mysteries.' As a result, baptism 'took on a miraculous colour' in time accruing names taken from pagan rituals of admission, namely enlightenment and initiation.[46]

However, Glover's views were challenged by Berkeley Collins who rejected the connexion between the sub-apostolic church and its religious environment. Rather, he sought to show that 'a candid examination and exegesis of the New Testament must lead to the conviction that from the beginning what is understood as sacramentarianism has had its foothold in the Church. There never was a time when baptism was regarded as a simple rite, having only symbolic significance. In the earliest documents it is represented as a genuine sacrament conveying various divine gifts to the recipients.' With the Lord's Supper 'it not only typifies but in some real sense effects redemption', a statement he supported with the

---

44   R. Birch Hoyle, a retired minister living in Kingston-on-Thames, 'What Happens in Baptism?', *BT* August 24, 1933, 572. This article built on an earlier one in which Hoyle had submitted that it was 'high time that more thinking was done on "what happens" at baptism, whether infant or adult', see his 'Baptism: As Others See It', *BT* July 13, 1933, 476.

45   A. Graham-Barton of Marylebone,'What Happens at Baptism?', *BT* September 14, 1933, 616.

46   T.R. Glover, *The Conflict of Religions in the Early Roman Empire* (1909), 158-59. Cf. his *Jesus and the Experience of Man* (1921), 164, where he rued the organization and sacramentalism linked with the Constantinian settlement of the church.

observation that this is clear 'from the close connexion between baptism and the gift of the Spirit which is everywhere assumed.'[47]

Without this renewed emphasis on the sacramental nature of baptism future ecumenical discussions and developments could never have taken place. E. Roberts-Thomson noted that without Wheeler Robinson and A.C. Underwood discussions between Baptists and the Churches of Christ could not have begun in 1942.[48] Further, without such developments the future of Baptist participation in the modern ecumenical movement could not have taken place, as their understanding of baptism and that held among paedobaptist denominations would have been so far removed from each other that any convergence would have been impossible, and the BU would have perhaps retreated into an extreme anti-ecumenical position, as some wanted it to, rather than the cautious yet committed position they have had.

Baptism and the Holy Spirit

The belief that baptism is a means of grace is inseparably linked to an identification of baptism with the working of the Holy Spirit. Perkin rightly observed that both Baptists and Paedobaptists during this period 'did not feel happy about the doctrine of the Holy Spirit, whether in connection with baptism or not' and that this constituted 'a serious lacuna in the theology of the period.'[49]

Perkin's research went up to 1920, but what he said equally applies up to the late 1920s, when this whole question of the relationship between the Spirit and baptism eventually began to be explored more seriously, principally by Wheeler Robinson. Other writers, of course, addressed this issue, but most of the references were scattered within the discussion of other themes and were thus all too often brief and underdeveloped. Such

---

47   Collins, 'The Sacrament of Baptism', 37. He defends this position in the whole of his three-part article, see *ExpTim* 27.1 (October, 1915), 36-39; 27.2 (November, 1915), 70-73; 27.3 (December, 1915), 120-23.

48   E. Roberts-Thomson, *Baptists and Disciples of Christ* (n.d., [1951]), 114-23, and especially p.122. On these discussions see below. The importance of Robinson, Underwood and the 1926 *Reply* in the development of Baptist theology away from the merely symbolic was also recognized by Ross, 'Theology of Baptism in Baptist History', 100-12. D.M. Thompson, 'The Older Free Churches', in R. Davies (ed.), *The Testing of the Churches, 1932–1982: A Symposium* (1982), 104-05, also identified Robinson and Underwood as the scholars responsible for the recovery of a sacramental doctrine among Baptists; and see also the discussion of them in I. Randall, *Evangelical Experiences: A Study in the Spirituality of English Evangelicalism 1918–1939* (PBTM; Carlisle, 1999), 193-94.

49   Perkin, 'Baptism', 13-14. Cf. the anonymous 'A Neglected Doctrine', *BT&F* January 16, 1914, 43.

glimpses simply evidence that the issue was only just beginning to emerge into the Baptist theological consciousness.

Several authors acknowledged that there was a connection between the Holy Spirit and baptism, but they did not proceed to develop this any further.[50] T.H. Robinson went beyond the bare statement of the existence of a connection, to state that baptism was ritual, whereas the baptism by the Holy Spirit was actual and permanent.[51] W.Y. Fullerton understood water baptism to be appropriate subsequent to the baptism of the Spirit of 1 Corinthians 12:13, which he saw as conversion, and that water-baptism is a means of grace which he described in terms of being filled in the Spirit.[52] Wheeler Robinson also linked the rite with the gift of the Holy Spirit,[53] but he developed this further. He stated that the church is the creation of the Spirit of God, for it is the Spirit who is the agent of regeneration which is the Godward side of conversion. Thus, there is no need to be surprised that the New Testament so closely links the gift of the Spirit with believer's baptism, indeed, it makes the experience of that gift the test of the rite. This, however, is not to be committed to any theory of baptismal regeneration. To focus on the external act and material means as the prescribed channel of the Spirit's activity would indeed result in sacramentarianism. But to focus on the internal conditions, the personal faith and conversion which are emphasized in believer's baptism, seeing them as the true realm of the Spirit, both guards against and prevents this. He continued, 'In fact, when we speak of Believer's Baptism, we mean that baptism in the Spirit of God, of which water baptism is the expression.'[54] E.C. Pike heartily concurred: immersion is the sign of the entire baptism into the Holy Spirit.[55] John Lewis sought to make it clear that it is not baptism 'into' or 'with' but 'in' the Holy Ghost.[56] The *Reply* declared that immersion was retained

---

50   E.g. F.B. Meyer, *Peter, Fisherman, Disciple, Apostle* (n.d., [1919]), 142; Glover, *Paul*, 112.

51   T.H. Robinson, *St. Mark's Life of Jesus* (1922), 17. For a biographical sketch of T.H. Robinson, see M.P. Matheney Jr, 'Teaching Prophet. The Life and Continuing Influence of Theodore Henry Robinson', *BQ* 29.5 (January, 1982), 199-216.

52   W.Y. Fullerton, *Souls of Men: Studies in the Problems of the Church To-day* (1927), 101-21, on the means of grace see pp.115-16.

53   Robinson, *Baptist Principles*, 13-14.

54   Robinson, *Baptist Principles*, 24-25. In his *Life and Faith*, 10-11, he wrote, 'Baptism signifies the entrance into a life of fellowship with Christ, which means a baptism of the Holy Spirit.'

55   Pike, *Some Unique Aspects*, 7.

56   Lewis, 'Baptised into Jesus Christ', 23. Unfortunately he said nothing beyond this.

'because this symbolic representation guards the thought of that inner baptism of the Holy Spirit which is central in Christian experience.'[57]

Baptists have always been vigorous opponents of baptismal regeneration, but on the new birth they were unanimous: it is by the Holy Spirit not baptism that a person is born again.[58] A distinction, therefore, is drawn by many between the baptism of the Spirit and water baptism,[59] which led Robinson to speak of the external act always being subordinate and secondary to the baptism of the Spirit.[60]

The belief that baptism is a means of grace led Underwood to conclude that in baptism the earliest Christians received a further endowment of the Spirit and further power to walk in newness of life. 'Their experience of union with Christ began at their conversion, but in the hour of their baptism it was deepened and enhanced to such a degree that the Apostle Paul could say that baptism united the believer to Christ and enabled him to put on Christ.' After quoting James Denney's comment that converts found that baptism 'in a high and solemn hour raised to its height the Christian's sense of what it is to be a Christian', Underwood continued: 'In a word, New Testament baptism was a definite means of grace, but never in a magical way, because it was administered only to believers, and what each got out of it depended upon the faith of his converted will.'[61] Wheeler Robinson said that by baptism, as well as by faith, the Christian is saturated in the Holy Spirit (1 Corinthians 12:13).[62] In his study of

---

57   *Reply*, 88. Similarly, Mountain, *My Baptism*, 17 and 182, acknowledged that the gift of the Spirit was spoken of by Peter, not as a substitute for the ordinance of baptism, but as an urgent reason for its immediate observance.

58   E.g. Phillips, *What Baptists Stand For* 14; Whitby, *Baptist Principles*, 15, 65-66; Clifford, 'The Baptist World Alliance', 59; Robinson, *Life and Faith*, 84.

59   Whitley, *Church, Ministry and Sacraments*, 51; Freeman, 'The Lambeth Appeal', 6-7.

60   Robinson, 'The Place of Baptism', 212, and *Christian Experience of the Holy Spirit*, 198.

61   Underwood, 'Conversion and Baptism', 30. Eleven years later, he reiterated his belief that 'in every baptism of a believer there is a bestowal of the Holy Spirit. Every water-baptism of a believer should be a Spirit-baptism too—and that in no magical fashion but in a manner thoroughly ethical, because the believer proceeds to baptism in virtue of his repentance and faith', see his 'Views of Modern Churches', 227, and 'Baptism and Regeneration', *BT* March 1, 1928, 144. Collins, 'The Sacrament of Baptism', 38, argued that 'From the beginning baptism was regarded as a "power."' What is said in the New Testament of baptism has reference only to the baptism of believers, repentance and faith always being assumed as the precondition of baptism. '*This means that the association of the Spirit with the rite might have some grounds in a genuine experience*', italics his.

62   H.W. Robinson, *The Christian Doctrine of Man* (Edinburgh, 1911), 125.

Ephesians 1:11-14, Flowers' main assertion was that the Spirit was given at baptism.[63]

At the 1926 Assembly, Rushbrooke called Baptists to self-dedication, 'a new baptism of the Spirit', if the denomination was to carry towards its completion the work of their fathers.[64] This comment in no way contradicted the understanding of the baptism of the Spirit held by the majority of Baptists at this time, for it used the term in much the same way as people nowadays call for revival, in no way suggesting a second re-birth. But there were other Baptists whose understanding of the baptism of the Spirit was vague. According to Lord baptism was the means whereby the believer could experience the power and blessing of the Holy Spirit. He elucidated his comment no further, nor based it on any passage of Scripture, but his comment does reflect many Baptists' unease and reluctance to say more than that the believer in some undefined way experiences some undefined blessing from the Spirit in baptism.[65] Even less satisfactory was the brief explanation given by Henry Wicks, who contented himself to equate water as a symbol of the Spirit in his cleansing power.[66] W.Y. Fullerton merely observed that the baptism with the Spirit needed to precede baptism in water.[67]

The only writer to draw the distinction which was found in Paul between the baptism of the Spirit and the fulness of the Spirit was Whitley. Discussing Acts 2:1-4, he observed the 'curious fact' that although the promise was to be baptized with the Holy Spirit (Acts 1:5) this metaphor was not retained by Luke in Acts 2:4 which recorded that they 'were filled with the Holy Spirit'. 'The one', he explained, 'implies their being surrounded with the Spirit as by an all-encompassing atmosphere in which they lived and moved; the other, their being taken full possession of and thoroughly imbued by Him. Both agree in the conception of the completeness of the influence exercised on them by the Spirit.' The 'slight' difference was that literal baptism could only be experienced once, and this unique Pentecostal experience was unique for each participant, whereas the same people could afterwards have a revival, being filled with the Spirit again, but not baptized again. 'So it is unscriptural to speak of a man or a church being baptised afresh in the Spirit: one baptism, many fillings; or, better still, one baptism, ever full.'[68]

There was one notable dissension from the above. F.B. Meyer suggested that the term baptism as applied to the Holy Spirit 'had better

---

63   H.J. Flowers, 'The Holy Spirit', 159, 161. It is a shame that Flowers' study was only exegetical and did not go on to apply his views to the contemporary situation.

64   Rushbrooke, 'Protestant of the Protestants', 83.

65   F.T. Lord, *The Great Decision: An Outline of Christian Discipleship* (1936), 17.

66   Wicks, 'Baptismal Regeneration', 22.

67   W.Y. Fullerton, 'A Baptised Church', *BT&F* April 27, 1917, 259.

68   Whitley, *Church, Ministry and Sacraments*, 118-19.

be confined to those marvellous manifestations of spiritual power which are recorded in Acts ii, viii, x, xix; whilst the word *filling* should be used of those experiences of the indwelling and anointing of the Divine Spirit which are within the reach of us all.'[69] He neither used 'baptism of the Spirit' in reference to the act of conversion nor in Rushbrooke's way of referring to revival. How widespread Meyer's views were is difficult to assess, but it is the only such comment to have been found in this period, and reflects a more Reformed position.

It was, however, Wheeler Robinson who developed this aspect of the doctrine most fully. It would be expected that his clearest thoughts on the relation between the Spirit and baptism would be found in the relevant chapter of his major work on the Christian's experience of the Spirit, but this is not the case. Here, the sacraments are described as the acts of believers, baptism supplying a visible parallel to the spiritual experience which Paul called the baptism of the Holy Spirit—the believer's death to sin and resurrection to newness of life.[70] Since the action corresponded to the spoken word, as with the prophetic symbolism of Israel's prophets,[71] therefore, there could be no question of 'mere symbolism' in baptism (or the Lord's Supper) 'for the act is the partial and fragmentary, but very real accomplishment of a divine work, the work of the Holy Spirit.'[72]

His clearest thoughts on the Spirit, however, are to be found in his other works, particularly his *Baptist Principles*,[73] in which he declared

---

69   F.B. Meyer, *John the Baptist* (n.d., [1900]), 85.

70   Robinson, *Christian Experience of the Holy Spirit*, 194. S. Clark, 'The shout which dislodged the avalanche of the Holy Spirit', *BT* October 21, 1999, 5 and 12, describes this work, p.12 (he also acknowedges Robinson's *Baptist Principles*), as 'a pioneer factor in awakening awareness to our need of the Holy Spirit.'

71   Robinson, *Christian Experience of the Holy Spirit*, 193.

72   Robinson, *Christian Experience of the Holy Spirit*, 194.

73   While *Baptist Principles* was first published as a separate volume in 1925, it was originally a contribution to Shipley (ed.), *The Baptists of Yorkshire* (1912), entitled 'Baptist Principles before the rise of Baptist Churches', 3-50. It has proved to be one of the, if not *the*, most influential books on Baptist principles in the twentieth century, and it was ground-breaking in that it moved Baptist discussion of baptism away from detailed discussion of the mode and subjects of the rite. Three points support this view of its influence: its reviews commended it highly, see Anon., 'Baptist Teaching', *BT* December 10, 1925, 904, also E.A. Payne's review of the German version, 'Baptische Grundsatze...Oncken Verlag, Kassel, 1931', *BQ* 6.2 (April, 1932), 95; it had become the standard replacement to Whitley's *The Witness of History to Baptist Principles* for the Lay Preacher's examinations by 1930, see A. Ellis, JP (ed.), 'The Lay Preachers' Column: "Baptist Principles"', *BT* October 31, 1929, 815; and copies were still available through the BU's Publications Department in the early 1980s—the present writer bought his copy of the 1960 3rd edn reprint from Baptist Church House in 1984.

that baptism is linked to the gift of the Spirit,[74] and then, when discussing the nature of the church as a spiritual society of the converted, he declared that the church was the creation of the Spirit, for he was the agent in that regeneration which was the Godward side of conversion. As the church in the New Testament was illustrated by the three metaphors of a spiritual house, God's family and a Spirit animated body, there was little surprise that the New Testament so closely linked the gift of the Spirit with believer's baptism, indeed making the experience of that gift the test of the rite.[75] Water baptism was thus the expression of the baptism in the Spirit.[76] It was this aspect, he admitted elsewhere, which Baptists had failed to emphasize.[77]

In the last chapter of this seminal Baptist work, Robinson proposed three conditions which would ensure for Baptist churches a great future, the second of which was the recovery of the New Testament emphasis on the Spirit of God.[78] It was this emphasis, more than any other single truth, which gave the New Testament its 'expansive and vital atmosphere, the sense of great things to be and do, and great powers with which to attain them.' The recovery of this would do much to meet the growingly insistent needs of the contemporary world—witnessing to 'a baptism of the Spirit which exhilarates, expands, purifies the whole personality, intellectual and emotional and volitional.'[79] In 1927, he called on Baptists to set themselves open-mindedly to the study of the New Testament references to baptism, for they might be surprised to find how closely baptism was related to the gift of the Spirit. A sharp distinction existed between John's baptism expressed as a moral decision and Christ's baptism which was with or in the Spirit. This he supported with reference to John 3:5 and 1 Corinthians 12:13. For Paul, baptism was not solely descent into the waters of baptism meaning death and burial with Christ and that mystical union with him which carried with it death to sin, but also ascent into new life, defined by Paul as newness of 'Spirit' (Col. 2:12). 'Thus, to be baptized into Christ is to put on Christ, i.e. to enter that realm of the Spirit over which Christ is Lord.' He dispelled any mechanical or quasi-magical connection between water- and Spirit-baptism, on the basis of Cornelius and his friends' Spirit-baptism preceding their water-baptism (Acts 10), and the Ephesian disciples in

---

74   Robinson, *Baptist Principles*, 13-14.

75   Robinson, *Baptist Principles*, 24.

76   Robinson, *Baptist Principles*, 25.

77   Robinson, 'The Place of Baptism', 214.

78   Robinson, *Baptist Principles*, 65-66. It is unclear as to what Robinson had in mind at this point, but it is more than unlikely that twentieth-century charismatic renewal would have met with his approval.

79   Robinson, *Baptist Principles*, 67.

Acts 19 who received the Spirit after the laying on of hands subsequent to their baptism.[80] He concluded his *The Life and Faith of the Baptists*:

> Most of all there is needed a new and clear teaching of the doctrine of the Holy Spirit, as against the rationalism that rejects all mystery, and the externalism which materializes mystery into manageable forms. The true emphasis is that of the New Testament—on personal faith as the human condition of divine activity, which is the truth supremely expressed in believer's baptism.[81]

To this can be added an earlier comment which pinpointed the fact that Baptist hesitation over the place of the Spirit in baptism was due, not to exegesis of biblical texts, but fear, even seventy to eighty years after the Tractarian movement, of baptismal regeneration and magical interpretations of the rite's operation and efficacy.

> But most of all, I want to urge that our peculiar denominational emphasis on believer's baptism should enable us to meet a great need of the religious life of to-day, I mean the recovery of the New Testament emphasis on the Holy Spirit. We have been unconsciously afraid of teaching the relation of the gift of the Spirit and water-baptism, because so much is made of it by those who believe in baptismal regeneration and appeal to the words, 'Ye must be born of water and the Spirit.' We have thrown our emphasis on baptism as a personal and human profession of repentance and faith. It is that, and that needed to be emphasised. But the uniquely ethical character of our baptism safeguards us from the risk of misunderstanding, and leaves full room for the more evangelical sacramentalism of the New Testament. The moral and religious experience of repentance and faith becomes the channel of the Spirit, and is psychologically reinforced by the definite expression of this experience in water-baptism. If we teach men that water-baptism is of real value on the human side—if it is not, we have no right to practice it—may we not teach that it is in the same way of value on the divine, possibly a real occasion, always a powerful declaration, of that baptism of the Spirit which is the true secret of Christian sanctification?

Baptism, thus understood, gave meaning to such passages as Ephesians 4:5, 1 Corinthians 6:11 and Galatians 3:27, and Robinson concluded that 'there could be no Christian baptism in the full sense before Pentecost.'[82]

Robinson also warned of the dangers of the Baptist position in that it tended towards individualism.[83] He asked, 'Does not baptism express much more than a personal act?', for he was trying to keep the individual and corporate dimensions together. Accordingly, Baptists stood for the

---

80   Robinson, *Life and Faith*, 175-76.

81   Robinson, *Life and Faith*, 179-80.

82   Robinson, 'The Place of Baptism', 216-17.

83   See Randall, *Evangelical Experiences*, 187-88, on Baptist individualism as typified by Glover and Clifford.

truth of a regenerated church membership expressed in believer's baptism, but he believed that their testimony of that would never be as effective as it ought to be until they had added to it 'a nobler Church-consciousness, and a profounder sense of the whole group, as well as the individual life, as the arena of the Spirit's activity.'[84]

Robinson succeeded in putting this matter firmly on the Baptist agenda, but he did not do so unchallenged. His views were not solely aired through books but also in the pages of the *Baptist Times*.[85] In 1914 he outlined the accepted position that New Testament baptism was an ordinance for believers only, a personal confession of faith, an act of obedience clearly symbolizing loyal devotion to Christ. But, he asked, was this the whole truth and was there another truth complementary to it on which Baptist witness was not equally clear? Did not baptism express more than a personal act? Was it not, by virtue of being that, also the entrance into a life of supernatural energies, that is, the surrender to the 'Law of the Spirit'? The baptism of Christ was sharply contrasted with that of John as a baptism with or in the Holy Spirit. To be baptized into Christ was to put on Christ, that is, to enter that realm of the Spirit under Christ's Lordship. The connection between water baptism and Spirit baptism was of no mechanical kind, for he rejected outright any notion of baptismal regeneration, which was precluded by the exceptions recorded in the Book of Acts, where all who were baptized were already believers, and he insisted that the moral and spiritual conditions of personal faith became the real channel of the Spirit's highest energies. Indeed, he said, it was the very divorce of baptism from personal faith which made sacramentarianism possible, and it was this against which Baptists rightly protested. But the energy of their protest brought its own peril, as they tended to become suspicious of any pronounced sacramental emphasis, even the genuine sacramentalism of the New Testament. They had so stressed the subjects of baptism that they failed to say

---

84 Robinson, *Life and Faith*, 172-74. Torrance, 'The Sacraments and Authority', 14, also recognized this when he admitted that, 'Our own Church emphasises Baptism, admittedly the Sacrament of the individual as the other [the Eucharist] is that of the group. Has not our emphasis been an under-valuation in another direction?' He criticized Baptists for having 'little or no "Church Consciousness"', then asked, 'But is this the price of our emphasis on Baptism...? It is rather clear to me that our failure is related to what we have done with the Sacraments.' While the 'Sacrament of the Table proclaims the necessity of the Church... Baptism...proclaims the reality of the individual in his decision to serve God. He is no longer a unit in a crowd but one in a fellowship.'

85 See H.W. Robinson, 'The Baptism of Power', *BT&F* January 16, 1920, 35-36, 'Baptism and the Gift of the Holy Spirit', *BT* March 29, 1928, 209-10, and 'Unto What Were Ye Baptised?', *BT* May 24, 1934, 384. In the first of these he asked, 'Do we make the ceremony of water-baptism symbolise the gift of the Spirit as clearly as we make it symbolise conversion?', p.35.

anything about baptism itself. In this respect, he admitted, 'we have much to learn from the sacramental Churches themselves.' Here, then, was an opportunity for Baptists to give a forceful testimony to the work of the Spirit on the believer. He continued:

> If any reader is afraid that this may mean a sacramentalism of the lower kind, where the channel of the Spirit is thought to be the material element, rather than the evangelical truth in the hearts of believers, let it be said distinctly that we are pleading for the connection of water-baptism with the Holy Spirit exactly in the sense in which we plead for its connection with personal faith. If the New Testament teaches the latter, it assuredly teaches the former, and Baptists are really committed to both. Let us tell that the Church is the home of supernatural powers, and not merely a human society, that faith is not a mere opinion, but a personal surrender to Him through whose Spirit these powers are to be experienced, and that baptism is not simply an act of faith, but 'the sign and seal' that that faith is answered by the Holy Spirit of God. So, and only so, will He Himself have led us into all the truth concerning New Testament baptism.[86]

Within a fortnight, Arnold Streuli voiced his appreciation of Robinson's article, but appealed for fuller teaching on the subject, particularly for the sake of younger people.[87] The following week George W. MacAlpine questioned whether the New Testament condition for the gift of the Spirit was baptism, or rather faith, 'of the operations of which baptism is only symbolical.' He felt that Robinson too strongly associated the gift of the Spirit with the act of baptism. Surely the Cornelius episode in Acts 10 established that the gift of the Holy Spirit was granted to faith? 'The Holy Spirit brings to the believer the new life, the life of the Spirit; and, precisely because baptism shows forth in symbol the rising believer to newness of life, it also symbolises the gift of the Holy Spirit. But we must ever keep clearly before us the fact that the moral and spiritual conditions of *personal faith* become the *real* channel of the Spirit's highest energies.'[88] Robinson's point was that by faith the

---

86   H.W. Robinson, 'Are Baptists Loyal to the New Testament Baptism?', *BT&F* June 26, 1914, 518.

87   A. Streuli of Peterborough, 'Are Baptists Loyal to the New Testament Baptism?', *BT&F* July 10, 1914, 576.

88   G.W. MacAlpine, 'Are Baptists Loyal to the New Testament Baptism?', *BT&F* July 17, 1914, 585. The italics were MacAlpine's, the words Wheeler Robinson's in his article. MacAlpine was an Accrington coal-owner and ardent supporter of the BMS, a few details on whom can be found in D.J. Jeremy, *Capitalists and Christians: Business Leaders and the Churches in Britain, 1900–1960* (Oxford, 1990), 364-65, especially n.31; I. Sellars (ed.), *Our Heritage: The Baptists of Yorkshire, Lancashire and Cheshire, 1647–1987* (Leeds, 1987), 54 and 72; B. Stanley, *The History of the Baptist Missionary Society 1792–1992* (Edinburgh, 1992), *passim*.

Christian had entered into possession of the energies of the Spirit—by that faith of which baptism was the symbol.

In his reply, Robinson agreed with MacAlpine that faith was the essential condition of entrance into the realm of the Spirit's energies as opposed to that work of the Spirit which preceded faith. However, he reiterated that his argument was that water-baptism in the New Testament symbolized not only this faith but also the reception of supernatural power by the believer, as MacAlpine had fully recognized. But further, he had argued that the present Baptist emphasis fell too exclusively on the personal act of faith and not adequately on the spiritual energies which that act of faith mediated. To the assertion that the normal condition for reception of these energies came before baptism, that is, with faith, Robinson referred to Acts 2:38: 'The manifestation of the Spirit's power (which, of course, does not exclude the preparatory work of the Spirit prior to repentance) is regarded as the sequel or close accompaniment of baptism. As men were made disciples (according to "the great Commission") before they were baptised, so, ordinarily, they were baptised before the Holy Spirit gave visible proof of His indwelling activity and power.' This was supported by Paul's statement in 1 Corinthians 12:13. Experience of the Spirit (like faith itself) was not simply an isolated event, but covered the whole Christian life. 'I am not afraid of the consequences of such loyalty to New Testament teaching, *so long as baptism is administered to believers only*. We may easily teach our candidates for baptism to expect too little; we can hardly lead them to expect too much from the Spirit of God. New Testament writers knew nothing of the distinction between the subjective (faith) and the objective (water) conditions of baptism which Baptists have felt compelled to urge, because the New Testament knows nothing of unbaptized believers, or of a water-baptism divorced from faith. The later abuse of water-baptism by its application to infants ought not to rob Baptists of the full meaning of New Testament baptism, as the expressive symbol of new powers underlying new life, as well as of the personal act of faith by which that new life is consciously entered.'[89]

MacAlpine replied immediately, but no new ground was covered.[90] His difficulty over Robinson's very carefully worded letters and writings can be taken as representative of Baptist dis–ease over the newly articulated Baptist sacramentalism. So entrenched were the anti-Catholic and anti-sacerdotalist feelings that anything that sounded like baptismal regeneration was greeted warily and, no doubt, many times with great hostilty.

---

89   H.W. Robinson, 'Are Baptists Loyal to the New Testament Baptism?', *BT&F* July 24, 1914, 601, italics his.

90   G.W. MacAlpine, 'Are Baptists Loyal to the New Testament Baptism?', *BT&F* July 31, 1914, 616.

The final comment within this brief yet revealing correspondence was sounded from a new participant. James Halliday was impressed that in New Testament times baptism was a portion of the process by which the individual received the Holy Ghost, for faith was not complete until it expressed itself in an outward act of avowal and confession—an outward and visible sign of an inward and spiritual grace. Without this addition to their doctrine of baptism, he claimed, other Christians interpreted Baptist baptism as a piece of unnecessary ritualism. The restoration of the true relation of the rite to the individual, in preaching and practice, would enable believers to know 'a deeper experience of the Spirit's power.'[91]

The 1937 *Report* highlighted an otherwise neglected aspect of the relationship between the Holy Spirit and baptism, namely the eschatological dimension, when it emphasized, 'Baptism not only looks backwards but also forwards. It looks forward to the fulfilment of that baptism of the Holy Spirit through which the believer receives the gifts and bears the fruits of the Christian life and fellowship.'[92]

The Subjective and Objective in Baptism

The subjective and objective dimensions of baptism can be divided, for convenience only, into two antitheses. The first raises the question of the internal and external aspects of baptism, the second the subjective and objective elements, but it will quickly become clear that they are, in fact, intimately related, as they are to the discussion of the sacramental aspect of baptism as a means of grace by the work of the Spirit.

The Internal and External Aspects of Baptism

There is clearly a link here with the definition of a 'sacrament' as 'an outward and visible sign of an inward and spiritual grace', but even those who would not wish to speak of baptism as a sacrament made a clear distinction between the internal and external aspects of the rite. Baptists have often been accused of being externalists or ritualists, a charge they have strongly repudiated, but of which they have often been guilty. Baptism, Mountain argued, was not to be understood as merely an external ceremony, but 'as an act of personal consecration to Christ; a divine service of the deepest spiritual significance and importance; and a perpetual ordinance expressly appointed by our Lord for the purpose of symbolising certain foundation facts and doctrines of the gospel.'[93] J.W. Ewing warned the 'young people of Nonconformity' to remember 'that

---

91   J.A. Halliday of Newcastle-on-Tyne, 'Are Baptists Loyal to the New Testament Baptism?', *BT&F* August 7, 1914, 635.

92   *Report of the Special Committee*, 5.

93   Mountain, *My Baptism*, 3.

no outward ceremony can ever enable us to dispense with the spiritual renewal in which we become "new creatures" in Christ!'[94] Whitby stated that a person could no more be saved by proxy than by any outward rite,[95] and Ford claimed that Baptists were not ritualists, because to ritualists the outward form was essential, but to Baptists the mere form was nothing apart from the faith and conviction which it expressed.[96]

In response, Baptists often argued that the move towards externalism or ritualism was what had led to the rejection of believer's baptism and the adoption of the non-scriptural infant baptism and its associated doctrines. Whitby spoke of the 'incurable weakness of human nature to turn from the spiritual to the external—to substitute outward observances for a change of heart.' This invariably led to errors such as the postponement of baptism until death was near or the doctrine of baptismal regeneration and the resulting practice of infant baptism.[97] Tymms also discussed this tendency of attaching undue importance to things outward, palpable, visible, audible, allowing these imperceptibly to replace the things inward and spiritual, unseen and silent. 'Symbols, emblems, forms of speech, rites and ceremonies are adopted and cherished at first for what they mean and are still clung to when their meaning has become vague or altogether changed, or lost. Was it not, then, antecedently probable, if not inevitable, that man's ritualistic tendency would operate to first exaggerate the value and ultimately alter the meaning, of baptism?'[98] H.G. Wood stated that it was the insistence on the intrinsic efficacy of the ritual act which had led to the tendency to regard conscious faith on the part of the recipient to be no longer essential.[99]

Speaking of the manner of administration of the rite as subordinate to the principle because it was to be administered only to believers, Wheeler Robinson maintained that it was not baptism which was essential but the thing signified.[100] That the dying robber on the cross could only repent and not be baptized confirmed Whitley's conclusion that 'what's essential is not baptism, the sign, but repentance, the thing signified.'[101] Cook

---

94   Ewing, *Talks*, 75.

95   Whitby, *Baptist Principles*, 93.

96   Ford, *Twenty-Five Years*, 10.

97   Whitby, *Baptist Principles*, 56-57.

98   Tymms, *Evolution of Infant Baptism*, 18-19. See also Robinson, *Baptist Principles*, 31.

99   Wood, 'BAPTISM', 392.

100   Robinson, *Baptist Principles*, 27.

101   Whitley, *Church, Ministry and Sacraments*, 100. He later wrote, p.160, 'The outward sign apart from the inward reality was valueless, and [Paul] plainly added that the inward reality apart from that outward sign was invaluable...' Flowers, 'The Holy Spirit', 161, observed that the act of baptism in the early church was not a mere formality, but rather 'corresponded to something very real in the inner life of the believer.' According

submitted that the ordinances were concrete and visible symbols of the facts on which the faith of the church fundamentally rested and, in partaking of them, believers accepted the truth they enshrined, once more by faith making it the basis of their lives.[102] Commenting that the name 'Baptist' was originally a nickname, Rushbrooke remarked that though it emphasized an external fact it ignored the inward and spiritual principle which alone gave significance and value to the external.[103] In one of his many studies on conversion, Underwood contended that 'Instead of working from the outside inward, we must work from within outward',[104] for, as Roberts had explained, baptism and faith are but the outside and inside of the same thing.[105] This was why Baptists had never regarded baptism as essential for salvation. The inward grace which alone saves someone is ratified or signified by the outward act.[106] What other outward act, Morris asked, could better express those experiences of the soul which were common to every believer than the act of immersion.[107] Baptism was, therefore, the outward confession on the part of the Christian.[108]

Whitley's comment that the Holy Spirit was not limited by outward acts, as in Cornelius' conversion,[109] quite probably reflected a common view of many at this time that baptism and the reception of the Spirit are separate experiences, a view which has often led to baptism being administered sometimes many years after conversion, rather than being seen as a part of the conversion process. But other writers believed that the New Testament regarded the outward and the inward as inseparably linked. Robinson was convinced that baptism in the New Testament sense did justice to both the inner experience and the external expression of it, 'which', he added in parenthesis, 'is always, in some form, necessary.'[110] Laws remarked how grand it would be if all Baptists were really baptized and not merely immersed. For him, immersion was simply the external sign. To have been baptized was 'to have been down with Christ into

---

to Child, 'The Baptist Contribution', 85, water-baptism expressed 'with incomparable fidelity' the inward surrender of the heart and will to God through Christ.

102 Cook, *Why of Our Faith*, 83.

103 Rushbrooke, 'Protestant of the Protestants', 62.

104 A.C. Underwood, 'The Place of Conversion in Christian Experience', *BQ* 6.4 (October, 1932), 161.

105 Roberts, *Christian Baptism*, 22.

106 See Meyer, *Peter*, 169; Mountain, *My Baptism*, 31; Whitley, *Church, Ministry and Sacraments*, 253.

107 Morris, *Thoughts*, 22-23.

108 Whitby, *Baptist Principles*, 64.

109 Whitley, *Church, Ministry and Sacraments*, 133.

110 H.W. Robinson, 'Review "The Psychology of Religion"', *BQ* 2.6 (April, 1925), 284.

death, to have put off the old man with his deeds, to have come out of the place of death to live in the power of an endless life, to have been pledged for ever against all sin, and to all holiness, to have ceased to be as a natural man, and to have become in actual truth a new creation in Christ. That is to have been baptized.'[111]

Wheeler Robinson sought to redress this Baptist aversion to ceremony. He contended that Jesus did not despise the outer ceremony, though his emphasis constantly fell on the inner meaning. There was, for him, a value in the outward and visible sign, 'for we simply cannot think of Him as participating in a perfunctory formalism.'[112] In support of this, Robinson and others, as has already been noted, brought the ethical aspect of the rite to the fore, speaking of moral holiness and consecrated character. 'This inward and ethical emphasis stands in contrast with the externalism of the older idolatry and the later legalism.'[113] For him, the external act of baptism was always subordinate to the conversion of the individual, his baptism of the Spirit,[114] which was, nevertheless, connected to water-baptism. Elsewhere he wrote, 'Baptism in the New Testament is so identified with the new experience it initiates that it is difficult to summarize its meaning without describing that experience itself.'[115] There is little wonder that the gift of the Spirit was linked with believer's baptism, in fact, the experience of that gift, according to Robinson, is the test of the rite.[116]

On 1 Peter 3:20-21, Whitley remarked that baptism itself does not save, but what it signifies does. On the divine side it pictures death and resurrection (cf. Romans 6:4), while on the human side it attests the candidate's desire to receive God's peace. Baptism only saved by the resurrection of Jesus Christ.[117] John MacBeath spoke of baptism as the grave at the entrance to the Kingdom of God, signifying how radical the experience is through which believers pass and how spiritual the society is into which Christians enter. It is an acted parable of the death and resurrection of Christ, but also of the believer. The old things have passed away and all things are made new. To surrender the outward act would run the risk of forfeiting the inward experience which it typifies. To modify the outward would be to run the peril of tempering the inward. 'What God has joined together let no man put asunder.'[118] The objective

---

111 Laws, 'Vital Forces', 19.

112 Robinson, 'The Baptism of Power', *BT&F* January 16, 1920, 35.

113 Robinson, *Life and Faith*, 12.

114 Robinson, 'The Place of Baptism', 212.

115 Robinson, *Baptist Principles*, 13.

116 Robinson, *Baptist Principles*, 24.

117 Whitley, *Church, Ministry and Sacraments*, 253-54.

118 J. MacBeath, 'The Catholicity of Our Faith', in W.T. Whitley (ed.), *Fourth Baptist World Congress* (n.d., [1928]), 120.

reality which these authors proclaimed was the givenness of grace in the death and resurrection of Jesus, which was grandly rehearsed in the baptismal act.

John Lewis gave as the reason for his address as 'to encourage that sense of dignity which responsibility recognised and accepted always brings, in this case a responsibility not merely for the outward symbol, but far more, for all that it symbolises.'[119] Later he observed that many who were very jealous for the outward form never seemed to see its implications, and those who did found it difficult to realize them.[120] Laws sounded a similar warning:

> ...we shall not be able to keep baptism if we make it merely an external rite, imposed as some kind of test. *We must emphasize its spiritual content.* As a piece of mere literal compliance with the letter it will not constrain the modern mind. But if we stress the spiritual antecedents, and the gift of grace brought through obedience, we shall be on ground where we can appeal to every instinct of a spiritual man. Make it a formal thing, or a little thing, and we shall not retain it. Make it an act of the soul rather than of the body, make it an act Christward rather than a church test, and we shall keep it alive.[121]

Subjective and Objective in Baptism

From their discussion of the relationship between the internal and external aspects of baptism, several Baptists also discussed the subjective and objective elements of the doctrine.[122] Though the objective clearly antecedes the subjective, as the grace of God precedes the response of the individual, yet for Baptists the focus of attention was on (and in many respects still is) the individual's act in baptism.

During this period there were few attempts to engage this issue directly. In the popular mind, baptism had always tended to concentrate on the subjective, emphasis often focusing on the public profession of the candidates' faith, what they were doing for God and what it meant to them personally, and the objective side often being little more than a rehearsal of what God had already done for them in the death and resurrection of Christ. There was seldom the notion that something actually took place in baptism, and this was the logical result of a

---

119 Lewis, 'Baptised into Jesus Christ', 15.

120 Lewis, 'Baptised into Jesus Christ', 21.

121 Laws, 'Vital Forces', 15, italics added.

122 It is first of all necessary to clarify what is meant by these terms. The subjective concentrates upon the action of the candidate and their personal testimony made at baptism. By objective is meant the givenness of God's grace and the objective rehearsing of death and resurrection.

Zwinglian memorialism, which writers like Robinson and Underwood sought to correct.

It will be quite clear that those for whom baptism was an ordinance, by which they stressed the element of obedience and little else, focus was directed upon the candidate. However, those who were seeking a return to the fuller New Testament doctrine began to redress the imbalance by emphasizing what took place in the rite and not simply what it meant to the baptized. Without doubt, the likes of Robinson and Underwood were greatly helped in this by the Psychology of Religion school of thought, and they tended to reflect a greater emphasis on the experience itself. And these two men were by no means alone. An influential group of writers sought to link together both the subjective and objective elements of baptism.

Perhaps the most clear, and certainly the most concise, statement of this was made by Underwood. In reply to the question as to what the outer act of baptism contributed to the inner experiences of forgiveness, regeneration, faith and fellowship with Christ, the only possible answer he could find was that Paul and the other New Testament writers never considered them apart in this detached manner. For Paul it was never a passive experience because it was no formal act, no mere symbol and never administered to any but believers. 'The outer act and the inner experience are always found together.'[123]

Wheeler Robinson too shared the concern that the two be held together, and he dealt with this matter in more detail than any other. In response to the same question as addressed by Underwood, Robinson provided the same answer, so much so that it is quite possible that Underwood abridged Robinson at this point. After declaring that the New Testament never considered these issues apart, Robinson added that the baptism of which it spoke was no formal act, but a genuine experience, and, in any case, the New Testament did not know of unbaptized believers. It was only later generations which separated the outer act from the inner experience, and this development had made possible the rise of sacramentarianism on the one hand and the entire rejection of the sacraments on the other. The later history of baptism was, he stated, in large measure, the history of this separation. He concluded, 'It became possible to administer baptism to unintelligent recipients only through the transference of emphasis from the moral and spiritual to the sacramental side of the rite.'[124] As has already been shown, according to Robinson the mode was not essential, only appropriate. To equate the practice with the principle was to stultify the principle itself, which emphasized the inner essential of faith, declaring that without it all

---

123 Underwood, *Conversion*, 111.
124 Robinson, *Baptist Principles*, 14-15.

outward ceremonies were valueless.[125] Baptists, he claimed, only value the external rite in so far as it emphasized the spiritual change wrought in human nature by the Spirit of God in Christ, implying both a profession of faith and a change of heart.[126] Thus baptism was the 'cardinal ceremony of union with Christ, the objective aspect of what is subjectively faith.'[127] Later, he outlined the triple aspect of baptism: it implied the historical events of the death, burial and resurrection of Christ, of which submersion was the suggestive symbol; it consisted of a series of acts on the part of the baptized, who went down into the water, was submerged and rose out of it; it supplied a visible parallel to the spiritual experience of the believer which Paul called the baptism of the Holy Spirit—his death to sin and resurrection to newness of life. 'All these three aspects are implied in the single series of visible acts, and they become sacramental to the participant for whom they have this implication.' Such significance was warranted in the light of prophetic symbolism, which was more than mere 'representation'. The charge of 'sacramental' magic could be dismissed because the person was a conscious believer, the efficacy of the rite depending on their conscious and believing part-icipation in it. Equally there was no question of 'mere symbolism', for the act was the 'partial and fragmentary, but very real accomplishment of a divine work, the work of the Holy Spirit.'[128]

In his contribution to the ecumenical volume, *The Ministry and the Sacraments*, Underwood asserted that there were many Baptists who could no longer accept that the baptism of a believer was 'merely declaratory', and given the representative nature of his contribution, suggests that though he and Wheeler Robinson were the chief advocates of this view, they were speaking on behalf of a growing number within the denom-ination. They stressed what God did in baptism, as well as what believers did, thereby avoiding the subjectivism which stressed what the baptized person did as though it were the only vital thing in the sacrament. For them, believer's baptism was more than a mere symbolic representation of conversion, much more than a picturesque and dramatic method of marking conversion and entry into church membership, but a definite means of grace.[129] He submitted that only when the two elements of the subjective and objective were held together that Baptists were truly able to reject the charge of being mere ritualists.[130]

R.L. Child expressed it thus: baptism declares the truth that God and people come together through Jesus Christ in a relationship which is

125 Robinson, *Baptist Principles*, 15.
126 Robinson, *Baptist Principles*, 7-8.
127 Robinson, *Christian Doctrine of Man*, 124.
128 Robinson, *Christian Experience of the Holy Spirit*, 193-94.
129 Underwood, 'Views of Modern Churches', 227.
130 Underwood, 'Conversion and Baptism', 27-35.

wholly personal. On the one hand, the rite demands of the candidate an individual apprehension of and assent to God's gracious purpose. On the other, baptism is the candidate's way of testifying to the fact that, in their personal repentance and faith, they have actually met God as Father and experienced his saving power. 'From both points of view the relationship between God and the believer is seen to be entirely personal, and one in which Faith and Grace are spiritually complementary, the one to the other.'[131]

At the end of his brief treatment of the unity of baptism, Flowers observed that, 'in the main, we can say that the attitude of the Church to baptism was uniform in the Apostolic period. It was one of the objective realities in which all shared.'[132] There was here a golden opportunity for Baptists to link the objectivity, the givenness, implied in baptism with its nature as an ordinance, that is, as a means of grace, instituted by Christ and to be observed by all believers—but it was not seized.

That Robinson, Underwood and the others were successful to a point, is clear from the remark in the 1937 Special Committee *Report* which acknowledged that as an acted creed and declaration of the gospel, baptism expressed faith in the power and grace of God in Christ to forgive, cleanse and re-create, showing forth the way of redemption by Christ's death, burial and resurrection, with which 'spiritually and mystically the believer is identified. *It testifies to the doctrine of grace and to the necessity for the complete surrender of self to God.* It is an appointed and an approved means of grace to the believing soul.'[133] They were also successful in that they paved the way for later scholars to develop a truly sacramental theology of baptism from a truly Baptist perspective.

Conclusions

The first four decades of the twentieth century witnessed a tremendous change within not just the Baptist denomination, but within the world church. The rise of the ecumenical movement meant that the principles held so dear for generations, or so it seemed, came under the theological microscope, and established practices were increasingly challenged from within and without. A great many of the denomination's theologians and ministers and, more gradually, lay people became exposed to ecumenical developments resulting in changes, sometimes marked ones, in emphasis and even conviction. The issue of baptism, perhaps more than any other doctrine because of its sectarian nature, became a focus of Baptist

---

131 Child, 'The Baptist Contribution', 85.
132 Flowers, 'The Unity of the Church', 350.
133 *Report of the Special Committee*, 6, italics added.

thinking. Wheeler Robinson eloquently declared that if believer's baptism was really central and fundamental enough to justify the existence of a distinct denomination to urge its claims, then Baptists should be able to show the great and permanent principles which were implied in it: personal conversion, the authority of Christ revealed in the New Testament and the doctrine of the church as the society of the converted.[134] Gilbert Laws similarly claimed that the Baptist witness within the ecumenical movement to both the 'Church-principle' and, no less, to the 'ordinance-principle' was a service for which the Baptists should be thanked.[135]

134 Robinson, *Baptist Principles*, 16-27.
135 G. Laws, 'The Church-Principle of the Baptists', *BT* October 14, 1937, 773.

CHAPTER FIVE

Ecumenical Developments 1938–1966

Introduction

The whole complexion of the baptismal debate was set to change when the Swiss theologian, Emil Brunner, delivered the Olaus Petri lectures at Uppsala University in 1937, instigating the beginning of the modern baptismal debate.[1]

Brunner's thinking was conditioned by his conviction that, in scripture, truth was always presented as something dynamic and personal, consisting of a divine–human encounter, a meeting between God and humanity, being God's revelation and humanity's response. He announced his rejection of the subject–object antithesis, which, he argued, had originated with Greek philosophy and had burdened the church ever since, denying that it represented the biblical understanding of truth with the consequence that 'much of our thinking and action in the Church must be different from what we have been accustomed to for centuries.'[2] On the sacrament of baptism, he contended that the antitheses he had identified were a misunderstanding of the New Testament:

> In baptism it is God, first and sovereign, who acts, who forgives sin, who cleanses man and regenerates him. But man too acts in baptism. He allows this cleansing of himself to take place, he lets himself be drawn into the death of Christ, he confesses his faith and his attachment to Christ. Baptism is not merely a gift to

---

1   E. Brunner, *Wahrheit als Begegnung* (Zürich, 1938), E.T. *The Divine–Human Encounter* (1944). It was later enlarged and re-titled *Truth as Encounter* (E.T. 1954). The original lectures were delivered after Brunner had returned from participating in both the Oxford and Edinburgh Ecumenical Conferences, where he had played an important role. Thompson, 'The Older Free Churches', 105, 'The debate about baptism took a new turn as a result of the challenge to infant baptism offered by Emil Brunner in 1938 and Karl Barth in a famous lecture given in 1943...' Overviews of the early period of this 'modern baptismal debate' include Payne, 'Baptism in Recent Discussion', 15-24; K. Runia, 'Recent Developments in Baptist Theology', *RTR* 20.1 (February, 1961), 12-23, and 20.2 (June, 1961), 47-49; D. Alten, 'Baptism in Recent German Theology', *ResQ* 7.3 (1963), 124-31.

2   Brunner, *Divine–Human Encounter*, 6.

man, but also an active receiving and confession on the part of man. Indeed baptism, precisely as this free confession of man, is the stipulation for the individual's joining the Church. Baptism is not only an act of grace, but just as much an act of confession stemming from the act of grace.[3]

When baptism was enjoined in the New Testament it was regarded as a 'two-sided happening', involving what he termed 'personal correspondence'. Baptism was not merely a gift to humanity, but also an active receiving and confession on the part of humanity.[4] From this base, Brunner, a paedobaptist Calvinist, launched his devastating attack on the doctrine and practice of infant baptism on the grounds of the inseparable connection between sacrament and faith. 'To be sure, faith does not produce the sacrament; but the sacrament is not accomplished, it is no true sacrament, without the faith.'[5] He proceeded by criticizing the covenantal arguments for infant baptism and attempted to meet objections to it by the introduction of the rite of confirmation. The sacrament, as the Reformation asserted, had no validity without faith, thus, by their retention of infant baptism, the Reformers had departed from their own principle.[6] This had severely damaged the image of the church, creating a discrepancy between two churches: one of the baptized and the other of those assenting to confession, and this, in its turn, was one of the chief causes of the present difficulties of the church in all places.[7] The irresistible conclusion was, therefore, that 'The contemporary practice of infant baptism can hardly be regarded as being anything short of scandalous.'[8]

However, despite his criticisms, Brunner remained a Paedobaptist. His views were first introduced to British Baptists by R. Birch Hoyle in an enthusiastic review of the book in 1938, which concluded with an invitation for Brunner to transfer his allegiance to the Baptists.[9]

The direct relevance and impact of Brunner's work on the British ecumenical scene was made explicit in Dr Frederick Cawley's 1945 review of the English version of Brunner's book. Cawley declared that this was an apologetic against infant baptism that was second to none and believed that such a fresh investigation served to reveal to Baptists how

---

3   Brunner, *Divine–Human Encounter*, 128. Traditionally, Paedobaptists have emphasized the objective side of baptism, the grace of God, while Baptists have stressed the subjective, the response of the believer.

4   Brunner, *Divine–Human Encounter*, 128.

5   Brunner, *Divine–Human Encounter*, 129.

6   Brunner, *Divine–Human Encounter*, 130-31.

7   Brunner, *Divine–Human Encounter*, 135.

8   Brunner, *Divine–Human Encounter*, 132.

9   R. Birch Hoyle, a former Professor at Western Theological Seminary, USA, 'Emil Brunner Vindicates the Baptist Position', *BT* June 30, 1938, 508.

impregnable their position was, anchored in the fundamental faith of the church of Christ. 'That being so', he confidently asserted, 'we have every right, and it is also our responsibilty, to stress that in any proposed union of the Churches, if and when such should take place, this principle of believers' baptism shall be openly acknowledged and endorsed by practice.' Further, 'We only ask that baptism shall be a real sacrament; that is, with the full consent of the believing heart.'[10]

What is surprising is that the impact of Brunner's work was at first completely missed and it was several weeks before Claydon Parry responded by arguing that the mode of baptism was a secondary matter, concluding that sprinkling should be the mode of baptism, especially for those who were afraid of water and older people. He advocated a United Free Church practising believers' baptism but left the mode to the candidate. He conceded to the obvious symbolism of immersion, but then dismissed the subject somewhat casually and quickly.[11]

Responses were not slow in coming. Elsie Halden expressed her inability to understand Parry's reason for the dread of immersion, remonstrating that Christianity was not a convenience, believing that sprinkling itself had originated as a convenience.[12] William Hitchcock felt strongly about the suggestion that there should be other modes of baptism, but made the concession that 'if for any reason a candidate cannot be immersed, let there be a forthright confession of faith.' He argued that Parry suggested the form of a corrupted ordinance be applied to a proper subject for baptism, and then posed the question, 'What could be gained by Church union through such a general retreat on the part of the Baptists?' Submission to baptism in its true form, he believed, was the outcome of the believer's full submission to the risen Saviour. R.H. Gostage confessed his failure to see how baptism for believers and immersion could be divorced from each other.[13] There is little to doubt that Mrs K. Willes spoke for the majority of Baptists when

---

10   F. Cawley, first a tutor then Principal at Spurgeon's College, 'Emil Brunner's Criticism of Infant Baptism', *BT* August 23, 1945, 7. W.H. Millard of School House, Benholm, Kincardineshire, 'Emil Brunner on Infant Baptism', *BT* September 6, 1945, 8, recounted a woman's shock when she discovered Brunner was still an Paedobaptist.

11   Mr L.C. Parry from Reading, 'Believers' Baptism and the Mode of Immersion', *BT* September 13, 1945, 6.

12   E.M. Halden of Wandsworth, 'Believers' Baptism and the Mode of Immersion', *BT* September 20, 1945, 6. 'A.C.', 'A Testimony to Immersion', *BT* October 4, 1945, 8, testified that he had been baptized by immersion in spite of a fear of water.

13   W.J.H. Hitchcock of Erith and Mr R.H. Gostage from St. Helens, 'Believers' Baptism and the Mode of Immersion', *BT* September 27, 1945, 8. Gostage favoured co-operation not unity, a view he again expressed in 'The Mode of Immersion', *BT* November 15, 1945, 7.

she simply asserted that the only baptism for Baptists was immersion upon a change of heart.[14]

That Brunner's book was beginning to make an impact on Baptist theology was first evidenced in an article by B.C. Shildrick on Baptists and the ecumenical movement.[15] Shildrick submitted that Baptists' first field of witness lay in the realm of theology, as it was here that so many issues were decided. Brunner's influence was reflected in Shildrick's statement that, 'Theology to-day is again in the melting-pot, and just as in the past theological thought has determined the main lines of Church development so it will be in the new ecumenical movement.' He continued, 'Our Baptist forefathers were theologians. It was their theology that made them Baptists. We need a Baptist theology now which is capable of presenting the issue of believers' baptism as something demanding the serious consideration of the world Church.'[16]

There is no doubt that Brunner's book set the tone for the most productive and varied period of baptismal debate since the rise of the Oxford Movement, and, as far as Baptists were concerned, it ignited what was to be the most fruitful and productive period of reflection and debate on the baptismal issue.[17]

From 1938 onwards the whole baptismal debate was in a state of flux, with a whole stream of writings flowing from the pens of international

---

14   K. Willes from Littlehampton, 'Believers' Baptism and the Mode of Immersion', *BT* October 11, 1945, 6. See the other letters in the same edition by F.G. French of Lee, London, A.S. Clement of Hearshall, Coventry, who noted that the mode did not ensure belief in the principle, M.G. Scroggie from Bromley, and A. Ives of Westminster Baptist church. See also G.E. Page of London, 'Baptism and the Mode of Immersion', *BT* October 25, 1945, 5; Miss M. Armstrong from St. Neots, 'Another Testimony to Immersion', *BT* November 22, 1945, 7.

15   B.C. Shildrick of Brighton, 'Baptist Witness and the Ecumenical Movement', *Frat.* 58 (September, 1945), 5-8. Six of his seventeen footnotes are from Brunner.

16   Shildrick, 'Baptist Witness', 5.

17   That Brunner's book marked the beginning of this modern debate was acknowledged by Payne, 'Baptism in Recent Discussion', 16-17; and Runia, 'Recent Developments', 12, who stated 'It started with Emil Brunner's "Wahrheit als Begegnung" in 1938...' His influence can also be seen, e.g., in N. Clark's 'Theology of Baptism', in Gilmore (ed.), *Christian Baptism*, 311-12; and most recently in C. Ellis, 'Baptism and the Sacramental Freedom of God', in P.S. Fiddes (ed.), *Reflections of the Water: Understanding God and the World through the Baptism of Believers* (Oxford, 1996), 38, 'Baptism may be seen as a focus of the divine–human encounter.' Brunner's importance is because a legacy of the Hyper Calvinism which dominated Particular Baptist theology in the eighteenth century was that it undermined the human dimension of faith, and Brunner contributed significantly to the rediscovery of this. See Fowler, 'Baptism', 91-93.

scholars of the highest calibre,[18] and also major reports from mainline denominations.[19] In fact, English Baptists kept up with all the wider discussions of baptism through frequent reviews and review articles,[20] and through the translation of important texts, most notably those by Karl Barth,[21] Kurt Aland and Rudolf Schnackenburg.[22]

---

18   Including K. Barth, M. Barth, F.J. Leenhardt, O. Cullmann, J. Jeremias, H.G. Marsh, D.G. Dix, K.E. Kirk, W.F. Flemington, P.Ch. Marcel, G.W.H. Lampe and K. Aland.

19   These included the Church of England and the Church of Scotland, as well as reports on the union discussions concerning the Churches of South and North India. On these reports and the writers mentioned above, see Payne's overviews in 'Baptism in Recent Discussion', 15-24, and 'Baptism in Present-Day Theology', in A.T. Ohrn (ed.), *Eighth Baptist World Congress, Cleveland, Ohio, U.S.A., July 22-27, 1950* (Philadelphia, 1950), 171-79; A. Gilmore, 'Some Recent Trends in the Theology of Baptism', *BQ* 15.7 (July, 1954), 311-18; *BQ* 15.8 (October, 1954), 338-45; *BQ* 16.1 (January, 1955), 2-9; W.M.S. West, 'Editorial', *BQ* 17.8 (October, 1958), 337-40; W.M.S. West, 'Editorial', *BQ* 18.4 (October, 1959), 145-47; G.R. Beasley-Murray, 'The Baptismal Controversy in the British Scene', in K. Aland, *Did the Early Church Baptize Infants* (London, 1963), 17-27.

20   E.g. E.A. Payne's review of H.G. Marsh, *The Origin and Significance of New Testament Baptism* in 'Baptism in the New Testament', *BT* May 1, 1941, 215; H.W. Robinson, '*The Origin and Significance of the New Testament Baptism*, by H.G. Marsh', *BQ* 10.6 (April, 1941), 349-51, and H.H. Rowley, '*The Origin and Significance of the New Testament Baptism*, by H.G. Marsh', *JTS* 44 (1943), 79-81. Seven years later W.F. Flemington, *The New Testament Doctrine of Baptism* was published, and in his review of it, E.A. Payne stated that his main exposition will confirm Baptists in the position they have taken up, *BT* December 30, 1948, 7. Also W.W. Bottoms, 'Christian Baptism', *Frat.* 78 (October, 1950), 40-43.

21   The importance of the publication of the English translation Barth's *The Teaching of the Church Regarding Baptism* (1948), a lecture originally delivered in Switzerland on May 7, 1943, is difficult to overestimate. The translation by Ernest Payne was based on the second German edition of *Die Kirchliche Lehre von der Taufe*, no.14 of the series of *Theologische Studien*, K. Barth (ed.), (Zürich, 1943). The book was critically acclaimed by R.L. Child in his review, '*The Teaching of the Church Regarding Baptism*, by Karl Barth', *BQ* 12.12 (October, 1948), 449, who stated that, 'Baptists in particular will be interested to read Dr. Barth's exposition, which is at once a plea for the vital significance of the rite, and a frank statement against Infant Baptism.' Its importance for the whole baptismal debate is emphasized by Runia, 'Recent Developments', 12, and Alten, 'Baptism in Recent German Theology', 124-26. The reason why Barth has been so influential on Baptist thought is because he separated water- from Spirit-baptism: the former being entirely a human work, an act of prayer and obedience, while the latter is entirely the work of God; however, in his later *Fragment*, he repudiated the sacramental character which he had previously held. See his *Teaching of the Church*, and *Church Dogmatics IV.4. The Doctrine of Reconciliation (Fragment)* (Edinburgh, 1960). See also J.E. Colwell of Spurgeon's College, 'Baptism, Conscience and the Resurrection: A Reappraisal of 1 Peter 3.21', in Porter and Cross (eds.), *Baptism,*

Baptists, then, were not unaware of the scholarly debate on baptism, in fact, from the mid-1950s to mid-1960s, several Baptist scholars were themselves to make important contributions, most notably H.H. Rowley, Neville Clark, R.E.O. White, G.R. Beasley-Murray and Alec Gilmore.[23] The debate within the denomination continued predominantly in response to the ongoing ecumenical developments in which Baptists played an important if ambiguous role.

'Official' Reunion Conversations

By the 1930s ecumenism had become an established part of the church throughout the Christian world. The F&O and Life and Work conferences had firmly established themselves, and the ecumenical dimension could no longer be ignored. The whole issue of baptism, then, was inextricably linked to this unstoppable movement. It was no longer possible for denominations to continue in their cherished beliefs and principles without re-examining and re-defining them in the light of the growing number of exegetical and theological studies which increasingly poured forth from individuals, groups and denominations. In Britain, as far as the Baptists were concerned, official reunion conversations took place on four fronts, each one running side by side and feeding one another and off each other. First, there was still the long-standing issue of Free Church union. That progress was being made on Free Church union was presupposed by the second series of conversations between the Free Churches and the Church of England. As these two were so intertwined, they will be dealt with together. Third, there was roughly a decade of exploratory discussions between the Baptists and the Churches of Christ. Fourth, there was the developing international dimension, originating in F&O which led to the formation of the WCC.

Free Church Union and Free Church–Anglican Reunion Conversations

The Joint Conferences between the Church of England and the FCEFC which had been suspended in 1925 recommenced in 1930, the fruit of

---

210-27; P.R. Clifford, 'Barth's Theology of Baptism', *BMJ* 259 (July, 1997), 11-13; Fowler, 'Baptism', 203-23.

22   K. Aland, *Did the Early Church Baptize Infants?* (1963), and R. Schnackenburg, *Baptism in the Thought of St. Paul*, (1964), both trans. by G.R. Beasley-Murray.

23   E.g. H.H. Rowley, *The Unity of the Bible* (1953), and several articles on the antecedents of Christian baptism, e.g. 'Jewish Proselyte Baptism and the Baptism of John', *HUCA* XV (1940), 313-34; N. Clark, *An Approach to the Theology of the Sacraments* (SBT, 17; 1956), and *Call to Worship* (1960); White, *Biblical Doctrine of Initiation*; Beasley-Murray, *Baptism in the New Testament*; A. Gilmore (ed.), *Christian Baptism.*

which appeared in February 1938 with the publication of three discussion documents, the most important of which was the *Outline of a Reunion Scheme*,[24] which was based on an earlier draft document prepared by the FoR on behalf of the churches represented by the Joint Conference, which the Canterbury Convocation commended to the attention of the churches. The *Outline*'s stated intention was to provide a basis for further work towards reunion by dispelling prejudices, pointing the way forward to fuller agreement and in time 'the union for which we pray.'[25] The official reply of the FCFC was submitted to the Joint Conference in September 1941,[26] but in the mean time the constituent denominations considered the reports.

Even before the *Outline* was officially released, Carlile gave notice of it in a front page editorial in the *Baptist Times* and argued that four major principles remained unsettled: the nature of the church, whether it was to be composed of those professing faith or those admitted by virtue of something done to them in infancy; baptism, on which the *Outline* seemed less than clear as to both its meaning and mode; the appropriate exercise of episcopacy; and the relationship of the church to the state.[27] In no time at all, the *Outline* became the chief topic of discussion. Hugh Martin stated that the understanding of the church as the fellowship of believers was safeguarded in the *Outline*, admitting that both forms of baptism would have to be permitted in a United Church. At the same time he recognized that, 'Those Baptists who refuse to consider the possibility of being in the same Church with those who practise infant baptism will object to this Scheme and to every other.'[28] Martin had been one of the four Baptist signatories to the *Outline*, the others being M.E. Aubrey,

---

24   For the text of the *Outline of a Reunion Scheme for the Church of England and the Free Churches in England*, see G.K.A. Bell, *Documents on Christian Unity: Third Series 1930–48* (1948), 71-101. A brief review of the *Outline* is to be found in *BQ* 9.1 (January, 1938), 66, which, noting who the Baptist representatives were, expressed the opinion that 'it is certain they would not unanimously agree that "Baptism may be administered in infancy or upon profession of faith".' For one of the few comments made on the *Intercommunion* document, see 'Inter-Communion', *BT* February 3, 1938, 82. The other two documents were *The Practice of Intercommunion and the Doctrine of the Church* and *1662 and To-day*. Fuller details of this whole controversy can be found in Cross, 'Hugh Martin: Part 3', 131-36.

25   *Outline*, 71-73.

26   *Reply of the Free Church Federal Council to the Joint Conference of Representatives of the Church of England and the Free Churches regarding the three documents presented to it by the Conference in 1938*, in Bell, *Documents on Christian Unity: Third Series*, 102-19. It should be noted that the FCEFC and the NFCC had amalgamated in 1940 to form the Free Church Federal Council (FCFC).

27   J.C. Carlile, 'Outline of the United Church', *BT* January 27, 1938, 71-72.

28   H.Martin, 'Outline of the United Church', *BT* February 3, 1938, 84.

Charles Brown and Gilbert Laws. However, each of the remaining three dissociated themselves from the Scheme.[29]

In his FoR booklet to accompany the *Outline*, Martin reasserted his support for the Scheme, but stressed that it was not being endorsed as a final basis of negotiations by anybody[30] and reiterated his previous arguments that such a reunion would be one of comprehension.[31] On the membership of the church the difficulty of baptism came to the fore, but he restated the Scheme's recognition of both infant and believer's baptism as permissible in the United Church, the former looking forward to and being completed by personal repentance and faith and instruction in the doctrines, privileges and duties of the church.[32]

It quickly appeared that Martin was alone in his ecumenical aspirations. Though this was not in fact the case, he became the focus of attention for the strong opposition within the BU to the unity schemes, chief amongst whom were the Baptist businessman, benefactor and member of the BU Council, R.W. Black, and Henry Townsend, Principal of Manchester Baptist College. Black asked whether Martin had been the only Baptist on the Committee which prepared the Scheme, while Townsend suggested that Martin had been acting on his own initiative and not representing the BU who, the previous November, had decided that organic union was not practicable, though they did desire the fullest co-operation with other Free Churches.[33]

A. Tildsley's suggestion that no more time should be given to the subject of reunion[34] clearly reflected the feeling of some that the exchange had got out of hand. Martin, who was deeply hurt by Black and Townsend's onslaught, defended both himself and his involvement in the preparation of the *Outline*, noting that the BU had not had to appoint him knowing his views on the issue, and asserted, 'I am always scrupulously

---

29   Laws, 'Outline of the United Church', *BT* February 3, 1938, 84, announced that his name had been appended to the document only because he had been a member of the Joint Committee at the time; while Brown and Aubrey informed the BU Council meeting on March 8 that they had not been consulted about the inclusion of their names, see 'The Council in Session', *BT* March 17, 1938, 208.

30   Martin, *Can We Unite? An Examination of the Outline of a Reunion Scheme issued by the Lambeth Joint Conference* (1938), 8.

31   Martin, *Can We Unite?*, 9-13.

32   Martin, *Can We Unite?*, 15-17.

33   R.W. Black, 'Outline of the United Church', *BT* February 10, 1938, 104. Black disapproved of the fact that the *Outline* admitted infant baptism on the grounds that it and episcopacy depreciated the Scriptures. It should not be forgotten that the *Outline* had been prepared by the FoR, within whose ranks Martin was proudly numbered, and in which he was a leading light. H. Townsend, 'Re-Union and Baptist Union Representation', *BT* February 10, 1938, 104.

34   A. Tildsley of Poplar and Bromley Tabernacle 'Re-Union', *BT* February 17, 1938, 124.

careful to distinguish, when necessary, between my personal views and those of the denomination as a whole. I fully realise that my views on reunion are those of a minority.' He underscored the fact that his actions had committed the BU to nothing, and expressed his belief that he had represented it in the 'Conversations'. 'I have put forward the Baptist view, and clear signs of that can be seen in all three documents.' Martin then went on the offensive, declining to apologise for his connection with the documents, of which he was proud, reiterating again his belief that it was along such lines that the United Church of the future would come. 'I shall deeply regret it if the Baptists stand out, but I have never said, in private or in public, that the Baptist Union was likely to agree with the Scheme.' Martin then stated his own convictions: 'I am a Baptist, and I glory in it, but I do not believe that our denomination has any monopoly of the truth... I do not believe in infant baptism, but I am certainly prepared to join a Church fellowship with those who do, on the basis of our common faith in our Lord Jesus Christ. Bigger issues than baptism are at stake in the world to-day, however important baptism may be in its own sphere.'[35]

The subsequent pages of the *Baptist Times* reveal the depth of feelings on the reunion issue, the majority being overwhelmingly against the pro-unity position whose figurehead was Hugh Martin,[36] though Martin was not without some support.[37] A paragraph from the *Outline*, noting the necessity of two forms of baptism in a United Church,[38] was submitted to

---

35   H. Martin, 'Outline of a Re-Union Scheme', *BT* February 17, 1938, 124. It is worth noting that Martin was for a long time in membership with the Hampstead Garden Suburb Free Church of which Dr Rushbrooke had been the first minister and which practised open membership.

36   See R.A.J. Cusden of Putney, 'Outline of a Re-union Scheme', *BT* February 24, 1938, 144, who, following earlier statements by Laws, recognized that to enter into a United Church would lead to separation from other Baptists throughout the world.

37   P.T. Thomson entered a plea for generosity and tolerance to be displayed within the controversy, and M.F. Hewett of Norwich called for positive letters instead of negative ones in the debate and observed that all varying interpretations of scripture were secondary to love for God which should be shown among Christian people, 'Re-Union', *BT* March 3, 1938, 164; R.S. McHardy of Chorley Wood and T. Edmunds of Leicester, 'Re-Union', *BT* March 10, 1938, 184. Edmunds agreed with Townsend, but felt it necessary to say 'one word of support' for Martin's appeal, namely, the common desire 'to see the Church of Christ on earth a unity', and noted that this required Baptists to make 'public the basis upon which we desire to see unity attained.' McHardy expressed his appreciation for an earlier artcile by F.C. Bryan, 'Unity, Uniformity and Union', *BT* February 24, 1938, 149, who had drawn attention to each denomination's responsibility to preserve the truth entrusted to it, but that equally all denomninations had a responsibility to manifest their unity in Christ to the world.

38   The paragraph runs, 'Baptism may be administered in infancy or upon profession of faith. Where baptism is administered in infancy, communicant status shall

a number of ministers in-pastorate, who were all but unanimous in their opposition to the proposals in the Scheme.[39]

Townsend launched another stinging attack. He believed that instead of glorifying God, as Martin maintained, Baptist involvement in the Scheme would mean confusion. Townsend wanted to draw a sharp distinction between organic unity and close co-operation, and that the Scheme's ideal of the former was at odds with truth and history. In a tone reminiscent of Glover's opposition to Shakespeare in the early 1920s, Townsend wrote, 'The ideal and the fact of unity in the New Testament were based on truth. Any departure from the truth of the Gospel which imperilled the local church or churches was quickly dealt with by Paul... Paul...did not begin with the ideal of unity and make all sorts of compromises to attain it or keep it.' Townsend was unprepared simply to accept Martin's statement that Baptists did not have a monopoly of the truth, a statement with which he would no doubt have agreed in general terms, but with reference to the *Outline* it was one he was committed to disputing. He underscored the fact that 'one of the biggest issues in this Scheme is baptism', observing that the Scheme insisted on every member of the church being baptized, that Anglo-Catholics and others believed infant baptism to be essential to salvation and that every person had to be baptized before they could partake of the Lord's Supper. 'In the Baptist Union', Townsend continued, 'we have open membership and open communion churches... This Scheme kills the open communion and the open membership church. There are bigger issues than baptism because Baptists do not believe that baptism is necessary to salvation.'[40]

When the BU Council met in March, two resolutions brought before the meeting dealt directly with the *Outline*. The first, moved by Gilbert Laws and seconded by Wilson Black, stated:

---

be attained only upon a profession of faith following upon due instruction and sealed in a public service of Confirmation or such other service of attaining communicant status as shall be agreed upon', from *Outline*, 75.

39   Under the heading 'A United Church: The Question of Baptism', these included the open membership advocate, R.G. Ramsey of Ferme Park and R.W. Waddelow of Adelaide Place, Glasgow, *BT* February 10, 1938, 108; F. Buffard from Yeovil and H.W. Janisch from Northampton, *BT* February 17, 1938, 133; T.M. Bamber of Rye Lane, Peckham and W.J. Grant of Watford, *BT* February 24, 1938, 153; M. Evans of Muswell Hill and H.H. Pewtress of Fillebrook, Leytonstone, *BT* March 10, 1938, 193. However, R.L. Child of Broadmead, Bristol, *BT* February 17, 1938, 133, gave the Scheme some benefit of the doubt by allowing two possible interpretations of the proposal: either the two baptisms would be regarded as alternative modes of the same rite, of which he disapproved believing that believers' baptism would be bound to disappear, or that Baptist and Paedobaptist churches would take their place side by side within one new denomination, a proposal with which he would not feel the same initial objection, as this would appear to be what would happen in a federal union.

40   H. Townsend, 'Bigger Issues Than Baptism', *BT* February 24, 1938, 148.

That the members of the Council of the [BUGB&I], cannot, in consistency with the beliefs of Baptists as to the nature of the Church, the ministry of the Word, and the Ordinances of the Gospel, which beliefs they hold as a sacred trust, (1) recognise infant baptism as an alternative to believers' baptism, (2) admit the necessity of Episcopacy..., (3) accept a sacerdotal interpretation of the pastoral office. The Council are therefore compelled to state that organic unity on the basis of the 'Outline of a Reunion Scheme...', is not possible for Baptists...

Further progress, in the expression of Christian unity, it was believed, would only be made by 'unreserved mutual recognition.' Explorations into federation of equal and autonomous churches would, however, find the approval and support from the Council. As such, the resolution was in total harmony with previous declarations made by both the Council and the Baptist Assembly. 'Let it be made known throughout all the Churches that Baptists are not in the market selling their principles, neither are they behind closed doors agreeing to compromises that would destroy their effectiveness.' The motion was carried with four dissentients.[41]

The second resolution, moved by Rushbrooke, was carried un-animously. It called for the documents on Christian unity under discussion to be referred to a Special Committee with instructions to draw up a statement incorporating the earlier resolution of the Council, setting forward the position of the BU as expressed in the *Reply to the Lambeth Appeal* of 1926 and dealing with any other matters the Committee deemed appropriate.[42] A second report of the Council meeting recorded Black's opposition, when he said that, after re-reading the document, he was surprised that 'any Baptist could consider it, for it recognised infant baptism as an alternative to believers' baptism.' Martin had responded asserting that at the Lambeth conversations he had repeatedly stated the Baptist position with regard to baptism, the lay administration of the sacraments and other matters discussed. In fact, he agreed with most of what Gilbert Laws had said, but maintained that if he had felt that the Scheme of reunion involved all that had been read into it, he himself would not touch it.[43]

But Laws fired another salvo against the reunionists. Making explicit reference to pamphlets from the FoR and Free Church Unity Group, he again denounced those who proposed following the pathway to organic union. 'They believe it as earnestly as I and others believe the contrary.'

---

41   A detailed account of this Council meeting, including a lengthy quotation of Laws' speech, is to be found in Townsend, *Robert Wilson Black*, 103-08.

42   J.C. Carlile, 'Baptists and Church Union. Declaration by the Council', *BT* March 17, 1938, 201-02. The Committee was chaired by Wheeler Robinson and included R.L. Child, P.W. Evans, C.T. Le Quesne and F.T. Lord.

43   'The Council in Session', *BT* March 17, 1938, 208; Townsend, *Robert Wilson Black*, 108.

Five areas were highlighted by him as areas in which Baptists could not give ground: episcopacy, infant baptism, the ministry, the authority of the scriptures and a national church.[44]

It can be seen, then, that in the weeks leading up to and immediately after the Council meeting on March 8, the reunion movement, and in particular Hugh Martin, were on the receiving end of an intense onslaught from the anti–reunionists. The effect on Martin was considerable. In a doleful letter, he announced his resignation from the Joint Conferences and expressed his hope that this correspondence was now concluded.[45] And, with the exception of the BU's official reply to the three documents in November 1938, cease it effectively did.[46]

When it came, the official BU *Reply* acknowledged receipt of the documents, but, 'with profound regret', stated that Baptists did not regard the *Outline* 'as affording a basis for organic reunion', the reasons already being laid out in the 1926 *Reply to the Lambeth Appeal*.[47] Baptism in the New Testament, the 1938 *Reply* reiterated, was the immersion of believers, thus Baptists were unable to accept the subsequent extension of the rite to infants. This position was itself based

---

44 G. Laws, 'Re-Union', *BT* March 17, 1938, 211.

45 H. Martin, 'Re-union', *BT* March 17, 1938, 204. He wrote, 'Will you kindly allow me space enough to say that, in view of the resolution of the Baptist Union Council...I have resigned my position as a member of the Joint Conversations at Lambeth. The Outline Scheme was put forward, as it clearly states, not as a final document, but as a basis for discussion... I do not believe for a moment that it involves the positions attacked in the Council resolution... The sub-committee has only been appointed to formulate more fully the reasons for its total rejection. Many Baptists will share my profound regret at this attitude. With this letter, so far as I am concerned, this correspondence ceases.'

46 The only remaining contribution to the reunion discussion that year was a paper read by R.L. Child to the FoR conference on May 3, 'The Ministry and the Sacraments. A Free Church Point of View', *BQ* 9.3 (July, 1938), 132-38. Here Child rehearsed the common ecclesiology of the Free Churches of the fellowship of believers, and on ministry, he observed the practice of lay administration of the sacraments. Discussing baptism, he sought to provide a consensus of the Baptist view on the mode, the subjects and meaning of believers' baptism: as a personal testimony, an expression of the moral and spiritual union of the believer with Christ, as also an experience of the baptism of the Spirit, i.e., a means of grace, and its link with entrance into church membership. Child also discussed Baptist opposition to infant baptism as the latter 'is an unscriptural practice which veils the essentially personal nature of the issue between the soul and God', p.136.

47 *Reply of the Council of the Baptist Union of Great Britain and Ireland to the letter of the Federal Council of the Evangelical Free Churches, conveying the three documents which had been issued for the consideration of the Churches by a Joint Committee of Anglicans and Free Churchmen*, in E.A. Payne, *The Fellowship of Believers: Baptist Thought and Practice Yesterday and Today* (2nd edn, 1952), 148-49.

upon the conviction that the essential meaning and value of baptism according to the New Testament was changed or obscured when administered to those who lacked the cardinal requirements of repentance and faith. Because Baptists recognized the church as a fellowship of believers they could not recognize infant baptism as an alternative form of admission into the united Church of England.[48] The *Reply* concluded acknowledging the value of intercourse and discussion among different traditions 'for the promotion of mutual understanding of firmly held beliefs which is the necessary condition of fruitful co-operation', believing 'that increased loyalty to such convictions on the part of all, coupled with the willingness to learn from each other..., will bring all the Churches nearer together and nearer to the will of their...Lord and Saviour...'[49]

When the FCFC was formed in 1940[50] proposals were tabled for the mutual recognition of members and ministry, which would also allow mutual participation at each others' communion services and permit freedom of transfer between the churches. This, however, was opposed by Black, who claimed that such would infringe Baptist autonomy on baptism.[51] In the following years the whole issue of the reunion movement and discussions moved out of the forefront of the denomination's consciousness as the looming threat and then terrible reality of the war occupied people's energies.

It reappeared in November 1946, when the new Archbishop of Canterbury, Dr Geoffrey Fisher, preached his famous sermon at Cambridge University in which he suggested that the path of intercommunion could be explored with potentially greater benefit than organic union, but only if the Free Churches were prepared to take episcopacy into their systems, adapting it as needed. The sermon, naturally, aroused much interest and sparked off another round of conversations between the Anglican and Free Churches, though after two years Ernest Payne reported that no real advance had been made since the first discussions which had begun in 1920.[52]

---

48 *Reply of the Council of the Baptist Union*, 149.
49 *Reply of the Council of the Baptist Union*, 151.
50 The formation of the FCFC took place in Baptist Church House on September 16, 1940. W.M.S. West, 'Future sees new role for Council', *BT* September 27, 1990, 13, suggested four reasons for the formation of the FCFC: the need for one representative to speak on behalf of the Free Churches to government and country; the need to integrate local and national Free Church action; to seek to develop a coherent expression of Free Church emphases; and to forward what many in 1940 hoped to see—Free Church Union.
51 Reported by Thompson, 'The Older Free Churches', 111.
52 For Payne's report see 'The Lambeth Conference Report', *BT* August 19, 1948, 3. See also Payne, *The Baptist Union*, 219. The text of the sermon, 'A Step Forward in Church Relations', can be found in *Church Relations in England. Being the report of*

The complicated question of intercommunion was not an innovation
from the Archbishop, as the F&O movement had been examining these
matters since 1939.[53] When it eventually appeared in 1950, the *Report*
explicitly refuted any idea that it was providing a pattern for intercommunion, rather it was seeking to work out and express the necessary
implications of the Archbishop's sermon, the final draft of which was
unanimously accepted by the delegates.[54] When the *Report* eventually
appeared, it was variously received.

Percy Evans made it clear whenever he spoke about the *Report* that he
felt that, though it deserved and required the most careful and sympathetic consideration, he did not believe that Baptists would or could go
very far along the lines set out by it.[55] R.E.O. White surveyed its contents
in order to draw out its practical implications. Though explicitly dealing
with intercommunion, he noted that the uncompromising distinction
drawn between episcopal and non-episcopal administration of the Supper
raised grave doubt over believers' baptism administered by ministers not
episcopally ordained.[56] Further, relegating problems of baptismal
theology to discussion at a later stage, 'where necessary', could hardly
satisfy Baptists who believed that believers' baptism was a witness of
supreme importance to both the gospel and the church. Added to this,
intercommunion would revive the open communion controversy, lay

---

*Conversations between Representatives of the Archbishop of Canterbury and
Representatives of the Evangelical Free Churches in England, together with the sermon
preached by the Archbishop of Canterbury on November 3rd, 1946, entitled A Step
Forward in Church Relations* (1950), 5-12. About this time, 1946–47, the Archbishop
invited a group of Free Church theologians, including R.L. Child, P.W. Evans and E.A.
Payne, to explore the subject of Protestant Catholicity, see R.N. Flew and R.E. Davies,
*The Catholicity of Protestantism, being a report presented to His Grace the Archbishop
of Canterbury by a group of Free Churchmen* (1950), which in several places discusses the
place of the sacrament of baptism in Baptist thought, pp.108-09.

53   See 'The Report of the Commission' in D. Baillie and J. Marsh (eds.), *Inter-
Communion: The Report of the Theological Commission Appointed by the Continuation
Committee of the World Conference on Faith and Order Together with a Selection from
the material presented to the Commission* (1952), 15-43, esp. pp.15-17 for the
background and origins of the Report. Of particular interest in this volume are the essays
by E.A. Payne on 'Intercommunion from the Seventeenth to the Nineteenth Centuries',
pp.84-104, and P.W. Evans, 'A Baptist View. (b) P.W. Evans (Great Britain)', pp.185-
195.

54   J. Derby and N. Micklem, 'Preface', in *Church Relations in England*, 3. The BU
was represented by Dr P.W. Evans, Principal of Spurgeon's College, E.A. Payne, tutor at
Regent's Park College, Oxford, and H. Ingli James, General Superintendent of the South
Wales Area.

55   See F. Cawley, 'Percy William Evans', *BQ* 14.4 (October, 1951), 150. The
whole of this article, pp.148-52, provides background on Evans' life and ministry.

56   R.E.O. White, 'Church Relations in England', *Frat.* 80 (April, 1951), 7.

administration of communion would have to be discontinued and such would run the risk of widening the gulf between British Baptists and other world Baptists. This led White to conclude that, 'As it is, the substance of the Report's proposals will appear to many of us to be, not intercommunion with a view to fellowship, but assimilation with a view to absorption.'[57]

Ingli James believed that White had misconceived certain points, among them the fact that the Report was not a draft of formal proposals for reunion, but rather a consideration and interpretation of suggestions aired in the Archbishop's sermon. The aim was not reunion but the achievement of intercommunion.[58] He further observed that Baptists differed among themselves on many issues, including their view of the sacraments and ministry, but such did not prevent their sitting down together at the Lord's Table.[59]

On receiving the 1950 *Report* in March 1951, the BU Council appointed a special committee, under the chairmanship of Dr Arthur Dakin of Bristol College, to consider it,[60] whose own *Report* expressed the belief that intercommunion between Christian churches should not be dependent upon episcopacy.[61] On the sacraments it stated that 'Baptists would have difficulty in binding the sacraments as closely to the official ministry as the report seems to suggest would have to be the case.' Along with the preaching of the Word, the administration of the sacraments was

---

57   White, 'Church Relations in England', 9. White, p.10, concluded his discussion thus: 'To pursue negotiations towards intercommunion, well-knowing that the declared conditions are unacceptable, and the implied goal of Reunion of doubtful value, seems slightly dishonest. Though it is pleasanter to "keep on speaking terms", further discussion might well cost us the loyalty of old friends without gaining us any new. Respectfully, and regretfully, we must, I think, reply that on these terms as submitted, further discussion is bound to be fruitless.'

58   H. Ingli James, 'Church Relations in England', *Frat.* 82 (October, 1951), 29.

59   James, 'Church Relations in England', 32. Note, however, the admission in the BU's report, 'Church Relations in England. *Report approved by the Council of the Baptist Union, March 1953*', in Payne, *The Baptist Union*, 298, that there were strict Baptist churches within the BU which only admitted their own members to the Lord's Table.

60   The Committee consisted of Dr A. Dakin, Rt. Hon. Ernest Brown, F.C. Bryan, R.L. Child, P.R. Clifford, K.C. Dykes, G.W. Hughes, C.T. Le Quesne and Mrs Angus McMillan, with H.I. James and E.A. Payne serving as consultants. The text, 'Church Relations in England. *Report approved by the Council of the Baptist Union, March 1953*', is in Payne, *The Baptist Union*, 292-303. The text was also published independently under the same title. However, the text in Payne's Appendix is the one being used here. A.W. Argyle provided a summary of the committee's report in 'Church Relations in England', *Frat.* 89 (July, 1953), 6-8. See also 'Church Relations in England', *BT* May 6, 1954, 6.

61   'Church Relations in England, *1953*', 296.

committed to those called out by the local church for such service, but they were not committed exclusively to the ordained ministry. Provided the person, male or female, was duly authorized by the local church, any church member could take them. When there was a pastor, they would administer the sacraments, but many Baptist churches depended on the services of lay preachers, who frequently administered the sacraments as well as conducting public worship.[62] The *Report* then acknowledged that complete intercommunion, 'or, better, "mutual communion", did not as yet exist among Baptists, as was evidenced by the various types of Baptist churches: those which admitted only their own members to the Lord's Table; those which admitted only those baptized as believers; those which gave an open invitation to all Christians; and, those which gave both an open invitation and practised open membership. The greater majority of Baptist churches belonged to the latter two categories, with very few of the first.[63] This meant that the conclusion was that the report *Church Relations in England* did not, as it stood, offer a plan of development which Baptists could either consider right or practicable to try to implement.[64]

For nearly a decade little happened between the Free Churches and Anglicans, and little resulted from continuing the Free Church union discussions, most of which only barely mentioned baptism.[65]

The exception to this was when, at the request of Professor T.F. Torrance, *The Fraternal* reviewed the Church of Scotland's first interim report on baptism in 1955,[66] which set out to defend infant baptism on exegetical, theological and historical grounds. The very fact of this request reflects the change in attitudes brought about by the whole ecumenical movement. The reply was penned by Dr Beasley-Murray, who offered a 'personal and spontaneous reaction', stating that it was 'the most impressive concise statement of the case for infant baptism'

---

62   'Church Relations in England, *1953*', 297. The administration of baptism by duly authorized people, whether ordained or lay, though usually the minister, is a deep-seated principle among Baptists, being the practical demonstration of the emphasis Baptists place on the doctrine of the priesthood of all believers, and as such was clearly a non-negotiable matter.

63   'Church Relations in England, *1953*', 298.

64   'Church Relations in England, *1953*', 299.

65   See A. Gilmore, 'Supplementary Membership', *BT* April 26, 1956, 8; W.W. Bottoms, 'A United Church: Report on Debate', *BT* September 27, 1956, 16; 'United Free Church. Baptist Reply to Moderator's Commission Report', *BT* November 29, 1956, 9; and W.W. Bottoms, 'Free Church Union Proposals', *BT* April 4, 1957, 9. See also 'Free Church Unity', *BT* March 21, 1957, 3; 'Free Church of England. Willesden FCC Plan', *BT* April 17, 1958, 15; G.S. McKelvie of Luton, 'Free Church Union: Commission to be Appointed. Conversations with Anglicans One Step Further Away', *BT* October 9, 1958, 1 and 8.

66   The second and third reports were issued in 1956 and 1957 respectively.

that he had ever read.[67] However, he challenged all six of the report's main arguments, concluding, 'Our denomination has much to learn of the theology of Baptism from our Scottish brethren. It is our shame that they have so little to learn from us. Yet that little is crucial: *To die and rise with Christ, and therefore to be baptised, is the prerogative of him who confesses, 'Jesus is Lord'—of him and of no other; for the Baptism wherein God acts is the Baptism wherein man confesses.* This is the one Baptism of the Apostolic Church. The New Testament knows no other. The Gospel allows no other. Any theology claiming the sanction of the New Testament must come to terms with the significance of this primitive Baptismal utterance. It is our earnest hope that our friends north of the border will yet do so.'[68]

At the meeting of the FCFC at the end of September 1959 statements on union from the four major denominations were discussed. It soon became evident that little real progress had been made in the nearly forty years since the *Lambeth Appeal*. The committee reported that it was clear that to attempt corporate union at the present time was not timely. Certain theological and ecclesiastical questions remained to be answered, specifically the nature of the church, ministry and the sacrament of baptism.[69]

Over the following two years matters did not progress. On October 5 1961, the *Baptist Times* reported that the recent meeting of the FCFC had concluded that any attempt to initiate a comprehensive scheme of union between Free Churches would not succeed. Half the local councils were indifferent, a quarter were opposed to it, and so it was felt that conversations between denominations would be more likely to succeed than through the FCFC.[70] The Editorial lamented that after fifty years this made sorry reading. More disturbing still was the apathy and indifference on the part of many members, churches and councils towards a United Free Church. Differing views on church organization, the nature of the ministry and the sacraments, especially baptism, were noted but, it was

---

67   G.R. Beasley-Murray, 'The Church of Scotland and Baptism', *Frat.* 99 (January, 1956), 7.

68   Beasley-Murray, 'The Church of Scotland and Baptism', 10, italics his. The Report was very critically reviewed by R.L. Child, 'The Church of Scotland on Baptism', *BQ* 16.6 (April, 1956), 244-51, who ended with the statement that infant baptism had endangered the very existence of the ordinance of baptism, p.251; and by A. Gilmore, 'The Scottish Report on Baptism', *Frat.* 102 (October, 1956), 16-19, who supplied notes for a study outline and bibliography following the major divisions of the report. Part II was also reviewed by Gilmore, 'Church of Scotland Report on Baptism', *BT* May 30, 1957, 6.

69   'Denominations' Views on Free Church Union', *BT* October 1, 1959, 11.

70   See *BT* October 5, 1961, 'Free Church Union: The Present Position', 1 and 6, 'Report on Free Church Union. Summary of Survey of Present Position', 10.

felt, should not be sufficient to prevent a Federated Free Church of England.[71] However, the writer of the editorial was in a minority. T.G. Green applauded the editorial but did so recognizing that it represented only a minority view, while R.J. Snell could not share the editorial's views.[72]

In his *Baptists and Unity*,[73] Dr Leonard Champion maintained that Baptists had five things to contribute to ecumenical conversations: their historical stability; geographical expansion; numerical strength; their divisions over the WCC which prevented them compromising truth as they understood it; and their theological emphases. Illustrative of the latter was their distinctive contribution: believers baptism. Without due and sympathetic examination by those who did not accept believers baptism any conversations would be limited. Further, attention would be drawn to the widespread acknowledgement among Paedobaptists that the existing practice of infant baptism had given rise to pastoral problems, including failure of godparents to fulfill their responsibilities and of those so baptized to come forward for confirmation.[74] Four distinctive emphases of Baptists presented truths inherent in the gospel which were needed within the world church: the theology and practice of believers baptism; the significance of the individual; the importance of the local congregation; and the Lordship of Christ.[75]

While all Christians accepted the baptism of believers, only Baptists held that this alone was what the New Testament meant by baptism and was therefore the only mode which should be practised.[76] Baptists made this exclusive claim on the basis of scriptural authority and it was fundamentally based on doctrines central to Christian faith. Believers baptism preserved the fact that grace is neither imposed nor mechanical, and that personal faith must not be identified with the faith of the church. These conceptions of grace and faith determined the conception of the

---

71   'Free Church Union', *BT* October 5, 1961, 5. The editor at this time was W.W. Bottoms.

72   Mr T.G. Green, 'Free Church Union', *BT* October 19, 1961, 6; Mr R.J. Snell, 'Free Church Union', *BT* November 2, 1961, 6.

73   See W.W. Bottoms' review, 'Books on Unity', *BT* December 27, 1962, 6. It was a one of the Star Books on Reunion, edited by the Bishop of Bristol.

74   L.G. Champion, Principal of Bristol Baptist College, *Baptists and Unity* (1962), 39-44. On Champion, see R. Hayden, 'The stillness and the dancing: An appreciation of Leonard G. Champion', in R. Hayden and B. Haymes (eds.), *Bible, History and Ministry: Essays for L.G. Champion on his Ninetieth Birthday* (Bristol, 1997), 1-8; R. Hayden, 'Leonard George Champion 1907–1997', *BQ* 37.5 (January, 1998), 211-12.

75   Champion, *Baptists and Unity*, 46-70.

76   It should be noted that this statement is not entirely true, as the majority of the Brethren and Pentecostal churches practice the baptism of believers, though, Champion was probably thinking about the historic and mainline denominations at this point.

church as the community, created by the Spirit, of those who trust God. Baptism is then to be understood as the outward and visible act proclaiming this personal experience of being in Christ which involves being in the church. For Baptists, then, the words grace, faith and fellowship are all personal words, being terms denoting reciprocity of personal response. The mode of immersion proclaimed the objective dying and rising with Christ and the subjective believer's death and resurrection to new life in Christ.[77]

With Beasley-Murray, Champion believed that a greater endeavour to make baptism integral to the gospel, to conversion and to church membership, would enable baptism in Baptist churches to become again 'what God has willed it to be.' Beasley-Murray's 'scholarly exposition of New Testament practice and theology is thus a call to all sections of the Church to consider afresh the meaning of baptism and to do this in obedience to the authority of Scripture and in response to the nature of the Gospel.' All Christians were concerned with questions about the nature of God's grace, the faith of the believer, and of the church. Baptists, however, understood these in personal terms and that was why they continued to maintain that Christian baptism was the baptism of believers. Champion then raised the issue of the existence of two forms of baptism in the church. Could they co-exist and if not, which ought to be retained? If believers baptism was to be rejected, on what grounds, and if so, would that imply the rejection of the personal understanding of grace, faith and the church which it implied?[78] Yet in all this, Baptists, Champion argued, should respect Paedobaptist convictions.[79]

The first British Conference on F&O held in Nottingham in September 1964 reignited the whole issue of reunion between all the churches in Great Britain. Organized by the British F&O Committee, it has proved to be a defining moment in modern British church history and has been described as 'the most important specifically British ecumenical conference ever to be held.'[80] Twenty eight Baptists connected with the BUGB&I attended, and only one subsection lacked a British Baptist participant. Its report, *Unity Begins at Home*, and resolutions were sent to all participants, all of which expended an enormous amount of time and energy in their detailed examination.[81]

---

77   Champion, *Baptists and Unity*, 46-53.

78   Champion, *Baptists and Unity* , 52-53. Champion was referring to Beasley-Murray's *Baptism in the New Testament*.

79   Champion, *Baptists and Unity*, 72-76.

80   Hastings, *History of English Christianity*, 541.

81   See *Unity Begins at Home* (1964), and the resolutions which were printed in Appendix 1 of *Baptists and Unity* (1967), 52-56. On the Conference, see also ch. 8 below.

The most important achievement of the conference was the call for the churches to unite by Easter Day 1980, a proposal about which Baptist feelings were mixed.[82] David Pawson, writing from a conservative evangelical position and as a member of the Baptist Revival Fellowship (BRF), expressed the opinion of many when he wrote of 'hesitation and even awkwardness in relation to the ecumenical movement', and in particular any notion of union by 1980.[83] However, John Matthews responded by asking whether Baptists shared the same faith in the same Christ with other Christians. Until such a dialogue as was being suggested took place 'we shall continue in our present spiritual dilemma of whether "the others" are Christian or not.' 'It is time that the whole matter was made a serious subject for the denomination as a whole.' At the very least, Baptists were being called to say by 1980 on what conditions they could join the schemes for unity.[84]

In contrast to Pawson's 'no compromise therefore no involvement' position was the position adopted by George Beasley-Murray. He too opposed any compromise of principle,[85] yet this did not preclude him from involvement within the British and international ecumenical movements.[86] Beasley-Murray openly admitted that the way of the ecumenical movement was a hard and long one, obstacles to its success being immense. Any attempts to minimise the obstacles did not serve the ecumenical cause, and for this reason he expressed his dismay over the proposed date of Easter Day 1980. He questioned the judgment that the time had been right for the reunion of churches forty five years ago,[87]

---

82   See the Editorial, 'Baptists and Unity', *BT* March 18, 1965, 5.

83   J.D. Pawson of Gold Hill, '1980: Must They Include Us In?', *Frat.* 136 (April, 1965), 9.

84   J.F. Matthews, assistant minister at Botley, 'The Contemporary Ecumenical Situation: A Comment on Recent Articles', *Frat.* 138 (October, 1965), 30-31.

85   G.R. Beasley-Murray, *Reflections on the Ecumenical Movement* (1965), 9, 13. So too was E.A. Payne, 'No, We Are Not Being Asked to Compromise', *BT* November 11, 1965, 16. See also Payne's 'The Reverend Dr. E.A. Payne', in R.D. Whitehorn (ed.), *The Approach to Christian Unity* (Cambridge, 1951), 26-27, '[Baptists] are as unlikely as any other communion to accept schemes of unity if they seem to prevent Baptists maintaining the truths in which they believe.' Baptists have throughout insisted that there should be no compromise of principle. See, e.g., C.W. Black, 'If I Were Dictator of the Baptist Denomination', *BT* March 28, 1940, 201; T.G. Dunning, 'Baptist Ecumenicity', *BQ* 10.2 (April, 1940), 86-87; H.W. Robinson, 'Expediency and Principle', *BT* December 11, 1941, 611 and 612; R.W. Black, 'A Frank Talk to Fellow Baptists' in Townsend, *Robert Wilson Black*, 98-99.

86   Beasley-Murray, *Reflections*, 8. For his involvement in F&O, see West, 'Baptists and Faith and Order', *passim*; and Cross, 'Service to the Ecumenical Movement', *passim*.

87   This was the opinion of Norman Goodall voiced at the Nottingham Conference reported by Beasley-Murray, *Reflections*, 12. He continued, 'the fact must be faced that it

and thus, by implication, that the situation had appreciably changed. W. Scott also believed that Baptists should continue their ecumenical involvement and that in so doing they should work to secure the reformation of the Christian doctrine of baptism, 'so that infant baptism may be seen to be not only scripturally unsound, but theologically untenable.' The most valuable contribution Baptists could make to the world church was in the doctrine of baptism.[88]

The chief obstacles continued to be the doctrines of the ministry and the sacraments. J.C. Askew reported with approval the comment made by John Weller to the effect that difficulties over believer's baptism were insufficient grounds for Baptists to stay out of the ecumenical movement, as different forms of baptism could exist together in a United Church.[89] Beasley-Murray, however, noted that if the negotiations between Anglicans and Methodists, as in those between Anglicans and Scottish Presbyterians before them, had made heavy weather on the doctrine of the ministry, then 'we Baptists are going to experience even more difficulties over the sacraments. Apart from the issues connected with the Lord's Supper, there has been no scheme of Church Union in any part of the world thus far that has satisfactorily solved the problems raised for Baptists by infant baptism, and the Churches have been talking about them for a long time.'[90] Contrary to Beasley-Murray, Alec Gilmore suggested that the plan of the Church of North India might provide a guide for Christian union in Britain.[91] This was followed by an editorial which criticized Baptist ecumenists, arguing that infant baptism created confusion about the nature of the gospel and the whole meaning of humanity's relation to God, and that it was naive to suggest that were

---

is *Churches* which have to be united, not simply enthusiasts for reunion, and it is by no means evident that the Churches are ready for reunion. This is not a question of unwillingness on the part of the uncomprehending to take obvious steps; there are genuine difficulties relating to the theology and practice of the Churches which remain to be solved, and Faith and Order and all the other related agencies of the Churches have an immense task ahead in sorting them out and finding satisfactory solutions', italics his.

88   W. Scott of Durham, 'The Spiritual and the Sacramental in the Theology of Baptism', *Frat.* 135 (July, 1965), 27. 'One thing...is certain, Baptists must make their voice heard in the ecumenical debate so that a doctrine of baptism true to the spirit and practice of the New Testament church may be adopted in a new and vigorous united church', p.28.

89   J.C. Askew from Campden Road, London, 'Baptism Reason Is Not Enough', *BT* March 11, 1965, 16. John Weller was a Congregational minister and secretary of the F&O department of the BCC.

90   Beasley-Murray, *Reflections*, 12-13. See also his 'I Believe in this Movement —But...The Way Will Be Long and Hard', *BT* March 11, 1965, 8.

91   A. Gilmore, 'Baptism and Christian Unity. N. India Plan May Give A Guide', *BT* March 11, 1965, 8. See the later discussion of this by J.B. Middlebrook, 'Baptism and Unity', *BT* March 25, 1965, 4.

paedobaptist churches to turn to the Baptist view of baptism there would be a revival of true religion.[92]

Yet, throughout all this, the question was again raised as to whether it was co-operation or unity that was being discussed.[93] Such uncertainty and confusion over precisely what the issues were and what was being talked about reflects the limited progress the ecumenical movement had made in over half a century of debate and conversation. That this was in fact the position within the denomination is further reflected by the concern voiced by the Advisory Committee on Church Relations (ACCR) to the BU Council in March to the effect that the denomination's position needed further clarification.[94]

Baptists and the Churches of Christ

The relationship between Baptists and other believers' baptist traditions, specifically the Churches of Christ, was a concern shared by a number of Baptists, most notably R.W. Black. At the General Purposes Committee meeting in October 1941, Black suggested that informal conversations between representatives of the Baptists and his old denomination should be held. Without committing the General Purposes Committee or the BU, it was decided to authorize Black, Wheeler Robinson, P.W. Evans, C.T. Le Quesne and Gilbert Laws to 'confer in an informal way' with Churches of Christ representatives.[95]

By 1944 a limited measure of progress had been achieved which enabled Laws to claim that, 'It is believed that a better knowledge of one another is a necessary preliminary towards further progress', and the Baptist representatives in the conversations, under Laws' chairmanship, were also re-appointed for a further term.[96]

---

92   'The Church and Baptism', *BT* May 27, 1965, 5.

93   Mr J. Hough, 'Is the Goal Co-operation or Unity?', *BT* June 17, 1965, 2, being a report on the Whitsuntide Conference of the BCC.

94   'Baptists and Church Unity. Need to make their position clearer', *BT* March 18, 1965, 8.

95   *BH* 1944–45–46, 272. This concern for Baptist unity was to reappear in the Merseyside Baptist Declaration and correspondence linked to it. See below. The beginnings of this process can be seen in the inclusion of articles on baptism in both the *BQ* and *BT* by Dr William Robinson of Overdale College, Birmingham, and a leading Churches of Christ scholar, 'The Nature and Character of Christian Sacramental Theory and Practice', *BQ* 10.8 (October, 1941), 411-20; 'Baptism and Faith', *BT* July 23, 1942, 366. See also W. Robinson, 'The Mode of Baptism', *BT* February 25, 1943, 4. supporting a previous one from E. Price of Church of the Redeemer, Birmingham, 'The Mode of Baptism', *BT* February 11, 1943, 6, who advocated that the mode of immersion should be in the kneeling position and forwards.

96   G. Laws, 'Baptists and Churches of Christ', *BT* October 12, 1944, 4. Laws reported that the Annual Conference of the Churches of Christ had approved the

In his address delivered on the occasion of the reception of Bootle Baptist Church into the BU in 1944, Hubert L. Watson asserted that apart from faith baptism was meaningless. As a confession of faith it was personal and was retained as a personal expression of faith in Christ. As it spoke of an experience it was also declaratory, thereby providing opportunity to proclaim to others 'whose we are and whom we serve.' Following Romans 6, it was also symbolic of the believer's death to the old life of sin and self and resurrection to a new life of fellowship and service. Further, it was a means of grace, and this was not to imply that it was a magical power. 'But we do believe that God meets us in our obedience to His command, and so ministers to us of His grace and enriches our whole life.'[97] On this address, Harold Densham made the perceptive observation that, in view of the approaching interchange of views with the Church of Christ, 'let us not be surprised if we are faced with more emphatic interpretation of this sacrament than we have been presenting for some time.'[98]

In the spring of 1946, P.W. Evans represented the BU at the 100th Annual Conference of the Churches of Christ in Birmingham. During the course of offering greetings from the BU Council, Evans argued that the time had not yet arrived when concrete proposals could be put forward by either side for closer union. He believed that there was need for consideration of the position of children within the believing congregation and that the practice of dedication needed to be carefully thought through. He confessed that he would be glad to see the revival of the word 'ordinance' which had, by this time, been largely supplanted by the word 'sacrament', so that due emphasis could be given to the fact that

---

recommendations which the BU Council had earlier accepted to the effect that a note would be inserted in the *BH* mentioning the conversations along with some particulars relating to the Churches of Christ. Second, that discussions concerning their common witness should be arranged where possible at district level. Third, that delegates from each tradition should take fraternal greetings to the other's Annual Assembly. Fourth, that the *BT* and *The Christian Advocate* should exchange articles, and the reading of the journals should be encouraged on both sides. It was reported that William Robinson was to be the Churches of Christ delegate to the next Baptist Assembly and that the Baptist delegate would be appointed shortly. See *BH* 1944–45–46, 272-73. In January, 1945, it was confirmed that William Robinson would attend the Spring Baptist Assembly, and announced that Laws would represent the BU at the Churches of Christ Assembly to be held in the autumn, G. Laws, 'Baptists and the Churches of Christ', *BT* January 25, 1945, 2.

97   'The New Birth and Baptist Belief', *BT* January 25, 1945, 6.

98   Mr H. Densham of Plymouth, 'The New Birth and Baptist Belief', *BT* February 8, 1945, 6. This shrewd observation was based on the fact that generally speaking the Churches of Christ held a 'higher' doctrine of baptism to the mainstream of the Baptists.

baptism was something commanded. It was reported that the Conference clearly regarded Evans' words as an outstanding pronouncement.[99]

In an article published in the *Baptist Times*, William Robinson observed that Baptists were very strongly evangelical and that it was perhaps for this reason that they had not yet developed a strong interest in the *doctrine* of baptism which characterized the Churches of Christ, as they feared making baptism an *effectual* sacrament. However, he welcomed the growing numbers of Baptist scholars and ministers who were showing a greater interest in such matters and remarked that it would be difficult to distinguish H.W. Robinson's and A.C. Underwood's doctrine of baptism from that of his own tradition. Likewise he reported a growing feeling towards making the Lord's Supper the centre of Christian worship, all of which would aid the ongoing discussions.[100]

By the November meeting of the BU Council, it was clear that the existence of open membership Baptist churches was a major obstacle to further progress. Laws suggested several possible avenues which would perhaps lead to the solution of this difficulty, which included united meetings, discussion groups and weekend conferences, united action by which Baptist witness concerning baptism might be made more effective, the interchange of speakers on suitable occasions, the reading of one another's literature and the issue of a joint manifesto.[101]

Eventually, however, the discussions did produce something visible. Evans and Townsend co-operated with William Robinson in writing the slim volume *Infant Baptism To-day*, a joint publication by the newly amalgamated Carey Kingsgate[102] and the Berean Presses. In his forward, Laws claimed that an 'extensive area of common ground'[103] existed between the two traditions, but the booklet, as its title made plain, dealt directly with infant baptism, providing a joint refutation of the practice,

---

99   G.J. Hammond, 'Churches of Christ', *BT* August 15, 1946, 11.

100   W. Robinson, 'The Baptist Churches', *BT* August 22, 1946, 7.

101   See G. Laws, 'The Churches of Christ', *BT* November 28, 1946, 6-7. In 1947 the delegate to the Churches of Christ Annual Conference was Henry Townsend, and, in contrast to the high aspirations earlier expressed by Laws for increased interest and contact, the *BT* contented itself by simply reporting that fraternal greetings were sent. See *BT* July 31, 1947, 5.

102   The Carey and Kingsgate Presses were formerly merged into one publications department on in April 1948. See 'CAREY KINGSGATE PRESS', *BT* March 25, 1948, 6, and F.T. Lord, 'The Carey Kingsgate Press', *BT* April 15, 1948, 1.

103   P.W. Evans, H. Townsend and W. Robinson, *Infant Baptism To-day* (1948), 5. The following year William Mander of Leicester contributed an article from the Churches of Christ perspective on 'Baptism To-day', *BT* December 15, 1949, 9, and this was followed the next year by G. Laws' description of Baptist–Churches of Christ relationships in the United States, 'Baptists and Disciples of Christ in America', *BT* December 14, 1950, 8. For details of these American conversations see also E. Roberts-Thomson, *Baptists and Disciples of Christ* (n.d. [1951]), 147-53.

there being no attempt to elucidate the claimed common ground beyond this. Though proposals for union were never discussed, either between the two denominations or with others, the three authors sought to express common attitudes towards infant baptism. William Robinson contributed the first two chapters which were comprised largely of quotations from Paedobaptist writers who recognized that believers' baptism was the New Testament baptism and their dis-ease with the practice of indiscriminate infant baptism. In the remaining two chapters, Evans examined the doctrinal issues involved in infant baptism's deviation from the New Testament rite, while Townsend investigated the difficulties that infant baptism had with the ethical dimension of the rite.

The flagging discussions gained a final fillip in 1951 with the publication of E. Roberts-Thomson's *Baptists and the Disciples of Christ*. In his appreciative review, Child conceded that as far as Britain was concerned, 'greater accord between the two denominations is unlikely to be achieved until much more intercourse has taken place between them than has so far been the case, and until painstaking efforts at mutual interpretation have enabled the exact character of each other's views and practices to be thoroughly grasped.'[104] Laws concluded that 'Baptists would honour themselves if they could show the sincerity of their plea for Christian unity by taking all possible steps to a closer union with our nearest relatives.'[105]

Roberts-Thomson provided a particular service in his historical and theological discussions, and this was nowhere more apparent than in his treatment of the understanding of baptism and attitudes to the reunion movement within the two traditions.[106] However, he identified a number of difficulties which faced any union between the two denominations. First, Baptists were generally suspicious that the Churches of Christ believed in baptismal regeneration, and this despite the bridging work done by Wheeler Robinson and Underwood. Second, the Churches of Christ could not agree with the by now widespread practice among Baptists of open membership.[107] Though delegates were sent to each other's assemblies that year[108] with the deaths within a few months of each other of the two brothers, J.W. Black and R.W. Black, who had been the chief architects and driving forces behind the conversations, the momentum was all but lost, and by the following year the discussions had

---

104 R.L. Child, 'Baptists and Disciples of Christ', *BQ* 14.4 (October, 1951), 189.

105 G. Laws, 'Baptists and Disciples of Christ', *BT* February 22, 1951, 7.

106 Roberts-Thomson, *Baptists and Disciples of Christ*, esp. 114-23, 142-47, 157-60.

107 Roberts-Thomson, *Baptists and Disciples of Christ*, 161-69. Other stumbling blocks included differences over the ministry, the Lord's Supper, the name of a united church and the place of creeds and the Bible, pp.169-83.

108 See 'Churches of Christ Conference', *BT* August 16, 1951, 7.

effectively drawn to a close and by mutual consent were concluded.[109] Though there was a suggestion that conversations should be reopened and informal discussions did take place in April 1956, by the following April the BU Council rejected the project for closer cooperation without giving any reason.[110]

Faith and Order and the World Council of Churches

By January 1938 details of the Edinburgh F&O Conference were beginning to filter into the denomination's consciousness. Hugh Martin's popular account of the conference had been published in October 1937,[111] and this was followed in January by reports from Aubrey and Laws, both of whom had attended the Conference, both concluding that at the present time reunion discussions were at an impasse.[112]

Addressing the Northern Convocation at York, Aubrey explained that many Baptists could not accept the validity of the baptism of infants who were incapable of personal faith, in the same way that many Anglicans had a problem with the validity of Baptist ministry and sacraments. 'We respect your hesitations. We are coming to see how they arise. We ask that you should sympathetically study ours.' He then admitted, with reference to the conversations which had begun in 1932, that Baptists could not see how they could enter into organic union with Congregationalists and Presbyterians, adding, 'though in real Christian unity we are constantly working together.'[113]

Laws provided a detailed account of the proceedings of the Conference, paying particular attention to Section III on the 'The Ministry and the Sacraments'.[114] Here the differences which divided Baptists from other traditions became very apparent, nevertheless, Laws felt that progress had been made. He reported that on baptism it stated: 'The reunited Church will observe the rule that all members of the visible Church are admitted by baptism; which is a gift of God's redeeming love to the

---

109 See Thompson, *Let Sects and Parties Fall*, 186; Payne, *The Baptist Union*, 221.

110 See Thompson, *Let Sects and Parties Fall*, 185. A report appeared in 1954 reporting the 108th Churches of Christ annual assembly, *BT* August 5, 1954, 6. The irony is that in 1981 the Reformed Association of the Churches of Christ joined the paedobaptist United Reformed Church (URC), though it does mean that the URC has to practise both believer's baptism and infant baptism.

111 H. Martin, *Edinburgh 1937: The Story of the Second World Conference on Faith and Order held in Edinburgh August 3rd–8th, 1937* (1937).

112 M.E. Aubrey, 'What Edinburgh Meant to Me', *BT* January 20, 1938, 42-44; G. Laws, 'The Edinburgh Conference: What Was the Good of it?', *BQ* 9.1 (January, 1938), 21-29.

113 Aubrey, 'What Edinburgh Meant to Me', 43.

114 On which see also Martin, *Edinburgh 1937*, 57-71.

Church; and administered in the name of the [Trinity], is a sign and seal of Christian discipleship in obedience to the Lord's command.' To this the Baptist delegates had secured a note stating that the just quoted statement could be accepted by them only if understood to apply to believer's baptism and they drew attention to a principle enunciated in one of the preliminary documents[115] which recognized that the 'necessary condition of receiving the grace of a sacrament is the faith of the recipient.' The note also expressed the Baptist belief that children belonged to God and that no rite was needed to assure for them his grace.[116] Discussing the report's section on admission to Holy Communion, Laws reported that some delegates had been unable to understand how Baptists were able to accept the non-baptized into membership, which had led to the gibe, 'Baptists are people who are so strong on baptism that they dispense with it!'[117]

Laws' conclusion, however, was negative: 'The conceptions of church, ministry and sacrament are so different that it is hard to see how any union can ever be looked for while opinion remains as it is.' The difficulties, therefore, facing Baptists were enormous. 'On the question of baptism our position is so distinct, and to the many so unacceptable, that I see no way of overcoming the difficulty short of equating believer's baptism with infant baptism. This would seem to me to make infant baptism the standard and believer's baptism a sort of tolerated exception. It is not likely that more than a very few Baptists would ever think of consenting to such an equation. It is a very painful thing to have to say to those who set store by infant baptism that we regard it as a perversion of an ordinance of Christ, a substitution of man's devising for a positive institution of the Lord. Yet nothing less than this is the true Baptist position, and as one holds it I see no way, except at the cost of truth, of organic union with other Churches.'[118]

The incompatibility of the two forms of baptism, though repeatedly attacked by a not insignificant number of pro-unity advocates, most notably Hugh Martin and later Alec Gilmore, was reiterated forcefully time and time again, and it has been this expressed incompatibility which has dominated, as is shown by the lack of real progress that has been

---

115 *The Report of the Commission*, 27, cited by Laws, 'The Edinburgh Conference', 24.

116 This was also reported by Martin, *Edinburgh 1937*, 58-62.

117 Laws, 'The Edinburgh Conference', 25.

118 Laws, 'The Edinburgh Conference', 29. Laws developed his opposition to the implications of any movement seeking the organic unity of the Churches in his article, 'Baptists and the Ecumenical Movement', *BT* February 3, 1938, 89, and he reiterated his belief that in a United Church believers' baptism would be a tolerated exception to the standard practice, and infant baptism and believers' baptism 'could no more permanently live together than the red and the grey squirrels.'

actually made towards either a United Free Church or a United Church in England. Some argued for an infant service with water which was essentially a dedication service and therefore not incompatible with the Baptist service of infant dedication/presentation.[119] Suggestions of a federally organized United Free Church were occasionally made,[120] but this idea was evidently losing its appeal as it was never again seriously considered.

A further response to the 1937 F&O and Life and Work conferences was the setting up of two commissions in preparation for the sixth BWC in Atlanta, Georgia, in 1939, the second of which examined 'The Baptist Contribution to Christian Unity' and was prepared by Wheeler Robinson.[121] Presenting the report to the Congress, W.H. Coats underlined baptism as an acted creed. Baptist loyalty to scripture and to the scriptural form of baptism went hand in hand, but it was not the letter but the spirit of scripture which preserved the scriptural form, and the form itself helped in the conservation of the spirit. The second section of the report, he emphasized, called for a 'higher' doctrine of baptism and for Baptists to make more of baptism not less.[122]

---

119 E.g. P.H. Jones of Bampton, Devon, 'Upon What Basis Should Baptists, Congregationalists and Presbyterians Unite in One Denominational Organisation?', *BT* January 20, 1938, 53.

120 E.g. O. Henderson of Wimborne, 'Upon What Basis Should Baptists, Congregationalists and Presbyterians Unite in One Denominational Organisation?', *BT* January 20, 1938, 53, argued that in such a federated United Free Church a spirit of fellowship would be fostered between the denominations, while church extension would take place either in the form of Union churches or by the establishment of open membership churches where believer's baptism was optional and infant dedication was observed for those wishing to associate their children with the church.

121 For the text of the report, see 'Report of Commission No.2. The Baptist Contribution to Christian Unity', in J.H. Rushbrooke (ed.), *Sixth Baptist World Congress: Atlanta, Georgia, USA, July 22–28, 1939* (Atlanta, 1939), 115-21, section II, pp.117-18. As well as compiling the second report, Robinson also prepared the questionaire on which it had been based. The nucleus of this commission comprised Robinson as chairman, P.W. Evans and W.H. Coats, Principal of the Baptist Theological College of Scotland. The first report dealt explicitly with 'The Reports and Findings of the Oxford and Edinburgh Conferences'. Robinson repeated his call for more to be made of baptism, see his 'Five Points of a Baptist's Faith', *BT* October, 9, 1941, 490. These were faith, baptism, fellowship, freedom and evangelism. Of baptism he said it was in (or into) the name of Jesus, marking a transition into the authority and power of a new Lord. Both baptism and the Lord's Supper, regarded spiritually, were definite means of grace and he followed this with the challenge, 'if we do not make *more* of baptism than we are doing, it will go.' The full text of this address was reproduced in the *BQ* 11.1&2 (January/April, 1942), 4-14.

122 W.H. Coats, 'Introductory Remarks in Presenting the Report of Commission No. 2', in Rushbrooke (ed.), *Sixth Baptist World Congress*, 122. On Coats, see D.B.

The report itself underscored the Baptist testimony to the necessity of personal faith as the prerequisite for baptism; that baptism is an acted creed; that Baptists are the only tradition which can maintain baptismal grace in the New Testament sense; that baptism should be made more of within Christian experience, and it criticized the inadequacy of much baptismal instruction. In the light of this, the report recognized that there were truths in the possession of other churches which Baptists needed to learn and apply. In itself this was an argument for closer co-operation, but, 'We may be permitted to doubt...whether it is an argument for organic reunion of the kind which would subordinate truths to institutions.' The report made clear that there was little inclination among world Baptists for closer incorporation with other branches of the church.[123]

One of the most significant dates for the church in the twentieth century is August 1948, when the work of almost half a century came to fruition in the formation of the WCC in Amsterdam.[124] Wisely the WCC did not become immediately embroiled with the baptismal question.[125]

Though many Baptists had strong reservations about the formation of the WCC, and many Baptist conventions, most notably the Southern Baptists, remained outside of it, Henry Cook, addressing the BWA the previous year, had called for active Baptist participation. 'I am, myself, a Baptist through and through, and I would not be speaking on this subject to-day if I thought for a moment that it was likely to jeopardise our Baptist testimony or weaken our influence among our own people.' Later, he expressed again his conviction that Baptists were in danger of risking their own position if such contacts involved the sacrifice of principle, however, he did not believe that such relationships would be jeopardized by entering into friendly association with other Christian bodies: 'on the contrary, I think that we lose a good deal by keeping apart; and I am quite persuaded in my own mind that we can do far more

---

Murray, *Scottish Baptist College: Centenary History, 1894–1994* (Glasgow, 1994), 41, 44-45.

123 H.W. Robinson, 'The Baptist Contribution to Christian Unity', 115-21, quotation from p.120. See also E.A. Payne, *Baptists Speak to the World: A Description and Interpretation of the Sixth Baptists World Congress, Atlanta, 1939* (1939), 48-50.

124 The opening service was held on August 22, 1948. Representatives from forty four different countries and 147 churches attended, among them M.E. Aubrey, P.W. Evans, C.T. Le Quesne and E.A. Payne on behalf of the BU, with Dr T.G. Dunning, Ernest Brown and Hugh Martin as alternates, see Payne, *The Baptist Union*, 219.

125 On the founding of the WCC see H. Martin, 'Amsterdam 1948', *BT* June 10, 1948, 2; E.A. Payne, 'Report from Amsterdam', *BT* September 2, 1948, 1-2; Payne, 'Second Report from Amsterdam', *BT* September 9, 1948, 9-10.

for Christ by showing a united front than we can by remaining aloof.'[126] Cook then added that Baptists would have to ensure that in joining the WCC they did not weaken their devotion either to their own particular testimony, specifically believers' baptism and the doctrine of the church of believers independent of state support and control, and their own particular fellowship, namely in the BWA with other Baptists.[127]

It was against the backdrop of the renewed Anglican–Free Church conversations and the imminent establishment of the WCC that the report 'The Baptist Doctrine of the Church' was published. Adopted by the BU Council in March 1948, and, though based to a certain extent on the earlier 1926 *Reply to the Lambeth Appeal*, it was a new document prepared under Percy Evans' chairmanship and included the participation of Ernest Payne.[128] Surprisingly, there was little interest shown in the report in the pages of the *Baptist Times*, but there can be little to doubt the importance of the report, especially as it was later included in a volume of papers presented to the F&O Commission in preparation for the Lund Conference in 1952.[129]

The report forcefully reiterated that the Baptist doctrine of the church rested on the central fact of evangelical experience: that when God offered his forgiveness, love and power the gift had to be accepted in faith by each individual. From this conception of ecclesiology came the Baptist teaching on believers' baptism. The report then concluded, announcing the Baptist contribution to the church: 'Gratefully recognizing the gifts bestowed by God upon other communions, we offer

---

126 H. Cook, 'Baptists and the World Council of Churches', in W.O. Lewis (ed.), *Seventh Baptist World Congress: Copenhagen, Denmark, July 29–August 3, 1947* (1948), 56 and 58. It is clear that some within the BWA, notably Southern Baptists, wanted to criticize the proposed formation of the WCC by referring the decision of any national BU to join the WCC to the Executive Committee of the BWA. Payne successfully opposed this move, drawing attention to its unconstitutional nature, see West, *To Be A Pilgrim*, 66-67.

127 Cook, 'Baptists and the WCC', 57-58.

128 See West, *To Be A Pilgrim*, 82.

129 'The Baptist Doctrine of the Church. *A Statement approved by the Council of the Baptist Union of Great Britain and Ireland, March, 1948*', *BQ* 12.12 (October, 1948), 440-48. All references will be taken from this edition of the report. The *Statement* was also printed in R.N. Flew (ed.), *The Nature of the Church: Papers Presented to the Theological Commission Appointed by the Continuation Committee of the World Conference on Faith and Order* (1952), 160-68; in Payne, *Fellowship of Believers*, 152-62; R. Hayden, *Baptist Union Documents, 1948–1977, with an introduction* (1980), 4-11; and extracted in H.L. McBeth, *A Sourcebook for Baptist Heritage* (Nashville, 1990), 368-71. The importance of the *Statement* for F&O was brought out by E.A. Payne, 'Faith and Order Discussions', *BT* July 28, 1949, 7.

these insights which He has entrusted to us for the service of His whole Church.'[130]

While the WCC was becoming established, the work of F&O continued. The Report of the Third World F&O Conference meeting in Lund, Sweden, in 1952, was welcomed by the BU, whose response noted that the section on baptism (p.21 lines 3-5, p.35 para. (f) and p.43) suggested that a thorough-going examination of baptism by the Commission was necessary, a view which in time would be realized, as is evidenced by the many baptismal documents produced from the 1970s onwards.[131]

During this time, the European Commission on F&O had met in August 1956. The subject of baptism was singled out for special consideration over the coming years, and Baptist participation was called for in such discussions.[132] This was followed up in 1958 by the Youth F&O Consultation on Baptism and Confirmation held at Hilversum, Holland, in which Alec Gilmore participated. The purpose of this meeting was to consider these doctrines with regard to the integration of young people into the church's life. In a brief article, Gilmore outlined the four major questions which were considered: whether baptism was necessary; whether there was any difference between infant baptism followed by confirmation and infant dedication followed by believers' baptism; the place of children in the church, and whether baptism was related to integration. He concluded with the by now oft repeated call that it was of 'the utmost importance that we should be able to state a case for believers' baptism, and to ensure that Baptists speak on this subject with a common mind—a fact by no means certain at the moment.'[133]

Reporting to the BU Council in March 1962 on the proceedings of the Third Assembly of the WCC at New Delhi the previous year, Dr Leonard

---

130 'The Baptist Doctine of the Church', 447.

131 *The Response of the Baptist Union of Great Britain and Ireland to the Report of the Third World Conference on Faith and Order* (November, 1953), 6. The Lund conference is discussed by W.M.S. West, 'Baptists in Faith and Order', 60-61. West, along with E.A. Payne, C.T. Le Quesne, K. Dykes and H.I. James (who represented the BU of New Zealand) were the 5 British representatives among 14 Baptists attending the Conference. Godfray Le Quesne was a visitor and unofficial youth delegate.

132 'Baptism Study by Church Leaders', *BT* October 18, 1956, 3. In September the following year, the North American F&O Study Conference at Oberlin, Ohio, examined 'The Nature of the Unity We Seek'. In reporting this, R.F. Aldwinckle sought to demonstrate that the fundamental difference between the churches was one of ecclesiology, and also criticized Baptists for having sundered baptism from faith, thereby throwing the true nature of the church into obscurity and confusion, see 'Christians Discuss Baptism', *BT* November 21, 1957, 8.

133 A. Gilmore, 'Some Baptismal Problems', *Frat.* 109 (July, 1958), 15. The need for further clarity on baptism for the sake of the 'Don't knows' within Baptist churches was also expressed by the army padre, E.G. Evans, 'Baptism? Never Heard of it!', *BT* October, 9, 1958, 3, 10.

Champion strongly urged that Baptists should share within ecumenical developments,[134] a position supported by Hugh Martin, who denied that either the WCC or the BCC were trying to commit the churches to some kind of reunion scheme.[135]

Reviewing two F&O reports, 'The Divine Trinity and the Unity of the Church' and 'The Meaning of Baptism', Maurice Williams encouraged Baptists to continue participation in the ongoing ecumenical debate, as the publication of these reports were 'a testimony to the Spirit of truth who will guide us into all the truth by creating the conditions in which it can be heard and done, and a challenge to listen as the same Spirit declares unto us the things that are to come.'[136]

The Reunion Debate Discussed

Throughout all these developments there were a number of important figures who expressed their views in some of the most important Baptist books of the period. These works themselves, the effect they had and the discussion they stimulated, need to be examined.

Hugh Martin's *Christian Reunion*[137] undoubtedly returned the whole reunion issue to the forefront of the denomination's thought which had, for the first few years of the War been otherwise occupied, and it is the finest and fullest expression of Martin's views on reunion.[138] Expressly written for 'the general membership of the churches, ministerial and lay',

---

134 L.G. Champion, 'Baptists Should Share in Ecumenical Movement', *BT* March 22, 1962, 9.

135 H. Martin, 'Gaining a Richer and Fuller Faith: "The Ecumenical Movement"', *BT* April 19, 1962, 9.

136 M.F. Williams of South Street, Exeter, '*One Lord, One Baptism*—Reports of the Faith and Order Commission of the World Council of Churches, with a Preface by Oliver Tomkins', *BQ* 19.5 (January, 1962), 237-38.

137 H. Martin, *Christian Reunion: A Plea for Action* (1941). *The Religious Book Club Bulletin* No.24 (September, 1941), 6, included a page and a half of 'Questions for Discussion' (pp.7-8) on the book. Martin was editor of the RBC, on which see Cross, 'Hugh Martin: Part 1', 37-38. The anonymous reviewer (the editor, S.J. Price, perhaps?) for the *BQ* concluded 'This *Plea* deserves careful study... We do not recall another which deals so competently and fairly with the various issues involved.' However, the review began with the admission, 'Mr. Martin is the flaming apostle of Christian Reunion, although when he thinks of the indifference of the average church member he may feel himself a voice crying in the wilderness', and later included the discouraging remark, 'He is an optimist, however, if he thinks that Baptists will accept that "the total action in infant baptism and confirmation is the same as in believer's baptism"', see '*Christian Reunion. A Plea for Action*, by Hugh Martin', *BQ* 10.8 (October, 1941), 460. See also 'Reunion', *BQ* 10.8 (October, 1941), 410.

138 Martin's *Christian Reunion* is discussed at length in Cross, 'Hugh Martin: Part 3', 136-38.

he sought to present 'the great importance of Christian Reunion' before as many as he could, 'and to make clearer how matters stand to-day and the nature of the issues at stake.'[139] He conceded that differences of opinion existed among Christians on important matters of belief and practice, but believed that behind all Christian divergences there was a large measure of unity of faith and spirit which was denied by organizational divisions.[140] He asserted that those working for Christian unity were not longing for uniformity: 'We abhor compromise. It is comprehension we seek.'[141] The ministry and apostolic succession, he believed, were the chief stumbling-blocks to reunion, and that problems of the ministry and sacraments 'could be settled only by prior agreement on the nature and purpose of the Church.'[142] In his discussion of 'The Basis of Unity: Creed and Sacraments', he made a statement most Baptists would have refuted outright: 'A common plan of unity is gradually emerging out of the prolonged and intimate discussions of recent years.'[143] Differences of opinion which were recognized as legitimate within the present denominations, Martin claimed, would not be made a barrier against union between them, and he suggested that, on the sacraments, though there were few areas over which misunderstanding was more rife, yet there was by no means such wide disagreements as appeared on the surface, and there was no necessary ground for continued disunity.[144] As far as Baptists at least were concerned, he could not have been more wrong, as Shakespeare had been before him.

On baptism, Martin acknowledged that it was a problem only for Baptists. 'Writing as a Baptist', he continued, 'I am anxious to advance a reconciling point of view in a realm where most Baptists feel no reconciliation is possible.' The consensus of scholarly work on baptism,

---

139 Martin, *Christian Reunion*, 7. The practical case for unity, according to Martin, pp.15-29, could be stated under three headings: the state of the world called for it; it was demanded by the need for efficient Christian service; and the mission field called for it.

140 Martin, *Christian Reunion*, 46-47.

141 Martin, *Christian Reunion*, 50.

142 Martin, *Christian Reunion*, 65.

143 Martin, *Christian Reunion*, 104. This was followed by four assertions which he maintained could be made as to the nature of a United Church. Its unity would be based upon a common faith; acceptance of the sacraments of baptism and the Lord's Supper; a form of church order comprehending episcopal, presbyteral and congregational elements; and freedom from state control in spiritual affairs, principles on which, he declared, substantial agreement had been achieved, see pp.105-06. He proposed to use as a text, what he called, 'the agreements' registered in the 1938 *Outline*, though he admitted that the 'substantial agreement' of which he so freely spoke existed only between representatives in the reunion discussions, and even this was not wholly the case, as was indicated by three out of the four Baptist representatives to the Lambeth Joint Conferences having distanced themselves from the *Outline Scheme* itself.

144 Martin, *Christian Reunion*, 108 and 116.

he observed, was that New Testament baptism was the immersion of
believers upon profession of faith. Yet some scholars held that though
there was no explicit reference to infant baptism it could nevertheless be
assumed that there were unmentioned ones, for example, in the
household baptisms of Acts. Despite such arguments, Martin at least
nailed his colours to the mast when he wrote that it could at least be
maintained that the words of Paul on baptism were meaningless except as
applied to believers. 'The New Testament theory of baptism and so far as
the records go, the practice also, assume faith in the recipient.' The
Baptist conception of baptism, he affirmed, involved three elements
(though in fact he proceeded to list four). The first was the candidate's
personal testimony to their faith in Christ, a sign of conversion and not a
means to it. Second, it affirmed moral and spiritual union with Christ in
dedication to his service and repudiation of sin. Immersion in water
symbolized burial to sin and a rising again to newness of life. Third,
baptism was seen as a means of grace and a baptism of the Spirit in
response to the candidate's and church's prayers. And fourth, the
sacrament spoke of entrance into church membership. These convictions
Baptists derived from the New Testament which they held as the ultimate
authority and it was not in the competence of the church to modify the
rite in a way which obscured its essential New Testament meaning, as
when it was administered to those lacking the cardinal requirements of
repentance and faith.[145]

What paedobaptist churches had done was to divide the New Testament
practice in two, as baptism, on any theory, was incomplete without the
response of faith, before or after. Hence the rise of confirmation. Martin
then asked, 'Can it not be said that the total action, if that phrase may be
permitted, in infant baptism and confirmation is the same as in believer's
baptism, as the *Scheme* suggests?'[146] Infant baptism emphasized the
grace of God, believers' baptism expressed the response in repentance,
faith and obedience.[147] Martin proceeded, 'I believe that the Baptists are
right in holding to the New Testament practice, but I do not agree that
this necessitates their refusal to enter into church unity with others who
do not. I do not believe that this issue lies at the heart of the Gospel. The
real nature of the Baptist witness concerns the doctrine of the Church and
its composition; it is only incidentally concerned with the rite of baptism.
We maintain that baptism should be the baptism of believers.' Immersion

---

145 Martin, *Christian Reunion*, 118-19. Martin's own personal convictions on
baptism were further made clear in two later articles, both of which showed him to be in
agreement with Baptists generally on the doctrine, 'Judson on Baptism', *BQ* 13.1
(January, 1949), 25-28, and 'Baptism in the Fourth Century', *BQ* 13.8 (October, 1950),
370-72.
    146 Martin, *Christian Reunion*, 120.
    147 Martin, *Christian Reunion*, 121

preserved the true Pauline symbolism, and a baptismal service was a moving proclamation of the gospel, but the mode was a secondary matter. Baptist baptism was not *adult* baptism, rather it was the faith of the recipient which mattered. 'Our fundamental contention is that the Church is composed of believers only.'[148] The place of faith in relation to baptism and church membership, he concluded, demanded much careful examination if reunion was to make progress. Baptists, however, needed to consider more sympathetically the real beliefs of Paedobaptists.[149]

In his biography of R.W. Black, Townsend noted how Black seized every opportunity during his presidential year, 1941, to 'quicken loyalty to the convictions which he held so firmly.'[150] On a visit to Liverpool, Black found a group of young ministers[151] who were concerned that current tendencies towards union or reunion would weaken or betray Baptist principles, so he encouraged them to make public their convictions. In *A Baptist Declaration*, they welcomed the formation of the FCFC 'as a means of achieving the closest possible co-operation between the Free Churches.' However, 'At the same time, we are convinced that any attempt to achieve the organic union of the Free Churches is neither wise nor practicable.' As Baptists, they declared their firm resolution to hold fast and proclaim the fundamental doctrine of the church of those only who personally believe in God through Christ as Lord and Saviour. By no means an extreme group,[152] the Merseyside ministers singled out baptism as the principle which they felt most threatened by the whole ecumenical movement. They affirmed that baptism apart from faith in Christ was unknown in the New Testament, therefore, to proclaim that baptism could precede faith was to invert the order of spiritual experience in the apostolic church. World circumstances, they believed, demanded definite Baptist testimony that the

---

148 Martin, *Christian Reunion*, 122.

149 Martin, *Christian Reunion*, 124. At the same time as *Christian Reunion* appeared in 1941, *An Appeal for Free Church Union* was published, 16 Baptist ministers and one layman included among its signatories. In a critical notice in the *BQ*, the reviewer doubted whether a huge, uniform United Free Church was desirable, and he closed by asking the 17 Baptist signatories whether they had given any thought to the pressing problem of union among Baptists? See 'Reunion', *BQ* 10.8 (October, 1941), 410. A copy of this has not been located.

150 Townsend, *Robert Wilson Black*, 110.

151 They were E. Buckley of New Brighton, K.C. Dykes of Wavertree, G.W. Hughes of Princes Gate, W.E. Moore of Page Moss Lane and H.L. Watson of Richmond, Liverpool, see Townsend, *Robert Wilson Black*, 112.

152 From 1949, Dykes was Principal of Manchester Baptist College, from 1956 Moore was a tutor at Rawdon, Watson became General Superintendent for the North Western Area in 1949, while Buckley moved into an educational appointment in 1962, as did Hughes in 1961, who also served as Secretary of the Baptist Historical Society from 1947.

'sacraments' apart from faith in Christ were not his ordinances. They therefore pledged themselves 'to preach the truly High Church doctrines of believers' baptism and of the living presence of Christ in the Communion service to all who participate in faith.' They expressed their conviction that a doctrine of the sacraments which ignored the New Testament demand for faith had weakened the authority and power of the church by cutting at the root of the Christian ethic, as personal faith was the dynamic of all genuine Christian life. It was, then, evident that infant baptism not merely obscured but subverted the character of the church as the fellowship of believers. The urgent task to which they called their fellow Baptists was to seek at once organic unity with all who accepted Baptist principles.[153] To try to go beyond this would deeply divide the denomination and make further progress impossible. They concluded, 'Our highest service to the larger Christian fellowship of which we feel ourselves a part, and to the extension of the Kingdom of God, is to hold fast the sacred trust committed to us.'[154]

A copy of the *Declaration* was sent to all Baptist ministers with a letter from the Merseyside ministers inviting all who were willing to add their signature to the *Declaration* to do so with a view to publication in the *Baptist Times*.[155] On publication,[156] the five ministers claimed that a proportion of roughly 5:1 of those who replied were in support of their position.[157]

---

153 This last comment was directed to the Churches of Christ and sections of the Strict Baptists, according to the groups' letter to the editor, 'Baptists and Free Church Union', *BT* November 13, 1941, 555. It was during 1941 that discussions with the Churches of Christ began.

154 The text of the *Declaration* is to be found in Townsend, *Robert Wilson Black*, 113-14, and 'Baptists and Free Church Union', *BT* November 13, 1941, 555.

155 The letter is printed in Townsend, *Robert Wilson Black*, 111-12.

156 'Baptists and Free Church Union', *BT* November 13, 1941, 555. The text of the *Declaration* was printed on November 13, with a total of 125 minsters trained since 1918, 140 ministers trained before 1918, 4 College Principals, 5 College lecturers and 68 theological students, a total of 342 in all, excluding the 5 original signatories. Many had said they would sign a slightly modified form of the *Declaration*, while several had hesitated over the phrase 'the purity of the Church', on the grounds that it was no more evident among Baptists than anywhere else.

157 Townsend interpreted the *Declaration* as a means of countering the effects of the 1938 *Outline Scheme* and any FCFC attitudes or initiatives towards organic union. Black himself sent out over 800 copies of the *Declaration* and he received many letters back. The Merseyside Fraternal had provided him with yet another opportunity to win others to his convictions on Baptist principles. If ministers replied saying that they could not sign the *Declaration*, they received two or more letters from Black trying to persuade them to do so. Though disappointed with those who assented to 9 of the 10 points but refused to sign, he was well satisfied that so many had signed it. See Townsend, *Robert Wilson Black*, 114.

Needless to say the *Declaration* aroused great interest.[158] Though
many clearly supported the *Declaration*,[159] it was not without its opponents, some of which were due to its choice of language.[160] Sylvester
Peat accused the *Declaration* of seeking to erect artificial barriers which
would hinder the real work of relating 'our message and witness to the
urgent needs of our time.' Garwood Tydeman believed that a clause in
any United Free Church constitution which maintained believers' baptism
by immersion as the only baptism, but which allowed people into
membership on profession of faith would be sufficient to satisfy Baptist
convictions. G.D. Hooper wondered whether some were over-
emphasizing baptism, while Arthur Gabb requested that the sponsors of
the *Declaration* answer four questions: by refusing to accept any other
form of public declaration of faith in Christ, were they saying there was
no salvation except through baptism?; would reunion with other baptist
sects really be a forward move or would it allow theological and religious
views into the denomination which Baptists did not accept?; were open
membership churches to be treated as heretics?; and, were not real
Christians to be found within all sects and was it not the grace of God that
really mattered?[161]

---

158 See the letters columns of the *BT* for the immediately following weeks.

159 E.g. the 342 signatories to the Declaration; P.H. Crunden of Slough, 'Unity
With All Who Accept Baptist Principles', H. Edwards of Newport, 'Obedience and
Example', C.H. Stockdale, 'Fifty Years of Committees and Resolutions', *BT* December
25, 1941, 639.

160 E.g. the use of the word 'subverts' by the Merseyside ministers, 'An Old
Baptist', 'A Baptist Declaration', *BT* November 20, 1941, 564. The original section of
the *Declaration* read, 'It is evident to us that the practice of infant baptism not merely
obscures, but subverts the character of the Church as the fellowship of believers', in
Townsend, *Robert Wilson Black*, 113. In defence of the word, 'From the Authors of "A
Baptist Declaration"', *BT* December 25, 1941, 639, attention was drawn to the use of the
very same word in the 1926 *Reply to the Lambeth Appeal*, which was itself quoted in the
1937 *Report of the Special Committee* of the BU, and that the word 'subversive' had been
used by H.W. Robinson in his *Baptist Principles*. 'We therefore make no apology', the
five declared, 'for using a word which has been cited with approval by one of our leading
Baptist scholars and has twice appeared in documents presented to the Baptist Union
Assembly and confirmed thereby.'

161 See Mr S. Peat, President of the Leeds Baptist Council, 'The Need is Christians
Not Denominationalists', G.S. Tydeman of the Union Church, Godmanchester, 'The
Experience of a Union Church', Mr G.D. Hooper, Secretary of the Essex Association, 'Is
Baptism Over-Emphasised?', and A. Gabb of Kingsteignton, 'Important Questions', all
in *BT* December 25, 1941, 639. See also Mr S. Hardy, secretary of Seven Kings, Essex,
E.W. Price Evans of Pontypool, S.B. John of Salcombe and Mr A.H. Calder of St Albans
and Treasurer of the Baptist Historical Society, under the heading 'A Baptist Declaration',
BT December 4, 1941, 588 and 603, who expressed disapproval of the *Declaration* and
were for the unity movement.

There were, however, a third group of Baptists, committed to Baptist principles and practice, but at the same time open and actively involved in the ecumenical forum. One such was Sydney Morris, who, in his presidential address to the 1943 Baptist Assembly, reasserted the need for conviction regarding those truths which Baptists, as Protestants and Free Churchmen, held distinctively. He rejoiced in the increasing friendship between the various denominations, 'Yet', he warned, 'the cause of union is hindered rather than helped by any attempt to deny that on certain matters we are divided. Our duty as Baptists is to teach the things that we hold dear, and to teach them clearly, and positively... There is an urgent need for explicit, charitable, positive teaching on our distinctive ordinance.' However, these views did not lead him, and an increasing number of Baptists, into a narrow denominationalism, and it is possible that, in what he proceeded to say, he had Hugh Martin particularly in mind. 'In all that I have said concerning our distinctive testimony, there is need for us to exercise charity. There are those among us who feel that the font and the baptistery may be housed under one ecclesiastical roof, and who earnestly desire to hasten the day. It is not for us to question their loyalty to Baptist principles, or to deny their claim to the name we are proud of.' He concluded with two suggestions: first, that Baptists should draw more closely together. Not that they should sacrifice their cherished and valuable independency but foster and deepen interdependency. Second, that Baptists should unite with every other branch of the Christian Church—and failing this, with every other family of Protestant believers.[162]

In 1947, R.L. Child examined the subject of Baptist suspicions over church union from the point of view of their love of liberty, fear that union would lead to the sacrifice of principle and their lack of conviction that organic union was actually the mind of Christ.[163] But he did not leave matters there, for he went on to suggest how best Baptists could serve the cause of unity.[164] First, he proposed they continued involvement in the Anglican–Free Church conversations and joint worship and communion. Second, by attending to Baptist divisions. Third, by holding true to the doctrine of the church. 'Finally', he impressed, 'let us recognise that the real hindrance to Christian unity today lies, as always, not in the presence or absence of any outward organisation nor in the possession or otherwise of various types of ministry or sacraments. It lies

---

162 S.G. Morris, former General Superintendent of the Metropolitan Area and scretary of the LBA, 'The Church Faces the Future', *BT* May 6, 1943, 9.

163 It was later published as R.L. Child, *Baptists and Christian Unity* (1948), see 3-8.

164 He had already made the distinction between 'union' and 'unity', explaining that Baptists viewed the former with caution but whole-heartedly pursued the latter, Child, *Baptists and Christian Unity*, 7.

in the absence of any genuine desire among the followers of Jesus to draw closer to one another in mutual commitment and service.'[165]

In spite of opposition and personal attacks, Hugh Martin continued in his advocacy of the reunion cause.[166] As Moderator of the FCFC, he preached at St. Paul's and again pleaded for a closer co-ordination of the churches. Many Free Churchmen, he maintained, were agreed that episcopacy would be a valuable element in any united church, but they could not agree that any one form of church order was essential to the validity of the ministry and the sacraments. Mutual authorization for a wider ministry was quite another matter from the re-ordination of those

---

165 Child, *Baptists and Christian Unity*, 8-14, quotation from p.14. Child's pro-ecumenical position had become clear earlier, see his paper read to the FoR conference in May 1938, 'The Ministry and the Sacraments. A Free Church Point of View', *BQ* 9.3 (July, 1938), 132-38. Here Child rehearsed the ecclesiology common to the Free Churches of the fellowship of believers, and on ministry, he observed the practice of lay administration of the sacraments. Discussing baptism, he sought to provide a consensus of the Baptist view on the mode, the subjects and meaning of believers' baptism: as a personal testimony, an expression of the moral and spiritual union of the believer with Christ, also as an experience of the baptism of the Spirit, i.e., a means of grace, and its link with entrance into church membership. Child also discussed Baptist opposition to infant baptism as the latter 'is an unscriptural practice which veils the essentially personal nature of the issue between the soul and God', p.136. In July 1941, Child again addressed the issue of the reunion movement, 'Baptists and the Reunion Movement', *BQ* 10.7 (July, 1941), 393. He noted that many Baptists had been involved in the developments which had taken place since the missionary conference in Edinburgh 1910 and isolated four reasons which, he believed, accounted for the signal failure of the reunion movement so far: WWI, the defective character of the proposals, denominational caution and the lack of interest of the majority of Christians. Nevertheless, the widespread decay of denominationalism and the needs of the modern world, he contended, ruled out of court any idea that the denominations could hope to operate successfully in isolation, p.395. So what was to be done? If the path to corporate union was blocked, what other ways were there for realizing Christian unity? He advocated three, the first of which was self-education. Baptists needed to understand and better appreciate their history and principles. In particular, Child felt the need to further examine the Baptist doctrine of the church, something that was to be realized in 1948 and 'The Baptist Doctrine of the Church'. Both the sacrament of baptism and the place and authority of the church meeting were bound up with the fundamental idea of the church, and a fresh re-think of these 'would do us all good.' Second, Baptists should play their part in the creation of a common mind among Christians. This would involve learning more about each others' traditions, worshipping, studying and serving together. Third, there was the path of Free Church Federation, a prospect more real since the establishment of the FCFC, pp.396-9. This latter point claimed the support of E.R. Tribbeck, 'Baptists and Reunion', *BT* September 25, 1941, 468.

166 H. Martin, 'Baptists and the Great Church: or Independency and Catholicity', *BQ* 14.7 (July, 1952), 310-19, which is further discussed in Cross, 'Hugh Martin: Part 3', 141-43.

who were already ministers of the Word and sacraments. 'At this point', he concluded, 'sincere Christian men seeking unity have not yet been able to find agreement, but however baffled for the moment we must not give up trying.'[167]

Two years later in his presidential address to the Baptist Assembly, Principal Child observed that the focus of attention in recent years had been upon corporate reunion, while hardly any attention had been given to the path of federation. He suggested, therefore, that the Free Churches should seek to discover ways of translating the federal principle in the cause of Christian unity.[168] However, the occasional reference apart, the federal option has never again been seriously debated.

More significantly, Alec Gilmore set out the difficulty which a United Church would face if the two forms of baptism were to co-exist. In 1917, P.T. Forsyth had made such a suggestion, claiming that neither form would hold the monopoly,[169] however, Gilmore noted, that a difficulty would arise when a child's parents decided to baptize them in infancy, thereby robbing them of the privilege of believer's baptism should they later desire it. 'In other words, believer's baptism would only be a possibility for those whose spiritual welfare had been left uncared for at birth.' Thus an impasse would be reached. The only solution, he proposed, was for a fervent call to the full and complete adoption of believer's baptism as the church could produce. Recognizing the impossibility of this, he remarked that all the church could do was to pray that God would lead them to a fresh doctrine of baptism so as to cover both forms. 'The only way open at present seems to be that infants where one or both parents are Church members would alone be baptized at birth; the rest would await personal decision. But if this practice were not to lead to more difficulties than it solved, then the interpretation of the rite would have to be so simple as to be almost meaningless.' Indeed, there were already those who maintained that infant baptism was a very different rite from believer's baptism, and such would be even more the case if one doctrine were to embrace both methods. 'Either it would not be a sacrament at all or it would be something quite different from what we have had in the past.'[170]

---

167 H. Martin, 'Dr. Hugh Martin at St. Paul's', *BT* May 14, 1953, 5.

168 R.L. Child, 'The Church's Commission Today', *BT* May 6, 1954, 2.

169 P.T. Forsyth, *The Church and the Sacraments* (1917), 214-16.

170 A. Gilmore of Northampton, 'Some Recent Trends—II', *BQ* 15.8 (October, 1954), 345. R.F. Aldwinckle, Assistant Professor at McMaster University in Canada, 'Believer's Baptism and Confirmation', *BQ* 16.3 (July, 1955), 123-24, raised the possibility of whether Baptists could recognize the service of confirmation as an alternative and legitimate way of securing a fellowship of believers. Even though the promises made at an infant's baptism were made by proxies, did this really matter, for if, in the service of confirmation, those vows were to become the expression of personal

R.C. Walton recognized the present state of the church as divided on the matter of initiation and therefore focused his views upon the essence of believers' baptism as a profession of a real faith in Christ. Baptists, he contended, had no desire to unchurch anybody, so when approached by those from other traditions who wished to join in membership of a Baptist church, they should insist only that they should have fulfilled the conditions of membership in their own communion and that they should have made a profession of repentance towards God and faith in Christ. 'Thus, because Christendom is divided, we could accept as members those, who, baptised as infants, have, in Confirmation, expressed in another though less scriptural form, the essential requirement of personal acceptance and personal faith in Christ and His benefits which is sacramentally expressed in Believers' Baptism.'[171] There is little doubt that for most Baptists such a position was untenable. Whether baptized as an infant or sprinkled as an adult, baptism according to the New Testament was the immersion of believers. Thus to be immersed as a believer could not be considered in any way as rebaptism.[172]

After critically assessing the theology and practice of infant baptism, Neville Clark was unable to endorse Baptist practice, as here too, confusion reigned. 'The Baptist communion bids fair to become the only major branch of the Christian church where baptism is not of universal observance—a somewhat curious basis from which to attempt to justify a separate denominational existence.'[173] He illustrated this confusion by the separation of baptism and first communion and the rebaptism as believers of those baptized in infancy, a practice which, he judged, 'constitues a blow at the heart of the Christian faith. As there is one Lord, and one faith, so there is but one baptism.' To the very end, baptism had to remain true to its christological pattern, standing under the *ephapax*

---

faith, what more could be expected? 'Baptists would not wish to question the reality of faith in such a candidate whose Confirmation obviously expressed his personal repentance and faith.'

171 R.C. Walton, formerly minister at Victoria Road, Leicester, at the time General Secretary of the SCM in schools, *The Gathered Community* (1946), 166-67.

172 See, e.g., Channon, *Much Water*, 60-61. That this had been the traditional Baptist view was confirmed by a comment by A. Gilmore, *Baptism and Christian Unity* (1966), 77, 'For years Baptists have cheerfully baptized those who previously had been baptized in the Church of England or in one of the other Free Churches.' He then added, 'To call a halt to such a practice would surely lead to an impoverishment of the Baptist understanding of the sacrament.'

173 Clark does not make any reference to either the Society of Friends or the Salvation Army, neither of whom practice either of the sacraments. After working for the SCM, Clark became minister at Rochester then Amersham-on-the-Hill Free Church, then tutor and Principal at the South Wales Baptist College. The role of the SCM in forming the ecumenical convictions of the likes of H. Martin, Clark and R.C. Walton should not be underestimated.

of redemption: 'The whole meaning of the rite hinges on its once-for-allness, its unrepeatability.' The assertion of the partial nature of infant baptism and the serious theological distortion involved in it does not carry with it the 'unqualified dismissal of it as "no baptism"; rather does the eschatological nature of the rite forbid so negative a verdict.' No baptism, he argued, lacked the proleptic element, as every baptism pointed forward to its completion and fulfilment. Such an unqualified denial of infant baptism could only be theologically justified if Baptists were prepared to unchurch all paedobaptist communities and to view themselves as the only true church. 'Can we, in this day and age, follow our forefathers to so radical a conclusion.'[174]

The matter came into starker relief in the discussions during 1964 on church union in North India and Pakistan, when the Baptists demanded to 're-baptize', as it was claimed, those baptized in infancy.[175] Two years later, Child confirmed that infant baptism was regarded by the majority of Baptists as no baptism at all, so the rebaptism issue, as charged by Paedobaptists, was not an issue for most Baptists. But such a position was not likely to satisfy everybody. Baptists could not be content with this position, as in the eyes of others they *were* practising rebaptism. However, he continued, revealing the very real dilemma facing Baptists in the present ecumenical situation, should this position deter Baptists from doing what was in their eyes equally a matter of conscience, even if others regarded it as encouraging disloyalty to church orders. Child, in the end, provided no answer to the vexed question, though he recognized that the contemporary situation made the matter very real. No general answer was applicable because the matter was not an abstract one. A person's infant baptism could mean little or nothing, but if the new respect between churches meant anything at all, then it lay on all Christians the obligation to evaluate issues in a new light.[176] Such a position, George Beasley-Murray sought to provide, as White had attempted twenty one years earlier.

---

174 N. Clark, 'The Theology of Baptism', 325-26. A comment by Gilmore in his 1966 *Baptism and Christian Unity*, 14, shows that Clark's views received a mixed reception, in some quarters being hailed 'as the dawn of a new age; by others it has been mourned as the end of an old era.'

175 'Is Re-Baptism Possible? Canon Questions Baptists' Demand', *BT* October 15, 1964, 9. A more open attitude was held by E.L. Wenger of Norwich, a former missionary, 'Is Re-Baptism Possible?', *BT* October 29, 1964, 4.

176 R.L. Child, 'Should Baptists Re-Baptise?', *BT* November 10, 1966, 8. In stark contrast, according to W.J.H. Hitchcock of Surbiton, 'Re-Baptism', *BT* November 17, 1966, 4, what mattered was to do the Lord's will. Thus, Baptists dare not refuse believer's baptism to anyone who asked for it, for they had to obey God not people. Donald Bridge from Sunderland thanked Child for his timely article, but expressed surprise by the lack of subsequent comment, 'Re-Baptism', *BT* December 22, 1966, 4.

Addressing the Commission Conference on Doctrine at the eleventh BWA Congress in June 1965, Beasley-Murray opened with the important statement that, 'Generally speaking, Baptists do not by their rejection of infant baptism call into question the standing of their fellow Christians who have not received baptism as believers, nor do they desire in any way to impugn the character of churches that practice infant baptism.' Further, most Baptists outside the USA had no hesitation in recognizing other churches' baptism when applied to those who confessed their faith. He explained that the chief hesitancy for Baptists was over the administration of infant baptism by sprinkling or pouring instead of immersion.[177] Then, after discussing and criticizing, among others, the work of Karl Barth, F.J. Leenhardt and N.P. Williams, Beasley-Murray declared that the situation in the church was that, 'We have two baptisms, one for infants and the other for confessors of faith.' He continued, 'If it be asked wherein the unity of the church does lie, if not in one baptism, the answer, surely, must be: *in the common confession of that to which biblical baptism points*, namely, the redemption of God in Christ and participation in it through the Holy Spirit by faith.' Later, he developed this further: 'Accordingly, *the crucial point is not the mode of entry into the church but the fact that the church exists, and that people enter it and in Christ by the Holy Spirit participate in redemption, despite varying modes of initiation or none at all* (vide the Quakers).'[178] From this overview of the baptismal issue, Beasley-Murray offered his conclusion:

If the churches were to recognize the point I have labored to make, namely that two baptisms have developed in place of one, far-reaching reforms in baptismal thought and practice would almost certainly ensue, and the ecumenical situation would radically change. Indeed, I cannot think of any step that would more materially assist the renewal of the church than this one. It would change the Baptist relations with other churches, for the Baptist resistance to infant baptism lies precisely in the claim that infant baptism is the baptism of the Bible and that it possesses the significance of New Testament baptism. Naturally Baptists are aware that there are needs which infant baptism seeks to meet and which ought to be met by some means or other. Their own service of infant blessing or dedication has been instituted in recognition of this fact, and I have little doubt that other churches could improve on it.[179]

---

177 G.R. Beasley-Murray, 'Baptists and the Baptism of Other Churches', in J. Nordenhaug (ed.), *The Truth That Makes Men Free: Official Report of the Eleventh Congress, Baptist World Alliance, Miami Beach, Florida, U.S.A., June 25–30, 1965* (Nashville, 1966), 261-62.

178 Beasley-Murray, 'Baptists and the Baptism of Other Churches', 268, italics his.

179 Beasley-Murray, 'Baptists and the Baptism of Other Churches', 269. See also R.P. Martin, 'Baptismal Disgrace', *The Christian and Christianity Today*, July 22, 1966,

What, then, he asked, should the Baptist attitude be to baptisms administered in other churches? First, where baptism had been administered to a believer on profession of faith, unreserved recognition should be given to it, whatever the church or mode. Second, where someone had received infant baptism and been duly admitted into membership on profession of faith, whatever the rite of admission may have been, they should be welcomed into membership of a Baptist church in the same way as if they came from another Baptist church, namely by transfer, this being grounded on the reality of their membership in the church of Christ. Third, where infant baptism had not been followed by a subsequent confession of faith or church membership, they should be baptized and join the church as any other convert would from without or within their own ranks.[180] Beasley-Murray commenced his closing paragraph realistically enough, then issued the challenge: 'I appreciate that this exposition is unlikely to meet with the approval of all. It is clear, however, that an immense adjustment in the thought and practice of baptism is required in the churches.'[181]

Alec Gilmore's *Baptism and Christian Unity* appeared at the same time as Beasley-Murray's *Baptism Today and Tomorrow*. According to Gilmore, 'Baptism is clearly more than Baptists have traditionally understood by it', so the traditional Baptist tacit rejection of infant baptism did not merit serious discussion. In fact, both forms of baptism as presently practised 'are defective, and progress is possible only if we are prepared to acknowledge that we each have a rite called baptism and a responsibility to go forward in an attempt to understand it together.' This led to the inevitable conclusion, 'It is this recognition that requires us to refuse baptism to those who are baptized already on the grounds that baptism cannot take place twice.'[182] Though the problem of rebaptism was by no means a new one, 'the practical way in which it presents itself is quite modern.' The ecumenical movement had achieved drawing denominations closer together, and increased population mobility had made the matter particularly acute.[183] The problem came into sharper focus in four ways: on new housing estates; in older areas; in union churches; and in church union schemes like those in Ceylon and North India.[184] As both Baptists and Paedobaptists believed that baptism was only possible

---

11, 'The facts are that, side by side in uneasy relation to each other, two forms and understandings of baptism exist in the Church today.'

180 Beasley-Murray, 'Baptists and the Baptism of Other Churches', 270-71, and these points are elaborated on pp.271-72.

181 Beasley-Murray, 'Baptists and the Baptism of Other Churches', 272. Cf. also his *Baptism Today and Tomorrow*, 145-72.

182 Gilmore, *Baptism and Christian Unity*, 76-77.

183 Gilmore, *Baptism and Christian Unity*, 77-78.

184 Gilmore, *Baptism and Christian Unity*, 78-80.

once,[185] the issue was, in fact, whether the sprinkling of an infant constituted baptism.[186] This, Gilmore was prepared to concede: 'It is better to acknowledge that infant baptism, though partial in its expression of the truth and though involving serious theological distortion, is nevertheless baptism, and cannot therefore be followed by believers' baptism being administered to the same person.'[187] Two points should be noted from such a position. First, this was in effect no different from Baptists expecting episcopalians to acknowledge their ministry, and, second, Gilmore recognized the inconclusiveness of the arguments both for and against the two forms of baptism.[188]

Gilmore then drew attention to the fact that believers' baptism was not the only principle on which Baptists had taken their stand, for they stood also for religious freedom, arguing that it would be a pity if in their enthusiasm for one principle they lost sight of another. If Baptists were to recapture this spirit 'it means that so long as those who practise infant baptism are convinced that this is the will of God for them, Baptists ought not to question their conviction of its validity.' Mutual recognition, then, was the way forward, and though not entirely satisfactory it would be 'a common platform from which together we can discern the will of God.'[189] Implementation of such mutual recognition would require of Paedobaptists 'much careful thought' to the question of the candidate

---

185 Gilmore, *Baptism and Christian Unity*, 80-81. The unrepeatability of baptism was asserted by Channon, *Much Water*, 37; N. Clark, 'The Fulness of the Church of God', in Gilmore (ed.), *Pattern of the Church*, 95.

186 This most Baptists were still unwilling to accept. W.D. Jackson, General Superintendent of the Metropolitan Area, 'One Lord, One Faith, One Baptism', in A.T. Ohrn (ed.), *Baptist World Alliance Tenth Baptist World Congress, Rio de Janeiro, Brazil, June 26–July 3, 1960* (Nashville, 1961), 62, stated what must be considered as the general Baptist position under the heading, 'There is one Baptism': 'That was true when Paul wrote, but it is not true now. Other baptisms have been invented. Infants are baptized by sprinkling... To some, this sprinkling is only a pretty extra to infant dedication. Among Roman Catholics and Anglo-Catholics it is a magic ceremony in which (so it is alleged) a child is regenerated. But the baptism wherewith we were baptized is the baptism by immersion of believers in Christ.' His next paragraph continued: 'Which of these is the one baptism? Baptism belongs to the resurrection side of the gospel... The baptized are those who in Christ have passed from death to life. They declare that they themselves have committed their hearts to Christ as risen Saviour, and submitted their wills to Christ as exalted Lord. Their baptism is the baptism of believers by immersion in water, wherein they are buried with Christ and raised with Christ. It is the baptism of risen men, risen with Christ. This is the only baptism known in the New Testament. It is the one baptism. It alone is worthy to be set alongside one Lord and one faith.' A second account can be found in W.D. Jackson, 'One Lord, One Faith, One Baptism', *BT* June 30, 1960, 8.

187 Gilmore, *Baptism and Christian Unity*, 81.

188 Gilmore, *Baptism and Christian Unity*, 81-82.

189 Gilmore, *Baptism and Christian Unity*, 83-84.

for baptism, and to Baptists the encouragement of those who came to question their infant baptism to reaffirm their baptismal vows, but if this were not agreeable, then concessions would have to be made for freedom of individual conscience.[190]

In February 1966, K.C. Dykes wrote an article which looked forward to Easter Day 1980, the date proposed for church union by the Nottingham F&O Conference.[191] Dykes recognized that the baptismal issue was an obstacle to union, but then proposed, 'It goes without saying that infant baptism and believer's baptism will have to lie side by side in a united Free Church. This should not worry us for, to refer to Uzzah..., we need not tremble for the safety of the ark of believer's baptism.' He suggested that Baptists were presumably ready to consider infant baptism as practised by the Free Churches and when followed in the years of discretion by confession of faith as the equivalent of the Baptist's one rite of baptismal initiation. He recognized that such infant baptism could not carry such a rich symbolism as did believer's baptism, nor be as potent in conveying grace to the believer, but the two stages were essentially the same thing. He drew attention to the fact that in talking to Free Church brethren, Baptists were not up against sacramentarianism or any suggestion that infant baptism worked *ex opere operato*, rather, they were confronted by the declaratory view of baptism, the affirmation of God's prevenient grace which was ultimately little different from what was witnessed to in infant dedication. It was when baptism and regeneration were viewed as identical that to baptize as a believer somebody who had been baptized as an infant was anathema to many.

Responses were not long in coming. Geoffrey Whitfield disagreed that infant baptism followed by a later profession of faith was equivalent to Baptist baptism, and called for Free Churchmen to admit that infant baptism was an antiquated, unscriptural and irrelevant doctrine which

---

190 Gilmore, *Baptism and Christian Unity*, 84-89. Gilmore had anticipated some of the arguments he put forward in his book in an address to the Baptist Board on 'Some Problems of Believers Baptism', see 'Baptist Board Discusses Baptism', *BT* December 31, 1959, 6. He also raised the issues of open membership, the relation of baptism to first communion, and made the point that for some Baptists baptism had degenerated into a subjective ordinance.

191 K.C. Dykes, Joint Principal of Northern College with Dr David Russell after the amalgamation of the Manchester and Rawdon Colleges, '1980—The Next Step for Baptists? Should it be a United Free Church?', *BT* February 3, 1966, 9. This was followed in January 1965 by a Conference held at Swanwick on 'The Baptismal Life'. It had been conceived two years previously by the Council of 'Parish and People', and Baptists were represented on it by A. Gilmore, N. Clark and S.F. Winward. The results of this consultation was published by SCM, each of the Baptist representatives contributing short articles. See A. Gilmore, 'Baptism and Creation: Comment', 62-64; N. Clark, 'Baptism and Redemption', 71-75; S.F. Winward, 'Baptism, Confirmation and the Eucharist: A Comment', 123-27, all in B.S. Moss (ed.), *Crisis for Baptism* (1965).

should be discarded forever.[192] Stanley Shackleton voiced the fear of many that believer's baptism would be lost in a United Free Church. Drawing attention to the first Baptist Principle he stated that the heart of the gospel could not be compromised. A unity which demanded the surrender of the very beliefs that were fundamental would never work. Unity not uniformity was what was wanted. John Bennett argued that there were more differences between Baptists and Paedobaptists than just baptism, including the doctrine of the church. Even a diluted doctrine of infant baptism, he contended, when practised alongside believer's baptism would present a confusing contradiction. To do such would give tacit acceptance to the validity of tradition lying alongside scripture and church belief and practice, an implication that would be unacceptable to many Baptists.[193] George Stirrup was startled by Dykes' article, and asked why discussions were not being opened up with 'closer brethren', such as the Open Brethren, Pentecostals and F.I.E.C. churches.[194] Brian Wilson was less temperate. Infant baptism was an offence to the gospel, and this was shown by the fact that he himself and other Baptist ministers baptized those who had been baptized in infancy, thereby showing that infant baptism was no baptism at all.[195] Yet Dykes' plea for a United Free Church could be justified. Wilson asked, which was the greatest offence to the Gospel—infant baptism or disunity. The justification for a United Free Church lay in the gospel being more effectively preached.[196]

---

192 G. Whitfield of Brighton, 'United Free Church', *BT* February 17, 1966, 4.

193 'United Free Church', letters by S.W. Shackletone and J.W. Bennett, *BT* February 24, 1966, 4.

194 G. Stirrup of Wanstead Park, London, 'United Free Church', *BT* March 3, 1966, 4.

195 That this was common Baptist practice is reflected in Channon's, *Much Water*, 48, who remarked that he was prepared to baptize those who came to him while still attending a paedobaptist church, and that this did happen was confirmed by E.A. Payne, 'Baptism and Church Membership among Baptists', *Theology* 55 no.383 (May, 1952), 171. See also V.F. Moss of Loughborough, 'Loaning the Baptistery', *BT* October 7, 1954, 7, who remarked that it was not unusual for Christians to apply to Baptists for baptism without seeking membership within the Baptist fold, and within the exercise of this freedom Baptists were willing to consider any such candidates for baptism, this being a suggestion made to him by R.G. Fairbairn of Reading. See also W.D. Jackson, 'One Lord, One faith, One Baptism', 63; 'Not Baptists But Baptised', *BT* June 23, 1960, 16. Child, *Conversation*, 100, added that there were a growing number of ministers who disliked this expedient, Child, implicitly being one of them. D.S. Russell, 'The Ministry and the Sacraments', *BT* May 5, 1955, 2, condemned the baptizing of those who had no intention of becoming church members, stating, 'There are no such things as private sacraments.'

196 B.E. Wilson of Church, Lancashire, 'United Free Church', *BT* March 17, 1966, 4.

Alec Dunn agreed with much that Dykes had called for, but not that the two baptisms could live side by side, and that this was not just a practical matter but a matter of doctrine.[197] Others were more positive and supported Dykes' position. J.B. Taylor was in favour of Free Church union, but could not contemplate joining with the Church of England.[198] He suggested that in a United Free Church a Baptist minister could get a Paedobaptist from outside to administer infant baptism.[199] The two forms could exist side by side until a more widespread acceptance of believer's baptism came about. Taylor drew attention to the fact that there were already a number of Midland Baptist churches which had covenants recognizing both forms of baptism. Sadly he did not mention which ones. Stan Hardy believed that Baptists ought to begin conversations with Congregationalists and Presbyterians immediately.[200] However, the suggestion was not pursued, though it had been briefly discussed three years earlier, when Leslie Stringer drew attention to the similarities between Baptists and Congregationalists, asking why it was not possible to talk about closer relationships at home and abroad, supporting his case with his understanding that half the churches affiliated to the BU were open membership and therefore baptism was not really a barrier.[201] John Nicholson agreed, noting that the two denominations were one on all matters of faith and church order except baptism, and that the existence of many open membership Baptist churches and a few Union churches which already practised both infant and believers baptism showed that those differing on this issue could work and worship within one local church.[202] E.K. Breakspear, a Congregationalist who had transferred to an open membership Baptist church in Coventry, endorsed Stringer's letter, though recognized that many Baptists would have trouble with the baptismal issue.[203]

---

197 A.G. Dunn of Woodbridge, Suffolk, 'United Free Church', *BT* March 6, 1966, 4.

198 J.B. Taylor of West Bromwich, 'United Free Church', *BT* March 3, 1966, 4. H.H. Bryant of Cotham, Bristol, also expressed pleasure with Dykes' article, *BT* March 3, 1966, 4.

199 This was indeed to become the practice when Baptists became involved in LEPs, as it was already the general practice within Union churches.

200 Mr S. Hardy of Ilford, 'United Free Church', *BT* February 24, 1966, 4. It is worth noting that the previous year the Congregationalists and Presbyterians had published a joint document in which it was proposed that baptism would be administered either to adults on profession of faith or to the children of believing parents. When it was infant baptism, membership would be confirmed on public confession of faith, see 'Outline of a United Church', *BT* March 11, 1965, 1.

201 L.A. Stringer of Crouch Hill, 'Congregationalists and Baptists', *BT* February 28, 1963, 6.

202 J.F.V. Nicholson of Manchester, 'Congregationalists and Baptists', *BT* March 21, 1963, 6.

203 E.K. Breakspear, 'Congregationalists and Baptists', *BT* March 28, 1963, 6.

Ernest Payne offered the important observation that those appointed to the BWA Commission on the Doctine of Baptism set up in 1950 to prepare the address on 'Baptism in Present-Day Theology' had not been able to agree upon even a brief statement as to the theology of baptism.[204] What was true of the BWA was equally true of churches and members within the BU.

All this had implications for the whole discussion of intercommunion. Donald Hudson raised the question of what significance infant baptism should have for Baptists, noting the usual answer that it was invalid and no baptism at all. However, it was necessary to take account of the baptism, and not just the faith, of other Christians. Two alternatives were possible for Baptists. First, the strict view, that infant baptism was no baptism and therefore only those baptized as believers were entitled to commune. The merit of this was consistency. Second was the broad view that infant baptism administered by other communions was undeniably Christian baptism and entitled those so baptized to come to the table. Most, he remarked, would probably wish to take up a position somewhere between the two. What puzzled Hudson, however, was how such a position could be theologically possible without denying that sacraments are essential to the church, that they are related to each other, the denial of which being a denial of New Testament teaching. Was the broad view possible, then? Hudson argued that it was when infant baptism was seen to have some validity (but not complete validity) as a witness to the prevenience of grace, and with confirmation as recognizing the importance of the individual's faith. As administered by the church it was undeniably a Christian sacrament, though Baptists could not accept it as in accord with the mind of Christ concerning his ordinance. If Baptists could take this line then the difficulty of intercommunion disappeared. If they could not, then how could they reconcile their advocacy of intercommunion with the denial of all validity to the baptism of those with whom they wished to communicate?[205]

Paul Ballard took up Hudson's point, agreeing with Neville Clark in his contribution to *Christian Baptism*,[206] that Baptists could not lay exclusive claim to truth. Baptists, he noted, criticized infant baptism on its departure from the New Testament, its theological emphasis and seeming indiscriminate use. However, he sought to draw attention to the important fact that the church had been broken and therefore every section had been disfigured and needed insights from others. Baptists had insights to

204 E.A. Payne, 'Believers' Baptism in Ecumenical Discussion', *Foundations* (January, 1960), 36.

205 Dr W.D. Hudson, lecturer in Philosophy at Exeter University, 'Inter-Communion and Infant Baptism. Can we have one without recognising the other?', *BT* January 1, 1960, 10.

206 N. Clark, 'The Theology of Baptism', 326.

press, but also much to learn from others. Baptist baptism was also partial, so 'in our divided state we must be gracious enough to accept all Christian baptism while still pressing our claims.'[207]

A week later, William Powell suggested that in a united church anyone baptized in infancy but wishing to express belief by deliberate acceptance of baptism should have their desire granted, and in so doing dissented from the views expressed by Hudson and Ballard. Validity, he declared, hardly seemed a valid conception to use. How could infant baptism have some validity but not complete validity. Surely, it was either valid or invalid?[208]

In March, 1963, Dr Champion reported on the Anglican–Methodist report on reunion. He contended that this new situation would make the distinctive Baptist emphases even more significant and needed, asking when it would be that Baptists would submit themselves to the same searching experience of such conversations with other churches. The evangelical interpretation of the Christian faith and its truth implied believers baptism as the only genuine Christian baptism. How could this evangelical interpretation ever be reconciled with Catholic interpretation? 'We dare not compromise about truth! Not even for the sake of unity! Yet is there a unity, not yet discussed, which will properly comprehend what is true in both interpretations? Until it is found we must remain in this tension of loyalty to the truth and longing for the oneness of all Christians.'[209] In August, reporting on the recent F&O Conference, Champion again reiterated his call that Baptists should be sharing more in the process than they were.[210]

J.E. Ennals advocated the possibility of Baptist churches adopting different modes for baptism, dependent on the wishes of the candidate so as not to cause an unnecessary obstacle to their being baptized, and that this would also aid progress towards Christian unity, 'if we could be known to stand for the great evangelical principle of faith as the basis of

---

207 P.H. Ballard, at the time working for SCM, 'Recognising Infant Baptism', *BT* January 21, 1960, 6.

208 W. Powell of Weston Favell, Northampton, 'Baptism and Church Membership', *BT* January 28, 1960, 6.

209 L.G. Champion, 'Anglican–Methodist Report "Raises Unity Problems for Other Churches"', *BT* March 7, 1963, 9. E.A. Payne noted that schemes of reunion often involved dangerous ambiguities and compromises and that Baptists found these unacceptable, see 'The Baptists', in R.J.W. Bevan (ed.), *The Churches and Christian Unity* (1963), 142. In November, E. Roberts, 'Baptism', *BT* November 28, 1963, 16, reported R.E.O. White's address, 'Baptism and the Responsibilities Involved', in which he analysed four areas of responsibility: responsibility to the truth itself; to the candidate; to the church; and to our fellow churches.

210 L.G. Champion, 'Dr. Champion Sums Up the Faith and Order Conference', *BT* August 8, 1963, 7.

all Christian experience, while leaving the actual method of expressing that faith in baptism to the conscience of the individual.' This, he believed, would involve no sacrifice of principle, but though no response was forthcoming, there can be little to doubt that this eccentric view would have received little to no support.[211] Ennals was yet another Baptist writer who failed to note that the divergence on the baptismal issue was not so much over the method or subject of baptism but over its meaning, and that though a change in mode might superficially appear to break down barriers, nevertheless it was the different theologies of believers' and infant baptism which kept Baptist and Paedobaptist communions poles apart.

Union Churches

From 1938–1966 there appears to have been little or no increase in the number of Union churches, and very little was written about them, though there were two periods of some debate carried on through the pages of the *Baptist Times*.

In 1946 'Enquirer' raised a number of issues concerning the running of Union churches. Did a Baptist minister have to practise both infant dedication and christening? Further, what were the conditions of membership in such a church, was it necessary for Trust Deeds to be altered when such a union took place, were there any examples of ministers belonging to two separate churches, Baptist and Congregational, and, if so, how did they operate and were such ministers recognized by the BU?[212]

A reply was published the following week from Keith Preston, the minister of Wells United Church. He explained the situation there was that the minister was alternately Baptist then Congregationalist. When under a Baptist minister all christenings were performed by a neighbouring Congregational minister who would exchange services with the Baptist. On membership, he explained that, 'The essential conditions of membership are confession of faith in Jesus Christ as our Lord and Saviour: a resolution to live day by day in all the engagements of life according to His spirit and teaching; and a willingness to uphold the honour, discipline, work and worship of this Church by the consecration of individual gifts of time, talent and means.' In his opinion, involvement

---

211 J.E. Ennals, 'Our Baptist Witness: Baptism in Practice', *BQ* 20.4 (October, 1963), 183-86, quotation from p.184. Ennals had gone out to South Africa early in his ministry, see H.J. Betts, *The Story of 100 Years, 1820–1920 being the History of the Baptist Church in South Africa* (Cape Town, n.d., c.1920), *passim*.

212 'Enquirer', 'The Baptist Minister in a Union Church', *BT* September 26, 1946, 8.

in Union churches was 'possible for Baptists without the sacrifice of any essential principle of their faith.'[213]

Edwin Newton wrote of his eight and a half years experience in Louth Union Church, Lincolnshire, which had been formed twenty seven years previously. There infants were dedicated and christened, in the latter instance another Free Church minister was brought in to conduct the service. The condition for membership was the same as an open membership Baptist church, receiving applicants on profession of faith, though the Baptist minister would ask them to consider baptism. Newton added that as a 'convinced Baptist' he had remained such and met 'no serious difficulty.'[214]

Union Churces were again the focus of discussion in 1959, when G.S. McKelvie described his ministry in the Baptist and Congregational Loughton Union Church, which also included Presbyterians, Methodists and Anglicans, all of whom were represented on the diaconate. While all monies were divided between Baptist and Congregational funds, the minister was always a Baptist who was only required to baptize believers, a local Congregational or Methodist minister being brought in for infant baptisms, and he noted that often infant dedication was preferred by non-Baptist parents. McKelvie's purpose in writing was to encourage work towards Free Church Union, in which he maintained the Baptist witness would not be swamped, as, he believed, his personal experience demonstrated. As there were a large number of Baptist ministers in training, something which was not the case in other denominations, there would be a great number of Baptist ministers in a United Church and it would be

---

213 K.M. Preston, 'The Baptist Minister in a Union Church', *BT* October 3, 1946, 8. In reply to Enquirer's other question he explained that the church was in membership with the BU and CU, the Bristol Baptist Association and the Somerset CU, receiving a small grant from central funds by which both Unions supported the ministry irrespective of their denomination, and the church contributed equally to the BMS and London Missionary Society. In Wells the old Congregational chapel had been sold and they worshipped in the Baptist chapel, therefore there was a baptistry, a Congregational school room having been added to the premises. Regarding the buildings, the Bristol Association and the Somerset Union remained the trustees of the respective properties, and Preston added that the necessity for any alteration of the Trust Deed surely depended upon its wording when such a union took place. As for the minister, they had to be accredited by their own denomination. He added that the church was a happy one and that, without such an amalgamation, it was probable that both causes would have died or been too small to support their own ministers or contributed effectively to the religious life of the city. In his opinion, such amalgamation was undesirable in larger places, but in smaller centres of population it 'promotes the extension of the Kingdom of God...'

214 E.H. Newton, 'The Baptist Minister in a Union Church', *BT* October 17, 1946, 8. He further commented that a Union Church was a very happy arrangement both economically and spiritually for utilizing the resources of smaller communities.

the duty of every sincere minister to put the claims of believer's baptism to every membership class.[215]

The experiences of others involved in Union churches, however, were mixed. In early February, 'L' and his wife spoke of how a few months previously they had joined Hutton (and Shenfield) Union Church after many years in membership in a Baptist church. Such had been their experience that they called for the BU and County Associations to come forward with positive policies for the establishment of more Union Churches.[216]

This called forth a response from 'Baptist Principles', who claimed on behalf of those like him/her to be deeply concerned about such Union churches as Hutton (and Shenfield) lest Baptist principles and practices should be lost sight of.[217] Such sentiments were also shared by 'Experienced' who was involved in an undisclosed Union Church, who reported that believer's baptism outside of families of confirmed and ardent Baptists were very rare, and that there was no proselytizing for fear of giving offence. In thirteen years only two believers' baptisms had taken place.[218] 'Inexperienced' replied arguing that 'Experienced' had no monopoly of experience regarding Union churches. As the assistant minister and minister-in-charge of an associated daughter church, his experience of thirteen years was completely different. He had found no difficulties in asserting believer's baptism in that it was a dramatic portrayal, a preaching sacrament. As both modes of baptism existed alongside each other in the church universal, he argued, why could such not obtain in a local church?[219] Later, Aubrey Moore voiced his disapproval of Inexperienced's acceptance of two modes of baptism side by side.[220]

---

215 G.S. McKelvie, 'How Do Baptists Stand in the Matter of Free Church Union', *BT* January 22, 1959, 10. Among the reasons for such unity, McKelvie included the number of struggling causes and the scarcity of ministers. McKelvie went to Blenheim, Luton, in 1959 after 9 years at Loughton. On the church in Loughton see V. Lewis, *Come With Us: Loughton Union Church, 1813–1973* (Loughton, 1974); J. Lawrence, *Churches Working Together in Loughton, 1944 to 1994* (Loughton, n.d., [1994]), on how the Loughton Union Church has related to the other churches in the town and particularly to the preparation of a local covenant for the Churches in Loughton (1985, see p.9 and Appendix IV), the Loughton Council of Churches (1988, see Appendix V) and the formation of Churches Together in Loughton (1994).

216 'L', 'Church Union', *BT* February 5, 1959, 6. In the same column, 'E.M.' reported a Presbyterian church which had been served by a Baptist minister for 25 years and who had not been required to baptize infants.

217 'Baptist Principles', 'Union Churches', *BT* February 12, 1959, 6.

218 'Experienced', 'Union Churches', *BT* February 26, 1959, 6.

219 'Inexperienced', 'Union Churches', *BT* March 12, 1959, 6.

220 J.A. Moore of Hindhead, Surrey, 'Union Churches', *BT* March 26, 1959, 6.

Others, however, continued to speak positively. While at Pinner United Free Church from 1947–56, Douglas Stewart had baptized sixty six people, over half of whom had been from non-Baptist families, and he claimed that in Union churches many adopted the Baptist position.[221] This was followed by B. Ince-Jones, then of Brentwood, but previously a member and ex-secretary of Hutton (and Shenfield) Union Church for over 30 years. Over the last eight years, he reported, there had been nine baptisms by immersion, including some from non-Baptist traditions. Though Baptists made up less than a quarter of the membership, Home Work Funds and missionary collections were divided equally. Under the last Baptist pastorate all applicants for membership had been given full opportunity to make their profession by baptism.[222]

'Experienced' rejoined the debate asking what happened when a Union Church had five years of a minister teaching believer's baptism only to be followed by a minister teaching infant baptism?[223] No reply was forthcoming, and the whole issue closed with a brief letter from the Secretary of a Union Church with a Baptist minister, who had been a member for sixty years, who simply wrote that the Baptist minister was not fettered in his testimony to believer's baptism, and believed that such churches were needed especially in smaller centres.[224]

The period closed with a short discussion of Union churches by Alec Gilmore. Here, he noted that provision was generally made for both forms of baptism and there would be a large baptistry for immersion and a font for christening, though the above correspondence shows that this was not always the case. Links with the headquarters of both denominations and both missionary societies were preserved and the ministry would be open to recognized ministers of either Union and these would frequently be alternated,[225] during which 'inevitably the emphasis tends to have swung to and fro according to the particular allegiance of either the minister or the leading officers. At some periods of the church's history believers' baptism has been preached and practised, at other periods the baptism of infants; and in some cases the result has been that no real attention has been given to baptism at all.'[226]

The main problem, according to Gilmore, arose for those who were born into one situation and grew up in another. For instance, a child might have been christenend under a Congregationalist's ministry, but

---

221 D. Stewart, 'Union Churches', *BT* March 5, 1959, 6.

222 B. Ince-Jones, 'Union Churches', *BT* March 19, 1959, 6.

223 'Experienced', 'Union Churches', *BT* March 26, 1959, 6.

224 'The Secretary', 'Union Churches', *BT* April 23, 1959, 6.

225 Again, the above discussion and that for the period 1900–1937, shows that this was also not always the case in practice, e.g., at Pill Union church, where the minister has always been a Baptist, though this was not the intention.

226 Gilmore, *Baptism and Christian Unity*, 79-80.

when a teenager under a Baptist's ministry had become converted along with youths of formerly Baptist parents who were not present for infant baptism. 'Is the Baptist minister right to baptize them all in the same way? Should he encourage the one who has been baptized already to be baptized again? Or, even if such a person wants to be baptized like the others, should the minister endeavour to dissuade him on the grounds that it would be wrong to do so?'[227] Gilmore's eventual answer acknowledged the complexity of such matters. For him, concessions had to be made to the freedom of individual conscience, and, from the Baptist side, some attempt needed to be made to overcome such situations and a possible way forward could be through a service of the reaffirmation of baptismal vows, which could also be used for the return of a lapsed baptized believer.[228] This he proposed in the light of his belief that there was room 'in the providence of God for both forms of baptism to co-exist, and might not this inconclusiveness be one means by which God is seeking to lead His Church into something richer than our forefathers ever dreamed of?'[229]

---

227 Gilmore, *Baptism and Christian Unity*, 80.

228 Gilmore, *Baptism and Christian Unity*, 87-89.

229 Gilmore, *Baptism and Christian Unity*, 83. Similarly, on p.82 he wrote, 'If, in the interests of the unity of the Church, it is felt that the episcopalian should accept the Baptist ministry, even though he believes that it has not got all that the true ministry requires, then by the same argument the Baptist must be ready to accept infant baptism even though he believes it has not got all that true baptism requires.' This reflects development in Gilmore's thinking, for 13 years earlier, 'Some Recent Trends—II', *BQ* 15.8 (October, 1954), 338-45, he had been more cautious, pointing out the problems of practising two forms of baptism, and, as rebaptism was not possible, he had called for 'as full and complete adoption of believer's baptism as the Church can produce.' Prior to this, there seems to have been only one solitary voice calling for the acknowledgement of some validity to infant baptism, as opposed to a few others who called for the mutual recognition of the rite. Shakespeare, *Cross-Roads*, 55-56, outlined three beliefs common to the Free Churches. First, that the church was composed of the born again and was not co-extensive with the State; second, that the internal life of the church was a spiritual fellowship, totally different from any secular relation of parishioners; and third, that the church's authority was vested under Christ himself as opposed to any clerical or sacerdotal hierarchy. These three positions represented the common ground, though each Free Church gave a different emphasis, was free to vary its form of government, and to 'witness to the common truth by a form of baptism.' Thus while the confining of the church to believers, the separation of church and state, and the spiritual relationship that bound member to member under the authority of Christ were essential marks of the church, forms of baptism could reflect legitimate diversity.

CHAPTER SIX

The Baptist Response

With the rise of the modern debate on baptism it was not long before Baptists realized that their preoccupation with the mode and subjects of baptism and dated arguments were inadequate to face the new demands of the wealth of scholarly studies on baptism, supplemented by important reports from some of the major denominations, notably the Church of England, Church of Scotland and Methodists. In response, calls quickly began to be made that Baptists should again re-examine all aspects of their own theology and practice of baptism.

In his review of the H.G. Marsh's book, *The Origin and Significance of the New Testament Baptism*, Ernest Payne lamented, 'It is surprising, and not to our credit, that Baptists have left to a Methodist the writing of a thoroughly competent modern study of the origins of the New Testament rite from which they get their name. In other generations we could boast exhaustive and scholarly examinations of the origin and significance of Christian baptism, but we have unfortunately produced little of recent years worthy to set beside this modest but most useful volume.'[1] In this, Payne was not alone. In 1938, Thomas Philpot had called for 'intensive and systematic instruction...on the principles and practices of the Baptists', and had highlighted the ordinance of baptism as a specific area in need of such treatment.[2]

Such wishes began to see fulfilment when, in September 1943, a modest collection of sermons from some of the leading Baptist preachers was published under the title *Concerning Believers Baptism*. Though in certain places clear differences of opinion between the contributers were evident, nevertheless their agreements were believed to be 'deep and fundamental.'[3] Intended primarily for ministers and others with special responsibilities for baptism, the book was the first of a considerable number of books in this period which dealt both directly and indirectly

---

1   E.A. Payne, 'Baptism in the New Testament', *BT* May 1, 1941, 215. See H.G. Marsh, *The Origin and Significance of the New Testament Baptism* (Manchester, 1941).

2   T. Philpot, a retired minister from South Woodford, London, 'Baptist Teaching', *BT* March 3, 1938, 171.

3   'Preface', in Bryan (ed.), *Concerning Believers Baptism*, 5.

with baptism, and part of the *raison d'être* for the book no doubt lay behind the comment in the preface that 'There are wanting signs to-day, in some of our churches, that baptism is in danger of falling into desuetude. We have endeavoured, therefore, in these sermons to show how integrally it is related to those things that are characteristic of our witness, viz., the necessity for the response of personal faith to God's grace mediated in Christ, the character of the Church as a fellowship of believing people, the evangelical presentation of the Gospel as grounded in the Cross and Resurrection, the liberty and responsibility of the Christian man in respect of his religious acts and decisions, and so forth.' Though the authors held different views on reunion, all agreed that no incorporation in a larger body would be possible for Baptists which did not leave them free to maintain their witness to believers' baptism.[4]

The following month Luther Walker asked whether it was not time that Baptists 'spoke out plainly once again about the evil attending the prevailing notions of infant baptism?' as 'the superstition that surrounds the rite is appalling.'[5] This was shortly followed by the observation from Percy Evans that more was needed from those advancing the cause of reunion than side-lining the issue of baptism, either in the hope that it would not greatly matter, or that it could be solved as discussion proceeded, or that opposed views could be ecclesiastically synthesized. 'Controversy', he noted, 'may have been declined less out of brotherly love than through timidity, as if Christian men could not be trusted to express their honest disagreement without quarrelling. Thereby we neither serve truth, foster charity nor promote unity.' To this end, Evans set out to reconsider whether infant baptism could be justified, with the words of P.T. Forsyth in mind, 'It is strong Churches that make real union, Churches that believe in themselves and look also on the things of others.' Evans' intention was to preserve just such a spirit.[6]

In March 1944, a special meeting of the BU Council was set aside to consider the spiritual welfare of the denomination. A group of Council members were appointed whose brief was to examine the situation. In the

---

4   'Preface', in Bryan (ed.), *Concerning Believers Baptism*, 6. The book was warmly received by H.V. Larcombe, *'Concerning Believers' Baptism'*, *BT* September 23, 1943, 2. J.B. Middlebrook, Home Secretary of the BMS, similarly declared that any scheme of reunion which did not permit the maintenance of believers' baptism would 'never win [Baptist] interest or attachment', see his 'Baptism as Entrance into the Church and its Relation to the Lord's Supper', in Bryan (ed.), *Concerning Believers Baptism*, 56.

5   Mr L. Walker of Flitwick, 'Infant Baptism', *BT* October 14, 1943, 6.

6   P.W. Evans, 'Can Infant Baptism Be Justified?', *EvQ* 15 (1943), 292, quoting Forsyth, *Church and the Sacraments*, 139. See the earlier companion article by D.M. Baillie, 'The Justification of Infant Baptism', *EvQ* 15 (1943), 21-31, and the review 'Principal Evans on Infant Baptism', *BT* November 25, 1943, 7.

resulting *Speak—That They Go Forward*, Henry Cook declared that 'New Testament Baptism is a vital part of the Gospel, and we should make more of it.' This meant more than simply refusing to baptize infants, for Baptists needed to expound their doctrine of baptism in relation to the whole life and purpose of the church.[7]

This need for more Baptist teaching on baptism was again expressed by Tait Patterson, the Baptist liturgist. After reading *Concerning Believers Baptism* 'with great pleasure', he remarked, 'surely this slender volume is not our last word on baptism to this generation.' Earlier in the war, Patterson explained, he had taught the doctrine of the Lord's Supper and baptism to a class of missionary students as an emergency locum. For this he had undertaken an examination of the literature on the subject and reported his astonishment 'at the poverty of the literature; much of it was neither good exposition nor good apologetic, and there was a real lack of understanding when it came to the historical background!' Baptism, he insisted, was entitled to have a prominent place in Baptist contributions to Christian doctrine. 'We need a thorough examination of the doctrine by one of our New Testament scholars.' He offered his opinion that Wheeler Robinson's *Baptist Principles* was the best book of his own generation, but was limited in its historical outlook. 'It is strange that a Church that boasts, quite rightly, of its New Testament origins has failed in these latter days to produce an outstanding New Testament scholar.'[8]

At this time another contribution to the better understanding of Baptist principles appeared. Dr Arthur Dakin's *The Baptist View of the Church and Ministry*[9] had been intended to be published on behalf of the College Principals, though not necessarily endorsed by them, and the preface was supplied by M.E. Aubrey.[10] However, a proof copy had fallen into the possession of Ernest Payne, Senior Tutor at Regents' Park College, who read it with growing dismay, believing it to be an incomplete presentation

---

7   H. Cook, *Speak—That They Go Forward: A Report on the Spiritual Welfare in Churches of the Baptist Denomination* (1946), 13. Extracts of this report are reprinted in McBeth, *Sourcebook*, 390-94.

8   D.T. Patterson of Droitwich, 'Concerning Believers' Baptism', *BT* April 13, 1944, 6.

9   A. Dakin, Principal of Bristol Baptist College, *The Baptist View of the Church and Ministry* (1944). There were two reviews of this: A.C. Underwood, 'The Baptist View of the Church and the Ministry', *BT* May 4, 1944, 10; L.G. Champion, minister in Rugby, '*The Baptist View of the Church and Ministry*, by A. Dakin', *BQ* 11.8-9 (January–July, 1944), 241-45. Both reviews displayed an appreciation to Dr Dakin, but also a dis-ease with it. On Dakin, see W.W. Bottoms, 'Herald of God. An appreciation of Dr. A. Dakin', in L.G. Champion (ed.), *The Communication of the Christian Faith* (Bristol, 1964), vii-xiv; and L.G. Champion, 'Arthur Dakin (1884–1969)', *Frat.* 155 (January, 1970), 5-8.

10   See Aubrey's 'Note by the General Secretary of the Baptist Union', Dakin, *Church and Ministry*, 4.

of the Baptist tradition on both the church and the ministry. As far as he was concerned, Dakin failed adequately to recognize the fact that many contemporary Baptist practices and difficulties were the result of nineteenth-century individualism and reaction to the Oxford movement.[11] He felt that Dakin's account of things needed to be challenged, and so, under considerable pressure of time and, it would appear, emotion, Payne wrote a reply. He showed a proof to both J.O. Barrett and Wheeler Robinson, the latter providing him with a cover letter to send to Aubrey. The suggestion was that Payne's work should be published as soon as possible and should have as much or as little backing from the BU as Dakin's book was to have. Only so could it be made clear that the Baptist tradition was more varied and complex than Dakin's work suggested. Though the manuscipt never saw the light of day, it appears that Payne had, at least to some extent, the sympathy of Aubrey, but there was no way that such a controversial attack on Dakin, who was to be nominated as Vice-President of the BU in 1944, was going to be printed. However, the Kingsgate Press did agree to accept a book on a similar subject, provided there was no obvious attack on Dakin's views. With a title suggested by Percy Evans, Payne, that same year, published his *The Fellowship of Believers*, a far more detailed study of Baptist principles than Dakin's slimmer volume.[12] Here, Payne confirmed that

---

11   In this Payne was not alone, for many others recognized that the Baptist doctrine of baptism was impoverished by modern individualism/subjectivism. See S.F. Winward, 'Towards A Doctrine of the Church. II', *Frat.* 55 (September, 1944), 3-4, who referred to 'three centuries of individualism' which had weakened Protestantism, people believing that religion was a matter between the individual and God, and that 'This distortion appears in much of our preaching and literature, and makes impossible a true doctrine of the Church.' Later he made this explicit in relation to baptism in which 'we are baptized into Christ Jesus and into the one Body'; Walton, *Gathered Community*, 127, and p.161 where he opposed the individualism which was characteristic of so many Baptists and exemplified in Dakin's *Church and Ministry*, 34, who had written, 'It should be noticed...that while [baptism] takes place in the fellowship, the blessing is conceived as being to each member separately. That is to say, Christ is thought of in the ordinances as related not primarily to the Church as a body, but first to each believing individual, and so to the church.' See also T.G. Dunning, 'A Baptist Oxford Movement', *BQ* 11.14-15 (July–October, 1945), 413; R.L. Child, *Baptists and Christian Unity* (1948), 13.

12   E.A. Payne, *The Fellowship of Believers: Baptist Thought and Practice Yesterday and Today* (1944). This outline of the episode is taken from West, *To Be A Pilgrim*, 60-61. As well as West's biography of Payne, see 'In Honour of Ernest A. Payne: Christian Scholar, Administrator and Statesman', *BQ* 22.3 (July, 1967), and also the whole issue of the *Frat.* 145 (July, 1967). It is interesting to note that Payne was nominated late in 1943 for the vice-presidency of the BU, but declined when he heard that Dr Dakin was also nominated. Of interest is A.C. Underwood's discussion of Dakin's *Church and Ministry* and Payne's *Fellowship of Believers*, 'Whither?', *BT* May 24,

the most distinctive feature of the Baptists was their doctrine of the church, from which he proceeded to claim that precisely because of this, Baptists were likely to have an important contribution to make to the modern ecumenical debate.[13]

Still calls were being made for a book on baptism, or at least the Baptist position on the rite and related doctrines,[14] and they were in part answered by the publication on behalf of a group of Baptists of *The Gathered Community* (1946) by Robert C. Walton,[15] the revised edition of Robinson's *Life and Faith of the Baptists* (1946),[16] the third edition of Henry Cook's *The Why of Our Faith* (1947) and, the same year, the first edition of his *What Baptists Stand For* (1947). Though the latter two books did not deal with the ecumenical issues of the time, Walton's book, which focused primarily upon the doctrine of the church, recognized that the attempt to rediscover the true significance of the church would inevitably lead each denomination to emphasize afresh its own insights. Baptists, then, would render no small service to the 'One Catholic Church' if it minimized the contribution which God had given them to

---

1945, 7. He wrote, 'Some [Baptists] see in believers' baptism a mere symbol [Dakin]; others find in it a genuine means of grace.'

13   Payne, *Fellowship of Believers*, 11.

14   G.H. Davies, tutor at Bristol Baptist College, 'His Baptism and Ours', *BT* June 6, 1946, 8, called on the Kingsgate Press or the Carey Press or a united Baptist Press to commission men like S.I. Buse, whose earlier article Davies was commending (see S.I. Buse, 'His Baptism and Ours', *BT* May 23, 1946, 6), to state the doctrine of baptism and so 'lift His baptism and ours into the context of His Incarnation and our redemption where they rightly belong.' What influence Davies' article had in the eventual publication of *Christian Baptism*, can only be speculated upon, but it is worthy of mention that Buse was among the contributors. Also S.A. Gray of Gloucester suggested that the Kingsgate Press produce a symposium under the title 'As Others See Us', see 'Helping Our Baptist Apologetic', *BT* February 6, 1947, 9. On G.H. Davies, see J.I. Durham, 'Gwynne Henton Davies. A Biographical Appreciation', in J.I. Durham and J.R. Porter (eds.), *Proclamation and Presence: Old Testament Essays in Honour of Gwynne Henton Davies* (1970), xiii-xvii.

15   The members of the group which initiated this book were W.W. Bottoms of New Road, Oxford, F.E. Hemmens of Melksham, N.S. Moon of Small Heath, Birmingham, Walton himself, S.F. Winward of Higham's Park, Walthamstow, Emlyn Davies, a tutor at South Wales Baptist College, Gwenyth Hubble, Principal of Carey Hall from 1946–60, Marjorie Reeves, later an historian and Oxford Don, W.H. Weston of Earl Shilton and Thurlaston, Leicester, E. Ford of Clarence Road, Southend-on-Sea, L. Moon of Elland, Yorkshire, D. Stewart from Heath Street, Hampstead, and Mr Alex Wilson, see Walton, *Gathered Community*, 10.

16   Reviewed by A. C. Underwood, *BT* May 22, 1947, 7; G.W. Hughes of Kingston-on-Thames, in his review, '*Life and Faith of the Baptists*, by H. Wheeler Robinson', *BQ* 12.6-7 (April–July, 1947), 228-29, who, p.228, welcomed the reappearance of Robinson's book, which, he suggested, relieved in some measure 'the present famine of literature dealing with the principles and history of the Baptists in this country...'

make to Christianity as a whole. 'Indeed', he continued, 'our best contribution is to rethink our doctrine of the Church, the Ministry and the Sacraments.' To this end, therefore, it would be to the enrichment and not the impoverishment of the universal church for Baptists to share with other Christians in the ecumenical movement.[17]

In what was to prove to be his most influential and long-lasting contribution to Baptist thought, Henry Cook argued that the Baptist contribution to 'the New Day' (that is, the post War world) was their direct appeal to the New Testament and their bold declaration of their conception of the church.[18] He defended the notion of unity as opposed to uniformity,[19] and in his discussion of reunion insisted that not all differences were really unimportant, stating that 'Baptists would be false to their deepest convictions if they did not say so.' Then, after rehearsing the Baptist opposition to a state church, their rejection of episcopacy and episcopal (re)ordination, Cook set down the Baptist conviction that the only baptism taught in the New Testament was that of believers, and that infant baptism was not only unscriptural but contrary to the essential character of the church as Christ conceived it.[20] In line with the 1926 *Reply to the Lambeth Appeal*, Cook accepted the possibility of a federation of equal and autonomous churches and followed this with the statement that the likelihood of Baptists surrendering or compromising their distinctive witness with regard to baptism was extremely unlikely.[21]

A few months before the eighth BWA met in Cleveland, 1950, a Commission on the Doctrine of Baptism was set up under the chairmanship of Ernest Payne. A week before the Congress, the Commission met and prepared a preliminary report which was accompanied by a questionaire and bibliography which were to be sent to the constituent unions of the BWA. In presenting the report to the Congress, Payne presented a celebrated address entitled 'Baptism in Present-Day Theology', in which he outlined the contemporary debate and stressed the necessity of Baptist existence as a separate denomination. Despite the conclusions reached by the scholars like Brunner, Barth and Dix, paedobaptist studies were still defending the rite, most notably Cullmann, Jeremias, Manson, Baillie and Flemington.[22] 'Let us not

---

17   Walton, *Gathered Community*, 112. See the review by L.G. Champion, '*The Gathered Community*, by Robert C. Walton', *BQ* 12.6-7 (April–July, 1947), 223-25.

18   H. Cook, General Superintendent of the Metroplitan Area, *What Baptists Stand For* (1947), 8-9.

19   Cook, *What Baptists Stand For*, 48-52.

20   Cook, *What Baptists Stand For*, 52-53.

21   Cook, *What Baptists Stand For*, 57.

22   Brunner, *Divine–Human Encounter*; Barth, *Teaching of the Church*; D.G. Dix, *The Theology of Confirmation in Relation to Baptism* (1946); O. Cullmann, *Die Tauflehre des Neuen Testaments* (1948, E.T. *Baptism in the New Testament*, 1950); J.

think', Payne urged, '...that our case is universally conceded and that there is no longer need for our continued existence as a group of Christians who maintain and practise believers' baptism. We have notable allies today in our contention that baptism should witness to the response of faith to the offer of God's forgiving love in Christ. But there are still many theologians who do *not* hold this position, and there is as yet little evidence that the mind of the church as a whole has so changed that there is likely to be any immediate abandonment of the practice of infant baptism.'[23] Rather, he impressed, the modern baptismal debate showed that there was still much patient argument necessary and much steadfast witnessing required before Baptists could regard their theological and practical tasks as discharged. 'We have still to guard the insights and heritage received from our fathers.'[24] Payne then issued the same frank challenge to the gathered BWA that he was shortly to issue to British Baptists:[25]

> It is hardly to our credit as Baptists that so many of the best books on Baptism have come of recent years from non-Baptist scholars, so few from within our own ranks. And it must be confessed that there are many matters connected with baptism about which we ourselves are far from clear, and some on which we are divided. We may hope that the Commission on the Doctrine of Baptism...will be able to make some contribution to the modern discussion and also help us as Baptists to a clear understanding of the rite which gives us our name. We greatly need to share

---

Jeremias, *Hat die Urkirche die Kindertaufe geübt?* (1949); Manson, 'Baptism in the Church'; Baillie, 'Justification of Infant Baptism'; Flemington, *Origin and Significance.*

23   E.A. Payne, 'Baptism in Present-Day Theology', in *The Doctrine of Baptism: An Address. A Report. A Questionaire. A Bibliography* (1951), 7. The address is also reproduced in Ohrn (ed.), *Eighth Baptist World Congress*, 171-79. It does not appear that this work progressed any further, no follow up having been traced.

24   Payne, 'Baptism in Present-Day Theology', 8.

25   See Payne, 'Baptism in Modern Theology', *BT* August 24, 1950, 9-10, 'It must be confessed that there are many matters connected with baptism about which we ourselves are far from clear, and some on which we are divided. There are matters to be set in order in our own house, both as to practice and doctrine. We have things to learn as well as teach. There are questions posed by the evidence of the New Testament which are not easy for any of us to answer.' Two years later he wrote in similar fashion, 'Baptism and Church Membership among the Baptists', 173, 'Like other Christians, Baptists are growingly aware that their own practice has not been without inconsistencies. Both the doctrine and practice of baptism are under reconsideration by Baptists as by others. But Baptists have always held firmly that those only should be baptized and recognized as members of the church who make a credible profession of faith; that the repentance and conversion symbolized in water-baptism are the gift and work of the Holy Spirit; that the Christian life is a corporate one, involving privileges and mutual responsibilities within that fellowship of the Spirit, of which a gathered church is the local expression; and that the mediation of the grace of God does not depend either on outward rite or on priestly succession.'

information and counsel. There are matters to be set in order in our own house, both as to practice and doctrine. We have things to learn as well as teach. There are questions posed by the evidence of the New Testament which are not very easy for any of us to answer.[26]

By trying to answer the many questions which the doctrine and practice of baptism raised, Payne believed that Baptists would not only greatly increase the depth and effectiveness of their own witness, but also give to the church universal a service which was surely laid upon Baptists by the very name they bore.[27] He concluded, 'As Baptists we must make no exaggerated claims for baptism. But these things we must continue unfalteringly to declare and faithfully to practise.[28] And with all other Christians we must give ourselves to a renewed study of the New Testament.'[29]

In 1950, William Channon added his voice to the now almost over-used cry that baptism was the Baptists' distinctive doctrine and therefore it 'should be proclaimed with no uncertain sound.' In relation to church union, he ruled out any notion of sacrificing New Testament principle, even if the goal, church union, was desirable. 'Truth must stand. As I have said so often, we are Baptists essentially, but not exclusively. "We are all one in Christ Jesus."'[30] Pronouncements such as this, though popular and oft repeated, did not really serve to further the denomination's thinking on the relationship between Baptists (particularly so far as their views on baptism were concerned) and the ecumenical movement, for they tended to come within fairly traditional Baptist expositions of believer's baptism, of which Channon's *Much Water and Believers Only* is a representative example, for it does not interact in any serious way with the whole wave of recent studies from across the denominational and theological spectra. However, 1950 also saw two important Baptist contributions on the subject, one from Ernest Payne, who, by this time, was emerging as a leading scholar and ecumenist, and R.E.O. White, who

---

26   Payne, 'Baptism in Present-Day Theology', 8-9.

27   Payne, 'Baptism in Present-Day Theology', 9-10.

28   By 'these things' Payne meant that the gospel sacraments required scriptural authority, indeed dominical authority, and that the very nature of the gospel itself demanded that it be conceived as a personal encounter between God and man, another reflection of the influence of Brunner, 'Baptism in Present-Day Theology', 10-11, quote from p.11.

29   Payne, 'Baptism in Present-Day Theology', 11. In 1954 in a review of R.S. Wallace, *Calvin's Doctrine of the Word and Sacrament*, A. Dakin also expressed the opinion that 'we Baptists need very much to clarify our minds on these very issues [Word and sacraments] as indeed the discussions on inter-communion have shown', '*Calvin's Doctrine of the Word and Sacrament*, by Ronald S. Wallace', *BQ* 15.6 (April, 1954), 282.

30   Channon of the Metropolitan Tabernacle, Spurgeon's church, *Much Water*, xv, 93-94. The book comprises the substance of baptismal addresses.

was similarly beginning to establish himself within the academic elite of the denomination.[31]

In 'Baptism in Modern Theology',[32] Payne sketched the rise of the intense contemporary debate on baptism which, he declared, was 'one of the main theological interests of our time.' He noted that this was especially so among Reformed Churches (influenced by Brunner and Barth) and the Church of England, but also other communions. After briefly discussing these various contributions,[33] he noted that none of them had become Baptists, despite the implications of their conclusions for the practice of infant baptism. He then reiterated the challenge he had made to the BWA, concluding that much patient argument from Baptists was necessary and much steadfast witnessing was required. The matters which required their attention included the relationships between Christian baptism and that of John, and John's baptism to Jewish proselyte baptism.[34] Further, had Baptists adequately stressed the truth

---

31   See G.W. Martin, 'Biographical Sketch: Revd R.E.O. White', in Porter and Cross (eds.), *Baptism*, 18-32, and the brief account of his work as first tutor then Principal of The Baptist Theological College of Scotland, in Murray, *Scottish Baptist College*, 47 and 49.

32   Payne, 'Baptism in Modern Theology', *BT* August 24, 1950, 9-10. There are similarities here between this article and Payne's later forward, 'Baptism in Recent Discussion', in Gilmore (ed.), *Christian Baptism*, 15-24.

33   Principally the work of Brunner, Barth, Dix, the Joint Commission of the Convocations of Canterbury and York (which had recently produced two interim reports).

34   It is worth noting that at this time Baptists provided a number of valuable articles and chapters of books dealing with the antecedents of Christian baptism. H.H. Rowley wrote a number of the most important studies, see his 'Jewish Proselyte Baptism and the Baptism of John', *HUCA* 15 (1940), 313-34, a revised version of which was included in his collection of essays *From Moses to Qumran: Studies in the Old Testament* (1963), as was 'The Qumran Sect and Christian Origins', pp.239-79; 'The Origin and Meaning of Baptism', *BQ* 11.12-13 (January–April, 1945), 308-20; 'The Christian Sacraments', in Rowley, *Unity of the Bible*, 149-87, being the first Whitley lecture in 1951; 'The Baptism of John and the Qumran Sect', in A.J.B. Higgins (ed.), *New Testament Essays in Memory of Thomas Walter Manson, 1893–1953* (Manchester, 1959), 218-29. Other studies include S.I. Buse, 'His Baptism and Ours', *BT* May 23, 1946, 6; A. Dakin, 'Christian Baptism and John's Baptism Contrasted', in Bryan (ed.), *Concerning Believers Baptism*, 39-44; H. Martin, 'Baptism and Circumcision', *Theology* 53 no.362 (August, 1950), 301-03, and no.365 (November, 1950), 423-24; H. Martin, 'Baptism and Circumcision', *BQ* 14.5 (January, 1952), 213-21; Champion, *Church in the New Testament*, 68-70; and the reviews of J. Schneider, a German Baptist, *Baptism and Church in the New Testament*, (E.T. by E.A. Payne, 1957), by H.H. Rowley, 'New Testament Baptism', *BT* January 31, 1957, 7, and Anon. (presumably the editor G.W. Hughes of Huddersfield), '*Baptism and Church in the New Testament*, by Johannes Schneider', *BQ* 17.3 (July, 1957), 129-30. See also, A. Gilmore, 'Jewish Antecedents', in Gilmore (ed.), *Christian Baptism*, 54-83; chs. 1 to 5 of White, *Biblical Doctrine of Initiation*, 13-89, see also pp.188, 319-22, and ch. 2 of White's *Invitation to Baptism*,

that Christian baptism was baptism into Christ's death and resurrection and that the benefits of this were unmerited gifts of God to the whole human race? Was baptism primarily an individual matter, a personal confession of faith, or was it primarily a means by which God contrived that there would always be a church to witness to his name? Were all these aspects or elements to be expressed in the administration of the rite? Should the subjects and the mode be distinguished, making the latter subsidiary and less binding? What meaning and authority had the New Testament rite of the laying on of hands? Were Baptists clear on the relationship between the doctrines of baptism and the church, and baptism and the Holy Spirit? What was the right relationship between baptism, church membership and the first sharing in the Lord's Supper? What should be the nature and extent of fellowship with those who did not agree with Baptists on baptism? 'None of these questions admits of a very easy answer. But they cannot honestly be evaded.' The attempt, he believed, would not only increase the depth and effectiveness of Baptist witness, but would also render to the church universal a service which was incumbent on Baptists by their very name. Most Baptist discussions paid little attention to Christ's baptism and baptism as a positive act by which the believer followed the example of the Lord. 'It would indeed be of value to us all and to our friends in other communions if some young Baptist scholar would collect from Baptist literature personal testimonies as to what the rite has meant to men and women who have thus "put on Christ".'[35] Water baptism was a conscious act of obedience to the Lord, an acted parable of union with Christ in his death, burial and resurrection, and of the believer's dependence for salvation on these acts of Christ.[36]

In his article on 'Advance and Reunion', White observed that after half a century of ecumenical developments Baptists were confronted by 'the painful dilemma of two apparently contradictory challenges.' On the one hand were the calls for Baptist advance, epitomized by the Forward Movement, launched in 1936.[37] On the other hand, was the much wider and bigger challenge of the ecumenical movement. Keen 'Advancists', as

---

19-26; and ch. 1 'The Antecedents of Christian Baptism' of G.R. Beasley-Murray, *Baptism in the New Testament*, 1-44, also pp.329-44. These studies were considerable improvements on previous treatments of the subject which amounted, very often, to little more than brief and unsatisfactory references to the antecedents of baptism.

35   The closest to such a study is A. Pain, 'Dying and Rising with Christ: A Study of the Baptismal Practice of Sutton Coldfield Baptist Church, 1978–1998' (Westminster College, Oxford, MTh, 1998), which is based on questioning the baptized about their baptism and the meaning they attach to it.

36   These are essentially the same questions as the ones Payne posed in his address to the BWA Congress. See Payne, 'Baptism in Present-Day Theology', 9.

37   On the Forward Movement see Payne, *The Baptist Union*, 203, and Townsend, *Robert Wilson Black*, 74-83.

White called them, such as J.H. Rushbrooke, had asked whether advance for Baptists would mean retreat from their historic and distinctive positions? Was their ideal of the gathered church outmoded? Would they have to revise their witness as to relations with the state? Was ecclesiastical fusion the necessary expression of Christian unity? 'Reunionists', White noted, would reply that the Baptist position was mainly negative, never having emerged from nineteenth-century individualism, and so they were ill-prepared, ill-informed and ill-organized to face the age of collectivism.[38]

Baptists were, therefore, constrained by the duty of defining their attitude and vindicating their place in the modern church, and justifying their continued existence either as a clearly defined group within a reunited church or as a separate denomination. For this purpose, White stressed, appeal to the authority of scripture was insufficient, for it was this authority of scripture over the church in so changed a situation that was in dispute. The only way forward for Baptists to vindicate the retention of their identity, within or without a reunited church, was dependent upon 'the permanent spiritual value of their principles', which had to be shown to be expressions of essential gospel truths. This was especially so in the case of believers' baptism. For Baptists themselves, appeal to the scriptural basis for believers' baptism was sufficient, but in the contemporary baptismal debate and ecumenical climate, the question of origins was less important than the question of value. Therefore, it was the question of the value of believers' baptism which would justify its continuance in the church. It was this issue to which White addressed himself. Like the Lord's Supper, believers' baptism anchored the church firmly to the fundamental historic facts upon which her message was based. The church's authority and power lay in her faithful witness to the definite, historic, concrete and unalterable act of God, and the baptismal pool and Lord's table repeatedly reminded the church of this. They also testified that saving grace was mediated through the one who died, was buried and rose again, and that the church's present fellowship and future life centred in that risen and living Saviour to whom the baptized were personally committed in conscious faith and obedience. At the pool and table, every incoming member was faced with the heart of the Christian gospel. Recalling the foundation of faith in the dying and rising Saviour, baptism yet left believers free in successive generations to interpret afresh the meaning of his redemptive work, thus preserving the church from mere subjectivism, from vague 'religiousness', spiritual decay and bringing believers back again and again to the scriptures.

---

38   R.E.O. White, minister at Rutherglen, Glasgow, 'Advance and Reunion', *BQ* 13.8 (October, 1950), 341-42.

Believers' baptism thus nourished the love of the Bible and loyalty to evangelical faith.[39]

Believers' baptism preserved the belief in the necessity of personal conversion. In this Baptists were not alone, but their practice of the rite kept the belief at the forefront and they did not obscure the doctrine by a rite of admission which denied its necessity.[40] More importantly, however, were the implications of all this for Christian ethics and the doctrine of grace. In fact, believers' baptism was the only form of baptism which was primarily an ethical act on the part of the baptized. Thus, Baptists were alone in the Christian church in being able to make the moral appeal to the implications of having been baptized which the New Testament repeatedly made, 'for no really moral appeal to the adult person can be based upon that which others did to him, by force, as an unconscious infant. Believers' Baptism consciously commits the candidate to the mastery and ownership of the Christ into whose Name and possession he is being baptised; the faith he is confessing is expressly a faith in a Master whose ethical demand and perfect example are before him, and Whose right to command is already being acknowledged in the act of Baptism itself.' This, obviously, had supreme importance for the whole meaning of Christian discipleship. The deliberate practice of a baptism that had neither moral conditions nor moral significance was both dangerous to the character of the church and disloyal to the whole revelation of God's will.[41]

Finally, believers' baptism preserved for the world church an indispensable element of the true doctrine of grace. Any form of baptism which removed the conception of grace from the personal realm where God meets people in spiritual communion, replacing it instead by a magical or mechanical 'something' which is conveyed or imposed by ceremony or priest, inevitably corrupts the gospel. 'A true doctrine of the grace of God finds expression and defence only in a form of admission to the Church where voluntary faith and surrender are expressed in conscious obedience to the Master Himself.' Believers' baptism, thus justified itself by its fruits and intrinsic worth, for involved in it were some of the deepest and most urgent doctrinal and practical issues facing the church and which would face any united church of the future.[42]

Underlying White's insistence on the baptism of believers, of course, lay the conception that everything in the Christian life depended upon the personal experience in which the individual soul confronted the Lord. This was the doctrine of the church as composed of regenerate believers. 'Whatever happens about reunion, we must go on insisting that you can

39   White, 'Advance and Reunion', 342-43.
40   White, 'Advance and Reunion', 343.
41   White, 'Advance and Reunion', 343-44.
42   White, 'Advance and Reunion', 344-45.

never obscure the spiritual nature of the Church without in the end obscuring the truth of the Gospel, and the whole Church will need our witness to the truth of the Gathered Church set humbly but firmly over against the world.'[43]

White concluded, observing that reunion discussions often seemed to proceed upon the assumption that no significant differences of principle remained to separate the various churches, and whatever the reason for such an assumption, he stressed, 'it is wrong.' Baptists, he stated, 'have much that is distinctive and important', and while they might desire unity, they could have little faith in a unity which overrode genuine differences, which would only give way, sooner or later, to a second Reformation. 'In one respect our position is peculiarly embarrassing; just because the things for which we stand seem to us to be matters of faith and theology, not accidents of history or preferences of method, compromise seems betrayal... All we know is that we have received a charge and a commission, and we must bear faithful witness and set faithful example.'[44]

As the 1950s progressed and calls continued to be made that Baptists ought to be emphasizing and contributing to the ongoing baptismal debate,[45] scholars from paedobaptist traditions, particularly in Europe,

---

43   White, 'Advance and Reunion', 345.

44   White, 'Advance and Reunion', 349. Five years later at the Jubilee Congress of the BWA, F.T. Lord again noted the Baptist refusal to equate brotherly co-operation with the sacrifice of essential principle, 'The Baptist World Alliance in Retrospect and Prospect', in A.T. Ohrn (ed.), *Baptist World Alliance Golden Jubilee Congress (Ninth World Congress), London, England, 16th–22nd July, 1955* (1955), 67.

45   So A.S. Clark in his presidential address to the Baptist Assembly, 'Worship the Lord', *BT* May 1, 1952, 2, 'We do not make enough of the sacrament of believers' baptism by immersion'; R.A. Mason, an assistant at West Ham Central Mission, 'The Theology of Baptism', *Frat.* 90 (October, 1953), 6, 'Yet while little has been said by our own community, there has come a wealth of thought and writing in defence of the theology of infant baptism'; B.G. Hastings of Adnitt Road, Northampton, 'An Outline of the History of Baptism', *Frat.* 90 (October, 1953), 31-32, 'our own conception of what is entailed in baptism is often very confused. Now is the time, surely, to review the roots and implications of our own precious heritage, so that we may have a clear account to give of our convictions.' In 1957, H.W. Trent, minister of Great Shelford, Cambridge, based his study on 'Ourselves and the Ordinances', *BQ* 17.1 (January, 1957), 10-11, 21, on the fact that Baptists had 'failed to make convincingly plain our convictions. Let us face it; we have been content to deal with our distinctive sacrament on pamphlet level. We have hidden our light under a bushel.' The 'dearth of works by competent Baptist scholars...is to a large degree responsible for the general ignorance of our theological position regarding the Sacraments, to say nothing of our practice. We have been content to rebut the arguments of those who have differed from us without making any positive contribution to the subject, and it is a sad reflection on us, that most of the matter, if not all that has been written in recent years on the Sacraments, has come from pens outside

continued to publish defences of infant baptism, which did not go without discussion by Baptist scholars.[46] Of note among these studies, was a proposal from the Swiss theologian, F.J. Leenhardt, for the reformation of the practice of infant baptism. In his review of this work, Alec Gilmore stated that the question which arose for the Baptists in a day when church union was to the fore, was whether in a united Free Church 'we would be willing to accept some method of reformed infant baptism' along the lines suggested by Leenhardt.[47] Gilmore pointed out that such a view was a long way from any doctrine of infused grace, but equally far from believers' baptism. 'Nevertheless, is it possible for us to accept it as being a possible interpretation of baptism to be administered alongside the baptism of believers, or are we to stand firm and admit of no alternative whatever?'[48] In a similar fashion, one of D.R. Griffiths' suggestions for questions that minister's fraternals and other groups should consider was, 'In the event (a most unlikely one) of a scheme of Church union being devised, on the basis of the abandonment of both infant baptism and believers' baptism, in favour of reception into Church membership by

---

the Baptist denomination.' This lack of interest in the ordinances not only had repercussions outside but also within the denomination as well. Trent concluded 'that we have no grounds to be complacent in our attitude towards the Sacraments and that there is room for closer thought and renewed interest in sacramental theology and practice within the denomination.'

46   See the reviews of the Methodist H.G. Marsh, *The Origin and Significance of the New Testament Baptism* by E.A. Payne, 'Baptism in the New Testament', *BT* May 1, 1941, 215; H.W. Robinson, *BQ* 10.6 (April, 1941), 349-51; and H.H. Rowley, *JTS* 44 (1943), 79-81. See also R.E.[O.] White, 'Theological Issues Involved in Baptism', *ExpTim* 62.4 (January, 1951), 124, a reply to an earlier article by the Presbyterian J.K.S. Reid, 'Theological Issues Involved in Baptism', *ExpTim* 61.7, (April, 1950), 201-04; E.A. Payne, 'Professor Oscar Cullmann on Baptism', *BQ* 14.2 (April, 1951), 56-60; D.R. Griffiths, 'An Approach to the Theology of Baptism. Some Comments on Mr. Flemington's Article', *ExpTim* 63.5 (February, 1952), 157-59, being a response to W.F. Flemington, 'Living Issues in Biblical Scholarship. An Approach to the Theology of Baptism', *ExpTim* 62.12 (September, 1951), 356-59; A. Gilmore, 'Leenhardt on Baptism', *BQ* 15.1 (January, 1953), 35-40; H.H. Rowley, 'Marcel on Infant Baptism', *ExpTim* 64.12 (September, 1953), 361-63, see also Rowley's 'Additional Note' in *The Unity of the Bible,* 189-90, on Marcel's *The Biblical Doctrine of Infant Baptism*; R.E.O. White, at the time minister of Grange Baptist Church, Birkenhead, 'Theology and Logic. A Logical Analysis of the Exegetical Method of the Church of Scotland's Interim Report on Baptism', *BQ* 16.8 (October, 1956), 356-64.

47   This reformed practice involved those who administered the rite to the unconscious infant in accepting the responsibility of making the child aware of what God had done for him/her and how this had already been symbolized on the child's behalf. In short, a form of discriminate infant baptism. See Gilmore, 'Leenhardt on Baptism', 39.

48   Gilmore, 'Leenhardt on Baptism', 40.

public profession of faith alone—what would be the chief gains and losses to be considered?'[49]

While Free Church union proposals were once again being discussed through the mid–late 1950s, the Robert Hall Society in 1959 debated the issues and concluded that Baptists as a denomination were guilty of woolly thinking, the only thing they seemed sure about being baptism. Yet having stated that, of the six points discussed, the second was that among Baptists there appeared to be no clarity or concensus about the meaning of the sacraments and the nature of grace, either in the sacrament or outside it. Talk of reunion was not possible while among themselves there was so much woolly thinking. Baptists needed first of all to know what they believed and why, before any progress could be made.[50]

Over the years the number of calls for more work to be done by Baptist scholars on baptism continued to increase, and they eventually bore fruit when, in early 1959, the volume *Christian Baptism* appeared.[51] Described as 'a landmark',[52] this book was to prove to be one of the most important Baptist works on baptism, and without doubt the most controversial.[53] Work on it had begun in 1955 by four ministers, but it had grown as had the number of contributors. Edwin Robertson noted that as no one person could speak for the Baptists, it was a joint project[54]

---

49   D.R. Griffiths, 'Baptism in the New Testament', *Frat.* 90 (October, 1953), 25.

50   Roger Hayden of Fitzwilliam House, and David Swinfen of St. Catherine's College, reported in 'Free Church Union', *BT* February 19, 1959, 6. The Robert Hall Society is the Baptist society at Cambridge University.

51   It was widely and generally enthusiastically reviewed: Dr N.H. Snaith, the Methodist scholar, 'Christian Baptism', *BT* April 30, 1959, 10; E.H. Robertson, Study Secretary for the United Bible Societies, 'Christian Baptism', *BT* May 14, 1959, 10; L.G. Champion, Principal of Bristol Baptist College, '*Christian Baptism*, edited by A. Gilmore', *BQ* 18.3 (July, 1959), 135-40; D.S. Russell, Principal of Rawdon College, 'Christian Baptism I', *Frat.* 113 (July, 1959), 5-8; E.F. Kevan of London Bible College, 'Christian Baptism II', *Frat.* 113 (July, 1959), 8-12; H.H. Rowley, '*Christian Baptism*', *ExpTim* 70.10 (July, 1959), 301-02; N.B. Jones of Waterbarn, 'Christian Baptism III', *Frat.* 115 (January, 1960), 18-23. *Christian Baptism* is discussed in detail by Fowler, 'Baptism', 122-47.

52   'Editorial', *Frat.* 113 (July, 1959), 4, which commented that 'apart from some useful translation work, a small book or pamphlet, a trenchant chapter or article here and there Baptists have taken an undistinguished part in the contemporary theological debate on baptism.'

53   W.M.S. West, 'Editorial', *BQ* 18.5 (January, 1960), 194, referred to the considerable interest aroused by its publication both inside and outside the denomination, though deferred comment for the time being because 'the debate on Baptism which was sparked off by the book within the Baptist denomination is still proceeding.'

54   E.H. Robertson, 'Christian Baptism', *BT* May 14, 1959, 10.

by many of the denomination's foremost up-and-coming ministers and scholars.[55]

Christian Baptism was never intended to be a statement on Baptist principles, but rather a careful criticism as well as justification of the Baptist position. This, Norman Snaith, declared, the writers achieved, it being an excellent book, almost wholly dispassionate.[56] Some months later, in his defence of the book, George Beasley-Murray stated that the concern of the authors had been 'to put before Baptists the picture of ideal baptism, as it is portrayed in the apostolic writings, in the hope that we may strive to recover it or get somewhere near it.'[57] In his preface, Gilmore observed: 'Whilst realizing that the subject of baptism was rapidly becoming of increasing importance in the ecumenical world, [the writers] were conscious also of the paucity of recent Baptist writing on the subject.'[58] The ecumenical importance of the work was highlighted in Dr Champion's review: 'Since the Baptist position is presented in this careful, scholarly manner the book may be regarded also as a contribution to ecumenical discussion and it will no doubt be studied with much interest in those areas of the world where Baptists are considering schemes for church unity.' The book, however, did not simply provide a challenge to Paedobaptists, but also to Baptists, raising questions which arose from contemporary Baptist theology and practice.[59] The Baptist

---

55   Of the contributors two were already Baptist College Principals, G.R. Beasley-Murray at Spurgeon's and D.M. Himbury in the Baptist College of Victoria, Melbourne, while three were to become Principals, W.M.S. West at Bristol, N. Clark at Cardiff and R.E.O. White at Glasgow. Four were existing College lecturers, A.W. Argyle and West at Regent's Park, S.I. Buse at the University College of North Wales, D.R. Griffiths at Cardiff. The remaining two were to become well-known ministers and authors within the denomination. After leaving the pastorate in West Worthing, A. Gilmore was to serve as Editorial Secretary of the United Society for Christian Literature from 1975–76, then as its General Secretary from 1976–93, as well as being Director of Feed the Minds, 1984–93, while S.F. Winward became a lecturer at the Selly Oak Colleges, Birmingham, from 1966, while also serving two churches in Sutton Coldfield—Victoria Road from 1967–77, and then Four Oaks from 1980.

56   N.H. Snaith, 'Christian Baptism', *BT* April 30, 1959, 10.

57   G.R. Beasley-Murray, 'The Spirit Is There', *BT* December 10, 1959, 8. Beasley-Murray continued, 'To insist on keeping our impoverished version of baptism would be a tragedy among a people who pride themselves on being the people of the New Testament'.

58   A. Gilmore (ed.), 'Preface', in Gilmore (ed.), *Christian Baptism*, 7. Jones, 'Christian Baptism III', 23, asked for 'a simple pamphlet, written in untheological language, which will make clear some of the riches uncovered in [*Christian Baptism*]', for the sake of those who had to interpret the doctine of believers' baptism to lay people.

59   Champion, '*Christian Baptism*', 135. These challenges were the specific concern of Champion's review. That *Christian Baptism*'s potential in the wider baptismal debate was realized can be seen by the references made to it in subsequent

contribution to ecumenical discussion was also in mind when Morris West concluded his *Baptist Principles* with the challenge that 'being Baptists by conviction, we should seek every opportunity of ecumenical encounter, so that we may set before all Christians the things we so surely hold.'[60]

R.E.O. White's *The Biblical Doctrine of Initiation* was the second major theological work published by Baptists within two years, showing that up and coming biblical scholars had risen to the challenge that had so often been aired for substantial contributions to both the Baptist and the ongoing international and ecumenical debate on baptism. R.L. Child heralded the book as 'a major contribution to [improving Church relations].'[61] Quoting Jim Perkin, White agreed that, 'There can be no doubt that sooner or later the church will have to settle the question of baptism, which threatens to become one of the major stumblingblocks in the path of the ecumenical conversations.'[62] White, along with many others before him, expressed concern over the inadequacies of the Baptist position on baptism, commenting, 'one sometimes fears that current practice of believer's baptism is scriptural on the single point of reserving baptism for believers and on very little else.'[63]

---

writings, e.g., C.F.D. Moule, *Worship in the New Testament* (1961), *passim*; A.B. Crabtree, *The Restored Relationship: A Study in Justification and Reconciliation* (1963), the Whitley lectures for 1961, e.g., p.65; J.D.G. Dunn, *Baptism in the Holy Spirit: A Re-examination of the New Testament Teaching on the Gift of the Spirit in relation to Pentecostalism today* (1970), *passim*. The essays also figured prominently in Beasley-Murray's own important study *Baptism in the New Testament, passim*. That it is one of the most important Baptist contributions this century to the theology of baptism cannot be doubted.

60   W.M.S. West of Dagnall Street, St. Albans, *Baptist Principles* (1960), 44 (all quotations in this and ch. 7 are from this 1st edn). On West, see H. Mowvley, 'Morris West—An Appreciation', in J.H.Y. Briggs (ed.), *Faith, Heritage and Witness: A Supplement to the Baptist Quarterly Published in Honour of Dr. W.M.S. West* (*BQSup*, 1987), 4-12; 'Morris West dies at 77—"a Baptist gift to the ecumenical family"', *BT* November 4, 1999, 2; Dr R. Ellis, 'The Revd Dr Morris West', *BT* November 18, 1999, 14; 'The Revd Dr W.M.S. West', *BQ* 38.5 (January, 2000), 211. A fuller tribute is to be paid to him by the Baptist Historical Society, to be entitled *Baptists Together* (Didcot, 2000). West's convictions on the need for ecumenical involvement are clear in his FCFC Congress address 'Relationships—in the Church', *Free Church Chroncile* 36.2 (Summer, 1981), 8-16.

61   R.L. Child, 'The Biblical Doctrine of Initiation', *Frat.* 118 (October, 1960), 18. Fowler, 'Baptism', 147-55, also discusses it in detail. Its abiding influence is reflected in the contributions to the Festschrift for White, see Porter and Cross (eds.), *Baptism*.

62   White, *Biblical Doctrine of Initiation*, 279, the source of the quote from Perkin was not noted and has not been found.

63   White, *Biblical Doctrine of Initiation*, 279-80.

In his detailed and sensitive discussion of the value of infant baptism,[64] White noted that infant baptism was a form of baptism prevalent in the modern church which was very much unlike that of the New Testament in form, content and theological significance, yet enshrining certain values and insights which in any final reappraisal of the rite would have to be preserved and prized. While infant baptism witnessed to these values and insights in a confused and ambiguous way, believer's baptism also sometimes obscured them altogether.[65] If it were to be asked why both forms of baptism could not exist side by side in the modern church the answer would be that the study of New Testament baptism showed a richness of meaning which neither current practice commonly possessed 'and to maintain two impaired baptisms does nothing towards recovering biblical initiation.' Further, the price which would have to be paid for the measure of truth which paedobaptism preserved would be too high, as 'the criticisms which must be levelled against it are far more serious than anything that can be said in its favour.'[66]

That October, White re-emphasized the fact that baptism was the most significant ecumenical stumblingblock. After criticizing Baptist confusion over baptism, particularly some unbiblical Baptist practices[67] and especially the individualistic view of baptism,[68] he wrote,

If in fact we are standing out from our brethren in other denominations, refusing the path of unity, because we prize a real sacrament of Christian experience, a valid scriptural emphasis upon the baptism of the believer into Christ, into the Spirit, and into the church, then we may be justified in our stand. We can do no other, though we do it with humility, and even with regret.

But if in fact we are standing out from our brethren in other denominations because we want to retain a bit of traditional symbolism, a somewhat self-righteous and very theatrical way of telling the congregation that we have come to the opinion that the gospel is true, then we are abandoning most of the New Testament teaching about baptism, and other denominations have every right to protest; and we are

---

64   White, *Biblical Doctrine of Initiation*, 281-96, he criticizes infant baptism on pp.296-305.

65   These include the prevenience of grace, the biblical doctrine of covenant, the corporate and objective aspects of salvation, and God's action within the soul.

66   White, *Biblical Doctrine of Initiation*, 295-96.

67   R.E.O. White, 'Baptism: The Domestic Debate', *Frat.* 118 (October, 1960), 14, noted that some baptismal practices among Baptists were defended as traditional or evangelical but in actual fact had little theological or scriptural justification: these he listed as baptism on the minister's (or evangelist's) sole say-so, baptism without preparation, baptism followed by reception into membership, and even by enquiry as to membership, as 'obvious examples.'

68   White, 'Baptism: The Domestic Debate', 16.

inflicting a grievous wound on the unity of the church *for no good reason.* Believers' baptism as sometimes practised is not worth contending for, and the contention is damaging to the whole ecumenical movement, and so to the body of Christ. This is no appeal for compromise, or for the tolerance of two baptisms in a united church, but for honest recognition of the fact that when all the church seems out of step except ourselves it might conceivably be because we—ourselves—are dragging our feet.[69]

White believed that the debate among Baptists had to continue until the meaning and spiritual value of believers' baptism were clarified afresh. It is clear, then, from White's writings and the various contributors to *Christian Baptism*, that a growing number of writers directly associated the need for Baptist re-appraisal of baptism with the broader ecumenical debate on baptism, and that this necessitated continuing Baptist participation within it.[70] He underlined the need to define Baptist baptismal doctrine when he contended that 'The time has come to move forward from the position held for 300 years, simply insisting that baptism is for believers only, to making it clear *why* this is so, and why it is important.' Ecumenical relationships challenged the Baptists' view of

---

69   White, 'Baptism: The Domestic Debate', 16, italics his.

70   R.E.O. White, 'New Baptismal Questions', *BT* April 13, 1961, 9. White also recognized the unavoidable fact that ecumenical relationships challenged Baptists and their views of baptism's importance and meaning. At this time Baptists continued to keep apace with the latest theological writings on baptism. See the following reviews, E.A.Payne, 'Baptism in the Early Church' [review of J. Jeremias' *Die Kindertaufe in den ersten vier Jahrhunderten*], *BT* April 2, 1959, 7; G.R. Beasley-Murray, 'New Voice in the Debate on Infant Baptism' [J. Jeremias, *Infant Baptism in the First Four Centuries*, and K. Aland, *Die Sänglingstaufe im Neuen Testament und in der alten Kirchen*], *BT* April 27, 1961, 8; N. Clark, 'In the Study', *BQ* 19.2 (April, 1961), 86-87 [reviewing the E.T. of Jeremias''s *Infant Baptism in the First Four Centuries*]; A.W. Argyle, 'Joachim Jeremias: *Infant Baptism in the First Four Centuries*', *BQ* 19.4 (October, 1961), 190-91. See also the later English translation of K. Aland's *Did the Early Church Baptize Infants?* (1963, E.T. by G.R. Beasley-Murray, who also included a lengthy 'Introduction. The Baptismal Controversy in the British Scene', pp.17-27, which is a most helpful and insightful survey of the recent debate in its own right. Aland's book was also reviewed by N. Clark, 'In the Study', *BQ* 20.3 (July, 1963), 133-35, and G.W. Rusling, 'Baptism in the Early Church', *BT* August 1, 1963, 6. Beasley-Murray also translated the Roman Catholic Rudolf Schnackenburg's *Baptism in the Thought of St. Paul* (1964). L.G. Champion, 'Baptism Without Faith—"Unimaginable"', *BT* February 11, 1965, 7, agreed with Beasley-Murray's statement on Schnackenburg's work that 'no treatment known to me of Paul's teaching on Baptism is so profound as that contained in these pages'; see also N. Clark, 'In the Study', *BQ* 21.2 (April, 1965), 82-83, who expressed appreciation for the translation of Schnackenburg's 'significant study in the field of baptism.' Another useful overview and survey was supplied by E. Roberts-Thomson, at the time Principal of the Baptist Theological College of New South Wales, Australia, *With Hands Outstretched: Baptists and the Ecumenical Movement* (1962).

baptism's importance and its meaning, therefore, reunion 'conversations' also made necessary the redefinition of Baptists' attitude to infant baptism.[71]

In his Whitley lectures, George Beasley-Murray stated his intention 'to offer a Baptist contribution to the discussions on baptism that are taking place throughout the Christian world.'[72] The first five chapters (305 pages) were devoted to the antecedents of Christian baptism and a detailed exegesis of all the passgaes explicitly relating to baptism, culminating in a chapter on the doctrine of baptism, while the last chapter was given over to a discussion of the rise and significance of infant baptism, followed by a postscipt on baptismal reform and inter-church relationships (a further 90 pages). Throughout, Beasley-Murray interacted with Paedobaptist and Baptist scholarship. Irenic in tone, he recognized that there was some hope of a closer rapprochement between Paedobaptists and Baptists if the former would limit baptism to the families of those actively Christian, encouraging the Church of England to set out the wholeness of the rite by combining baptism, confirmation and communion for those who came to the church in maturer years, and that some of the Anglican baptistries built for immersion be used for such. Baptists, he exhorted, ought to refrain from baptizing those baptized in infancy except where asked for explicitly by the applicant.[73] To Baptists,

---

71   R.E.O. White, 'New Baptismal Questions', *BT* April 13, 1961, 9.

72   Beasley-Murray, *Baptism in the New Testament*, v-vi. It was widely reviewed, though often none too enthusiastically, see 'Dr. G.R. Beasley-Murray on Baptism. Dr H.H. Rowley reviews an important book on Baptism by the Principal of Spurgeon's College', *BT* August 30, 1962, 6, who recommended that ministers and laymen should give it wide attention, regarding it as more than a defence of the Baptist position, being irenic not polemical in purpose. G. Every (an Anglican clergyman and historian), 'G.R. Beasley-Murray: *Baptism in the New Testament*', *BQ* 20.1 (January, 1963), 42-43, commended its thoroughness, especially in 'his full and weighty discussion of every text' in the New Testament, but argued that Beasley-Murray had not fully understood some of the nuances in the practice of infant baptism within the early church from the second century onwards. C. Morrison (a Reformed theologian), '*Baptism in the New Testament*, by G.R. Beasley-Murray', *JBL* 72.3 (September, 1963), 339-41, similarly criticized his knowledge of many problems regarding ancient life and thought, while overall regarding it as 'a highly informative and stimulating contibution to the current discussion.' A.R. George, 'Baptism', *ExpTim* 74.4 (January, 1963), 106, criticized Beasley-Murray's discussion of children in Christian families for not considering such questions as the spiritual development of children, the nature of the Christian church or the value of a *Volkskirche*. Finally, George believed that it would be unfortunate if Beasley-Murray's keen interest in ecumenical discussion overshadowed the earlier exegetical work. N. Clark, 'In the Study', *BQ* 20.2 (April, 1963), 82-84, bluntly wrote, 'My difficulty is that I cannot see where Dr. Beasley-Murray stands, and am not at all sure that he stands with consistency anywhere', p.83. See also Fowler, 'Baptism', 155-62.

73   Beasley-Murray, 'Postscript', *Baptism in the New Testament*, 387-95.

Beasley-Murray laid down a challenge: 'A call for reform according to the Word of God has to be heeded first by those who issue it. In this connection there is room for improvement in our own administration of the rite of initiation.'[74] There is no doubt that *Baptism in the New Testament* is the single most important and lasting contribution made by any Baptist this century to the baptismal debate, and more than adequately fulfilled the hopes of the many who had for so long called for a major Baptist work to be published.

A year later, *The Pattern of the Church*, edited by Alec Gilmore, with contributions from Morris West, Neville Clark and Stephen Winward, appeared. 'Our purpose', the Foreword explained, 'has been to clarify and elucidate our own denominational beliefs, especially with regard to church and ministry, and to seek the road of reformation for the churches of our faith and order from the ecumenical perspective, and within the immediate ecumenical context.'[75] The writers looked forward to reunion, but noted that even intercommunion would be nothing more than a mockery until 'we have steadily, realistically, and finally purposed visible union through denominational crucifixion and resolved to give ourselves in love for each other and the one Church of God.'[76]

The final chapter directly addressed the issue of church union, beginning with the statement, 'Preceding chapters have explicitly been concerned with problems of denominational life and denominational reformation; but implicitly the questions of church reunion have all the while been posed... For denominational reform and movement towards church union in England are but two sides of a single coin. They inescapably involve each other. They cannot be separated.' No effective move towards union, it declared, was possible apart from denominational reform 'precisely because many of the contemporary obstacles are bound up with distortions within our own life.' But equally, no ultimate denominational reform was possible apart from reunion 'because of the inevitably partial vision of the "separated".'[77] Three obstacles stood in the way: inertia and complacency, confessionalism on a world scale, and

---

74   Beasley-Murray, *Baptism in the New Testament*, 393.

75   Gilmore (ed.), *Pattern of the Church*, 10. See M.F. Williams, 'A. Gilmore (ed.): *The Pattern of the Church: A Baptist View*', *BQ* 20.4 (October, 1963), 188-90; 'Book About the Church by Baptist Authors', *BT* May 2, 1963, 7; L.G. Champion, 'A Baptist View of the Church', *BT* May 16, 1963, 6, who was unconvinced about the strongly sacramental emphasis of the book.

76   N. Clark, 'The Fulness of the Church of God', in Gilmore (ed.), *Pattern of the Church*, 112.

77   'Towards Church Union', in Gilmore (ed.), *Pattern of the Church*, 157-58. The author of this final chapter is not named, but presumably the chapter speaks for all four contributors. The style would suggest Neville Clark as its author.

fundamentalism.[78] Action was therefore demanded, including the need to re-initiate conversations in Great Britain, not just among the Free Churches but with the Anglican communion as well, though the authors recognized four burning problems hindering such progress—tradition, *episcope*, initiation and the question of church and state.[79]

A unity that was understood in terms of the sacramental rather than the liturgical could not evade the question of initiation, the question of the catechumenate and its relationship to incorporation into the body of Christ. Preoccupation with baptism as the flag of unity exalted secondary issues of the method of administration and the identity of the separated and the saved upon whom the rite could correctly be performed. Rather, 'It is the meaning of baptism that is the crucial problem. And this inexorably directs us towards a fuller apprehension of that into which we are baptized.' The reality is Christ in his church, and baptism is incorporation into the body of Christ. The church cannot neatly seal her boundaries nor define them. She must take seriously her visibility, decide on the terms of incorporation and ensure that it is gospel reality that is sacramentally expressed. 'But this is surely where the ecumenical discussion must begin.'[80] The authors did not set out to try to meet this agenda, but stated, 'Even this brief assessment of the obstacles that confront us makes clear the magnitude of the endeavour for which we plead. Only clear vision, deep faith, and untiring hope are likely to prevail.'[81]

In his dialogical *A Conversation about Baptism*, R.L. Child also set his book firmly within the ecumenical context, expressing his own conviction that he did not believe that denominations were wrong nor that the merger of separate communions into one vast ecclesiastical system should take place. However, unity certainly did mean accepting the fact that Christ created the church and meant it to be a society of persons united to him and to one another in faith and love, but he gave no further comment on how this could be worked out in practice.[82] All he would say was that he believed that what was really involved in the controversy

---

78 'Towards Church Union', 158-60.
79 'Towards Church Union', 163-64.
80 'Towards Church Union', 166-67.
81 'Towards Church Union', 168.
82 R.L. Child, Emeritus Principal of Regent's Park College, *A Conversation about Baptism* (1963), 87. It was reviewed by D.H. Sparkes, 'R.L. Child: *A Conversation about Baptism*', *BQ* 20.4 (October, 1963), 190; W.W. Bottoms, 'Conversation about Baptism', *BT* August 1, 1963, 6. Extracts were printed in the *BT* under the title 'What is Baptism for?', see August 15, 6; August 22, 6; August 29, 6; under the title 'The Future of Baptism', September 12, 6; September 19, 7; and elicited a letter from W.F. Webber of Kenton, 'Baptism', *BT* November 7, 1963, 4-5.

between Baptists and Paedobaptists was a differing conception of the nature and constitution of the church.[83]

Throughout the early 1960s Baptists continued to interact and assess the work of paedobaptist scholars. Concluding his review of Kurt Aland's reply to Joachim Jeremias, Beasley-Murray wrote, 'The lesson I deduce from this latest contribution of one of the most learned instructors of the Church of our day is the dire necessity for the witness of our denomination to continue and abound throughout the whole Church of God.'[84] Such a sentiment would have received the near unanimous support from within the denomination, as evidenced by Leslie Moon: 'We Baptists rightly claim that our distinctive contribution to the Universal Church is our teaching on Believers' Baptism, with the necessity for personal faith and personal committal to Him as Saviour and Lord that Believers' Baptism emphasises and helps to safeguard.'[85] However, W.H. Kennedy responded to Moon, even citing the sentence noted above, and cautioned that Baptists should not therefore regard the baptismal debate as closed. He stated, 'Without starry-eyed absorption in the possible wonders of a united church, we must go on testing our conception of Baptism and enquiring whether it is really and ultimately irreconcilable with that of paedobaptist Christians.'[86] While believers' baptism incorporated individuals into the partnership of the Body of Christ, it was also a divisive factor among Christians. Within the Baptist denomination itself sharply divergent views of baptism were held and 'between Baptists and other denominations the difference of understanding is so great as to make genuinely close co-operation hardly possible. This does not mean that we must thoughtlessly deny our history or foolishly relinquish the insights granted us; it means rather that under the tutelage of the one Lord we must seek greater light on the one Baptism.'[87] When Baptists invited the unbaptized to the Lord's table were

---

83   Child, *A Conversation*, 94.

84   G.R. Beasley-Murray, 'Debate on Infant Baptism', *BT* January 2, 1964, 7. Beasley-Murray also reviewed J. Ysebaert's *Greek Baptismal Terminology: Its Origins and Early Development* (Nijmegen, 1962), in *JTS* ns 15 (October, 1964), 381-84.

85   L.J. Moon of Perth Road, Ilford, 'Partnership', *Frat.* 132 (April, 1964), 20.

86   W.H. Kennedy of South Shields, 'Incorporate in Christ', *Frat.* 133 (July, 1964), 23.

87   Surprisngly few Baptists this century have discussed Ephesians 4:5's 'one baptism'. One who did during this period was Dr H.H. Williams of Bloomsbury, 'Unity in Christ', *ExpTim* 75.11 (August, 1964), 348-49, who, following O. Cullmann, *Baptism in the New Testament*, and J.A.T. Robinson, 'The One Baptism as a Category of New Testament Soteriology', *SJT* 6 (1953), 257-74, saw this one baptism as the life, dying and rising of Christ 'and any one baptized [unspecified in terms of subjects and mode] acknowledges this way as the way of life', p.349. Cullmann's and Robinson's views and their refutation by W.E. Moore, 'One Baptism', *NTS* 10 (1963–64), 504-16, are discussed by A.R. Cross, '"One Baptism" (Ephesians 4.5): A Challenge to the Church',

they breaking the wholeness of the gospel, or when they received them at the table were they implicitly recognizing their baptism as infants?[88]

Others too recognized that Baptists were a body holding divergent views, not least upon baptism, and so there were those who drew attention to the need of greater denominational unity.[89] Yet this did not deter many from maintaining that Baptists should be actively involved within the ecumenical movement. Leonard Champion did just this in his presidential address to the Baptist Assembly,[90] as did Dr Payne in his exploration of the contemporary situation and issues at the second denominational conference at the Hayes, Swanwick, in May.[91] Here, Payne acknowledged that on the matter of union with other Christian bodies Baptists had always been extremely cautious, 'primarily because of their determination to remain loyal to their understanding and practice of the rite of baptism.'[92] He noted that there were only four sets of union conversations in which Baptists were playing a part: in Ceylon, North India, between the American Baptist Convention and the Church of the Brethren, and finally in discussions between the Free Churches in Wales. 'Ought Baptists to be involved at more points than this? Perhaps neither we nor others are yet ready, and we must wait in general for more light

---

in Porter and Cross (eds.), *Baptism*, 183-84. See also the brief discussion by L.J. Kreitzer, *The Epistle to the Ephesians* (Peterborough, 1997), 118-23.

88   Kennedy, 'Incorporate in Christ', 25.

89   See 'Baptists and Union', *BT* February 20, 1964, 7, where G.H. Williams of Bishop Stortford (apparently not Gwilym Henry Williams of Merthyr Tydfil and apparently not a minister), suggested that there was no longer justification for the continued separation of Baptists, Strict Baptists, Old Baptists, Churches of Christ, Brethren or Pentecostalists, whereas R.J. Avery of Harpenden claimed that just because the Church of England and Methodists, Presbyterians and Congregationalists were involved in conversations, that did not mean that Baptists needed to look around for possible organic union with other groups. Later, W.M.S. West, 'Call for Denominational Unity', *BT* May 7, 1964, 1 and 3, argued that party labels within the denomination should be dropped, and that to Baptists baptism was a symbol of personal identification with Christ. H. Whyte of City Road, Bristol, 'Call to Denominational Unity', *BT* May 28, 1964, 4, focused on conservative evangelicals, and this letter called forth a response from Mr G.W. Dixon, secretary at Calne, Wiltshire, [it is incorrectly spelt Colne in the *BT*, which is in Lancashire), 'Call to Denominational Unity', *BT* June 11, 1964, 4, who contended that all those who confessed Jesus Christ as Lord were Christian brothers and that as there would be no party labels in heaven, so there should be none on earth.

90   'Dr. Champion's Plea to the Assembly', *BT* April 30, 1964, 1 and 9.

91   E.A. Payne, *Baptists and Church Relations* (1964), number 2 in the *Live Issues Booklets* published by the BU. See also 'Baptists and Church Relations', *BT* May 28, 1964, 8, and 'New Series of Booklets', *BT* October 1, 1964, 2.

92   Payne, *Baptists and Church Relations*, 7.

from the theological discussions on baptism in which our own and other scholars are engaged.'[93]

There was still, however, a considerable body within the denomination which viewed any such involvement as that advocated by Drs Beasley-Murray and Payne with caution and even hostility. Mr F. Jarman was outright against the union movement, and Mr P. Cook believed that unity was an unlikely 'dismal sham'.[94] White, on the other hand, in concert with Beasley-Murray and Payne, argued against the compromise of principle but nevertheless for the involvement of evangelicals in ecumenical conversations. 'Is it "interference" to suggest to paedobaptists that their rite is unscriptural? Are we, in fact, to bear witness to our convictions only to those who already agree with us?'[95]

The Pattern of the Church had set itself firmly within the ecumenical context, believing that all examinations of the issues of church, ministry or the sacraments by whatever denomination would have to consider the ecumenical dimension. But this book did not go unchallenged. Its 'sacramental' and 'ecumenical' tone called forth a strong rebuttal from the Baptist Revival Fellowship (BRF), a conservative evangelical group within the BU.[96] The Study Group responsible for the production of the booklet *Liberty in the Lord* was signed by sixteen ministers[97] who insisted that the churches of the New Testament were already thought of as one

---

93   Payne, *Baptists and Church Relations*, 9.

94   F. Jarman of London, and P. Cook, 'Baptists and Unity', *BT* March 5, 1964, 4.

95   R.E.O. White, *An Open Letter to Evangelicals: A Devotional and Homiletic Commentary on The First Epistle of John* (1964), 182-94, but especially 185-89, quote from p.188.

96   In 1956, three members of the BRF Committee, had discussed the church union proposals for India and Pakistan and called for revival not reunion, T.M. Bamber of Rye Lane, Peckham, G.R. King of Croydon and T.A. Steen of Old Basford, Nottingham, 'Not Reunion but Revival', *BT* April 26, 1956, 7. A brief outline of the origins and theological stance of the BRF can be found in T.M. Bamber, 'The Baptist Revival Fellowship', *Frat.* 89 (July, 1953), 29-31.

97   Bamber, Pastor Emeritus of Rye Lane, Peckham, B.H. Butt of Dudley, A.M. Derham, editorial secretary of Scripture Union, J.A. Eaton of the Good News Trailor Missionary Fellowship, R.M. Frost of Godalming, P.L. Jones of Woking, King who concluded his pastorate at West Croyden Tabernacle in 1964 to take up office as Commissioner for Evangelism of the LBA on a part-time basis, D.P. Kingdon Principal of the Irish Baptist College, Belfast, E.M. Kirk of Sidcup, S.E.L. Larwood of Welling, R.S. Luland of Wootton, S.G.H. Nash of Leigh on Sea, I.J.W. Oakley who moved from Aylesbury to a tutorship at the Irish Baptist College in 1964, H.G. Owen from Reading, Steen and H.E. Ward of Kingston upon Thames. The Study Group was made up of Derham, Kingdon, Luland, Nash, Oakley, Ward and, according to Samuel Nash in a personal conversation, David Pawson of Gold Hill, who declined to have his name printed in the Foreward. The papers submitted to the group which formed the basis for the sections which were finally published were written by Kingdon and Luland.

church of Jesus Christ, 'with no suggestion that this will be more true if and when they are corporately organized. This is a fundamental fact often overlooked in the plea for organic union (even within a denomination) as the fulfilment of Christ's prayer for unity.'[98] Later, they again expressed considerable reservations about the contemporary ecumenical movement, noting under the heading 'General Trends Among Liberals', first, that theologically the doctrines of baptism and the church had in particular been subjected to searching scrutiny and re-examination, and this had resulted in traditional Baptist principles being rejected or modified, opening the way, it would seem, for the kind of compromise which would allow for some element of paedobaptist practice. Second, the ecumenical movement with its objective of a united church adopted ambiguous statements, its basis of faith allowed freedom of interpretation and there was a lack of machinery for disciplining members. 'The broad impression given, rightly or wrongly, is that organic union is a way to doctrinal understanding and unity; an approach which is in direct contrast to that which evangelicals believe right.' The third point focused on administrative matters, while the fourth recorded their belief that there was a liturgical trend which over-emphasized the sacraments which had led to the shift in Baptist thinking on baptism.[99] These trends called for evangelicals to deal with them theologically. *Liberty in the Lord*, then, provided a clarion call for further and fuller evangelical thinking on these and other trends within Baptist life, but in clear opposition to the studies being made by the likes of Gilmore, West, Winward and Clark.

Liberty in the Lord itself called forth a mixed response, from the critical,[100] to the approving.[101] Neville Clark, however, noted that it was interesting that two groups of conservatives (the BRF and he and his co-authors of *The Pattern of the Church*), working from the same dogmas about scripture, christology and atonement, came up with quite different doctrinal conclusions about church order and baptism, concluding that 'Perhaps Scripture is not that simple after all.' Clark also noted *Liberty in the Lord*'s criticism of baptismal incorporation into Christ with the comment, baptismal incorporation undermining *sola fide* and *sola gratia* (did St. Paul ever realise his inconsistency?).'[102]

---

98   *Liberty in the Lord: Comment on Recent Trends in Baptist Thought* (1964), 13.
99   *Liberty in the Lord*, 34-36.
100   W.W. Bottoms, 'Where Are Baptists Going? Plea for re-examination of trends of Baptist thought', *BT* May 7, 1964, 10.
101   Mr P. Tucker of East London Tabernacle, 'Liberty in the Lord', *BT* May 21, 1964, 4.
102   N. Clark, 'In the Study', *BQ* 20.7 (July, 1964), 327 and 328, reference to *Liberty in the Lord*, p.38.

The end of the second phase of the twentieth-century baptismal debate was marked by the publication of two important books, both by active participants in the ecumenical movement: Gilmore's *Baptism and Christian Unity* and Beasley-Murray's *Baptism Today and Tomorrow*.[103] Gilmore's was a passionate plea that Baptists should reconize the validity of infant baptism, drawing to attention the stress of recent exponents of infant baptism on the importance of faith for all modes of baptism.[104] He argued that if Baptists were to recapture the spirit of toleration, then people should be able to believe and worship according to their own understanding of scripture and knowledge of God: 'it means that so long as those who practise infant baptism are convinced that this is the will of God for them, Baptists ought not to question their conviction of its validity.'[105] Concessions had to be made to the freedom of individual conscience.[106] In his review, Beasley-Murray took Gilmore to task on arguing from this that Baptists should allow infant baptism, therefore making way in a united church for both forms of baptism.[107] The question that needed to be addressed was, according to Beasley-Murray, '*how* is faith operative in infant baptism?' He concluded,

> Mr Gilmore's motives are impeccable. I wish I could be persuaded his arguments were equally impeccable. The way forward in Church relations is a painful one for everybody, and the pain is greatest where convictions are strongest. Somehow we *must* go forward, with truth and love always in company. It is possible that increased illumination given by the Holy Spirit will mean a heavier cross for the churches. I share the belief that part of that cross will be a reform in baptismal doctrine and practice difficult to be carried through; but it will mean one thing for Baptists and another for Paedobaptists. In this sphere it is imperative to distinguish the things that differ.[108]

For his part, Beasley-Murray acknowledged that 'Baptists...are the most intransigent group in inter-Church discussions; they believe that in their adherence to the primitive pattern of baptism God has entrusted

---

103 Both books were reviewed by W.E. Moore in *BQ* 21.8 (Oct, 1966), 382-83, and along with Basil Moss's *Crisis for Baptism*, by R.P. Martin, 'Baptismal Disgrace', *The Christian and Christianity Today*, July 22, 1966, 11; Gilmore's book was reviewed by Beasley-Murray, 'The Validity of Infant Baptism', *The Christian and Christianity Today*, July 15, 1966, 18; while John Norman reviewed Beasley-Murray's, 'A Jolt About Baptism', *BT* March 10, 1966, 6. Fowler, 'Baptism', 162-68, discusses Gilmore's work.

104 Gilmore, *Baptism and Christian Unity*, ch. 2, 'Faith and Baptism', 17-39.

105 Gilmore, *Baptism and Christian Unity*, 83-84. Gilmore adduced the support of E. Leslie Wenger as expressed in his 'The Problem of So-called Re-Baptism', in *Church Union: News and Views*, May 1958, 23.

106 Gilmore, *Baptism and Christian Unity*, 87-88.

107 See Gilmore, *Baptism and Christian Unity*, 16.

108 Beasley-Murray, 'The Validity of Infant Baptism', 18.

them with a treasure for the whole Church, and that it would be a betrayal of the Lord and of His Church to forsake it. Accordingly they find it difficult to enter into negotiations for the uniting of Churches in a given area.'[109] Later on, he reiterated the position he had outlined at the BWA the previous year, stating that for Baptists infant baptism was not the baptism of the New Testament, and the reality of the present day situation was that there were two baptisms.[110] He wrote, 'concurrence concerning the Biblically oriented theology of baptism is one thing, but concurrence about baptism as it exists in the Churches today is another.'[111]

---

109 Beasley-Murray, *Baptism Today and Tommorrow*, 80.

110 Beasley-Murray, *Baptism Today and Tommorrow*, 145-58. On the present day situation, p.158, he wrote, 'We do not have one baptism. We have two baptisms, one for infants and the other for confessors of faith.'

111 Beasley-Murray, *Baptism Today and Tommorrow*, 160.

CHAPTER SEVEN

The Consolidation of Baptist Sacramentalism

In 1944 Ernest Payne described the Baptist position on baptism thus: 'We do not find here, any more than on other matters, complete unanimity of view. Divergences as to the nature and meaning of sacraments in general inevitably affect thought and practice in regard to baptism as well as the Lord's Supper.' He later added, 'The very considerable variety of practice in regard to baptism from the very beginnings of Baptist witness down to our day is naturally reflected in differences of interpretation. Moreover, Baptist apologetic has inevitably tended to concentrate far more on questions of the subject and mode of baptism than on questions of meaning.'[1]

This situation, however, had to change when an increasing number of Paedobaptist scholars, from Brunner and Barth onwards, with the notable exceptions of Oscar Cullmann and Joachim Jeremias, accepted that New Testament baptism was the baptism of believers by immersion, but who nevertheless retained infant baptism on the basis of theology and tradition as opposed simply to scripture.[2] For Baptists, such a position was wholly untenable because of their understanding of scripture, its authority and their loyalty to it. This shift of viewpoint of some Paedobaptist authors forced Baptists to a reconsideration of their theology of baptism, so much so, that George Beasley-Murray, at the close of this period, wrote on 'Steps to a Revival of Apostolic Baptism', addressed specifically to a Baptist readership.[3] In 1960 Beasley-Murray had criticized existing Baptist practice of baptism, stating that it was not apostolic baptism. 'If the churches—including our own people—desire to have a baptism as rich as that of the Apostolic Church, much courageous thinking requires to be done.' He concluded:

---

1   E.A. Payne, *Fellowship of Believers* (1st edn, 1944), 63 and 70.

2   See, e.g., the surveys of Paedobaptist apologetic provided by Payne, 'Baptism in Present-Day Theology', 171-79; G.R. Beasley-Murray, 'Introduction. The Baptismal Controversy in the British Scene', 17-27.

3   Beasley-Murray, *Baptism Today and Tomorrow*, 89-98. He stated that the 'first step required for Baptists to recover the fulness of apostolic baptism is *humility*', p.89, italics added.

But have not we Baptists a duty to set our own house in order? For too long we have regarded it as our vocation to demonstrate *who* are the proper recipients of baptism, but have been unable to supply a coherent account from the Scriptures of *what* that baptism is that must be administered to the right persons. Anyone acquainted with our churches knows that there exist in them traditions as stereotyped as can be found in any other churches, and we are as dangerously near to mistaking our own popular traditions for the Word of God as are the rest. We Baptists pride ourselves on being churches of the New Testament. It behooves us to take our own medicine—to cast aside our pride, search afresh the Scriptures, submit ourselves to their teaching, and be prepared for reform according to the Word.[4]

Baptists were beginning to realize and challenge other Baptists, questioning whether their own doctrine of baptism was an adequate expression of New Testament baptism and whether there was not much that they could and should learn from Paedobaptists.[5]

This fundamental shift can be seen by the move away from writings which were dominated by the discussion of the mode and subjects of baptism to the theology and practical outworking of that theology.

With but a few exceptions, Baptists were unanimous that the New Testament mode of baptism was immersion and that this was binding for the present day church.[6] Its value lay in its appropriateness by virtue of its symbolism, and this was reinforced by the emphasis on the death, burial and resurrection of Christ and the believer's participation in these events by faith. This was not, however, to say that baptism was merely symbolic. For a long time Baptists had been content with such statements as that made by Dr Arthur Dakin, that even baptism by immersion was 'quite useless apart from faith in the recipient, and it is thought of, first,

---

4   G.R. Beasley-Murray, 'Baptism in the New Testament', *Foundations* 3 (January, 1960), 29-30.

5   Most notably Clark, 'Theology of Baptism', 316, 'if the Paedo-Baptist case is exposed to grave objections and harbours serious weaknesses, the Baptist position in many ways fits even more uneasily with Biblical theology. Its preoccupation with the recipient and the mode of baptism at the expense, so often, of the meaning and purpose of the rite, has constantly exposed its supporters to the charge of tithing mint and anise and cummin whilst neglecting the weightier matters of the law'; p.325, Clark spoke of confusion reigning in Baptist practice. White, *Biblical Doctrine of Initiation*, 279-80, listed Baptists' own difficulties with believer's baptism, concluding a long list of such difficulties, 'There is much in the Lukan, Petrine and Pauline expositions of baptism that finds little place in contemporary Baptist thinking; one sometimes fears that current practice of believer's baptism is scriptural on the single point of reserving baptism for believers and on very little else.' See also pp. 295-96, 306.

6   So Clark, 'Theology of Baptism', 325, 'We have no warrant for making any one mode obligatory; but to give to immersion a normative place is to recognize the importance for sacramental practice of the closest possible correspondence between sign and signification.' In practice, and in exceptional circumstances, Baptists have been willing to baptize by affusion.

as a means of grace to the believer, and then as his witness to His Lord',[7] but an increasing number of scholars and ministers had already recognized the inadequacy of such a position when compared with the teaching of the New Testament and other non-Baptist scholars.

R.E.O. White launched perhaps the most stinging attack on the merely symbolic understanding of believers baptism.

> It must be repeated that some upholders of believer's baptism are as much at fault in minimising what baptism does as the paedobaptists are in applying their more adequate sacrament to the wrong subjects. The view that baptism merely symbolises, declares, a spiritual experience, prompts the same question as does infant baptism: to whom is the declaration made? If it is the pledge of a good conscience addressed to God, does God not answer it? The symbolic, declaratory view of baptism negates much that is undoubtedly present in the primitive rite: the sense that baptism is a real event within the dispensational scheme, a real entrance upon the messianic sign, a personal experience of the actual fulfilment of the promises of the gospel. When the rite is thus impoverished, the claim to dominical authority becomes inexplicable. Did Jesus really require of His followers a religious exercise merely symbolic, devoid of profit, efficacy or result? Moreover, if baptism is no more than a symbolic profession of faith, why should it not be performed at every crisis of religious experience—why is it once only?[8]

White accepted that baptism by immersion vividly recalled the death and burial of Jesus and as vividly suggested the death and burial of the Christian, though not in the same sense, but the notion that baptism was merely a mimed symbol, an acted parable expressing a spiritual attitude not necessarily connected with any outward act 'is unfortunately the view of believer's baptism most widely held. But it is not Paul's view.' Rather, according to Paul, baptism points to the moment when the Christian actually ethically died with Christ to sin. 'Paul's statement [in Colossians 2-3 and Romans 6] is that they *were* baptised into His death, they *did* die with Christ, they *were* buried with Him by baptism into death... Together with the other great Pauline affirmations concerning baptism, that thereby believers are washed, justified, cleansed, sanctified, receive the Spirit, enter the church and the New Age, such statements leave no doubt that in Paul's mind baptism *accomplishes* things. It does not merely represent them, express them figuratively, or impose the obligation that what is here illustrated ought to be accomplished at other times and places.'[9] Baptism is effective and not theatrical or illustrative, because it is the act of responsible and comprehending believers in the kerygma and it is this fact which controls the meaning of Pauline sacramentalism. 'The notion of baptism's effectiveness apart from such response of faith and moral

---

7   Dakin, *Baptist View of the Church and Ministry*, 31-32.

8   White, *Biblical Doctrine of Initiation*, 306.

9   White, *Biblical Doctrine of Initiation*, 215-17.

obedience is utterly foreign to Paul's thought.'[10] Any idea that such a view is mechanical is both unnecessary and untrue as, according to Paul, baptism is dynamic, because the sacrament of which he writes is essentially an act of obedient faith accepting personally and responsibly all that Christ offers in the gospel.[11] To speak of Paul's sacramentalism is possible so long as it is remembered that the efficacy of baptism belongs not to the ceremony of baptism as such but to the action of God, by the Spirit, within the convert's soul who at that time and in this way is responding to the grace offered in the gospel. 'There is no dualism here between faith and baptism simply because for Paul baptism is always, and only, faith–baptism: given that Paul is emphatically a sacramentalist.'[12]

Writing over a decade earlier, H.H. Rowley had expressed matters similarly:

> Baptism is a symbol, and it is the constant teaching of the whole Bible that the symbol has no meaning without that which it symbolizes. As a mere external act it is as dead as the sacrifices which the prophets condemned... The symbol is of less importance than that which it symbolizes. It is of importance that Baptists no less than others should remember this. What matters most is not that a man has been voluntarily immersed, any more than that he has been baptized in infancy, but that he has truly died with Christ and been raised again to newness of life in Him, so that his life is now hid with Christ in God. The symbol is worthless without that which it symbolizes. It must be the organ of the soul's approach in faith and surrender to God before it can become the organ of God's approach in power to him.[13]

It was this meaning of New Testament baptism that an increasing body of Baptist scholars and ministers were striving to rediscover.

Stephen Winward concurred. A sacrament, he submitted, was both symbol, an enacted symbol, and yet much more than a symbol, for while

---

10   White, *Biblical Doctrine of Initiation*, 218.

11   White, *Biblical Doctrine of Initiation*, 220-21.

12   White, *Biblical Doctrine of Initiation*, 226. See also White's, *Invitation to Baptism*, ch. 4 'Baptized into Christ Jesus', 37-43, where he argued that baptism was more than a symbol in that it was an experience of Christ.

13   H.H. Rowley, Professor of Hebrew Language and Literature at Manchester University, 'The Christian Sacraments', in H.H. Rowley, *The Unity of the Bible* (1953), 172-73. Later, pp.185-86, he reiterated the same point: 'It is meaningless without that which it symbolizes, but it may be a channel of blessing to those who know the experience which it symbolizes.' When a symbol became an end in itself the symbol was worthless, yet, the Bible, did not despise 'symbols when they are charged with meaning.' On Rowley see E.A. Payne, 'H.H. Rowley, 1890–1969', *Frat.* 155 (January, 1970), 9-12; F.F. Bruce, 'Obituary. Harold Henry Rowley', *PEQ* 101 (1969), 134; R.E. Clements, 'The Biblical Scholarship of H.H. Rowley (1890–1969)', *BQ* 38.2 (April, 1999), 70-82. Clements, however, fails to make any reference to Rowley's *Aspects of Reunion*, a point corrected by Nicholson, 'H.H. Rowley', 196-99. Rowley discussed the sacraments in some detail in *Aspects of Reunion*, 66-88, and the issue of membership, pp.107-22.

a symbol represented, a sacrament conveyed. 'A sacrament is a means of grace, an instrumental symbol, an act of God. In baptism and the eucharist, this act of God is related to the gospel... To separate either sacrament from the proclamation and acceptance of the gospel, is to pervert it.' Accordingly, significance and conveyance, that which people apprehended and that which God gave, were neither to be equated nor divorced, for the sacraments were for those who saw and accepted that which they signified, and yet also believed that 'God does "immeasurably more than all we can ask or conceive".'[14] In short, baptism was both a sacrament and a symbol.[15]

It was neither the quantity of water[16] nor the actual performance of a rite, for Baptists denied the charge of being merely ritualists, some even arguing that the mode itself was a secondary matter.[17] A.C. Underwood, for example, criticized those Baptists who stressed what people do in baptism rather than what God does, thereby reducing it to a mere sign or a bare symbol. When viewed only as a symbol of an inward experience of conversion or surrender to Christ, of the experience of dying to the old life and rising to newness of life in Christ, as an utterance of a new purpose to live for him and join his people, as a public profession of faith and dedication to Christ and his service, it was true as far as it went, but it did not go far enough. It failed to do justice to the actual experience of those baptized as believers, making the baptism of a believer merely declaratory, reducing the sacrament to a mere sign and a bare symbol, turning all Baptists into ritualists. However, a return to the New Testament doctrine would remove any such misunderstandings, and this would be

---

14   S.F. Winward, *The Reformation of Our Worship* (1964), 69-71.

15   Beasley-Murray, *Baptism Today and Tomorrow*, 13-41.

16   R.L. Child, 'The Ministry and the Sacraments', *BQ* 9.3 (July, 1938), 136, 'it is a mistake to suppose that our distinctive convictions are concerned mainly with the amount of water which is used in the act of baptising'; M.E. Aubrey, 'In the Service of the Churches', *BT* April, 30, 1942, 212, 'It is not the quantity of water but the quality of belief that matters. If we immerse, it is because we think that mode safeguards a truth. The truth, to put it in modern terms, is that when a man gives himself to Christ, he is committed to total warfare. The submerging of the whole body is a symbol of the surrender of the whole life. That is our ideal for church membership. That is our conception of the Church. We say it every time we hold a baptismal service. That is what makes us Baptists, and we need not be ashamed of the nickname.'

17   Robinson, 'Five Points of a Baptists Faith', 11, though he believed that the New Testament mode provided a truer symbolism than any other, yet it was not essential to the spiritual reality. As has already been noted, a considerable number, predominantly ecumenists, went further than this, advocating the possibility of a variety of modes, e.g., A. Gilmore, 'Some Problems of Believer's Baptism', *BT* December 31, 1959, 6, asked whether Baptists were justified in refusing baptism to those incapable of receiving immersion, e.g., the invalided and crippled, or whether affusion was also permissible.

achieved by returning baptism to its New Testament place with conversion and the reception of the Holy Spirit.[18]

Thus, there was a growing number of writers who sought to bring together both the inner and outer aspects of baptism. Wheeler Robinson contended that the fullest and clearest of the Apostle Paul's associations of the outer sign and seal with the inner and invisible grace was made in Romans 6:3-5, where the act of water-baptism was said to unite the believer with the dying, buried and risen Lord on the one hand, and on the other with the new obligations and new resources of a penitent and risen life in Christ. In 1 Corinthians 12:13, the visible act of water-baptism was into the name of Jesus and expressed and mediated the invisible baptism into the Holy Spirit. The context of this verse indicated that Paul was thinking of the common act of water-baptism by which alone there is entrance into the visible Body of Christ, and with this he closely associated the invisible experience as the normal accompaniment. This was supported from the book of Acts (especially Acts 2:38) where water-baptism and Spirit-baptism are intimately linked.[19] Winward wrote, 'The washing of the body with water is the outward and visible sign of the inner and invisible cleansing of the life from all sin. In conversion and baptism we receive through faith in the Saviour the forgiveness of all sin.'[20] This position was confirmed by George Beasley-Murray: 'For Paul the inner and outer acts of the decision of faith and its expression in baptism form one indissoluble event.'[21]

---

18   A.C. Underwood, 'What Mean Ye By This Service?', 58-59 and 60-61.

19   Robinson, 'Five Points of a Baptist's Faith', 8.

20   Winward, *New Testament Teaching on Baptism*, 26-27. See also his *Reformation of Worship*, 59, 'In baptism the *kerygma* was enacted and embodied. And not only the gospel, but the faith of the candidate, was declared and embodied in sign and symbol, in ritual act and sacrament. Here also the outer and the inner, the sacramental act and personal confession...are one.'

21   G.R. Beasley-Murray, 'Baptism in the Epistles of Paul', in Gilmore (ed.), *Christian Baptism*, 130. See also R.L. Child, 'The Practice of the Apostolic Church. Baptism on Profession of Faith', p.17, and 'The Significance of Baptism to St. Paul. Union with Christ in Baptism', p.24, and R.G. Ramsey, 'Baptism and the Gospel. The Perspective and Emphasis Proper to Baptism', p.32, all in Bryan (ed.), *Concerning Believers Baptism*; W. Powell of West Haddon, 'Baptists and Baptism', *BT* September 29, 1949, 9, 'The inner belief necessary to salvation is made definite by its expression in baptism, so that it is even said baptism saves us'; P.R. Clifford, *The Christian Life* (1954), 21-22; E. Shackleton from Barrow-in-Furness, 'The First Epistle of Peter. On Baptism. 1 Peter 3:13 to 4:6', *BT* November 19, 1959, 9; White, *Biblical Doctrine of Initiation*, 125, 'Certainly Jesus criticised merely ritual religiousness—the observance of religious ceremonial without the corresponding religious character and spirit. But when it truly expressed the inward attitude of soul, the outward act of piety received His clear approval and even His command...', and also in 'New Baptismal Questions—II', *BT*

The next logical step was to address the objective and the subjective, the Godward and the human aspects of the rite. Traditionally, Baptists had tended to focus on the subjective, what the believer did in baptism, omitting reference to the activity of God in and through the rite. Baptists were not slow to recognize this. In 1938, Dakin had recognized the lack of attention paid by Baptists to the activity of God in baptism,[22] and it was no time at all before the first of an increasing number of writers addressed this deficiency. Just three months later, Guy Ramsey asked, 'Can we have a purely subjective experience of the Grace of God? Or must there be a continuous interplay of objective reality and subjective reaction in our apprehension of God?'[23] Wheeler Robinson continued to challenge fellow Baptists, arguing that if his interpretation of the New Testament was sound, 'then there is something yet to be done if Baptists are to substantiate their claim to be fully loyal to the New Testament. Baptism is there not only a necessary profession of repentance and faith; it is also a sacrament of grace...'[24] The number of those who took up this matter quickly increased.[25]

August 24, 1961, 2, White spoke of believer's baptism not only expressing but illustrating, objectifying and enshrining the faith which saves.

22   A. Dakin, 'Calvin's Doctrine of Baptism', *BQ* 9.3 (July, 1938), 164. See also his 'Christian Baptism and John's Baptism Contrasted', 39-44.

23   R.G. Ramsey of Horfield, Bristol, 'The Means of Grace. A Personal Confession', *BQ* 9.4 (October, 1938), 213.

24   H.W. Robinson, 'Believers' Baptism and the Holy Spirit', *BQ* 9.7 (July, 1939), 395.

25   See E. Davies, who moved from North Finchley to the position of Welsh Secretary of the SCM and tutor at South Wales Baptist College in 1942, 'Our Baptist Genius. A Reply to Principal Whale', *BT* February 12, 1942, 75, (referring to J.S. Whale's *Christian Doctrine*), and Charles Brown of Chorley Wood, 'Dr. Whale and Infant Baptism', *BT* February 19, 1942, 88, both asserted that baptism was not only the act of Christ but also of the baptized; Champion, *Church of the New Testament*, 70-71, later Champion declared that Baptist baptism, like Jesus', centred on the divine initiative, 'Baptism of Jesus', *BT* March 2, 1961, 5, see also his *Baptists and Unity*, 11; H. Cook, *Why Baptize Believers Only?* (1952), 6; Rowley, 'The Christian Sacraments', 167-68, 'Surely it is hard to suppose that these passages [Acts 8:37, 16:31, 33, Mt. 28:19 and Rom. 10:9] mean that the New Testament writers eliminated the act of God in salvation and made the decision of the believer do all that was necessary.' Later he continued, 'If, then, faith is held to be necessary to baptism, it does not for one moment imply that faith is all that is necessary, and that God can be dispensed with, or that baptism is merely the act of the person who is baptized, or even of the Church and that person. In the context of Biblical thought we may say that if baptism is to be charged with meaning and power it must be both a divine and human act', see also p.185; J.B. Skemp of Durham, 'A Scottish Letter. Report on Baptism', *BT* November 3, 1955, 7, endorsed William Whyte's, minister at Portobello, earlier call ('A Scottish Letter. Report on Baptism', *BT* October 27, 1955, 7) for a reasoned reply to the first interim Report of the Church of Scotland on baptism, saying the fear of sacramentalism was so strong that

George Beasley-Murray wrote: 'the idea that baptism is a purely symbolic rite must be pronounced not only unsatisfactory but out of harmony with the New Testament itself.' Apostolic writers made free use of baptism's symbolism, but they went beyond this to view the act as a symbol with power, that is, a sacrament. The grace available to people in baptism included forgiveness of and cleansing for sins, union with Christ, particularly union in his death and resurrection, participation in Christ's sonship, consecration to God, membership in the church, possession of the Spirit, that is, regeneration, grace to live according to the will of God, deliverance from the powers of evil, inheritance of the Kingdom of God, and the pledge of the resurrection of the body.[26] In this, there was no claim for the magical operation of the baptismal rite, rather the grace offered was nothing less than the gracious action of God himself,[27] and this was possible only because baptism is the divinely appointed rendezvous of grace for faith.[28] 'Faith is needful *before* baptism, that Christ and his Gospel may truly be confessed in it; *in* baptism, to receive what God bestows; and *after* baptism, in order to abide in the grace so freely given and to work out by that grace what God has wrought within.' And this theology of faith–baptism is founded on the presupposition that baptism is administered to converts.[29]

Baptists had so stressed individual conversion that they failed to see that baptism re-stated the truth about God's mighty working which made it possible for conversion to occur; West, *Baptist Principles*, 32.

26   Beasley-Murray, *Baptism in the New Testament*, 263-64.

27   Beasley-Murray, *Baptism in the New Testament*, 264-66. In this he was in total agreement with Walton, *Gathered Community*, 164, whom he quoted in a footnote, pp.265-66 n.4, the full quotation of which is, 'As the Church is created by God, so Believers' Baptism is primarily God's act. It is not, first of all, our act of obedience—an ordinance—but God's redemptive activity—a sacrament. Here Christ gives Himself in all his fullness to those whom He has chosen and called. Yet in this matter, the spiritual liberty of the Christian man is involved.'

28   Beasley-Murray, *Baptism in the New Testament*, 273, but see his whole discussion from pp.266-75.

29   Beasley-Murray, *Baptism in the New Testament*, 274, italics his. He added, 'In the New Testament faith *comes* to baptism; the idea of baptism creating faith is not on the horizon', p.274. He later wrote, 'That salvation is of God is an axiom of Biblical religion. The Gospel declares what God has done in Christ for the redemption of the world. The sacraments are embodiments of that Gospel, deriving significance from their relation to the acts of God in Christ', p.344. 'For the Apostle, and for his contemporaries, baptism was for *faith*. They never envisaged it being administered to any but believers', p.352. In his 'Baptism in the Epistles of Paul', 136, he stated, 'We have therefore to recognize a tension in Paul's thought concerning the relation of Christ's redemptive acts and the believer's response thereto in baptism... It is that work of grace which gives baptism any significance.' On p.138 he said, 'the subjective aspect has [not] been made the starting point, nor has it been exalted above the objective

This was in agreement with the work of White two years earlier, who had argued that

> The obvious objections to a sacramental interpretation of infant baptism are assumed to lie equally against believer's baptism—which is nonsense. The dynamic, or existential, sacramentalism of the New Testament seizes upon the fact that divine activity and human response meet in sacramental *actio*... efficacy belongs strictly neither to the element, nor to the rite, but to the action of God within the soul of the baptised who at that time, in that way, is making his response to the grace offered to him in the gospel. The sacrament consists not in the thing done, but in *the doing* of that which gives expression to faith in appointed ways. On the one side, the faith of the person doing the appointed thing invests the rite at that moment, for himself, with sacramental meaning; on the other side, God, accepting this response, in fulfilment of His promise in the gospel invests the rite at that moment, for that convert, with sacramental power.[30]

Neville Clark was another explicitly to criticize much of Baptist teaching on baptism as being inadequate because it focused on the subjective element of the rite, again asserting that 'the inseparability of divine action and human response must never be denied.'[31] Correcting such excessive subjectivism, Clark impressed that 'Baptism is a sacrament of the Gospel, not of our experience of it; of God's faithfulness, not of our faithful response to Him; and any theological formulation which

---

redemption history: on the contrary, the personal experience has been grounded upon the objective redemption.' Then, p.148, he quoted with approval W.H.P. Hatch, *The Pauline Idea of Faith and its Relation to Jewish and Hellenistic Religion* (1917), 43, 'Faith and baptism go together, as is clear from the following passage (Gal 3:27)... The two constitute a single act of which faith is the subjective and baptism the objective side.' See also 'Baptism in the New Testament', 28, where he pressed, 'from the human side, faith is viewed as the operative power of baptism.' From the evidence of his exegetical study, he concluded that 'If God gives his gracious gifts to faith *and* baptism, he gives them in association, i.e. he gives them to faith in baptism, or (which amounts to the same) to baptism *in faith*', italics his, p.28. See the whole of his discussion of the relation of faith to grace in baptism, pp.27-29. In *Baptism Today and Tommorow*, 66, writing of baptism, the gospel and faith, he developed his earlier statements, maintaining that rightly understood baptism also avoided the perils of extremes: 'It harmonizes the objective and subjective elements in Christianity, the personal and the corporate, the relationship with the Lord of the cross and resurrection, and the relationship to members of His body.'

30   White, *Biblical Doctrine of Initiation*, 308, italics his. See his earlier contribution on this matter, his *BT* prize essay, 'The Baptist View of the Sacraments', *BT* March 29, 1945, 6, 'In these days of religious subjectivism it is no small gain for the Church to be thus repeatedly reminded that she sprang from a concrete, historic act of God, unalterable and definitive...'

31   Clark, 'The Theology of Baptism', 311-12. He developed this further on pp.313-14.

lends itself so readily to an interpretation of the rite primarily in terms of a public confession of faith must at once be suspect.'[32] Several years earlier H.W. Trent had argued the same point, asking, 'do the Ordinances testify to what we do or to what God has done, or both? The present writer has the feeling that we have been inclined to make the Sacraments man-centred rather than God-centred and the contribution which man makes has overshadowed God's work in redemption. We must regain our perspective and regard the rites of Baptism and the Lord's Supper as essentially indicative of what God has done and continues to do in Christ for man in the first place and how men respond in the second... If we emphasise the Godward aspect to the exclusion of the other we must arrive ultimately at paedo-baptism and infant Communion. And vice versa if we glorify the manward we arrive at a position when Baptism becomes purely a sign of our faith and the Lord's Supper a memorial rite with little other meaning.'[33] This led to his first conclusion, that Baptists had no grounds to be complacent towards the sacraments and that there was room for closer thought and renewed interest in sacramental theology and practice. 'We ought to emphasise at all levels that the Ordinances are the Gospel in action, and the important thing is that they testify to what God in Christ has done and is doing for men rather than what we ourselves do. The part that faith plays is in receiving the benefits of which they speak and in making them effective for us. Faith does not condition the primary act of God though it is necessary for the reception of its benefits.'[34]

Stephen Winward admitted, 'Speaking of our churches as a whole, it can hardly be denied that at present many of our baptismal services give a distorted picture of the meaning of baptism. The stress is usually laid upon that which is being done by the candidates. This itself is often over-simplified and represented only as an act of witness.' Other aspects of baptism needed to be stressed. First, in baptism God acts, through Christ in the Spirit. Second, baptism is an act of God by which believers are admitted into his church. Third, baptism is a confessional rite. 'In the Divine–human encounter of baptism, confession is the human response

---

32   Clark, 'The Theology of Baptism', 316. A similar criticism of the onesidedness of both Paedobaptist and Baptist baptismal theology was made by G. Hastings, 'An Outline of the History of Baptism', *Frat.* 90 (October, 1953), 31, 'there is a great difficulty in expressing the doctrine so that one side of its truth does not outshine another side. Men have stressed the working of the power of God in baptism until the faith of the one being baptised was forgotten. And perhaps men have looked so much upon the faith of the candidate, and the witness that he is making, that they have forgotten that God works wonders and miracles of grace through the sacrament.'

33   Trent, 'Ourselves and the Ordinances', 11-12.

34   Trent, 'Ourselves and the Ordinances', 21.

to the Divine activity.'[35] A year later, Winward again directly reflected the language of Brunner when he declared that 'Baptism is the encounter between the Lord and man, the place where the enacted word of God meets the enacted human response.'[36]

With the bringing together of the outward and inward and subjective and objective aspects of baptism the way was open for both the further development and consolidation of sacramentalist teaching within Baptist doctrine. Accompanied by an increasing number of other writers, the leading sacramentalist of the second half of the century has been George Beasley-Murray. Though the old antagonism still existed between those who wished to play off the sacramentalist against the anti-sacramentalist position, it is clear from the sources that in this period the sacramentalist understanding became not just acceptable to most Baptists but an indisputable part of the theology of those who wrote most extensively on the subject.

That conflict continued to exist, however, is illustrated by an interchange in 1948 between L.A. Read of Stapleton and Stoke Gifford, Bristol, and George Beasley-Murray, at the time minister of Zion, Cambridge, which fairly represents the positions on either side. In January 1948, Louis Read wrote a short article on 'The Ordinances', in which he observed that for many members of Baptist congregations there was the feeling that the ordinances were needless or for select souls. 'This has caused such concern that we now often hear pronouncements which seek to awaken people to the place and meaning of these rites and in these they are most often termed sacraments and stated to be "means of grace". Here I am concerned to show why I feel these to be wrong emphases, unlikely to solve the problem of instructing our people in attendance at the more intimate meetings of the church fellowship.'[37]

First, Read examined the word 'sacrament'. Such a term, he contended, could be used if its meaning could be established which fitted the Baptist view of ceremonies and which was isolated from its history and use by other communions. 'As things are it generally conveys a meaning alien to our thought or is so nebulous as to mean nothing.' Not least did Read disapprove of the definition which allowed all of life to be considered sacramental in the sense of being able to mediate God to people.[38]

After a tentative use of the word 'sacrament' in the early days, Baptists substituted for it the word 'ordinance', a word lacking ambiguity and being self-explanatory, implying quite naturally the institution of both

---

35   S.F. Winward, 'The Administration of Baptism', *Frat.* 123 (January, 1962), 8-10.

36   S.F. Winward, 'The Church in the New Testament', in Gilmore (ed.), *Pattern of the Church*, 69.

37   L.A. Read, 'The Ordinances', *Frat.* 67 (January, 1948), 8.

38   Read, 'The Ordinances', 8.

ordinances by Christ, a fact which provided sufficient reason for their continued observance.[39] To claim that baptism and the Lord's Supper were means of grace was far from satisfactory, 'For it would seem that people come in the mood naturally engendered by this conception of the ceremonies and when they do not at once perceive some benefit, conclude they have been misled.' Justification for the claim of a means of grace was usually found in Augustine's phrase about being an outward and visible sign of an inward and spiritual grace, but this Read dismissed as redundant, as signs had to be outward and visible and grace in the religious sphere could only be inward and spiritual.[40]

Read understood the two ordinances primarily as opportunities for the expression of dedication and gratitude to God. To interpret them as occasions chiefly for the bestowal of grace was selfish, untrue and unbiblical. Any benefit which might be claimed from observance of the ordinances was secondary to Christ's desire for the believer's remembrance and worship. 'We should gather, not primarily to gain some good, but to offer praise to Him Who is our Redeemer and has already gained for us in that the greatest good.' This was not to deny that grace was received by the worshipper, for the Spirit was always present when any met in sincerity and truth to worship their God as he had directed. 'But we must emphasise not our private desire for gain but our submission to our God Who first loved us and redeemed us for Himself.' The purpose and meaning of the ordinances, therefore, lay in the fact that through them believers dedicated themselves to the master, initially by baptism and then by constant and frequent renewal at the Lord's Supper. 'It is our response to His goodness and a vivid portrayal of the means of our redemption, evoking in us praise and worship. We are blessed in that inevitably, and certainly receive more than we give; yet this must remain the prime meaning. We give ourselves because He asks it of us. So these have a distinctive character, marking them off from all other meetings of the church.'[41]

Beasley-Murray responded with 'The Sacraments'. His aim was not to defend the use of the term 'sacrament', though, he stated, its loose use by some was scarcely an adequate reason for its rejection. He did, however, 'deplore that a fellow-Baptist, in a discussion on the nature of the sacraments, should write with scarcely a reference to the Scriptures.' The general emphasis in discussion of baptism among Baptists, he reported, undoubtedly fell on its value as a means of confession and that other significations were subordinated to this main idea. Baptism was normally held to make no difference to the condition of the baptized, its value

---

39   Read, 'The Ordinances', 9.
40   Read, 'The Ordinances', 9-10.
41   Read, 'The Ordinances', 10.

lying in the expression of spiritual realities already appropriated. This was the position presented by Read and the many non-sacramentalists who maintained that, 'Baptism is our act for God, our response to His appeal for obedience.' But, without denying baptism's confessional value, Beasley-Murray argued that this was secondary not primary, for 'In every explicit mention of Baptism it is regarded as the supreme moment of our union with Christ in His redemptive acts for us and our consequent reception of the life of the Spirit', as in Romans 6:4-8, Galatians 3:27 and 1 Peter 3:21, where each implied that outward expression and inward experience should coincide, and where the act mediated the experience of receiving.[42] He failed to see how exegesis of these passages, along with Titus 3:5 and 1 Corinthians 12:13, could lead to the assertion that the important thing in baptism was what we gave God. 'Without minimising the necessity of faith and confession of Christ, such a view is tantamount to esteeming our act of surrender to God as of greater value than His gift of Himself to us.' Objections to this position were usually made on other than exegetical grounds. Free Churchmen were disinclined to believe that a sacrament could have such significance, that baptism could be operative not symbolic, postponing the operation and gift of the Spirit from the submission of faith to the reception of an outward ordinance. Beasley-Murray identified the word 'postpone' as the key to the problem, for the New Testament knew nothing of postponing a baptism after conversion.

> Every recorded baptism takes place immediately upon profession of faith, the instances are too well known to require statement. In the primitive Church conversion and baptism are so indissolubly linked together that they may be regarded as a unity. In such a context to speak of a Christian dying and rising with Christ and receiving the Spirit of Pentecost in baptism is no magical concept, for the submission to the rite was the occasion of surrender to Christ. This is no setting of a sacrament over against repentance and faith, as though Baptism made conversion unnecessary, but the intertwining of the two so that baptism is a part of conversion. It is only when the primitive relationship is separated that sacerdotalism creeps in and *opus operatum* becomes the watchword instead of the New Testament principle *nulla sacramentum sine fide*.[43]

In dividing the unity of conversion and baptism Baptists had become almost as culpable as others, and in so doing had become accustomed to introduce a probationary period between profession of faith and confession of faith in baptism and joining the church, baptism thereby effectively becoming a kind of promotion in discipleship, instead of initiation into Christ and the Christian life. The reason offered in defence

---

42   G.R. Beasley-Murray, 'The Sacraments', *Frat.* 70 (October, 1948), 3.
43   Beasley-Murray, 'The Sacraments', 4.

of this separation was the necessity of giving a new convert instruction so as to establish them in the faith. 'We grant that this is necessary, but who said it should precede baptism? Contrary to popular opinion and practice, the whole New Testament set-up of doctrine and organisation is based on the assumption that instruction in doctrine is for the baptised Christian, not for the enquirer.' If this seemed like putting the cart before the horse, he continued, this was only because Baptists had not become used to the fact that *kerugma* precedes *didache*, the gospel before doctrine.[44]

If Baptists feared to baptize converts straightaway, Beasley-Murray continued, then they needed to recognize that in doing so they had changed the nature of baptism. The New Testament declared that it was the transition of the believer from one world to another, from life estranged from God to life in Christ, and whatever else baptism might bring a year after conversion, it could not bring that. To teach that would be to head for Romanism. But once baptism was once more regarded as part of conversion, the moment of supreme surrender rather than the expression of a believer's obedience, Baptists would again be free to teach the New Testament doctrine of baptism.[45] His discussion concluded noting the irony if the present generation witnessed New Testament baptism being championed by paedobaptist theologians, while Baptists lapsed into a sub-theological view of the rite. 'If we are to take that opportunity, which Wheeler Robinson foresaw a generation ago would come, of leading the Body of Christ to the true view of Baptism, we shall do it only if we rise to a clearer apprehension of it than we appear to possess to-day.'[46]

It was most important to Beasley-Murray that baptism was a part of the conversion experience. Addressing the fourth session of the Baptist Assembly in 1959, he elucidated his views that part of the conversion experience was turning to God in repentance and faith which came to definitive expression in baptism. The regular procedure of Baptists to separate conversion and baptism was not New Testament practice, where faith found its goal in baptism.[47] He reiterated the point on numerous occasions,[48] and in this he played an invaluable part in a process which

---

44   Beasley-Murray, 'The Sacraments', 4-5.

45   Beasley-Murray, 'The Sacraments', 5, and see also his 'The Church of Scotland and Baptism', *Frat.* 99 (January, 1956), 9, where he accepted the report's claims that baptism was a dying with Christ, a union with him, a recreation in him, a subjection to his total Lordship over body and soul, only on the condition that 'baptism and conversion be viewed as an indivisible unity of experience.'

46   Beasley-Murray, 'The Sacraments', 5.

47   G.R. Beasley-Murray, 'The Saving Experience', *BT* May 7, 1959, 8-9.

48   E.g. G.R. Beasley-Murray, 'The Spirit is There', *BT* December 10, 1959, 8, 'For...the New Testament writers, baptism was nothing less than "*the climax of God's dealing with the penitent seeker and of the convert's return to God*"', italics his. Equally

had begun before him,[49] but which grew largely as a result of his advocacy.[50]

---

as axiomatic for a proper theology of baptism as baptism administered to converts is conversion and baptism being inseparable, if not indistinguishable, for in the primitive apostolic church baptism was 'conversion-baptism', *Baptism Today and Tomorrow*, 37.

49   H.V. Larcombe, 'Our Specific Contribution', *BT* January 13, 1944, 6; Walton, *Gathered Community*, 27; Cook, *Theology of Evangelism*, 111, who understood baptism to be an essential element of the Pentecostal testimony, being to Peter the completion of all that was involved in repentance, concluding, 'that all true evangelism must aim not only at conversion but at conversion that leads directly to baptism and church membership'; A. Gilmore, 'Some Recent Trends in the Theology of Baptism', *BQ* 15.7 (July, 1954), 311, 'baptism and conversion are very closely linked and that, in fact, baptism is the recognised declaration of an inner change in the heart of man', see his whole discussion of baptism and conversion, pp.311-18.

50   Commenting on the at times heated correspondence sparked off by the publication of *Christian Baptism*, S.W. Ford of London, 'Christian Baptism', *BT* November 5, 1959, 6, observed that most of the correspondents seemed to have shut out the Holy Spirit from baptism, and this separation of baptism from conversion thereby rendered baptism unnecessary. West, *Baptist Principles*, 32, explained that 'it will help if we recognise that baptism is a part of a total conversion experience', but then added, '—an experience which may be short in terms of time, or long.' Though not mentioning baptism as a part of conversion, Payne and Winward, *Orders and Prayers*, 131-32, ascribed to baptism the benefits of conversion. White, *Biblical Doctrine of Initiation*, 116, 'To claim His authority, the form of initiation must express the terms upon which Jesus offered men salvation. Christian baptism may be the concomitant of repentant faith: it may be its earliest symbolic expression: it cannot in any event with His authority be accepted as its substitute'. See also G.E. Shackleton, 'Conversion and Discipleship: 13—The Place of Baptism', *BT* May 17, 1962, 11; W. Scott, 'The Spiritual and the Sacramental in the Theology of Baptism', *Frat.* 135 (July, 1965), 25, 'It is only when we lose sight of the New Testament pattern of personal commitment to Jesus Christ, expressed and confirmed in baptism that insuperable difficulties are created', and, 'The fact cannot be gainsaid that in Paul's estimation of it, baptism was an event closely woven into the texture of the conversion experience, intimately connected with repentance and faith, and identified with commitment to Christ as its concrete expression. Baptism was into the body of Christ.' C.J. Pike, *Under Christ's Control* (1950), 12, was vaguer when he said that in New Testament times baptism 'generally took place on the same day as conversion.' Channon, *Much Water*, 52, remarked that the search for any long period between conversion and baptism in the New Testament would be in vain. The difficulty of trying to translate this belief of the place of baptism in conversion into actual Baptist practice was reflected in two separate works by Dr Jim Perkin of Hale Road, Altrincham. At one point he rued the fact that the old view which believed that baptism and church membership were two different things was gaining ground, one of the consequences being conversion and baptism were separated, 'The Principles and Practice of Believers' Baptism', *BT* June 4, 1959, 10, whereas in the introduction to his *Divine Encounter: An Outline for Discussion of Believer's Baptism* (1965), 3, material written for baptismal preparation, he wrote, 'It is some time since the candidates were brought to the point of decision; now they are to seal their allegiance to

In his *An Approach to the Theology of the Sacraments*, Neville Clark set aside the question of the recipients of baptism, thereby enabling him to address directly the theology of baptism. 'There is little doubt', he wrote, 'that the New Testament view of baptism is of a rite that is effective rather than merely symbolic. It brings the disciple into a union with Christ too deep and realistic for words adequately to describe it; it has objective significance.'[51] In the last resort baptism is not 'into the death of Christ but baptism into Christ, the incarnate, crucified, risen and ascended Redeemer. In baptism the disciple enters into the whole redemptive action of his Lord, so that what was once done representatively for him may now be done in actuality in him; he is incorporated in order that he may be crucified.'[52] In his review, Beasley-Murray agreed, saying that this was well said and in the line of thought of an increasing number of Baptists—not least those who were to combine to produce *Christian Baptism*—'Its provocativeness is an advantage, for it demands a constant questioning of presuppositions, and anyone who can disturb us from platitudinous thinking deserves our gratitude.'[53] Clark concluded: 'At the opening of the Christian way stands the sacrament of Christian initiation. In the baptismal rite we are offered forgiveness of sins, engrafted into the mystical body of the Christ, incorporated into the manhood of the Son. Receiving the gift of the Holy Spirit and made sons of God by adoption, we participate in the life of the blessed Trinity. Reborn of water and the Spirit, we are, henceforth, those who have died and risen with Christ.'[54]

---

their Lord and his Church in baptism.' Frequently, however, the exact relationship between conversion and baptism went unspecified, e.g., the 1948 'Baptist Doctrine of the Church', 442, 'The basis of our membership in the church is a conscious and deliberate acceptance of Christ as Saviour and Lord by each individual... It is this vital evangelical experience which underlies the Baptist conception of the Church and is both expressed and safeguarded by the sacrament of Believers' Baptism'; Winward, *New Testament Teaching on Baptism*, 13, 'God gives to us His Holy Spirit in conversion and baptism...'

51   Clark, *An Approach*, 32.
52   Clark, *An Approach*, 31
53   G.R. Beasley-Murray, 'Theology and the Sacraments', *BT* May 24, 1956, 10.
54   Clark, *An Approach*, 84. Three years later, Clark, 'The Theology of Baptism', 306, continued his thoughts on baptism, linking it to the pattern and limits of salvation history (*Heilsgeschichte*): 'Its foreshadowings lie in the past, its consummation in the future; but its theology must be written round the two poles of the baptism of Jesus at the Jordan and its fulfilment in His death, resurrection and ascension.' He reiterated that there was a threefold emphasis of New Testament baptismal theology: it effects the forgiveness of sins, initiation into the church and the gift of the Spirit, each stemming from John's baptism and Jesus' participation in it, each being transfigured by the fulfilment that the cross and resurrection provide, and each being marked by the eschatological tension between the 'now' and the 'not yet' which characterizes the Christian era,

It was not long before Clark was attacked for his views. G. Thompson Brake heralded Clark's book as 'excellent', but possessive of 'disturbing features.' He accused Clark of having been over-influenced by Catholic and Anglo-Catholic writers such as Dom Gregory Dix, A.G. Herbert and L.S. Thornton in his attempt to reconcile Catholic incarnational theology with evangelical views. When Clark wrote, 'In so far as the Church is the extension of the incarnation, the sacraments are the extension of the atonement',[55] Brake insisted that he could not have it both ways. The danger of seeing the church as an extension of the incarnation was that it inevitably led to a Catholic conception of the church and the sacraments. The implications of Clark's book was that the Lord added to the church those who were being baptized, not those who were saved. Any reference to baptism being effective rather than symbolic came under Brake's strictures. Again and again, he claimed, while reading the book the reader had to substitute the word 'salvation' for 'baptism' and he accused Clark of advocating baptismal regeneration. 'We cannot share his enthusiasm for the catholic categories of thought. It is very much to be hoped that he does not remain as enthusiastic.'[56]

Jim Perkin, having just finished his doctorate on baptism at Oxford, was quick to Clark's defence, suggesting that Brake had misunderstood Clark's main purpose which had been to deal with fundamentals of sacramental theology and not denominational views or practices. Perkin claimed that Clark was one of the few writers who had turned first to the New Testament in order to draw out what baptism and the eucharist really meant. 'Not since J.H. Shakespeare', Perkin concluded, 'has anyone called [Baptists] so loudly to examine their basic tenets.'[57]

Clark's second defender was Harry Trent, who challenged Brake's contention that Clark was over-influenced by Catholic writers. Did it follow, he queried, that just because a book was written by a Catholic that its contents were necessarily suspect? Further, Clark did not always quote such authors with approval, and Trent also charged Brake with taking passages out of their contexts. Concerning baptism as an effective rite, Trent asked whether, in the light of Romans 6 and other passages, it was possible to conclude otherwise? Using twentieth-century categories such a conclusion was possible, however, in New Testament terms it was not. The

---

pp.308-09. Clark also touched on baptism in 'The Fulness of the Church of God', 79-113, and in his *Call to Worship*, 54-59, returning to the eschatological dimension most recently in his 'Baptism and Eschatology', in Porter and Cross (eds.), *Baptism*, 337-49.

55   Clark, *An Approach*, 74.

56   G.T. Brake, minister at Halstead, 'The Theology of the Sacraments', *BT* June 28, 1956, 7. Brake was initially a Methodist, entering the Baptist ministry in 1955 and serving two Essex Baptist churches, Halstead and Avenue, Southend-on-Sea, before re-entering the Methodist ministry in 1971.

57   J.R.C. Perkin, 'The Theology of the Sacraments', *BT* July 5, 1956, 6.

act of baptism had become so far removed from the 'salvation experience' which it had accompanied in the New Testament that it was inevitable that Baptists had lost something of its meaning. 'To assert that a rite is effective does not mean that it is so *apart from* active faithful participation.'[58] It was because spiritual experience and sacramental symbolism went hand in hand in the early church that Clark was justified in assessing the New Testament rite as effective rather than merely symbolic. As to how baptism effectively accomplished the believer's union with Christ, a point frequently stressed by Baptists,[59] Clark had answered in terms of initiation into the church. 'It is here', Trent declared, 'that I feel the author makes a valuable contribution for it is not an uncommon attitude or belief in our Denomination today that Church membership is something different and unconnected with Baptism', a position which had led to the anomalous position of coming across folk baptized but not received into the church, or when the word of a minister was sufficient for baptism, for the church had to have its say before the candidate could enter church fellowship.[60]

It was the inability of most Baptists to keep in biblical tension the various aspects of the New Testament rite that led the likes of Clark and White to write what they did, but especially Beasley-Murray, who wrote what are undoubtedly the most eloquent, theologically balanced and important contributions any Baptist has made to the baptismal debate, contributions that span six decades, but which focus down upon three major writings.[61] While clearly the foremost Baptist sacramentalist,

---

58   H.W. Trent, 'The Theology of the Sacraments', *BT* July 12, 1956, 7, italics added.

59   See Child, 'Significance of Baptism to Paul', especially pp.23-25; Winward, *New Testament Teaching on Baptism*, 46, on Romans 6:1-4, 'we are *united* with him in his death and resurrection. This union is entered into through faith and baptism'; Trent, 'Ourselves and the Ordinances', 13; Crabtree, *Restored Relationship*, 65, what Paul means by being 'in him' is being 'united with the crucified and risen Christ through faith and baptism.'

60   H.W. Trent, 'The Theology of the Sacraments', *BT* July 12, 1956, 7.

61   Beasley-Murray, 'Baptism in the Epistles of Paul', *Baptism in the New Testament* and *Baptism Today and Tomorrow*. M.J. Walker, 'Baptist Worship', in Clements (ed.), *Baptists in the Twentieth Century*, 24, claimed that Beasley-Murray's *Baptism in the New Testament* and White's *Biblical Doctrine of Initiation* 'revolutionized the Baptist understanding of the intiating sacrament.' J.J. Brown reiterated this conviction, 'George Raymond Beasely-Murray. A Personal Appreciation', in P. Beasley-Murray (ed.), *Mission to the World: Essays to Celebrate the 50th Anniversary of the Ordination of George Raymond Beasley-Murray to the Christian Ministry (BQSup,* 1991), 15. Cf. also R.A. Culpepper, 'George R. Beasely-Murray', in George and Dockery (eds.), *Baptist Theologians*, 576, who referred to *Baptism in the New Testament* as 'the definitive work on the subject for years to come.' (See also the biographical appreciation, W.H. Gloer, 'Editor's Preface', in W.H. Gloer (ed.), *Eschatology and the*

Beasley-Murray was by no means alone. The most important book on this matter was the collaborative *Christian Baptism*. Together, the articles provided both a response to the many calls for a major Baptist contribution to the baptismal debate and a powerful argument for the sacramental nature of baptism.[62] In this regard two articles in particular stood out. The first, and to a lesser extent, was the concluding article on 'The Theology of Baptism' by Neville Clark. In 1956, he had written, 'Any attempt to state and analyse the Pauline theology of baptism is confronted with immediate difficulties.'[63] This task of developing an adequate exegesis of Paul's teaching on baptism was taken on by Beasley-Murray, and it was this article more than any other which caused a debate which was to last nearly a year and a half, and centred around the same kind of charges Clark had faced three years previously and was to a lesser extent to face again with his 'The Theology of Baptism'.[64]

George Beasley-Murray had defended the biblical sacramentalist view of baptism in 1948, but in his essay 'Baptism in the Epistles of Paul' he expounded the position that for Paul baptism was a sacrament of the gospel and that this fact was basic to all the apostle's utterances on the subject. This proved the most controversial work on baptism by any Baptist this century. He argued that behind and in baptism stood 'the Christ of the cross and resurrection, bestowing freedom from sin's guilt

---

New Testament: Essays in Honour of Goerge Raymond Beasley-Murray (Peabody, MA, 1988), vii-x, and 'World pays tribute as George Beasley-Murray dies at 83', *BT* March 2, 2000, 1-2.) However, Walker's statement cannot be accepted just as it is, because, even though Beasley-Murray and White produced what are without doubt the most important, detailed and eloquent examinations of baptism in this period, their impact has been limited in both grass-roots baptismal theology and the actual practice of the rite, a fact borne out by the observation that much of what they said has either not been read by many Baptists, including ministers (not least because of their length), or have been read but not understood, or have been read but ignored.

62   See the discussion of the book and the responses to it by Fowler, 'Baptism', 122-47.

63   Clark, *An Approach*, 22. At the time of writing 'The Theology of Baptism' Clark moved from Rochester to Amersham-on-the-Hill Free Church.

64   The editorial in the issue of *Frat.* which had two articles devoted to *Christian Baptism* anticipated that it would be Clark's essay which would displease some, 'Editorial', *Frat.* 111 (July, 1959), 4. D.S. Russell noted the complexity of Clark's language, 'Christian Baptism I', 7. The reason that Clark's work on the sacramental nature of baptism caused less of a stir than Beasley-Murray's can only be conjectured. However, it would not seem unreasonable, particularly in the light of Russell's remark, to suppose that in large measure it is due to the complexity of both Clark's style and thought, which would put off everyone except the most determined and theologically adroit readers. E.F. Kevan was particularly critical of Clark's essay, 'Christian Baptism II', 10-11. Clark responded in 'Christian Baptism Under Fire', *Frat.* 114 (October, 1959), 16-18.

and power, and the Spirit who gives the life of the age to come in the present and is the pledge of the resurrection at the last day.' But Paul went further than any of his predecessors and contemporaries, seeing baptism as the sacrament of union with Christ. Because of this, baptism involved union with him in his redemptive acts, both in the rite and in subsequent life, and union with his body, the church, making the believer a living member who partook in the life of the whole. 'Baptism was thus an effective sign; in it Christ and faith come together in the meeting of conversion.'[65] Whether baptism was conceived of as a sacrament of the gospel or of union with Christ, 'in either case faith is integral to it', and this was the decisive issue between Baptists and Paedobaptists. He continued: 'The Gospel exercises its radical influence in a man's life when he receives it in faith; he becomes one with Christ when he submits to Him in faith; for Paul the decisive expression of such faith is baptism.'[66] That faith and baptism went together was consistently maintained by Paul in his baptismal teaching, setting forth a unified baptismal theology where the presence of faith is *presumed*, operative as the 'instrument of surrender' of the convert.[67] Therefore, when Paul's teach-

---

65   Beasley-Murray, 'Baptism in the Epistles of Paul', 148. He was not alone in understanding baptism as an effective sign. See also Gilmore, 'Jewish Antecedents', 62; White, *Biblical Doctrine of Initiation*, 98, 'Never, with Jesus' baptismal experience before us, can we reverently say that "nothing happens" in baptism. In Jesus' experience water-baptism proved to be Spirit-baptism, not only coincident in time but causally related... Henceforth, true baptism is inseparable from the gift of the Spirit'; pp.263-64, 'Men are saved by faith: but faith too can degenerate into a transient mood of the soul unless it be given body, substance, objectivity, in the overt acts of believing men. Faith needs to be "objectified" in the sacramental experience of the believer, and this involves no inconsistency, because for John, [whose writings White had just examined] as for the whole New Testament, "sacrament" *means* "faith-sacrament". There is no tension, dualism, or contradiction in requiring faith and sacrament, because baptism *is* believer's baptism... Tension arises when baptism...[is] divorced from faith and then set over against it', italics his, and p.294, 'Where baptism is faith finding expression, there divine truth is made known and divine things happen in the soul.' See also pp.273 and 305. Also, White, *Open Letter*, 262, 'sacraments attest and confirm to believers the abiding effect of the life and death of Christ'; R.L. Child, 'What Happens in Baptism?', *BT* February 2, 1960, 8, 10; Jones, 'Christian Baptism III', 22, 'baptism will be the climax of [the] conversion experience, and that through his new faith he will die with Christ and rise with new power to newness of life. This can be real for him providing that the time from the initial conversion experience is not too long. Baptism will be an effective sign, the outer and the inner experience will be one'; Winward, *Reformation of Our Worship*, 71. Such a position, however, was vigorously opposed, e.g. by Kevan, 'Christian Baptism II', 9-10.

66   Beasley-Murray, 'Baptism in the Epistles of Paul', 148.

67   Beasley-Murray, 'Baptism in the Epistles of Paul', 148-49, citing Rom. 6:1-11; 10:9-10; Gal. 3:27; Col. 2:11-12; 1 Cor. 6:11, italics added.

ing about baptism is applied to infants incapable of such faith violence is done to exegesis. 'Nor is there evidence that Paul possessed another baptismal theology which he applied to infants.'[68]

The first reactions to his work, and to the volume as a whole, were very positive, Beasley-Murray's contribution being hailed as 'a most scholarly and convincing assessment of the evidence' which stressed baptism as an act of personal faith thereby ruling out any magical notions being attached to the rite.[69] What criticisms there were, were initially directed towards Clark's essay.

The controversy began inconspicuously enough when Robert Clarke from Jordanstown, County Antrim, Ireland, a Presbyterian who had become a Baptist, expressed his concern about comments in *Christian Baptism* which he understood to support baptismal regeneration, notably Clark's statement that 'Baptism effects initiation into the life of the blessed Trinity and all the blessings of the new "age".' He asked, 'Aren't those who trust in the Lord Jesus Christ as Saviour and who are born again of the Holy Spirit partakers of the divine nature, and in possession of the divine life, before they are baptised?' He had always believed Baptist teaching to be that believer's baptism symbolized union with Christ, making it more real and through it bringing spiritual blessing, but that it did not effect such union.[70]

Clarke was quickly followed by L.J. Stones who expressed grave concerns about what he called the 'new sacramentalism' which was gain-

---

68   Beasley-Murray, 'Baptism in the Epistles of Paul', 149.

69   So Russell, 'Christian Baptism I', 6. The book was described as excellent and almost wholly dispassionate by the Methodist scholar Dr Norman Snaith, 'Christian Baptism', *BT* April 30, 1959, 10, while E.H. Robertson, 'Christian Baptism', *BT* May 14, 1959, 10-11, lauded Beasley-Murray's work, stating that it called Baptists back to the Pauline conception of baptism which conveyed the fulness of meaning ascribed to it.

70   R. Clarke, 'Christian Baptism', *BT* August 13, 1959, 6, quoting Clark from 'The Theology of Baptism', 309, but he did not mention Clark, p.313, where he had written, 'Baptism effects regeneration and new birth because and only because it sets us at Golgotha and the empty tomb.' It is clear here that the reason for Clarke's difficulty with the 'effective rite' position was due to the fact that in Baptist tradition baptism had become separated from conversion where, in the New Testament, it was the climax and initial and initiating rite. Clarke's comments are consonant with Irish Baptist conservative evangelicalism, and also reflect the lingering Baptist revulsion of the doctrine of baptismal regeneration, so associated with Catholicism, on which see the ensuing debate and note especially the misunderstandings that arose from language such as 'effective sacrament'. But see also Frank James, who appears to have been a retired minister in Crawley, who wrote, 'Christian Endeavour Topic for May 1. Church Ordinances', *BT* April 28, 1938, 332, that 'no rite, ordinance or sacrament, by whatever name we call it, can convey to us the grace of regeneration', citing in support Henry Townsend. What Clarke and others feared was that the authors of *Christian Baptism* and those who defended them were sliding into this doctrine.

ing rapid ground among ministers. For him baptism was a symbol, a witness to grace not for the reception of it, and he believed that the recent baptismal service televised from Falmouth, the contributors to *Christian Baptism*, and R.C. Walton and those whose views were expressed in *The Gathered Community* were returning to the position of baptismal regeneration.[71]

Alec Gilmore replied to Robert Clarke's letter pointing out that A.C. Underwood had understood baptism to be more than a symbol,[72] but this was not to Clarke's satisfaction, who was disappointed that Gilmore did not unequivocally repudiate baptismal regeneration, again implicitly accusing the contributors to *Christian Baptism* of upholding this doctrine.[73] A fortnight later Elwin Shackleton entered the fray, quoting Wheeler Robinson to the effect that outer and inner experience were never considered apart in the New Testament, only later generations had separated them, which was what the opponents of *Christian Baptism* had done. When this happened it made it difficult to account for much New Testament teaching. In the New Testament, he reasserted, baptism was a part of the conversion experience, and *Christian Baptism* was a genuine attempt to understand what the New Testament said about believer's baptism and it was not a Baptist manifesto attempting to justify existing practice.[74] This was shortly followed by S.W. Ford who observed that most of the correspondence had shut out the Holy Spirit from baptism and criticized the separation of baptism from conversion, thereby making baptism unnecessary.[75]

Dr N. Beattie expressed amazement at what he described as some of the mischievous statements made in the book and denied Shackleton's contention that baptism was a part of the conversion experience. For him, baptism was merely the first step in obedience by the believer and the blessings of it were a new found joy, peace and satisfaction, asserting 'by grace we are saved through faith...' When the writers of the book gave the impression that the outward symbolic act played even some part in conversion they were guilty of pandering to the popular superstition that

---

71   L.J. Stones of Bristol, 'Sacramentalism Among Baptists', *BT* September 10, 1959, 6. A report of the Falmouth service was carried in 'Baptismal Service Televised', *BT* July 9, 1959, 1. The brief report concluded with Alan Gibson's (the son of a Baptist minister) summing up saying that it was a sacrament in which those baptized were confirmed into their new life in Christ.

72   A. Gilmore, 'Christian Baptism', *BT* September 24, 1959, 6, referring to A.C. Underwood, *A History of English Baptists* (1947), 268-74.

73   R. Clarke, 'Christian Baptism', *BT* October 8, 1959, 6.

74   G.E. Shackleton of Barrow-in-Furness, 'Christian Baptism', *BT* October 22, 1959, 6.

75   S.W. Ford of London, 'Christian Baptism', *BT* November 5, 1959, 6.

something done to us, for us or by us, was essential or demanded, so that we might be saved.[76]

In a series of studies on 1 Peter, Elwin Shackleton, the very next week, examined 1 Peter 3:13–4:6 and warned that in their anxiety to disclaim the doctrine that baptism was essential to salvation Baptists should not hesitate to accept all that New Testament teaching implied. Baptism was not just something that happened in the flesh, but a spiritual experience involving one's moral and spiritual life and relationship with God. The experience of baptism involved a moral transformation which enabled a person to repent, receive forgiveness and be restored to God's fellowship. Again following Wheeler Robinson, the outer act and the inner experience were never considered apart, so baptism took into its scope the whole of the gospel. Baptism was not *something* like dying and rising again, it *was* a real participation in Christ's resurrection. 'It is unfortunate that after centuries of division in the church over infant and believer's baptism, we tend to adapt our interpretation of the New Testament to the pattern of the practice we accept. There can be no doubt, that Peter is here referring to believer's baptism, and his words are not a defence but a description. It is as a helpful description that we should use them.'[77]

In December, D.R. Griffiths denied that Robert Clarke's quotation from his contribution on 'The Fourth Gospel and 1 John'[78] implied baptismal regeneration, and did so by quoting another passage[79] which read, 'a feature of the sacramental teaching in general, which safeguards it from the materialistic, the magical' was the persistent stress on the Holy Spirit in Johannine teaching.[80]

Feeling a sense of responsibility as one of the contributors to *Christian Baptism*, George Beasley-Murray sought to answer the alleged charge that the contributors believed in and advocated baptismal regeneration.[81] The answer suggested by some through the letters column of the *Baptist Times* was that this was precisely what they were doing, but he stated clearly that if this question was put to them, their answer would be the words of Paul's favourite expression, *'Me genoito!* ("Not on your

---

76   Dr N. Beattie, a medical doctor from Dr Beasley-Murray's first church in Ilford, 'Christian Baptism', *BT* November 12, 1959, 6.

77   G.E. Shackleton, 'The First Epistle of Peter. On Baptism. 1 Peter 3:13 to 4:6', *BT* November 19, 1959, 9.

78   D.R. Griffiths, Lecturer in Biblical Studies at University College Cardiff, 'The Fourth Gospel and 1 John', in Gilmore (ed.), *Christian Baptism*, 158.

79   Griffiths, 'The Fourth Gospel and 1 John', 170.

80   D.R. Griffiths, 'Christian Baptism', *BT* December 10, 1959, 6. See R. Clarke, 'Christian Baptism', *BT* October 8, 1959, 6.

81   G.R. Beasley-Murray, 'Baptism Controversy. "The Spirit is There"—Declares Dr. G.R. Beasley-Murray', *BT* December 10, 1959, 8.

life!").' But were a different question put to them, namely, 'Do you believe that baptism is a means of grace?', the answer would be, 'Yes, and more than is generally meant by that expression. In the Church of the Apostles (please note the limitation) the whole height and depth of grace is bound up with the experience of baptism. For to the New Testament writers baptism was nothing less than *"the climax of God's dealing with the penitent seeker and of the convert's return to God".'* This he supported from some of the pertinent New Testament statements about baptism.

First, baptism was of the Spirit. In Matthew 28:19 the significance of baptism was the handing over by a convert of himself to God and the appropriation of the convert by the Triune God. Symbolism and confession were subordinated to this all important aspect of dealing between God and humanity in baptism. Such was presupposed of baptism in the book of Acts. The plain import of Acts 2:37-38 was that repentance and baptism would be answered by God with the bestowal of forgiveness and the Spirit. An unprejudiced reader of Acts 22:16 would interpret the command as meaning that in baptism Paul would wash away his sins, not that the water accomplished this but that in baptism the Lord and Paul would have dealings with that result.[82]

Second, baptism was union with Christ. According to Galatians 3:26-27 the faith that received and the baptism that united were indissoluble, and no explanation of Romans 6:1-11 had validity if it failed to recognize three inseparable elements associated with the baptismal experience: the convert was united with the Lord in his dying on the cross and rising from the tomb; the convert was transferred from existence out of Christ to life in Christ; and the convert renounced their old life to begin a new one for the glory of God. That this was so was supported by the authentic commentary on Romans 6 provided in Colossians 2:12, the latter part of which stated that through baptism the convert is raised with Christ in baptism. In 1 Peter 3:21 baptism was basically an appeal for a clear conscience, that is, the occasion for asking for it from God.

Finally, modern baptism was a reduced baptism. 'The teaching of these scriptures seems to me to be unambiguous. It militates unreservedly against the reduced baptism championed of late by so many correspondents of this paper.' Beasley-Murray, then, was at pains to emphasise

---

82   For those who defended the non-sacramentalist interpretation of baptism, the Holy Spirit was in no way involved in baptism, see, e.g., *Liberty in the Lord*, e.g. pp.35-36, and R. Clarke, 'Christian Baptism', *BT* January 7, 1960, 6. This position, however, could not accord with the many New Testament statements which explicitly brought the Holy Spirit and baptism together, chiefly 1 Cor. 12:13, Acts 2:38 and Tit. 3:5. And so many, before and after, but never more eloquently or convincingly than Beasley-Murray, built on the growing emphasis throughout the period 1900 to 1937 that baptism and the Holy Spirit were related.

that 'this teaching relates to *baptism in the apostolic Church*, not to baptism in the average modern Baptist church. Where baptism is sundered from conversion on the one hand, and from entry into the Church on the other, this language cannot be applied to it; such a baptism is a reduced baptism.'[83] Objectors to *Christian Baptism*, he continued, were guilty of transferring the theology applying to apostolic baptism to that which they had known and was still fostered in their churches. They had, therefore, misunderstood Beasley-Murray and his co-contributors. 'My concern, along with my colleagues, is to put before Baptists the picture of ideal baptism, as it is portrayed in the apostolic writings, in the hope that we may strive to recover it or get somewhere near it. To insist on keeping our impoverished version of baptism would be a tragedy among a people who pride themselves on being the people of the New Testament.'

J.G.G. Norman was quick to express thanks to Beasley-Murray, but asked for a further article which would clarify questions which arose from it.[84] Others, however, were not so pleased. Robert Clarke wrote again, denying the Holy Spirit's presence in baptism either to effect or consummate regeneration, but rather to bless and empower the already regenerated and forgiven believer.[85] This third letter of Clarke's highlights the dialectic in which the two sides of the debate were involved. The contributors and defenders of *Christian Baptism* were deliberating on the theology of New Testament baptism, where baptism was part of conversion, and not on the contemporary situation as it prevailed among twentieth-century Baptists where baptism had been separated from conversion. This fact was noted by A.J. Matthews who described the problems which were arising as twofold: first, due to the way conversion and baptism had been separated by months, even years, and second, that the Spirit's movements, like the wind, refuse to be organized and tidied up to suit our convenience. Matthews' letter was published at the same time as S.B. John's, which expressed dissatisfaction with Beasley-Murray's article, disapproval of Shackleton's letter and accused both of advocating baptismal regeneration.[86] There can also be little doubt that the clear statements made by Beasley-Murray and the other contributors,

---

83   G.R. Beasley-Murray, 'Baptism Controversy. "The Spirit is There"—Declares Dr. G. R. Beasley-Murray', *BT* December 10, 1959, 8, italics his.

84   J.G.G. Norman of Erdington, 'Christian Baptism', *BT* December 31, 1959, 4, these questions were: What was meant by 'means of grace'?; Did Acts 2:37-38 mean repentance with baptism equalled conversion?; and, finally, What does it mean to be 'united with Christ'? These, he believed, would help the understanding not only of baptism but New Testament thought generally.

85   R. Clarke, 'Christian Baptism', *BT* January 1, 1960, 6.

86   A.J. Matthews of Cheam, and S.B. John from Gloucester, 'Christian Baptism', *BT* January 14, 1960, 6.

to use his phrase from 1966, concerned 'faith-baptism',[87] yet consistently those who accused them of presenting a form of baptismal regeneration misunderstood this or ignored it. This can again be illustrated by the objection of S.F. Carter who claimed that it was faith not baptism which was for conversion.[88] Dr N. Beattie disclaimed baptism to be in any way 'initiation' which he understood as 'a non-scriptural word, associated with evil pagan superstitious ceremonies!'[89] However, Beattie did this in the face of the vast array of ministers and scholars from across the theological spectrum who did recognize baptism as the initiatory rite, the door of entrance into the church.[90]

In the same issue of *The Baptist Times*, R.L. Child answered the question whether anything transcendent or supernatural happened in baptism

---

87   Beasley-Murray, *Baptism Today and Tomorrow*, 46, where he wrote that union with Christ took place 'through faith–baptism'.

88   S.F. Carter of Truro, 'Christian Baptism', *BT* January 28, 1960, 6.

89   N. Beattie, 'Christian Baptism', *BT* February 4, 1960, 6. In this letter, Beattie was most critical of A. Gilmore's 'Some Problems of Believer's Baptism', *BT* December 31, 1959, 6, and W.D. Hudson, 'Inter-Communion and Infant Baptism. Can we have one without recognising the other?', *BT* January 7, 1960, 10.

90   Robinson, 'Five Points of a Baptist's Faith', 9; Dakin, 'Christian Baptism and John's Baptism Contrasted', 39; Underwood, 'What Mean Ye By This Service?', 62; Walton, *Gathered Community*, 31, 159; Channon, *Much Water*, 78; Cook, *Theology of Evangelism*, 109; Clark, *Theology of the Sacraments*, 24, 33, 84, also his, 'The Fulness of the Church of God', 89 and 94, and 'Christian Initiation. A Baptist Point of View', in *SL* 4.3 (Autumn, 1965), 156-65; Trent, 'Ourselves and the Ordinances', 13-14; West, *Baptist Principles*, 31; Beasley-Murray, *Baptism in the New Testament*, 279-84; Winward, *Reformation of our Worship*, 59 and 69, and also in his 'Embodied Worship', in R.C.D. Jasper, *The Renewal of Worship* (1965), 54; Perkin, *Divine Encounter*, 6. More cautious was White, *Biblical Doctrine of Initiation*, 155, who noted that baptism might 'mark initiation without being precisely coincident in time with it', a caution which he continued later, pp.192-95. In his discussion of the Lukan development of initiation, he asked, p.192, 'What if, in the nature of things, the total event of Christian initiation *cannot* be systematised, nor its "rationale" consistently and universally defined? Luke's variety of representation faithfully reflects the variety of religious experience, the freedom of the Spirit which bloweth where it listeth. No order or pattern of actions or events can be devised which will infallibly bring about the desired spiritual result.' This, however, did not prevent him from recognizing that in the Pauline letters, the idea that baptism brought the believer into the church was assumed in Eph. 5:25 and 1 Cor. 1:13-14 and explicitly affirmed in 1 Cor. 12:13. However, the fact that baptism is initiatory was implicit within White's title.

A number rejected altogether that baptism was in any way initiatory, e.g., H.H. Pewtress, 'A United Church. The Question of Baptism', *BT* March 10, 1938, 193, on the grounds that it was a sign of having already entered the church; 'Another Northern Baptist', 'Baptism and Church Membership', *BT* March 24, 1949, 8; and *Liberty in the Lord*, 38.

by appeal to baptism as a means of grace.[91] If nothing happened, then what did Baptists make of Romans 6:3-4, Galatians 3:27 and Titus 3:5? The true response to a false sacramentalism '(better called "sacramentarianism")' was not to abandon the category of the sacramental but to use it with more discrimination. As baptism was in the name of the Trinity, it was, therefore, an act of the church. Individuals did not make baptism, rather they came to it and received baptism at the hands of the church. This removed baptism from the private and individual sphere and set it within the context of the believing church.[92] It was for this reason that baptism was a part of the public worship of the church.[93]

---

91   This paragraph discusses the views of R.L. Child, 'What Happens in Baptism?', *BT* February 4, 1960, 8 (and p.10), and inserts the views of others. There were basically two ways in which Baptists used the phrase 'means of grace'. First, as no more than a blessing of the baptized. So, Channon, *Much Water*, 32-33, 'Let the newly-baptised offer the prayer of expectancy that they may receive *something* for others that shall make their life more fruitful—more fragrant—in the service of God', italics added, and on p.66 baptism was described as 'a quickening of interest in things spiritual'. [There was also a non-specific and, therefore, vague usage, e.g., T.A.H. Getley of Gorleston-on-Sea, 'Baptism and Discipleship', *BT* February 22, 1945, 6; A.J. Barnard, who moved from Windsor to Hall Green, Birmingham, in 1947, 'The Use of Symbols in the Baptist Church', *Frat.* 64 (April, 1947), 13.]
    Second, as a sacramental means, that is, an 'effective rite' which effects what it symbolizes and this because it is an expression of faith. So, H. Townsend, '"Ilico" and Baptist Theology', *BT* January 6, 1938, 13; Child, 'The Ministry and the Sacraments', 137; A.C. Underwood, 'Why Be Baptised? An Imaginary Conversation', *BT* September 1, 1938, 675, and also his 'What Mean Ye By This Service?', 62; the 1938 *Reply of the Council of the Baptist Union*, in Payne, *Fellowship of Believers*, (2nd edn, 1952), 149; M. Evans, 'My Faith in the Sacraments', *BT* February 6, 1942, 67; Robinson, 'The Five Points of a Baptist's Faith', 9; F.C. Bryan, 'The Sacraments', in F.C. Bryan *et al, Things Most Surely Believed* (1944), 70-71; Walton, *Gathered Community*, 161; 'The Baptist Doctrine of the Church', 445-46; R.A. Mason, 'The Theology of Baptism', *Frat.* 90 (October, 1953), 8-10; Clifford, *Mission of the Local Church*, 49; Winward, *New Testament Teaching on Baptism*, 47, also his *Reformation of Our Worship*, 69, and 'Embodied Worship', 52-53; White, *Invitation to Baptism*, 75.
92   Though Baptists have tended to individualize baptism, e.g., R.G. Ramsey, 'Baptism and the Gospel', 32, 'the decision about our individual attitude to...baptism is between Christ and our own souls', and his 'Baptism and the Great Commission', 37, 'The individual's responsibility for responding personally to the claims of Christ... Believers' Baptism emphasises that responsibility.' In marked contrast was the position advocated by R.L. Child, 'The Practice of the Apostolic Church', 18, 'the baptized believer is on the way to discover a right and true relationship to his fellows in the society of Christ's people. *Believers' Baptism exhibits the true spiritual constitution of the Church* as a company of the faithful, who are knit to their invisible Head by the ties of personal faith and obedience', italics his. See also, S.F. Winward, 'Towards a Doctrine of the Church', *Frat.* 55 (September, 1944), 3-5, p.4, 'Of course Christian life is a personal relationship with the Lord Jesus Christ, but it is a personal relationship

What happened, then, in baptism was an enacted proclamation of the gospel, symbolizing not what people do but what God did once for all in Christ for salvation and also what he promised to do and would do in the present. No single compact phrase could describe it. It depended on two factors, one constant and unvarying, the other variable and uncertain, one divine the other human. It was, therefore, an efficacious sign (Calvin), moving towards the accomplishment of that to which it pointed. For this, the personal response of faith on the part of the candidate in baptism was not only desirable but indispensable.[94]

The following week, Beasley-Murray wrote again expounding the sacramental view, defining 'sacrament' as the word of God in action, further clarifying the interpretation of baptism for which he and others were contending.[95] In a sacrament two worlds were in contact in an effective fashion. In Acts and Paul baptism was entrance into the Christian life, and this baptism was immediately on profession of faith, thereby making it possible to speak of being baptized as the means of becoming a Christian, as 'becoming a Christian and getting baptised were inseparable experiences. Naturally, the Spirit's work began before baptism, but it led to baptism and was definitively experienced in it. In retrospect the process was seen as indivisible, as indeed it was.' In Romans 6 it was not baptism that was in view, 'but the work of the Spirit under the baptismal image.' The suggestion that such was 'magic' amazed Beasley-Murray. 'If baptism be the vehicle of confession of Christ, prayer to Christ and surrender to Christ, how can it be other than

---

corporately mediated..... In baptism we are baptized into Christ Jesus and into the one Body', and his *New Testament Teaching on Baptism*, 'The Sacrament of Unity', 44-45; Walton, *Gathered Community*, 167, 'Because Baptism is the means of entrance into the Church and of access to the Lord's Table, it is more than a private transaction... It is an act of God through His Church; it is a sacrament of the community'; 'The Baptist Doctrine of the Church', 442, 'The...sacramental observances...are congregational acts of the whole church', and p.444, 'It is the church which...celebrates the sacraments...'; Mason, 'The Theology of Baptism', 10-11, 'Baptism has its New Testament significance only when it is set in the context of the believing fellowship of the Church and is connected directly with entry into that fellowship by Church Membership... Baptism which is not closely connected with entry into the Church is no more Scriptural than the Baptism of Infants'; Clifford, *Mission of the Local Church*, 50, 'If the sacraments are sacraments of the Church..., then the sacraments must...have a corporate significance.' See also White, *Invitation to Baptism*, ch. 6, 'Baptized into one Body', 51-58 and his 'New Baptismal Questions—II', *BT* August 24, 1961, 2; L.G. Champion, J.O. Barrett and W.M.S. West, *The Doctrine of the Ministry* (1961), 10; L.J. Moon, 'Partnership', *Frat.* 132 (April, 1964), 20; Beasley-Murray, *Baptism Today and Tomorrow*, 63.

93   So Perkin, *Divine Encounter*, 3.

94   R.L. Child, 'What Happens in Baptism?', *BT* February 4, 1960, 8.

95   G.R. Beasley-Murray, 'Baptism and the Sacramental View', *BT* February 11, 1960, 9-10.

critically significant for the baptised?' This in no way clashed with the doctrine of justification by faith, where 'God gives his salvation to faith and faith alone—as he gives the sacraments to faith and faith alone. We are not contending that God justifies by faith but gives the Spirit and unites to Christ by baptism, as though baptism were a "work" alongside faith. That would be a perversion of the Gospel. Our plea has been that in the New Testament baptism is inseparable from the turning to God in faith, on the basis of which God justifies, gives the Spirit, and unites to Christ.' 1 Corinthians 6:11 and Titus 3:5-7 implied that in the baptismal experience God gave to faith his declarative and recreative work which justified. 'Union with Christ' was therefore to be interpreted 'in terms of *koinonia*.' Using the concept of corporate or inclusive personality, the believer, through baptism, was there with Christ on Golgotha's cross, participating in 'our Representative's acts.' Such an exposition of what God had willed baptism to be, said not a word as to what God did when baptism was misapplied or absent, as in state churches, the Salvation Army or Quakers. 'That the Churches have lost immeasurably and suffered corruption through the loss of believer's baptism cannot be denied... Yet the Spirit is undeniably there...' At this point, Beasley-Murray exited the debate, and, surprisingly, no comments were made concerning this final article.

While R.J. Snell was to acknowledge that Child had granted all that the most extreme anti-sacramentalist could ask for—baptism as a confession of repentance, a testimony to God's grace and a challenge to bear fruit worthy of repentance,[96] S.B. John was less appreciative, thanking Beasley-Murray for his article but discounting it as an answer to his critics, again accusing *Christian Baptism* of maintaining an *ex opere operato* position on baptism. For him, D.R. Griffiths' comment that '*entrance into the kingdom of God is impossible except by means of the rebirth in baptism which is both water-baptism and a bestowal of the Spirit*' was heresy.[97]

From this point, the controversy took on a new slant focusing on the nature of symbol in reference to baptism. Peter Cowling entered the fray, observing that no-one in the debate, so far as he could remember, had sought to define what a symbol was. He offered the definition that a symbol involved the two worlds of the physical and the spiritual. On the earthly and physical level, baptism was our testimony to the justifying grace of God and what he had done in Christ, but on the spiritual level it was incorporation into Christ. In baptism, then, testimony was given to God's grace and a mystical union with Christ in death, burial and thereby incorporation into his Body.[98] Later, Cowling defended baptism as part

---

96   R.J. Snell, 'Christian Baptism', *BT* February 18, 1960, 4.

97   S.B. John, 'Christian Baptism', *BT* February 25, 1960, 6, referring to Griffiths, 'The Fourth Gospel and 1 John', 158, italics original.

98   P. Cowling of Buckhurst Hill, 'Symbolism and Baptism', *BT* April 14, 1960, 6.

of conversion as the New Testament norm,[99] but on both occasions S.B. John responded, first of all arguing that a symbol was simply an outward sign of an inner grace which already existed, if otherwise it would be a symbol no longer but an agent,[100] then simply disagreeing with Cowling,[101] and here the controversy ended.

What all this meant was that the Baptist understanding of baptism was taking on a deeper and fuller, and it must be said a more biblically theological, content. While there were throughout this period those who continued to resist all notions of 'sacrament', insisting that it was nothing more than an ordinance,[102] an ever increasing number were prepared to

---

99   P. Cowling of Leeds, 'Symbolism and Baptism', *BT* May 26, 1960, 6. The reason for his change of address is unknown.

100   S.B. John, 'Symbolism and Baptism', *BT* April 28, 1960, 6.

101   S.B. John, 'Symbolism and Baptism', *BT* June 16, 1960, 6.

102   H.D. Hilliard of Penge, 'The Beginning of the Forward Movement', *BT* 1938, 366; J.B. Middlebrook, 'Towards a Doctrine of the Church', *Frat.* 55 (September, 1944), 8; Dakin, *Baptist View of Church and Ministry*, 28; 'The Ordinances', *BT* January 24, 1946, 4, being excerpts from R.A. Laidlaw's 'Baptism and the Lord's Supper', the precise nature of which (tract, pamphlet, booklet?) is unknown, as is who Laidlaw was, but whether a Baptist or not, the inclusion in the *BT* of the excerpts reflects the belief of many that baptism signified nothing more than union with Christ and other believers; L.A. Read of Nailsworth, '"Ordinance" Rather than "Sacrament"', *BT* September 12, 1946, 10, who referred to Dr P.W. Evans' preference for 'ordinance' in his visit to the 100th Annual Conference of the Churches of Christ in Birmingham in August, agreeing that 'ordinance' was proper to Baptist faith and order, while repeating the dislike of many for 'sacrament' and 'means of grace', see G.J. Hammond, 'Churches of Christ', *BT* August 15, 1946, 11; Pike, *Under Christ's Control*, 9; G.H. Davies, 'What Baptists Stand For', *BQ* 15 (April, 1954), 278-79, a review of Henry Cook's book of the same title in which Davies contested Cook's claim that 'sacrament' better described baptism than 'ordinance'" and Davies kept up his use of the latter in his review of '*An Order for Holy Baptism. The Church in South India*', *BQ* 16.7, (July, 1956), 331; F.T. Lord, 'The Baptist World Alliance in Retrospect and Prospect', in A.T. Ohrn (ed.), *Baptist World Alliance Golden Jubilee Congress* (1955), 65; the Radlett Fellowship, *Faith and Life: Practical Lessons in Christian Living* (1966), section on 'Baptism', n.p.. The 1964 BRF's *Liberty in the Lord*, was written to counter in particular the authors of *The Pattern of the Church*, and against the sacramentalist position in general. The opposition of the Radlett Fellowship and BRF demonstrate that it was mainly conservative evangelicals who opposed the 'sacramental' views, though Dr Henton Davies would perhaps be an exception which shows that such was not a hard and fast rule. This does *not* mean, however, that only or even mainly liberals maintained the sacramental position, as G.R. Beasley-Murray and R.E.O. White prove, each of them known evangelicals. Opposition to White's New Testament sacramentalism, as expressed in his 'New Baptismal Questions', *BT* April 13, 1961, 9, and its sequel, 'New Baptismal Questions—II', *BT* August 24, 1961, 2, came in the form of letters by S.B. John, 'New Baptismal Questions', *BT* April 27, 1961, 6; W. Beattie of Chigwell, 'New Baptismal Questions', *BT* May 18, 1961, 6, to which White defended himself, 'New Baptismal Questions', *BT*

see the rite as both an ordinance and a sacrament,[103] and in general it must be noted the ease and comfort with which Baptists could now refer to baptism simply as a sacrament.[104]

Two corollaries of biblical baptismal sacramentalism were the growing recognition of the role of the Spirit and the eschatological dimension. From relative obscurity within the first forty years of this century, the work of the Holy Spirit in baptism became increasingly recognized as central to a truly biblical theology, not least through the untiring advocacy of Wheeler Robinson and A.C. Underwood, who continued to contribute work on the subject.[105] Prior to the publication of *Christian Baptism*, a growing number of references to the Spirit in baptism are to

---

May 18, 1961, 6, which called forth S.B. John's self-defence, 'Baptismal Controversy', *BT* June 15, 1961, 6.

103 In his *Theology of Evangelism*, 109, and *Why Baptise Believers Only?*, 5, H. Cook had no difficulty referring to baptism as an ordinance, but this did not preclude the sacramental understanding of baptism, which, Cook argued, was to be preferred over 'ordinance', so *What Baptists Stand For* (1st edn, 1947), 69-74. A.J. Barnard, 'The Use of Symbols in the Baptist Church', *Frat.* 64 (April, 1947), 13, used 'ordinances' but spoke of them as 'means of grace'. That this was now widely the case can be illustrated by the following references to both 'ordinance' and 'sacrament' by the same author in the same work: F. James, 'Christian Endeavour Topic for May 1. Church Ordinances', *BT* April 28, 1938, 332; M. Evans, 'My Faith in the Sacraments', *BT* February 6, 1941, 67; Bryan, 'Preparation, Administration and Visitation', 70 and 75; Payne, *Fellowship of Believers* (1st edn, 1944), 60; P.W. Evans, *Sacraments in the New Testament with Special Reference to Baptism* (1947), 8; Walton, *Gathered Community*, 158; 'The Doctrine of the Church', 441-42; Channon, *Much Water*, xv and 5; Winward, *New Testament Teaching on Baptism*, 42-43 and his *Reformation of Worship*, 27; Beasley-Murray, *Baptism in the New Testament*, 113 n.3 and 122.

104 So Child, 'The Ministry and the Sacraments', 132, and his *Conversation About Baptism*, ch. 1, 'Symbols and Sacraments', 10-15; H. Townsend, '"Ilico" and Baptist Theology', *BT* January 6, 1938, 9; Ramsey, 'Baptism and the Gospel', 31; Underwood, 'What Mean Ye By This Service?', 58-64, and *History of English Baptists*, 274; T.A. Bampton, 'The Sacramental Significance of Christian Baptism', *BQ* 11.10-11 (October-December, 1944), 273-74; R.E.O. White, 'The Baptist View of the Sacraments', *BT* March 29, 1945, 6, also his *Biblical Doctrine of Initiation*, 274-78; Walton, *Gathered Community*, 25; R.L. Child (ed.), *The Lord's Supper* (1951), 9; A. Gilmore, 'The Sacrament of Baptism', *BT* July 2, 1953, 2; Rowley, 'The Christian Sacraments', 149-90; Clifford, *Mission of the Local Church*, ch. 3, 'The Sacraments', 47-60; Winward, *Reformation of our Worship*, 69-72.

105 See H.W. Robinson's, 'Believers' Baptism and the Holy Spirit', *BQ* 9.7 (July, 1939), 387-97, 'The Five Points of a Baptists Faith', 8-9, and 'Report of Commission No. 2. The Baptist Contribution to Christian Unity', 117-18, while his importance in this matter was highlighted in the obituary contributed by the Very Rev. W.R. Matthews, Dean of St. Paul's, 'H. Wheeler Robinson', *BQ* 12.1-2 (January–April, 1946), 1946, 8, who commented that, 'The theology of Wheeler Robinson is, first of all, a theology of the Holy Spirit'; and Underwood, 'What Mean Ye By This Service?', 61.

be found, ranging from the cautious observation that, 'The New Testament clearly indicates a connection of the gift of the Holy Spirit with the experience of baptism which, without making the rite the necessary or inevitable channel of that gift, yet makes it the appropriate occasion of a new and deeper reception of it',[106] to the more definite views like those expressed by Rex Mason who emphasized that the New Testament spoke of baptism as the occasion when the gift of the Spirit was imparted and that what made a sacrament a means of grace was the Holy Spirit working through it.[107] From his study of the book of Acts, S.I. Buse concluded that, 'Baptism is regarded as important, but not as absolutely essential. It is not necessarily bound up with the gift of the Holy Spirit' but was administered only to 'those capable of repentance and confession.' But in Paul's letters (chiefly 1 Cor. 12:13 and Gal. 3:27-28) Beasley-Murray denied the interpretation that a Spirit-baptism existed distinct from water-baptism, and that 'through the activity of the Spirit in baptism the rite becomes an initiation into the One Body.' Clark wrote, 'Baptism, in this normative period [New Testament times], implies, embodies and effects

---

106 'The Baptist Doctrine of the Church', 446. Such vagueries, no doubt, can be explained by the fact that 'The Baptist Doctrine of the Church' was a document intended to be representative rather than controversial. This equally applies to West's *Baptist Principles*, 32, '[Baptism] is an occasion upon which the Holy Spirit is active towards the person baptized.' Cf. D.S. Russell, 'The Ministry and the Sacraments', *BQ* 17.2 (April, 1957), 72, baptism 'is not just a symbol, it is a sacrament; it is not just a declaration of faith, it is an experience of grace through the Spirit. The evidence of the New Testament is not always clear when we try to find the exact relation between Baptism and the gift of the Spirit, but the relation is there. It is an experience in which the Holy Spirit, who was given to us at our conversion, deepens still further the experience of God's grace.'

107 Mason, 'The Theology of Baptism', 8-9. See also M. Evans 'My Faith in the Sacraments', *BT* February 6, 1941, 67; 'Symbols of the Holy Spirit', *BT* May 29, 1941, 261-62 (an anonymous front page article, possibly by J.C. Carlile the then editor); W.H. Coats, 'Introductory Remarks in Presenting the Report of Commission No. 2', 122; Child, 'The Practice of the Apostolic Church', 19; Dakin, 'Christian Baptism and John's Baptism Contrasted', 42; H.H. Rowley, 'The Origin and Meaning of Baptism', *BQ*11.11-12 (January–April, 1945), 314-15; Walton, *Gathered Community*, 29-31; Evans, *Sacraments in the New Testament*, 25-26 (though by 1955 Evans appears to have become less certain of the coincidence of water- and Spirit-baptism, see his 'Sealing as a Term for Baptism', *BQ* 16.4 (October, 1955), 174-75); Channon, *Much Water*, 90-91; H.J. Charter (whose identity and whereabouts are unknown), 'Christ's Baptism and Ours', *BT* August 17, 1950, 2; Champion, *Church in the New Testament*, 74-75; H. Clarkson, 'The Holy Spirit and the Sacraments', *BQ* 14.6 (April, 1952), 265-70; H.F. Peacock, 'Baptism and the Holy Spirit. An Exegetical Study of Titus iii,5', *Frat.* 85, (July, 1952), 17-20; Winward, *New Testament Teaching on Baptism*, 54-55; A. Gilmore, 'Some Recent Trends in the Theology of Baptism (concluded)', *BQ* 16.1 (January, 1955), 2-9; Clark, *An Approach*, 23-24, 34; G.R. Beasley-Murray, 'The Holy Spirit, Baptism and the Body of Christ', *RevExp* 63 (1966), 177-85.

forgiveness of sin, initiation into the church and the gift of the Holy Spirit... The gift of the Holy Spirit, which descended upon Christ at His baptism, is poured out by the ascended and glorified Lord upon His people, and those who respond to the Gospel proclamation receive the power and presence as they, too, share in the baptismal experience.'[108] Such persuasive advocacy as this unquestionably provided the basis for further examinations and enunciations of this truth and for its widespread acceptance,[109] and criticized much evangelical, including Baptist, teaching which lacked any 'specific point at which the gift of the Spirit to the believer may be expected to take place.'[110] This rediscovery of the Spirit's operation in faith-baptism was expressed with such eloquence and power by the various writers of *Christian Baptism* and others that the few denials which remained lacked both cogency and theological foundation.[111]

Recognition of the role of the Spirit led necessarily to the recovery of the eschatological dimension of baptism. As John's baptism was essentially an eschatological rite, so Jesus' baptism took place within that context, and Christian baptism was thus an entry into the eschatological order of the new creation. The possession of the Spirit brought with it a forward look, this finding biblical support in the intense expectation of the early chapters of Acts, the eschatological context of baptism and the laying on of hands in Hebrews 6:1-2, 'the confession of our hope' in Hebrews 10:23, the eschatologically full doxology opening 1 Peter 1:3-5, and not least John 3:5's confidence that those baptized in water and the Spirit would receive the Kingdom of God. This eschatological dimension of baptism in the Spirit was deepened as baptism was understood as into Christ's death and resurrection (so Rom. 6:8, Col. 3:3-4). The believer's union with Christ was the assurance that he would rise with him on the last day. As the Spirit was the 'first instalment' of the Kingdom, bestowing its powers in the present age, so resurrection in Christ was the 'first instalment' of the resurrection unto the consummated kingdom. Beasley-

---

108   Buse, 'Baptism in the Acts of the Apostles', 128; Beasley-Murray, 'Baptism in the Epistles of Paul', 142; and Clark, 'The Theology of Baptism', 308-09.

109   E.g. J.R.C. Perkin, 'The Principles and Practise of Believers' Baptism', *BT* June 4, 1959, 10; Payne and Winward, *Orders and Prayers* 131; White, *Biblical Doctrine of Initiation*, 203-05, 254, 315, see also his *Open Letter*, 73, and *Invitation to Baptism*, ch. 7, 'By one Spirit we were all baptized', 59-70; Beasley-Murray, *Baptism in the New Testament*, 275-79, and *Baptism Today and Tomorrow*, 52-60; A.W. Argyle, *God in the New Testament* (1965), 33, 141, 166.

110   R.E.O. White, 'Baptism: The Domestic Debate', *Frat.* 118 (October, 1960), 17.

111   So, e.g., the rejection of the Spirit in *Liberty in the Lord*, 33, 35-36, appeared in the form of mere assertions which were both uncorroborated from scripture and unconvincing. See also R. Clarke's attacks on *Christian Baptism*, especially 'Christian Baptism', *BT* January 7 1960, 6.

Murray summed up this aspect of biblical teaching, so neglected by Baptists, stating that '*the beginning of God's dealing with us, which is the true beginning of Christian experience, bears within itself the assurance of our immortality*. As the grace of God in the Gospel gives unfaltering promise to the believer, so the grace of God in baptism gives sure and certain hope to the believer concerning his final destiny. Dying with Christ the believer has been justified before the bar of God; rising with Christ he has entered the new creation; possessing the Spirit he has the first fruits of the Kingdom of God; a member of Christ, he shares his sonship and his inheritance.'[112]

It is clear, then, the central contribution *Christian Baptism* and especially George Beasley-Murray made in consolidating the sacramental interpretation of baptism within Baptist thought, providing for it a firm biblical basis and, at the same time, some of its leading advocates. *Christian Baptism* was by no means the first in this area, but it was certainly the most important as well as controversial expression of this understanding of the rite, and is rightly understood as a watershed in twentieth-century Baptist thought. What it achieved was that it focused all previous work in one major volume and set the tone and direction for future studies. The present widespread acceptance of the language of 'sacrament', is due in no small measure to the contributors to *Christian Baptism* and particularly Beasley-Murray.

---

112 Beasley-Murray, *Baptism in the New Testament*, 290-96, quotation from pp.295-96, italics his. He had earlier, but more briefly, noted this in his essay, 'Baptism and the Epistles of Paul', 142. Other contributors to *Christian Baptism* likewise noted this aspect of the rite, see Buse, 'Baptism in Other New Testament Writings', 181, and Clark, 'The Theology of Baptism', 308-09, 317-18. Clark also developed the understanding of baptism as a rite of inaugurated eschatology in his *An Approach*, 26, 80-85, and in his 'Christian Initiation. A Baptist Point of View', 160, 162. See also H. Townsend, '"Ilico" and Baptist Theology', *BT* January 6, 1938, 13; Trent, 'Ourselves and the Ordinances', 14-15; White, *Biblical Doctrine of Initiation*, 185-86, 205-06, 272-73.

CHAPTER EIGHT

Ecumenical Developments 1967–1999

The period from the early 1960s to 1999 witnessed greater ecumenical activity and advancement than any other time in the history of the church. Within this movement, Baptists have continued to play a major if ambiguous role. To illustrate this and the place of debates about baptism within this development, five key 'processes' will be examined: the developments leading up to and following the publication of the report *Baptists and Unity*, the *Ten Propositions*, the F&O document *Baptism, Eucharist and Ministry*, the Inter-Church Process, and Local Ecumenical Projects/Partnerships.

It becomes increasingly clear that the baptismal question is so bound up with other ecumenical issues that it has come to have a subordinate place to them.[1] It has often become subsumed to the ecumenical process itself, in its various phases, and therefore cannot be separated from these broader developments. It will also become clear that the majority of Baptist writing and discussion of baptism has occurred within the ecumenical context. This has led to polarized positions on baptism within the BU. Non-ecumenical Baptists have stayed largely where they were, seemingly content with what has been written on baptism in previous generations, whereas those Baptists involved ecumencially have developed their baptismal understandings, evincing a growing charity towards Paedobaptists and those Baptists who have become more open towards regarding the two forms of baptism as complementary. As such, it is true that the Baptist discussion of baptism has become one in which only a relatively small number of writers and Baptist churches have been involved, and the context for the overwhelming majority of them has been ecumenical in one form or another.

---

1   This is reflected in the marginal role which baptism occupies in D. Butler, *Dying to be One: English Ecumenism: History, Theology and the Future* (1996).

Baptists and Unity: Before and After

The Nottingham F&O Conference has been rightly recognized as a watershed date in modern British ecumenism with its call for church unity by Easter 1980,[2] though, at first, it was barely acknowledged among Baptists.[3] However, in time, it came more and more to the fore.[4] In November 1964, the BU Council referred the matter of the Nottingham recommendations to the Advisory Committee on Church Relations (ACCR) which drew up an interim reply which was considered by the Council on March 9, 1965.[5] It commented that before long Baptists would have to 'give clearer indication than they have so far done as to their attitude to some of the major questions involved in the movement for the greater unity among the Christians of this and other lands', and acknowledged the 'considerable divergences of view among Baptists' which made it 'the more important that they study and face together the questions raised at Nottingham.' In view of this, the ACCR asked the Council to empower it to prepare a comprehensive statement to help clarify and shape Baptist opinion and policy regarding both the changing pattern of church relations and the more general question of Christian unity 'and to ensure by careful consultation that the statement takes account of the different theological and ecclesiastical opinions within the denomination.'[6] It recommended that Baptists, as asked by the BCC resolutions, should again consider the issues of open and closed

---

2   Among the most recent literature, see J. Matthews, *The Unity Scene* (n.d., [1986]), 81-96; T.F. Best. 'Local Ecumenical Projects', in N. Lossky *et al* (eds.), *Dictionary of the Ecumenical Movement* (Geneva, 1991), 628; E. Welch and F. Winfield, *Travelling Together: A Handbook on Local Ecumenical Partnerships* (1995), e.g. p.5, but implicitly throughout the book; R. Nunn, *This Growing Unity: A handbook on ecumenical development in the counties, large cities and new towns of England* (1995), 1 and 15.

3   Notification of it was given in August, see 'The Unity We Seek', *BT* August 20, 1964, 7, and 'Church Union By 1980?', *BT* August 27, 1964, 1-2, and then afterwards by R. Cowley of Tyndale, Bristol, 'Sense of Urgency is Felt in Unity Discussions', *BT* October 29, 1964, 2.

4   See the editorial, 'Baptists and Unity', *BT* March 18, 1965, 5; 'Baptists and Church Unity. Need to make their position clearer', *BT* March 18, 1965, 8; J. Hough, 'Is the goal Co-operation or Unity?', *BT* June 17, 1965, 2; R. Cowley, 'Unity Movement Speeding Up', *BT* November 4, 1965.

5   See Appendix II 'Report on the Resolutions of the Nottingham Faith and Order Conference Adopted by the Council of the Baptist Union, 9th March, 1965', in *Baptists and Unity* (1967), 57-60. On the prehistory of the report see 'Terms of Reference', *Baptists and Unity*, 4. On the origins of *Baptists and Unity* see West, *To Be A Pilgrim*, 140-41.

6   'Report on the Resolutions', 58.

membership and open and closed communion, on which the Council had
issued a report in 1937, but that this time closer attention be paid to the
theological issues involved.[7] It argued that Baptists be fully represented in
such consultations and 'that they will share with others in the consultation with sympathy and a recognition of the problems which face all
the Churches in this field.'[8]

The resulting document, *Baptists and Unity*, was presented to the
Council in November, 1966,[9] and adopted, though by no means
unanimously, in March 1967.[10] The report highlighted baptism, local
church autonomy, episcopacy, communion, creeds and confessions, and
church-state relationships as the major areas of disagreement, and advised
against pressing for organic union by 1980 as it would damage denominational unity and witness.[11] On baptism, it stated that the 'maintenance
of baptism as a rite to be administered upon a personal profession of
faith is generally regarded as the distinctive characteristic of Baptists.'

In assessing whether the rigid maintenance of believer's baptism was a
ground of separation from other Christian traditions, three issues needed
to be borne in mind: the widespread desire to overcome the difficulties
raised by indiscriminate infant baptism; new theological and practical
insights into the rite of Christian initiation and the general acceptance of
the validity of the Baptist position; and the fact that most modern union

---

7   'Report on the Resolutions', 58. See 'Section II.2—Worship' where all BCC
member churches were asked to re-examine and clarify their practice and regulations about
intercommunion and reconsider the theology underlying them, see Appendix I 'British
Council of Churches First British Faith and Order Conference, September 12th-19th,
1964. Texts of Resolutions from the Sections Passed at the Conference', in *Baptists and
Unity*, 53. The 1937 report was *The Report of the Special Committee* appointed to
examine Baptist, Congregational and Presbyterian union.

8   'Report on the Resolutions', 59. 'Section III.1—Membership' had requested
consultations to deal with the varying doctrines and practices of Christian initiation and
the problems arising for member Churches, 'Texts of Resolutions', 54.

9   'Baptists and Church Relations', *BT* November 24, 1966, 9. See *Baptists and
Unity*, 4-5, for an outline of the process leading up to its publication. The ACCR was
made up of its chairman, G.R. Beasley-Murray, Principal of Spurgeon's College, Dr L.G.
Champion, Principal of Bristol College, W. Davies, Area Superintendent for South
Wales, W.J. Grant, Area Superintendent for the East Midlands, R.L. Child now retired in
Oxford, A.S. Clement, Home Secretary of the BMS, Dr W.M.S. West of St. Albans, and
four laymen, H.F. Gale of Bedford, E.E. Ironmonger of Oxford, J.G. Le Quesne, QC, of
Hampstead, and Miss M. Russell of Hitchin.

10   'Not Yet Ready For Unity', *BT* March 16, 1967, 1 and 8. The report was
presented to the Council by Dr Beasley-Murray. At the meeting, Leslie Larwood, of West
Croydon, believed that official adoption of the report would jeopardize denominational
unity, to which Dr Champion responded by reminding the Council that it was the answer
to the Nottingham Conference and a Baptist answer was needed.

11   *Baptists and Unity*, 20-21, and 8.

schemes provided recognition of both believer's and infant (or sponsored) baptism, insisting that in the latter case full membership depended on a later personal profession of faith. So-called 'rebaptism' was then identified as the primary sticking point: 'It is clear that at the present time Baptists are not all of one mind as to how far for the sake of greater Christian unity it is or might be right to go in recognising infant baptism in this modified or supplemented form. Most Baptists feel an additional hesitation if it is insisted that the recognition of both current forms of baptism must exclude the baptism on profession of faith of anyone baptized as an infant.'[12]

After a brief study of the biblical and theological principles concerning the unity of the church,[13] the report admitted, 'There is probably no other major denomination in which there is such widespread doubt concerning the present desire and movement to recover the unity of the Church.'[14] Three proposals, then, required consideration. The first distinguished between the concepts of the unity of the church and the union or reunion of the churches: the former being a gift from God, the latter a work of his people resulting in organizational structures. Second, Baptists needed to take more seriously the fact that Paul set baptism in the context not only of faith, but also unity. Beyond the faith confessed in baptism lay the fellowship and mission of the church. 'The unity of the Spirit is known in mission activity, and the wholeness of the baptismal understanding of unity requires the continued participation in mission.' Third, it is in the local church that Baptists find their Christian life centred. If these statements genuinely reflected Baptist convictions, then within them lay the challenge to face up to contemporary events. If this truly was what the Spirit was doing in the present, then 'ought it not to be of concern to us?' Clearly opinions differed as to how the church's unity is known and expressed, thus participation in the discussions was called for, 'that we may together learn the mind of the Spirit for the Church to-day.'[15] This led to the conclusion, 'That Christian unity is of great importance, urgency and complexity', and that Baptists needed to give much closer thought to the issues involved. That no plan of church union or scheme had to date been put forward to which Baptists could assent,[16] 'their close

---

12   *Baptists and Unity*, 23-24.

13   *Baptists and Unity*, 42-44.

14   *Baptists and Unity*, 45.

15   *Baptists and Unity*, 45-48.

16   This was an echo of G.R. Beasley-Murray's contribution to the BU's Living Issues booklets in which he admitted that reunion presented special difficulties as no scheme in any part of the world had to date satisfactorily solved the problem of infant baptism for Baptists, see *Reflections on the Ecumenical Movement* (1965), 12-13, and also his 'I Believe in this Movement—But...The Way Will Be Long and Hard', *BT* March

study of current discussions and negotiations, whether as official "observers" or not, is of great importance.' The report believed that it would be a mistake for the BU, and perhaps some others, to press for organic union by 1980 'lest it endanger denominational unity, and thereby seriously weaken the witness Baptists have to make.' Nevertheless, 'Baptists are right in sharing in the exploration of what co-venanting together might mean and the conditions on which it might become possible for Baptists.'[17]

Baptists and Unity was formally received and adopted by the Council in March 1967.[18] It advocated cautious yet continued involvement, a position which received considerable support,[19] though many believed it should have pressed for unity,[20] while others, most notably the conservative evangelical BRF, opposed both positions, for which they

---

11, 1965, 8. He also expressed dismay at the proposed date of 1980 on the grounds that it was churches not simply enthusiasts which needed to be reunited.

17   *Baptists and Unity*, 49-50. The call for the preservation of denominational unity recurred a number of times, e.g., E.E. Ironmonger, 'Unity of the denomination', *BT* October 12, 1967, 7.

18   The Council agreed that *Baptists and Unity* should be sent to the churches and Associations for careful study, and to the BCC and member churches of the BWA. The ACCR was also instructed to review the situation in a year in the light of the responses received and the progress of discussions by the BCC, and to report back to the Council no later than November 1968, see *Baptists and Unity*, 51. The importance of *Baptists and Unity* was indicated by reference to it in J. Huxtable's chapter on 'Key Documents on Unity', *A New Hope for Christian Unity* (Glasgow, 1977), 101-02. Huxtable, citing sections of the 1948 'Baptist Doctrine of the Church', sought to call Baptists to full participation in the ecumenical movement, challenging them to participate in what the Spirit was doing in 'drawing churches out of isolation into discussion and activity together', p.102. Comments on *Baptists and Unity* had to be submitted by the first week of April, 1968, see W.W. Bottoms, 'We Cannot—And Shall Not—Go Back to Rome', *BT* April 11, 1968, 8.

19   Editorial, 'Baptists and Unity', *BT* March 16, 1967, 5, which highlighted the lack of consensus over baptism and the place of children in the life of the British church as major factors. See also the report of the BU Council debate, 'Consider these points, Unity Report Urges Baptists', *BT* March 16, 1967, 9; R. Hayden of Northampton, 'Baptist Unity Report is Ahead of Us', *BT* April 20, 1967, 4, and also his contribution to 'Baptists and Unity', *Frat.* 146 (October, 1967), 24-26.

20   E.g. Mr R. Browne, 'Baptists and Unity', *BT* March 23, 1967, 4 (this was not Rev Robert D. Browne of West Bromwich); so too the letters of H. Howland of Woodford Green, Essex, and A. Thatcher of Bristol, *BT* April 20, 1967, 4; and a group of ten from Manchester who believed denominational unity would not be jeopardized and that Baptists had a valuable contribution to make to a United Church, 'Astonished and distressed', *BT* March 30, 1967, 3, the group being J. MacFee, R.S. MacFee, G. Creer, R. Wilkinson, E. Blakeley, S.J. Lockwood, Enid Welford, M. Welford, A.D. Redhouse and M. Redhouse. W. Bennewith of Watford, 'Baptists and Unity', *BT* April 13, 1967, 3, declared that he would have signed with the Manchester group given the opportunity.

were themselves taken to task by J.A. Anderson who accused them of threatening to split the denomination, a claim renounced by Theodore Bamber.[21]

While many favoured continuing ecumenical participation,[22] there were also those who refused to accept assurances that full union would not be the outcome and so called for withdrawal from the movement.[23] But there were also those who believed in unqualified participation in everything that was happening ecumenically and that the official BU report did not go far enough. Most prominent of these were a group of five ministers from the West Midlands who, after meeting together over a six month period, produced their own response, *Baptists for Unity*.[24]

The group noted that those Baptists fully committed to the ecumenical movement had no such unifying organization as the BRF and also

---

21   J.A. Anderson, a deacon from Epsom, 'Revival or Dissidence?', *BT* December 14, 1967, 3-4; T.M. Bamber of Paignton, 'Evangelical Doubts About Questions of Unity', *BT* January 4, 1968, 4. Bamber noted that since the last BU Council meeting in November, six churches had withdrawn from the BU. See also D.P. Kingdon, *Baptists at the Crossroads* (1968), details of which are reported by W.W. Bottoms, 'But at Which Crossroads Do Baptists Stand?', *BT* February 29, 1968, 6. This was an address given in 1967 but published in pamphlet form by the BRF in early 1968. In it, Kingdon severely censured the BU for lack of theological rigour, and was himself heavily criticized by Bottoms. For his review and defence of the BU's position, Bottoms was himself applauded by Mr K.L. Savage of Watford, 'Baptists at Crossroads', *BT* March 14, 1968, 5, but denounced by D.S. Floodgate of Portsmouth, 'Baptists at Crossroads', *BT* March 7, 1968, 4; J.C. Beyer of Sheffield, 'Baptists at Crossroads', *BT* March 14, 1968, 5; R.S. Luland of Bedford, *BT* March 21, 1968, 4; and H. Willmer of Leeds, 'Baptists at Crossroads', *BT* March 28, 1968, 3. S. Voke of Walton-on-Thames, 'Baptists and Unity', *Frat.* 146 (October, 1967), 26-27, criticized the report for not having contained a single representative from the conservative evangelical wing who had serious reservations about ecumenical involvement, and for being 'beclouded by a sacramental emphasis which can easily send us off in another direction', as was evidenced, he believed, in the absence of reference to the substitutionary atonement.

22   E.g. Dr R. Brown of Upton Vale, Torquay, 'Cool It—This subject needs light—not heat', *BT* April 4, 1968, 6 and 8; W.W. Bottoms, 'We Cannot—And Shall Not—Go Back to Rome', *BT* April 11, 1968, 8, who viewed the Baptist contribution to the life of the true church as essential.

23   F.S. Fitzsimmonds, a tutor at Spurgeon's College, 'Should we now pause in our progress towards unity?', *BT* March 14, 1968, 7, who argued against ecumenism's proceeding in a way which would compromise principles, believing that Baptist independence in ecumenical matters did not imply non–co-operation, though personally he did not think the ecumenical movement was the way forward.

24   The booklet was prepared by Michael Taylor of Hall Green, but had grown out of written contributions by members of the group. They were R. Brown of Hearsall, Coventry, P. Coleman of Coseley, R. Nunn of Walsgrave and Shilton, and D. Smith of Birmingham Bible Institute. The group had received encouragement and help from Principal K.C. Dykes of Northern Baptist College since 1967, and Alec Gilmore.

criticized *Baptists and Unity*'s caution for reasons of denominational unity.[25] For them, discussion of ministry, sacraments and the relation of church and state, were scarcely of any interest.[26] The church should be talking to the world, and instead of being concerned with its own life, it should be concerned with the lives of those to whom it is sent. 'It is in this sense that we have no great interest in questions about valid ministries and sacraments, in baptismal controversy and debates about Church order.' They doubted whether preoccupation with F&O questions would ever provide the road to church unity and renewal, and that entry into deeper truth would be attained not by arguing out an agreed basis for co-operation, but by actual co-operation.[27]

The group regretted the emphasis on church unity and truth which implied there could be no such unity until all agreed about doctrinal statements or about questions of ministry, membership and church government,[28] advocating instead a more pragmatic line. Obstacles could best be removed, not by solutions to problems, but by temporary working agreements which readily admitted the existence of problems thus enabling Christians to live with them and work together. 'We are all aware, for example, that Church unity will wait for ever if the issue of baptism has to be settled first, but already many Christians see the wisdom of letting different baptismal practices live side by side in the one fellowship.'[29]

There followed a suggested 'Agenda for Baptists', which fell into two sections,[30] the second of which dealt with temporary working agreements which included polity, episcopacy, ministry, membership (including

---

25   They declared, 'We believe that...we can wait too long before joining the conversations', and that, 'Denominational unity, insofar as it can be regarded as an isolated issue, cannot therefore be an overriding concern...', *Baptists for Unity* (1968), 8-9 (the final draft of the book was Taylor's work, p.5).

26   *Baptists for Unity*, 15-16, citing approvingly the work of Albert van den Heuvel, *The Humiliation of the Church* (1967), 188-89.

27   *Baptists for Unity*, 16.

28   *Baptists for Unity*, 17 and 19.

29   *Baptists for Unity*, 20. This is a clear allusion to LEPs.

30   *Baptists for Unity*, 22-24. The first included practical steps which they recommended the BU should take immediately. First, the Baptist Assembly should empower the BU to inform the BCC that Baptists would join other churches in a covenant 'to work and pray for the inauguration of union.' Second, the Assembly should authorize the BU to enter negotiations for union with the Congregationalists, Presbyterians and Churches of Christ, and that this would be aided if, like the CU, the BU should become the Baptist Church and that the BU Council and the Associations should thereby take decisions on behalf of the local churches. Third, local Baptist churches should act together 'in all matters except those in which deep differences of conviction compel them to act separately.'

baptism) and worship (including communion).[31] In seeking to reach a working agreement on baptism three groups of people had to be kept in mind: fully committed believers; those not committed but who had been drawn into the life and worship of the church—the catechumenate; and those outside the church altogether. In the case of children belonging to the third group, they saw no objection to a service called 'The Blessing of Infants' to which all could be brought indiscriminately.[32] To aid this, indiscriminate infant baptism should be stopped and children should be admitted to the catechumenate at a service for the dedication of infants, but infant baptism should be accepted as an alternative practice. Children of Christian parents clearly belonged to the catechumenate, and for these infant baptism would admit them into the church, while for Baptists a service of dedication would admit them to the catechumenate. This would require that both infant and believers' baptism would exist side by side, and that those who became members of the church by admittance to the catechumenate followed by believers' baptism or those admitted by infant baptism followed by an affirmation of personal commitment to Christ 'should be equally acceptable to all.' Those in the catechumenate should be baptized into membership when they had reached the age of personal moral responsibility and committed themselves to Christ, and those infant baptized should also recognize that personal commitment was an essential part of church membership. In both cases, the person would enter the first group, the committed fellowship of believers, and in both instances the laying on of hands and admittance to communion would follow.[33]

They believed that Baptists should be as discriminating over rebaptism as they wished others to be over infant baptism.[34] Such a church in which two forms of baptism existed, they believed, would 'continue for a very long time', though this did not mean that it would be a permanent solution to the problems. It remained to the Spirit 'to increase our understanding of the baptismal experience and of what it means to be members of Christ's Church, in order that we may unify our baptismal practice.'[35]

---

31 *Baptists for Unity*, 24-31.

32 In this, the group agreed with the views of Gilmore, *Baptism and Christian Unity*, 100-03, and the 1966 report *The Child and the Church*, 33-34.

33 *Baptists for Unity*, 28-29. The issues surrounding children and communion (and baptism) was later discussed by S.F. Winward, 'A Baptist Point of View', in R.C.D. Jasper (ed.), *Worship and the Child: Essays by the Joint Liturgical Group* (1975), 47-50.

34 *Baptists for Unity*, 30, 'If we are to accept both forms of baptism and have respect for differing ways of entering the Church whilst at the same time rejoicing that it is one Church into which all are baptised, then it seems to us that we ought not to deny these things by re-baptising those baptised as infants.'

35 *Baptists for Unity*, 30. They further believed that wider acceptance of the catechumenate as an essential part of the church, together with the understanding that

Baptists for Unity concluded that Christian unity must be outward and visible, though they recognized that it might not happen, and questioned whether the will for it existed among Baptists. They then suggested that perhaps it was time for local Baptist churches wishing to move ecumenically either to enter local schemes of union or seize the initiative and apply for membership in the proposed United Reformed Church.[36] Many joined with them in pressing for organic union with the Congregationalists, Presbyterians and Churches of Christ,[37] while others claimed that following *Baptists for Unity* would mean Baptists losing their distinctive witness.[38]

This was followed by the official report *Baptists and Unity Reviewed*, which was presented to and adopted by Council in March 1969.[39] From

---

membership is more concerned with commitment to Christ and his mission than sealing personal salvation, were most important witnesses to the missionary nature of the church.

36   *Baptists for Unity*, 32-33. This was reviewed by W.W. Bottoms, 'An Agenda for Baptists for Unity', *BT* April 11, 1968, 8, who also noted that the pro-unionists had nothing like the BRF for making their views known. He warmly received their contribution but warned that the views expressed were potentially divisive.

37   E.g. Mr B.G. Cooper of Coventry, 'Not Organic Union—then what can it mean?', *BT* April 4, 1968, 3; Dr H.H. Williams of Bloomsbury, 'Baptists for Unity, *BT* May 9, 1968, 4; E.F. Clipsham, 'Could this, at last, be the way forward?', *BT* May 16, 1968, 6, who advocated federal union.

38   F.V. Mildred of Middlesborough, 'Baptists for Unity', *BT* April 25, 1968, 4. The BRF continued to try to ensure that the interests of ministers and churches were safeguarded against the BU's membership of the BCC and WCC, see T.M. Bamber, 'Why Revival Fellowship took its decision', *BT* January 15, 1970, 3. Such views were answered by D.S. Russell, 'Baptists and inter-Church relations...', *BT* October 22, 1970, 2. *Baptists for Unity*, however, did prove to be the catalyst for a meeting of eighty ecumenically committed Baptists at Hothorpe Hall, Market Harborough, in December 1968, which led to the formation of the Baptist Renewal Group (BRG). See A. Gilmore, 'Now "unity" Baptists get together', *BT* December 5, 1968, 16; 'Now Baptist Unity Group Formed', and A. Gilmore, 'Unity Baptists Slip Into Gear', *BT* December 26, 1968, 1 and 2 respectively. At the centre of the BRG were Gilmore and P.R. Clifford.

39   'Baptists and Unity' Reviewed (1969), 10; 'Council Endorses Unity Report'; and 'What the Review Says', *BT* March 20, 1969, 1 and 8, and 8-9 respectively. It was accompanied by an Assembly resolution which would endorse the conclusion of the 1967 report, specifically continuation of membership in both the BCC and WCC, with an added clause recognizing the liberty of each church to either engage in or refrain from participation. Similarly, the decision whether or not to share in areas of ecumenical experiment was to be left to the local church or Association. Of those who responded to the 1967 report, many remained cautious yet committed, while many others were reported as anxious for co-operation at the local level, especially in mission, see *Baptists and Unity Reviewed*, 3-4 and 9. The composition of the ACCR, had by now changed since the 1967 report, the two Superintendents having been replaced by J.H.G. Adam of the Eastern Area and G.W. Haden of the Metropolitan Area, Mr H.F. Gale and Miss M. Russell

the responses received, it appeared that the majority of churches agreed with the conclusion of the 1967 report.[40] In presenting the resolution to the Assembly, Dr George Beasley-Murray noted that Baptists felt the ecumenical tensions more than others,[41] and the Assembly went on to endorse the report.[42]

The same year, the BCC's *Report of the Inter-Church Enquiry into Baptismal Practice* surveyed the baptismal practices among participating churches, optimistically concluding that, 'it appears that there is now no obstacle to the mutual recognition of baptisms among churches which use the Trinitarian formula.'[43] This assessment was clearly premature. That no broad basis for such a conclusion existed is also illustrated by the BCC's 'Common Certificate of Baptism', jointly published with SPCK in 1972, which was intended for use either for infants or adults, simply stating that a person had been baptized with water in the name of the

---

also having departed, replaced by Mr J.V. Beaumont and Mrs S.C. Crowe, and Frank Goodwin who in 1969 became the Director of Evangelism of the LBA, and S.E.L. Larwood of West Croydon increased the number of ministers from three to five. The others remained the same.

40   *Baptists and Unity Reviewed*, 9. The conclusions are set out in *Baptists and Unity*, 49-51, and *Baptists and Unity Reviewed*, 14-15. The review document was drawn up on the basis of submissions from 655 of a total number of 2,214 BU churches, 17 Associations, several minister's fraternals and a number of individuals, so p.3. Roughly a third of the churches and half the Associations had replied, see also the Editorial, 'Baptists and Unity', *BT* March 27, 1969, 5.

41   'Baptists feel ecumenical tensions more acutely than other Christians', *BT* May 8, 1969, 2.

42   'Unity Report Endorsed', *BT* May 1, 1969, 1 and 16. 1,125 voted for it, 356 against, and this meant continued Baptist involvement in the BCC and WCC. However, those who had opposed it did make their voices heard, e.g. D.K. Blades of Alperton, London, A.D. Edwards of Thornbury, and J.W. Clarke of Great Baddow, Essex, all voted against it, 'Assembly Debate on Baptists and Unity', *BT* May 15, 1969, 4. The letters both for and against kept coming in to the *BT* for quite a while after the vote. Their fears were not assuaged by Sir Cyril Black who, in preparation for becoming BU President, expressed his hope that he could help people see the value of both ecumenical discussion and co-operation, see 'Crusader...', *BT* April 23, 1970, 6. See also the account of his Assembly presidential address, 'Love, Truth, Unity', *BT* April 30, 1970, 6. On Black, see H. Kingsley, *Crusader: The Life and Times of Sir Cyril Black* (privately published, 1996).

43   Cited by R.M.C. Jeffery, *Ecumenical Experiments: A Handbook*, (1971), 5, quoted by J.M. Cassidy, 'Membership of the Church with Special Reference to Local Ecumenical Projects in England' (draft copy of a Birmingham University PhD), Part 1 'The L.E.P.s', 'Introduction', 4. I am grateful to Father Cassidy for supplying me with several draft chapters.

Trinity. Though it was endorsed by nineteen major British churches,[44] it was rejected by the Baptists and the Orthodox Church.[45]

In 1965 it was reported that the proposals for the Congregationalist–Presbyterian union envisaged baptism administered either to adults on profession of faith or to children of believing parents, who would be received into membership after a public profession of faith.[46] These moves towards Congregational–Presbyterian union, prompted Ernest Clipsham to ask whether Baptists might not find a place within the URC. While there would be no way infant baptism would be abandoned, he commented that there were no exclusive claims being made for infant baptism, in fact the process of initiation was incomplete until infant baptism was ratified by an affirmation of faith in Christ and commitment to the church. Baptists, he urged, had a responsibility, even obligation, at least to consider the possibility.[47]

The *Ten Propositions*

In early October 1972 the Congregationalists and Presbyterians finally united to form the United Reformed Church (URC).[48] The impact of this

---

44   Including the Church of England, Church of Scotland, Methodists, Congregationalists and Roman Catholic Church in England and Wales.

45   On the Common Certificate, see, 'Churches agree on single certificate of Baptism', *BT* August 24, 1972, 1, and 'Common Certificate of Christian Baptism', *Voyage* July/August 1971, 5. In 1979 a BCC proposal recommended consideration of the possibility of a common certificate of church membership, but this was rejected by the Baptists, Church of England and Roman Catholic Church, see the CTE *Baptism and Church Membership with particular reference to Local Ecumenical Partnerships* (1997), 10-11.

46   'Outline of a United Church', *BT* March 11, 1965, 1. It must be recognized that this practice was nothing new in paedobaptist communions which have never denied believer's baptism for new converts.

47   E.F. Clipsham, who, from 1964–67, had charge of the Ministerial Recognition of the BUGB&I, from 1967–70 Director of Studies and Librarian for the BU, 'Could we have a place in this church?', *BT* May 25, 1967, 6. Of the URC proposals Clipsham wrote, 'Indeed after a careful and sympathetic consideration of this document and its implications, many may well ask the question; dare we any longer stand apart?'

48   Notification of this was given under the heading 'New Church is formed—with someone knocking at the door', *BT* October 12, 1972, 2, referring to the interest of the Churches of Christ, the irony being that after having broken off union talks with the BU in the early 1950s because they regarded the Baptist doctrine of baptism as too low, they were eventually to ally themselves with two paedobaptist communions in 1981. In order for the Union to take place, the Congregational Union had had to become the Congregational Church. This included reorganization due to constitutional changes, one of the effects of which was to bring to an end the oldest united association in the country, that of the Bedfordshire County Union of Baptist and Congregational Churches, which

long awaited union was quick to follow. Cyril Black admitted that Baptists were being challenged by the newly formed URC and the merging of three Methodist bodies into the Methodist Church in 1932. These had caused many to ask with whom the Baptists should unite, but for Black this question remained rhetorical until someone could solve the problem of how such a union could be brought about and answer the question of how far ecumenical enthusiasts were really willing to go. He believed that when the terms were eventually spelled out they would be unacceptable to the majority of Baptists. Of the enthusiasts he asked: 'Are they prepared to accept a weakening of our insistence that the baptism of believing penitents is the only baptism known in the New Testament, by accepting infant sprinkling as an alternative form of baptism? Further...would they accept, as would quite likely be required, a limitation on our right to baptise those who have been the unconscious recipients of sprinkling in infancy, but...have become convinced that they ought to go through the waters of believers' baptism?' Black believed that in all probability all these principles would be sacrificed.[49]

The following week, Peter King reported that the URC was being urged to ask the Church of England and other Free Churches on what terms they would be prepared to negotiate for union. The call originated in an unofficial unity conference held in Oxford the previous week in which Dr David Russell had participated. This had led to the establishment of a Consultative Committee of representatives from churches willing to be involved, recommendations to be taken to the participating churches by the summer of 1974. At the initial meeting Russell had pleaded that conversations should have in mind 'visible unity' and not necessarily 'organic union'.[50] At the March meeting of the Council, George

---

had to form separate denominational unions, see 'The Union that was formed in 1779...', *BT* August 29, 1968, 11-12.

49   C. Black, 'Are We Dragging Our Feet?', *BT* January 11, 1973, 8. P. Clements-Jewery of Botley, 'Yes, we are dragging our feet', *BT* January 25, 1973, 4, responded, asserting that the separation of believers was sin, that it was not truth that divided but 'sheer, stubborn rigidity', and that in any case, the compromise spoken of by Black was hypothetical. Mr S. Hardy of Ilford came out in support of Black and his position on believer's baptism in 'Where are we going?', *BT* January 25, 1973, 4.

50   See P. King, presumably of Cecil Road, Enfield, 'Churchmen call for unity moves', *BT* January 18, 1973, 1 and 12. Other addresses at the conference were given by A. Bonser, the East Midland Area Superintendent, who asked that any future scheme should provide a real and genuine choice with regard to believer's baptism, and W.M.S. West, since 1971 President of Bristol Baptist College, who, on the basis of *Baptists and Unity*, declared Baptist willingness to share in discussions on ways to further mission and unity. Russell later reiterated the point that union talks were not the only way to demonstrate church unity at the September meeting of the 'talks about talks'. He again cautioned against either organic or structural union, see 'Church union? Talks team will point to other ways...', *BT* September 27, 1973, 1 and 12. The talks were attended by the

Beasley-Murray urged that it was vitally important that the BU be involved from the outset so that they would be able to help form the agenda of future conversations.[51]

In May, the URC formally issued an invitation to the Roman Catholics, Anglicans, Methodists and Baptists to attend talks about talks.[52] The need for Baptist participation continued to be pressed[53] and in time the Churches Unity Commission (CUC) was set up.[54] Progress reports were published,[55] until, in January 1976, *The Ten Propositions* were finally issued.[56]

Church of England, Methodists, BU, URC, Roman Catholics, Churches of Christ, Congregational Federation, Independent Methodists, Countess of Huntingdon Connexion, Moravians and Wesleyan Reformed Church.

51   'Big vote for unity talks', *BT* March 22, 1973, 6. Beasley-Murray's report to the Council was supported by Dr West, Chairman of the ACCR, and the motion carried with only five abstentions.

52   'Unity: Come and Talk', *BT* May 17, 1973, 1.

53   E.g. 'Commit yourselves to unity, churches urged', *BT* February 14, 1974, 1 and 12; 'Council Supports Unity Commission', *BT* March 21, 1974, 6-7, the resolution put to the Assembly is reported on p.7; 'BU council calls for support for commission', *BT* March 28, 1974, 3. The Assembly debated the proposal on April 30, and voted overwhelmingly to send representatives to the Commission. The resolution was put by Dr West and seconded by Mr William Booth who reiterated the point that Baptists should play their part and make their distinctive contribution, see S. Clark, 'Baptists Will Support Unity Commission', *BT* May 2, 1974, 8.

54   The decision for Baptist membership in the CUC was approved at the March 1974 BU Council meeting, see *A Statement to the Churches in membership of the Baptist Union of Great Britain and Ireland* (March, 1976), n.p., but p.1.

55   E.g. 'Unity Talks Have Made Progress', *BT* April 3, 1975, 12; and D.S. Russell, 'An Ecumenical Bird's Eye View', *Frat.* 175 (February, 1976), 5, noted these explorations into 'visible unity' were part of a process which would include an examination of what constituted Christian initiation and how this related to the mutual recognition of members and ministers, adding, 'Already in these discussions the question of baptism has been raised and a sympathetic hearing given to the claims of believers' baptism.'

56   They are set out in *Local Church Unity: Guidelines for Local Ecumenical Projects and Sponsoring Bodies* ([1975], revised edn 1985), Appendix F 'The Ten Propositions', 58 (with a 'Foreword', pp.1-2, by D.C. Sparkes, at the time of publication Moderator of CCLEPE as well as Deputy General Secretary of the BU). Proposition 4 sought the mutual recognition and welcome to communion without condition of communicant members in participating churches. Proposition 5: 'We agree that, as from an accepted date, initiation in the covenanting Churches shall be by mutually acceptable rites.' Proposition 6: 'We agree to recognize, as from an accepted date, the ordained ministries of the other covenanting Churches, as true ministries of word and sacraments in the Holy Catholic Church,...'. Proposition 7 agreed that the covenanting churches would 'respect the rights of conscience, and to continue to accord to all our members, such freedom of thought and action as is consistent with the visible unity of the Church.'

The propositions were published with explanatory notes, stating on proposition 5 that mutual recognition of membership was dependent on the prior agreement on Christian initiation, envisaging this possibility that baptism was a complex reality which needed to be considered in its totality. 'The whole meaning and effect of the baptismal rite itself cannot therefore be tied to the moment of its performance.' Baptism looked forward to the future in which God's purposes were brought to victory. As the sacrament of faith it should be regarded as a pattern of divine address and human response. 'The total process of Christian initiation includes the washing with water and sharing the bread and wine: it is baptism reaching its conclusion in the Eucharist.' As each tradition stressed the importance of instruction either before believer's baptism or in preparation for confirmation or its equivalent rite, the commentary argued that, 'On such understandings movement from one covenanting Church to another, though properly requiring appropriate admission to fresh rites and responsibilities, would not involve any supplementing of the "initiation" already received.'[57]

The proposals marked a shift away from previous schemes for a United Church, and instead invited churches to consider whether mutual recognition of membership and ministries, accompanied by a declaration of intent to build upon this, might not be a more productive way forward. It was this basic change of approach which lay behind *The Ten Propositions*.[58]

Morris West presented the document to the March BU Council, recommending it be sent to every church.[59] This was agreed to and January 31, 1977, was selected as the final submission date, after which the Council would then be informed of the churches' responses and a reply to the Commission would accordingly be made. West explained:

> The approach to visible unity is now not through union schemes but through the making visible of the unity which all believers have by being in Christ together. The motivating purpose is not to create one united structure but to see how the

---

57 'Unity Commission spells out a challenge: The Propositions', *BT* January 8, 1976, 5. This understanding of baptism as a process which would have made possible the mutual recognition of initiatory rites, though eventually failing at this point, was later to reappear in the *Called to be One* process and the 1996 BU document *Believing and Being Baptized: Baptism, so-called re-baptism and children in the church* (1996).

58 This was in line with the earlier suggestion of D.S. Russell, 'Towards a New Era?', *BT* March 18, 1976, 1, 'whether mutual recognition of membership and ministries, accompanied by a declaration of intent to build upon this, might not open up the way at once to table fellowship, closer relations and more effective mission.' The words are those of Dr West, see his advocacy of the Propositions below.

59 W.M.S. West, 'The New Approach', *BT* March 18, 1976, 7-8. Details in this paragraph are from p.7. Copies of the *Ten Propositions* were sent to all churches along with a statement from the BU's ACCR, see 'Towards a New Era?', *BT* March 18, 1976, 8.

needs of the local church may best be met in the developing relationships and in their mission to the world: not structural union but realise and manifest unity in Christ in the congregations in their worship and on the frontiers of their mission is their aim.

The way ahead envisaged in making visible the unity is through mutual recognition of members and ministries, a sharing of table fellowship and by a declaration of intent by all those Churches willing to build on such a foundation towards closer relationships and more effective mission.

West commented that Proposition 5 'sets out what is implied by the present practice of most of our open membership churches.' He further sought to clarify that 'the phrase mutually acceptable rite does not mean one common uniform rite', but rather that 'Christian initiation is understood to be a process made up of various elements, for example instruction in the faith, confession of it and later baptism in the name of the Trinity, reception into church membership—and so on—elements which may vary in order and timing but which are essential before the process is completed. What will turn out to be mutually acceptable to all those seeking to be involved in furthering Church relations remains for further discussion.' Over the past twenty five years, he remarked, Baptist participation in ecumenical developments had moved believer's baptism 'more and more into the centre of the discussion', and Proposition 5 reflected that development. He acknowledged the difficulty such a position on initiation would have for closed membership churches, and asserted that their views needed to be respected.

In *A Statement to the Churches*, the BU set before the churches the propositions accompanied by notes. On Proposition 5's 'mutually acceptable rites' three notes were made. First, this phrase did not mean 'one uniform common rite.' Second, the understanding of initiation as a process would involve Baptist willingness to recognize and receive members who had passed through the initiatory process of other churches, adding, however, that, 'A proper freedom must be maintained for Christian judgment over so-called re-baptism to be exercised in the living pastoral situation.' It was later noted that Proposition 7 was an attempt to preserve freedom of conscience, particularly relevant to Baptists on the matter of 'rebaptism'. Third, this would require closed membership churches to give careful consideration to admitting members of other denominations.[60]

---

60   *A Statement to the Churches in membership of the Baptist Union of Great Britain and Ireland* (March, 1976), n.p., but pp.2-3.

The responses from the churches were collated and reported by Jim Wisewell in April 1977,[61] and the BU Council debated its response at its November meeting. The first denominational body to do so, it was reported that after detailed debates within the Council, painstaking study by the ACCR and the responses of the churches, the BU could not unconditionally recommend that the churches accept the *Ten Propositions*. Morris West told the Council, 'It may well be that for us the end of the road of the Churches' Unity Commission is in sight, as indeed the commission's life comes to an end next year, but that does not mean the end of the journey.' At present, he explained, 'We haven't sufficient agreement...to join the Covenant road. Too many questions remain unanswered.'[62] It was, however, the ACCR's judgment that even so, Baptists ought to continue to walk with other churches in the truth of the gospel, highlighting the main difficulties for Baptists as unity, membership, ministry, covenanting and the local and universal understanding of the church. On unity, Baptists believed in unity in life and mission, not structure.[63] One of the documents by the CUC had described mutually acceptable rites, but for Baptists the matter revolved around whether or not a faith-response to the gospel was being made by an individual. Many Baptists felt that the CUC appeared 'to be papering over the cracks of a fundamental disagreement on baptism which really needs to be brought right out and discuss[ed] frankly.'[64]

Visible Unity in Life and Mission was applauded at the Council meeting. Paul Rowntree Clifford, another committed ecumenist, recognized that the reply represented the majority, but urged that the CUC be informed that there were 'different minds amongst us.' He also felt that as a tradition, Baptists should humbly acknowledge their own

---

61   J. Wisewell, Secretary of the Sussex Association, 'Unity...it's sure to divide!', *BT* April 21, 1977, 7. From 1,749 sent the *Propositions* and accompanying ACCR document, 962 churches replied. When the larger churches had been taken into acount, this meant that some 70% of the BU membership had responded. The replies, in general, were cautious. By a two to one majority, churches had welcomed the suggestion that 'instead of trying to work-out a blue-print of a United Church there should be a mutual recognition which would involve both ministers and members.' Many churches had also reported that they were already involved in co-operating at a local level, but even among these there was suspicion of denominational or national schemes.

62   This paragraph is taken from 'We Cannot Say Yes', *BT* November 17, 1977, 1 and 6.

63   This fact provided the title to the official BU reply, *Visible Unity in Life and Mission. Reply by the Council of the Baptist Union of Great Britain and Ireland to the Ten Propositions of the Churches' Unity Commission* (1977), probably edited/compiled by Neville Clark.

64   'We Cannot Say Yes', *BT* November 17, 1977, 6.

weakness: 'Believers' Baptism witnesses to a regenerate church membership but it does not guarantee it. We ourselves have problems.'[65]

Visible Unity, it was claimed, represented the views of the majority of Baptist churches, though it recognized that there would be some who would have wished it went further and others who would have wished it had not gone so far. While unable to make an unqualified recommendation to the churches, the report was careful in its attempt to offer some constructive indications as to the kinds of understandings upon which a covenant might in fact be possible. This involved asking questions of other members of the CUC, most notably on baptism, the historic episcopate, freedom of conscience and the doctrine of the church. It concluded expressing the clear determination of Baptists 'to remain in close fellowship and consultation with other Churches.'[66]

Proposal 5 invited agreement that no supplementary rites of initiation should be sought of those moving from one covenanted church to another. In itself this would not prove a stumbling block to Baptists, nevertheless clarification would be needed on what grounds and within what context progress at this point could be made. 'Most Baptists would approach the issue of the recognition and reception of members of paedobaptist Churches by reference to whether or not a faith response to the Gospel of the grace of God in Christ had in fact been made.' On the negative side, no automatic recognition of infant baptism as true baptism could necessarily be given. 'We do however believe that it would be costly delusion to imagine that the creation of mutually acceptable rites of initiation indicates profound theological agreement on the baptismal issue.'[67]

Concerning Proposition 7's 'rights of conscience', questions of baptism pointed to but one of many areas in which difficulties might arise, and baptism provided a test case. If the covenant included the practice of mutually acceptable rites of initiation, then covenanting Baptist churches would have to observe the commitment they had freely

---

65   Hugh Cross, 'It may be the end of this road but it's not the end of the journey', *BT* November 17, 1977, 6, welcomed the report, but added, 'we have not yet shown that local ecumenical projects warm our hearts', while Mr John Beaumont encouraged member churches to use the document to let others know how Baptists felt and thought. John Beaumont, at the time a member of the BU Council representing the LBA, later became chairman of the General Purposes and Finance Committee. P.R. Clifford's ecumenism is reflected in both the title and contents of his autobiography, *An Ecumenical Pilgrimage* (West Ham Central Mission, 1994). The Roman Catholics and Congregational Federation also stepped out of the covenant scheme. This is an important correction to, e.g., Matthews, *Unity Scene*, 83, who mentioned only the withdrawal of the Baptists and Catholics.

66   *Visible Unity*, 'Preface' and p.1.

67   *Visible Unity*, 2-3.

accepted. However, on so-called rebaptism, if any Baptist church which covenanted as proposed continued to preach believers' baptism on grounds of conscience, it would negate the covenant relationship itself whenever they urged believers' baptism on individual paedobaptists seeking the transfer of their membership. Therefore, such an issue of conscience needed to be faced and settled before entry into covenant. 'However, we could not commend to our churches any covenant which involved a bar to the administration of believers' baptism in the case of a paedobaptist whose conscience might lead him or her to the conclusion that fidelity to Scripture and the Gospel required such baptism.'[68]

Rejection of the *Ten Propositions* was clearly not the end of Baptist ecumenical involvement, merely the rejection of the scheme as put forward by the CUC at this time. A considerable number of ministers, a few laymen and a number of churches were deeply distressed by the negative official reply to the *Ten Propositions*. David Rowland believed that the starting point ought to be that God makes no distinction between Christians on grounds of methods of initiation, denomination or rites of ordination and stated that assent to the *Ten Propositions* would not have implied a scheme of organic union.[69]

On January 14, 1978, forty Baptists met at the Selly Oak Colleges, Birmingham, feeling that the Union's report did not adequately represent them and that the CUC should be informed about this as knowledge of their support might influence future decisions about covenanting together. They believed that the *Ten Propositions* did form a promising basis for the mutual recognition of ministers and members and that many others wished to be associated with such views. They therefore invited interested parties to write to Rodney Ward of Alvechurch, Birmingham.[70]

---

68 *Visible Unity*, 3. The report concluded expressing the wish to remain in close fellowship and consultation with partner churches and believing that the model of diversity in unity adopted by the CUC constituted the most promising avenue for further advance, p.9.

69 D. Rowland of Oxford, 'No distinction', *BT* December 1, 1977, 5.

70 'We Want to Covenant', *BT* January 26, 1978, 5. Among the thirty six signatories were Dr M. Ball of Pontypridd, P.R. Clifford, President of Selly Oak Colleges, Hugh Cross of Grove Hill and Highfield, Hemel Hempstead, who was to become Ecumenical Officer for England for the BCC from 1979, N. Fairbairn from Penarth, M. Taylor, Principal of Northern Baptist College, D. Tennant, General Secretary and Director of Training of the Birmingham Council of Christian Education and Tutor in Christian Education at Westhill College, Selly Oak, and David Wilcox of Abingdon. It is clear that Birmingham ministers and the Selly Oak Colleges played an important role throughout this period in maintaining Baptist interest and involvement, even if in an observer capacity, in the ecumenical developments at this time.

Support for the group was not long in coming.[71] The final meeting of the CUC in Birmingham recommended that a Churches' Council for Covenanting in England (CCC) should be established comprising representatives of the churches still interested in pursuing a covenant scheme.[72] Five of the denominations were prepared to do so: the Anglicans, Churches of Christ, Methodists, Moravians and URC, while the BU, Roman Catholics and Congregational Federation maintained observer and consultative status.[73]

While the denominational leadership was giving a cautious yet committed response to the ecumenical state of affairs, stressing the importance of denominational unity,[74] the pro-ecumenists[75] launched the

---

71   E.g. E.F. Clipsham, now of Warrington, 'Covenant Welcomed', *BT* February 2, 1978, 5. At a meeting arranged by the Working Group on LEPs and the BRG at the Baptist Assembly, David Savage, chairman of the Group and the Merseyside Ecumenical Officer, reported the disappointment of Baptists involved in LEPs over the official BU response. Speakers at the meeting included H. Cross, J.F.V. Nicholson, at the time the BCC's Ecumenical Officer for England, D. Wilcox, M. Ball and D.S. Russell. Roger Nunn was chairman of the BRG. See 'Spell out unity issues, call', *BT* May 11, 1978, 12. On this meeting see also D. Savage, 'Unity: next steps', *BT* November 9, 1978, 6, which also announced that a day conference was going to be held at the Selly Oak Colleges on January 13, 1979. The meeting, however, did not take place until later in the year. The autumn CCLEPE conference passed the resolution to go to the CUC declaring that in LEPs the churches had already begun covenanting, see H. Cross, 'Unity? Churches are already covenanting', *BT* September 21, 1978, 1-2.

72   'Set Up Unity Council, Churches Told', *BT* September 28, 1978, 1.

73   W. Bottoms, 'Five churches are ready to take next step', *BT* November 23, 1978, 4. The final report of the CUC was published the week after its last meeting, and it anticipated that the most controversial element would be Proposition 6—the recognition of one another's ministries, see *Final Report on the Churches' Response to the Ten Propositions*, details are from Bottoms' article. Meeting about the same time, the BU Council was addressed by the new chairman of the ACCR, Neville Clark, a tutor of South Wales Baptist College, who said, 'Our concern for unity in mission should positively drive us to continue this involvement.' The Council agreed to participate fully in further developments, see 'Unity: we must still be involved, Baptists urged', *BT* November 23, 1978, 5.

74   This is reflected in two addresses to the Baptist Assembly, one by D.S. Russell reported in, 'Strengthen your unity, Baptists urged', the other by Morris West, who had been one of the denomination's representatives on the CUC, 'My Plea', both in *BT* April 26, 1979, 8 and 10 respectively.

75   A group of twenty eight pro-unity Baptists had met in Bristol in 1979 under the chairmanship of Ron Cowley, General Superintendent for the Western Area. At the meeting John Nicholson reported that the CCC had decided to draw up a covenant which it would submit to the churches in 1980. This gave the group the impetus to form an organization of Baptist churches and individual members who were committed ecumenically. Its fivefold task was to define the contribution which Baptists could make to the future shape of the English church; to create groups to work on the issues which

'1980 Group'. The Group convenor was one of the emerging leaders of Baptist ecumenism, Roger Nunn of Manvers Street, Bath.[76] When the 1980 Group was dissolved in the autumn of 1981[77] it was succeeded by the Fellowship of Baptist Churches for Covenanting (FBCC).[78]

While the CCC continued its work, committing itself to reach a decision by mid-1982,[79] Baptist involvement continued in two forms. The first was in the presence of official observer-consultants,[80] the second through the

---

required such redefinition; to share in negotiations with churches following the outcome of the CCC in 1980; to encourage commitment to visible unity; and to produce a scheme to enable churches to remain in formal association with each other and the BU. For this purpose, a group was appointed to bring the organization into being during the Nottingham Baptist Assembly in 1980. This group was made up of Vivien Baggs, Free Church Chaplain at Birmingham University, H. Cross, David Dale (details of whom are unknown), K. Lamdin of Devizes, R. Poolman, Pastor-Secretary of the Northamptonshire Association, and R. Nunn, see H. Cross, 'Baptist group take forward step in search for unity', *BT* October 4, 1979, 12.

76 J. Tall, 'Call for wider commitment', *BT* May 22, 1980, 2. Its aims were based on the desire to see formal shape to wider church commitment and to make plain that they were prepared to share in schemes for visible unity while remaining loyal to their Baptist views and remaining in fellowship with both the BU and their local Baptist associations. The Group was comprised of 150 men and women and twelve churches, and set up regional groups to examine various subjects (the Midland Group looking at baptism) in order to discuss them more fully at a day conference at the time planned for Birmingham in October. Another of the group, Dr David Rowland, wrote an article on his ecumenical commitment in which he stressed his belief that it was important that baptism was not made a precondition to sharing communion, 'Confession of an Ecumaniac', *BT* August 7, 1980, 4.

77 B. Cooper, 'Move on unity planned for autumn', *BT* May 14, 1981, 4. The major problems continued to be identified as episcopacy, 'rebaptism' and lay presidency at communion. The 1980 Group had been initially set up for a trial period of twelve months, after which the Group was willing to be disbanded if there was no good reason for its continued existence, an outcome they did not at the time envisage.

78 It was formed at a meeting in Birmingham on October 31, which included 170 people and fifty four churches, see 'Baptists form a new group', *BT* November 5, 1981, 1. 'Unity and the Baptists', *BT* July 8, 1982, 2, a week before the Church of England rejected the covenant, stated that thirty churches had joined the FBCC. Which figure is correct is uncertain. The FBCC's constitution stressed the desire of its churches to remain in full membership of the BU while seeking to share in the steps towards covenanting being taken by other denominations. The FBCC's first moderator was Chris Ellis of Swindon Central Church, supported by David Good of Sutton as secretary and Simon Dalwood of Christ Church, Cotham, as treasurer. Ten others were elected to the Council, and three BU representatives could be co-opted, underlining the desire to remain within the BU.

79 J. Tall, 'It's the best way forward, say churchmen', *BT* June 26, 1980, 6. The CCC published *Towards Visible Unity: Proposals for a Covenant* (1980), and continued to work for visible unity not organic union.

80 W.M.S. West, 'Now the crunch', *BT* January 29, 1981.

1980 Group, who believed that the door still remained open for Baptists to join in the covenanting if they wished.[81] At the March 1981 meeting of the Council, P.R. Clifford described *Visible Unity* as 'not a significant contribution', even though it had kept the Union committed in company with other churches to the search for visible unity, while George Beasley-Murray again repeated that Baptists had a responsibility to the whole church and needed to continue their participation.[82]

It soon became evident that the fate of the covenanting scheme rested heavily on the Church of England's decision due in the summer of 1982. Neville Clark described as engaged in 'wishful thinking' those who imagined that the rights of conscience provision would resolve any of the problems, with the possible exception of the case of insistent pressure from an individual for so-called rebaptism. What still awaited final clarification was whether and in what way Baptist congregations could in the end relate to the covenant currently under consideration. Clark further saw moves to limit covenanting to national churches as liable to exclude those bodies, such as the BU itself, which were comprised of associations of local churches.[83]

The covenant scheme, though endorsed by the URC and Methodists, was narrowly rejected by the Church of England, and the covenant discussions came to an end.[84] Addressing the annual meeting of the Bristol Baptist College, Morris West said that the initiative for any further developments now lay with the Anglicans.[85] By December 1983, even Roger Nunn was speaking of unity by national covenanting as dead in

---

81   H. Cross, 'Church of England says yes to next step on unity', *BT* March 5, 1981, 8.

82   P. Wortley, 'Unity: we have a responsbility to the whole Church, the council is told', *BT* March 19, 1981, 4. The importance of the Baptist contribution continued to be regularly raised, e.g. H. Cross, 'Where do we stand now?', *BT* July 16, 1981, 2, and P. Wortley, 'Unity: they want to have their cake and eat it...', *BT* February 18, 1982, 1 and 3, who said that Baptists should have a say in the ongoing conversations 'not least on Christian initiation and ministry', p.3. The Council also received a further document whose intention was to prompt and assist the discussion of the covenanting proposals: *Baptists and Visible Unity: an interim statement* (1981), cited by N. Clark, 'Visible unity: where do we go from here?', *BT* October 15, 1981, 7.

83   N. Clark, 'Visible unity: where do we go from here?', *BT* October 15, 1981, 7.

84   H. Cross, 'Covenant for unity: church votes yes by a whisker', *BT* May 27, 1982, 1 and 6; 'Unity: now the second church says yes', *BT* July 8, 1982, 1; H. Cross, 'No! By a whisker to the unity proposals', *BT* July 15, 1982, 8-9.

85   W. Bottoms, 'Next unity move "up to CofE"', *BT* October 14, 1982, 3. Ruefully, Ruth Matthews of the Grove Hill LEP, Hemel Hempstead, 'Covenanting', *BT* November 11, 1982, 11, remarked that if Baptists were afraid that their particular insights, such as baptism and the place of the local church, would be lost if they joined in then perhaps they were not trusting enough in God who would lead people into truth.

England.[86] Nevertheless, interest in unity continued. Bill Hancock, the South Eastern Area Superintendent, reported a renewal of Baptist interest in local co-operation since the covenant scheme had folded,[87] a view supported when Hugh Cross reported that Baptists were presently involved in eighty LEPs and that this was the way forward ecumenically, though it did not hide areas of difficulty, particularly the on-going issue of rebaptism.[88]

Twice in a decade, then, the BU had taken soundings among the churches as to the ecumenical movement and the level of Baptist involvement. In 1967, *Baptists and Unity* affirmed that fidelity to scripture compelled the search for a more adequate visible expression of the God-given and God-intended unity of Christ's church. In 1977, *Visible Unity* had to take into account two new factors: the increase of Baptist involvement in LEPs and the influence of the charismatic movement. Hesitations on the *Ten Propositions* had focused, as in previous generations, primarily on matters of baptism and episcopacy, but, with the development of LEP's in the mid-1960s, the issue of rights of conscience had also become a very real issue. Since the 'official' rejection of the *Ten Propositions*, Baptists had had only consultant observer status.[89]

What, then, had been achieved through all this? When George Beasley-Murray presented *Baptists and Unity* to the 1967 Baptist Assembly he stressed the importance of Christian unity and that Baptists needed to answer what part they should play in it and that problems that still needed to be faced included baptism. For him, the point was what outward expression union should take, and noted that as far as Baptists and ecumenism were concerned nothing new had happened since 1888, the year of the Lambeth Quadrilateral.[90] The situation was summed up in

---

86   R. Nunn, 'When the churches can become signs of hope', *BT* December 8, 1983. The pages of the *BT*, e.g., reflected this. Only a series of four articles on baptism appeared throughout the whole of 1983, all by R.F.G. Burnish from Powerscourt Road, Portsmouth, a series extracted from his Nottingham PhD which he had recently completed. See R. Burnish, 'Early risers in the Early Church', *BT* August 18, 1983, 4; 'Inquisitors or Befrienders?', *BT* August 25, 1983, 4; 'Backwards or forwards?', *BT* September 1, 1983, 4; 'White robes told of new life', *BT* September 8, 1983, 4. Each article examined various early church practices and drew lessons from them for contemporary practice. His thesis was published as *The Meaning of Baptism: A Comparison of the Teaching and Practice of the Fourth Century with the Present Day* (Alcuin Club Collections, 67; 1985).

87   'Baptists taking keener interest in unity', *BT* January 26, 1984, 1.

88   Margaret Jarman, 'Unity? "To be real it must be local"', *BT* November 29, 1984, 6.

89   N. Clark, 'Visible unity: where do we go from here?', *BT* October 15, 1981, 7.

90   'No "Selling Out" to Rome', *BT* May 4, 1967, 1-2. For Beasley-Murray, ecumenical discussions should go on, but not to Rome. Of this address, A. Noles of Bow,

1980. Now that Easter 1980 had arrived, 'The scene does not appear to have changed much.'[91] But would the developments in the 1980s bring about a new situation, especially through the work of the F&O branch of the WCC?

Baptism, Eucharist and Ministry (BEM)

The origins of the *BEM* text have been well documented in a number of publications and need only the barest mention here in order to set the present discussion within its proper context.[92] The Third F&O Conference at Lund in 1952 had marked a significant shift in approach to the ecumenical task, moving from comparative study to seeking convergence on vital theological issues.[93] The suggestions and emphases coming out of Lund led to the establishment of four theological commissions whose final reports were presented to the 1963 Montreal F&O Conference.[94] In preparation for this, the commission on 'Christ and the Church' found itself more and more involved with the issue of baptism. A preparatory study was carried out on that subject by the European section of the Theological Commission, the result of which was presented to the Working Committee of the F&O Commission at New Haven, Connecticut in 1957.[95] Further work continued up to 1959 in both the

---

London, 'Baptists and Unity. Unpersuaded', *BT* May 11, 1967, 3, wrote that it would cause many to be pro-ecumenical, but that many, like the writer, remained unconvinced.

91   J.H.Y. Briggs, 'When the Quest for Church Union Pointed to a Day Sixteen Years On...', *BT* April 3, 1980, 9. This article was incorrectly attributed to Briggs, who had not attended the Conference at Nottingham in 1964 as the article stated, but was written by Paul Ballard of University College Cardiff. Information from J.H.Y. Briggs. Briggs was Senior Lecturer in History at Keele University until 1997 when he became Principal of Westhill College of Higher Education, now University of Birmingham, Westhill. On Prof. Briggs, see 'John Briggs to head Westhill', *BT* April 10, 1997, 3.

92   The substance of this sketch has been gleaned from five of these sources, G. Gassmann, *Documentary History of Faith and Order, 1963–1993* (Geneva, 1993), especially vii-ix, 6-9, 22-25, 104-05; *Baptism, Eucharist and Ministry, 1982–1990: Report on the Process and Responses* (F&O Paper 149; Geneva, 1990), 3-16; West, 'Towards a Consensus on Baptism?' (being a slightly amended form of an article published in the American journal *Midstream*), 225-26, and his 'Baptists in Faith and Order', 68-74; M. Thurian, '*Baptism, Eucharist and Ministry* (the "Lima text")', in Lossky *et al* (eds.), *Dictionary of the Ecumenical Movement*, 80-83.

93   This is conveniently set out by Gassmann, *Documentary History of Faith and Order*, 7, and also discussed by W.M.S. West, 'Lund Principle', in Lossky *et al* (eds.), *Dictionary of the Ecumenical Movement*, 633-34.

94   These commissions examined 'Institutionalism', 'Christ and the Church', 'Worship' and 'Tradition and Traditions'. Gassmann, *Documentary History of Faith and Order*, 7, lists the titles of the published interim and collected papers.

95   For details see West, 'Baptists in Faith and Order', 62-63 and nn.17-19.

USA and Europe, during which time it became clear that something needed to be said about the meaning of baptism and its relationship to the unity of the church. The report *The Meaning of Baptism* was prepared by a joint meeting of the two theological commissions and went before the Working Committee meeting in Spittal, Austria, in 1959.[96] *The Meaning of Baptism* was then taken before the full F&O Commission at St. Andrews, Scotland, in 1960, to which Dr Leonard Champion had by now been appointed, where it was presented by Neville Clark. It now formed the second part of the larger document *One Lord, One Baptism: The Meaning of Baptism* (1960), to which George Beasley-Murray had contributed.[97] A sub-committee was set up at St. Andrews to look at the meaning of baptism and the comments made by Clark and this committee pointed to the necessity for further work. These included points which were taken up and re-emphasized in *BEM* some twenty years later.[98]

The Fourth World Conference on F&O in Montreal was divided up into five sections whose reports drew on those of the four earlier theological commissions and much additional material. Section IV on 'Worship and the Oneness of Christ's Church' included ecumenical perspectives on baptism and the eucharist. This received further reflection at the 1971 commission meeting in Louvain, Belgium, which produced *Baptism, Confirmation and Eucharist* (1971) Here it became clear that there was the possibility if not of consensus then of convergence, not only on the meaning but also on the actual practice of baptism. With this sense of hope it was agreed that the member churches of the WCC should receive the document and be invited to comment on it.[99] Consideration of

---

96 E.A. Payne played an important role at this meeting, having been appointed to the F&O Commission with C.T. Le Quesne in 1952. At the F&O Commission in Spittal, Payne presented a 'Study of the Implications of Baptism for Christian Unity', *Encounter* 21.3 (Summer, 1960), 311-16, which placed baptism within the renewed interest in Christian initiation, p.311. See also 'Faith and Order Commission Paper 27: Minutes of the Working Committee, 1959, Spittal, Austria', 12-16, cited by West, 'Baptists in Faith and Order', 63-64, for the discussion of the baptismal issue.

97 For an outline of *One Lord, One Baptism*, see West, 'Baptists in Faith and Order', 65-66. Clark's role in this is discussed by West, pp.66-67.

98 'Faith and Order Commission Paper 31: Minutes of the Faith and Order Commission 1960, St. Andrews, Scotland', 122-23, cited by West, 'Baptists in Faith and Order', 67-68.

99 See West, 'Towards a Consensus on Baptism?', 226. Though no British Baptists had been present at Louvain, the Baptist presence was in the person of Dr Günther Wagner, Professor of New Testament at the International Baptist Theological Seminary, Rüschlikon, Zürich. The importance of the Louvain meeting is stressed and outlined by West, 'Baptists in Faith and Order', 70-71, most importantly being the decision that there needed to be a consideration as to whether there could be a consensus document prepared on baptism, eucharist and ministry. At Louvain West was elected to

the responses took place at Accra, Ghana, where the document *One Baptism, One Eucharist and a Mutually Recognized Ministry* (1974) was produced. West has noted the general agreement on the definition of baptism itself and the implications of the sacrament, but commented that the document spoke 'too glibly of a common baptism which unites us all in Christ.' As a result of Baptist concerns over this phrase it was agreed that the 'Introduction' should make clear that the document was not a consensus of all that was in the text but rather a summary of shared convictions and perspectives to help lead the churches closer together.[100] The final document was *One Baptism, One Eucharist and a Mutually Recognized Ministry* (F&O Paper 73; 1975). West has also drawn attention to the fact that this document was 'the outcome of a new ecumenical process—that of consultation with Churches and response.'[101]

F&O Paper 73 was discussed at the Fifth WCC Assembly at Nairobi and became known as *BEM* before this was adopted for the 1982 Lima text. To this the BU responded suggesting that there was need for genuine, rather than apparent, agreement and indicated that the cracks had been plastered over at certain points. Also, there was a failure to recognize that at the heart of the issue of infant and believer's baptism were ecclesiastical differences. Finally, the document over-simplified the question of so-called rebaptism.[102] Nairobi was followed by a consultation at Crêt Bérard, Switzerland, in 1977, where further responses of the churches were considered and a way forward was planned. The report *Towards an Ecumenical Consensus: Baptism, Eucharist, Ministry—A Response to the Churches* (F&O Paper 84; 1977) was the fruit of these deliberations, among which was the recommendation that the F&O Commission should initiate a consultation with Baptists 'to explore the issues involved in the debate on infant baptism and believer's baptism which remain many and complex and need to be addressed at this time if we are to move forward in the agreement on baptism.' This recognized that one approach in seeking a way forward was to confront positively the two practices of baptism and to see how far within the two practices there was a possibility of movement towards consensus and mutual recognition.[103]

An important landmark on the way to *BEM* was the Louisville Consultation on Baptism, held at the Southern Baptist Seminary in 1979, the BU being represented by George Beasley-Murray, Morris West and

---

the then Working Committee of F&O, being the only Britain among eight Baptists on the F&O Commission.

    100 West, 'Baptists in Faith and Order', 71-72.
    101 West, 'Towards a Consensus on Baptism?', 226.
    102 Sketch taken from West, 'Baptists in Faith and Order', 72.
    103 West, 'Towards a Consensus on Baptism?', 226.

John Nicholson.[104] The importance of this meeting lies in the fact that it was the first time that an equal number of believer-Baptist and paedobaptist scholars had met to try and find some kind of consensus in the understanding and practice of baptism.[105] Keith Clements has rightly noted that this consultation coincided with a heightened debate on Christian initiation and church membership among British churches.[106]

Towards an Ecumenical Consensus had listed points which it was believed showed an emerging agreement, so West, who had been present at Crêt Bérard, formulated a series of questions which needed addressing so that there could be some clarification as to how near to or how far from consensus the two traditions were.[107] These covered the meaning of baptism, the ecclesiastical differences underlying baptismal differences, seeing Christian initiation as a process which included baptism in water in the name of the Trinity, instruction in and confession of the faith, the activity of the Holy Spirit, participation in the Lord's Supper, what similarities in Christian nurture revealed about the differences over baptism, including discussion of the catechumenate, and the question of the authority and justification for baptism.[108] West further noted that guidance was needed on whether the consensus process would be promoted through the co-existence of the two forms of baptism. This would, then, raise the issue of 'rebaptism', problems over which were beginning to become evident in the Church of North India (established in 1970).[109]

---

104 Nicholson was chosen because of his experience of LEPs in England in which both forms of baptism were practised, see Nicholson, Association Minister of the Lancashire and Cheshire Association, 'Baptism in Context', 275.

105 K.W. Clements, 'Editorial', *BQ* 28.5 (January, 1980), 195, saw in the Consultation 'a sign of our ecumenical times that discussion of the theology and practice of baptism means much less of a sectarian or partisan confrontation.'

106 K.W. Clements, 'Baptism', in C. Davey (ed.), *British and Irish Churches respond to BEM: Analysis and Implications of the British and Irish Churches' Responses to the Lima report on Baptism, Eucharist and Ministry* (1988), 9-10. He also drew attention to the Common Certificate of Baptism used by some churches, and also the 1983 BCC's Division of Ecumenical Affairs working party which reported on the whole question of Christian initiation and membership in *Christian Initiation and Church Membership*, as well as the British churches' responses to *BEM*. The importance of Louisville to British Baptists was reflected in the number of articles about the consultation and that the report was published in the *BQ*.

107 W.M.S. West, 'Toward A Possible Agenda', *RevExp* 77.1 (Winter, 1980), 13-20.

108 West, 'Toward A Possible Agenda', 14-17.

109 In October, 1970, A.S. Clement, Home Secretary of the BMS, 'Churches Unite in India and Pakistan—Baptist will be one of the first bishops', *BT* October 29, 1970, 2, had reported that one of the first bishops in the newly united Church of North India and Pakistan was to be a Baptist, J.K. Maharty. The church's baptismal policy included both

Beasley-Murray set out the evidence for believers' baptism, in which he primarily discussed the difficulties which Baptists commonly experienced in ecumenical conversations, with the secondary intention of shedding some light on these matters to the others involved in the consultation.[110] After a discussion of the authority for believer's baptism from Matthew 28:19, the nature of baptism itself, the issue of the relationship of faith and baptism and between the faith of the individual and that of the community, the ecclesiological implication of the baptism of believers, the place of children and the role of the catechumenate, and finally the issue of rebaptism, Beasley-Murray concluded, on the one hand, by encouraging the possibility that Baptists could accept others on the grounds of their initiation into the body of Christ, rather than their infant baptism. On the other hand, if infant baptism could not comprehend the significance of baptism as expounded in Galatians 3:25, Colossians 2:12 and 1 Peter 3:21, and was therefore a different baptism, then application of baptism '*at the time of profession of faith* of one who has been baptized as an infant' was at least arguable. Such, he believed, should be allowed in paedobaptist churches, when requested, 'and could

---

infant and believer's baptism, but ruled out rebaptism. See also E.W. Burrows, 'Understanding of Baptism in Baptist Traditions, with Special Reference to Modern Trends', *IJT* 26 (1977), 27. By 1978 it had become clear that church union schemes were not operating as Baptists had hoped when it came to the issue of so-called 'rebaptism'. The Constitution of the Church of North India stated that the situations of believers baptized in infancy but seeking believer's baptism were to be referred to the Bishop. However, the Bishop of Patna had forbidden pastors to carry out such requests, see A. Clement, 'Bishop turns down "re-baptism" request', *BT* June 22, 1978, 1. For some of the background of the Church of North India from a Baptist participant and focusing specifically on the matter of rebaptism, see L. Wenger, a retired missionary living in Norwich, 'Faith, baptism and church order', *BT* February 8, 1996, 11.

110 G.R. Beasley-Murray, 'The Authority and Justification for Believers' Baptism', *RevExp* 77.1 (Winter, 1980), 63-70. This was preceded by a paper on 'The Authority and Justification for Infant Baptism', by J. Eagan, S.J., 47-61. For their contributions, both Beasley-Murray and Eagan were criticized by C. Ellis, 'Relativity, Ecumenism and the Liberation of the Church', *BQ* 29.2 (April, 1981), 89, as typifying the traditional approaches adopted by apologists for each respective position—Eagan mainly being concerned with a theological defence of the development of infant baptism in the post-New Testament church and its appropriateness for the contemporary church, while the Baptist contribution was primarily an exegetical examination of the relationship of faith to baptism in the New Testament. 'Bluntly put', he asserted, p.88, '*the difference can be said to rest upon the acceptance or rejection of Tradition as a valid and authoritative norm over and against Scripture*', italics his. However, Ellis's criticisms of Beasley-Murray and Eagan lose much of their force when it is recognized that Beasley-Murray's intention was, first and foremost, to explicate the Baptist position and the difficulties they encountered in ecumenical discussions.

be understood sympathetically when such people confess Christ in Baptist churches.'[111]

The final report, as well as the published papers, show that no such consensus was possible.[112] Clear signs of bridge-building from both sides were evident, and for some the bridge was sufficiently complete to allow mutual recognition of each others' practices, while for others the gap had narrowed sufficiently to allow mutual respect and facilitate growing understanding. Five significant areas of agreement emerged.[113] First, that the most clearly attested practice in the New Testament was of believer's baptism. Second, the statement that the personal faith of the recipient and continuous life of the church were essential for the full fruit of baptism. Third, that both forms of baptism required similar and responsible attitudes to Christian nurture and a serious development of the concept of the catechumenate. Fourth, that the pressures of contextuality always bore down on the understanding and practice of baptism. Fifth, that indiscriminate baptism was an abuse to be eliminated.[114]

The Consultation's success also lay in the fact that it had happened at all[115] and many positive suggestions were made as to the way forward. West wrote of it: 'the impression gained...was not only a real striving to mutual understanding but a search for perhaps a new approach to bridge the baptismal divide.' Glimpses of this new approach, he continued, appeared when neither infant nor believer's baptism were the starting point for discussion, but rather, for example, God's activity in Christ initiating the gospel, or of the community of God's people receiving and communicating that gospel, or the response of the individual within that community to the gospel, 'then the issue of baptism, whether infant or believer's, looks rather different. Maybe the baptismal issue needs to be approached by all Churches in this overarching perspective of God, His community, and the individual responding within that community and world.'[116] Later, when he reflected on the consultation, West remarked

---

111 Beasley-Murray, 'Authority and Justification', 70.

112 'Editorial Introduction', *RevExp* 77.1 (Winter, 1980), 3. The papers and the final report were all reproduced in this issue of *RevExp*. The consultation resulted from and was concerned with F&O Paper 84, *Toward an Ecumenical Consensus: Baptism, Eucharist, Ministry*. The final report, 'Baptism: Report of the Faith and Order Consultation, Louisville 1979', was published in *BQ* 28.5 (January, 1980), 232-39.

113 'Report of the Consultation With Baptists', in *RevExp* 77.1 (Winter, 1980), 101.

114 'Report of the Consultation With Baptists', 101-02. This report continued by outlining the Consultation's discussion on authority and justification for baptism, sacrament and faith, ecclesiology and contextuality, pp. 103-07.

115 West, 'Towards a Consensus on Baptism?', 230.

116 West, 'Towards a Consensus on Baptism?', 231-32.

that it had got the questions right and had also been right to emphasize the issue of contextuality.[117]

This latter issue was taken up by John Nicholson, who had been involved in the discussions on contextuality and so he limited his reflections on the consultation to this issue. He had also earlier been involved in the conference on Christian initiation sponsored by the BCC at Damascus House, Mill Hill, three weeks before Louisville,[118] which had identified four factors as affecting baptismal practice: theology; law, including both canon law and Baptist Trust Deeds; pastoral concern; and the social context.[119] Reflection on both consultations led Nicholson to realize that the English context for the baptismal dialogue was unique in several ways. First, probably the majority of Baptist churches were open membership and did not require baptism as a condition of membership. In addition, many other churches while still legally closed membership, allowed other Christians the privileges and reponsibilities of membership as much as they could. Open membership churches were (and still are) rare among Baptists in the rest of the world.[120] Second, there were between fifty and sixty congregations in membership with the BU and at least one other denomination, twenty of which were Union churches founded before the 1969 Sharing of Buildings Act, being joint members of both the BU and CU. Third, the *Ten Propositions* had challenged the English churches to recognize each others' members and ministers. Though the BU had not been able to proceed with the covenant, if the churches involved in the CCC did manage to reach agreement on such a

---

117 West, 'Baptists in Faith and Order', 73. See the whole of his article, 'Towards a Consensus on Baptism?', 225-32.

118 Nicholson, 'Baptism in Context', 276. The Damascus House meeting had been set up in response to requests from CCLEPE, the BU Council in its response to the *Ten Propositions, Visible Unity*, 'Preface', n.p., and the F&O Commission's invitation for churches in certain regions to discuss together their response to *One Baptism, One Eucharist and a Mutually Recognised Ministry*. Nicholson's input is reflected in the final report's reference to the practice of an unnamed Oxford LEP (possibly Blackbird Leys) which included both paedo- and believer-baptists, and which held a service for the celebration of new life including opportunity either for infant baptism or for infant blessing with or without the dedication of the parents, 'Report of the Consultation With Baptists', 107.

119 See Nicholson, 'Baptism in Context', 276-77, citing *Christian Initiation*, BCC Department of Ecumenical Affairs duplicated report, March 1979, and *Baptism: Some Historical and Social Considerations*, BCC Department of Ecumenical Affairs, duplicated paper, March 1979.

120 Nicholson, 'Baptism in Context', 277. According to Nicholson the questionaire sent out by the BU in 1976 concerning the *Ten Propositions* had contained a question on the conditions of membership, and the clear majority of those churches responding claimed to practise open membership—but it was difficult to ascertain the exact proportion.

covenant, this would renew the challenge to Baptists to reconsider their attitude to Paedobaptists and to define more closely what they understood by 'diversity in unity'. Fourth, there was the charismatic factor which raised the whole question of the relationship between water- and Spirit-baptism. Nicholson concluded: 'For me therefore the most valuable lesson from Louisville was its stress on contextuality, because that has helped me to see the particular elements in our English context which we have to face in our teaching on, and practice of, baptism.'[121]

The Lima text of *BEM* is a considerably revised form of the Accra document.[122] Its greatest challenge to Baptists lay in its call that 'Any practice which might be interpreted as "re-baptism" must be avoided.'[123] Churches were also invited to regard infant and believers' baptism as 'equivalent alternatives'.[124] *BEM* also admitted that, while the possibility that infant baptism was also practised in the apostolic age could not be excluded, 'baptism upon personal profession of faith is the most clearly attested pattern in the New Testament documents.'[125] Though this did not go far enough for Baptists, it nevertheless demonstrated that their ecumenical presence and contribution had made an impact.

---

121 Nicholson, 'Baptism in Context', 277-79, quotation from p.279. Nicholson spoke of the 'English' situation because 'the historical, cultural and ecumenical context is quite different for Baptists in Scotland, Ireland and Wales', p.276. A second study on contextuality was that of Ellis, 'Relativity', 81-91, which provoked a response from his brother, Robert Ellis of Bletchley, 'How Relative Should Theology Be?', *BQ* 29.5 (January, 1982), 220-24, which discusses baptism in some detail.

122 See Gassmann, *Documentary History of Faith and Order*, 8, 23 and 104-05; L.A. Hoedemaker, the Dutch Reformed theologian from the University of Groningen, 'Toward A Consensus on Baptism, Eucharist and Ministry', *RevExp* 77.1 (Winter, 1980), 7-9. This comes out most clearly in the comparative study of the Accra and Lima texts by G. Wagner, 'Baptism from Accra to Lima', in M. Thurian (ed.), *Ecumenical Perspectives on baptism, eucharist and ministry* (F&O Paper 116; Geneva, 1983), 12-32.

123 *BEM*, 4, 'IV Baptismal Practice', §13. See also the section on 'Towards Mutual Recognition of Baptism' (§15-16), p.6.

124 *BEM*, 5, 'Commentary 12'. In order to overcome their differences, believer baptists were encouraged to seek to express more visibly the fact that children were placed under the protection of God's grace, paedobaptists were called to guard against indiscriminate baptism and take more seriously their responsibility to nurture children to mature commitment.

125 *BEM*, 4. In his study guide issued to students of Bristol Baptist College, Keith Clements remarked that 'over the years, our understanding of believers' baptism has been moving more and more into the centre of the discussion and has become more and more recognised as being true both to the biblical understanding and to the practice of the Early Church', 'Baptism, Eucharist and Ministry' (unpublished, Bristol Baptist College, 1983), 2.

Through *BEM* the F&O Commission invited all churches to consider and then respond to the *BEM* text by the end of 1984.[126] The BU, therefore, asked Associations, ministers' fraternals, Superintendents, Colleges, church meetings and diaconates and a number of individuals to consider *BEM* and to submit their replies to the General Secretary, Bernard Green, by November 1983.[127] These were then analysed and drawn together for the ACCR by its chairman, Neville Clark.[128] This was then taken to the BU Council and approved by it in November 1984.

---

126 *BEM*, x. In Britain, *BEM* was accompanied by a study guide prepared for the BCC by J. Matthews, *Baptism, Eucharist and Ministry: Seven Studies by John Matthews based on the Faith and Order Paper No.111 of the World Council of Churches 1982* (n.d., probably 1982–84). Its use was recommended, e.g., by B. Green in his 'Foreword' to *Baptism, Eucharist and Ministry: The response of the Council of the Baptist Union of Great Britain and Ireland to the Faith and Order Paper No.111 of the World Council of Churches, 1982* (1985), n.p.. In 1983, M. Thurian and G. Wainwright edited *Baptism and Eucharist: Ecumenical Convergence in Celebration* (F&O Paper 117; Geneva, 1983), which brought together a wide selection of liturgies of baptism and the eucharist with commentaries on the traditions and texts included, for the purpose of aiding current understanding and practice of the two sacraments. 'The Baptist Tradition', pp.66-74, included an order for believer's baptism from Payne and Winward's *Orders and Prayers*, and orders for 'Christian Initiation' and 'Infant Dedication and Thanksgiving' from A. Gilmore, E. Smalley and M.J. Walker (eds.), *Praise God: A Collection of Resource Material for Christian Worship* (1980), 129-36, and 'A Baptist Service of Thanksgiving on the Birth of a Child' (1980), 73-74, from Morris West.

127 According to the supplement from the ACCR included with the official BU response, 'Baptist Union of Great Britain and Ireland', in M. Thurian (ed.), *Churches Respond to BEM: Official responses to the 'Baptism, Eucharist and Ministry' text, vol.1* (F&O Paper 129; Geneva, 1986), 74-75, comments were received from 16 Associations, the Superintendents' Board, two Baptist Colleges, and a number of other groups. Several such study documents have been traced. In March 1983, students at Bristol Baptist College, under the supervision of Keith Clements, received a 5 page, typed preparation document to aid their discussions, 'Baptism, Eucharist and Ministry'. The LBA appointed a six man team to respond to *BEM*, G.R. Beasley-Murray (from the language, probably the author of the section on baptism) and R.C. Dalton, of West Wickham and Shirley, commenting on baptism, see 'London Baptist Association Response to "Baptism, Eucharist and Ministry"', *Free Church Chronicle* 39.1 (Spring, 1984), 13-18. Also the EMBA produced their own study guide, *Growing Together. I—Baptism: A Study Guide to Baptism, Eucharist and Ministry* (n.d., c.1983), prepared by K. Hobbs of Grimsby, being the result of the EMBA's own ACCR.

128 Clark has been an important, though quiet, Baptist ecumenist and his contribution has been frequently overlooked, but is noted in Cross, 'Service to the Ecumenical Movement', 114 and 118, and his ecumenical views can be found in two of his *Invitation to a Conversation* (both Cardiff, 1998): *11. Baptist Churchmanship* and *12. Ecumenical Dilemma*, both of which discuss baptism in this context.

In its official response, the BU declined to comment on the minutiae of *BEM*, but drew attention to major points of difficulty or hesitation.[129] It began by agreeing with the five strands setting out the essential meaning of baptism, noting the significant place accorded to faith and recognizing the danger of indiscriminate infant baptism.[130] Three specific reservations, however, emerged, the first and last both highlighting the ambiguity surrounding *BEM*'s use of 'baptism'. First, attention was drawn to the language which marked all subsequent discussion where, 'We are told that baptism *is...gives...initiates...unites...effects....* It has to be asked what is meant by "baptism" where this sort of language is constantly used.' Second, *a priori* consent could not be given to a universal bar on *BEM*'s 'any practice which might be interpreted as "re-baptism" must be avoided.' The BU stated that this was 'wholly unacceptable in its present form since, on some interpretations, nothing could pass through so restrictive a sieve.' For 'where the individual involved is convinced out of an instructed conscience that Christian obedience requires believer baptism', Baptists maintained that person's right to be so baptized irrespective of accusations of 're-baptism'.[131] Third, the response noted that 'a total process of Christian initiation wherein, at some point, all the necessary elements—including responsible faith-commitment—find a place' offered the most promising path toward mutual recognition of

---

129 *Baptism, Eucharist and Ministry: The response of the Council of the Baptist Union.* It was subsequently published under the title 'Baptist Union of Great Britain and Ireland', in Thurian (ed.), *Churches Respond to BEM*, 70-77. It is from this later version that all subsequent quotations and references are taken. The BU's response to *BEM* was whole-heartedly supported by D. McBain, Superintendent for the Metropolitan Area, in 1991, 'Worthy of Trust', in M.I. Bochenski (ed.), *Evangelicals and Ecumenism—When Baptists Disagree* (Didcot, 1993), 30-31.

130 'Baptist Union of Great Britain and Ireland', 70. The five-fold meaning was participation in Christ's death and resurrection; conversion, pardoning and cleansing; the gift of the Spirit; incorporation into the body of Christ; and the sign of the kingdom. See *BEM*, 'II. The Meaning of Baptism', 2-3. In this it is important to realize that *BEM* achieved a great deal of theological convergence but there was no such convergence on the practice of baptism.

131 On this see the similar comments made by N. Clark and P. Beasley-Murray at the BU Council when it received the ACCR's response to *BEM*, 'All one body we...but we bump a bit', *BT* December 4, 1984, 7. The subtitle of the article is also informative, 'Council is told, young people don't care about discussions like these'. Also, the BU's Working Group on LEPs (WORGLEP), a sub-group within the ACCR, later commented: 'In two swift sentences it prescribes a universal sacramental norm', adding, 'Two immediate comments can be made: it requires a considerably longer commentary; it does not work.' See 'Rebaptism in Local Ecumenical Projects', undated and anonymous two page document used at the October 1989 meeting of WORGLEP.

baptism, but this fact underlined *BEM*'s 'arguable ambiguity in its references to "baptism".'[132]

Similarly, Morris West highlighted two issues. He believed that *BEM* had not thoroughly dealt with the issue of authority, which for Baptists rested with scripture and from which infant baptism is not a valid development, and the doctrine of the church from which baptism is derived.[133] He also criticized *BEM*'s lack of clarity on whether baptism was an act which achieves the believer's participation in the death and resurrection of Christ, or just symbolizes it, and its absolute prohibition of rebaptism was unacceptable, as for Baptists an individual's conscience has priority over ecclesiastical discipline. He concluded that while it marked considerable progress 'much yet remains to be thought through.'[134]

BEM had requested that all churches consider four specific questions. To the second of these,[135] the BU responded that, more important than whether the BU could recognize the text as an 'expression of the apostolic faith', was the extent to which the text enshrined 'a basis for mutual recognition.' *BEM*'s 'Preface' spoke of 'consensus' and 'convergence', but it was felt that what required keener debate was what measure of articulated baptismal and eucharistic agreement and agreement on patterns and orders of ministry was necessary for 'living in communion with one another'. No clear and coherent answer was offered, but the reply acknowledged that 'the question presses upon us particularly in relation to the issue of baptism.'[136] Finally, in response to question four,[137] it stated that further work on baptism could be usefully done

---

132 'Baptist Union of Great Britain and Ireland', 70-71, italics original. There are two typographical errors on the first and second point, where reference in *BEM* is purportedly at 'B1' and 'B13'. *Baptism, Eucharist and Ministry: The response of the Council of the Baptist Union*, 1, rightly locates the references at 'I.1' and 'IV.13'. On the third point, Keith Clements, in his overview of the responses to the baptism section of *BEM*, 'Baptism', 15-16, explained Baptist hesitancy over the apparent tendency of *BEM* to make baptism itself operative of that which it signifies. This ambiguity became especially problematic for Baptists when it was not clear whether 'baptism' meant a rite of water-baptism per se, or that rite together with the faith-commitment of the person baptised. 'Baptist Union of Great Britain and Ireland', 75, described as an inevitable feature of ecumenical statements this ambiguity of language allowing formal assent in the teeth of suspected unbridged disagreement.

133 W.M.S. West, 'Baptism, Eucharist and Ministry: A Baptist Comment', *One in Christ* 20.1 (1984), 26.

134 West, 'Baptism, Eucharist and Ministry', 26-27, quote from p.27.

135 This read: 'the consequences your church can draw from this text for its relations and dialogues with other churches, particularly with those churches which also recognize the text as an expression of the apostolic faith', *BEM* x.

136 'Baptist Union of Great Britain and Ireland', 73-74.

137 This read: 'the suggestions your church can make for the ongoing work of Faith and Order as it relates the material of this text on Baptism, Eucharist and Ministry to its

only in the wider context of Christian initiation.[138] David Russell[139] recognized that *BEM* had achieved 'a goodly measure of "convergence",... [but] this falls short of "consensus", not least in the report's interpretation of baptism and the nature of the Church to which baptism testifies.' It made claims for the 'rite' of baptism 'which, in the Baptist mind, belong to the total process of Christian initiation which includes a responsible faith-commitment on the part of the one baptised.'[140]

A supplement, prepared by the ACCR, was appended to the official BU response. On baptism, it identified the unanswered question of 'What is a Christian?' as lurking behind *BEM*'s discussion of baptism. Baptists, once again, found themselves effectively in a dialectic with their ecumenical partners. Baptists based their faith and practice on scripture, much of the debate reflected in *BEM* was based on scripture *and* tradition, and this was reflected in how the supplement continued. 'If the starting point is a New Testament inseparability of conversion and

---

long-range research project "Towards the Common Expression of the Apostolic Faith Today"', *BEM* x. On Baptist participation in this see K.W. Clements, 'Towards the Common Expression of the Apostolic Faith Today. Baptist Reflections on this Faith and Order Project', *BQ* 33.2 (April, 1989), 63-71, and also his 'A Response to the Faith and Order Commission Document No.140', in Brackney and Burke (eds.), *Faith, Life and Witness*, 48-53.

138   'Baptist Union of Great Britain and Ireland', 74. Many of the BU's responses were noted in the volume *Baptism, Eucharist and Ministry, 1982–1990. Report on the Process and Responses* (F&O Paper 149; Geneva, 1990), 21, 37, 39, 42 n.15, 48-49, 59 n.16, 60 n.18, 65, 102 (the section on 'The Responses to the Baptism Section', 39-55, was prepared by W.M.S. West and Dr Mary Tanner of the Church of England). In its warm reception of F&O Paper 149, 'Comment. Our voices must be heard...', *BT* August 16, 1990, 2, reiterated the BU's response to *BEM*, that while there was a growing convergence, 'agreement on fundamentals there is not.' On *BEM*'s assumption that the two practices of baptism concerned only differences of understandings of baptism, the commentator stated that 'in reality they reflect basic differences on the doctrine of the church, its membership and on the Christian life itself.'

139   Russell's ecumenical involvement included work with the BCC and as a member of the WCC's Central Committee from Uppsala in 1968 to Vancouver in 1982, so D.S. Russell, 'The Ecumenical Role of Baptists', in F.H. Littell (ed.), *The Growth of Interreligious Dialogue 1939–1989* (TST, 46; Lewiston, NY, 1989), 112-131. On Russell himself, see J.H.Y. Briggs (ed.), *Bible, Church and World: A Supplement to the Baptist Quarterly Published in Honour of Dr. D.S. Russell* (Baptist Historical Society, 1989), and on his ecumenical involvement especially G.W. Rusling, 'David Syme Russell: A Life of Service', 15-17, and D.M. Thompson, 'Baptists and the World Fellowship of the Church', 61-62. See also his autobiographical *In Journeyings Often* (1981), based on his privately published 'Roots and Branches: Unprofound reflections on a full life' (privately published, n.d.).

140   Russell, 'Ecumenical Role of Baptists', 130. A later study based on *BEM* is that by P. Beasley-Murray, 'Celebrating the Faith in Baptism', *BMJ* 244 (October, 1993), 11-14, who used it as a foil for his discussion of Baptist distinctives in worship.

baptism, certain conclusions may arguably follow. If the starting point is tradition, the implications may be importantly other. It may be objected that such questions are falsely posed because they proceed from a starting point which is not that of the report. *It must be retorted that this is in fact the baseline from which many Baptists by conviction move.*'[141] In conclusion they wrote:

> In its Preface, the BEM report states: 'If the divided churches are to achieve the visible unity they seek, one of the essential prerequisites is that they should be in basic agreement on baptism, eucharist and ministry.' Comment from our Baptist constituency makes clear that this apparently self-evident statement conceals as many questions as it answers. What understanding of visible unity is here intended? What measure and kind of basic agreement is here required? Part of the felt difficulty with the total presentation of both baptism and eucharist is a sense that these sacraments are being filled with an exclusive theological weight which is more properly attributed to the deeper realities of which they are the visible signs and to which they bear witness, and that it is upon these deeper and more pervasive realities that unity is properly founded.[142]

The Inter-Church Process (ICP)

The real starting point of the Inter-Church Process (ICP) was the 1984 Spring Assembly of the BCC, though it was not until May 1985 that the ICP was formally launched[143] with the circulation of an introductory document eliciting twenty six responses which were published in 1986.[144] For the next few years, the Baptist constituency was fully updated.[145] The

---

141 'Baptist Union of Great Britain and Ireland', 75-76, italics added. This interpretation is supported by Clements, 'Baptism', 18, who wrote, 'To explore the nature of the gap between the two approaches to baptism, which churches on both sides feel still exists despite BEM, it is evident that some recognition of differing *basic presuppositions* on both sides will be necessary', italics added. He then proceeded to discuss the basic unanswered question, 'What is a Christian?'

142 'Baptist Union of Great Britain and Ireland', 77.

143 The 1984 BCC Assembly resolved to consult all member churches and national Councils of Churches on their readiness to share in 'a process of prayer, reflection and debate together centred on the nature and purpose of the church in the light of its calling in and for the world'. It was heralded as a 'Major boost towards church unity', *BT* May 23, 1985, 3.

144 The resulting study booklet was called, *REFLECTIONS—How Churches view their life and mission* (1986).

145 This was done by means of the *BT*, the BU Annual Reports, the Baptist Assembly popular report, letters circulated to every church and *The Fraternal*. See the notes above and below. See, e.g., the letter which B. Green wrote to all the churches in his capacity as BU General Secretary, asking that the BU's proposed membership of the ICP be fully discussed in every Baptist church and that they make their own response to

findings of the three regional conferences for England, Scotland and Wales held in 1987, were sent to the British and Irish Conference at Swanwick. It was this conference which issued the Swanwick Declaration,[146] and has proved to be yet another ecumenical landmark, marking a shift in emphasis from declared co-operation between churches towards commitment.[147] Swanwick was significant, not simply for the Declaration, but because it was felt to be a conviction arrived at by Christians of all denominations and at all levels and not the result of a dialogue between church authorities.[148]

The build up to the 1989 Leicester Assembly was tense,[149] some feeling that matters were progressing with undue haste,[150] which prompted a

---

the matter. Dated December 1987 it stated, 'On the basis of the initial responses we shall send provisional comments to the Inter-Church Steering Group and initiate a full debate in the November BU Council 1988. The final proposals will be available by the end of December 1988. The March 1989 Council will then need to prepare proposals for a major debate and decision in the 1989 Baptist Assembly.' A process of consultation was also set up in the regional Baptist Associations, and further documents were circulated. 1988 was marked by study, discussion, prayer and initial responses. In September 1988 a four page document was sent to all churches setting out practical steps for local churches to follow in discussing the issues, and later *Questions and Answers*, another four page document, was sent to every church, in which B. Green addressed ten major questions raised during the preceding few months. The book *Churches Together in Pilgrimage* (1989) being sent to each BU church in January 1989 along with a four page commentary compiled by the ACCR containing revised proposals for the ICP. See also *The Next Steps for Churches Together in Pilgrimage: Including definite proposals for ecumenical instruments* (1989), and 'Churches Together in Pilgrimage. A Commentary by the Baptist Union Advisory Committee for Church Relations on the revised proposals of the Inter-Church Process' (January, 1989). The former dealt largely with practical and structural issues, no reference to baptismal policy or theology was included.

146 The Swanwick Declaration is reproduced in, among other places, *Not Strangers But Pilgrims: Report of the Swanwick Conference, 31 August to 4 September 1987* (n.d., [c.1987]), 3-4, and *Called to be One* (1996), 1-2. Fifteen BU representatives attended.

147 'It is our conviction that, as a matter of policy at all levels and in all places, our churches must now move from co-operation to clear commitment to each other...', *Not Strangers But Pilgrims*, 4.

148 So the WORGLEP document *After Swanwick, Practical guidance for Baptists seeking Christian unity* (unpublished, n.d., c.1987), n.p., but p.1.

149 E.g. M. McGill of Green Street Green, 'No', and M. Bochenski of Blackburn, 'Yes', *BT* March 9, 1989, 10-11; and 'The Inter-church debate', 'Yes', M. Bochenski, 'No', M. McGill, *BT* March 16, 1989, 8-9.

150 'Members uneasy at pace of inter-church process', *BT* November 17, 1988, 8, reporting N. Clark, chairman of the ACCR, who spoke of the 'unseemly haste of the process', yet concluding an inconclusive BU Council debate saying more time would not help.

number of denominational leaders to try and calm fears.[151] In all this, baptism was hardly mentioned,[152] if at all. The Assembly vote took place on April 19, 1989,[153] and allowed dissenting churches to write and indicate this to the General Secretary,[154] though the BU Council, advised by the ACCR and its chairman, John Briggs of Keele University, who presented the resolutions, strongly backed participation in the ICP,[155] it being stressed that the BU had not entered into any form of organic union, that each local church remained free to respond as it felt led, and that Baptist representatives were continuing to maintain a clear and unashamed Baptist witness in which mutual respect for one another's conscience and integrity were of paramount importance.[156]

On August 31, 1990, the BCC ceased to exist,[157] and the following day in the Roman Catholic Cathedral in Southwark, Churches Together in England (CTE) was inaugurated.[158] A vital principle accepted by all in-

---

151 E.g. D. Sparkes, 'We Baptists have so much to gain', *BT* February 16, 1989, 8; C. Marchant, BU President, 'We don't compromise our principles by working with others', *BT* March 2, 1989, 5; J.H.Y. Briggs, 'It's a serious matter', *BT* March 16, 1989, 5; W.M.S. West, 'So what if the Assembly says yes and my church says no?', *BT* March 23, 1989, 5, who, citing the last phrase of the first Declaration of Principle, stated clearly that an Assembly yes-vote would not commit local churches to be involved, and similarly that a no-vote would not prevent local churches participating. The bulk of the article, however, was to try and dissuade those against the ICP not to leave the BU if the decision was in favour of it.

152 The majority of references to baptism in the *BT* in both 1989 and 1990 came in the form of accounts of baptismal services, often accompanied by photographs. The specific references, e.g., to the theology of baptism or the baptismal issue within the ecumenical context were few indeed and usually very brief.

153 By the decision of the BU Council, the Leicester vote had been altered from a simple majority to a two thirds majority if the proposal were to be carried. See 'Council gives strong backing to Inter Church Process', *BT* March 23, 1989, 1 and 13, and 'BU continuation in CTE proposed', *BT* February 9, 1995, 2. In fact, 73.97% voted in favour of membership (1035 for, 364 against), see *Baptist Union Annual Report 1989* (Didcot, 1990), 10.

154 According to *FAB* 7 (n.d., [Autumn, 1992]), 10, by 1992, eighty churches had written to the General Secretary expressing their dissociation from the decision, while 'more than 25 churches' had resigned membership of the BU before the Bournemouth Assembly in April 1991. On p.2, these figures were confirmed by David Coffey in his answers to FAB questions.

155 'Council gives strong backing to Inter Church Process', *BT* March 23, 1989, 1 and 13.

156 A letter from B. Green to all BU churches dated September 1990.

157 The BCC's final assembly was noted by D. Hall, 'Future hopes as BCC flame is put out', *BT* April 5, 1990, 1 and 6.

158 Brenda Forward, 'Going forward in faith and mission', *BT* September 6, 1990, 1 and 13. This was followed a week later, August 8, with the inauguration of the Council of Churches for Britain and Ireland (CCBI). A transcript of the televised service was

volved was that each denomination would continue to operate according to its own creed or confessional basis and within its normal authority structures. Thus the BU's participation in no way compelled individuals or churches to participate.[159]

One outcome of the 1989 Assembly vote was the formation of an anti-ecumenical group which developed around the FAB newsletter and the figure of David Rushworth-Smith of Crich, Derbyshire.[160] With regard to the place of baptism within the ICP, some Baptists have tended to retreat from constructive dialogue into dogmatic assertion and implicit denunciation of anyone, Baptist or otherwise, who disagrees with them. This position is nowhere better illustrated than in a FAB booklist distributed at the Baptist Assembly in 1991, recommending Terry Griffith's *The Case*

---

published by the members of Days Lane Baptist Church, Sidcup, Kent, accompanied by a commentary which sought to expose what they considered to be the unbiblical nature of all that was going on, *Advances in Ecumenism in 1990 or The End of Protestantism?* (n.d.), prefaced by S. Pendrich, who personally resigned his membership of the BU. The church, too, eventually left the BU because of its staying within the ICP. The booklet was distributed and sold by FAB

159   The mechanisms for review of membership of the ICP were built into it, and for the BU this was initially to be in 1993. However, in practice, this did not prove possible and it would not be until 1995 that the BU reviewed its commitment to CTE and CCBI. This delay of two years came under condemnation from *FAB*, see no.6 (n.d., [Spring 1992]), 1-2.

160   All *FAB* and later *It's FAB* newsletters and leaflets include the statement of the following words or something similar: 'A newsletter linking those evangelical Baptist Churches in Britain which are unhappy about "Churches Together" (that is CTE, CYTUN & ACTS).' A brief note on its origins is included on the back page of *FAB* 8 (n.d., [Spring 1993]), n.p., but p.8. Rushworth-Smith stated that his views, as editor, why Baptists should not be involved were: '(i) Because the very nature of the [ICP] precludes Baptists—it is not the kind of movement that Baptists should be involved with; (ii) Baptists, by their very calling and beliefs, cannot identify with confusion and vague doctrines—they are "'those who live by the Bible".' It is clear from reading their material that another reason, perhaps even the major one, was that, in distinction from the BCC, Roman Catholics were now involved. A fundamentalist, almost 'hyper' Protestant and reformed emphasis permeates much of the FAB newsletters and the books and booklets they distribute and endorse. Their concern was that the WCC and ICP were both allegedly linked with New Age syncretism and the movement towards One World and a One World Church. Seldom does any theological argumentation occur or is any desire expressed for open dialogue. FAB representatives have held a number of discussions with David Coffey on various issues. The origin of the name 'FAB', evidently arose when a young Pastor rang Rushworth-Smith in September 1990, and said that their opposition to the Leicester vote was 'fab' (fabulous), and it stuck, *FAB* 7 (n.d., [Autumn 1992), 12. Their active campaign for Baptist withdrawal from the ICP has included mailing all ministers on several occasions advocating their views and threatening resignations from the BU if matters did not go their way. However, after the 1995 vote to remain within the ICP, FAB was disbanded.

for Believer's Baptism (1990). The accompanying endorsement stated that the booklet 'makes it abundantly clear that baptism by immersion for believers is the biblical standard. What has happened at Milton Keynes, in the ecumenical experiment, could not have taken place if the teaching in this book had been accepted by everyone on the committee in charge.'[161] In other FAB literature the issue of baptism has only rarely surfaced, for example when Rushworth-Smith contended that the Baptists' special role in the contemporary church included the assertion that 'the biblical form of initiation into the visible Church is through baptism by immersion into water of those who have been justified', believing that the modern ecumenical movement would challenge this special role and put an end to Baptists being set apart from other denominations. If such occurred, he asserted, it would not be long, 'following integration', before the subject of the initiation of believers, among other doctrines, would become a point of disagreement and lead to a breakaway group forming.[162]

In response to those within the BU who were discontented with the Union's position, David Coffey, the BU General Secretary, through the Faith and Unity Executive (FUE, formerly the ACCR), convened a consultation at Fairmile Court, Cobham, Surrey, in December 1991, when six ministers from churches which dissented from the Leicester vote met with six representatives of the BU.[163] Six of the papers, three from each side, were published in March 1993 and entitled *Evangelicals and Ecumenism—When Baptists Disagree*.[164] Though baptism does figure in

---

161 'Books on the Subject of the Inter-Church Process and Matters which are Connected' (Crich, n.d.). FAB also made numerous references to and often cited C.H. Spurgeon's attitude towards ecumenism, as, e.g., when they quoted, 'If we could find infant baptism in the Word of God, we should adopt it... But, we have looked well through the Bible, and cannot find it, and do not believe that it is there; nor do we believe that others can find infant baptism in the Holy Scriptures, unless they themselves first put it there', from Spurgeon's autobiography, *The Early Years*, quoted in *FAB* 8 (n.d., [Spring 1993]), 4.

162 D. Rushworth-Smith, *Baptists have a special role* (Crich, n.d., [post 1989]).

163 Those in favour of membership of the ICP but who did not contribute to the resultant publication were J.H.Y. Briggs and T. Hubbard, former Area Superintendent of the North Western Area. Those against membership were A. Argile of Leyland, A. Bailyes of Bethel English Baptist Church, Tonypandy and representative of the East Glamorgan Association on the BU Council, and N. Walker of Dereham Road, Norwich, see 'Introduction' to Bochenski (ed.), *Evangelicals and Ecumenism*, 11.

164 Those in favour of participation, M. Bochenski of Dagnall St., St Albans; Mrs. Faith Bowers a member of Bloomsbury Central, London, and sub-editor of the *BQ*; D.G.T. McBain, General Superintendent of the Metropolitan Area; and David Coffey; and against, R.J.M. Amess of Duke St., Richmond; Dr J. Balchin of Purley, formerly a tutor at LBC; A.R. Green of Upton Vale, Torquay. Many of Robert Ames' views had been expressed earlier in his book *One in the Truth: Fighting the Cancer of Division In The*

the book, it does not hold a prominent place and references to it are often brief, descriptive and illustrative, in keeping with Andrew Rigden Green's concluding study in which he discussed 'Levels of Truth', dividing primary truths from secondary ones. In the former he listed Christ, salvation, authority and the church, in the latter types of church government, differences on the parousia, and baptism, 'where Evangelicals clearly disagree and yet co-operate.'[165] This relegation of baptism into 'adiaphora'[166] reflects the marginal place baptism has come to hold in much contemporary ecumenical debate which starkly contrasts with the central place it has held throughout the larger part of the twentieth century.[167]

During the winter of 1992–93, the FUE solicited the views of ministers and churches on the working of CTE, and, as agreed, the CTE Review Group was set up in September 1993. In June 1994, this Group completed its report which encouraged continuation in the ICP while attempting to dispel fears that uniformity was the movement's goal.

CTE's first residential Forum met in July, 1991, a short time after the Seventh Assembly of the WCC in Canberra where an agreed portrait of the unity of the church had been produced. However, it quickly became clear in the Forum that the differing interpretations of what was meant by 'the visible unity of the church' was leading to considerable misunderstanding and frustrating attempts at deepening unity. This led, in 1993, to the establishment of the 'Called to be One' process, the purpose of which was to discover precisely what the member churches of CTE understood

---

Evangelical Church (Eastbourne, 1988), as had D. Coffey's in *Build That Bridge: Conflict and Reconciliation in the Church* (Eastbourne, 1986). In neither book did baptism figure prominently.

165 A.R. Green, 'The Anti-Ecumenical and the Pro-Ecumenical Mind', in Bochenski (ed.), *Evangelicals and Ecumenism*, 52.

166 Literally 'matters of indifference', i.e., those beliefs or practices which the sixteenth-century Reformers regarded as being tolerable, thus allowing them to adopt a more pragmatic approach thereby avoiding undesirable confrontation.

167 This impression is supported by the discussions held towards the end of 1991, in which D. Coffey, then newly appointed General Secretary, met with FAB representatives and replied to questions submitted by those associated with FAB. These were eventually published, after a short delay, in the autumn of 1992. Questions 16 and 18 elicited mention of baptism, but only briefly so. See *FAB* 6 (n.d., [Spring, 1992), pp.7-8 respectively. Here, p.2, Coffey stressed his firmly held evangelical convictions but believed that it was important to participate in ecumenical discussions and that this involvement did not imply compromise.

by the phrase 'the visible unity of the church'.[168] This resulted in the book *Called to be One*.[169]

A provisional Baptist response was drawn up by the FUE and sent on their behalf to Canon Martin Reardon, Convenor of the Working Party, by Keith Jones in October 1994. Again baptism did not figure prominently in the response. Four models on how 'visible unity' was understood were tentatively offered, reflecting the diversity of Baptist opinion: the mutual recognition of other denominations at every level, including faith, conversion, baptism, eucharist, ministry, mission and ecclesiology; a unity between local communities who recognized in each other a sufficient amount of the true church to share in mission and to commend members and ministries, allowing diversity of practice around the core of faith in Christ and the gospel sacraments of baptism and communion; such unity would be expressed by 'Christian unity' rather than structural, ecclesial, denominational or church unity, in a similar way to the Evangelical Alliance; and post-denominational fellowship in which there was mutual acceptance of each other's members, ministers, sacraments and statements of faith.[170]

From the time the BU first committed itself to join CTE and CCBI in 1989, baptism was rarely prominent in the discussions, yet again illustrating the peripheral place the rite has come to hold within Baptist thought and reflection on ecumenical developments, and this despite the BU's initiative, linked to the series of consultations called *Towards 2000*, which sought to encourage Baptist identity.[171] Taking the letters column

---

168 To this end Seven Questions were distributed to the twenty two member churches of CTE, thirteen of which responded, the BU among them, as did twenty three of the fifty county ecumenical bodies in association with CTE.

169 Details in this paragraph are taken from *Called to be One* (1996), vi-vii and 1-5. Two Baptists served on the Working Party which produced the text of the book, having met nine times between August 1994 and October 1995—Roger Nunn, Field Officer (South) of CTE who was based at Baptist House in Didcot, and Dr Hazel Sherman, tutor at Birmingham University, formerly a tutor at Bristol Baptist College. Of the five substantial papers presented to the Working Party which prepared *Called to be One* during this three year period, 'Christian Initiation and Church Membership' was prepared by Morris West. The texts of the Swanwick Declaration and Basis and Commitment of Churches Together in England are included in *Called to be One*, 1-2. An accompanying popular study booklet was published in the summer of 1996, compiled by Helen Lidgett, *Called to be One: The Workbook* (1996), followed by a video *Called to be One* (1996).

170 *Churches Together in England: 'The Called to be One' process. Provisional Answers to the Seven Questions* (October, 1994), n.p., Question 3, Models A-D.

171 On *Towards 2000* see ch. 9 below. Baptism also received only the briefest of mentions in a review document circulated to all the churches in preparation for the spring 1995 Plymouth Assembly debate on whether to remain in CTE and CCBI. The questionaire comprised 10 questions, which themselves contained subsections. Question 6 asked, 'in what areas [of ecumenical involvement] are there joys/enrichment or

and articles in the *Baptist Times* as a barometer reflecting the importance attached to baptism in relation to ecumenical developments or Baptist life as a whole, it must be concluded that baptism has dropped from any prominent place in the denomination's agenda and a more pragmatic approach to the issue has been adopted.[172]

The run up to the Baptist Assembly in Plymouth 1995 where the decision whether to remain within the ecumenical instruments or not was to be decided was marked by a whole array of articles and letters discussing the pros and cons of Baptist commitment to CTE and CCBI, but only a few ever mentioned the issue of baptism,[173] and fewer still did more than simply refer to it.[174] The proposal to remain within the ecu-

---

tensions/difficulties?', and rather vaguely asked for positive or negative comments on six areas one of which was 'Issues around baptism', see 'Review of our membership of *Churches Together in England* and the *Council of Churches for Britain and Ireland*' (1994), n.p., but p.3. The background to this questionaire was that during the winter of 1992–93, the FUE had solicited the views of ministers and churches on the working of CTE, and, as agreed, the CTE Review Group was set up in September 1993. In June 1994, the Review Group completed its report which encouraged continuation in the ICP while attempting to dispel fears that the movement was moving towards uniformity, and it was this that immediately preceded the questionaire sent to all churches on the pattern of their involvement with ecumenical bodies with a view to drawing up the wording for the Plymouth Assembly proposal.

172 Following the 1995 decision to remain within CTE and CCBI, A. Gilmore, 'Ecumenism: New Rules of Engagement?', *BT* June 1, 1995, 5 and 13, expressed his opinion that matters of faith and doctrine within the ecumenical context had either been settled or that Baptists had learned to live with them, existing problems having more to do with power and administration, quote from p.5. I. Burley, 'Baptists and Unity', *BT* July 6, 1995, 8, criticized the statement as pragmatically true in much ecumenical life, asking, 'What has been settled? By whom? With what have we learned to live? With what consequences? For whom?'

173 See P. Clements-Jewery of Liverpool, 'Unashamed Ecumaniac', *BT* January 19, 1995, 6; in a negative letter regarding ecumenical involvement, G. Finnie of Portsmouth, 'Questions on the road to unity', *BT* February 16, 1995, 9, implicitly mentioned baptism through reference to the 'doctrines of regeneration and ecclesiology (lying at the heart of our faith)'; 'BU Council to decide CTE proposal for Assembly', *BT* March 2, 1995, 3; Mrs Rita Armstrong of Clevedon, wife of R. Armstrong a retired minister, 'Let's tackle the prejudice and misunderstanding', *BT* March 16, 1995, 10.

174 These included D. Coffey, 'It's Time to Cross Some Bridges', *BT* March 30, 1995, 7 and 11, in which he argued for continued involvement, referring to the article 'Evangelicals and Catholics Together: The Christian Mission in the Third Millenium', in which leading American Evangelicals and Catholics expressed their growing common resolve about Christian faith and mission. In the lists of differences and disagreements were whether sacraments and ordinances were symbols or means of grace, and whether baptism was a sacrament of or a testimony to regeneration. Coffey later remarked, 'In our own Union...there is a diversity of viewpoint on sacraments and ordinances', quote from p.7. D. Coffey and K.G. Jones made the same point in 'Misunderstandings and

menical instruments was vigorously opposed,[175] and alternative proposals were tabled,[176] only to be defeated.[177] At the Assembly itself, two identical amendments were proposed, one for CTE, the other for CCBI,[178] only to be rejected when the Assembly's morning session on May 6 ratified membership of the two bodies with an increased majority.[179] In spite of the vigorous and often heated debate, it is again worth noting the increasingly marginal place accorded to baptism. Of the three articles specifically on baptism published in the *Baptist Times* during 1995 only

---

Disagreements', *Baptist Leader* 11 (Spring, 1995), 1-2. See also Coffey and Jones, 'Committed, But Critical' in *SecCheck* 11 (Spring, 1995), 2, 'Because so much of our understanding of the Gospel is enshrined in believers baptism, the link between Baptism and belief cannot be compromised', further observing that the nature of ecclesiology and ministry required lengthy debate and that co-operation necessitated a strong trinitarian basis. (*SecCheck* along with the *Baptist Leader* are the official mailings from the General Secretary and Deputy General Secretary of the BU to ministers and church secretaries sent out about three times a year. The first editions came out in the Autumn/October 1991.) D. Rushworth-Smith responded to Coffey's article in 'The Inter-Church Process: A bridge too far?', *BT* April 20, 1995, 15, pointing to the BU's continuing ecumenical involvement as disruptive of Baptist unity, a position also expressed by G.B. Jones of Burnham-on-Sea, 'More Heat—and even a little light', *BT* April 6, 1995, 7.

175 'BU continuation in CTE proposed', *BT* February 9, 1995, 2. The report was challenged by D. Gardner of Burwell, Cambridgeshire, 'CTE Review: Painting a Different Picture', *BT* February 23, 1995, 11, who believed that the simple five point summary of the 1994 Review Group's report was insufficient and was actually pushing Baptists into ecumenical involvement, and that the questionaire circulated had not asked the direct question whether Baptists wanted to continue membership with CTE and CCBI, a response to 'BU continuation in CTE proposed', *BT* February 9, 1995, 2. According to R. Nunn, the lengthy 1994 report does not make any reference to baptism, in a letter to the author dated April 4, 1995.

176 See, e.g., I.D. Burley of Huddersfield, 'Constructive proposal from FAB', *BT* February 23, 1995, 11, and F.R. Cook of Govilon, Gwent, 'Assembly proposal "divisive"', *BT* March 16, 1995, 11.

177 'Council affirms continuing Baptist membership of CTE', *BT* March 16, 1995, 2. At this meeting, J.H.Y. Briggs and Ruth Bottoms, chair of the Church Relations Committee, proposed and seconded the proposal which, after debate, was carried. At the same meeting, K.G. Jones reported that 91 churches still in membership with the Union had registered as having opted out.

178 'Amendments tabled to Assembly resolution on CTE and CCBI', *BT* April 27, 1995, 3. See also I.D. Burley, 'The Plymouth Vote', *It's FAB* 13 (December, 1994), n.p., but pp.1-2, and 'The Plymouth Assembly', *It's FAB* 14 (April, 1995), n.p., but p.1, which sets out the amendments.

179 'Assembly confirms CTE and CCBI membership"', *BT* May 11, 1995, 1, and 'Baptists plan active role in inter-church process', *BT* May 18, 1995, 3. For CTE the voting was 986 Yeses, 107 Noes, 28 Abstentions, with 22 Welsh Abstentions, and for CCBI 924 Yeses, 213 Noes and 30 Abstentions. This represented an increase of the majority over 1989, 90.21% for CTE and 81.27% for CCBI.

one was by a Baptist, Robert Burt, a deacon of the church at Newcastle-under-Lyme,[180] the remaining two by a Methodist,[181] yet it is manifestly clear that most of the contentious theological issues surrounding baptism are no nearer resolution now than they were at the beginning of the century, despite some of the excellent theological work that has been done by Baptist and other scholars.

The fruit of nearly three years work, *Called to be One* was published in early 1996. In three major chapters the various understandings of the meaning of the words 'Church', 'unity' and 'visible unity' in the participating denominations were comprehensively discussed, setting out the differences and also convergences and challenges.[182] Apart from descriptive references to the place of believer's baptism within BU churches,[183] baptism was only dealt with at any depth in Appendix B on 'Christian Initiation and Church Membership', which was the work of Morris West.[184] Though common ground with Paedobaptists lies with acknowledgment that baptism is a 'once-for-all sign of entry into the Christian church', it reported that some Baptists see infant baptism as at best incomplete, but by most as no baptism at all, thus requiring true baptism for the first time by immersion. Some Baptists were prepared to regard

---

180   R. Burt, 'Questions About Baptism?', *BT* March 16, 1995, 13.

181   G.T. Brake, a former Baptist minister who returned to the Methodist ministry in 1971, 'Baptism: Symbol of Grace', *BT* August 3, 1995, 9, and 'Baptism and the Activity of God', *BT* August 10, 1995, 7. He also wrote the 'Open Line' column 'Methodist Questions', *BT* July 27, 1995, 6, which dealt with baptism within, chiefly, Methodism. One is left only to wonder why the editor had to turn to a Methodist for two articles on baptism.

182   These were followed by chapters on the participants' experiences of unity, models of unity, the way forward, and five appendices on church and mission, initiation and membership, eucharistic communion, ordained ministry, authority and decision-making, concluding with suggested rules of good practice.

183   Such as the mention of the second BU Declaration of Principle that baptism is of believers in the name of the Trinity, *Called to be One*, 17; that Baptists include baptism along with the Bible and agreement in faith as visible elements or bonds of unity, p.19; the value placed on the sacraments of baptism and the eucharist (interestingly not using the word ordinance), but recognizing the difficulty that a major emphasis on the sacraments as a focus of unity would have, p.22; recognition of the tension in LEPs between infant and believer's baptism and the development of understandings within them on baptism and membership, pp.24 and 34; that while most Baptists did not regard infant baptism as proper and complete baptism, most Baptist churches did not require someone baptized in infancy to be baptized before admission into membership, p.51; an outline of the Baptist pattern of entry into the church by baptism on profession of faith, p.68; and, that most Baptist churches practised open communion, only a very few restricting it to baptized believers, p.71.

184   Appendix B on 'Christian Initiation and Church Membership', *Called to be One*, 67-70.

infant baptism as part of a process of salvation which needed completion through an act of personal profession of faith but not necessarily by baptismal immersion in water.[185] Yet in the whole matter, Baptists pressed for the rights of conscience of each candidate for baptism and a minister's obligation to baptize a candidate who had been baptized in infancy, whether confirmed or not, should they feel strongly that this was God's will.[186]

It was acknowledged that the words 'baptism' and 'membership' clearly did not mean the same thing in all churches, so *Called to be One* issued four challenges 'if they are to make their baptismal unity more visible'. First, the meaning of the word baptism and the nature of sacrament and symbol needed further exploration. Second, mutual understanding of one another's processes of initiation, of which at least four patterns had been identified.[187] Third, churches should discuss their understanding of the church and membership to see whether they are mutually exclusive or complementary. Fourth, the possibility should be invesitigated of belonging to more than one church.[188] To believer-baptist churches the cessation of admitting into church membership those never baptized was suggested; the refraining of baptizing by immersion those baptized in infancy, brought up in and having confirmed their faith; re-consideration of the sense in which children belong to the church; and the suggestion to all churches that a suitable rite of re-affirmation of vows should be developed for those already either infant or believer-baptized.[189] It was further noted that the BU 'is not happy to speak of infant and believer's baptism as a *common baptism*.'[190] It would appear, then, that recognition of a 'common baptism' is a goal of the ICP, or at least, a significant majority within it.[191]

---

185 This is probably a reference to *Believing and Being Baptized*.

186 *Called to be One*, 67.

187 See *Called to be One*, 68: baptism on profession of faith; baptism and chrismation followed by communion; baptism, usually of infants, accompanied by profession of faith from parents/godparents, followed by a later confirmation and reception into membership; and the experience of transformation by the Spirit not marked by any outward rite.

188 *Called to be One*, 69-70.

189 *Called to be One*, 70.

190 *Called to be One*, 68, italics theirs, though the report does say that the four challenges issued to the churches should not be seen as enough in themselves 'to assure the churches that there is a *common baptism*', p.70, italics theirs.

191 Initial responses to *Called to be One* were published from four ecumenically committed Baptists, two of whom briefly mentioned baptism. The text of these reviews was published in *SecCheck* 14 (Summer, 1996), 2-3, and *Ecumenical News* 4 (June, 1996), 3-8. The former is the source used here. Dr Hazel Sherman highlighted challenges to the churches, among which she included 'do you need to think again about how those who were baptised as infants might be welcomed as believers in your church, while doing

Local Ecumenical Partnerships (LEPs)[192]

Baptismal Policy in LEPs

More significant than the call for church unity by Easter 1980,[193] the Nottingham F&O Conference gave birth to the concept of 'areas of ecumenical experiment',[194] which became known as Local Ecumenical

justice to the baptism administered by another Christian church?' In this she did not deny the freedom of conscience, but rather wished Baptist churches to consider the question. Tony Peck, minister-secretary of the YBA, was encouraged by the seriousness with which the different understandings of baptism were taken. Michael Cleaves, Baptist Team Minister in the Ecumenical Parish of Stantonbury, Milton Keynes, merely queried the generalization and asked for substantiation of the statement on p.51 section 6.28 vii, that 'most Baptist churches...do not require someone, already baptised as an infant, to be baptsied as a believer before being admitted into membership'. A fourth review was included by Alan Bailyes, Moderator of the Church Relations Committee and minister at Bethel English Baptist church, Tonypandy, but this did not discuss the baptismal issue. On the debate on 'common baptism', see chapter 9 below.

192 An LEP exists where 'there is at the level of the local church a formal written agreement affecting the ministry, congregational life and/or buildings of more than one denomination, and a recognition of that agreement by the appropriate denominational authorities', *Local Church Unity*, 4.

193 One of the reasons why the Covenant for unity by Easter 1980 never materialized was because, 'no one did sufficient work to follow it up', so R.M.C. Jeffery, *Case Studies in Unity* (1972), 45, cited by Matthews, *Unity Scene*, 82. Bi-lateral unity negotiations which were under way at this time proved to be another reason for the covenant failure. In 1964 the Congregational Union had become the Congregational Church, a necessary step towards the formation of the United Reformed Church (URC) with the Presbyterian Church in England in 1972, though a number of churches did not so unite, forming the Congregational Federation. The URC was joined by the Reformed Association of Churches of Christ in 1981. In 1972 an insufficient vote in the Synod brought the scheme for union between the Church of England and the Methodist Church to an end, as did the later attempt at union between the Methodists, Moravians, URC and Church of England in 1982. These failed negotiations led to a shift of emphasis within the ecumenical movement from schemes striving for organic union to local schemes, a fact reflected in the increasing number of LEPs. For details of the above, see Matthews, *Unity Scene*, 82; Welch and Winfield, *Travelling Together*, 4-5; brief details concerning the negotiations up to 1977 between the URC and the Churches of Christ, specifically relating to the baptismal issue, are to be found in D. Bridge and D. Phypers, *The Water That Divides: The Baptism Debate* (1977), 200-01 [unless otherwise indicated all subsequent references are from this 1st edn], citing the Joint Committee Interim Report, *The negotiations between Churches of Christ and the United Reformed Church* (1975), e.g., p.3.

194 The Nottingham Conference passed the following resolution: 'Recognising that visible unity will only be realised as we learn to do things together...as congregations, this Conference invites...member Churches...to implement the Lund call to "act together in all matters, except those in which deep differences of conviction compel them to act separately." In particular it requests them... 3. To designate areas of ecumenical

Projects in 1973, this being changed to Local Ecumenical Partnerships in 1994.[195] LEPs superceded Union churches, which were affiliated to both their Unions, practised believer's and infant baptism and were served by ministers of one or other denomination. Though considerable discussion took place in the 1930s and again in the early 1950s as to whether it would be possible or desirable to establish further churches of this kind, the discussions proved inconclusive. Little resulted until in the mid-1960s when Union churches were established on a new estate at Ramsgate and Bristol, and when Arundel Baptist and Congregational churches united.[196]

The growth of LEPs has been greatly aided by the comity agreements between the main denominations in Britain (Anglican, Free Church and Roman Catholic) which often owed their origin to negative factors such as land restrictions in both new towns and older areas,[197] financial and property considerations, and diminishing congregations.[198] Localized co-

---

experiment, at the request of local congregations, or in new towns and housing areas. In such areas there should be experiments in ecumenical group ministries, in the sharing of buildings and equipment, and in the development of mission', taken from 'Introduction. Churches Together in England Consultation on the Future of Local Ecumenical Projects, Swanwick, 21-23 March, 1994', in *Pilgrim Post* 21 (May–June, 1994), 15. Both the Nottingham and Lund conferences discussed primarily theological matters, but both also realized that progress towards visible unity would only take place if theological convergence was accompanied by local action.

195   Welch and Winfield, *Travelling Together*, 4-5 (though it ought to be noted that the change to 'Partnerships' is wrongly dated as 1995 on p.5); Nunn, *This Growing Unity*, viii.

196   See *Baptists and Unity*, 13 n**. *With Charity and With Conviction. Report of the Working Group on Local Ecumenical Projects of the Baptist Union of Great Britain and Ireland* (1984), 6-7, noted that, after the formation of the URC in 1972, some Union churches were then in partnership with the URC, others with the Congregational Federation, and added that, although they were often still referred to as Union churches 'there is no doubt that in type they are indistinguishable from a local ecumenical project and should be regarded as such.' Consistent with this position, *With Charity and With Conviction*, 18-21, included Union churches in its section on LEPs in partnership with Congregational or United Reformed Churches.

197   So T.G. Dunning, 'Instant Unity', *Frat.* 148 (April, 1968), 7, 'Land [in some of the new housing estates] because of its scarcity and cost must be carefully allocated. Readiness is shown in some cases to set aside one or two sites for the christian church. It would be foolish to contend in such circumstances that every denomination should have the right to a site... These are certainly special cases but surely they call for instant united action rather than no action at all.'

198   See *Baptists and Unity*, 38. St. Thomas's Anglican church and Mulehouse Road Baptist Church in Crookes, Sheffield, began joint worship in 1977 when the Baptist church was very small and in financial difficulties and the Anglican church was undergoing extensive refurbishment, the LEP eventually being inaugurated in October 1982, see R. Warren, *In The Crucible: The Testing and Growth of a Local Church* (1989), 7 and 144; 'DCP', *Wendover. Our God Reigns* (1993), n.p., but 1-2, mentions the

operative evangelism has also led to the development of LEPs, where variations in doctrinal stand on baptism and faith-commitment has not been seen as a barrier to co-operative evangelism and even church planting.[199] The most important factor enabling the growth of LEPs has been the 1969 Sharing of Buildings Act.[200] Prior to this, Baptist LEP involvement had been hindered by Trust Deed stipulations which made such sharing difficult if not impossible. However, the Act has enabled different traditions to share the same building.[201]

Baptists and Unity stated that the BU should share 'whenever possible, in co-operation with local Baptists, in the designation of "areas of

---

financial situation that both the Baptist and URC churches were in, both also having buildings in need of costly structural work.

199 Such co-operative ventures have taken place in Milton Keynes, Telford, Mosborough and Swindon, see K.G. Jones, 'Baptist Evangelistic patterns and Inter-church Relations. A perspective from the United Kingdom' (unpublished BWA Commission on Baptist Doctrine and Inter-Church Cooperation paper, July 1994), 3-4. Advocates of LEPs are quick to stress that the major reasons for their formation are positive, chiefly missionary, 'that the world may believe', e.g. K.G. Jones, *From Conflict to Communion* (Didcot, 1996), 9, 'it is in the very working together of diverse communities who trust in the same Jesus, that the mission of God finds response in people of faith.' Later, p.25, he warned that it was 'normally unwise to come to the point of sharing a building simply on the basis of cutting costs in order to survive. You cannot move into such a relationship with much hope of success unless there is also a positive mission vision and a desire to get to know more and share more with other traditions of Christians.' Also F. Crix, *Tap Roots No.15: Anglican–Baptist L.E.P. in Milton Keynes* (n.d., c.1980), n.p., but p.1, 'The reason [for the LEP] was to enable the Church [with a captial C] to engage more effectively in mission to a rapidly expanding area within the new City of Milton Keynes.' 'Tap' stands for 'Teams and Projects', a CCLEPE group. Jones, 'Baptist Evangelistic patterns and Inter-church Relations', 4-5, dismissed objections that this kind of evangelistic co-operation only led to a message reduced to the lowest common denominator and that it was impossible to evangelize with those not sharing the same theological and ecclesiological determinatives. In contrast he asserted four benefits: '1. The attractiveness to those evangelised... 2. There is an enhanced confidence and vision of those who participate... 3. It is possible to develop more attractive and better publicized programmes... 4. There are more insights to draw upon.' These could clearly be labelled pragmatic considerations not matters of principle and no mention was made of baptism.

200 Details of which are set out in the CCBI/CTE/CYTUN book *Under the Same Roof: Guidelines to the Sharing of Church Buildings Act 1969* (1994). See also *The Sharing of Church Buildings Act 1969: Guidelines prepared by legal representatives of the Church (Revised 1983)* (1983), published for CCLEPE by the BCC. See also Welch and Winfield, *Travelling Together* 44-45; and *Local Church Unity*, 30-31.

201 The Act's purpose had been to enable congregations of different traditions to use the same building for worship at different times, and could not have foreseen the ecumenical developments for which it has been used, making possible the partnership between churches well beyond what was originally envisaged by the legislation.

ecumenical experiment".'[202] *Baptists and Unity Reviewed* recommended that the decision to participate in areas of ecumenical experiment and the sharing of church buildings were matters for the local church or the Association. When such involvement was decided upon, the BU's role should be to supply advice and safeguard Baptist property.[203] This policy of encouraging active participation was reasserted in the 1984 report *With Charity and With Conviction*, which recommended that any LEP applying for BU membership should be examined by the ACCR who would ensure that Baptist interests would be safeguarded. It further noted that whether a Baptist minister was present or not, the Baptist element would want the freedom to teach and advocate believers' baptism.[204]

The first detailed examination of so-called rebaptism and baptismal policy in LEPs was by Keith Jones, General Secretary of the progressive and pro-active YBA.[205] Jones' *Baptismal Policy in LEPs* sought by reference to past experience in LEPs to act as an interim contribution and

---

202 *Baptists and Unity*, 50. This was endorsed by *Baptists and Unity Reviewed*, 15. The BU's Working Group of the Church Relations Committee later welcomed the 1975 *Guidelines for Local Ecumenical Projects*, stating that its implications for procedure would be examined and adequate machinery for dealing with them would be devised, noted in *Local Church Unity*, 44.

203 *Baptists and Unity Reviewed*, 10, reference being made to the 'Report of the Ad Hoc Group on Areas of Ecumenical Experiment', approved by the BU Council in November 1968. Any attempts by the BU to direct such matters could be interpreted as interference with the independence of the local church. The affairs of LEPs are overseen by the Sponsoring Bodies, most of which have now been absorbed into what are called 'Intermediate Bodies'. Baptists are usually represented by the Area Superintendent and/or the Association Secretary and perhaps other local representatives of the Baptist community who may sit on a formal council with elected and appointed representatives from the various denominations. See Jones, *From Conflict to Communion*, 35-36. For further and more detailed information on the Sponsoring Bodies, see Welch and Winfield, *Travelling Together*, 47-55; Nunn, *This Growing Unity*, 15-30; *With Charity and With Conviction*, 10-11. All of the participating denominations in an LEP like to ensure that the constitutions protect key elements of denominational identity, but for Baptists, several further steps are appropriate. The BU's Local Ecumenical Committee examines and approves all LEP constitutions and some Associations also share in this, particularly if they are trustees of the Baptist church involved, see Jones, *From Conflict to Communion*, 37.

204 *With Charity and With Conviction*, § 41 on p.12, and §49 on p.14. This was produced by WORGLEP, whose parent body was the ACCR, chaired by N. Clark, and was compiled by D.C. Sparkes. The BU Council recommended that General Superintendents and Associations be encouraged in their active participation in sponsoring bodies and in the support offered to Baptists in LEPs, and invited other Baptist churches to consider whether participation in such a project might be God's will for them, see p.5.

205 It is not surprising that Baptists were the first to directly tackle the thorny issue of rebaptism for the simple reason that Baptists are the only ones who, because of their practice of believer's baptism, create the 'problem'.

discussion starter to the on-going baptismal debate.[206] He noted that the agreements and constitutions produced at the inauguration of LEPs often stated that the baptismal issue would be dealt with as a 'pastoral concern', which invariably meant that decisions were taken by the ministers *in situ*, usually with little or no reference to the constituent churches in the LEP or denominational agencies.[207] Frequently it had been reported that Methodist, URC and Anglican clergy had issued a blanket veto on the baptism as a believer of anyone who had been baptized, in whatever circumstances, as an infant.[208] Dissatisfied with this state of affairs, Jones insisted that 'a proper debate on the local and practical pattern of Baptism in LEPs must be held and guidelines incorporated into new LEPs at their commencement.'[209] This he set out to do.

Jones identified three Baptist inconsistencies which presented real difficulties to their ecumenical partners. First, on baptism and church

---

206 K.G. Jones, *Baptismal Policy in LEPs: A Discussion Document* (Leeds, 1983, revised 1989), 'Introduction'. It was first compiled in 1982 for the Commission of Christian Witness in order to assist Baptist churches who were contemplating entering LEPs, then published a year later. It is from the 1989 edition that all quotations have been taken. The importance and usefulness of this document is shown by its recommendation as 'A good airing of the issues' by the 2 page document 'Ecumenical Pack Mini Index', circulated at the May 23, 1988, meeting of WORGLEP.

207 This practice was indirectly confirmed by *With Charity and With Conviction*, §55, p.14, which suggested that in order to avoid unnecessary distress, the LEP and the principal representatives, including the General Superintendent, 'ought to anticipate before a particular request [for rebaptism], what factors should govern the response... Meanwhile the LEP, the sponsoring body and the denominational leaders should endeavour to discover how such difficulties in other LEPs have been resolved to determine what progress can be made in the given instance.'

208 Jones, *Baptismal Policy in LEPs*, 1. He noted that united constitutions often dealt with baptism in a formula on the lines of 'We shall use the rites and customs of our respective churches', or 'Baptism and re-baptism shall be regarded as a pastoral issue.' He continued, 'this seems to mean that the Ministers of the constituent denominations agree in private the course of action to be followed which generally results in a blanket exclusion of the possibility of believers baptism to anyone who has, at some stage, been baptised as an infant.'

209 Jones, *Baptismal Policy in LEPs*, 2. On p.1 he had already expressed this: 'The proposition of this document is that agreement on Believers' Baptism needs to be reached *before* a constitution is agreed for a project and a sharing agreement effected. Basic ground rules of decision-making and the possibilities for "re-baptism" must be set out in principle to avoid later heartache in the situation.' That Jones' views have been acted on is shown by the observation that now in LEPs which include Baptists, a working agreement on baptismal practice has to have been worked out beforehand and incorporated into the LEP's constitution. In practice, this can take various forms, the importance of which is reflected in the detailed discussions in *Believing and Being Baptized* and the *Called to be One* process and book. See also its discussion in Welch and Winfield, *Travelling Together*, 19, 27 and 60.

membership, the oddity of baptism without requiring membership, or the admission to membership on 'profession of faith' without requiring any form of baptism at all. Such practices would need to be abandoned in an LEP. Second, Paedobaptists often regarded as arbitrary the Baptist refusal to baptize under a certain age and question the underlying theology. Abolition of such exact prescriptions might be required, provided it did not lead to a false division between baptism and membership of the believing community. Third, in their advocacy of infant dedication, Baptists tended to use paedobaptist arguments, which was why some Baptists had replaced this with a simple service of thanksgiving for the child's birth without any substantial promises. In so doing, Baptists did not recognize that children of believers relate in a different way to the church family than the children of outsiders. Though he did not believe that the debate could be settled in so short a compass, Jones maintained that in reaching agreement with others, Baptists needed to be aware of their own problems.[210]

After summarizing the positions on baptism of the Baptists' major ecumenical partners, Jones set out his most important work towards a possible agenda for agreement. Developing the views of the likes of Professor James Dunn of Durham University,[211] who linked baptism-conversion-initiation, he suggested that Baptists should recognize the rite and see its forms as practised by others as different in sequence and order in time. In LEPs Baptists needed to acknowledge the churchmanship of others. From this starting point, a possible baptismal agreement could be established around the following elements. First, in each shared building there needed to be a font and baptistry. Second, baptism should be understood as both an act of God and a response of the church and individual and, thereby, part of the conversion-initiation rite. In the case of believers it would always be linked to church membership, in the case of infants it would need to be completed in confirmation and reception into full membership. Third, three models of baptismal practice were possible. 'Model A: Denominationalism' involved a shared church/LEP which agreed that those of other denominations could be baptized as believers even if baptized in infancy provided they transferred to the Baptist roll. 'Model B: Complete Ecumenism' where, in a shared church/LEP, once baptized meant always baptized, so Baptists could only baptize as believers those who had never received any baptism. 'Model C: The Baptismal/Initiation Rite' in which a shared church/LEP agreed that if someone had been infant baptized, but not confirmed and received into the church, the baptismal rite was regarded as incomplete. Such a person

---

210 Jones, *Baptismal Policy in LEPs*, 3-4.
211 J.D.G. Dunn, *Unity and Diversity in the New Testament: An Inquiry into the Character of Earliest Christianity* (1977).

could seek the complete rite of baptism-initiation as a believer by either baptism or confirmation. Were B or C to be adopted, Baptist membership of an LEP should note that their freedom of conscience was put within limits and that to break the pattern would be to cast the whole of the LEP's constitution into disarray. He also recommended the availability of both services of infant baptism and infant thanksgiving, the Baptist church refusing to accept anyone on profession of faith who had never been baptized, the responsibility to nurture children within the church and to bring them to complete the baptismal-initiation rite, the development of a service for the renewal of baptismal vows for those who never completed the full baptismal-initiation rite, and that the Baptist church carefully consider the inclusion of the laying on of hands as part of the service of baptism and reception into membership and communion.[212]

As well as pioneering work on the theory of baptism, the YBA has also led the way with work on baptismal practice.[213] As Jones had previously made clear, his work was in part based on the actual experience of Baptists in LEPs. Along with the late Methodist minister of the Girlington LEP, John Shaw, Jones worked on some embryonic ideas[214] which were discussed with regard to the LEPs in Rawdon and Beeston Hill. Later, with the Methodist minister, Ivan Selman, these were clarified in the con-stitution ultimately negotiated for Girlington Methodist/Baptist church, formed in 1979 when the two congregations moved in to share the Methodist building. Negotiations had taken several years before they were finally completed when the constitution was agreed in November 1984, a process which had been greatly aided by the options discussed by Jones' *Baptismal Policy in LEPs*.

---

212 Jones, *Baptismal Policy in LEPs*, 5-6.

213 The YBA also produced its *Position Paper of the Yorkshire Baptist Association Council on Baptist Church Planting in an Ecumenical Context* (Leeds, 1989). This paper concluded that there was a place for Baptist church planting if the emphases they wished to contribute to the whole church were not evident in an ecumenical congregation or in the existing congregations of other denominations (8), but they did so asking Baptists to appreciate the anxiety of other denominations over what they call "rebaptism"' (9a), and for other denominations to understand the emphases that Baptists wished to bring to the church's witness in any local situation (9b).

214 This information is from a letter from K.G. Jones, 25 April 1996. John Shaw died in 1982. According to Tony Peck, Shaw's successor as minister of the church in 1984, then Secretary of the YBA and now a tutor at Bristol Baptist College (details from a telephone conversation held on April 1, 1996), the reason for Shaw and Jones' solo work was due to the failure of the Methodist Church to suggest any strategy on baptism in LEPs. According to Mrs June Rossington, treasurer of Girlington Baptist Church, in a letter of June 18, 1996, numerous approaches were made to the Methodist Church to which no specific guidance was offered, so the church 'finally worked it out between us and then submitted it for acceptance.'

Everything in the Girlington constitution flows from the fact that individuals shall be members of either the Methodist or Baptist church (3.(a)).[215] On baptism it declared the church's intention to maintain the integrity of both Methodist and Baptist understandings and practices of baptism (8a (i)) by adopting a 'flexible approach' (8a (ii)). After setting out the usual practice of the Methodists and Baptists (8b (i) and (ii)) it declared that it would be left to the Baptist church's discretion whether they baptized as believers any previously infant baptized in other churches, 'but in the interests of the unity of the congregation this should not be applied to Methodists' (8c), unless the candidate maintained the desire so to be baptized, in which instance they would transfer their membership to the Baptist roll (8d (ii)). All this took place within the policy that, whatever form of baptism, it was such an important step that candidates or parents of infants 'should proceed with the full knowledge of all the options that are available to them' (8e).[216]

The importance of the work towards baptismal policy agreement is reflected in the minutes of WORGLEP where 'rebaptism' was a constantly recurring matter which received considerable discussion.[217] One of their documents stated, 'Lightly to perform what many will see as "rebaptism" will appear to strike a destructive blow at the church-manship of ecumenical partners; it is a shallow basis for the fruitful movement into unity. On the other hand, blanket refusal to respond to a request for believers' baptism made by a convinced and instructed conscience that has seriously weighed the issues may seem to deny

---

215 *Girlington Methodist/Baptist Church Constitution* (1984). All references will be to the relevant section and point. This method will be followed in discussions of all constitutions and all references will be contained in the main text in parentheses.

216 In practice, Mrs June Rossington, letter dated June 18, 1996, admitted that the prohibition on 'rebaptizing' one of the Methodists in the church 'does not work out as we know several Methodists who have been baptised by total immersion as believers whilst at college or university or 3 in the River Jordan...and they are all remaining within the Methodist membership.' The LEP has received permission to instal a baptistry and when baptisms take place both Methodist and Baptist ministers take part in the service and the communion which follows, during which candidates are received into the Baptist membership. Prior to the installation of the baptistry other local Baptist churches were used and the Methodist members went along too. Mrs Rossington added that the Baptists in the LEP 'would have no objections at all to young Methodists being baptised as believers as a sign of their personal response to Christ, and remaining Methodists.' According to the Baptist minister of the church, Brian Tucker, letter dated April 2, 1996, there have been no developments since his arrival in 1993 and no Methodist infant baptisms. He added, 'Oddly, the only baptism of a believer that has taken place, which I conducted, was of a girl whose reception into church membership was to be at a different Methodist church.'

217 I am grateful to Dr Paul Sheppy of Barnoldswick for access to these minutes which cover the period 1988–1991.

Baptist convictions and damage discipleship.'[218] A later discussion stated that 'behind the baptismal controversy was the theology of the nature of the church and whatever resolution of the ['rebaptism'] issue was adopted there would be a need to avoid "unchurching" others.'[219]

In April 1987, WORGLEP sent a letter of enquiry to seventy one LEPs, forty one of which replied, and these constitute the largest and most detailed source of information concerning 'rebaptism' in LEPs with Baptist involvement, bearing testimony to the fact that baptismal practice has been very much developed at local level. Only two replies failed to answer the question, three indicated that it was not a live issue, two that it was currently not an issue but could become one, while one referred such requests to the nearest non-participating Baptist church. Five churches indicated that rebaptism was not practised, of which only one was opposed in principle, one had had a rebaptism but was presently reconsidering its attitude in future, another offered the renewal of baptismal vows by immersion following the New Zealand rite,[220] two churches

---

218 'Baptists and LEPs', n.d., and anonymous, n.p., but p.1, written before the May 23, 1988, meeting of WORGLEP.

219 Minutes of the WORGLEP meeting April 26, 1989, c). The apparent 'unchurching' of paedobaptists was a regular concern for Baptist's discussing these issues, see, e.g., *With Charity and With Conviction*, §54, p.14.

220 The only other place in the world to have LEPs similar to those in Britain is New Zealand, where they are known as co-operative ventures, see Best, 'Local Ecumenical Projects', 628-29. Here, those baptized in infancy but wishing to express their faith are not 'rebaptized' but offered a service of renewal of baptismal vows using the symbolism of immersion in water. This service has been adopted by a number of LEPs with Baptist involvement, including the LEPs at Southgate, Bury St Edmunds, Binley Woods and Whaddon Way, Milton Keynes (this was their practice in 1987 as expressed in response to the WORGLEP enquiry of April 1987, see minutes entitled 'The "Rebaptism" Controversy' (January, 1988), 1 and 3), and Swaleside prison (see D. Taylor, 'The Baptism of Believers and Church Membership' (TCDTBW; August, 1999), 6). However, many have felt, to say the least, uneasy about this rite. So 'Ecumenical Pack Mini Index' (WORGLEP, n.d.), p.2. At their meeting May 23, 1988, they admitted, 'it must be said that many Baptists, as well as others, are distinctly uneasy about its use.' A more open view of the New Zealand rite was expressed by Dr Paul Sheppy, 'Life-Cycle Liturgies', a lecture given to the JLG's Sarum Conference: Life Cycle Liturgies (September 24, unpublished 1996), 4: 'Its restatement of the baptismal vows and its invocation of the Spirit seem to many to question the original baptism; but it is, in my judgement, a more sophisticated response than its critics allow.' Later he added, 'Baptists are not unfamiliar with this sort of procedure, and I cannot be the only Baptist minister to have reminded those previously baptised who are present at the baptism of a new believer of their opportunity "at this time, in this hour" to consecrate themselves afresh to Christ.' The BCC's Division of Ecumenical Affairs appended the note to the New Zealand rite that they had a number of reservations about its use: that it would be understood by many as baptism, as suggested by one of the questions put to the candidate (Question 5), the individual nature of the rite itself might strengthen the danger that it would be confused

distinguished between those infant baptized and not confirmed and those so baptized and confirmed, and twenty five stated that rebaptism was possible. Of these twenty five, in three churches rebaptism meant becoming a member of the Baptist church with no possibility of multiple membership, most referred to the importance of counselling and rebaptism only as a concession to persistence in the request, three deferred the decision to the church (one of which also said the matter was referred to the Sponsoring Body), two left the decision to the minister though one questioned this practice, three particularly referred to indiscriminate infant baptism affirming that where this had occurred rebaptism could be administered with a clear conscience, while one church reported that applicants had to be interviewed by two interviewers representing both persuasions.[221]

In January 1990, CCLEPE published its *Constitutional Guidelines* for LEPs. On 'Baptism and Membership' it stipulated that 'Baptism shall be administered according to the rite and practice of each denomination, and shall be set, in normal circumstances, within an act of congregational worship.' However, the accompanying note (4b) observed that where a Baptist church was involved, 'consideration will need to be given to the procedures to be adopted where there is a conflict of practice.' It further

---

with baptism, and that those who rejected their infant baptism might also reject this service in view of its emphasis that it is not baptism, see 'Order of Worship: Rite of Renewal (Authorised by the General Assembly of the Presbyterian Church of New Zealand, November 1977, for use in congregations)', (a 3 page sheet which included a 'B.C.C. Division of Ecumenical Affairs Note', n.d.). Such a view was not put forward in the WORGLEP document, 'After Swanwick. Practical guidance for Baptists seeking Christian unity', 3, 'there is everything to be said for holding a Service of Renewal of Baptismal Vows, and this could incorporate the symbolism of immersion so long as the words used leave no doubt as to what is intended.' Such a rite as the New Zealand reaffirmation has also been discussed in the CTE report *Baptism and Church Membership*, 7 and 30, the latter stating that 'The Working Party was very clear that such services of re-affirmation should not make use of water in such a way that they could be confused with baptism.' On p.30 it recommended the holding of ecumenical services of the renewal of baptismal vows, but states that the wording should be such that the service is not confused with baptism, also referring to the JLG's *Confirmation and Re-affirmation of Baptismal Faith* (1992).

221 Details extracted from the summary by D.C. Sparkes, 'The "Rebaptism" Issue' (January, 1988), which noted that Baptists were involved in over eighty LEPs. See also 'The "Rebaptism" Controversy', compiled by D.C. Sparkes (January 7, 1988). A later WORGLEP document reported that 'in about two-thirds of the churches who replied rebaptism occurred', and classified the conditions as fourfold: only Baptist membership was possible; there could be no question of multiple membership; only in line with the "conscience clause of the 1980 proposals; there might be referral to the Sponsoring Body; where there has been "indiscriminate" baptism', 'Rebaptism in Local Ecumenical Projects' (n.d., but discussed at the October 9, 1989, meeting of WORGLEP).

noted that where 'rebaptism' was an issue, LEPs and their Sponsoring Bodies had evolved various conditions and interim solutions, 'e.g., that only Baptist (not multiple) membership is possible, that the applicants have not made a previous Profession of Faith at a Confirmation, etc..'[222]

After several years of work, WORGLEP and the Methodist Church Ecumenical Committee finally published what has become known as the *Concordat* in 1991[223] which, as in the Girlington constitution, has sought to maintain the integrity of both the Baptist and Methodist theologies and practices of baptism while adopting a flexible and sensitive approach to this delicate pastoral issue (A i) and ii)) which has the potential to destroy LEPs. The *Concordat* was not only modelled on, but in its wording is almost identical to, the Girlington baptismal policy.[224] It stipulated that should a Methodist decide to be 'rebaptized' this can only happen if his/her name is transferred to the Baptist roll (C.4).

---

222 *Constitutional Guidelines for a Local Ecumenical Project* (1990), 5, model 'Constitution', section '4 Baptism and Membership, 4a NOTE and 4b NOTE'.

223 *Baptist/Methodist Agreement on Baptismal Policy Within Local Ecumenical Projects* (n.d., [1991]). From this point on referred to as the *Concordat*. The text is also to be found in Welch and Winfield, *Travelling Together*, Appendix 5, 107-09, and *Baptism and Church Membership*, 48-50.

224 The work on the *Concordat* had recommenced in 1988, see WORGLEP minutes May 23, 1988, p.2, when the Methodist Ivan Selman suggested that the possibility of such an agreement should be re-examined. However, it is not known when the idea had been first put forward, though it is known that a draft 'Concordat for Baptist/Methodist LEPs' existed in May 1988 as a WORGLEP document, though this was to be considerably revised for its final form. From October 1989, M. Bochenski and David Staple, Secretary of the FCFC, did a great deal of work on the text on behalf of WORGLEP, see WORGLEP minutes for the meeting held at Inter Church House, London, October 9, 1989. Four draft Constitutions went before this meeting of WORGLEP, entitled 'Model Constitutions for Local Ecumenical Projects', which was based on and amplified paragraphs 79-81, 'Decision Making Processes', of *With Charity and With Conviction*, 17. Model A represented shared decision making between a Baptist and another Free Church; Model B a developed form of constitution for a Baptist church making decisions in common with at least two other Free Churches; Model C was for a Baptist church involved with an Anglican parish church; Model D demonstrated the relationship between four major denominations—Baptist, Methodist, URC and Anglican. On the second page of this document, it was stated that 'Each of the constitutions...provides for some measure of common decision making on baptismal policy. In some [LEPs] the topic of Infant and Believers baptisms is not constitutionalised, but left on one side as a matter of pastoral practice. Where this is done it is normally by advice from the regional sponsoring body. These models are all taken from sponsoring bodies who prefer to have some clarity of view on baptismal policy in the approved constitution.' It is not known what happened to these four draft constitutions, though some material was clearly used in the *Concordat*.

In 1996 a Baptist–URC policy was agreed,[225] and presented something similar to the *Concordat* as 'the simplest baptismal policy' for LEPs which have separate Baptist and URC membership rolls (6). However, it presented an alternative which underlines the exceptional nature of 're-baptism', and differs from the *Concordat* in that it permitted recourse to outside persons when agreement cannot be reached. Only if a service for the renewal of baptismal vows and/or personal confession of faith (7c.iii) is refused will the request be granted provided the minister(s) and church meeting(s), after consultation, agree that the applicant is willing to transfer their membership to the Baptist roll. Should disagreement arise, help and advice is to be sought from the intermediate bodies and the Baptist General Superintendent and URC Provincial Moderator (7d).

The negotiations on these two policy-documents were aided by the fact that the two sides, the Baptists on the one and the Methodists and United Reformed Churches on the other, were facing two separate problems. The Baptists were seeking to preserve the freedom of the person infant baptized, subsequently coming to faith and wanting to be baptized, while the Methodists and URC's problem was that believer's baptism was being asked for by their own members in good standing.[226]

A third[227] way of handling requests for rebaptism was suggested which distinguished between those only baptized and those also confirmed. It stated that 'it would be inappropriate to re-baptise those who were baptised in infancy and who have already made a personal and public profession of faith in confirmation or formal admission to church membership.' Any so baptized but not confirmed who 'out of an instructed conscience' request baptism as believers 'should be placed under Baptist discipline and practice prior to baptism as believers and to reception into Baptist membership.' Where congregations worship separately, the use of the *Concordat* was encouraged as the framework for baptismal policy and practice.[228]

---

225 *Baptist Union of Great Britain/United Reformed Church Agreed Guidelines for Baptismal Policy in Local Ecumenical Partnerships* (n.d., [1996]). The agreement has also been printed in full in *Ecumenical News* 3 (April, 1996), 2-4, and *Baptism and Church Membership*, 50-53.

226 I am grateful to Prof. John Briggs for this observation.

227 That there are only three ways of handling such requests was also acknowledged by *Baptism and Church Membership*, 26-27, which admitted, pp.27-28, 'Our working Party has not thought of any other sort of track, apart from these three, which might provide a way forward agreed by both [Paedobaptists and Believer-Baptists].' This is the pattern set out on the BU's official website, http://www.baptist.org.uk/baptism.htm, e.g., February 28, 1998, 'What makes a Baptist?', under the section 'Questions people ask coming from another tradition.'

228 'Report of Group 1: Baptism and "Re-Baptism"', version agreed by the final plenary session on March 23, *Pilgrim Post* 21 (May–June, 1994), 16. This came from

The 1994 CTE 'Consultation on the Future of LEPs'[229] also recommended the establishment of a high level group to explore 'a deeper
understanding of baptism and to search with urgency for more
comprehensive guidelines.'[230] The group first met at Inter-Church
House, London, on Friday January 27, 1995, and their last meeting was in
December 1996. A number of Baptists have been actively involved,[231]
including Dr Morris West as a consultant.[232] The final report was
published in 1997.[233]

In his paper, West contended that while the churches might come to a
short-term *modus vivendi* on one or more of the immediate points of
ecumenical tension, any long-term solution would depend on tackling the
fundamental issues.[234] Elsewhere, in a discussion of the Lund Principle,

---

the March 1994 Swanwick CTE 'Consultation on the Future of LEPs' and is also printed
in *Baptism and Church Membership*, 54. This suggestion, obviously predated the
Baptist/URC guidelines. Group 2, dealing with church membership, noted that most
churches recognized that incorporation involved 'a baptismal process expressing the
faith of the church and of the individual.' It also reported that many joining LEPs
combining Anglican and Free Churches sought membership of more than one tradition,
'Multiple Membership', defined as 'through a joint Initiation or Confirmation Service,
certain denominations [generally Anglican, Baptist, Methodist and United Reformed and
sometimes others, but not Catholic] can confer full initiation and communicant status on
the same candidate simultaneously', see 'Report of Group 2: Church Membership',
Pilgrim Post 21, 17. (The *Pilgrim Post* was edited by Roger Nunn.) When annual returns
are sent to the participating denominations, those on separate denominational
membership rolls are reported accordingly, while the total of those having multiple
membership are to be divided especially by the number of traditions in the LEP. In the
'Vision for the Future of LEPs', agreed in the final plenary session in March 1994, it was
stated that 'Reconciliation will express the mutual acceptance of all members, ministries
and sacraments in a form we cannot yet see in detail...', *Pilgrim Post* 21, 15.

229   'Churches Together in England Consultation on the Future of Local Ecumenical
Projects, Swanwick, 21-23 March 1994', *Pilgrim Post* 21, 15-18. It was at this meeting
that LEPs were re-designated Local Ecumenical *Partnerships*.

230   *Pilgrim Post* 21, 16.

231   C.J. Ellis of Cemetry Road, Sheffield, Dr P.S. Fiddes, Principal of Regent's Park
College, Dr R. Hayden, General Superintendent for the Western Area, and K.G. Jones.

232   Among the many papers considered by the Group were a number of Baptist
documents, the *Concordat*; G.R. Beasley-Murray's 'The Problem of Infant Baptism: An
Exercise in Possibilities', in *Festschrift Günther Wagner*, edited by the Faculty of the
Baptist Theological Seminary, Rüschlikon (Berne, 1994), 1-14; a draft of the Baptist–
URC agreement; *Believing and Being Baptized*; and, from its first meeting, Dr West's
report on 'Christian Initiation and Church Membership'. The meetings were chaired by
Canon Martin Reardon, General Secretary of CTE.

233   *Baptism and Church Membership*. On its origins see pp. 3-5.

234   W.M.S. West, 'Churches Together in England: Called to be One. Christian
Initiation and Church Membership. A Report', (1995), 1-2. A slightly revised form of
this paper is 'Ecumenical Notes and Documentation. Churches Together in England:

he expressed his belief that the question of the churches acting together except where deep differences of conviction compel them to act separately is still being asked, adding the positive impression, 'I have a feeling that, particularly locally, it is being dodged and fudged rather less than it used to be.'[235]

The issue of LEPs was also taken up in *Believing and Being Baptized* which advocated the adoption of the *Concordat* as providing the way forward most in tune with its own position.[236] In such an LEP, the Baptist partner had already accepted the restraints of working through a process of consultation and counselling rather than acceding immediately to the enquirer's request and such voluntary restriction of baptismal liberty could be extended to the participating Baptist congregation declining to baptize those who had already received both infant baptism and confirmation within their own tradition.[237] Such restraint, however, could not be adopted as a general Baptist policy for LEPs, for its imposition could not be made on a Baptist congregation, though it could be adopted if the congregation so wished. If this was to happen the BU working through its Local Ecumenical Committee should still approve the constitution and baptismal policy.[238] The importance of this liberty of con-

---

"Called to be One". Christian Initiation and Church Membership: a Report', *One In Christ* 32.3 (1996), 263-81 (it is from the latter that quotations are taken). These fundamental issues, are surely an echo of the 1952 Lund F&O Conference, at which, so B. Till, *The Churches Search for Unity* (Harmondsworth, 1972), 239, noted the question was asked, 'Can we go on for ever and ever, round and round in the same circle explaining ourselves to one another?' It was at Lund that frustration over this circularity surfaced, resulting in the emphasis changing from discussion of peripherals to essentials, known as the Lund Principle which questioned 'whether they [the participating churches] should not act together in all matters except those in which deep differences of conviction compel them to act separately', cited by Nunn, *This Growing Unity*, 13, and Matthews, *Unity Scene*, 22. Matthews, also noted that it was from Lund onwards that 'conversations' for union became the adopted way forward in place of 'acting together', p.22. Lund marked Morris West's introduction into the international ecumenical scene as a Youth Delegate on behalf of the BU, see his 'Baptists in Faith and Order', 60.

235 W.M.S. West, 'Swedish milepost on the road to unity', *BT* August 13, 1992, 6.

236 *Believing and Being Baptized*, 30-31, see also p.26, guideline 'c)'.

237 In this, the committee were following the Swanwick Proposals, see *Pilgrim Post* 21, 16, and *Believing and Being Baptized*, 51 n.8.

238 *Believing and Being Baptized*, 31-32. The role that the BU's Local Ecumenical Committee has taken on, in approving church constitutions and policy documents, runs the risk of quasi-presbyterianism, something foreign to Baptist ecclesiology. It should be noted that both of the official baptismal agreements concerning LEPs have referred to the BU's official rejection of *BEM*'s position that 'any practice which might be interpreted as "re-baptism" must be avoided', such being 'wholly unacceptable in its present form since, on some interpretations, nothing could pass through so restrictive a sieve...we cannot agree that an *a priori* universal bar should operate.' In so doing, they

science, to pursue baptism or not, also emerged in *Called to be One*, which notes that some Baptists see infant baptism as at best incomplete,[239] but by most as no baptism, thus requiring 'true baptism for the first time' which would be by immersion. It then noted how some Baptists were prepared to regard infant baptism as part of a process of salvation which requires completion through an act of personal profession of faith but not necessarily by immersion baptism in water. Yet in the whole matter, Baptists press for the rights of conscience of each candidate for baptism and a minister's obligation to baptize a candidate who has been baptized in infancy, whether confirmed or not, should they feel strongly that this was God's will.[240]

These proposals amount to a 'flexibility of approach to baptism', the theological basis for which is the belief that 'baptism cannot be claimed to be *essential* either for salvation or for membership in the Universal Church of Jesus Christ.' Such a position, they believed, was consonant with historic Baptist convictions, following on from the basic conviction that those baptized as believers 'will *already* have come to personal faith in Christ and be in the way of salvation.' The confession of Jesus Christ as Lord is of the essence of Christianity, taking priority over all symbolic acts however much such acts are vehicles of grace. The committee recognized that Christian initiation is a confused matter and 'what really

---

have highlighted the importance of the freedom of the individual's 'informed conscience', see *Concordat*, B.iv), and *Baptist/United Reformed Church Agreed Guidelines*, 3.

239 An e.g. of this was Jonathan Edwards, Baptist minister of the Southgate Church, Bury St. Edmunds (Baptist, URC and Anglican). The church was founded in 1970 when a church worker was appointed and what meetings there were took place in a school. Regular worship began in 1974, and the building (part of the community centre) was opened in 1976. The church was founded when David Harper was pastor of Garner Street, Bury St. Edmunds. Baptism was left out of the original setting up of the church, where, originally, membership was organized so that people were accepted provided they had been initiated at one of the other town churches—either christened or baptized. Edwards commented that the baptismal policy was mixed, respecting the conscience of those who attend. He also stated that though a Baptist minister, he personally administered infant baptism because he was the pastor of the people, confessing he did not believe it was wrong, though he believed it was not best. Information from J. Edwards speaking to probationary ministers at an Eastern Area Probationer's Day, organized by the Eastern Area General Superintendant, David Harper, at the Southgate church, May 22, 1990. Edwards admitted that the church's policy was not con-stitutionalized, but followed the ethos of the fellowship. They did rebaptize those christened, it being left to the minister's discretion whether to do so or not. Edwards also noted the existence of the New Zealand rite of the renewal of baptismal vows, though this had not been adopted by the church.

240 *Called to be One*, 67, Appendix B on 'Christian Initiation and Church Membership', B4 p.67.

matters is the Christological and Trinitarian *centre* of the acts of initiation.' This is not to imply that baptism is optional, for it is necessary for genuine discipleship. The obedience of discipleship, however, has always to be set within the context of salvation, and salvation is a process. Even when conversion has taken place a long time before, baptism can still 'be a moment of renewal and growth in the Christian life.' But when someone has been baptized in infancy, then other factors involved in discipleship have to be weighed against this, 'namely a concern for the oneness of the Body of Christ which is broken by disagreement on this issue, and respect for the way that fellow members in the Body of Christ have heard the call to discipleship. It is in an attempt to resolve these claims of discipleship, and not because baptism is thought to be unimportant, that believers' baptism should not be insisted upon.'[241]

Keith Jones argued that within unity there is space for diversity of practice, variety in the form that Christian communities may take and discussion on important issues,[242] and that churches, including the BU, need to move from competition through co-existence to co-operation, and this for the purpose of going and making disciples.[243] In LEPs, he wrote, there will always be provision for believers' baptism, stating that 'Our freedom as local Baptist communities means that we are less restricted than most in reaching local agreements on these matters.'[244] He continued: 'We will always want to secure the place of believers' baptism.' 'Constitutions must make provision for the Baptist community to be able to baptise as a believer someone previously baptised in infancy. However, this issue needs to be handled with sensitivity.'[245]

---

241 *Believing and Being Baptized*, 34-35, italics theirs.

242 Jones, *From Conflict to Communion*, 9.

243 Jones, *From Conflict to Communion*, 18.

244 Jones, *From Conflict to Communion*, 26.

245 Jones, *From Conflict to Communion*, 26. He noted the agreements already reached on baptismal policy with the Methodists and URC and mentioned that discussions were underway with other traditions. The baptismal issue, Jones rightly noted, pp.30-31, also has relevance to the issue of ministry. In team ministries, which allow a differentiation of tasks, problems over baptism could be overcome, but in single ministries, if the minister is a Baptist, then others have to be brought in to perform an infant baptism, 'as Baptist ministers sign the Declaration of Principle...which precludes them conducting infant baptismal services.' This limitation on what Baptist ministers are able to do has implications for the mutual recognition of ministry. As the full and mutual recognition of ministers would compromise the issue of baptism, Baptist ministers could, e.g., only seek 'Authorised' status from the Methodist Church not 'Recognised and Regarded'. This despite the fact that ministers of other traditions are treated as if they were Baptist ministers, their names appearing in the BU Directory, they are entitled to attend the Assembly, be elected to the BU Council and be involved in Union life as if they were fully accredited Baptist ministers.

Baptismal Practice in LEPs

While all these official discussions have been taking place, much has been happening at grass-roots level within local churches.[246] It is important to note that LEP constitutions are not static but developing, learning and changing according to experience and also as some of the sponsoring denominations produce official guidelines on baptismal procedure.[247]

An ecumenical landmark took place in August 1965 when Baptists and Congregationalists united to form what was effectively the first LEP in Cotham, Bristol.[248] The following January, the Methodists joined and Christ Church, Cotham Grove was formed.[249] In the spring of 1968, the Provisional Sponsoring Body, set up after the Nottingham Conference, reported on proposals for a new ecumenical experiment in Donesholme in Corby, involving Anglicans, Baptists, Congregationalists and Methodists. In it, new members would be admitted by baptism (whether immersion, affusion or sprinkling) and by a public confession of faith, accompanied by the laying on of hands and participation in communion. Participation of believer-baptists created anomalies which could only be overcome by mutual forebearance and charity, so parents in the church

---

246 Up until 1994 LEPs have been classified into four types: 'Local Covenant', abbreviated to LC, previously known as 'ecumenical Parishes'; 'Shared Building' [abbreviated to B]; 'Shared Congregational life' [abbreviated as C]; 'Shared Ministry' [abbreviated as M]. See *With Charity and With Conviction*, 9, following the CCLEPE document, *A Pattern for Local Ecumenism* (1984), 5, D.26. See also Welch and Winfield, *Travelling Together*, 12-15. This classification continued to be used up until 1996, when the sixfold classification, which was the result of the work of a small working party set up by the 1994 CTE Group for Local Unity in 1994, was adopted: congregations in covenant (signified 1); single congregation partnership (2); shared building partnership (3); chaplaincy partnership (4); mission partnership (5); education partnership (6), see Jones, *From Conflict to Communion*, 19-22, which reproduced details from the earlier *Ecumenical News* 2 (February, 1996), a BU newsletter for Association Ecumenical Officers. The new classification was first used in the *BH* 1996–97, 47, but because this new classification is less familiar the old classification has been used in the references below.

247 This development can be seen by comparing, e.g., the development at the Whaddon Way Church, and Central Church, Swindon. See North Bletchley LEP (Anglican/Baptist), *Interim Policy on Baptism* (1984) with *The Whaddon Way Ecumenical (Anglican/Baptist) Church Constitution* (24th February 1994); and Central Churches, Swindon, *Living with two forms of Baptism* (1976) with Central Church, Swindon, *Constitution* (February, 1995). Details of the developments will not be mentioned here, but sufficient examples concerning baptism and membership are discussed below.

248 'Two Bristol Churches Unite', *BT* August 5, 1965, 1.

249 'Free Churches Unite', *BT* January 6, 1966, 16.

would be free, it was announced, to choose either baptism or dedication for their infants.[250]

In these early days, individual LEPs exercised considerable freedom in the procedures they adopted, though these always had to be ratified by the Sponsoring Bodies, and these tended to focus on providing rites for infants. For example, in 1968 the United Church of St. Luke at Billingham on Teeside (Baptists, Anglican, Methodist and Presbyterian), replaced the service of infant baptism with a 'Service of Thanksgiving, Naming and Blessing of a Child'.[251]

In 1981, Michael Quicke remarked that in the search for a way forward on the baptismal question there had been 'both pragmatism and Charity.'[252] An example of such pragmatism can be seen in Central Churches, Swindon, which in 1976 produced an interim statement which claimed that it was possible for two forms of baptism to co-exist, though that it helped 'if nothing is written down. Our experience is free to grow if we agree about what we are going to do but are not tied down to written policies.'[253] In other LEPs the problem had either never been encountered or the issue remained unresolved. For example, membership of Wendover Free Church (Baptist/URC), part of Wendover LEP,[254] 'shall

---

250 'One-Church Scheme for New Era', *BT* April 18, 1968, 1 and 12.

251 'United Church Decides Against Christenings', *BT* October 3, 1968, 9. Similarly, Baptists and Congregationalists in Sydenham, London, came together in January 1969, and their agreement included one service for infant presentation followed by reception into the church family, or, if requested, infant baptism. There was also one service of believer's profession of repentance and faith and reception into membership. See F.H. Smith, 'Working for Unity', *BT* April 10, 1969, 12. Subject to the solving of Trust Deed problems, the Baptist church was going to be sold and the Congregational site redeveloped.

252 M.J. Quicke, minister of St. Andrew's Street, Cambridge, 'The Current Debate on Baptism: a background paper', in W.M.S. West and M.J. Quicke, *Church, Ministry and Baptism: Two Essays on Current Questions* (1981), 19, published after the *Ten Propositions* and at the time of the covenant proposals.

253 Central Churches, Swindon, *Living with two forms of Baptism*. When the churches became Central Church, Swindon, in 1978, this policy was adopted, and ratified in October 1981. Describing itself, the interim statement said, 'What follows, therefore, is a statement how far we have got. It should not be seen as a statement of what we think will always be the case.' On consititutions, Warren, *In the Crucible*, 149, after commenting that baptismal practice was an issue which needed to be considered in any constitution, remarked how they were 'advised not to tie the hands of future generations by making this document too full and detailed.'

254 Wendover LEP is Baptist, Anglican, URC and Roman Catholic, B, C and M. Wendover Free Church was formed in April 1983 when the Baptist and URC joined together and at Advent in 1985 they moved into the Roman Catholic Church, a Sharing Agreement being signed in January 1987, the Anglicans joining in July 1992—details from 'D.C.P.', *Wendover. Our God Reigns* (April, 1993).

be upon profession of faith normally sealed by Baptism of believers by immersion or sprinkling, or Confirmation of Baptism previously administered to infants', candidates having been examined and recommended by visitors (3. Membership b) iii.). However, in 1996 the minister, Ruth Bottoms, chair of the BU's Church Relations committee, wrote that, though the church would have a problem with someone from Wendover Free Church (and presumably the Anglican church too) seeking 'rebaptism', 'perhaps somewhat illogically', the church would not have a problem with someone in the same position requesting believer's baptism but from outside of the Wendover church. Though she recounted that this latter situation had in fact occurred, at that time, only once in her two years at the church, nevertheless the church's constitution had nothing to say on the matter.[255]

The best known example of the co-existence of the two forms of baptism as a matter of Christian charity, is the seventeenth-century Bunyan Meeting Free Church, Bedford. Its constitution stated, 'Baptism either by Immersion or sprinkling is administered as occasion may require, according to announcement.' The church secretary, Brian Stevens, wrote, 'It is an informal agreement that the minister is prepared to administer both forms of baptism.'[256] Similarly, when in 1988 the newly formed Waterloo United Free Church (Baptist–URC), Liverpool, stated, 'There are no particular theological problems ahead. We will practise two forms of baptism. One difficulty we are overcoming is finding hymns with which we are all familiar.'[257]

Many LEPs set out from the point of first inquiry what the options are when parents approach them for infant baptism. Central Churches, Swindon, offered the parents infant baptism, a service of thanksgiving for

---

255 R. Bottoms, in a copy of a letter to Martin Reardon, dated June 17, 1996. She then expressed her expectation that the church will work through the Baptist–URC agreement.

256 Mr B. Stevens in a letter dated September 7, 1996. Membership there was open—'Admission to the Church is made as simple as possible consistent with the assurance that those who join are trusting in Christ, and are seeking to walk in holiness of life'—and letters of transfer, certificates of membership and other such credentials from the applicant's previous church are taken as satisfactory for admission into the church. So, 'Rules for the Government of the Church, approved and adopted at a Church Meeting held on April 2nd, 1958 and amended at the Church Meetings held on November 27th 1991 and September 29th 1993'. *Constitution of the Ferndown United Church, Wimborne Road, Ferndown, Dorset* (n.d., but probably 1985), accepted believers in membership with other Baptist or United Reformed churches by letters of transfer or commendation with the approval of an ordinary church meeting (Membership.5.), while a letter of commendation followed by a visitation from two church members was required for those from other churches (Membership. 6).

257 'Members will be strangers no longer', *BT* February 18, 1988, 3.

the birth of the child and of dedication of themselves as parents,[258] while
other LEPs also add a service of naming which require no promises from
the parents.[259] Ruth Matthews has acknowledged that this kind of
procedure provides a point of tension for Baptist ministers in LEPs who
are expected to practise and prepare parents for infant baptism.[260] What is

---

258 Central Churches, Swindon, *Living with two forms of Baptism*; North Bletchley
[Whaddon Way Church, B and M] LEP (Anglican/Baptist), *Interim Policy on Baptism*,
section (1). 'Whaddon Way Ecumenical (Anglican/Baptist) Church' is known by its
shorter 'Whaddon Way Church'. It became an area of ecumenical experiment in July
1973, see *The Whaddon Way...Constitution*, 1, for its history, also 'C of E to link up
with Baptists', *BT* November 15, 1973, 12. Since the 1994 Constitution parents are
offered a Service of Thanksgiving, or Infant Dedication or Infant Baptism (4.5.1), p.5.
Bowthorpe LEP, Norwich, (Baptist, Anglican, Methodist, URC, Roman Catholic and
Quaker, being a LC, B, C and M), has used an explanatory leaflet for parents, 'Bowthorpe
Babies'. This invited parents to a simple Dedication Service, explaining, there is also a
growing number who *are* convinced Christians (such as Baptists) who prefer a Dedication
Service for their babies. They believe baptism should wait until the children are old
enough to decide for themselves to follow Christ.' Only after this is infant baptism
mentioned, details in Quicke, 'Current Debate on Baptism', 19. Further details about the
church are contained in R. Simpson, Anglican minister of the LEP, *How We Grew A Local
Ecumenical Project* (Grove Pastoral Series 17; Bramcote, 1984), especially 10, 20-21.
The LEP was formed c.1977–78, see p.7, which unfortunately does not give a precise
date, though the building was opened in January 1979, p.9.

259 At Blackbird Leys, Oxford, (Baptist, Anglican, Methodist, URC, B, C and M,
established as an area of ecumenical experiment in 1974), all parents of new-born infants
were invited to a session in which the three choices were offered them—standard infant
baptism, thanksgiving for the child and dedication of the parents with the same promises
as in infant baptism, or a naming and blessing service with no commitment from the
parents, all three occurring in a liturgy for the 'Celebration of the gift of life', see
Quicke, 'Current Debate on Baptism', 19, who noted that the majority still (in 1981)
opted for infant baptism. D. Rowland, 'Grass-roots Ecumenism', *Frat.* 206 (January,
1984), 24, wrote of Blackbird Leys that it seemed 'to many from both Baptist and
Catholic traditions that functionally there was a close parallel between infant baptism
and infant dedication as also between Confirmation and Believer's Baptism', and equally
a marked distinction between infant and believer's baptism. 'There was also a strong
agreement that infant baptism or blessing could not be linked primarily with the faith of
the parents, as a sort of vicarious faith for the child, but should be firmly grounded in the
action of God in Christ and the faith of the church. In the service at Blackbird Leys it is
the church which declares its faith and the parents are asked if they wish their children to
enter the fellowship of those who share this faith. Promises are made by parents after the
blessing or baptism as a response to the free gift of God's love, not as a condition of its
sacramental expression.' Bowthorpe LEP rejected indiscriminate infant baptism, and so
offers non-church families a service of blessing and dedication which incorporates
elements of the Jewish and Baptist services and of the *Alternative Service Book*'s service
of Thanksgiving for Childbirth, see Simpson, *How We Grew A LEP*, 20.

260 R. Matthews, 'What is different about LEP Ministry?', in *Ministry in Local
Ecumenical Projects* (CCLEPE, 1985), 14. In the same volume, Margaret Mascall (a non-

clear is that the process of accommodation within LEPs has not always been for Baptists to give ground on infant baptism, as, for example, the Bingley Woods LEP (Anglican–Baptist) has adopted a service of thanksgiving as its normal practice.[261]

Where there is no question of rebaptism, baptism is often set out as being administered along denominational lines or an ecumenical rite. For example, Grove Hill Church (Anglican/Free Church) adopted only a provisional constitution which stated, 'Baptism shall be administered according to the rite and/or practice of one of the constituent denominations, or according to an ecumenical rite approved by the Sponsoring Body, and shall be set, in normal circumstances, within an act of congregational worship.'[262] According to its December 1995 standing orders, Central Church, Swindon, arranges a meeting between those seeking to become members by confessing their faith in baptism and/or confirmation with the pastoral minister who organizes preparation classes for them.[263] Ferndown United Church accepts both believers' and infant baptism, provided infant baptism is seen as the initial step in the process of Christian initiation to be followed by a personal and public confession of faith and commitment to Christ before entering membership (Membership 1.).[264] Here, when the minister is a Baptist, any infant baptisms are conducted by a URC minister brought in for the occasion, and *vice versa* (Membership. 3.).[265] Whaddon Way Church offers adult converts not baptized in infancy the choice of baptism with confirmation or

---

Baptist), 'Theology of Ministry in LEPs', 30, included in her summary of key issues in ecumenical ministry (which had emerged from the previous essays) the implications of baptismal and eucharistic diversity in practice and interpretation. Such are further highlighted when the second Baptist Declaration of Principle, which has to be assented to and signed by all Baptist ministers seeking accreditation, is remembered, which seems to preclude any other forms of baptism: 'That Christian Baptism is the immersion in water into the Name of the Father, the Son, and the Holy Ghost, of those who have professed repentance towards God and faith in our Lord Jesus Christ...'.

261 Information from J.H.Y. Briggs.

262 Information from the church in a letter dated October 5, 1996. All information concerning Grove Hill is taken from this letter unless otherwise stated. Grove Hill was set up when the shared building was opened in 1977 and consists of two united Anglican/Free Church congregations and a Roman Catholic congregation which shares the building with one of the Anglican/Free Church congregations.

263 *Central Church, Swindon—Local Ecumenical Project Standing Orders* (December, 1995), 3.2.1.

264 *Constitution of the Ferndown United Church*, the church, Baptist and URC, was formed in 1985, being a LC, but also a shared ministry, a fact not recorded in the *BH* 1995–96, 121, the ministry usually alternating Baptist–URC (Ministry. 1.).

265 At Christ Church and Upton, Lambeth, the practice in the 1940s was that when a Baptist minister was in pastorate, e.g., Theo Valentine, the church secretary conducted any infant baptisms. Information from J.H.Y. Briggs.

believers' baptism (2).[266] To facilitate the two forms of baptism and the corresponding two modes, many LEPs have both a font and a baptistry,[267] but this is not true of all of them.[268]

Anticipating the *Concordat* by over a decade, and therefore also the Yorkshire LEPs and the work of Keith Jones by a few years, Central Churches, Swindon, in 1976 agreed that rebaptism was only possible, though in no case necessary, on the grounds of conscience, and that any such applications would be looked at with four considerations in mind. First, was the infant baptism undertaken by believing parents who sought to keep their vows or was it indiscriminate? Second, had there ever been an outward profession of faith by the candidate, and if so, why was a second public profession now considered important? Third, what considerations led to the request? Fourth, what would be the effect of such a baptism on the fellowship of the churches involved?[269] According to its February 1995 Constitution,[270] Central Church now states that baptism shall be administered according to the rite and practice of each participating denomination (4.1). In the case (4.1.1) of someone baptized in infancy who, after pastoral consultation, maintains their wish to be

---

266 North Bletchley LEP (Anglican/Baptist), *Interim Policy on Baptism*, and this practice has continued, see *The Whaddon Way...Constitution*, (4.5.2), p.5.

267 E.g. Bunyan Meeting Free Church, which has a covered baptistry and a table font which is brought out when required; Christ Church, Westminister Bridge, had a baptistry and font installed in the new building erected in the 1950s. Previously, during F.B. Meyer's pastorate, a baptistry had been installed in the school-room. Christ Church, Cotham, Bristol, had a baptistry installed into the Methodist building, both reported by I. Mallard, 'The Administration of Baptism', *Frat.* 171 (September, 1974), 39-40; the new Anglican–Baptist Emmanuel church building in Weston Favell, Northampton, sited both the font and open baptistry together, see 'Baptistery Beside the 18th Century Font', *BT* January 9, 1975, 1; Church of Christ the Cornerstone (Baptist, Anglican, Methodist, Roman Catholic and URC, B. C and M), Milton Keynes, dedicated in March 1992; Grove Hill Church; Abbeydale, Christchurch LEP, Gloucester (being Baptist, Anglican, Methodist and URC, shared B, C and M), has both in their new building built in 1995.

268 E.g. St. Luke's LEP, Sheffield (Baptist, Anglican, Methodist, URC, B, C and M), meeting in the former Anglican church which had no baptistry, see 'First baptism' (being in a hydrotherapy pool), *BT* May 24, 1990, 3; Ferndown United Church, which had to hire a portable baptistry for the two believers baptized *BT* December 5, 1996, 16. The church, however, has subsequently had a baptistery built into the floor infront of the platform. Understandably it has often been the case that it has taken time for LEPs using a paedobaptist building to install a baptistry. E.g., concerning the LEP made up of Higham Hill Baptist Church and St. Andrew's Parish Church, Walthamstow, it was reported in 1987 that, after three years of their partnership, they were still working out their baptismal policy and planning for the inclusion of a baptistry, 'Baptists move in with Anglicans', *BT* May 21, 1987, 6.

269 Central Churches, Swindon, *Living with two forms of Baptism*.

270 Central Church, Swindon, *Constitution* (December, 1995).

believer's baptized, the church follows the procedure of the *Concordat* (C.2 and C.4). If a URC member is involved, the same kind of pastoral consultation takes place as in C4 of the *Concordat*, the Provincial Moderator of the URC also being consulted. If a second baptism takes place the URC member's name is transferred to the Baptist roll. Clearly aware of the Baptist–URC discussions on the matter, the following was added: 'This procedure shall be superseded in the light of any national agreement on baptism which is subsequently made between the Baptist Union and the United Reformed Church.' Similarly, other LEPs will explore other options which will often include a public confession of faith,[271] believer's baptism only being permitted after a full consultation between the individual and the minister(s), church council and church meeting(s).[272] However, certain LEPs reject the possibility of such a 'rebaptism' because 'it would deny the validity of their infant baptism.'[273]

---

271 E.g. Grove Hill/Woodhall Farm LEP, Hemel Hempstead, 'Policy to be followed when a person baptised as an infant requests baptism by immersion', agreed at Church Council September 19, 1995.

272 E.g. Grove Hill/Woodhall farm LEP, 'Policy to be followed...'.

273 North Bletchley LEP (Anglican/Baptist), *Interim Policy on Baptism* (1982), (3), 'To those who have been baptised in infancy *and* confirmed, or who have been baptised as believers, but who subsequently have a conversion experience, we will offer a service of Renewal of Baptismal Vows', italics added. However (4), converts infant baptized but *not* confirmed 'will be offered Confirmation, preferably according to an Ecumenical Rite. However, if they ask for Believers' Baptism that request is open to agreement in the usual way by the Baptist Membership'—such people will not be eligible for Anglican membership. The prohibition of 'rebaptism' of those infant baptized and confirmed has been ratified, *The Whaddon Way...Constitution*, (4.5.4), pp.5-6. Mr F. Crix, a member of the ministerial team at Whaddon Way Church, *Anglican–Baptist L.E.P. in Milton Keynes*, n.p., but p.2, records the first occasion when the church's agreement to prohibit the rebaptism of someone infant baptized and confirmed actually became tested. Both the Anglicans and Baptists wished to accede to the lady's wish, but the Bishop rejected it. She was baptized in another Baptist church but was received into the membership at Whaddon Way. Some LEPs seem to lurk in a twilight zone between allowing 'rebaptism' and rejecting it. E.g. R. Simpson of Bowthorpe, *How We Grew A LEP*, 21, wrote, 'Our leaders felt we must have a place for freedom of conscience, and have no pastoral "no–go areas", but that we must find an option other than "re-baptism".' He then recounted how a group from the church returned from the Dales Bible Week which had propagated 'rebaptism' and stated they had to be baptized by Simpson or go elsewhere. So, at a joint evening service at a neighbouring Baptist church, Simpson joined the minister in baptizing the people, 'but when we came to those who had already been baptized as infants, I used the words "I renew your baptism", and made clear that, as far as I was concerned, this was no more than a renewal of the original baptism.' Later, some of those so baptized left and joined a house church.

The general practice has become that when so-called 'rebaptism' has taken place, the candidate is transferred to the Baptist membership roll.[274] Many LEPs have a single membership and a single membership roll, in which case their denominational allegiance is recorded next to their entry on the single register,[275] while others have a common roll and also denominational rolls.[276] It is the hope that when members move from an LEP they will be able to be accepted as full members of, in the case of Whaddon Way Church, the Anglican or Baptist churches they go to.[277]

In many LEPs all candidates for membership are trained together, whether coming through infant baptism and confirmation or believer's

---

274 So Central Churches, Swindon, *Living with two forms of Baptism*. 'Rebaptism', as such, is also possible at Emmanuel, Mosborough (Baptist, Anglican, Methodist, URC, LC, B, C and M), and Beaumont Leys, Leicester (Baptist, Anglican, Congregational Federation, Methodist and URC, B, C and M), mentioned by Quicke, 'Current Debate on Baptism', 19.

275 E.g. *The Whaddon Way...Constitution*, 4.4, p.4. It is important to note the changes that have taken place in the Whaddon Way Church's constitution. Denominational allegiance is now shown only if the person requests it or 'as a result of Believer's Baptism of a person baptised in infancy, when the person shall be identified as a Baptist.'

276 North Bletchley LEP (Anglican/Baptist), *Interim Policy on Baptism* (1982), (10), 'The name of each member of the integrated congregation shall appear on a joint membership roll, and, where applicable, on a denominational roll as well'—there will be some new converts who do not have and do not wish to have any denominational affiliation, who simply want to be members of the LEP. Their names only appear on the common roll. Section (10) continues by noting that in the case of someone baptized in infancy and later baptized as a believer 'he/she shall be entered on the denominational roll as a Baptist.' This is also reported by Crix, *Anglican–Baptist L.E.P. in Milton Keynes*, n.p., but p.1. In the Panshanger LEP in Hertfordshire, established in 1971 or 1972 (Baptist, Anglican, URC and Methodist), those coming to faith for the first time and who become members either through believer's baptism or by confirming the vows made for them in infancy become 'common' members, see Jenny Price, 'Grass-roots Ecumenism', *Frat.* 206 (January, 1984), 18-19. See also Central Church, Swindon, *Living with two forms of Baptism*, ratified October 1981, then in 1995, *Central Church, Swindon...Standing Orders*, 3.2.1, which noted that new members 'will be received into Central Church and thereby into each of the participating Churches (Methodist, Baptist & URC), their names being entered on the Central Church roll and each of the denominational rolls', i.e., multiple membership. For denominational statistics each multiple member counts as one third of a member when calculating the number of each denominational roll. The *Constitution*, 4.6 states, 'There shall be a Common Roll, including multiple members, and a separate roll of members shall also be kept for each denomination, multiple members being included on each roll.' Grove Hill Church has a joint membership, and those who have been members of a church elsewhere are welcomed into membership and a record is kept of their previous denomination.

277 *The Whaddon Way...Constitution* (4.5).

baptism,[278] and frequently joint baptism and confirmation services are held.[279] Reception into membership can then take place immediately[280] or at the next communion service.[281]

Generally, those involved in LEPs do not suspend their membership of their own denomination, rather they worship in LEPs as Anglicans, Baptists, etc., their membership, therefore, is not suspended through belonging to an LEP.[282] More broadly within LEPs, Baptist believers are able to share in a number of forms of membership.[283] 'Multiple membership' is possible where through a joint initiation (including believers' baptism) and confirmation service in which certain denominations (including Baptist, Anglican, Methodist and URC) can confer full initiation and communicant status on the same person simultaneously.[284] 'Extended membership' is conferred without any further initiation rite

---

278 So Central Churches, Swindon, see H. Dunscombe, *Footprints of Faith: A History of Central Church, Swindon* (Swindon, 2nd edn, 1990), 115. The 1995 *Constitution*, 4.3, stated, 'All candidates for membership who are becoming full members of a local church for the first time shall be instructed in the traditions of all the participating denominations.'

279 Central Churches, Swindon, see Dunscombe, *Footprints of Faith*, 115; Grove Hill Church, where baptism is immediately followed by confirmation along with those being confirmed after having been infant baptized, those baptized and confirmed this way become joint members; Bowthorpe, Simpson, *How We Grew A LEP*, 16; *The Whaddon Way...Constitution*, (4.5), 'Whaddon Way Church affirms the validity of both the Anglican and Baptist traditions. Services of both Baptism and/or Confirmation will normally be held according to an ecumenical rite with both Anglican and Baptist participation.'

280 'Four denominations receive new members', *BT* October 24, 1996, 15, reported such a joint service at Kingston Park, St. John the Evangelist LEP (Baptist, Anglican, Methodist and URC, being a single congregation partnership), Newcastle-Upon-Tyne, in which one Baptist was fully immersed, while another was baptized but not by immersion, then the seven new members were confirmed into full membership of the four (Baptist, Anglican, Methodist and URC) denominations, and this was followed by communion, the elements being distributed by the Methodist and URC ministers, while the Baptist (Jenny Price) and Anglican ministers blessed the younger children. The LEP was formed in 1986, and the Baptist church only joined in 1996.

281 E.g. Central Church, Swindon, see Dunscombe, *Footprints of Faith*, 115.

282 See *BH* 1995–96, where, at the beginning of its list of churches notes, 'In Local Ecumenical Partnerships the number in brackets below the number of Baptist members indicates the total number of church members in the LEP.' So, e.g., the LEP at Girlington records 38 Baptist members, under which, in parentheses, occurs the number within the whole LEP fellowship (87), see *BH* 1995–96, 141.

283 These are outlined by Welch and Winfield, *Travelling Together*, 62-63.

284 That this pattern is followed is confirmed by Jones, *From Conflict to Communion*, 27.

on members of LEPs whose denominations allow it.[285] When it comes to membership returns,[286] in the instance of a sharing agreement separate membership rolls are required for each denomination. Many LEPs keep one list, but identify the person's tradition alongside their name. In other instances the membership is divided equally between participating churches for the purpose of denominational returns. So, for instance, Ferndown United Church reports those on the Baptist roll and URC roll separately, while the total with multiple membership are divided by two and that figure is sent back to the central bodies.[287] In other LEPs[288] everybody on the electoral roll is counted as a member of all the denominations involved, or the list is divided according to the tradition from which a particular person or family comes. The initiation practice reflects this. The person joining the church is welcomed into that particular community. Cassidy noted that the confirmation/reception into full membership/believer's baptism is more often than not a joint service with all participating traditions involved, and this after a course of preparation based on the local church, thereby expressing the full entry into the local church and the Christian church.[289] As yet, however, there is no national agreement on the shape, content and timing of membershp returns.[290]

---

285   The many issues surrounding 'extended membership' are thoroughly examined in *Baptism and Church Membership*, 30-34.

286   Welch and Winfield, *Travelling Together*, 63-64. 'Multiple membership' affords to every LEP member not previously in membership with any church the right to be a member of each denomination involved in the LEP. 'Extended membership' would enable every LEP member previously in membership elsewhere to be regarded as a member by every other participating denomination in the LEP. Such provisions would not apply when the member left the LEP to join a single denominational church elsewhere. Jones, *From Conflict to Communion*, 27-28, noted that extended membership had been discussed over the past twenty years as a possible option where Free Churches were involved, though none of the major Free Churches had taken the initiative on the issue.

287   Information from G. Butler, Baptist minister at Ferndown since 1996.

288   According to Cassidy, 'Membership of the Church', 'Part 1: The L.E.P.s', ch. 3 'The Ecclesiology of Local Ecumenical Projects', 37, where in n.175 he ascribed this to information from clergy involved in such situations, though he made no mention as to whether any Baptists are involved in these situations.

289   Cassidy, 'Membership of the Church', 'Part 1: The L.E.P.s', 37, recorded having been told of one church with a Baptist presence, in which the anomalous situation had occurred of the admission to communion of children as yet to receive believer's baptism, because their peers, baptized in infancy, had been admitted under the rules of another participating denomination.

290   A problem does, however, arise for those converted and brought up solely within an LEP when they leave that fellowship and go to a different area without an LEP church. Then the problem arises as to which denomination they belong to, a matter made

Finally, reference needs to be made to the results of a 1994 BU questionaire in which churches were asked to indicate the level of their ecumenical co-operation at every level. Though an undisclosed number did not reply, of the returns 81% were involved in sharing worship, 61% shared in house groups, 59% in evangelism, 40% in social action and 58% in joint prayer. Though the exact percentages of churches who responded and those that did not is not mentioned, this shows an increased involvement of Baptist churches within the ecumenical movement.[291]

What Baptist churches involved in LEPs have learnt, then, is a pattern of accommodation in which two forms of baptismal theology and practice have come to be practised side by side. The importance of the ecumenical context of Baptist life is shown by the observation that *Believing and Being Baptized*, the most recent BU document dealing with baptism, is addressed specifically to Baptists in LEPs, as it seeks to develop policy for LEPs, but it is not relevant to non-LEP Baptist congregations.

The Way Forward

In December 1996 the FUE Committee held a special consultation to reflect upon the submissions from the churches, Associations and colleges to *Called to be One*, so that a draft response could be drawn up for consideration by the Executive in January and by the BU Council in March 1997.[292] The CTE Forum in July 1997 would then discuss all the responses.

A 'first version of our provisional response' was published in January 1997, and it is important to note the direction it took.[293] The Executive examined the suggested models of unity (6.11-19) and understood Baptists to be most at ease with the pattern of *'Unity in reconciled diversity'* (6.17). Acknowledgment (6.9) was made that some within the ICP 'believe we now share a common baptism', remarking that 'This is

---

all the more significant when the person was baptized in the LEP as a member of that church without any previous membership. So Cassidy, 'Membership of the Church', 'Part 1: The L.E.P.s', ch. 3 'The Ecclesiology of Local Ecumenical Projects', 36.

291 Jones, *From Conflict to Communion*, 39 n.9.

292 See *Ecumenical News* 3 (April, 1996), n.p., but p.1, and *Ecumenical News* 5 (October, 1996), n.p., but p.1.

293 'Draft Response of the Council of the Union to the Report *Called to be One* of Churches Together in England Prepared for the Forum of CTE in July 1996', in *Ecumenical News* 6 (January, 1997), n.p., but pp.1-6. This is divided up into sections corresponding to the chapters and sections of the *Called to be One* report, and these will be followed in the main text, referring to both *Called to be One* and the 'Draft Response'.

not true for all member bodies of CTE and must be addressed in an honest way.' Several times, Baptist inconsistencies in their own practice of baptism were noted[294] and the Executive asked other members of CTE to 'consider the starting point of visible unity—"our common faith in Jesus Christ"—rather than baptism' (6.9).[295]

On *Called to be One*'s Appendix B, 'Christian Initiation and Church Membership', the draft stated, 'We are anxious not to comment at too great a length', directing attention to what is said in *Believing and Being Baptized* (B). In a manner reminiscent of the BU's response to *BEM*, much agreement was found with what baptism means theologically 'but we note how this is often divorced from the practice of CTE member bodies. We want to challenge paedo-Baptists to clarify what they mean by the word "signifies". Are we to understand that at the moment of infant baptism an infant is regenerate and salvation is secured?' (B7).[296] Awareness of the CTE's 'Working Party on Baptism and Church Membership', which examined the subject of children and communion, comes out in the statement that children not baptized as believers are not usually encouraged to take communion (B16iii). Finally, 'We see no objection to the use of a suitable service of re-affirmation for those who wish to re-affirm their baptismal vows', a practice which finds parallels to the annual covenant renewal service which some Baptist churches have, which contains elements of personal rededication (B17).

The final report of the CTE's 'Working Party on Baptism and Church Membership' was published in 1997 as *Baptism and Church Membership*. The Working Party focused their attention primarily on the issues of 'rebaptism' and 'extended membership', but also on the admission of children to communion, as these were the most pressing issues within LEPs which include both believer's-baptist and paedobaptist churches. Each of these subjects are examined, some of the fundamental

---

294 These inconsistencies being the unacceptability that Baptist churches admit the unbaptized to membership, noting that more reflection is needed on the link between baptism and membership in the body of Christ, referring to the discussion in *Believing and Being Baptized* (6.28vii). This is reiterated in B16i, to which is added acknowledgment that the baptism of some has not led to membership, and 'We recognise the failure of our churches in these respects but, in calling their attention to this, it must be understood our ecclesiology is such that each congregation is independent. It can be encouraged but not coerced into a uniform practice.' B16ii noted the move among Baptist churches to refrain from baptizing by immersion those already baptized in infancy, brought up in the faith and who have already professed that faith either in confirmation or some other way. However, Baptists feel obliged to baptize such a person if they strongly feel this is God's will for them.

295 See also 'Council affirms "unity in recognized diversity"', *BT* April 3, 1997, 2.

296 Reference here is to the comment, 'Baptism signifies the rebirth of a person as a Christian by the grace of God. It is therefore a once-for-all event' (*Called to be One*, B7, p.68).

theological questions underlying them are considered and ways forward are proposed. Three principles are recommended which are believed to be important for any satisfactory arrangement in an LEP: first, that before a new LEP's constitution is drawn up there should be discussion of these three issues and that clear agreement should be established on how they will be handled. Second, that the same process should happen when existing LEPs are reviewed. Third, that pastoral sensitivity and a measure of flexibility should always be exercised in difficult cases in consultation with the Sponsoring Body or appropriate representatives, and that details in constitutions should be amended to include this.[297] The report notes three ways of handling a request for 'rebaptism' and expresses the fact that no further proposals suggested themselves:[298] the Baptist–Methodist *Concordat*; the 1996 *Baptist–United Reformed Church Agreed Guidelines* and the Swanwick Proposal.[299] From these the Working Party made the following recommendations: that Anglicans and Baptists try to agree bilateral national guidelines on so-called 'rebaptism'; that as a short term measure, LEPs, in agreement with their church authorities, should be given freedom to decide on which of the three approaches they will adopt; and that national churches whose congregations share in LEPs commit themselves to finding together a long-term way forward on 'rebaptism'.[300]

On 'extended membership', the group recommended that churches explore the issues involved and suggested the reintroduction of the catechumenate and that the Free Church concept of asssociate membership might provide possible ways forward. They also recommended each denomination consult on permitting extended membership within their own understandings and practices of church membership.[301] Finally, on the admission of children to communion, they invited all denominations to take the situation of LEPs into consideration as they discuss this matter and added their own recommendation that only those baptized should normally be so admitted.[302]

While CTE has concluded that at present there are no alternatives to either the *Concordat*, the *Baptist–United Reformed Church Agreed Guidelines* or the Swanwick Proposal, I have explored the possibility of a

---

297   *Baptism and Church Membership*, 25-26.

298   *Baptism and Church Membership*, 27-28.

299   *Baptism and Church Membership*, 26-27. On p.28, it noted that in open membership Baptist churches people have been accepted into membership on the basis of a personal profession of faith, and concurred with *Believing and Being Baptized*, 25 and 29, which urged the non-acceptance into membership of persons as yet not initiated in any way into the church of Christ.

300   *Baptism and Church Membership*, 27-29.

301   *Baptism and Church Membership*, 33-34.

302   *Baptism and Church Membership*, 34-35.

fourth way in a study of Ephesians 4:5's 'one baptism'. While noting the history and developments of ideas going back as far as the Bunyan tradition,[303] I suggest that the growing scholarly recognition of New Testament baptism being conversion-initiation, conversion-baptism,[304] offers the possibility of a return to the 'one baptism' of the New Testament.[305] The CTE route, however, maps the more likely paths to be followed.

---

303 Cross, '"One Baptism"', 197-206.

304 Cross, '"One Baptism"', 173-93.

305 Cross, '"One Baptism"', 206-09. While I am not sanguine enough to think that this route is likely to be taken up, I nevertheless believe that it is a theologically valid possibility. However, in practical terms, I believe that the mutual recognition of the two forms of baptism is the practical and most realistic way ahead. Hence my positive review of the argument for the co-existence of the two baptisms by the South African Baptist, K. Roy, *Baptism, Reconciliation and Unity* (Carlisle, 1997), e.g. p.13, see A.R. Cross, 'K. Roy, *Baptism, Reconciliation and Unity*', *BQ* 38.4 (October, 1999), 202-03.

CHAPTER NINE

New Perspectives and Developments in the Theology of Baptism

With the covenanting proposals and particularly the inception of LEPs in the early 1960s, the importance and influence of the ecumenical movement has become an increasingly powerful and prominent factor in British church life, which has led, among many other things, to new developments in the baptismal debate and new perspectives on old baptismal issues. Six examples have been selected to indicate these developments and perspectives in Baptist baptismal theology, after which three potentially landmark studies, all from 1996, will be examined as they may prove to be indicators as to possible directions in which Baptist thought will develop into the twenty-first century.

Introduction

Baptists have continued to draw attention to the impoverished nature of Baptist baptismal theology. Dr Haddon Willmer of Leeds University wrote, 'no-one who knows Baptists can pretend that all is well on our side: anti-sacramentalists, believing it is of the essence of faith not to be ritually embodied, are countered by advocates of Pauline sacramental realism who, in turn, cannot carry with them many who value baptism highly only as an act of witness. Apart from the question of its divisive effect, our thinking and practice of baptism need reform if they are to build up Christians in the faith.'[1] A *Baptist Times* editorial in 1974 noted the renewed Anglican interest in baptism, commenting that one of the temptations among Baptists was to think they were so right about baptism that they had become convinced that no questions remained to be asked and that there was no need for the re-examination of their faith and practice. 'On the contrary, there are many questions that Baptists have

---

1   H. Willmer, 'Twice-Baptized Christians—A Way Forward for Church Reform and Unity', *Frat.* 175 (February, 1976), 12. Willmer's doctorate was on the patristic doctrine of baptism: 'Sealing and Enlightenments: Aspects of the Early Christian Doctrine of Baptism' (Cambridge University PhD, 1970).

not settled': the place of the infants of Christian families in the church, the relation between faith and baptismal action, should children be baptized and should the rite include the laying on of hands?[2] Paul Beasley-Murray admitted that time and again Baptists downgraded baptism to a simple witness to Christ, when it really involves commitment to Christ, his way and his people,[3] while at the close of the century, Christopher Ellis admitted that Baptists still have 'a wide range of views about baptism', and the differences 'begin when it is asked: "What does *God* do in baptism?"'[4]

Christian Initiation

The most significant development in the debate has been the shift from the either–or of believer's baptism or infant baptism, which had effectively come to an impasse as arguments were repeated with no suggestion of any possibility of the convergence of views, to discussion of the broader subject of Christian initiation.

It is difficult to pinpoint just when the baptismal debate developed into the broader discussion of Christian initiation. Morris West tentatively located it in the 1950s in the BCC's 'Consultation on Entry into the Church'.[5] West also identified it in the F&O Theological Commission on *Christ and the Church* which met in the 1950s.[6] Ernest Payne comment-

---

2   'Baptism', *BT* October 17, 1974, 2. The editor at this time was Geoffrey Lodes.

3   P. Beasley-Murray, 'We are really not so scriptural about baptism...', *BT* April 19, 1984. The impoverishment of Baptist baptism was also highlighted by F. Cooke, who retired from Andover in 1990, 'Post-Easter people', *BT* April 26, 1990, 14, who added that 'most Baptists are afraid of New Testament baptism.' Many preparing for baptism are told firmly not to expect anything to happen. 'We are so afraid of full New Testament baptism that we have created a folk religion which accepts the separation of water and spirit baptism (which the New Testament never does) and have down-graded it to be public declaration of a decision to follow Christ.'

4   Ellis, 'Baptism and the Sacramental Freedom of God', 23. He reiterated this, p.27: 'It is no easy task to present Baptist teaching on baptism... [T]here is a wide spectrum of interpretation about the meaning of the rite, and a survey of Baptist writings on baptism will show that many contributors have been concerned with polemical issues over and against the rest of the Christian church.' He proceeded with the comment, 'They have been primarily concerned with *who* is a proper subject of baptism—i.e. a believer as opposed to an infant—and the *method* of baptism—i.e. baptism by immersion rather than sprinkling.'

5   West, 'Churches Together in England: a Report', 263-64, and his 'Editorial', *BQ* 17.8 (October, 1958), 337. The 'Consultation on Entry into the Church' was arranged by the BCC's F&O Secretary, David Jenkins, later Bishop of Durham, and met under the chairmanship of the Methodist Dr Marcus Ward.

6   So West, 'Baptists and Faith and Order', 61-63, where he noted that a preparatory study was made by the European Section of that Commission whose report was

ed that 'in this whole matter of Christian initiation the greater casualness of recent generations is being reversed', and he located the beginning of the turnabout among Baptists with the introduction of a service of infant dedication/presentation, followed by the work of Wheeler Robinson and his plea for the recovery of the New Testament emphasis on the Spirit. Further impetus came from the infant baptism controversies of the 1930s and onwards, though Baptists were slow in recognizing what was taking place in other denominations.[7] This development from the traditional discussion of baptism to that of initiation has been a gradual and partial one, for the old form of the debate has continued despite this and other developments in the line of approach taken to the issues.

Baptist developments on initiation, according to Payne, were led by Neville Clark, the contributors to *Christian Baptism* and *The Pattern of the Church*, and Alec Gilmore,[8] and was being worked out through F&O,

---

presented to the F&O meeting at New Haven, Connecticut, in 1957. The Commission itself was the response to a suggestion made at Lund that such a Commission should be set up to discuss christology and ecclesiology. Thompson, 'Baptism', 85-86, reported that the beginning of this approach is to be located a decade earlier when he noted that 'the language of "Christian Inititation" to cover the cycle of rites which begins with baptism and ends with first communion, and did much to popularize this approach to the problem', was adopted by the Church of England's Joint Committee reports in the 1940s: *Confirmation Today* (1944) and *Baptism Today* (1949).

7   E.A. Payne, 'Baptists and Christian Initiation', *BQ* 26.4 (October, 1975), 154. Among the developments in other traditions Payne listed the works of Brunner and Karl Barth, followed by his son Markus Barth, the Anglican Joint Committees of the 1940s, D.G. Dix, G.W.H. Lampe, the Methodists H.G. Marsh and W.F. Flemington, the Church of Scotland Commissions and the work of T.F. Torrance, and also F&O and the negotiations leading to the United Churches of India, pp.154-55. He added, p.155, 'Baptists have been impelled to do some fresh theological thinking about their position and to examine their practice.' An e.g. of this debate is the review of two reports on Christian initiation by the Church of England and Church in Wales reviewed by R. Nunn, 'Upheaval in Christian Initiation', *Voyage* January/February 1972, 13-14.

8   E.g. Clark, *An Approach*, and editorship with R.C.D. Jasper of the JLG's *Initiation and Eucharist* (1972), and Gilmore's *Baptism and Christian Unity*, so Payne, 'Baptists and Christian Initiation', 155-57. See Clark's assertion that baptism and eucharist are theologically inseparable, *An Approach*, especially pp. 71-85. In his essay on 'The Theology of the Sacraments', 234, Clark wrote, 'It is the response to the Word which the Spirit empowers that makes baptism Christologically congruous and ethically meaningful. Existence in Christ is churchly existence, that is to say, baptismal and eucharistic existence.' He insisted that the general pattern of initiation in the primitive church was baptism, laying on of hands and first communion, and that this pattern should be restored. This is not to say that Baptists did not use this terminology earlier, as many Baptists have been prepared to see baptism as initiatory into the church, simply to say that Clark appears to have been the first (or at least among the first) to use it in this modern way. See also Clark's *Invitation to a Conversation 2. Baptism and Church Membership* (Cardiff, 1995).

Baptist involvement in the Church of North India, the BWA's discussions with both Lutherans and Reformed Churches, and in LEPs. The challenge of this shift in emphasis was 'to give careful thought to what Christian initiation should include and imply, and to guide our churches to more satisfactory procedures. Once it is recognized that the ceremony of baptism is only one part of a process or progress, we shall find ourselves not only closer to our founding fathers, but closer also to many of our fellow Christians of other traditions.'[9]

Christian initiation first surfaced as a major issue for Baptists when, in 1967, Victor Hayward[10] proposed that as there were two ways of entering the church in the New Testament (by conversion or by birth into a believing family), so there were two baptisms and two types of faith (personal decision and that of parents). 'In either case, the local church has the responsibility of satisfying itself of the presence of faith, whether avowed, or given by prevenient grace through birth into a godly household.'[11] He believed that it was New Testament principles not practice that is determinative for the contemporary church, maintaining that basic differences between New Testament times and the present needed to be recognized as pertinent to the discussion, and that certain principles were to be found in the New Testament in a germinative, undeveloped form. There were, therefore, three fundamental differences between New Testament times and the present day: modern individualism stood at odds with the corporate psychology of both the Old and New Testament; the New Testament was uninterested in the personality of little children; and the New Testament church existed in a missionary situa-

---

9   Payne, 'Baptists and Christian Initiation', 156-57, quote from p.157.

10   His article was originally intended to be a letter to G.R. Beasley-Murray, prompted by his dissatisfaction with Beasley-Murray's answer to his questions on the Baptist–Paedobaptist controversy and the Baptists' impoverished theology of infants and children in Christian households, as expressed in *Baptism Today and Tomorrow*, and the BU report *The Child and the Church*. See V.E.W. Hayward, then of the Division of Studies of the WCC, 'Can our Controversy with the Paedobaptists be Resolved?', *BQ* 22.2 (April, 1967), 50. Hayward has been cited by paedobaptist apologists in support of their practice and as evidence that some Baptists accept the legitimacy of infant baptism, e.g. M. Reardon, *Christian Inititation—A Policy for the Church of England. A Discussion Paper* (1991), 12. On Reardon's views see J.F.V. Nicholson, General Superintendent of the North Eastern Area, 'Infant Baptism—a rite in search of a theology?', *BT* June 20, 1991, 6, who noted Reardon's reference to Hayward. That infant baptism is a practice in search of a theology had earlier been argued by Clark, 'The Theology of Baptism', 320. In all this, Hayward, 'Can our Controversy', 51, as many in a similar position had before him, asserted his loyalty to Baptist convictions, but that he parted company with them in seeking to do justice 'to the facts regarding children of believing parents.'

11   Hayward, 'Can our Controversy?', 63.

tion.[12] From these he argued for the likelihood that infants were included within household baptisms, that the concept of vicarious faith confirmed this belief and that this was confirmed by faith found in little children.[13]

The logical conclusion of Hayward's views, according to G.R. Beasley-Murray, was that 'Baptists ought not only...soften their attitude to infant baptism..., but they should introduce it into their own churches forthwith, without waiting for reunion schemes...'[14] 'The peculiarity of baptism in the New Testament lies in its embodiment of *both*....—grace and faith, redemption and repentance. The real issue here is not between Baptists and Paedobaptists, but between a view of grace that takes seriously the role of faith and the essentially Catholic view of grace which sees it as operative through the means that God has given his Church, irrespective of the condition of the receiver.'[15] If Hayward was right about vicarious faith then 'what reason is there for limiting the significance of infant baptism' and not pouring into it '"the whole Gospel in its entirety"'?[16] But, he asked, 'where is there in the whole New Testament a single line that suggests a modified doctrine of baptism, formulated with a view to its application to infants?'[17] Hayward's speculative argument from silence was unacceptable to Beasley-Murray because there was no evidence for it in the apostolic records, 'whereas there is a great deal of evidence in those records for the administration of baptism to men who repent and believe, and a fairly consistent doctrine of the significance of that baptism. That this leaves ragged edges in our doctrine and practice regarding the place of children in the Church should not be permitted to justify making the position worse by confusing the doctrine and practice

---

12　Hayward, 'Can our Controversy?', 52-53.

13　Hayward, 'Can our Controversy?', 53, 54-58 and 58-60 respectively. Reviewing Hayward's article, W.W. Bottoms, 'Faith, Baptism, and the Church', *BT* June 29, 1967, 6, echoed his call for Baptists to 'reform the shocking readiness of many of their congregations to receive into full membership Christians who have never been baptized.' He further denounced the omission of the laying on of hands and claimed that there should be no distinction between baptism and public entry into membership, criticisms of Baptist practice also made by Hayward, 'Can our Controversy?', 63.

14　G.R. Beasley-Murray, 'I Still Find Infant Baptism Difficult', *BQ* 22.4 (October, 1967), 225. Beasley-Murray examined household baptisms and the concept of solidarity, and the place of children in Baptist thought, pp.227-28, 228-31 and 231-35 respectively, and disagreed with Hayward's use of them in defence of his position.

15　Beasley-Murray, 'I Still Find', 233, italics his.

16　Beasley-Murray, 'I Still Find', 234, quotation from A. Schlatter, *Die Theologie des N.T.*, ii p.495, cited on p.231, where Beasley-Murray quoted Schlatter's statement: 'The blessing that is bestowed upon the baptised man does not consist in an individual gift of grace, nor in a particular religious condition, but in a union with Christ, by which the totality of God's gifts are obtained. For which reason the baptismal preaching consistently uses the whole Gospel in its entirety for the interpretation of baptism.'

17　Beasley-Murray, 'I Still Find', 235.

of baptism.' The chief difference between the two men was that Hayward put 'the two baptisms into the primitive Church and I view [infant baptism] as a later ecclesiastical development.' There is no possibility of putting the meaning of believer's baptism into infant baptism. 'I feel that the confusion of having two baptisms in the Church is so great, I could wish that infant baptism were abolished and replaced by some sort of service of infant blessing, whereas Mr. Hayward feels infant baptism to be desirable.'[18]

Christian initiation was a major factor in the F&O consultations at Crêt Bérard and Louisville, preliminary to the issue of *BEM*.[19] At Louisville, Beasley-Murray admitted that Baptists no more believed in rebaptism than other Christians did, but he explained, 'Where...it is believed that faith is integral to baptism, it is not unnatural for it to be held that such baptism is deficient of that which makes it the baptism instituted by Christ. Infant baptism is then viewed as an ecclesiastical rite, performing an important function within the Church, but it is not to be claimed as biblical baptism. To baptize on profession of faith one who has received infant baptism is regarded as the the first application of the baptism commanded by Christ in the Great Commission.'[20]

Morris West believed that real progress towards the co-existence of both forms of baptism could be made if agreement could be reached on the issue of the initiation process. If one accepted that such a process contained infant baptism, would Baptists be saying that infant baptism was 'of itself baptism or am I simply accepting that others see it so and that I accept the sincerity of that belief about infant baptism without thereby accepting the practice?' He asked whether the consensus process could be furthered through the co-existence within the church of two forms of baptism, noting, for instance, the pastoral problem of 'rebaptism' in the Church of North India. From the point of view of

---

18   Beasley-Murray, 'I Still Find', 235-36. In his reply, Hayward protested that Beasley-Murray had ignored his contention that he was arguing for 'discriminate' infant baptism, 'that only those infants should be baptized of whom at least one parent is a communicant member in good standing, able to give a reliable promise of real Christian nurture.' Accepting Beasley-Murray's criticisms of his argument for 'vicarious' faith, Hayward changed his language to that of 'derived' faith, see Hayward, 'Infant Baptism: A Further Comment', *BQ* 22.6 (April, 1968), 313-14.

19   The notion of Christian initiation underlies the whole of the baptism section of *BEM*, 2-7, and is reflected, e.g., in its assertions that the '*need to recover baptismal unity is at 'the heart of the ecumenical task*', see Commentary (6), p.3, and it is used as an example of church union schemes including believer-baptist and infant-baptist traditions where 'it has been possible to regard as equivalent alternatives for entry into the Church both a pattern whereby baptism in infancy is followed by later profession of faith and a pattern whereby believers' baptism follows upon a presentation and blessing in infancy', Commentary (12), p.5.

20   Beasley-Murray, 'Authority and Justification for Believers' Baptism', 69-70.

believers' baptism there had been no baptism and therefore it was no rebaptism. While a number of Baptists would hesitate to rebaptize if the person had already completed the process of initiation, West rightly stated that 'probably a much greater number would baptize such a person without any qualms of conscience.' This presented paedobaptist churches and churches where the two forms co-exist with very real problems.[21] Within the context of the Louisville Consultation, 'this is a situation which is being lived with in a number of contexts but which require much further and frank discussion as to the best way forward.'[22] Later, West wrote:

> The idea that Christian initiation is a process which includes baptism in water in the name of the Trinity, instruction in the faith, confession of faith, activity of the Holy Spirit, reception of Holy Communion, has been canvassed much over the past 30 years or so. The argument is that, whilst there is a variety of order within the various Churches in their initiation processes, there is nevertheless a recognition that in an acceptable process all the elements are involved. What is different is simply the order of the various elements in the process. But it may well be that such an approach begs certain questions, notably that of the doctrine of the Church. It may be argued that those who practice infant baptism and those who practice believers baptism start from different 'models' of the Church. Those practicing infant baptism see the Church as an ontologically given community into which a child is incorporated, whereas Baptists and those practising believer's baptism, view the Church as a community which is constituted by the activity of God on the individual who responds consciously and believes and so becomes a participating member of the community.[23]

---

21 On inititaion as a process and the question requiring consideration, see West, 'Toward A Possible Agenda', 14-15. On the possible co-existence of both forms of baptism, see p.17.

22 West, 'Toward A Possible Agenda', 17.

23 West, 'Towards A Consensus on Baptism?', 227. That this is·recognized from the paedobaptist view is reflected in the comments of M. Reardon, *Christian Initiation— a Policy for the Church of England* (1991), cited by J.[F.V.] Nicholson, 'Infant baptism—rite in search of a theology?', *BT* June 20, 1991, 6, who reported, 'Reardon acknowledges that Anglicans come to different conclusions on baptism because of their different understanding of the nature and boundaries of the Christian community', adding his own comment that, 'This is where the fundamental difference lies between Anglicans and Baptists, and this is where theological dialogue needs to start.' This was supported by the Synod's 1991 decision to continue to practise 'indiscriminate infant baptism', on which see J. Capon, 'Chester CoE clergy reject indiscriminate baptism', *BT* June 20, 1991, 2, and J.[F.V.] Nicholson, 'Infant baptism remains "open" to all', *BT* July 18, 1991, 9.

Michael Quicke concurred: 'any act of initiation presupposes an eccles-iology and Baptists have a fundamentally different understanding of the Church from paedo-Baptist communions.'[24]

Alec Gilmore noted the variety of practice among Baptist churches concerning the relationship between baptism and church membership. Some churches treated baptism and membership as two different things, while some open membership churches regarded baptism as unnecessary. Still others accepted young candidates for baptism but saw no need of it for older believers. Others used sprinkling instead of immersion when there were problems over the latter. Some closed membership churches waived baptism if a doctor's certificate was presented, others insisted on believer's baptism whatever the situation. 'If you have seen all these variations in approach...there can therefore surely be no reason why members of other communions should listen to us.' He admitted, 'the fact is that our Baptist doctrine of baptism has always been in a bit of a mess if by that we mean that it has been enormously varied...' Gilmore opposed 'rebaptism' by Baptists and advocated the mutual recognition of initiation as proposed by the CUC. Total baptism, he continued, is all four elements: immersion, individual response to what God has done, reception of the Spirit and entry into membership, but there existed considerable variety among the churches in weighting them though there was 'a basic common understanding.' 'If we could begin here, instead of from the old infant baptism/believer's baptism controversy, we may soon begin to see that other Christian communions are nearer to us than we think.'[25] D. Beaumont believed that if God accepted Anglicans, Salvation Army or Quakers, then, who were Baptists to reject them? When open membership was practised conscientiously it was a valid solution, the matter not being that of baptism, but whether one was a Christian.[26]

The traditional line was expressed by Dr Paul Beasley-Murray who believed Baptists were being pressured into equating believer's baptism with infant baptism and confirmation, and asserted that only when Jesus' Lordship was being confessed by faith was baptism really baptism. By all means, he agreed, Baptists should recognize each others' standing in Christ, but the dishonest use of scripture for the sake of unity would be to sell the Christians' birthright. The authority of scripture needed to be

---

24   Quicke, 'The Current Debate on Baptism', 16.

25   A. Gilmore, 'Baptism: Gateway to the Church', *BT* July 22, 1976, 4. Gilmore's overview of the variety of Baptist procedures concerning baptism and membership demonstrate the fact that still, after nearly four centuries of discussion, apologetic and heated argument, the issues remain the same and the positions unreconciled.

26   Mr D. Beaumont of Dinas Powis, South Glamorgan, 'Membership', *BT* February 24, 1977, 5. He suggested that a letter of transfer from a previous church, of whatever tradition, ought to be acceptable, but where none was provided, a suitable confession of faith should suffice when supported by reports from church visitors.

asserted over tradition. The baptismal service was a great evangelistic event, though, with the realization that it was also a church event, many churches had unfortunately come to link it with communion. While theologically there was much to commend this, evangelistically, he believed, it was a retrograde step. Above all, he contended, baptism ought to be a Spirit event, as it clearly was in the New Testament.[27]

In his capacity as consultant to the 'Called to be One' Process, Morris West reflected on forty years of personal involvement within the ecumenical movement when he spoke of the 'tendency to maintain the *status quo*' which had characterized the quest for unity. The net result of four decades of dialogue had been that most paedobaptist churches had come to see believer's baptism and infant baptism as two alternatives existing side by side, but never as a both/and.[28] This period had seen a growing mutual recognition of each others' baptism, a fact marked principally by *BEM*, but West asked whether participating churches in the 'Called to be One' Process could affirm the statement, 'Mutual recognition is but a staging post on the road to the visible unity of the Church.'[29]

West identified five issues as arising from the contemporary context of the Christian initiation debate which 'direct urgent and pertinent questions to the process upon which we are engaged.' First, the existence of LEPs exerted pressure towards closer unity. The application of locally agreed processes of initiation leading to membership raised serious questions by their inability to develop beyond the local situation. Second, there was the kind of ecumenicity based on a defined doctrinal basis, such as the Evangelical Alliance and charismatic networks, and not on the answer to the questions which have traditionally occupied the ecumenical process such as 'Called to be One' itself.[30] Third, there was the question

---

27 P. Beasley-Murray of Altrincham, 'Make the most of baptism', *BT* October 23, 1980, 12. P. Coleman of Watford, 'Making the most of baptism', *BT* November 13, 1980, 5, disagreed, arguing for the link of baptism with communion, and that the most obvious way for baptism to be made a Spirit event was to adopt the laying on of hands. Such a service, he believed, would be theologically right, liturgically right and made the most of baptism for the candidate, the church member and the outsider.

28 West, 'Churches Together in England: a Report', 263-64.

29 West, 'Churches Together in England: a Report', 264-65, quote from p.265.

30 These were noted by A. Gilmore, now retired and serving as Ecumenical Officer for the Sussex Baptist Association, in his critical appraisal of the document *Called to be One*. In 'An establishment view of church unity?', *BT* April 18, 1996, 10, Gilmore stated, 'if you really want to know how far we have come [in 50 years of ecuemnical activity], the only conclusion to be drawn is "not very far".' He criticized *Called to be One* as 'an in-text for professional establishment ecumenists, who have a set agenda, often reflecting their problems not ours, problems on which they wish to focus our attention', these being the church and visible unity, ministry and ordination, initiation, eucharist and membership, authority and decision making, renewal and mission.

of the relationship between bilateral conversations (such as the Anglican–Methodist talks) and the multilateral debate (such as *BEM* and the many BCC and WCC reports). Fourth, additional to denominational diversity, there was now cultural diversity, such as the Black majority churches. Fifth, since *BEM* and the response volumes associated with it, great efforts had been made to define the theological issues which lie at the heart of unresolved differences. Perhaps these and other documents which point beyond mutual recognition could help future developments.[31] In the present situation, West proceeded, at least four different patterns of entry into the church exist, therefore, the concept of baptism and membership clearly did not mean the same thing in all churches, though there had been a growing mutual recognition of each other's baptism.[32]

To test the present position on mutual recognition, West had sought responses from the participating churches in 'Called to be One' and presented the findings in his paper. Ten denominations had responded.[33] The Baptist response noted that open membership churches were generally willing to accept letters of transfer from other Free Churches, but not in the same way from an Anglican church, and certainly not from a Catholic or Orthodox one. In the latter cases, a profession of faith from the person would be required and an acceptance of the ethos of the receiving church. Baptism, however, would not be the inevitable requirement for membership. In closed membership churches, no-one would be accepted into full membership without believer's baptism, though many such churches have associate memberships which allows those from other traditions virtually all the advantages of membership except voting on matters stated within the Trust Deed.[34]

However, the issues confronting the churches are different: church planting, the Toronto Blessing, women priests/ministers, 'gays in the Forces', concluding, 'This is not a local church document. It is establishment.' His second article raised other grass-root issues, 'Building Pyramids', *BT* April 25, 1996, 15, e.g., problems between charismatic and traditional churches, and the question of church decline and survival.

31   West, 'Churches Together in England: a Report', 265-69.

32   West, 'Churches Together in England: a Report', 270. First, baptism upon personal profession of faith, which was the practice, among others, of the Baptists. Second, baptism and chrismation, usually of infants, followed by communion, with no later profession of faith. Third, baptism of candidates, usually infants, accompanied by a profesion of faith by parents or godparents, with confirmation later, as in Anglicanism and Roman Catholicism. Fourth, among Pentecostal churches there is also required evidence of baptism in the Spirit.

33   These are set out by West, 'Churches Together in England: a Report', 271-76. These were the BU, Church of England, Congregational Federation, Methodist Church, Moravian Church, Orthodox Church, Roman Catholic Church, URC, Salvation Army and Society of Friends.

34   West, 'Churches Together in England: a Report', 271-72.

These results led West to conclude that such mutual acceptance of baptism is widespread, giving added credence to the concept of 'common baptism'. However, some responses also indicated that beyond mutuality of baptism consensus became divergence which in turn became difference, and herein lay the seeds of continuing divisions on the whole process of Christian initiation. Therefore, if 'Called to be One' were to be a serious exercise in ecumenical exploration it would have to embark on potentially demanding journeys, exploring ecclesiology, sacramentality and the sources of Christian authority. Four basic issues, he proposed, could surely be agreed upon. First, mutual acceptance of baptism on the basis that it is in water in the name of the Trinity. While some Baptists did not accept such mutuality, others questioned the necessity of baptism for membership. Second, the meanings of sacraments and sacramentality were used differently between Western and Eastern churches, and within the West between Catholic and Protestant. Third, the doctrine of grace was differently perceived by the churches, and could not be separated from consideration of the Holy Spirit in relationship to both sacraments and grace, which were the basic issues underlying the merely symbolic and the quasi-magical understanding of sacramental grace. Fourth, the issue of ecclesiology needed to be placed on the ecumenical agenda,[35] a point that was taken up in the 'Called to be One' process and book.

West concluded with discussion of what '*legitimate* diversity' means within ecumenical discussions, raising the matter of what range of issues and viewpoints are open for discussion and what those are for each participating church. Progress in the area of baptism and church membership, he believed, could only take place when this matter had been clarified. He suggested that a potentially fruitful context in which the baptism and membership issues could develop would be examination of the theology of the child,[36] for which there were three reasons. First, the subject had not yet occupied much ecumenical time and could therefore bring a fresh perspective to the debate. Second, the relationship of the child to the church had been raised already by the Church of England and Baptists, the latter now asking whether infant baptism says something to them and encouraging Baptists to draw the practice of infant dedication into the whole process of Christian initiation. Third, because this subject would also raise the related issues of grace, the Holy Spirit, eucharist, ecclesiology and conversion.[37]

Believing and Being Baptized adopted a different approach and was based on the premise that salvation is a spiritual journey in which the two elements of the grace of God and the faith of believers are active, in

---

35   West, 'Churches Together in England: a Report', 276-79.

36   It should be noted in this regard that G.R. Beasley-Murray's 'The Problem of Infant Baptism' was also considered by the Working Party.

37   West, 'Churches Together in England: a Report', 280-81.

which baptism 'is *normally* to be received near the beginning of entrance upon Christian discipleship.' For those who come to faith from outside the influence of the community of faith baptism will be located relatively close to conversion. However, those nurtured within a Christian family and the fellowship of the church 'will have grown through various stages of trusting Christ', so, for them, 'baptism marks the decisive point within their whole journey of salvation', providing a moment when they emerge from childhood into a clear profession of faith and discipleship, at which God bestows his Spirit graciously in a new way for new responsibility. Therefore, the 'image of baptism as a place of special encounter with God along the road of salvation, or as a high point on the journey of increasing wholeness, underlies the rest of this document.'[38]

The idea of both salvation and initiation as processes is to be found also in Christopher Ellis' study of the sacramental theology of baptism which is based on three observations, the first of which is that

> recent ecumenical studies of baptism have tended to emphasize the whole *process* of initiation, indicating that baptism is a focus of a larger process. The gift of the Spirit is seen as being at work in the reception of a child into the family of God, the nurture of a young faith, the confessing of faith, the commissioning in confirmation, and the ongoing discipleship and incorporation into the body of Christ.

The importance of this for Ellis is that it removes some of the historical pressure to identify the moment and means of God's activity, encouraging the view of baptism as a process of initiation for the believer and part of the ongoing life of the people of God. 'Baptism is not an isolated event but a focus of what is continually taking place.'[39] He argued that

---

38   *Believing and Being Baptized. Baptism*, 10-12, italics theirs. See the whole of section II 'Baptism and the journey of new life: or "Pilgrim's Progress"', 9-12.

39   Ellis, 'Baptism and the Sacramental Freedom of God', 36. The other observations are that seeing baptism as a part of a process enables the broadening of the understanding of baptism as a sign. While only part of the whole, baptism should never be referred to as 'only a sign', as, through baptism, the understanding of the freedom of God acts as a pointer to his activity elsewhere; and, baptism is both subjective and objective, as the very symbolism links the believer and the church with that which it signifies, pp.36-37. C.J. Ellis, *Baptist Worship Today* (Didcot, 1999), 37, believed that the open membership practice of welcoming people into membership because of their being Christians, not because they have been initiated in a certain way, 'is an important clue in understanding Baptist spirituality and the nature of Baptist worship. It is in the inwardness of prayer, rather than performative sacraments that we will need to look for the Baptist sense of spiritual reality. Or perhaps we should distinguish between those actions which are expressive of inner realities, such as the laying on of hands or the raising of hands in praise and those which are seen to be performative and effectual.'

the activity of God is not restricted to the sacraments,[40] leading to his overall conclusion that, 'The freedom of God means that He is free to work through the means of grace that He has given to His church', and that the Spirit operates beyond as well as within the church. 'Again, baptism becomes a focus of divine activity but not its entirety: the act is Christocentric, and its fulness is in its centre—not its boundary.'

In his examination of 'Baptism and Creation', Paul Fiddes investigated five motifs connected with water: birth, cleansing, conflict, journey and refreshment, followed by consideration of the communication and scope of grace.[41] Different traditions have tended to overstress one of the five motifs at the expense of the others, Baptists stressing baptism as a boundary marker for believers, the fifth motif, 'a moment of separation from past life and commitment to new kingdom values.' Despite its potential for a richness of meaning, Baptists have sometimes narrowed it to an act of obedience.[42] Baptists have traditionally claimed that only believers' baptism has been able to adequately draw upon the whole range of water-symbolism, so Fiddes challenged them to explore such imagery as 'descent into the womb' to understand and value more the prevenient grace of God involved in the nurture of a child in the Christian community before it comes to 'birth' and 'this may lead them to affirm some of those aspects that are vividly presented in...infant baptism. A reflection upon the strong element of initiation in these motifs may also lead Baptists more consistently to practise the sequence followed in other Christian churches, that a person must be baptized before sharing in the Eucharist.'[43] Earlier Fiddes had written:

> Baptists should in fact be quite willing to recognize that there are elements of *both* faith and divine grace in the act that is called infant baptism. There is the prevenient grace of God, already at work deep in the being of the child, giving life and wholeness, and enticing it towards a personal response of faith to Himself in due time. There is the faith of parents and the Christian community, supporting and nurturing the child as it grows. Most Baptists will also recognize that the completed sequence of infant baptism and later personal faith in Christ sealed in

---

40   Ellis, 'Baptism and the Sacramental Freedom of God', 35. This position Ellis defended by reference to the book of Acts which 'testifies to the untidiness of the Holy Spirit.' In Cornelius' case the Spirit was given before baptism, but after in the case of the Samaritans evangelized by Philip, p.33. On p.35 he concluded, 'A constant theme is that God is not restricted by the sacraments as the only means whereby He may graciously work in the lives of men and women. Any theology that is developed concerning baptism as a means of grace must make room for this inconvenient, yet gloriously inspired, belief in the freedom of God.'

41   P.S. Fiddes, 'Baptism and Creation', in Fiddes (ed.), *Reflections*, 47-57 and 57-61 respectively.

42   Fiddes, 'Baptism and Creation', 61-62.

43   Fiddes, 'Baptism and Creation', 62.

confirmation constitutes initiation into the church as the body of Christ, and many Baptist churches in Britain do not therefore require baptism of believers in this situation. When salvation is seen as a process or a journey, [as in *BEM*], many Baptists can readily perceive different combinations of grace and faith at different stages of the journey and can find various ceremonies appropriate to mark the stages.[44]

In a paper for the Institute for Ecumenical Research in Strasbourg, the American Professor Mark Heim examined the difficulties Baptists have with the practice and theology of infant baptism, but offered a possible way forward in recognizing baptism as a part of the process of Christian initiation which includes instruction, personal confession of faith and participation in the eucharist. In his review of this and other essays of the theme, Mike Smith of Skelmersdale asked, 'If these elements are all present in any tradition, even if not in the same order, could this provide a way forward towards the mutual recognition of Christian initiation including baptism?'[45]

Liturgically this shift of emphasis to that of initiation was explored by Neville Clark,[46] who presented a baptismal eucharist which, he proposed, was the 'goal towards which the catechumenate moves', having already stated 'The two sacraments belong together. Baptism, laying on of hands, and first Communion, is the pattern of Christian initiation.'[47] In this he was followed by the orders in the three most recent ministers' manuals. Payne and Winward deliberately and consecutively set out orders for the dedication of children, believer's baptism, the laying on of hands, reception into church membership and the Lord's Supper,[48] stating in the rubric at the beginning of the baptismal service, 'Since we are baptized

---

44   Fiddes, 'Baptism and Creation', 60.

45   M. Smith, 'Baptism and Unity: a way forward?', *BT* December 31, 1998, 11, discussing S.M. Heim, 'Baptismal Recognition and the Baptist Churches', in M. Root and R. Saarinen, *Baptism and the Unity of the Church* (Grand Rapids, 1998), 150-63, e.g. pp.162-63.

46   Clark had become involved in the work of the F&O Commission from the 1960 meeting in St. Andrews, on which see West, 'Baptists and Faith and Order', 65-68.

47   Clark, *Call to Worship*, 58-59 and 54 respectively. Clark had wrestled with these and related issues the year previously in his essay 'The Theology of Baptism', e.g., 324-25. White's *Biblical Doctrine of Initiation*, does not strictly come into this discussion of Christian initiation as it focused on New Testament baptism, though the second of his three criticisms of infant baptism was that it split 'the single New Testament initiation rite, so introducing endless and costly confusion', pp.300-02. As such R.L. Kidd is misleading to include it as an example of Baptist studies on Christian initiation despite its use of the word in the title, see Kidd, 'Baptism and the Identity of Christian Communities', in Fiddes (ed.), *Reflections*, 98 n.5.

48   Payne and Winward, *Orders and Prayers*, 123-61. Such consecutive arrangement of the services was not followed by either of the two later service manuals.

into the Church, it is desirable that Baptism should, *if possible*, be followed by the Lord's Supper, at which the reception of new members should take place.'[49] Gilmore, Smalley and Walker entitled their baptismal section 'Christian Initiation', which opened, 'Among Baptists of late there has been a growing tendency to bring closer together the act of baptism, reception into membership and admission to communion', while other denominations had moved towards seeing 'the wholeness of Christian initiation in terms of strengthening the links between baptism, confession of faith (or confirmation) and communion.' 'One result of this theological discussion for Baptists is that the act of baptism as a confession of faith is increasingly seen as a part of a larger act of initiation which often then finds expression in one service of baptism and communion.'[50] They identified five essential elements in the whole process of initiation: the reading of scripture and the reasons for engaging in Christian initiation; profession of faith and commitment; prayers; baptism in the name of the Trinity, possibly with the laying on of hands; and reception into membership and admission to communion.[51] The most recent manual similarly states: 'Believers' baptism, reception into membership at the Lord's Supper, and the laying on of hands, all relate to our *one initiation* into the Body of Christ. These elements *may* take place within a single act of worship, or they may be divided between morning and evening services, or two Sundays.'[52]

According to Morris West, the debate on Christian initiation has achieved two things.[53] First, it has forced Baptists to take seriously what they do throughout the Christian life, from infancy, through conversion and profession of faith, to baptism and membership of the local church, and to communion. However, it must be acknowledged that Baptists have

---

49   Payne and Winward, *Orders and Prayers*, 127, in the original the whole of the rubric is italicized, but this was altered in order to highlight the 'if possible', which reflects the position of many, perhaps even the majority, of churches which would not follow this pattern.

50   Gilmore, Smalley and Walker, *Praise God*, 137. To support this position they provided a baptismal eucharist at which the baptized were accepted into membership, p.138.

51   Gilmore, Smalley and Walker, *Praise God*, 137.

52   *Patterns and Prayers for Christian Worship: A guidebook for worship leaders* (Oxford, 1991), 93, italics added. See also P. Beasley-Murray's discussion of this pattern of baptism followed by communion at which the baptized are received into membership, and its traditional alternative of 'Gospel proclamation' which is not followed by communion, the latter being the pattern he prefers, though on the pragmatic grounds that the service is best used for evangelistic purposes, *Faith and Festivity*, 103-16. He had earlier expressed these views in his 'Make the most of baptism', *BT* October 23, 1980, 12.

53   W.M.S. West in a conversation on March 5, 1997. To his basic outline details have been added to exemplify both the positive and the negative aspects of the debate.

not been able to find an agreed pattern for this process either in theory or practice. Second, it has misleadingly suggested to their ecumenical partners that infant baptism followed by confirmation is equivalent to believer's baptism and membership. Clearly, discussion of Christian initiation has provided another perspective through which to see old questions and has raised new ones. The old questions include infant baptism and sacramental interpetation of baptism, the new ones include the charismatic debate and the movement towards common baptism.

Infant Baptism

Many Baptists have continued to dismiss infant baptism outright. For them, because it has no basis in scripture, it is invalid[54] and therefore the issue of rebaptism is a non-issue.[55] However, not least because of the new perspective of Christian initiation and the formal and informal developments in baptismal practice within LEPs, some Baptists have been encouraged to look afresh at infant baptism. Some have rejected infant baptism but recognized the right of all believers to follow their con-

---

54   So, e.g. D. Pawson, 'Cross-Examination', in D. Pawson and C. Buchanan, *Infant Baptism Under Cross-Examination* (GBMW, 24; Bramcote, 1974 [a sequel to C. Buchanan, *A Case for Infant Baptism* (GBMW, 20, 1973)], 5-18, who, from the outset declared, 'the case must be established within the bounds of Holy Scripture', p.5; B. Milne, tutor at Spurgeon's College, '*Children of Promise: The Case for Baptizing Infants* by Geoffrey W. Bromiley', *BQ* 29.5 (January, 1982), 235-36; T. Griffith, 'Look, Here Is Water', *Mainstream Newsletter* 27 (January, 1988), 3, and his *Case for Believers Baptism*, 11-27, where he dismissed the historical, scriptural and theological arguments put forward for infant baptism.

55   E.g. A. Jones of Millom, Cumbria, 'Baptism and christening', *BT* July 23, 1992, 8. Jones admitted that he had moved from a Methodist church to an open membership Baptist church where he was welcomed into membership on profession of faith, 'but it was made clear that this was out of respect for my conscience' as the church did not recognize his christening. He concluded, 'I do not practise rebaptism. However, I will gladly baptise (once!) any who profess faith in the Lord, regardless of what ceremonies they have been through in infancy.' Also C. Stutton of Chatham, 'Queries on Baptism and Eucharist', *BT* July 30, 1992, 13, 'infant baptism is not really baptism at all in the eyes of Scripture. Consequently, to be baptised as an adult, having repented and believed, is not rebaptism but merely scriptural baptism.' There is little doubt that these views acurately represent the majority of non-ecumenically involved Baptist ministers and churches this century, but the issue remains a live one, not least because of the increased involvement of Baptists, and, in recent years, more Baptists have come to acknowledge the legitimacy of infant baptism, as reflected in the extended debate in the *BT* between November 1997 and April 1998, see, e.g. the full page of views *BT* December 11, 1997, 12, and Mr G. Bennett of Ashford and H. Doyle of Highams Park, 'Arrogant to think ours is the only true baptism', *BT* January 8, 1998, 13.

science.[56]   Others have adopted a more conciliatory position which has set both forms of baptism side by side, largely because they have been writing for a general Christian readership, though it is usually obvious which form they advocate.[57] There have been, however, an increasing number of Baptists willing to part company with the traditional Baptist rejection of infant baptism. A few examples will indicate the variety of approaches adopted.

The pattern of the mutual recognition of the two forms of baptism is the commonest way Baptists have lived with the reality of two forms of baptism.[58] Prior to the establishment of the CUC, David Russell voiced Baptist concern over the practice of indiscriminate infant baptism, declaring that it was a stumbling block even to Baptists who were prepared to accept infant baptism with confirmation as an alternative pattern of Christian initiation.[59] Walter Bottoms similarly viewed indiscriminate infant baptism as a cause for concern for Baptists who continued to press solely for believer's baptism. However, he believed that recognition of their own principles need not alienate Baptists from Paedobaptists, citing several Baptist church covenants which allowed both

---

56   E.g. D. Pawson, *Water Baptism* (1992), 59-64, where, after dismissing the purported scriptural basis for infant baptism, he answered the question, 'what is to be done about those who come to repentance and faith, ask for baptism, but are refused because they were "christened" as a baby?' He later wrote, 'While respecting the views of other Christians and churches, the answer must be sought from the Lord himself. This means searching the Scriptures..., asking the Spirit of truth to say whether what is there said about it has happened or has not yet happened', p.63. In this, Pawson can be taken to be speaking for a great many Baptists, though the wording might well be different.

57   E.g. R.P. Martin, *The Worship of God: Some Theological, Pastoral, and Practical Reflections* (Grand Rapids, 1982), 124-44; B. Milne, *Know the Truth: A Handbook of Christian Belief* (Leicester, 1982), 232-35; N.G. Wright, *The Church* (1984), 'Infant Baptism and Confirmation', 21-22, and 'Believers' Baptism', 22-24; P. Beasley-Murray, 'Should Babies be Baptized?', 'Yes' p.238, 'No' p.239, in D. English *et al* (eds.), *An Introduction to the Christian Faith* (new edn, 1992), originally published in 1982 as *The Lion Handbook of Christian Belief*.

58   Mutual recognition is the logic of open membership and, to a lesser extent, closed membership churches which have a supplementary roll. Mutual recognition, of course, does not legitimize those open membership churches which allow into membership those never baptized by any means.

59   'Indiscriminate baptism "an obstacle to unity"', *BT* September 28, 1972, 1-2, being the report of an address to a Leaders' Conference in Birmingham. Russell's views are also to be seen in 'Church Union? Talks team will point to other ways...', *BT* September 27, 1973, 1, where he told the church unity talks about talks that union was not the only way to demonstrate church unity.

forms of baptism and which 'have existed happily in this way for centuries without compromise of principles.'[60]

In their concluding chapter, the Baptist–Anglican writing team of Donald Bridge and David Phypers explored 'a working compromise', asking Christians on either side of the dispute to make concessions to each other.[61] Three considerations would point the way forward. First, recognition of the principle of regenerate membership would entail 'baptists' recognizing that there would always be some Christians who wished to baptize their children, and paedobaptists recognizing that indiscriminate infant baptism debased the rite and scandalized their brethren.[62] Second, the belief that all Christians in good standing with other denominations needed to be confirmed was to be eschewed. Third, all baptists should relax their demand for rebaptism when admitting Christians in good standing with paedobaptist churches, for 'If baptists would be excused confirmation they must likewise excuse rebaptism.'[63] The authors believed that 'Christians must work together while the problems are being solved.'[64]

Michael Quicke[65] believed that 'The possibility of the two patterns [of initiation] enjoying a rich theological relationship rooted in the breadth

---

60   W.W. Bottoms, 'Baptism', *BT* December 7, 1972, 11, a comment on the reprinting of Beasley-Murray's *Baptism Today and Tomorrow*. Bottoms believed it to be a timely re-issue because of the new situation in inter-church relations and any suggestion of talks with Baptists and the URC. Beasley-Murray personally disagreed with Baptists who recognized the validity of infant baptism, but argued that Baptists should refrain from demanding baptism of those baptized in infancy who wished to join a Baptist church. Bottoms, however, was mistaken and the book was never reprinted. Information from Dr Beasley-Murray.

61   D. Bridge of Frinton Free Church, and D. Phypers, an Anglican teacher in Derby training for the auxiliary pastoral ministry, *Water That Divides*, 191-95.

62   Bridge and Phypers, *Water That Divides*, 196-97.

63   Bridge and Phypers, *Water That Divides*, 197-98. Like *Baptists for Unity* before them, Bridge and Phypers admitted that a problem existed with no final solution and argued for the priority of mission, similarly arguing that baptists recognize a complete initiation complex involving instruction, confession of faith, baptism and the laying on of hands in any order, *Water That Divides*, 199. In all this, the Church of North India was held up as a source of hope and inspiration as to what could be achieved, pp.199-200.

64   Bridge and Phypers, *Water That Divides*, 199.

65   Quicke, 'Current Debate', 11-23 (reprinted in *BQ* 29.4 (October, 1981), 153-68). This was written at the request of the ACCR in response to the 1979 BCC Assembly in Belfast request that churches 'consider how far the two classic patterns of Christian initiation can be seen as acceptable alternatives', see p.11. Quicke listed the two patterns of initiation as: first, infant baptism, nurture in the Christian community, confirmation/reception into full membership on profession of faith and admission to communion; second, thanksgiving for childbirth and dedication of parents, nurture in the Christian community, baptism upon profession of faith and admission to communion.

of man's experience of God and response to him gives us a new perspective and opens up several possibilities for both sides to work through.'[66] In 1996, the four English College Principals argued that the Declaration of Principle's phrase 'That Christian baptism *is* the immersion in water...' is open to two possible interpretations. The verb 'is' could be understood as narrowly exclusive, or it 'could provide a strong centre whilst also allowing space on the boundaries for other possibilities.' Baptists, they believed, need 'a genuine openness to others.'[67] *Reflections on the Water* included in its introduction the statement that, 'Though this is not...a polemical volume, the Baptist essayists do believe that the reflections *can be best seen* when it is believers who are baptized.'[68] Paul Fiddes urged Baptists to recognize 'that there are elements of *both* faith and divine grace in the act that is called infant baptism': the prevenient grace of God already at work in the child and enticing it in time towards a personal response of faith, and faith in the support and nurture of parents and the Christian community.[69] The growing acceptance by many Baptists of the existence of infant baptism was also reflected when Richard Kidd spoke of his inability to choose infant baptism for his children 'any more than I would expect someone baptized as an infant and responsibly exercising discipleship in another tradition to seek another baptism as a believer.'[70]

Two radical proposals are worth mentioning as they show the extent to which some Baptists have felt able to go. Frustrated by the impasse of what he called 'the weary and inadequate denominational apologetic', Haddon Willmer offered 'speculations' which might contribute towards the coming of 'a united church freer for the fulness of the Gospel.'[71] If

---

Somewhat surprisingly, Quicke did not include reception into full membership within the second pattern. Quicke believed that by setting the two patterns within their processes of initiation, the dilemma of rebaptism could be ameliorated if Baptists stressed the renewal of baptismal vows, though he recognized that, for most Baptists, pastoral considerations could not exclude totally the practice of so-called rebaptism, pp.20-23.

66   Quicke, 'Current Debate', 23.

67   Kidd (ed.), *Something to Declare*, 38. Later, the Principals wrote, p.38: 'In the current debate on infant baptism and so-called "rebaptism" (as in...*Believing and Being Baptized*...), we require a declaration that provides Baptists both with strength of principle and a genuine openness to others.'

68   'Introduction', in Fiddes (ed.), *Reflections*, 2, italics added.

69   P.S. Fiddes, 'Baptism and Creation', in Fiddes (ed.), *Reflections*, 60.

70   Kidd, 'Baptism and the Identity of Christian Communities', 97.

71   Willmer, 'Twice-Baptized Christians', 16. He recognized that 'on all sides...baptism is in a crisis...the bulk of theorizing about...baptism is still trapped by our divisions into apologetic for either paedobaptism or believers' baptism, although the baptismal crisis is plain to see on both sides of that divide. The theories do not overcome the crisis partly because they are developed within the terms laid down by the basic structures of the crisis.'

the proposed union between the URC and Churches of Christ were successful, 'a united church would come into being in which not only would infant baptism and believers' baptism be practised, but individuals might be allowed, however grudgingly, to be baptised both as infants and as believers.' This suggestion was momentous as it breached the centuries–long taboo against rebaptism.[72] He adduced a number of points in support. First, such a church would have to distinguish clearly between them without denying either and, second, in such a situation, infant baptism would no longer be loaded with all the meaning of believers' baptism.[73] 'The two baptisms cannot be telescoped into one without loss of clarity. Each requires the other: not one being dominant in one church, the other in another church, but both together accepted in one church, practised happily and offered freely to all Christians.'[74]

None of this, Willmer believed, infringed the principle of 'one baptism' as already it was accepted that many baptisms of different individuals were one baptism by virtue of the trinitarian name and water. 'We see that both infant baptism and believers' baptism are one': unity can be seen in the events of baptism–confirmation–first communion, despite their being divided over time; it can also be seen in the New Testament reports of many different baptisms and their varying inter-pretations 'which...cannot be brought to a simple unity in which all the meaning might be realized in one act. All this is to say that the unity of baptism does not depend, and has never depended, on a unity to be dis-covered in some feature of the event of baptism itself, or in inter-pretations which are part of the baptism, except in the name of God.' Willmer then asked: 'Then why should it be made to depend on its being performed only once to each person?', a position he justified with the argument that persons exist at two quite different levels: the unconscious, passive level of infancy and the conscious, purposive, individualized level of adulthood. 'People are neither one nor the other, but become both and remain both, and this is not helped by denial. 'Yet as churches, we make a claim for baptism as a complete initiatory rite—it suffices to make a man a Christian—only to refuse to administer it in a way that shows we have some understanding of the full scope of manhood. A united church with a reformed baptismal practice could do that.'[75]

---

72   Willmer, 'Twice-Baptized', 12. He believed that to manipulate baptisms merely to achieve unity was unprincipled and trivializing, for reform was needed too, but this could only come about 'in a united church which practises both forms of baptism, not merely allowing them but rejoicing in both, and conscientiously free to let Christians be baptised both as infants and as believers.'

73   Willmer, 'Twice-Baptized', 12-13.

74   Willmer, 'Twice-Baptized', 15.

75   Willmer, 'Twice-Baptized', 15-16.

Somewhat surprisingly, Willmer's views received neither support nor opposition.

Another controversial attempt has been implemented by Eric Blakeborough who believed that there is little hope of reconciling the two practices of baptism.[76] His church in Kingston-upon-Thames has 'no single understanding of baptism.' They agree with believers' baptism but not in rebaptism, which has led the church to recognize three kinds of baptismal experience. First, the baptism of believers by immersion on profession of faith is the usual mode. Second, those infant-baptized who wish to reaffirm their baptism are invited to dip their hand in the baptistry water and make the sign of the cross. Third, those impelled by conscience to be immersed are allowed to do so though it is made clear that this is reaffirmation not rebaptism.[77] For his views and practice,[78] Blakeborough, a self-confessed liberal/radical and probably the most controversial contemporary Baptist figure, was accused of having moved away from both scripture and the BU's Declaration of Principle.[79]

The greatest surprise to Baptists is the modified position on infant baptism adopted by George Beasley-Murray.[80] In his most recent work,[81]

---

76   E. Blakeborough, *Permission to Be* (1992), 50-51. For him, the difference between the two baptisms reflects a theological rivalry between those who stress the objective aspect of the sacrament and those who stress the subjective—infant and believer's baptism respectively.

77   Blakeborough, *Permission*, 53-55.

78   E. Blakeborough, 'Knowing God in Baptism and Eucharist', *BT* July 9, 1992, 10, being the second of four extracts from *Permission to Be*, which was reviewed by D. McBain, 'Journey towards wholeness', *BT* July 23, 1992, 12, who described John Bunyan Baptist Church, Kingston-upon-Thames, as 'arguably the least conventional and the most radical of all our Baptist churches today', the church being the base for the Kaleidoscope Project which provides residential, social and medical facilities for about 300 drug users. For his work there, Blakeborough was awarded the MBE. On his views on baptism, McBain remarked, 'there is a sense of appreciation of ecumenical variations in baptism and in the Lord's Supper.'

79   A. Jones of Millom, 'Baptism and christening', *BT* July 23, 1992, 8; by W. Andrews of Lincoln, and C. Stutton of Chatham, 'Queries on Baptism and Eucharist', *BT* July 30, 1992, 13.

80   The surprise will undoubtedly be lessened by four factors: first, many Baptists do not read very widely, particularly when it comes to academic books and articles; Beasley-Murray's views occur in a book neither readily available nor easily accessible in Britain; the fact that the book has not been reviewed in any British Baptist journal or paper, and appears to be comparatively unknown; and the relatively unimportant position the issue of baptism now appears to hold among British Baptists, except among ecumenically involved Baptists, many of whom will welcome Dr Beasley-Murray's shift in position.

81   Beasley-Murray, 'The Problem', 13. He wrote: 'for long I gave the answer "No" to the question [whether Baptists could acknowledge discriminate infant baptism]... This was due to my conviction that Paedobaptist apologetic for infant baptism depended too

he explored the 'possibilities' of a rapprochement between believer's baptism and paedobaptism when infant baptism is seen as attesting 'the commencement of the work of grace within the baptized with a view to its blossoming into fulness of life in Christ and his Body the Church as the individual's life progressively opens to Christ.'[82] This could be supported by recovery of the catechumenate, especially if focus is placed on 'initiation', that is, the whole process of leading individuals to Christ and into the church.[83] He pleaded 'that churches which practise believer's baptism should consider acknowledging the legitimacy of infant baptism, and allow members in Paedobaptist churches the right to interpret it according to their consciences.' Practically this would involve believer-baptist churches refraining from 'rebaptism'.[84]

The shift in emphasis to the perspective of Christian initiation and with it the associated view that salvation is a process[85] has enabled more

---

much on traditional interpretations, which appeared to me neither to face the realities of history..., nor to relate adequately to the New Testament theology of baptism.' His views were appreciatively welcomed by W.M.S. West, 'Baptist theology of the child', *BT* June 30, 1994, 6, who commented that Beasley-Murray was not suggesting the acceptance of the practice of infant baptism, for he maintained that the scriptural norm is the baptism of believers, but that, in West's words, 'we should, as Baptists, contribute more positively and actively to the wider debate which is going on about infant baptism and its place within the whole of Christian Initiation.'

82   Beasley-Murray, 'The Problem', 9, citing the Anglican, O.C. Quick, *The Christian Sacraments* (1932), 168-74, as an example of this point of view.

83   Beasley-Murray, 'The Problem', 13, following the suggestions made at the Louisville Consultation by the Jesuit, J. Eagan, 'The Authority and Justification for Infant Baptism', 60-61. For paedobaptists the catechumenate would involve infant baptism followed by an extended catechumenate leading to confirmation and adult entrance into the Christian community, or a religious ceremony for infants at birth. In believer-baptist congregations an extended catechumenate leading to baptism–confirmation–eucharist would have to be adopted.

84   Beasley-Murray, 'The Problem', 13-14. He remained, however, 'not sanguine enough to believe that members of believer-baptist churches will be convinced by the arguments within this essay', even though many groups of churches, most notably the Waldensians in Italy, have for centuries proceeded along these lines. He further drew attention to his sub-title, 'An Exercise in Possibilities', believing it to be 'at least in harmony with variations in the experience of baptism among the earliest believers recorded in the New Testament', the 'great lesson' of which 'is the freedom of God in bestowing his gifts', p.14 (citing Ac 2:37-38; 8:14-17; 10:44-48; 11:1-18; 18:24-19:6). His essay was received appreciatively by D.F. Wright, Senior Lecturer in Ecclesiastical History at Edinburgh University, 'Scripture and Evangelical Diversity with Special Reference to the Baptismal Divide', in P.E. Satterthwaite and D.F. Wright (eds.), *A Pathway into the Holy Scripture* (Grand Rapids, 1994), 265, 267-68.

85   That this view of salvation as a process is now firmly established among Baptists is to be seen in its acceptance in some of the most recent writings on baptism: see Quicke, 'Current Debate', 13 and 16-17; P.S. Fiddes, *Charismatic Renewal: A Baptist*

Baptists than ever before, in theory and practice, to develop a greater appreciation of infant baptism and to keep the way open for future possible ecumenical developments.

Sacramental Interpretations[86]

The work of scholars and ministers during the previous period (1938–1966) had opened up the way for the widespread acceptance by Baptists of the language and theology of 'sacrament', and the ecumenical climate had made the issue unavoidable, even if undesirable to some mainly conservative evangelicals who also tended to oppose all ecumenical involvement. Hence, Baptist sacramentalists constantly reiterated the necessity for personal faith in order to avoid an unbiblical sacramentalism. Baptists, David Russell asserted, stood for evangelical faith, renouncing 'all notions of sacramentalism which would see the sacraments as less than ethical acts and all notions of sacerdotalism...' Salvation is by grace through faith, and regeneration belongs to the realm of personal faith and commitment to Christ and is not to be contained within any rite of infant baptism however ecclesiastically and sacerdotally correct. Baptism testifies to the evangelical doctrine of salvation, being an ethical sacrament, associated closely with baptism of the Spirit, and a church sacrament by which the believer marks their entry into the fellowship of God's redeemed people.[87]

George Neal believed that the growing church unity movement ought to be leading Baptists to re-examine their beliefs and practices. However, this was not happening. Of the books written by Baptists, Neal commented that 'few Baptists seem either to have read the books or felt the impact of their rich and far-reaching conclusions.' He continued: 'In view of the fact that believer's baptism is the one main doctrine and practice that kept Baptists separate, we should do more serious work on this.' With all its theological and spiritual consequences, baptism 'is the supreme gift we can offer to a united Christendom.' In short, this was a plea 'for Baptists to adopt a true biblical and theological interpretation of baptism as a sacrament.' He observed, 'There seems to be an inability to unite FAITH AND *sacramental action* together.' An impartial and objective look at the New Testament showed baptism to be a rite that did things, that is, a sacrament. This fear of sacramental baptism was most

---

View (1980), 34; Beasley-Murray, 'The Problem', 12; *Believing and Being Baptized*, 9-12; Kidd (ed.), *Something to Declare*, 44-45; Ellis, 'Baptism and the Sacramental Freedom of God', 36; and Fiddes, 'Baptism and Creation', 60-61.

86   Many of the sacramental interpretations of baptism have been included in the discussion in other sections of this chapter. Therefore, to avoid repetition only several examples of baptismal sacramentalism need outlining.

87   D.S. Russell, 'Two Wings...?', *BT* October 1, 1970, 7.

unfortunate, as it revealed a failure to discern that Baptists alone could emphasize the sacramental nature of baptism without the danger of undermining the need for personal faith.[88]

In a second article, Neal expanded his views that in the New Testament baptism did something, for it was closely associated with the forgiveness of sins, regeneration, the gift of the Holy Spirit, union with Christ in his death and resurrection, indeed it was necessary for salvation. As such, the Roman Catholic sacramental interpretation was closer to scripture than the Baptist symbolic interpretation. But there was a mid-point, which was baptism with faith. 'It is only an unbiblical attitude and irrational fear that insists that the act of baptism is neither very important, nor part of God's way of channeling blessing into the lives of converts.' God had joined together repentance, baptism, forgiveness and the gift of the Spirit, so why should Baptists divorce them? The evidence of scripture was overwhelming that baptism was a sacrament, but the fact was that many Christians practised unbiblical baptism. If the teaching of the New Testament and its significance for the Christian was fairly faced 'we will do great service to the Catholic Church.' 'Because man is both body and spirit, and is impressed equally by the outward signs and the inner spiritual experiences, he needs both aspects in his religion for it to be completely satisfying to the whole man.' Baptists were able to provide both the inward and the outward, for believer's baptism alone adequately interweaved the inner experience and outward manifestation.[89]

Responses to Neal's article in large measure vindicated his views that many Baptists still refused to face up to the baptismal sacramentalism so eloquently and clearly set out from scripture by the likes of Beasley-Murray and White. Neal was accused of misinterpreting Romans 6:4-5 and John 3:5.[90] L.J. Stones expressed concern that baptism effected that which it symbolized. His problem over baptism as a sacrament was due to the delay of baptism until after conversion, rather than understanding it as conversion-baptism. 'The impossible situation is that if baptism is a sacrament we have to tell those who profess faith in Christ that they must

---

88   G. Neal of Sundon Park, Luton, 'Let's sort ourselves out on baptism', *BT* June 5, 1969, 6-7, emphasis and italics his. This appeared after the publication of *Baptists and Unity* and *Baptists and Unity Reviewed*. The books Neal was referring to were Beasley-Murray's *Baptism in the New Testament* and White's *Biblical Doctrine of Initiation*, in addition to which he recommended the use of Winward, *The New Testament Teaching on Baptism*.

89   G. Neal, 'The Bible is serious—and so clear about baptism—And we should be too', *BT* June 12, 1969, 9.

90   Mr C.B. Hyde of Stotfold, 'Does Baptism Separate Us?', *BT* June 26, 1969, 3, and B. Bowers of Bloomsbury, London, 'Repentance', *BT* July 3, 1969, 3, respectively.

wait for baptism before they can receive those blessings, such as forgiveness and regeneration.'[91]

On the relation of baptism to conversion, Paul Beasley-Murray contended that the traditional evangelical understanding of conversion was limited. 'Baptism is faith in action' and as the believer is buried and raised with Christ in it, therefore, 'Baptism is...no optional extra. It is part of the conversion process.' So far from being antithetical to grace and faith, as commonly held in Protestantism, 'baptism is the sacrament of justification by faith.' 'To say, "in Christ Jesus you are all sons of God through faith" is tantamount to saying "As many of you as were baptised into Christ have put on Christ".' This was a challenge to paedo-baptists, but equally it was a challenge 'to the many Baptists who are anti-sacramentalists at heart. Conversion involves faith expressed in baptism. A decision alone is insufficient.' Therefore a 'decision for Christ' which did not involve repentance, baptism and church membership 'is not true conversion.'[92]

In his survey of Baptist booklets on baptism between 1960–1980, Dr Raymond Burnish drew attention to the diversity of approaches to baptism as illustrating 'both the independency of Baptists, and their stress on the inward faith rather than the outward symbol, and upon God's work in the candidate's life before baptism, expressed in the baptismal rite, rather than upon what the sacrament accomplishes in itself.' He concluded: 'the Baptist theology of baptism and liturgy of baptism stress the importance of the personal faith and commitment to Christ of the candidate. Although they take the view that the inward and spiritual grace is more important than the outward and visible sign they still see baptism in sacramental terms, emphasizing the way in which baptism unites the candidate to Christ and grants his participation in the death and resurrection of Christ.'[93]

In 1996 George Neal returned to the subject, reiterating his earlier view that too often Baptists belittled the importance of the sacraments. One way for Baptists to take the sacraments seriously, he proposed, was to accept the word 'sacrament' over the use of the weaker and safer word

---

91   L.J. Stones of Stoke St. Gregory, Somerset, 'Is Baptism a Sacrament?', *BT* November 27, 1969, 3.

92   P. Beasley-Murray, 'The Big Decision', *Leadership Today* (October, 1988), 24-25. He also noted baptism's place in making disciples, that in the New Testament it is a rite of initiation, therefore a corporate act whereby a person enters the new community of the people of God and that baptism without church membership was, according to the New Testament, a nonsense.

93   Burnish, *Meaning of Baptism*, 160 and 166. Burnish also presented a paper to the Tyndale Fellowship Study Group on Biblical Theology and Christian Doctrine entitled 'Baptism in Ecumenical Theology' (unpublished, 1988).

'ordinance'.[94] Similarly, Christopher Ellis began his study on the sacrament: 'It may come as a surprise to many Christians that most Baptists do not refer to baptism as a sacrament.'[95] If applied to the contemporary British Baptist scene,[96] Ellis' comment does not reflect the contemporary situation. If applied to Baptists world-wide, however, it would be generally true. But contrary to Ellis, the evidence is overwhelming that the majority of Baptists are comfortable with the use of the word 'sacrament' applied to baptism and the Lord's Supper. This position is confirmed by the overwhelming evidence which points towards widespread Baptist acceptance and use of the term 'sacrament'. In fact, it is now difficult to find written sources which only use 'ordinance'.[97]

---

94   G. Neal, now retired in Devon, in an extended series of articles on worship, 'The Sacraments: more than mere symbols', *BT* July 18, 1996, 10. He later wrote: 'Baptists, of all people, need never be afraid of the sacramental principle because of their emphasis on personal faith before calling oneself a Christian. Because of this they should have no fear of something objective being done in Baptism and Communion.' It is necessary to make the most of baptism as it is only done once, something that can only be done when the sacramental note is emphasized 'believing that is that when we are baptised something great and wonderful happens, with the church community present also believing something mighty is happening by the grace of God and the power of the Holy Spirit.' This event includes the believer's ordination to service, provision of the Spirit, assurance of God's acceptance, forgiveness of all sins, baptism being 'the first real act of worship for the new Christian followed...by...first Communion...'

95   Ellis, 'Baptism and the Sacramental Freedom of God', 23.

96   The various contributors to *Reflections* 'tend to concentrate upon [the English] cultural context', see p.2. This study, however, is focused on 'British Baptists' by which is meant those Baptist churches in the BU, for which Ellis's comment is no longer true, though it was undoubtedly the case for the larger part of the present century.

97   One of the problems in all this is, of course, that most Baptists are not writers. Among those writers who use only 'ordinance' see, e.g., J.J. Brown of Dagenham, 'Baptists and Some Contemporary Issues', *Frat.* 153 (July, 1969), 7 and 8; F. Bacon, *Church Administration: A Guide for Baptist Ministers and Church Officers* (1981), 113 [repeated in the revised and enlarged 2nd edn of 1992, p.135], and also in the 'Modal Church Rules' (n.d.), section '4. Ordinances', reproduced in Bacon, pp.171-72; 'Modal Rules for a Baptist Church' (n.d.), in R. Poolman and J. Barfield, *Church Administration* (CTP, D4; 1989), Appendix II, sections 'II. Membership (a)' and 'III. Ordinances', pp.58 and 59; and somewhat surprisingly N. Wright, *Challenge to Change*, 174, who earlier mentioned baptism as part of the believer's initiation into Christ, p.80, as a sign of the outpouring of spiritual power, p.79, and as a sign of conversion, p.161. It is not clear from these passages whether these authors would reject the use of 'sacrament' to baptism, rather these sources *only* use ordinance in reference to the rite. Others, however, use 'ordinance' in a way that would seem to exclude any sacramental understanding of it, e.g. S. Ibbotson, 'The Variety of Worship', in D. Slater (ed.), *A Perspective on Baptist Identity* (Mainstream, 1987), 65; and G. Finnie of Northern Parade, Portsmouth, a member of the FAB Council of Reference, *What is the True Church?* (Crich, n.d., [early 1990s]). He claimed that the doctrine of regeneration supported by the ICP was flawed,

It is clear, then, that Baptists have generally accepted the word 'sacrament' and use it with comfort. However, this does not mean that Baptists have widely taken on board a sacramental interpretation of baptism. The evidence strongly suggests that there continues to be a divide between the most eloquent theological expressions of baptismal sacramentalism and the grass-roots view of the rite which continues to emphasize its subjective aspect, as a profession of faith, an act of witness and obedience and little more.[98] For instance, the caption accompanying the photograph of a baptism in Nepal which began 'Washing their sins away',[99] prompted the response, 'Surely we don't believe that, do we?' The correspondent continued, 'I...am confident that the washing away of the candidates' sins was gloriously granted first by their prior saving faith in Christ, and was a pre-requisite to their witnessing in baptism—not dependent upon it.'[100]

In the main, then, the sacramental aspect of baptism has been unaffected by the shift of focus to Christian initiation, except in the most recent studies. Two examples will show this, both from the volume *Reflections on the Water* which builds on the ideas of baptism as a journey and as a divine and human drama. Viewing salvation/conversion as a process is a key element which has enabled this broadening of the discussion to Christian initiation.[101] Christopher Ellis has sought 'to give meaning to a Baptist use of the word "sacrament" with regard to baptism', which clearly reflected his belief that previous attempts had not been successful.[102] Baptist anitpathy to the term 'sacrament', he argued,

---

and the presence within it of sacramentalists who suppose 'that by use of outward signs a saving grace envelopes his soul' was further reason for Baptist non-participation. This statement was followed by use of the term 'ordinance'.

98   E.g., a testimony from a recently baptized lady speaking at the Cambridgeshire Baptist Association annual assembly, June 1, 1990, who gave as her reason for baptism, 'Baptism is a thank you for what he [Jesus] has done'; a brief report in the New Road, Bromsgrove church magazine (March, 1995) which commented that the four candidates 'testified to their faith, and why they had chosen to be baptised'; the testimony of a Baptist man aged 38, 'Baptism was only a follow-up to giving my life which was the really wonderful thing', in J. Finney, *Finding Faith Today: How Does it happen?* (Swindon, 1992), 109. For other examples see the testimonies reported by S. Gaukroger, *Being Baptized* (1993), 2-9.

99   'Believers baptised in a bath', *BT* March 25, 1999, 4.

100   Mr D. Callis of Norwich, 'Baptism', *BT* April 15, 1999, 6.

101   E.g. Ellis, 'Baptism and the Sacramental Freedom of God', 36, 'seeing baptism as a part of a process enables us to broaden our understanding of how baptism may operate as a sign. While it may be only a part of the whole, it should never be referred to as "only a sign" since it provides a lens through which the Spirit's activity may be viewed in the world and in the ongoing life of the church.'

102   Ellis, 'Baptism and the Sacramental Freedom of God', 24. He defined 'sacrament', p.36, as suggesting 'the power of symbols to link us to the depths of reality, and points us to the use by God of material means to mediate His saving action.'

while in part due to a reaction against tractarianism, was predominantly a response to the Roman and Reformed Churches' institutional commitment to a comprehensive state church.[103] Baptists were free of this precisely because they understood baptism to be a divine–human encounter,[104] and the faith they see as essential to the rite 'is the recognition that faith involves trust and reliance upon the grace of God. Therefore, if faith becomes the key pivot of divine activity, that very faith looks to God's graciousness and offers not an anthropocentric but theocentric understanding of what happens in baptism.'[105]

Building on Ellis's idea of sacraments, Paul Fiddes stressed that sacraments are pieces of matter which God takes and uses as places of encounter with himself, grace transforming nature, grace being nothing less than God's gracious coming to his people and his world. Generally, Baptists have shied away from the 'stuff' of creation, despite the inherent potential of total immersion and the involvement of the person and the community at every level of this 'multimedia drama.'[106]

When the drama of baptism is properly arranged, 'the contact with the element of water should arouse a range of experiences in the person baptized and in the community that shares in the act', evoking a sense of descent into the womb, a washing away of what is unclean, encounter with a hostile force, a passing through a boundary marker, and reinvigoration. Water, thereby, becomes a place in the material world that can be a rendezvous with the crucified and risen Christ. Anticipating the accusation that such a kaleidoscope of natural motifs would suggest that baptism means anything and everything and therefore nothing in particular, Fiddes emphasized that the controlling event was the death and resurrection of Jesus.[107] The symbolism of water resonates on both the levels of creation and redemption, concerning both natural phenomena and human history.[108] When the baptismal candidate, or the witnessing

---

103 Ellis, 'Baptism and the Sacramental Freedom of God', 29-30. He maintained that within such state church systems, *ex opere operato* theologies objectify God's activity 'within the institutional processes of liturgical activity, thus enabling church and state to control the dispensing of salvation.'

104 Ellis, 'Baptism and the Sacramental Freedom of God', 38.

105 Ellis, 'Baptism and the Sacramental Freedom of God', 30. On p.38, Ellis wrote, 'Christians must acknowledge that faith itself is a gift and the human response is a part of the divine action.'

106 Fiddes, 'Baptism and Creation', 47-48. On p.48 he illustrated this reluctance to fully use the stuff of creation by reference to the concealing of baptistries, the emphasizing of the testimony over against the use of water, and the insulating of the minister from the water by the use of waders, a practice whose passing away he regarded as fortunate.

107 Fiddes, 'Baptism and Creation', 57-58.

108 Fiddes, 'Baptism and Creation', 59, 'There is no merely random collection of images here; they refer to the activity and self-disclosure of the God who relates Himself

community, encounters God anew through this particular water 'they will be the more aware of the presence of God in other situations where water is involved in birth, conflict, cleansing, journey, or refreshment.'[109] Though many Baptists 'can readily perceive different combinations of grace and faith at different stages of the journey and can find various ceremonies appropriate to mark the stages', Baptists nevertheless

> find important dimensions of baptism missing in the rite as applied to infants, so that it is hard to use the word baptism with any fulness of meaning. A Baptist will certainly find something lacking in the faith expressed there, as the infant himself or herself can vow no personal allegiance to Christ as Lord. But it is not only faith that lacks fulness. It needs to be understood in ecumenical conversations that a Baptist will also want to say that the scope of *grace* in such baptism is narrower than in the baptism of believers.[110]

Grace is not a supernatural substance but the gracious coming of God as supremely personal into relationship with his creatures. If salvation is understood not as a momentary event but a journey of growth, then baptism provides a point within the process when 'God draws near to transform persons in a special way. Salvation cannot be isolated within the act of baptism...but it can be "focused" there in the moment when the Christian believer is made a part of the covenant community of Christ's disciples. Using an element of His creation, water, God offers an opportunity in baptism for a gracious encounter which is rich in experience and associations.'[111]

Too often the church has narrowed the meaning of baptism, different traditions over-emphasizing one of the five motifs over the others. The Roman Catholic Church has majored on the imagery of cleansing, infant baptism being the washing away of original sin and original guilt, thus enabling a theology in which infants are seen as the 'proper' subjects of baptism. Baptists, on the other hand, have tended to emphasize baptism as a boundary marker for believers, stressing it as the moment of separation from past life and commitment to new kingdom values. Despite the rich potential of meaning, they have sometimes narrowed it to 'following Christ through the waters of baptism', a mere phase on a pilgrim journey.

---

to every dimension of the life of His universe. Baptism into the body of Christ means a new depth of relationship between the believer and Christ; it must also involve a new relationship between the believer and the whole community of those who are consciously in covenant partnership with God in Christ (the church—1 Cor 12:13). But further still, in the light of the commitment of the triune God to the body of the cosmos, baptism means a new relation of believers to as yet unredeemed humanity and to our whole natural environment.'

109 Fiddes, 'Baptism and Creation', 59.
110 Fiddes, 'Baptism and Creation', 60, italics his.
111 Fiddes, 'Baptism and Creation', 60-61.

Baptists like Fiddes, however, argue that 'only the baptism of believers at a responsible age can adequately draw upon the whole range of water-symbolism and enable the baptismal pool to be the focus for God's creative-redemptive process.' Baptists, he noted, should be more alert to the width of the range of significance. Reflection on the birth motif with its strong element of initiation, should lead Baptists more consistently to practise the sequence followed by other churches of baptism followed by eucharist.[112]

The Holy Spirit and the Charismatic Debate

The question of the relationship between baptism and the Holy Spirit is not a new one, but the charismatic movement has provided a new perspective in which to view it and has raised awareness of the role of the Spirit in baptism.

With its British origins in the early 1960s[113] the charismatic movement[114] has come to be a major factor and contributor to the 'ecumenical texture' of British church life.[115] As well as the establishment of

---

112 Fiddes, 'Baptism and Creation', 61-62. For Fiddes, p.63, believers' baptism underlines a final allegiance to Christ alone which is not worked out as a private individual but within the whole human community. It is the entrance to church membership which carries with it the responsibilities of active discipleship under the Lordship of Christ.

113 Its origins are set out by Bebbington, *Evangelicalism in Modern Britain*, 229-48. Later he argued that charismatic renewal is largely an expression of cultural modernism, p.275. He also observed how the presence of charismatic Christians within the Roman Catholic Church has served the ecumenical process by breaking down the Protestant–Catholic divide, p.256, something that it has also done within Protestant denominations. Bebbington dates the first contacts of the charismatic movement in Britain as taking place in 1963, p.229. See also Tidball, *Who Are The Evangelicals?*, *passim*. Tidball, p.53, agreed with Bebbington that the charismatic movement owes much to the influence of contemporary culture.

114 Here the 'charismatic movement' is used as an umbrella term which takes into account the various branches of the movement, including separated church networks including the charismatic house churches, restorationist churches, the new churches and other new wave churches, and also many mainline denominational churches which are also charismatic, e.g. charismatic Baptist churches, charismatic Anglican churches, etc..

115 P.S. Fiddes, 'The British Church Scene: Issues of Identity for Baptists in Discussion with Others' (BWA Commission on Baptist Doctrine and Inter-Church Relations paper, unpublished, 1991), 2: 'I want to suggest in this paper that beliefs about, and styles of, church and ministerial leadership within the charismatic movement have actually shaped Baptist response to ecumenical ventures. It is impossible to tear apart the woof and warp of the ecumenical–charismatic texture of life on the British church scene, in which questions of Baptist identity are posed.' This 'Ecumenical Dimension' is also discussed in the 'The Report presented to the Council of the Baptist

many new churches,[116] it has affected many churches within the traditional denominations, many Baptist churches among them,[117] sometimes for good and sometimes for the worse.[118] Not least, the charismatic movement has challenged Baptists who were 'in danger of losing sight of the charismatic dimension of the Christian life in general and of Christian initiation in particular.'[119] Many Baptists are key figures in the charismatic movement and have written much on the subject.[120] There is a great deal of evidence for charismatic inroads into Baptist life,[121] a

---

Union of Great Britain and Ireland, March 1978, on the movement for Charismatic Renewal', A. Gilmore (ed.), published in Fiddes, *Charismatic Renewal*, 7.

116   On these see, e.g. A. Walker, *Restoring the Kingdom: The Radical Christianity of the House Church Movement* (3rd edn, 1989), 23-121.

117   Fiddes, 'Issues of Identity for Baptists', 2, 'Baptist identity has been challenged and influenced strongly in recent years by the charismatic (or "renewal") movement and even by its associated fringe of "Restorationism".'

118   Tidball, *Who are the Evangelicals?*, 220, noted that, like the ecumenical and feminist movements, the charismatic movement has been a source of division. That it has also been a source of both numerical and spiritual growth has been demonstrated by P. Beasley-Murray and A. Wilkinson, *Turning the Tide: An assessment of Baptist Church Growth in England* (1981): this study itself comes from within the Church Growth movement (the third wave—see below).

119   'The Report', 6.

120   The most prominent of the 'Baptist' charismatic leaders is D. Pawson, formerly minister at Gold Hill and the Millmead Centre, Guildford, but involved in itinerant ministry since 1979, *Fourth Wave: Charismatics and Evangelicals: are we ready to come together?* (1993); N. Wright of Lytham St. Annes (1973–86), tutor in Christian doctrine at Spurgeons (1986–95), subsequently minister at Altrincham, *The Radical Kingdom: Restoration in Theory and Practice* (1986), *Lord and Giver of Life: An Introduction to the Person of the Holy Spirit* (CTP, C7; 1990), and with T. Smail and A. Walker, *Charismatic Renewal* (1993, 2nd edn, 1995); and R. Warner, former Religious Book Editor for Hodder and Stoughton, minister at Herne Hill (1989–1995), from 1995 a member of the ministry team at Queen's Road, Wimbledon, which has been a prominent church linked to the Toronto Blessing, on which he wrote *Prepare for Revival* (1995), see also his earlier *Rediscovering the Spirit* (1986). Another leader is the former Baptist minister Terry Virgo, who left the BU to set up a Restoration church in Hove, see Walker, *Restoring*, *passim*, and D. McBain, *Fire Over the Waters: Renewal Among Baptists and Others from the 1960s to the 1990s* (1997), 76-78. McBain's book gives details of Baptist involvement in the renewal movement and sets this against the background of wider developments in the renewal movement.

121   See P. Brierley (ed.), *Christian England: What the English Church Census Reveals* (1991). In the 1989 English Church Census Baptist overall strength was recorded as 199,400, see p.164 Table 61. 83% of this figure was BU, totalling 166,100, p.40 (the other Baptist traditions are also listed on p.40). Of the total Baptist strength, 22% classifed themselves as charismatic evangelicals, p.164 Table 61 (giving the figure a total of 43,000 Baptist charismatics, see p.162 Table 60), an increase of 13% from 1985 (see p.164 Table 62), which is the first year that such statistics were available.

process which has been greatly enhanced by the existence of Mainstream, which has drawn together evangelicals and charismatics.[122]

Analysts and participants of the movement have defined four 'waves' in its development. The first wave was Pentecostalism, the second the charismatic movement itself, the third was the signs and wonders movement associated with John Wimber and the Vineyard churches and the Church Growth movement coming out of Fuller Theological Seminary, California,[123] the fourth wave is the (hoped for) integration of charismatics and evangelicals.[124]

A key tenet of both the first and second wave has been that 'the baptism of/with/in the Holy Spirit' is an experience subsequent to

---

Though this four year gap between figures does not give an idea of the long-term trend (p.166), it does, for present purposes, indicate the strength of the charismatic movement among BU churches, as it is unlikely that the charismatic movement has made an impact of any note within the other Baptist bodies, except for the Jesus Fellowship [formerly Bugbrooke Baptist church, which is the only Baptist church ever to have been expelled from the BU, see 'Not what we regard as a Baptist church', *BT* November 27, 1986; the Jesus Fellowship is also discussed by McBain, *Fire Over the Waters*, 144-45, who also recorded their practice of rebaptizing all those they received into their fellowship, and the complaints the BU received about this from neighbouring Baptist churches], which consists of a total of 900 members (p.40, Table 10). Therefore, if we take the number of Baptist charismatics to be 43,000 out of a total of 166,100, then 26.4% of the BU is charismatic. The importance of the charismatic movement within BU churches is also reflected in 'The Report', 1-8. Cf. the earlier study by Beasley-Murray and Wilkinson, *Turning the Tide, passim.*

122 Its full title is 'Mainstream Baptists for Life and Growth' and was formed in 1979, and revolves around its *Mainstream Newsletter* and annual conferences. In 1993 Mainstream developed into 'Mainstream—a Word and Spirit Network'. One of its founders was Dr P. Beasley-Murray of Altrincham, see Bebbington, *Evangelicalism*, 268, to which McBain, *Fire Over the Waters*, 82-85, adds himself, Dr R. Brown, Principal of Spurgeon's, P. Grange of Kirby Muxloe, C. Roseweir of Redhill and Secretary of the Home Counties Association, and P. Goodland of Gorsley. See McBain's chapter on Mainstream and the Word and Spirit Network, pp.108-28. See also M. Bochenski, 'A Word and Spirit Network—the story so far', p.9, 'A Word and Spirit Network' by the Mainstream Executive (these are listed on p.18), pp.10-11, and M. Abernethy of Bushey Meads, 'Reflections on a Word and Spirit Network', pp.12-15, all in *Mainstream Newsletter* 50 (June, 1994).

123 McBain, *Fire Over the Waters*, 98-99, discussed Wimber's understanding of the baptism in the Spirit. The Toronto Blessing is a phenomenon which has come out of the third wave of the movement, originating in the 'Airport Vineyard Fellowship', Toronto. Pawson has also written a book on the Toronto Blessing, *Is the 'Blessing' Biblical? Thinking Through the Toronto Phenomenon* (1995).

124 See Tidball, *Who are the Evangelicals?*, 72-73; Pawson, *Fourth Wave*, especially 56-61.

conversion (a second blessing) and separate from baptism in water.[125] Paul Fiddes set the charismatic debate within the wider discussion of Christian initiation noting how their ecumenical partners have urged Baptists to accept that 'the relation between the prevenient grace of God and the response of human faith can be expressed in different ways' and that they ought 'to recognise the sequence of infant baptism and later confirmation as one of those ways.' He noted that the charismatic movement has also exercised an influence here 'in encouraging the view that spirit-baptism is a further stage beyond water-baptism.'[126]

The baptism in the Spirit first arose as an issue for Baptists in the early 1970s, prompted not least by the visit to Britain of the American leader of the Jesus People, Arthur Blessitt.[127] There were those who were persuaded by Pentecostalist and charismatic contentions that 'the baptism of the Holy Spirit' was a post-conversion experience,[128] while others called for leaders in the denomination to write on the subject.[129] In time, such teaching did appear.[130] In 1980 Fiddes rightly observed that accept-

---

125 See Walker, *Restoring the Kingdom*, e.g. 129, who writes, p.131, 'Restorationists are aggressively Baptist', stressing that believers' baptism 'is not an option for Christians but an essential part of the restored church', views which owe as much to Brethrenism as to Pentecostalism. 'Their view that the "baptism of the Holy Spirit" is a second experience quite separate from conversion is taken from classical Pentecostalism. They believe that the "baptism" is the initiation into the power of the Holy Ghost. Most Restorationists believe that the initial sign, or evidence, of the baptism is speaking in tongues. There is no dogmatic ruling on this, however.' See also Tidball, *Who are the Evangelicals?*, 27 and 112; and D. Bridge and D. Phypers, *Spiritual Gifts and the Church* (1973), 101-45, who discussed in detail 'The baptism of the Spirit and spiritual gifts', their own conclusion being that 'the baptism of the Spirit is not an experience subsequent to conversion but the initial conversion experience itself' with no necessary connection between this experience and speaking in tongues, p.117, summarizing their discussion on pp.109-16.

126 Fiddes, 'Issues of Identity for Baptists', 3, though he adds that this influence does not come in the rigid form of a 'second blessing' as in older Pentecostalism.

127 There were many reports of Blessitt's impact in the *BT* throughout 1972.

128 E.g. A.V.C. 'Baptism of the Holy Spirit', *BT* April 13, 1972, 3, who believed that the baptism was evidenced by the gift of tongues; whereas Mrs E. Constable of Cambridge, 'Baptism of the Holy Spirit', *BT* June 1, 1972, 3, urged Baptists to seek this blessing, but said that tongues was not essential to it.

129 So V.G. Tucker of Enfield, 'Holy Spirit Baptism', *BT* May 4, 1972, 3, being a response to the letter by A.V.C.. This call for more teaching was echoed by the BU's Working Group on the Charismatic Renewal in 1978, see the 'The Report', 6.

130 E.g. D. McBain, 'Baptism in the Spirit', *BT* June 19, 1975, 2, being the first of five articles over successive weeks which dealt with tongues, healing, deliverance, and concluding with the way forward. For details of McBain's articles and others before and after, see McBain, *Fire Over the Waters*, 81 and the notes on p.207. The most substantial BU response to this request was the 1978 'Report' from the BU's Working Group and Fiddes' *Charismatic Renewal* which was a commentary he provided to accompany 'The

ance of a two-stage initiation had led to the separation of water-baptism
from Spirit-baptism in Baptist churches, with the tendency to regard the
latter as the 'real thing', while the former was treated as an optional sign.
This had led to another reason for the anomalous situation of Baptist
churches having non-baptized members, it often being seen as 'more
important to be a believers' church than a baptised church.'[131]

Earlier, Michael Walker had written, 'It could be argued that because
we have emptied baptism of its sacramental character, because we have
been afraid to believe that God acts in grace and pours out His spirit in
water baptism, we now see the sundering of water and spirit. There is now
a "second" baptism, a "second" blessing, something more that has to
be done before we are brought fully to Christ.'[132] A *Baptist Times*
editorial explicitly noted the widespread neglect of the Spirit's place in
baptism,[133] a comment which reflects that so much of the work by Baptist
sacramentalists in previous decades had not penetrated the core of Baptist
thought.

Reviewing James Dunn's *Baptism in the Holy Spirit*, Neville Clark
sketched the author's indictment of Pentecostalism's separation of Spirit-
baptism from conversion-initiation, by claiming that Spirit-baptism was
an experience which followed conversion, separating water-baptism from
faith by understanding the rite as a confession of a commitment already
made. Rather, Dunn argued, the gift of the Spirit or Spirit-baptism was
the focal point of the conversion-initiation reality which was what made a
person a Christian. The implication of this, Clark noted, was that if
Dunn's case had been made, which he believed it had, 'then infant

---

Report'. For the background and origins of 'The Report', see D.S. Russell, 'Foreword',
n.p., and p.4. The Working group comprised D. MacKenzie, E. Heddle and G. Rusling of
representing the Ministry Department, Mr J.H.Y. Briggs and D. Black representing the
Mission Department, H. Logan representing the General Superintendents, and D.S.
Russell, General Secretary of the BU, see p.41.

131 Fiddes, 'Issues of Identity for Baptists', 3, who then added, 'It is a matter of sad
irony that because it has been regarded as "Baptist" to deny any meaning to infant
baptism at all, it has become supposedly "Baptist" to make baptism of believers an
optional matter!' Earlier, also p.3, Fiddes remarked that this two-stage theology among
paedobaptist churches, 'has tended to support the time gap between baptism of infants
and confirmation', but, 'The question that arises for Baptists therefore, is whether it is
really part of our identity to find *no value or meaning in infant baptism whatever*', italics
his.

132 M.J. Walker of Beckenham, 'How Sacramental is Baptism?', *BT* March 30,
1972, 4.

133 'The Neglected Spirit', *BT* May 18, 1972, 5. Throughout 1972 there were a
considerable number of letters on the related issues of baptism of the Spirit, spiritual
gifts, Pentecostalism and the Jesus People.

baptism must go. And a great many other contemporary views must go as well—or cease to pretend New Testament sanction.'[134]

It is probably true to say that the majority of Baptists follow the evangelical line which understands baptism in the Spirit to be conversion.[135] However, several have wanted to remain undogmatic about this. John Peck noted the ambiguous use of the phrase in scripture, claiming, 'The biblical argument is not water-tight enough for the idea to be a dogma.'[136] Nigel Wright rejected the interpretation of many but not all charismatics that baptism in the Spirit has to do with empowering and equipping, and with the mainline view that it is the Spirit's work of regeneration, that is, conversion. In their place he advocated a 'fluid interpretation' which recognized 'that in the New Testament the idea...is fuller than we realise. It is a fluid term which points to the life-changing reality of life in the Spirit of God.'[137]

---

134 N. Clark, 'Baptism by water and by the Spirit', *BT* November 5, 1970, 6. See J.D.G. Dunn, *Baptism in the Holy Spirit: A Re-examination of the New Testament Teaching on the Gift of the Spirit in relation to Pentecostalism today* (SBT, 15; 1970). Clark's conclusion included criticism of much Baptist practice and views of baptism, as well as paedobaptist ones. Dunn's book was also critically reviewed by R.E.O. White, *'Baptism in the Holy Spirit*. James D.G. Dunn', *BQ* 24.2 (April, 1971), 93-94.

135 So D. McBain, 'Baptism in the Spirit', *BT* June 19, 1975, 2; J. Balchin, *I Want to Know What the Bible Says About the Church* (Eastbourne, 1979), 61-63; Fiddes, *Chrismatic Renewal*, 35; D. MacKenzie, 'Frank questions on the Baptism of the Holy Spirit', *BT* December 13, 1984, 4, which discussed F. Cooke's presidential study booklet on Ephesians, *The World at One* (1984); R.P. Martin, 'Worship in New Testament Churches', *JSNT* 37 (1989), 71, and *The Spirit and the Congregation: Studies in 1 Corinthians 12–15* (Grand Rapids, 1984), 27; P. Beasley-Murray, *Radical Believers* (1992), 15, who described baptism as 'a believer's personal Pentecost'; G.R. Beasley-Murray, 'Baptism', in Hawthorne, Martin and Reid (eds.), *Dictionary of Paul and His Letters*, 60-66, especially p.63; Dr M.M.B. Turner, Director of Research and Vice Principal of London Bible College, *The Holy Spirit and Spiritual Gifts Then and Now* (Carlisle, 1996), 44-46.

136 J. Peck, a Baptist minister, at the time Head of the Koinonia School of Christian Practice and lecturer in Hebrew and Old Testament Theology at a Suffolk College, having been a tutor at the Bible Training Institute, Glasgow (1965–78), *I want to know what the Bible says about the Holy Spirit* (Eastbourne, 1979), 110. He identified, pp.126-27, three possible uses of the term: the gospel-norm was that Spirit-baptism took place at conversion; however, in practice conversion is often followed by a period marked by worldliness which is terminated by introduction into life in the Spirit which may take the form of a definite crisis/baptism in the Spirit; or it could be used of an experience of 'self-abandonment to God' and associated with tongues-speaking, usually emphasizing enduement with power.

137 Wright, *Lord and Giver of Life*, 61. On p.62 he observed that some argue 'that all Christians have been baptised in the Spirit (i.e., have entered into new life) and also that all Christians need to be baptised in the Spirit (i.e., to enter into the experience of the Spirit's power). This may sound like saying everybody is right. Actually it is saying

While the third wave focused on other matters, chiefly signs and wonders,[138] the fourth wave has returned to the matter of initiation chiefly, as
far as Baptists are concerned, through the writings of David Pawson.[139]
Pawson presented his fullest views in his argument that Christian initiation
is a complex of four distinct 'spiritual doors': repentance towards God,
believing in the Lord Jesus, water-baptism and receiving the Holy
Spirit,[140] arguing that all four are essential for entrance into God's
kingdom. This means that many 'Christians' have been badly 'delivered' (birthed), initiation either taking years to be completed or remaining
incomplete.[141] While heralded by some,[142] he has been strongly criticized, most notably by George Beasley-Murray, who rejected Pawson's
insistence that the book of Acts is the yardstick for understanding the gift
of the Spirit, his separation of the baptism of the Spirit from the experience of Christ in conversion and his use of the accounts in Acts 8 and 19
as normative rather than exceptional.[143] Pawsons views have not found
wide acceptance outside charismatic circles, and certainly not within the
BU.

In his *Fourth Wave*,[144] Pawson discussed what he considers 'probably
the most critical difference between charismatics and evangelicals, and the

---

that the truth about the Spirit is bigger than all of us. Those who disagree over this
subject may well be stressing different aspects of the total truth.'

138 Baptist examinations of signs and wonders include D. Bridge, at the time
Warden of the Garden Tomb in Jerusalem, *Signs and Wonders Today* (1985); and most
recently Turner, *The Holy Spirit and Spiritual Gifts*.

139 It should be noted, however, that having left the Baptist ministry in 1979 for an
independent, itinerant and cross-denominational ministry, Pawson stands very much on
the periphery of Baptist life, though he does command considerable support and is held
in high regard in churches of the evangelical-charismatic wing of the BU.

140 D. Pawson, *The Normal Christian Birth: How to give new believers a proper
start in life* (1989), the main thesis being set out in pp.11-90. His ideas received their
first airing in his *Truth to Tell* (1977), 99-108, and his most recent work is *Jesus
Baptises in One Holy Spirit: How? When? Why* (1997).

141 Pawson, *Normal*, 3.

142 E.g. M. Hooton, 'The Normal Christian Birth by David Pawson', *Frat.* 228
(October, 1989), 26.

143 G.R. Beasley-Murray, 'Christian Initiation—the discussions must go on', *BT*
December 14, 1989, 17; also by D. Slater of Kingsbridge, 'Pawson on Initiation',
Mainstream Newsletter 33 (July, 1989), 12-13.

144 Pawson seems to have been the originator of this term. He regards *Fourth Wave*
as a sequel to his *Normal Christian Birth*, so *Fourth Wave*, 12. He says that *The Normal
Christian Birth* attempted a synthesis between charismatic and evangelical insights on
the single issue of Christian initiation, while the later work arises from the former one,
which it briefly summarizes, but it broadens its discussion beyond the initiation issue to
include discussion of theology, prophecy, glossalalia, worship and holiness. Pawson's
views are also set out in his contribution to the 'Explaining' series of booklets, *Water*

one over which there may be the greatest reluctance to reconsider traditional positions', and he did so by focusing on the 'two greatest gifts of God': the objective gift of his Son and the subjective gift of the Spirit, and how they relate to each other.[145] In his attempt to bring the two groups together, he exhorted charismatics to understand that receiving the Spirit is not repeated (there is no second blessing), and evangelicals that believing in Jesus is not the same as receiving the Spirit.[146] Acceptance of these two facts, and the necessary adjustments in practice, Pawson believed, would serve the process of charismatic–evangelical integration.

Derek Tidball believed that Pawson has hit the nail on the head on initiation and the other areas he discussed,[147] but Rosemary Davis objected to Pawson's line of reasoning that those who have not experienced the baptism of the Spirit do not belong to Christ and thus are not saved. She further believed that he then contradicted himself by suggesting that those who believe in the Lord Jesus are on the 'Way' and, should they die, would go to heaven. 'Have I missed something, or is he trying to have his cake and eat it?'[148] It is too early to tell whether anything will develop from this fourth wave debate on initiation,[149] though Dr David Middlemiss's detailed assessment of the charismatic movement reflects the fact that discussion of the baptism of the Spirit no longer holds the important place it once did,[150] and this observation suggests that Pawson's attempt to return the initiation debate to the centre of the charismatic–evangelical agenda has not, to date, succeeded.

Baptism (1992), which was well-received by Michael Fanstone of Frinton Free Church, 'Helpful, refreshing treatment of baptism', *BT* November 5, 1992, 11. Pawson's views and ministry have been discussed at many points by McBain, *Fire Over the Waters*, *passim*.

145   Pawson, *Fourth Wave*, 89-90.

146   Pawson, *Fourth Wave*, 90-92 and 93-96.

147   D. Tidball, 'Clear exposition of charismatics and evangelicals', *BT* April 1, 1993, 6.

148   Rosemary Davis of Redhill, Surrey, 'David Pawson's "Fourth Wave"', *BT* April 15, 1993, 6, referring to Pawson, *Fourth Wave*, 96-97.

149   Therefore, Tidball's conclusion, 'Clear exposition of charismatics and evangelicals', *BT* April 1, 1993, 6, is correct: 'Whether the vision of the Fourth Wave—the phase during which evangelicals and charismatics are integrated—is fulfilled we wait to see.'

150   D. Middlemiss, *Interpreting Charismatic Experience* (1996), in which there are only a few references to baptism in the Spirit, most of which are descriptive. Middlemiss was formerly assistant minister at London Road, Lowestoft, and then minister at Portrack, Stockton-on-Tees.

The most detailed Baptist studies of the charismatic movement have been done by Paul Fiddes. In the earlier of the two[151] he agrees with the BU's Working Party that 'baptism in the Spirit' cannot be separated from a theology of water-baptism.[152] It is here, he believes, that Baptists have a contribution to make to the theology of the Holy Spirit, though they have often failed to do so because of an impoverished understanding of water-baptism 'as no more than a human witness to faith.'[153] The 1978 report recommended that 'more direct teaching on the Holy Spirit should be incorporated into baptism/church membership classes or their equivalent',[154] to which Fiddes added that this should be set in the context of the need to teach a fuller understanding of baptism, 'so that candidates should have a higher level of expectation about what they may receive from God in their baptism.'[155] For Fiddes, water-baptism in the New Testament is truly a sacrament because it is the God-appointed meeting place for the believer who comes in faith and God who comes in grace, and this possesses a corporate dimension, for 'baptism is immersion into the Spirit and into the Church as the body of Christ.'[156]

Fiddes then took into account the contextual issue, that while in the New Testament repentance, faith and baptism 'were so closely connected in time that they clearly formed one event of Christian initiation', this no longer pertains as 'The Church as a whole today...is in the situation of having separated initial faith in Christ more widely from the act of baptism.'[157] 'Some theological development is needed then to relate water-baptism to conversion', such thinking underlying both paedo-

---

151 The earlier commentary on 'The Report' is the most relevant to the present study, but in his later work, 'The Theology of the Charismatic Movement', in D. Martin and P. Mullen (eds.), *Strange Gifts? A Guide to Charismatic Renewal* (Oxford, 1984), 28-29, Fiddes examined the theology of the charismatic movement, concluding that it 'points to the need for the mysterious and hidden work of the Spirit to be focused in a particular objective event', though no conclusive theological arguments had been offered 'for that event's being other than the usual entry of believers into the community of faith through confirmation or believers' baptism. Moreover, the theologians of the Charismatic Movement have argued impressively that there is no reason why these events should not be called 'baptism in the Spirit', whatever process of salvation has already preceded them in time.' Fiddes, p.26, also pointed out the tendency of charismatic theologians to want to hold water- and Spirit-baptism together while at the same time holding them apart as well, 'adding that the original initiation in the Spirit needs to be brought to conscious awareness in a deliberate subsequent experience.'

152 Fiddes, *Charismatic Renewal*, 30, cf. 'The Report', 6.

153 Fiddes, *Charismatic Renewal*, 31.

154 'The Report', 6.

155 Fiddes, *Charismatic Renewal*, 31.

156 Fiddes, *Charismatic Renewal*, 31-32.

157 Fiddes, *Charismatic Renewal*, 33. He immediately continues: 'Nor does it seem possible now to make them simultaneous.'

baptism and believers' baptism, it being 'the conviction of Baptists that baptism *after* rather than *before* a conscious act of faith in Christ makes most sense of the lofty New Testament claims about the grace of God given in baptism.' To understand baptism, therefore, as a mere witness of what has taken place is a wholly inadequate view of baptism.[158]

It must be admitted that Baptists have not risen to the opportunity articulated by 'The Report' and Fiddes to provide either a fuller doctrine of the Spirit or doctrine of baptism. Baptist discussions of the role of the Spirit in baptism continue to be many and varied, and, it must be added, usually brief,[159] though many continue to draw attention to this weakness in Baptist baptismal theology.[160]

---

158   Fiddes, *Charismatic Renewal*, 33, italics his.

159   E.g. M.J. Quicke, *Baptist Beliefs* (Baptist Heritage series 2; n.d., c.1982 or after), 'The Holy Spirit is intimately bound up in the repentance, trust and action which is signified in believers' baptism'; P. Beasley-Murray, *Believers' Baptism* (Baptist Basics 2; 1993), who discussed baptism as a sign of the Spirit's presence and that candidates should expect God to bless them 'anew with His Spirit', and, in his *Radical Disciples: A Course for New Christians* (Didcot, 1996), 9, he said baptism 'is often associated with the gift of God's Spirit'; D. Monkom, *John's Portrait of Jesus* (CTP, 1992), 26, where Christian baptism is 'an experience in which [Christians] *may* look for a fresh infilling of the Holy Spirit', italics added; N. Clark, *Invitation to a Conversation 9. Life in the Spirit* (Cardiff, 1997). M.M.B. Turner's article on 'The Holy Spirit', in J.B. Green, S. McKnight and I.H. Marshall (eds.), *Dictionary of Jesus and the Gospels* (Leicester, 1992), 341-51, included brief discussion of the Spirit in baptism throughout this article, though he provided detailed discussion in his 'Jesus and the Spirit in Lucan Perspective', *TynBul* 32 (1981), 3-42; 'The Significance of Receiving the Spirit in Luke–Acts: A Survey of Modern Scholarship', *TrinJ* 2 (1981), 131-58; *Power from on High: The Spirit in Israel's Restoration and Witness in Luke–Acts* (JPTS 9; Sheffield, 1996). Also more detailed are R.E.O. White, 'Baptism of the Spirit', in W.A. Elwell (ed.), *Evangelical Dictionary of Theology* (Basingstoke, 1984), 121-22, and G.R. Beasley-Murray, *The Holy Spirit* (CTP C.7, n.d., mid-1980s).

160   E.g. the anonymous, 'The Principles We Uphold', *BT* July 29, 1976, iii, 'Not enough emphasis has been given to the belief that the Holy Spirit is present in baptism bringing joy and new power to the candidates. As they give themselves to God in Christ so He gives power to them, through the Holy Spirit, to rise and walk in newness of life.' Further, 'The main thing is not how much water is used, not the method, but the condition of the one baptised.' See also P. Beasley-Murray, 'Make the most of baptism', *BT* October 23, 1980, 12.

Common Baptism[161]

While the issue of 'common baptism' has been debated since the 1950s,[162] and has been discussed within national ecumenical schemes[163] and particularly within F&O,[164] it was not until 1996 that it became an issue for British Baptists when it was raised by Bishop Michael Nazir-Ali.[165] In response, Keith Jones maintained that churches did not agree on a common baptism, and, as a member body of the CCBI, the BU did not accept the infant baptism of other traditions, even though the matter was presently under discussion.[166] Later he added, 'As Baptists we remain unconvinced about the validity of infant baptism and have a strong conviction that faith in the Lord Jesus Christ is a clearer starting point.'[167] *Believing and Being Baptized* declared that, while commendable, recognition of a common baptism was 'hardly possible', and such a desire was better expressed by the recent focus on *koinonia*.[168]

Some Baptists, however, are willing to accept 'common baptism'. In his ecumenical theology, Christopher Ellis stated that 'In facing the

---

161 Though a very recent debate as far as Baptists are concerned, this subject is examined in detail because it will be one which will probably come to occupy more and more attention as an issue within ecumenism in the forthcoming years.

162 E. Lanne, 'Baptism', in Lossky *et al* (eds.), *Dictionary of the Ecumenical Movement*, 79-80.

163 'Common baptism' figured in 'The Covenant' considered in the final report *Covenanting for Union in Wales* in the early 1970s, section 4 (a) which stated, 'We recognise the members of all our churches as members of Christ in virtue of their common baptism and common calling to participate in the ministry of the whole Church', quoted by P.H. Ballard, 'Baptists and Covenanting', *BQ* 24.8 (October, 1972), 375.

164 See *BEM*'s discussion of incorporation into the Body of Christ, II.D.6, p.3: 'Through baptism, Christians are brought into union with Christ, with each other and with the Church of every time and place. Our *common baptism*, which unites us to Christ in faith, is thus a basic bond of unity', italics added.

165 M. Nazir-Ali, Bishop of Rochester, at the third biennial CCBI Assembly, '"Koinonia"—local, national and worldwide', *BT* March 7, 1996, 3 and 13.

166 This was an allusion to *Believing and Being Baptized*. See K.G. Jones, 'Deputy General Secretary reacts to Bishop's speech', and 'CCBI delegates find evidence against "ecumenical winter"', *BT* March 7, 1996, 2. According to the former report of the session, Jones received warm applause when he said that discussions of these issues should be treated with more care and people be asked to avoid implying that things had been resolved when they had not, requesting a greater willingness to face honestly the questions which divided the member bodies.

167 Jones, *From Conflict to Communion*, 20. He proceeded to recommend the discussion of *Believing and Being Baptized* on this point and made the same point in *Ecumenical News* 2 (February, 1996), n.p., but p.1.

168 *Believing and Being Baptized*, 23 and 21.

claims of its Lord, the church is encouraged to seek the unity which comes from sharing a common baptism in a common Lord.'[169] Leslie Wenger expressed the wish, 'Would it not be wonderful if we all, of various denominations, recognised that there is only "one Lord, one faith, one baptism, one body, one Spirit"...?'[170] In the autumn of 1996, CTE released a video also entitled *Called to be One*.[171] The video included an interview with Keith Jones in which he clearly set out the Baptist position on 'common baptism'. 'Baptists, like many other Christians believe in one baptism... But the question then is, What is our understanding of baptism, what is involved in baptism, when does baptism take place?... We believe there's still much work to be done between the different traditions.' After reference to *BEM* and acknowledging that Baptists could accept much of what it said about the meaning of baptism, he continued, 'we tend to want to say we're not agreed about baptism, we recognize that we must work at that and for present we'd rather talk about our one faith in Christ as the basis of our common action rather than our "common baptism" which is a phrase we don't believe yet we all adequately understand.'[172]

---

169 C.J. Ellis, *Together on the Way: A Theology of Ecumenism* (1990), 22. This was published by the BCC to coincide with the launch of the new ecumenical bodies and was a companion volume to J. Matthews' *The Unity Scene*.

170 L. Wenger, 'Denominations need one another', *BT* November 28, 1996, 6. Though not mentioning 'common baptism', his 'with differing insights into truth and practice', in the context of the theme of his letter suggests this.

171 *Called to be One*, the video (1996), quotations have been transcribed from the video. The script was written by Geoff Crago of Milestone Communications, producers of the video, working with Roger Nunn, see 'Defining a Common Baptism', *BT* September 26, 1996, 1. The fact that Nunn was presumably the chief source of information used in the script gives added credence to the admittedly few yet clear references to the goal of a common baptism in the video. Earlier, the *Ecumenical News* had reported the ten topics identified by *Called to be One* on which sufficient convergence was needed if progress is to be made, the seventh of which was 'Unity might be expressed in a common understanding of baptism', *Ecumenical News* 4 (June, 1996), n.p., but p.3.

172 The quotation is an accurate transcription of Jones' remarks in the video. This quotation, then, is different in that it is fuller than the one reported in 'Defining a Common Baptism', *BT* September 26, 1996, 1. In the video Jones continued, 'We're conscious much needs to be done', he then referred to *Believing and Being Baptized*, in which 'we're challenging our churches to look at the issues involved there and to reflect again on how we can be of help and sensitive particularly in [LEPs]. So work continues. We've not reached a conclusion. We're on a journey together.' In the same video, Dr Mary Tanner of the Church of England's Council for Christian Unity expressed her personal vision of the future in terms of a koinonia/communion made visible by local sharing and witnessing to a common faith, and sharing a common baptism and sharing the eucharist together, a community served by a single ministry with a ministry of oversight. That her words are included in an official CTE video add weight to the view that a common baptism is firmly on the agenda of CTE.

The *Baptist Times'* review of the video opened: 'Further progress by the churches in reaching a common understanding on baptism is one of the priorities on the road towards church unity, according to...Keith Jones.'[173] This rather provocative leader prompted David Gardner to challenge the ambiguity of Jones' position. 'I would have thought that all Baptists are unhappy with the phrase "our common baptism" as a basis for church unity.' Gardner, an opponent of CTE, did not believe that the process set in motion would change direction, believing that there would eventually be an 'agreement to a form of words which keeps the participants happy, but which will be given different interpretations by the various denominations involved—another ecumenical fudge!'[174]

In a JLG paper, Dr Paul Sheppy stated that probably the majority of Baptists did not regard paedobaptism as valid and so they '(re-)baptise on the grounds that the previous event has neither soteriological nor ecclesiological significance.'[175] However, 'Baptists who do immerse those who in infancy were signed with water in the name of the Holy Trinity are charged with aspersing...the validity of the sacrament practised by their sister Churches.'[176] The 'bland assertion of Lima that we all believe in one baptism', he continued, 'was only approximate to the truth, since the baptism in which we believe is variously defined, believed in, and liturgically celebrated.'[177] In his reply to Gardner, Sheppy assured him that in his forthcoming address to the Januray 1997 WCC conference on 'Becoming a Christian: Ecumenical Implications of our Common Baptism' he would 'challenge the bland assumption behind the phrase "our common baptism".' As a committed Baptist who was also ecumenically committed, he declared, 'The two are not mutually exclusive.'[178]

The traditional view which opposes any concessions to the validity of infant baptism and confirmation was reiterated by Gardner in his reply to

---

173 'Defining a Common Baptism', *BT* September 26, 1996, 1. It then quoted the section of Jones' contribution transcribed from the video and noted above.

174 D. Gardner of Burwell, Cambridgeshire, 'Common Baptism "a fudge"', *BT* October 17, 1996, 6.

175 Sheppy, Secretary of the JLG, 'Life-Cycle Liturgies', 2-3.

176 Sheppy, 'Life-Cycle Liturgies', 3-4. He continued: 'I hope you will not find it indelicate in me if I observe that a number of my friends who were Baptist ministers and now exercise their ministry in other places have had to be "re-ordained". The validity of our orders, of our sacrament, has been impugned no less. Our effort did not do the trick. Mind you, none of us really accept one another's orders.'

177 Sheppy, 'Life-Cycle Liturgies', 4.

178 Sheppy, 'No fudge on common baptism', *BT* October 31, 1996, 6. This whole issue has not been served by such vague comments as that made by M.J. Quicke, 'The World at One. Study No.20', *BT* November 29, 1984, on Ephesians 4:5, that 'no matter how many different emphases and understandings about entering the church they all add up to one baptism.'

Sheppy, and he drew attention to two articles which detailed the 15% drop in baptisms from 1994 to 1995.[179] Gardner noted how Baptists were being encouraged to co-operate 'with any and every church of all denominations whatever their theological persuasion', adding, 'and that means we rarely talk about, let alone proclaim, our biblical and Baptist distinctives.' Those who followed the Swanwick Declaration's aim to move 'from co-operation to commitment', he derided, 'want all to accept each other's membership and each others baptism.' This would lead, he believed, to anyone converted in a Baptist church, but christened/ baptized in infancy, not being encouraged to be baptized on profession of faith, which would result in an even greater drop in the number of baptisms. He further contended that the term 'evangelism' be rescued instead of the '"fudge" word "mission"', for 'we will need to remember that we practice believers' baptism. After all, the words of Jesus say, "Go into all the world and make disciples, baptising them..."'[180]

The contemporary ecumenical movement appears to operate under the assumption that once the issue of baptism and rebaptism has been sorted out then other matters relating to ecclesiology, eucharist and ministry will more easily fall into place. *Believing and Being Baptized* noted this with the remark that 'the direction in much ecumenical debate is *from* the act of baptism *to* the nature of the Church and ministry', a fact which has led to 'Bafflement...as to why Baptists will not apparently take what is widely seen to be the "easiest" step of recognising a common baptism as the basis for unity.' However, as Baptists 'our direction of thought is *from* the nature of the church *to* the meaning of baptism.'[181] According to Fiddes, ecumenical partners who have been steadily moving towards the position of a 'common baptism' received *Believing and Being Baptized* with consternation when they realized that the majority of Baptists were still unwilling and unable to accept infant baptism and confirmation as equivalent to believer's baptism.[182] The general grass-roots Baptist

---

179 'Annual Baptisms Drop Below 4000' and 'An Open Letter from the Evangelism Office', *BT* October 31, 1996, 1 and 5 respectively. According to the former of these reports, if current trends continued baptisms might decrease by a further 20% in 1996. D. Gardner, 'Drop in baptisms', *BT* November 14, 1996, 6, drew attention to the coincidence that these reports were published in the same issue as Sheppy's letter, implicitly suggesting a correlation between what he saw as a weakening of the Baptist position on baptism and the decline in its practice. Apart from Gardner's letter, the only letter on baptismal decline suggested a re-think on evangelism given the present situation of both church and society, Dr G. Walters of Ashford, Kent, 'Baptismal decline? Rethink evangelism!', *BT* December 12, 1996, 10.

180 D. Gardner, 'Drop in baptisms', *BT* November 14, 1996, 6.

181 *Believing and Being Baptized*, 22, italics original.

182 In a conversation at Regent's Park College on December 18, 1995. The committee which drew up *Believing and Being Baptized* can be taken to represent fairly

position on 'rebaptism' is that when a person baptized in infancy requests believer's baptism most Baptist ministers will agree to such a request on the grounds of Christian conviction and conscience. The majority will baptize such a person whether or not they have made a Christian profession or not, though ecumenically there is less of a problem when a person infant baptized has not made such a profession.

With all these considerations, was it possible to affirm still the 'one baptism' of the Nicene-Constantinopolitan Creed? If such were possible for Baptists, the report asserted that it must not be taken to mean that infant baptism and believers' baptism were simply the same act, or that someone could not undergo both rites, but it could be affirmed in the sense that there 'is still one immersion into the death and resurrection of Jesus through the Spirit.' This was how the committee interpreted Ephesians 4:5's 'one baptism', seeing confirmation in Jesus' understanding of his death as a baptism (Mk 10:38-39), this being the baptism believers share in union with Christ.[183] 'There is therefore, we believe, one baptism despite diversity of practice, and this need not be reduced to a notion of "common baptism".'[184]

---

the views of the denomination in that it sought to review three ways in which Baptists would respond to the question whether infant baptism was a valid kind of baptism. The three solutions were: 1/ The Lima solution, following the 1982 *BEM* document which proposed equal validity; 2/ believers' baptism as normative and infant baptism as possessing derived validity; 3/ that infant baptism can only truly be called baptism when it is completed later by personal faith. Though the majority of the committee would follow none of these proposals, several accepted derived validity for infant baptism, and only one accepted the Lima solution, see *Believing and Being Baptized*, 13-15. This indicates the committee was split 5–3–1 respectively, a view confirmed by Dr Fiddes. Because of this, p.16, '*This report will therefore reflect the variety of view represented by these two groups* (the majority and minority views between which it had become clear that there was "a considerable amount of common ground"), in an attempt to mirror the diversity of views held among Baptists more widely, and yet at the same time affirm what is distinctive about the Baptist understanding of baptism', italics original.

183   For a different interpretation of Eph 4:5, see Cross, '"One Baptism"', 173-209.

184   *Believing and Being Baptized*, 36. The idea of 'common baptism' is to be found in the only statement formally adopted by the Canberra Assembly of the WCC in 1991, the statement on unity, *The Unity of the Church as Koinonia: gift and calling*, in the second of four elements of visible expression of the church's unity, 'a common sacramental life entered by the one baptism and celebrated together on one eucharistic fellowship', see *The Report of the Canberra Assembly*, 173, quoted in *Called to be One*, 46. Paragraph 15 of Section iii of the report from the Fifth World Conference on F&O in Santiago, 1993, stated, 'A common baptism also expresses the paradigmatic nature of the Church in the world as an inclusive community where men, women and children of different cultures and races can participate freely on an equal basis, where social and economic inequality can be surmounted, and where there is respect for different traditions and capacities, confirmed by the bonds of love for brothers and sisters and in fidelity to the Triune God', quoted in *Called to be One*, 70. This is also the goal stated in *Called to*

Called to be One acknowledged that the words 'baptism' and 'membership' clearly did not mean the same thing in all churches and therefore issued four challenges 'if they are to make their baptismal unity more visible.' First, the meaning of the word baptism and the nature of sacrament and symbol need further exploration. Second, mutual understanding of one another's processes of initiation, of which at least four patterns have been identified.[185] Third, churches should discuss their understanding of the church and membership to see whether they are mutually exclusive or complementary. Fourth, the possibility should be investigated of belonging to more than one church.[186] To churches practising believer's baptism the report suggested the cessation of admitting into church membership those never baptized; refraining from baptizing by immersion those baptized in infancy, brought up in and having confirmed their faith; re-consideration of the sense in which children belong to the church; and suggesting to all churches that a suitable rite should be developed for those already either infant or believer's baptized to reaffirm those vows.[187] It was further noted that the BU 'is not happy to speak of infant and believer's baptism as a *common baptism*',[188] though the report did say that the four challenges issued to the churches should not be seen as enough in themselves 'to assure the churches that there is a *common baptism*.'[189]

Clearly, then, a recognition of a 'common baptism' is a goal of the ICP, or at least, a significant majority within it, and that at present the BU dissents from this position. The mainline denominational position was illustrated by Ruth Bottoms, minister at Wendover Free Church and Moderator of the FUE, in her opposition to a draft of the official message from the Eighth Assembly of the WCC in Harare which claimed that 'we are brought to this newness of life, bound to Jesus and to all others baptised in the name of the Holy Trinity.' She maintained that this was not the case and that member churches of the WCC were as divided over

---

be One, 70, which speaks of the move towards a common baptism. In contrast, the Baptist response to this is seen in G. Abraham-Williams and K.G. Jones, 'The Baptist Union of Great Britain', in Welch and Winfield, *Travelling Together*, 74. Also note that, by and large, Baptists do not accept infant baptism as a variant of believer's baptism.

185 See *Called to be One*, 68: baptism on profession of faith; baptism and chrismation followed by communion; baptism, usually of infants, accompanied by profession of faith from parents/godparents, followed by a later confirmation and reception into membership; and the experience of transformation by the Spirit not marked by any outward rite. These were those identified by West in his consultative paper discussed above.

186 *Called to be One*, 69-70.

187 *Called to be One*, 70.

188 *Called to be One*, 68, italics theirs.

189 *Called to be One*, 70, italics theirs.

baptism as they were over the eucharist. Rather, 'We Baptists would want to speak of our common faith in Jesus Christ as our basis for unity.'[190]

Baptist Identity

It is almost ironic that amid all the ecumenical developments since the 1960s and the corresponding developments and new perspectives on baptismal theology and practice, there has been a growing concern for Baptist identity most of which has been non-controversial.

From the late-1960s to the end of the 1970s interest in Baptist identity was served mainly by the continuing availability of some older works and the reprinting of others.[191] But from the 1980s this was to change as new material was published in a wide variety of sources. This process was instigated at the turn of the 1980s by a number of BU reports which fuelled calls for the re-examination of Baptist principles.[192] These bore fruit in the publication of several information packs which included leaflets on baptism as well as other Baptist principles and other materials

---

190 'Baptist concerns over baptism', *BT* December 17-24, 1998, 1, see also Hilary Bradshaw, 'Giving the deep fried caterpillars a miss', *BT* December 17-24, 1998, 12. Her stand was applauded by Mr P. Youngman of Swanage, 'Brave stand on baptism', *BT* January 21, 1999, 6, and she reiterated her views in R. Bottoms, 'Where does ecumenical commitment fit into the Consultation process', *BT* November 11, 1999, 11. The view that 'we all share in the one baptism' was also asserted by P. Ballard, 'Baptists and Baptism: A Socio-Ecumenical Issue', *BMJ* 260 (October, 1997), 21, for which he was censured by R.E.O. White, 'Baptists and Baptism', *BMJ* 262 (April, 1998), 17.

191 See, e.g., S. Clark, 'Why I think this book is still a treasure', *BT* December 31, 1981, 8, who discussed the merits and value of H.W. Robinson's *Baptist Principles*, editions of which were still being printed in 1966 and available for many years afterwards. This was advertised in the *BUD* 1973-74, 18, which also listed among the titles on Baptist principles available from the BU's Publications Department—F.B. Meyer, *Seven Reasons for Believer's Baptism*, H. Cook, *What Baptists Stand For*, R.E.O. White, *Invitation to Baptism*, S.F. Winward, *Your Baptism* and *New Testament Teaching on Baptism*. A third edition of W.M.S. West's *Baptist Principles* was published in 1975, while R. Hayden, *Baptist Union Documents, 1948–1977* (1980), made available to a wide readership some of the most important BU documents since 1948, beginning with the 1948 'The Baptist Doctrine of the Church'.

192 D.S. Russell, *A Call to Commitment: Baptist Christians through the 80s* (1980), 8, which included the challenge 'to know what it means to be "a Baptist Christian" today.' Among its many proposals for action was that literature be produced including material on discipleship, post-baptism and Baptist principles, p.9. Here, Russell, General Secretary of the BU, presented a 'strategy for action', p.1, arising out of the responses made to the report *Signs of Hope* (1979). Cf. also the review of the report by B.R. White, 'Shedding light on issues that Baptists need to debate', *BT* December 31, 1981, 2.

on Baptist heritage and identity.[193] Baptist principles have been directly and indirectly discussed in histories of the Baptists,[194] in the many pamphlets whose purpose is to introduce Baptist beliefs to newcomers or inquirers,[195] and Baptist writers who have contributed numerous articles to various dictionaries.[196] In 1982 the BU adopted a logo to support its

---

193 In 1982 the 'Baptist Basics Series' was produced including seven leaflets which included P. Wortley, *3. What is a Baptist Church?*, R. Mills, *5. For those Visiting Applicants for Church Membership*, and P. Beasley-Murray, *6. Why Baptism and Church membership?*, each of which included discussion of baptism. This was followed by the 'Baptist Heritage Series' (n.d., 1982 or after), which included M.J. Quicke, *2. Baptist Beliefs*. These packs were followed by 'Baptist Basics' (n.d., [1993], see 'Baptist Union prepares definitive new information pack', *BT* September 2, 1993, 1), which included P. Beasley-Murray, *Believers' Baptism*, B. Haymes, *Why be a Baptist?*, D. Coffey, *Church Membership*, K.G. Jones, *The Lord's Supper* and M.J. Quicke, *Visiting New Church Members*. This pack was accompanied by the 15 minute *Baptist Basics Video*.

194 These include the major new series of Baptist histories which were first planned under the editorship of Ernest Payne, but edited first by Dr Barrie White until his illness caused him to retire, when he was replaced by Dr Roger Hayden. See B.R. White, *The English Baptists of the Seventeenth Century* (1983, revised 1996 by J.F.V. Nicholson); R. Brown, *The English Baptists of the Eighteenth Century* (1986); J.H.Y. Briggs, *The English Baptists of the Nineteenth Century* (Didcot, 1994); and the final volume, in preparation, by I. Randall, *The English Baptists of the Twentieth Century* (forthcoming, 2005). See also R. Hayden, *English Baptist History and Heritage* (CTP, G3; 1990), especially 97-106.

195 E.g. 'What Baptists Believe' (n.d., [c.1980s]), a small leaflet; *Who'd be a Baptist?* (Didcot, 1995), a glossy brochure, see 'Brochure to explain "Who'd be a Baptist?"', *BT* May 4, 1995, 17; *Basix* (Didcot, 1996), a small booklet; and *5 Core Values for a Gospel People* (Didcot, 1998), a glossy brochure.

196 These include G.R. Beasley-Murray, 'Baptism, Wash', 143-54; S.F. Winward, 'Baptist Spirituality', in G.S. Wakefield (ed.), *A Dictionary of Christian Spirituality* (1983), 36-38; S.F. Winward, 'Baptism. 5. Baptist', pp.62-63, and K.W. Clements, 'Baptist Theology', pp.61-62, both in J.G. Davies (ed.), *A New Dictionary of Liturgy and Worship* (1986); J.H.Y. Briggs, 'Making Disciples—Baptizing Them', in R. Banks, J.H.Y. Briggs *et al* (eds.), *The Quiet Revolution* (Oxford, 1989, originally published as *Christianity: A World Faith*, (1985)), 66-71, which discussed Baptists on pp.67-69 [this was also published in booklet form under the same title, see J.H.Y. Briggs, 'The History of Baptists on the Move', *BT* September 3, 1985, 8]; G.R. Beasley-Murray, 'Baptism. 1 Biblical Theology', pp.69-71, and R.F.G. Burnish, 'Baptism. 2. Historical and Systematic Theology', pp.71-73, R. Brown, 'Baptist Theology', pp.75-76, all in D.F. Wright and J.I. Packer (eds.), *New Dictionary of Theology* (Leicester, 1988); G.R. Beasley-Murray, 'Baptism', in Hawthorne, Martin and Reid (eds.), *Dictionary of Paul and His Letters*, 60-66; R.E.O. White, 'Baptism for the Dead', and 'Baptize, Baptism', in W.A. Elwell (ed.), *Evangelical Dictionary of Biblical Theology* (Grand Rapids, 1996), 49 and 50-53.

new corporate identity, and this was refined in 1991.[197] This domestic debate on identity has been mirrored in the EBF[198] and the BWA.[199]

In 1991 the new General Secretary and Deputy General Secretary of the BU, David Coffey and Keith Jones, instigated a year-long series of consultations held throughout the regions.[200] After these 'Listening Days', the BU Council's first ever residential meeting gave their broad approval to a ten year programme entitled 'Towards 2000' which focused on mission and strengthening the Baptist family.[201] Part of this

---

197 The logo is used on all BU material. The main components of the logo are three Christian symbols: the cross above the baptismal waters beneath which is the fish sign, which 'speaks of the Baptist distinctive practice of believers baptism', the whole logo being drawn with one continuous line. In 1991 the logo was further developed by being made elliptical 'to demonstrate our place within the world community'. Details from a BU sheet giving details of the new logo and how it can be used in printing materials, n.d., c.1991. On the logo see, 'Baptists launch new identity', *BT* September 26, 1991, 2.

198 E.g. G. Overton of Newbury, who presented a paper on Baptist identity to the EBF, a copy of which has not been obtained, see 'Consultation on Baptist Identity', *BT* October 10, 1991, 5, gave notification of the European Consultation on Baptist Identity to be held in January 1992.

199 These discussions have gone on throughout the 1980s and 1990s, see the two volumes Brackney and Burke (eds.), *Faith, Life, and Witness*, which included papers from the Commission on Baptist Doctrine and Interchurch Cooperation', including K.W. Clements, 'A Response to the Faith and Order Commission Document No.140', 48-53, and the Commission on Baptist Heritage, which included J.H.Y. Briggs, 'Baptists and Higher Education in England', 92-115, and 'Towards a Baptist Identity: A Statement Ratified by the Baptist Heritage Commission in Zagreb, Yugoslavia, July, 1989', 146-49, prepared by J.H.Y. Briggs; and W.H. Brackney and L.A. Cupit (eds.), *Baptist Faith and Witness: The Papers of the Study and Research Division of the Baptist World Alliance 1990-1995* (Birmingham, Alabama, 1995). British Baptists have presented a number of papers to these Commissions, for instance: P.S. Fiddes, 'The British Church Scene: Issues of Identity for Baptists in Discussion with Others' (1991); P. Beasley-Murray, 'Celebrating the Faith in Baptism', published in the *BMJ* 244 (October, 1993), 11-14; M.J. Quicke, 'Developing the Debate on "Baptist Identity"' (unpublished, 1992), presented to the Commission on Doctrine and Interchurch Cooperation.

200 The 'Listening Day Process' led to the report *A Five Year Plan Towards 2000* (1991). Of this N. Wright, 'Baptist Identikit', *BT* February 27, 1992, 8, wrote that the proposal of the five year plan to establish a clearer Baptist identity risks being seen as yet another dose of '"oughtery and mustery", banging the big bass Baptist drum.' Wright nevertheless stressed the importance of this, suggesting that the theme of Baptist identity be transposed into the key of mission. 'Only a church which displays the need for personal conversion and commitment as is illustrated in believers baptism will be able to call people to this conversion. Infant baptism obscures the vital truth that we must enter the kingdom of God on our own account not be smuggled in on someone else's ticket.'

201 See 'At the Baptist Union Council', *BT* March 19, 1992, 7-10. The vision of 'Towards 2000', pp.8-9, used as key-words Mission, Identity, Associating and

programme was realized in the publication of *AIM 3*[202] and Paul Beasley-Murray's *Radical Believers*.[203] This process culminated in the 'Denominational Consultation' at Swanwick in September 1996,[204] which led to the setting up of a seven-strong Denominational Consultation Reference Group responsible for monitoring progress and clarifying the issues raised.[205] Throughout the 1990s, then, Baptist identity was an important part of Baptist life, though discussions of baptism were

---

Resourcing. For the initial report of the meeting, see 'Towards 2000: A Call to Prayer for a Baptist agenda for the 1990s', *BT* March 5, 1992, 8-9. This resulted in the report *A Ten Year Plan Towards 2000 incorporating the National Mission Strategy* (Didcot, 1993).

202 *AIM 3* (Didcot, 1992) was the final manual in the *Action In Mission* programme. *AIM 1* (1988) was a step-by-step evaluation survey for use in a local church and its neighbourhood and later condensed in what became known as *AIM 1—Simplified* (Didcot, 1990). *AIM 2—Mission* (Didcot, n.d.), provided material for churches to move on from *AIM 1*. This was accompanied by N. Wright and D. Slater, *A Theology of Mission* (Didcot, 1990). In their discussion of personal conversion, Wright and Slater described baptism as the initiation rite which 'marks the end of the process of conversion and is the sign of regeneration', though it is more than a human response and a mere symbol for it is the God-appointed occasion for 'the Holy Spirit to work into the life of the person being baptised those things symbolised by baptism', p.48. Later, p.49, they stated that 'Baptism in the Holy Spirit brings us into the Body of Christ', but did not explain how this relates to water-baptism. *AIM 3* (Didcot, 1992), prepared by Dr D. Tidball, was a discipleship course for the nurture of new believers. Section 2 Part 3 discussed believers' baptism and set out the basic biblical theology of baptism as traditionally interpreted by Baptists. For those with learning difficulties BUild (The Baptist Union Initiative with people with learning difficulties) produced 4 booklets which adopted a simple picture format where words were kept to a minimum: Susan Wright, *Joining the Church* (Didcot, 1991), discussed baptism and communion.

203 P. Beasley-Murray, *Radical Believers* discussed baptism at a number of points, but chiefly pp. 9-22. P. Beasley-Murray's *Radical Disciples* was a brief, Bible-study format follow-up booklet.

204 On this see, e.g., D. Coffey and K.G. Jones, 'The Denominational Consultation' in both *BaptistLeader* and *SecCheck* nos.13 (Winter, 1995), 1-2; 'Beyond 2000—What Kind of Union?', *BT* May 9, 1996, 7; 'Questions for Consultation', *BT* May 23, 1996, 1; K.G. Jones, 'What shape the Union?', *BT* July 4, 1996, 12; D. Coffey, 'My vision for 21st century Baptists', *BT* August 15, 1996, 2; D. Dewey, 'Mission Tops Consultation Agenda', *BT* September 12, 1996, 1, and various reports on p.2; and the *BT*'s guide to the 'Denominational Consultation', *BT* October 3, 1996, 7-10, which was also published separately and mailed to all churches via their secretaries; and D. Coffey and K.G. Jones, 'Guard the Vision' in both the *BaptistLeader* and *SecCheck* nos.15 (Winter, 1996), 1.

205 'Council agrees Consultation process', *BT* December 12, 1996, 2. See also the whole issues of the *Baptist Leader* and *SecCheck* nos.16 (Spring, 1997), which provided progress reports on the Consultation, and inluded details of the seven members of the Reference Group. The Consultation proposals were primarily if not exclusvely organizational, there having been no discussion of baptism or any other issues of theology to this point.

relatively few, and those that there were were largely undertaken within Baptist ecumenical commitment.[206]

However, not all of this discussion of Baptist identity was non-controversial. That the ecumenical situation provided the undeniable context even for Baptist discussion of its own principles is reflected in the 1989 YBA Bible study booklet *Fellowship in the Gospel*. Its fourth study, while based on the Declaration of Principle, used baptism to raise three questions: what it teaches about the nature of the church; the place of children in the church family, the Kingdom and at communion; and its significance for someone who has been a committed believer for many years.[207] Only the first of these cannot be said to have been an important subject within ecumenical discussion at the time.

The ecumenical climate also provided the background for the earlier *A Baptist View* series.[208] The volume on baptism by John Matthews included a summary of the traditional Baptist position on baptism which included the statement that the practice of infant baptism had no basis in scripture, confused the true meaning of baptism and was based on false understandings of the nature of faith and the church.[209] However,

---

206   E.g. the reports *Believing and Being Baptized*, which is concerned chiefly, not with baptismal theology *per se*, but the ecumenical dilemma of rebaptism, and Baptist involvement in the Called to be One process is also explicitly ecumenical. For the ecumenical dimension of *Something to Declare* and *Reflections on the Water* see below.

207   K.G. Jones (ed.), *Fellowship in the Gospel: A series of six studies on Baptist principles and practice in belonging to the Church* (Leeds, 1989), 19, prepared by the Doctrine and Theology Group of the YBA, which comprised J.F.V. Nicholson (Convenor), General Superintendent of the North Eastern Area, I. Collins of York, D. Morris of Headingley, A. Peck of the Central Bradford Fellowship, Susan Thompson of Sheffield, and Dr H. Willmer.

208   These appeared in 1976 and 1978 under the editorship of A. Gilmore with the assistance as advisory editors of Dr Rex Mason, Senior Tutor at Regent's Park College, and P. Saunders, a tutor at the South Wales Baptist College. The ecumenical context of the series was stated in the 'Editor's Introduction' which appeared at the beginning of each volume, which ended, 'We hope...to help Baptists to a new grasp of the traditions they have inherited and to inform others of what it is that makes Baptists the distinctive people that they are', e.g., in G.W. Martin, tutor in Church History and Theology at the Scottish Baptist College, *The Church: A Baptist View* (1976), which included throughout brief discussions of baptism, but which raises nothing new or controversial. The ecumenical dimension was highlighted in the review of the first four books in the series by R.S. Smart of Darlington, 'Authority; Baptism; Church; Ministry', *Frat.* 178 (January, 1977), 25-26. See also the review 'Studies in Baptist principles', *BT* July 29, 1976, vii, reviewing also B.R. White's *Authority*, G.W. Martin's *Church*, and J.F.V. Nicholson's *Ministry*. Fiddes' *Charismatic Renewal* was the last to be published in this series in 1980.

209   J.F. Matthews minister of Swindon Tabernacle, *Baptism: A Baptist View* (1976), 16-17, the point on infant baptism is on p.17.

Matthews' personal position was perhaps reflected in his earlier statements that in the household baptisms of the book of Acts children could
have been included and probably were, and that personally he opposed
indiscriminate infant baptism, suggesting he accepted discriminate infant
baptism.[210] Himself a committed ecumenist, Matthews accepted the
sacramental nature of baptism, maintaining that it was the combination of
the human response to divine action which made it so.[211] His position is
seen most clearly in his opposition to rebaptism. Neville Clark had proposed that it was not the practice of the early church which is determinative for present day practice but the theology of the early church.
From this Matthews argued that the church stands in between the announcement of the Kingdom of God in Jesus and the completion of the
Kingdom of God in the parousia. Its place in the middle meant 'that
everything the church does is in some sense provisional or interim', it
pointing backwards to the historical events of the cross and resurrection
and forwards to the fulfilment of those events, baptism being 'the sign
given to the church to show this inseparable link with Christ's own living,
dying and rising and also with the hope of a creation restored and
complete.' This did not mean the Baptist case was unassailable 'since
baptism is a sacrament of the gospel and not of our faithful response to
the gospel', and such a view clearly affected the Baptist view of
rebaptism. 'If baptism is interim and not final, if it always points beyond
itself to some future fulfilment, then one can hardly justify a second
baptism on the ground that the first was provisional to a greater
degree!'[212]

In his *Radical Believers*, Paul Beasley-Murray sketched Baptist beliefs
on baptism, for which he was highly commended by Brian Haymes,
though 'Not every Baptist will agree with the author's way of seeing and
saying things', though the book's style and temper was a 'welcome
invitation to a discussion about the church and Christian discipleship.'[213]
While it is unclear precisely which matters Haymes was thinking of,
clearly non-sacramentalists would be uncomfortable with Beasley-

---

210 Matthews, *Baptism*, 7 and 15 respectively. Matthews, with his wife Ruth, were
prominent leaders in the establishment of the ecumenical Central Churches Swindon.

211 Matthews, *Baptism*, 19. He continued, 'The promises of God meet with the faith
of the Christian community and with the personal faith of the believer and the whole is
signified in symbolic ritual. God has so ordered the life of his community that he does act
uniquely through baptism.'

212 Matthews, *Baptism*, 20-21, quotations from p.21, referring to Clark, 'The
Theology of Baptism', 306-26. Later, Matthews, *Baptism*, discussed rebaptism at greater
length, pp.24-26. Matthews also defended the connection between baptism and
membership and opposed their frequent separation in Baptist churches, pp.26-28.

213 B. Haymes, 'A Baptist voice with integrity and open-minded commitment', *BT*
December 3, 1992, 14.

Murray's association of baptism with the gift of the Spirit and its accompaniment with the laying on of hands,[214] while others would perhaps object to his assertion that baptismal practice should be so reformed that only in exceptional cases would it be possible to be baptized without becoming a church member.[215]

The most contentious treatment of Baptist principles was by Dr Brian Haymes,[216] in fact his work was the catalyst for a particular phase in the Baptist identity debate.[217] Haymes' discussion of baptism is almost entirely confined to two pages within his larger discussion of the doctrine of the church, as the former arises out of the latter.[218] He rejected the

---

214 P. Beasley-Murray, *Radical Believers*, 15-17.

215 P. Beasley-Murray, *Radical Believers*, 14.

216 B. Haymes, Principal of the Northern Baptist College, *A Question of Identity: Reflections on Baptist Principles and Practice* (Leeds, 1986). Haymes set out his thesis right from the start, p.1: 'I propose...to set forth and defend a thesis. It is in three parts; (1) that there are important features of Christian identity to which Baptists have born witness as a way of being Christ's Church. (2) that these features are worth developing and guarding because *it is for more than our own good* that Baptists be true to their inheritance. (3) that we are presently in danger of neglecting these features and in some instances actually betraying them.' The added italics shows consciousness of the ecumenical context in which Baptist identity has had to be discussed. On the same page he drew attention to his own ecumenical commitment and experience, then added, 'It is my personal experience and observation of others that ecumenical involvement does strengthen denominational awareness. My suspicion is that you will find the most convinced Baptists as Baptists in the various forms the ecumenical movement takes.' He then mentioned E.A. Payne and D.S Russell as examples, to which can be added the many leading figures discussed in Cross, 'Service to the Ecumenical Movement'.

217 So D. Slater of Kingsbridge and Secretary of Mainstream, 'Editor's Note', in Slater (ed.), *Baptist Identity* (Mainstream, 1987), 5, who reported that the papers included in that volume came out of the Mainstream consultation held in September 1987 organized by the mainstream Executive 'as a response to the debate about Baptist identity currently being raised within the denomination.' N.G. Wright, 'The Baptist Way of Being the Church', in Slater (ed.), *Baptist Identity*, 41, directly identified Haymes' work as sparking off this particular round of the discussion, which was encouraged by B. Green, General Secretary of the BU. Mainstream returned to the theme of Baptist identity at their January 1995 conference, see 'Rob White: "Baptist distinctives"', *BT* February 2, 1995, 14, though baptism was not mentioned in the report.

218 Haymes, *Question of Identity*, 6-12. Concluding his opening chapter he reiterated his position, p.5: 'My argument is that there is such a thing as Baptist identity and that it is important for the good of the whole church that it be preserved. I do not think that such identity consists in particular doctrines in themselves, such as believers baptism or the gathered church, but in their unity, a way of being Christ's church in the world.' Wright, 'Baptist Way of Being the Church', 41-45, challenged Haymes' ecclesiology by advocating a link between Baptist and Anabaptist ecclesiology, objecting to Haymes' use of 'the Baptist way of being the Church' with its openness to other ways of being the church, whereas Wright, an advocate also of restorationism, contended

charge that believers' baptism stressed more the human response while
infant baptism stressed God's grace, and described the Baptist interpretation of baptism as merely a personal act of witness to faith as
'selling the Baptist understanding short', for believers' baptism 'is an
affirmation of the saving grace of God. As such I think we Baptists ought
to be much bolder in thinking of the sacramental nature of the action.'
Baptism is a fruitful meeting point between God and his church, 'his
church' because more than the individual candidate is involved.[219] Of
closed membership, Haymes said '"in spirit Yes, in law no"', for the
former would make a religious rite the basis of Christian fellowship,
something which Paul rejected in his Galatian letter. The relationship between baptism and church membership 'is too important to be overlooked.' Those who stressed the individual nature of baptism offered an
unbalanced interpretation for there are no private deals with Jesus. To be
baptized into Christ is to be baptized into his body, making the baptized
members of his church, 'and for Baptists that always takes the form as the
local fellowship of believers.' He charged Baptists who baptize without it
leading to the privileges and responsibilities of membership as not having
grasped the full significance of baptism, the church or the fellowship of
Christ. 'When this happens we are in serious risk of loss of identity, not
just as Baptists, but as Christians.'[220]

Opposition came almost entirely from Mainstream.[221] What is surprising about this debate is the relatively marginal place baptism
occupied,[222] though Derek Tidball did criticize him for having given
insufficient attention to believer's baptism.[223] The reason for this is not

---

that, 'The New Testament presents us with a picture of variety in unity. The unifying
factor is not how the Church was organized in this or that particular culture but the New
Testament theology of the Church and its ministry', pp.44-45.

219 Haymes, *Question of Identity*, 9-10.

220 Haymes, *Question of Identity*, 10. On p.7 he referred to baptism as the sign of
entry into the church and as such is for believers only.

221 See Slater (ed.), *Baptist Identity*, which included contributions from D. Tidball,
Senior Pastor of Mutley, Plymouth, B.R. White, Principal of Regent's Park College, A.
Campbell, research student at Spurgeon's College, N.G. Wright, lecturer in Biblical and
Historical Theology at Spurgeon's, S. Ibbotson of Peterborough, and G.R. Beasley-
Murray, who was the one contributor from outside of Mainstream.

222 Evidently baptism was not among the contentious issues of this particular
debate, which was understood by Mainstream to be between a theological liberal,
Haymes, and themselves, conservative evangelicals, who believed they represented the
majority within the denomination, so Slater, 'Editor's Note', 5.

223 D. Tidball, 'A Response to "A Question of Identity"', in Slater (ed.), *Baptist
Identity*, 12. It can be said that the same applies to Mainstream's volume. While they, in
turn, might reply that they were responding to Haymes' discussion, it should be added
that the contributors frequently go beyond Haymes' work and had ample opportunity to
rectify Haymes' 'omission'. E.g., in only two other places did Tidball refer to baptism:

wholly obvious. It could be due to the relative absence of discussion of baptism by Haymes, or a reflection of its non-contentious status in what was an internal Baptist controversy, or a reflection of its declining importance in Baptist theology. Or it could be a combination of these.

1996: Three Important Studies

Three important studies appeared in 1996 which provide a fitting climax to Baptist thought on baptism in the twentieth century and each reflect the impact on Baptist thought of the Christian initiation debate.

Baptism and Rebaptism

Believing and Being Baptized has within in it the potential of being one of the most important documents of the twentieth-century on the Baptist understanding and practice of baptism. Building on nearly ten decades' discussion and development in the theology of initiation[224] it paves the way for future Baptist reflection both within the BU, the BWA and national and international ecumenism.[225] It was further intended to help ecumenical partners understand what is often perceived as Baptist awkwardness over baptism within ecumenical discussions, the majority of paedobaptists viewing the Baptist position as pedantic and disruptive of further developments. It stated, 'there remains a need to examine further

---

in mentioning Haymes' discussion of baptism and membership in one sentence, p.8, and in a discussion starter question on p.17 about whether believers' baptism will become optional if Baptist understanding of the church has a clear centre but blurred edges. The only discussion of baptism of any size is provided by Beasley-Murray's concluding essay, 'Confessing Baptist Identity', 83-84, which examined the contemporary situation with little reference to Haymes. He interestingly discussed baptism as the sacrament of the gospel of the Kingdom.

224   The very first line of the text reads, 'In this century Baptists have produced a good deal of material on the theology of baptism, *affirming that the fulness of baptism* is expressed when the person baptized is a believer making a conscious profession of faith', *Believing and Being Baptized*, 7. The italicized section reflects awareness of the ecumenical situation which is the context in which and for which this document was prepared.

225   The fruit of three years work by a group of nine members of the Doctrine and Worship Committee under the chairmanship (and editorship) of P.S. Fiddes, for the background and context of the document, see *Believing and Being Baptized*, 7-8. It was presented to and unanimously accepted by the BU Council on November 7-8, 1995. The committee comprised Dr Fiddes, Mrs Faith Bowers, Committee Secretary, G. Abraham-Williams, General Secretary of the Covenanted Churches in Wales, D. Coffey, ex officio, C.J. Ellis, B. Haymes, Dr P.A. Hicks, Director of Ministry at LBC, K.G. Jones, D. McBain and N.G. Wright, D. Rowland of Botley, was also part of the committee in the earlier days of the project.

the issues that arise when someone is baptized who has already been "baptized" as an infant. Is this "re-baptism", or baptism for the first time? Should it be encouraged, discouraged or even prohibited in an ecumenical situation? What is the relation of the two rites to each other, to salvation and to church membership?'[226]

While the majority of the committee were able to accept that grace and faith could be recognized as present at all stages of Christian nurture 'in different forms and proportions', they could not, however, 'regard anything but believers' baptism as *baptism* in the proper theological meaning of the term.' The rite of infant baptism, therefore, could not be regarded as 'baptism' because not enough of the New Testament understanding of baptism could be applied to it.[227] What the report did, then, was advocate the mutual recognition of initiation into the church of Christ of those baptized as infants and confirmed, while firmly dismissing the possibility of a 'common baptism'.[228] This marks a significant shift from that advocated throughout the larger part of the twentieth century, where the actual act of believer's baptism has been understood to be one of the major stumbling blocks to ecumenical progress, and this position

---

226 *Believing and Being Baptized*, 7. These issues are not new and have existed within Union churches since the seventeenth century, but among Baptists more intensely since the mid-1960s and the rise of LEPs. The immediate background to *Believing and Being Baptized* is also, more narrowly, the completed Baptist–Methodist *Concordat* of 1991 and the Baptist–URC baptismal policy discussions.

227 *Believing and Being Baptized*, 17, italics theirs. See the whole of pp.17-20, 'Dimensions of believers' baptism not present in infant baptism.' In the same way that believer's baptism was seen to be in accord with the New Testament rite of conversion-baptism (so p.10, 'the act of baptism is *normally* to be received near the beginning of entrance upon Christian discipleship', thereby, p.14, possesses 'normative status'), so too the method of immersion has normative status, though in exceptional cases such as 'age or infirmity or handicap' we 'must surely focus on baptism itself rather than the particular mode.' While immersion is normative because it portrays a 'going down' into death with Christ and a 'coming up' in resurrection, sprinkling can symbolize the pouring or anointing of the Spirit, p.29.

228 The key to the whole document is summed up in the statement that, 'Baptists can share in a *mutual recognition of others as being members of the Body of Christ*, regardless of the mode of initiation in their church tradition. Being in the Body of Christ, and not baptism itself, is the basis of unity. The work of the Holy Spirit, indwelling those who are in the Body of Christ, is recognized experientially in others through their exercise of faith and other spiritual gifts and by the production of Christ-like fruits of life, not by the evidence of having taken part in a particular ritual act', *Believing and Being Baptized*, 21. Later the committee affirmed, 'While we believe that the *proper* place for baptism is at the moment of making personal allegiance to Christ, we can affirm that God freely uses a variety of traditions to incorporate persons into the Body of Christ', p.22.

of mutual recognition of initiation is consonant with the BU's official involvement in CTE and CCBI.

The report's discussion is based on the assumption that Baptist churches practise open membership, the committee taking the opportunity to ask 'seriously whether a membership "closed" to all except those baptized as believers takes sufficient account of the work of God's spirit among all the Christian churches.' This again is indicative of another shift in emphasis since the turn of the century when open membership was widely regarded as an aberration and a betrayal of true Baptist principles. The committee acknowledged the constraints of churches' Trust Deeds, and clearly approved of closed membership churches' adoption of associate membership, asking them 'to consider how they might find creative ways to reduce the effect of this distinction between kinds of membership, as far as is possible within legal restraints.' They commended open membership or closed membership with a supplementary roll as a 'normative practice', though they recognized that different people would come to different answers to this matter and that 'what is not freely accepted may have little spiritual significance.' Open membership churches which accepted candidates who had never been baptized by any means were strongly criticized: 'What had originally begun as a desire not to "unchurch" others who had previously been members of other churches, has become a lack of conviction about baptism for the "unchurched".' There then followed an urgent appeal for the reappraisal of baptism within Baptist church life and practice, urging, 'that churches re-consider the place of baptism within Christian discipleship, and do not any longer accept without baptism those who have not as yet been initiated in any way into membership of the Church of Christ.'[229]

The net result of all this was that it needs to be 'openly admitted that we are living in a situation where there are two views of baptism, and where this is likely to be the case into the foreseeable future.' Therefore, Baptists, the committee believed, ought to live and work together with other Christians as sensitively and with as much mutual affirmation about baptism as possible, something possible only because 'the reality of the Church as the Body of Christ does not depend upon a particular practice of baptism', for baptism falls within what they describe as 'penultimate' as opposed to 'ultimate' issues.[230]

The implications of all this for pastoral practice are considerable, and the committee set out to provide guidelines based on the theological foundations they had set out which would take into account the many

---

229 *Believing and Being Baptized*, 28-29.

230 *Believing and Being Baptized*, 24. That baptism is a secondary conviction was also accepted by A. Campbell, 'Romans Through New Eyes: Part 2: The Real Issue', *BMJ* 243 (July, 1993), 13.

different backgrounds and spiritual needs of those who will seek baptism within a Baptist church. Five potential procedures were outlined. First, baptism followed by membership would apply to someone converted from a totally secular background. Second, someone infant baptized but never confirmed could also be baptized, though evidence of the Spirit's work since infancy might allow a profession of faith with the laying on of hands with membership following. Third, someone baptized in infancy and brought up in a Christian family and congregation would be offered an affirmation of the work of God with the laying on of hands in place of baptism, which would be allowed if the candidate persisted. Fourth, if the same situation as scenario three pertained but confirmation had also taken place, stronger encouragement would be given to recognize the work of God in the whole process of Christian nurture, and a further act of laying on of hands for a renewal of the Spirit and deeper union with Christ at the moment of reception into membership would be offered, though baptism could still be administered if the request was being made in all good consience. The only exception to this exercise of individual freedom of conscience would be where the local congregation had willingly and voluntarily accepted restraint in its baptismal practice due to ecumenical involvement. Finally, the request for baptism by one already believer's baptized, even though little meaning could be found within the original act, should be declined, and the minister should explain that baptism involved not solely the subjective faith of the believer, but the enabling grace of God. Here, the overt sacramentalism of the committee came to the fore as they explained that 'Whatever the degree of faith and trust the candidate might have, God can still use the act of baptism to begin to draw someone to himself, and a believer should be encouraged to look back and find that prevenient grace of God at work.' To such an enquirer, the minister and congregation should encourage a public confession of faith with the laying on of hands for a new filling with the Spirit.[231]

The committee defended itself against the charge that the middle three guidelines contradicted their previously declared position that believers' baptism alone was baptism in the fullest sense, on the grounds that the guidelines were offered 'because we recognize different stages in the

---

231 *Believing and Being Baptized*, 24-29, quotations from pp.27-28. On the fifth procedure, the committee defended their recommendations from the charge of inconsistency with the previous scenarios with the justification that, 'In the case of someone receiving believers' baptism there is at least the *potential* for exercising some personal trust in God', for, looking back later, a person may in fact incorrectly be judging the original baptism as 'empty' or 'meaningless'. 'Moreover, when God offers his grace in the baptism of someone of responsible age, rather than a very young infant, he gives "enabling grace" in the sense of helping someone to make personal decisions and to meet demands laid upon his or her life.'

journey of salvation and affirm the freedom of God to use whatever outward acts he will to draw people to himself' and 'we want to share in the healing of a broken church.'[232]

The reason why other Christian churches regard anything resembling rebaptism as scandalous is the connection of baptism with entrance into the church. To 'rebaptize' appears to un-church those baptized in infancy. Such problems, the committee believed, could only by met by pastoral sensitivity and the following of the guidelines they had set out. But, they maintained, there are other ways of belonging to the church than membership. Some may be 'in the Body of Christ' in a different kind of way, before being baptized as believers, and such need not be considered as excluded. Thus, incorporation also was to be understood as a process rather than as a single moment of crossing a threshold. 'The fact that we permit baptism, as believers, of those baptized in infancy (for those who request it) may well remain an offence, but it is an offence that derives from the sadly broken state of the Church Universal.'[233]

When Dr Fiddes presented the document to the BU Council in November, 1995, the ensuing debate revolved around the recognition that the document itself also marked a stage on a journey not the arrival at a destination.[234] Dr Arnold Baines expressed his appreciation for the report, speaking of baptism as a sign and a reality: the sign was of water which signified death and resurrection, the reality being justification by faith. The one negative comment reported came from Roger Nunn who argued that it was time that the assertion that infant baptism was no

---

232 *Believing and Being Baptized*, 28.

233 *Believing and Being Baptized*, 37-38. The issue of 'The child and the Church' is addressed on pp.39-47. The most recent discussion of this is W.M.S. West, 'The Child and the Church: A Baptist Perspective', in W.H. Brackney, P.S. Fiddes and J.H.Y. Briggs (eds.), *Pilgrim Pathways: Essays in Baptist History in Honour of B.R. White* (Macon, GA, 1999), 75-110, who discussed *Believing and Being Baptized* on pp. 107-09, but see also the earlier G.R. Beasley-Murray, 'The Child and the Church', C. Ingle (ed.), *Children and Conversion* (Nashville, 1970), 127-41, and 'The Theology of the Child', *ABQ* 1.2 (December, 1982), 197-202.

234 The view that baptism is a process and that faith is a journey has been taken up more and more by Baptist writers since the 1950s when the focus shifted to Christian initation, particularly those who seek to discuss baptism within the ecumenical context. E.g. Ballard, 'Baptists and Baptism', 22, 'The baptismal process has been...extended: a movement *that starts at birth and moves through to the consummation of the Kingdom.* There may be many stages, each appropriately marked—but *faith is a journey.*' The italicized phrases are those objected to by White, 'Baptists and Baptism', 17, on the grounds that on that principle baptism 'ceases to be the celebration of a wonderful revelation newly discovered and to be explored lifelong, and becomes merely the first, unconscious step on a long, vague, candle-lit pilgrimage in search of some truth to believe and hope to hold on to, that must constantly change to match the uncertain social and intellectual climate of the unbelieving world.'

baptism should be dropped, despite the findings expressed within the report itself. *Believing and Being Baptized* was unanimously accepted by the Council,[235] and can be taken as the 'official' position of the BU on the issues discussed.[236]

In his review, Alec Gilmore believed that *Believing and Being Baptized* marked progress in four areas. He praised the differences of approach to rebaptism, 'Opposition and argument have made way for understanding and sensitivity'; noted the pastoral exceptions in baptismal practice, remarking, 'Now it seems possible to distinguish theology and practice'; welcomed the 'positive encouragement to be more creative in the use of biblical metaphors to point towards different ways of belonging to the Church'; and that closed membership churches were urged to consider whether they adequately account for 'the work of God's spirit among all Christians', while open membership churches were urged not to permit the unbaptized into membership. Overall, however, Gilmore was disappointed on the grounds that 'there is so little fresh material and so little change in approach' in fifty years or so of conserted work.[237]

The Declaration of Principle

The four Principals of the English Baptist Colleges presented their contribution to 'the current debate on Baptist identity' and as a document to be considered in preparation for the Denominational Consultation in September 1996.[238] The Principals took up the language of covenant as

---

235 'Document on "re-baptism" marks a stage on the journey', *BT* November 23, 1995, 2. Dr Baines was representative of the Buckinghamshire Association. It is clear from the *BT* report that initially the Council was only being asked to 'receive' not 'accept' the report, but it is evident that after the intervention of A. Peck, Secretary of the YBA, and others, the Council, in the end, did accept it.

236 *Believing and Being Baptized* formed the basis for Faith Bowers, 'Baptism: A Baptist Perspective' (a paper presented to and circulated by the Society for Ecumenical Studies, 1996), and its treatment of infant dedication services was briefly discussed by D. Bridge and D. Phypers, *The Water That Divides: A survey of the doctrine of baptism* (Fearn, Ross-shire, 2nd edn, 1998), 157-58. It is also discussed, along with *Reflections on the Water*, by B. Haymes, 'Further Reflections on the Baptismal Waters' (CTS-NABPR; June 1999).

237 A. Gilmore, 'Baptism on the ecumenical agenda', *BT* April 9, 1998, 12.

238 The words are D. Coffey's, 'Foreword', in Kidd (ed.), *Something to Declare*, 6. The authors stated: 'We believe that the Declaration, as it stands, is an important affirmation. We have no desire to change it but wish that it be better known and understood because we believe something important is here for our present and future life.' The study was based on the current revised edition of the Declaration of Principle (1938). This was followed by Sparkes, *Constitutions*, which provided the history of the BU's constitutions and declarations of principle going back to the original constitution of 1813. In 1904, at the suggestion of J.H. Shakespeare, the Declaration of Principle had

the basis of the BU,[239] affirming that the Declaration is a 'covenant document' which was more than adequate as 'The Basis for this Union'.[240] While they declined to see the Declaration as a confession of faith[241] they did see it as theological, identifying an authentic expression of Baptist ecclesiology. 'We cannot fail but notice its crucial trinitarian reference to baptism as baptism into the life of God.'[242]

On the second Principle,[243] dissatisfaction was expressed with the standard threefold reasons offered for the significance of believers'

---

taken on the form of the threefold structure of the Great Commission (Mt. 28:18-20), see Sparkes, *Constitutions*, 21; Kidd (ed.), *Something to Declare*, 20-22. The pattern of the Great Commission is followed throughout the Principals' study, Kidd (ed.), *Something to Declare*, 27-52, which sets out their discussion of the three sections of the Declaration.

239 The use of covenant to explore the horizontal relationship of believer to believer was earlier used in *The Nature of the Assembly and the Council of the Baptist Union of Great Britain* (Didcot, 1994), prepared jointly by the FUE Committee and the Doctrine and Worship Committee. On the objections to this horizontal usage and its development, see *Something to Declare* 12-15. The concept of covenant had earlier been explored in *A Call to Mind: Baptist Essays Towards a Theology of Commitment* (1981), and *Bound to Love: The Covenant Basis of Baptist Life and Mission* (1985), both written by K.W. Clements, R.L. Kidd, P.S. Fiddes, R. Hayden and B. Haymes, who examined the theology of commitment and covenant respectively, neither of which, however, discussed baptism at any length. E.g., the 'Introduction' in *Call to Mind*, which referred to 'Christian initiation' as a 'means of identification *with* Christ by faith', p.8, italics original, while Haymes, 'On Being the Church', 59, discussed baptism as 'a fruitful sign', a meeting place between God and man; and in *Bound to Love*, Kidd, 'The Documents of Covenant Love', 48, who spoke of 'the sacramental worship of baptism.' Only two works had previously discussed explicitly the theme of covenant, K.C. Dykes, Principal of the Manchester Baptist College, 'The Biblical Doctrine of Church and Covenant', *Frat.* 76 (April, 1950), 16-18, and Ballard, 'Baptists and Covenanting', 372-84, though, again, in neither did baptism figure prominently.

240 Kidd (ed.), *Something to Declare*, 54. The Declaration of Principle opens 'The basis of this Union is:'.

241 Kidd (ed.), *Something to Declare*, 15-16 and 24-25.

242 Kidd (ed.), *Something to Declare*, 24. They continued, p.25: 'By Christ, and in the Spirit, we come to the Father. We are baptised into the life of the triune God and live to share God's mission.'

243 The Declaration's statement on baptism was taken by the Principals to be a fusion of Mt. 28:18-20, 1 Cor. 15:3 and possibly Acts 2:38. This section was prepared by M.J. Quicke, Principal of Spurgeon's College, though all the sections were agreed on by the whole group and finally edited by Kidd, Principal of Northern Baptist College. See 'Editor's Introduction', Kidd (ed.), *Something to Declare*, 8-9, for the background of the study. The authors noted that the ordering of the Declaration of Principle placed believers' baptism as a secondary issue dependent on the primary convictions of the absolute authority of Christ, the revelation of scripture and the liberty of each church under the Spirit: 'Our strongest Baptist distinctives lie in our ecclesiology which emerges from our obedience to Christ and our listening to Scripture. It is the radical view

baptism because Baptists so concentrated on Christ's command, Jesus' example and the practice of the early church that they failed to explain the connection between Christian baptism and the person and work of Christ: 'Practice can be emphasized at the expense of New Testament theology.'[244] The greatest strength of the second principle is that it combines Matthew 28:18-20 with 1 Corinthians 15:3's powerful christ-ological statement, which refused to allow this to happen: 'By all means we should begin with the Great Commission but it is essential that we move on into deeper places of the salvation of Christ and how this relates to baptism itself.'[245] Baptism is immersion in water '*into*' not just '*in*' the name of the Trinity, which, they believed, indicated 'how much Christian baptism is a personal movement with dynamic incorporation into fresh commitment.' The very word *into* strongly suggested a '"coming-into-relationship with". Something powerful is happening both to the individual concerned, but also to the whole community which itself belongs to the Name.' Baptism into 'the Name of the Father, and of the Son, and of the Holy Ghost' enabled seeing 'the act of believers' baptism in its profound dimensions as incorporation into rich fellowship with God. Here there is a participation in life in God, a sharing in divine life where water in baptism, and baptism in the Spirit clearly inter-weave.'[246] This baptism into the Name also provides evidence of ownership, and is also a profession of repentance towards God and faith in Christ, for 'Here is the totality of new birth and new life which im-mersion in the Name and by the power of the new owner demonstrates', it being a call to a new lifestyle.[247]

Use of 1 Corinthians 15:3[248] emphasizes that 'the christological heart of baptism is not related to any one single moment of Christ's life. Rather baptism relates to the whole redemptive action of God in Christ involving the cross with his dying for our sins, the burial, and the

---

of the church, rather than a particular view of baptism that is critical for Baptist principles. Only when we recognise the priority of the Baptist way of being church, can we then make a declaration about the significance of what believers' baptism means about belonging to Christ and joining his church', p.37. The Declaration of Principle has also been discussed by N. Clark, *Invitation to a Conversation 10. Belonging and Believing* (Cardiff, 1997), who did so with particular reference to baptism on pp. 10-13.

244   The fact that in the twentieth century there continued to be the maintenance and propagation of a depleted theology and practice of baptism reflects the distance that exists between the most eloquent theologies of baptism and grass-roots belief.

245   Kidd (ed.), *Something to Declare*, 39.

246   Kidd (ed.), *Something to Declare*, 40-41.

247   Kidd (ed.), *Something to Declare*, 41-42. It was this point in particular which was highlighted by G.R. Beasley-Murray in his highly commendatory review of the book, '*Something to Declare*', *BQ* 37.2 (April, 1997), 99-100.

248   Particularly 'that Christ died for our sins according to the Scriptures; was buried, and rose again the third day.'

resurrection.' The second clause of the Declaration uses this passage to define the nature of saving faith in Christ, for it widens the focus beyond just the repentance and faith of the baptized to embrace the whole work of Christ.[249] Baptism, then, is more than a sign, for 'We should anticipate that the Holy Spirit may both give and be given in baptism', as 'In Scripture, everything that is attributed to faith can be attributed to baptism also: union with Christ, participation in his death and resurrection, becoming a child of God, giving of the Spirit, inheritance of the kingdom and salvation.'[250] The Principals endorsed *Believing and Being Baptized*'s description of the interaction between grace and faith as a journey/process which varies from person to person. What is common to the development of all Christians is the three tenses of salvation: *have been* saved, *being* saved, *shall be* saved. 'Baptism is then regarded as a decisive moment in the process of being saved, whenever the process of salvation actually began.'[251] The Principals concluded that by its combining part of the Great Commission with the life and work of Christ 'this clause provides a dynamic basis for Baptists as we go on working and thinking through our baptismal life and witness together.'[252]

Nigel Wright applauded the study though he felt that it highlighted the deficiencies of the Declaration which he believed needed rewriting. On baptism he accused them of 'some fancy footwork to minimise the absolutism of this clause', which, at face value, leaves Baptists and others baptized as believers as the only genuinely baptized people in Christendom. Further, as it defined baptism as necessarily immersion the Mennonites were also excluded. 'Most of us would hold views more nuanced than this. But by a deft movement the Declaration is absolved of its absolutism by redefining the meaning of the word "is". So clause 2 becomes a norm rather than an absolute.'[253]

---

249 Kidd (ed.), *Something to Declare*, 43.

250 Kidd (ed.), *Something to Declare*, 44. The Principals concurred with *Believing and Being Baptized*, 9, which stated: 'As a person comes in faith to the baptismal pool, the triune God meets him or her with a gracious presence which transforms his or her life. Of course, a relationship between the believers and God has already begun before the moment of baptism, but this is now deepened in a special moment of encounter.'

251 Kidd (ed.), *Something to Declare*, 44-45.

252 Kidd (ed.), *Something to Declare*, 45.

253 N. Wright, 'Declaration of Principle', *BT* August 29, 1996, 6. The second part of this two-part examination of the book was by Dr E.J. Hale of Northampton, 'Declaration of Principle', *BT* August 29, 1996, 7 and 12, who criticized the booklet's position on covenant as unbiblical.

A Radical Departure

Reflections on the Water[254] is a radical departure as far as English Baptist work on baptism is concerned in that it is deliberately less biblical and more theological[255] in its approach,[256] its aim being to raise the question of what believers' baptism says about the nature of God and the world.[257]

---

254 Written by six Baptists and one Anglican, *Reflections* was the fruit of a six year period of discussion and mutual reflection, the essays having been designed as a sequence, though this did not mean the contributors agreed on everything, see Fiddes, 'Introduction', Fiddes (ed.), *Reflections*, 5. *Reflections* benefits from the addition of a reflection on the essays by the Anglican, Prof. Christopher Rowland of Oxford University, who described himself as in 'critical solidarity' with the contributions and himself 'an erstwhile crypto-Baptist who has never entirely shed these sympathies', p.6.

255 This departure from the norm of a biblical approach is made explicit by Fiddes in his 'Introduction', 2, 'Though this is not...a polemical volume, the Baptist essayists do believe that the reflections can best be seen when it is believers who are baptized... The writers are so enthusiastic about the richness of meaning and experience in believers' baptism, that they are bound to point out that this is why Baptists baptize believers *instead of* children, rather than *in addition to* children. In this way they hope to make a contribution to the ecumenical debate about baptism through a different strategy from the usual cross-currents of argument about scripture and tradition', italics his. The 'reflections' referred to in the first sentence of the quote are set out on p.1, 'As an event rooted in the material world and in human community, which expresses salvation in Christ and immersion into the very Spirit of God, baptism will reflect the image of the triune God, and it will reflect aspects of society and nature that are His creations. It is these implications that the writers want to follow up. They believe that baptism offers a crucial perspective on God, the natural world, the church, social groups, and politics.' Ellis, 'Baptism and the Sacramental Freedom of God', 43 n.5, also made this explicit: 'Here this exploration takes place within a discussion of historical theology, but a thorough treatment would need to interact more fully with the Bible.' If past experience is anything to go by, this admission will either/or or both/and limit the impact of the book among Baptists and be the cause of criticism.

256 As well as the contributions by Ellis and Fiddes discussed under 'Sacramental Interpretations' above, R. Hayden contributed a short history of what happens in the practice of believers' baptism, 'Believers Baptized: An Anthology', 9-21. B. Haymes, 'Baptism as a Political Act', 69-83, developed Fiddes' use of 'conflict' as one of five motifs connected with baptism, in his argument that baptism into Christ has ethical consequences which are both personal and social: an event with political significance. R.L. Kidd, 'Baptism and the Identity of Christian Communities', 85-99, explored how Baptists can overcome the exclusiveness of believers' baptism, developing his idea that as a 'living sign' and a mark of Christian identity baptism acquires new meanings in different cultural contexts. Hazel Sherman, 'Baptized—"in the name of the Father and of the Son and of the Holy Spirit"', 101-16, examined the implications of sharing in the life of a personal God. These were followed by C. Rowland, 'A Response: Anglican Reflections', 117-34, and Kidd's 'In Conclusion: Continuing the Dialogue', 135-37.

Its intended ecumenical significance was brought out by Roger Hayden's reference to the writers' attempt 'to speak about baptism in a different way from the usual ecumenical debate. We aim to place baptism in the context not only of the church but also of the wider society and the natural world, and we believe that this could prove creative, not just for Baptists, but for the whole Church of Christ.'[258]

The tone for all that follows is set by Fiddes and his remark that the first six contributors 'are all Baptist ministers, and they gladly affirm that for them the gracious activity of God and human response to His gift of salvation is *best* focused in the baptism of believers, that is, in the baptism of Christian disciples who can make their own profession of faith.'[259] The authors' position here reflects the minority though growing position among Baptists that believer's baptism is parallel to infant baptism and confirmation after conversion.[260]

Bridge and Phypers concluded their revised *Water That Divides* with a discussion of baptism in the postmodern world, which they characterize as altogether 'denying the reality of objective truth... If it feels good then it must be good. If it feels right, it must be right, for me, though not

---

257 Fiddes, 'Introduction', 1. He explained that these 'wider realities...can be seen *reflected in* these waters. As an event rooted in the material world and in human community which expresses salvation in Christ and immersion into the Spirit of God, baptism will reflect the image of the triune God, and it will reflect aspects of society and nature that are His creations', italics his. It is these implications which the writers follow up. A decade earlier Clements in 'Baptism', 20-21, had written, 'The exposition of baptism in BEM stresses the universal implications for the Christian and the church in the life of the world, the sign of a new life and a new world in the midst of the brokenness of the old, a liberation into a community where the old divisions are being transcended, and a way of life where the will of God is to be realized in every sphere of activity. Relatively few of the British responses have made explicit reference to these dimensions of baptism. The impression overall is that the chief concern about baptism lies in the traditional areas of the relation of the baptized to Christ and to the church, and of the churches to each other, rather than in relation of the baptized to the life of the world as a whole. None of the responses, it appears, reflected on what the ethical dimensions of baptism specifically are in Britain today in our own context of conflict, violence and deprivation... Perhaps reflection on the ethical dimension will be more evident in the "reception" process rather than the "response" stage.'

258 Hayden, 'Believers Baptized: An Anthology', 20.

259 Fiddes, 'Introduction', 1, italics added. This is immediately followed by, 'But in fact all denominations of the Christian Church, not just Baptists, practise the baptism of believers.' This is too absolute, as the Quakers and Salvation Army do not practise any form of baptism.

260 Fiddes, 'Introduction', 1, later writes, 'As society becomes more secular, or multicultural, many of those coming into Christian faith will inevitably be coming within the fellowship of the Church for the first time, and will be baptized as believers. It may well be that the *normal* mode of baptism will soon be as it once was in the early days of the Church, when it was a minority group in the pre-Christian Roman Empire.'

necessarily for everyone else.' They asserted that Christians must deny such postmodernist affirmations, yet admitted that 'we are deeply affected and half-consciously influenced by them', commenting on how important feelings have become in contemporary Christianity when compared with previous generations' (specifically the 1940s and 50s) search for sound doctrine.[261] Yet they found one positive contribution of postmodernism in that its 'distaste for the rational and the verbal, has nevertheless done a service by restoring the value of the visible, symbolic, tangible and sacramental', and it is at this point that the authors discuss *Reflections on the Water*. They began with Fiddes' statement that the 'Water in baptism is not merely a visual aid to help us understand various spiritual concepts; in its sheer materiality of "stuffness" it actually communicates the presence of the transcendent God. A created thing provides places and opportunities for a transforming encounter.'[262] Further, Bridge and Phypers believed that postmodernism encourages Christians to explore God's action in baptism anew, 'not in the old context of faith versus religious work, or national solidarity versus separated church, but in the categories crying out to be explored today', which include a society driven, dehumanized and enslaved by market forces, and for those marginalized for econmic, sexual, social or racial reasons.[263] As postmodernism mistrusts uniformity and regards diversity highly, Bridge and Phypers also welcomed Richard Kidd's proposal of a process of 'letting go' which might have the effect of releasing people 'to discover meaning in the diversity of baptismal principles and practices, and that enables them to celebrate that diversity rather than struggle against it.'[264]

However, Bridge and Phypers were by no means uncritical of post-modernism, for on its rejection of metanarrative (the big story) in favour of 'my narrative', they contended that baptism addresses both. They believed that 'we need to explore (together)...the way in which baptism brings together personal story and metanarrative.' In baptism 'we share our personal testimony. "This is how I found God, and this is how I (and my family?) intend to behave because of that." But also in baptism we re-affirm in words and symbol the Big story of Creation, Fall, Incarnation, Crucifixion, Resurrection, Ascension and Holy Spirit, which

---

261 Bridge and Phypers, *Water That Divides* (2nd edn), 171.

262 Bridge and Phypers, *Water That Divides* (2nd edn), 175, citing Fiddes, 'Baptism and Creation', 58.

263 Bridge and Phypers, *Water That Divides* (2nd edn), 175.

264 Bridge and Phypers, *Water That Divides* (2nd edn), 177, citing Kidd, 'Baptism and the Identity of Christian Communities', 87. See the whole of Bridge and Phypers' discussion of *Reflections* on pp. 175-80.

would still be true in the absolute sense, even were no-one to be found believing it at the moment.'[265]

It is impossible to predict the impact *Reflections on the Water* might have long-term on the future development of Baptist thought. However, on the basis of the basic direction of Baptist thinking towards a greater openness to discriminate infant baptism and confirmation as a legitimate alternative mode of initiation into the church, it possesses great potential. But if past experience is anything to go by, many Baptists, the majority of whom are conservative evangelical, are not likely to be happy with its progressive theological approach or its sacramentalism and could well regard it as a piece of esoteric theologizing and give little further thought to it.

Conclusion

Twentieth-century Baptist baptismal theology and practice, then, effectively concluded with three important studies, each of which clearly reflect the fact that Baptist thought on baptism has not only been influenced by ecumenical and theological developments, but has increasingly been seen to provide a Baptist apologetic for the continuation of believer's baptism within the context of the British church at the close of the twentieth century. *Believing and Being Baptized* is representative of the attempt by Baptists to address the major contemporary ecumenical problem which has arisen because of the diversity of views on Christian initiation, namely rebaptism, and it was written for those Baptists involved ecumenically, containing little that is likely to interest non-ecumenically-minded and involved Baptists. *Something to Declare* is evidence that Baptists are seeking to address the contemporary situation without losing their heritage or compromising their principles. Finally, *Reflections on the Water* is proof that Baptist theologians are not content to be merely reactive in their thinking on baptism, nor are they stuck in a timewarp simply restating the arguments of past generations, but that they wish and are able to think creatively, and therefore able to contribute towards the developments which will take place in both baptismal theology and practice in the twenty first century. It is also worthy of note that each of these volumes is the result of group study and reflection. The fact that many of the contributors to these three volumes have been involved in at least one of the others, and all of the writers are, to varying degrees, either actively involved in or open to ecumenical developments, further supports the contention that the ecumenical dimension has been and continues to be the primary in-fluence on Baptist theologies of baptism and it is ecumenically-minded

---

265   Bridge and Phypers, *Water That Divides* (2nd edn), 178-79.

Baptists who are producing what work there is on baptism. By the close of the century responses to the three documents have been minimal, which could suggest a relative lack of interest in baptism, despite the renewed interest in so-called 'Baptist Identity' being stressed by the BU in the mid-late 1990s, or it could simply be because all three are recent publications and there has been little time for any response.

CHAPTER TEN

The Practice of Baptism: 1900–1999

This chapter will seek to illustrate the extent to which the practice of baptism was affected by the theological and ecumenical developments which took place during the twentieth century.

Introduction

In 1910 W.T. Whitley rued the fact that, 'Our actual practice as regards baptism itself is not recorded in any history, but is traditional and handed down by eye-sight.' He continued: 'this is a singular omission, and a chapter on what really occurs, and on the variations in practice at various times and places, is badly needed.'[1] While there have been a number of essays and orders of service written discussing and setting out contemporary practices[2] such a study as Whitley envisaged has never been produced.[3] The result of all this is that there are many important

---

1   W.T. Whitley, 'The Baptist History We Need (Continued)', *Frat.* os 4.3 (September, 1910), 75.

2   G.P. Gould and J.H. Shakespeare, *A Manual for Free Church Ministers* (n.d. [1905]); F.B. Meyer, *Free Church Service Manual* (n.d. [c.1911]); Aubrey, *A Minister's Manual* (n.d. [1927], revised 1940); D.T. Patterson, *The Call to Worship: A Book of Services* (1930); Payne and Winward, *Orders and Prayers* ; Gilmore, Smalley and Walker (eds.), *Praise God*; *Patterns and Prayers*. It is worth noting that *Come Let Us Worship: A Book of Common Worship for Use in Free Churches*, published by the Kingsgate Press in 1930, with a preface by and so probably edited by F.C. Spurr, contained no service for baptism, though it did contain one for the Lord's Supper. This is surprising after the manuals by Gould and Shakespeare, and Meyer, each of which, though prepared for use in Free Churches, did include a baptismal service for believers. The first articles to deal with this issue were Bryan, 'Preparation, Administration and Visitation', 65-78; B. Green, 'The Authority for Baptising', *Frat.* 119 (January, 1961), 19-22; various parts of Gilmore (ed), *Pattern of the Church, passim*; J.R.C. Perkin, 'The Interviewing of Candidates for Baptism and Membership', *Frat.* 135 (January, 1965), 23-2. However, these articles discussed contemporary practice and alternatives not the history and development of the practice of baptism.

3   The only partial exception to this is Burnish, *The Meaning of Baptism*, especially pp.146-66. This study examined in detail Baptist catechetical material

questions which cannot be properly answered, leaving us with an incomplete picture of the pre-baptismal preparation, the service itself and post-baptismal care. The extant evidence is often incidental and has to be gleaned from a wide variety of sources. Therefore, a caveat on all statements must be made that the evidence adduced for any particular practice of baptism cannot necessarily be taken to have been normative. However, especial weight has been given to those writers whose position put them in a position to have widespread knowledge of denominational practices. Even the use of oral tradition has its limitations, as it too can be highly selective and subjective, and errors occur, particularly relating to date, especially the further back the memories go. With this in mind, however, an attempt has been made to indicate baptismal practice and how some Baptists have sought to apply their theologies of baptism.

Pre-Baptismal Preparation

There always appears to have been some sort of pre-baptismal procedure to ascertain the fitness of a candidate. In the twentieth century this took a number of forms. In 1928 R.W. Thomson[4] was interviewed by two deacons who ascertained his suitability for membership and the sincerity of his desire for baptism.[5] In other places the interview would have been taken by the minister. A different and probably complementary pattern was followed in the Downs Chapel, Clapton, which, every few years, held a series of special services lasting a week to ten days, intended to quicken and deepen the spiritual life of members, drawing outsiders in and bringing youngsters to a decision for baptism and church membership.[6]

---

produced between 1960 and 1980 and so partially filled the lacuna identified by Whitley, though it must be noted that Burnish used only a selection of the most common studies. Burnish's most recent historical study is 'Baptismal Preparation under the Ministry of St John Chrysostom in Fourth-Century Antioch', in Porter and Cross (eds.), *Baptism*, 379-401.

4   All recollections from R.W. Thomson, who was, after five pastorates, Minute and Committee Secretary of the BU from 1958–60, Assistant General Secretary of the BU from 1960–71 and Secretary of the Psalms and Hymns Trust from 1958–77, are taken from a recorded interview conducted in September 1990.

5   It was normal practice that interviews for church membership were conducted by several deacons, and it appears that this procedure was often followed with regard to an applicant's suitability for baptism. See A. Newton, Treasurer of the LBA, 'The Duties of Deacons and the Method of Their Election', *BT&F* July 11, 1913, 523.

6   West, *To Be A Pilgrim*, 9-10. Other meetings too were held, including mid-week Young People's Meetings and mid-week services, during which baptism was one possible subject among many. Shortly after his settling at Bugbrooke and Heyford, probably around early 1929, Ernest Payne himself organized a Wednesday evening young people's class which provided a steady procession of candidates for baptism and church membership, no doubt following the pattern of his earlier experiences of such groups. It

However, by far the most common procedure has been to use baptismal classes.[7] These have usually been led by the minister and once satisfactorily completed the baptismal service follows, though some have warned that attendance at such classes should not automatically lead to baptism.[8] Baptismal preparation classes have been undoubtedly the norm, though they have varied in length and content,[9] and the importance

---

is unlikely that Payne was alone in doing this, see West, *To Be A Pilgrim*, 39. While Baptists have always stressed that baptism is a dominical command, they have nevertheless tended to leave the decision to be baptized to the individual—a position which, though widespread, has seldom been written down—who then seeks the agreement of, usually, the pastor. See Dr R. Allaway of Wood Green, London, 'Why you should be a Church Member', *BT* September 16, 1999, 5, 'When you and they feel ready, we will welcome you by baptism (if you are not already baptised) and by fellowship in the Lord's Supper.'

7   R.W. Thomson believed that baptismal classes were not common early in the century. However, it should be noted that his knowledge is mainly of those areas in which he served as minister, in London and the north Midlands, and there is a certain amount of evidence which suggests that baptismal classes were more widespread than he and others believed, though exactly how widespread it is not possible to determine. E.g. in 1927 Robinson, *Life and Faith*, 93 and 98 n.1, spoke approvingly of baptismal classes, saying that they were held 'wherever a Baptist minister faithfully discharges his duty', though it was a duty often neglected by ministers. He pressed that they should be held occasionally when needed, giving instruction as to church membership and discipleship, baptism and the Lord's Supper, and in this the minister would follow 'no prescribed form.'

8   L.H. Marshall, 'Baptists and Church Membership', *BT&F* October 31, 1924, 712, warned against making the act of joining the church too easy, expressing his opinion that 'Compulsory attendance at a Church preparation class and baptism at a public service are obstacles that may quite reasonably be placed in the path of the young aspirant to fellowship with the Church of Christ.' It would seem reasonable to infer that the church preparation class spoken of by Marshall contained some teaching on the nature and importance of baptism.

9   Bryan, 'Preparation, Administration and Visitation', 67, expected such classes to last from 3 to 6 months, a view which had considerably changed twenty years later, when West, 'Baptist Church Life Today', 35, envisaged the need for only 3 to 4 classes before baptism and 'a greater number afterwards to make clear to the new church member the responsibilities of belonging to the Church.' Payne, 'Baptism and Church Membership among the Baptists', 172, noted the content of these classes as extending 'over many weeks', covering the main Christian doctrines, the principles of Christian conduct, the cultivation of personal religion and the special tenets of the Baptists. White, *Biblical Doctrine of Initiation*, 162-63, proposed that the capacity of the hearer should always govern the length of instruction, and that this would be followed by a course of more advanced instruction which would last indefinitely. In 1981, Burnish, *Meaning of Baptism*, xiii-xiv, surveyed 330 Baptist ministers on the material and practices they adopted. The subjects used in the 'syllabuses' either before or after baptism were set out on pp.146-47, and his breakdown of the responses revealed that the number of meetings held before baptism could vary from 1–4 to 10+ and that the duration of pre-

attached to them is reflected by the increasing number of study materials published[10] and privately prepared,[11] and also the care and innovation used.[12] Many of these studies have combined baptismal preparation with preparation for membership[13] and have often also included more general material on Christian discipleship.

While baptismal preparation classes have remained the norm, several have challenged them on the grounds that such a practice is unbiblical, and, in turn, have themselves been criticized.[14] George Beasley-Murray maintained that as in the New Testament baptism was the climax of conversion and, as the gospel preceded doctrine, so baptism should precede

---

baptismal classes could be between 1–6 months, with 'Others' (unspecified) also mentioned and others noting that they varied, p.223 n.4. Burnish, pp.146-66, also provided a detailed study of both the theology and liturgy of baptism as reflected in the most widely used Baptist catechetical material from 1960–1980.

10   The publication of such study materials appears to have arisen largely since the 1950s and has increased significantly in number over the last two decades as the Christian book market has grown rapidly. See Winward, *New Testament Teaching on Baptism* (1952), revised, updated and edited by M. Quicke as *Countdown to Baptism: The New Testament teaching on baptism in daily readings* (1995), and also Winward *Your Baptism: A booklet for the instruction of candidates for baptism and church membership* (1969); J.R.C. Perkin, *Divine Encounter: An Outline for Discussion of Believer's Baptism* (1965); White, *Invitation to Baptism* (1962), and *Christian Baptism: A Dialogue* (1977); *Church Membership* (1972) and *To Be A Christian* (1981), both published by the Education Committee of the EMBA; D.F. Neil, *The Way of Christ: A study booklet for new Church members* (1973); F. Rinaldi, *Stepping Out. Preparing for believer's baptism* (1985), a Bible Society 'Beginnings' study booklet; *AIM 3: AIM Discipleship* (1992); P. Beasley-Murray, *Radical Disciples* (Didcot, 1996). One of the most widely used booklets in baptismal preparation has been *Believe and Be Baptized* (1970) by the Brethren writer Victor Jack, see, e.g. J.J. Brown's endorsement of it, 'Booklets for Witnesses...', *BT* March 29, 1973, 4. See also S. Gaukroger of Stopsley, Luton, *Being Baptized*, which is a popular practical guide intended to help baptismal candidates in their personal preparation and also for ministers to use as a basis for preparation classes.

11   Burnish, *Meaning of Baptism*, 223 n.4, noted this practice of ministers preparing and using their own material.

12   E.g. R. Burnish, 'Early risers in the Early Church', *BT* August 18, 1983, 4, suggested that fresh ideas, perhaps drawn from the baptismal practice of the early church, might serve to make the preparatory period before baptism even more spiritually significant and encouraging to the candidates.

13   This was advocated by, e.g. West, 'Baptist Church Life Today', 34-35. Liturgically this is witnessed to by a service incorporating baptism with reception into membership at the Lord's Table, often accompanied with the laying on of hands. On this see 'Liturgical Developments' below.

14   West, 'Baptist Church Life Today', 35, 'Large numbers of Baptist members have come into the Church with all too little preparation. Some, it transpires, have been baptized without any preparation at all and have received little teaching afterwards.'

teaching.[15] Though a number have advocated and practised baptism immediately after conversion, they have been few, even though they have sought to be true to the New Testament.[16]

---

15   Beasley-Murray, 'The Sacraments', 3-7. He argued. p.5, that if Baptists feared to baptize converts straightaway, then they needed to recognize that in doing so they had changed the nature of baptism. The New Testament declared that it was the transition of the believer from one world to another, from life estranged from God to life in Christ, and whatever else baptism might bring a year after conversion, it could not bring that. To teach that would be to head for Romanism. But once baptism was regarded as part of conversion, the moment of supreme surrender rather than the expression of a believer's obedience, Baptists would again be free to teach the New Testament doctrine of baptism. L.J. Newman of Truro, 'A Baptismal Candidates Complaint', *BT* April 8, 1948, 6, concurred, urging that belief was the sole requirement for baptism. Preparation classes and visitation for church membership were necessary, but the test for believer's baptism was surely, 'If thou believest with all thy heart, thou canst.' Beasley-Murray developed his views on immediate baptism in his 'The Church of Scotland and Baptism', *Frat.* 99 (January, 1956), 9, where he accepted the report's claims that baptism was a dying with Christ, a union with Him, a recreation in Him, a subjection to His total Lordship over body and soul, only on the condition that 'baptism and conversion be viewed as an indivisible unity of experience.' See also his 'The Saving Experience', *BT* May 7, 1959, 8-9, 'The Spirit is There', *BT* December 10, 1959, 8, and *Baptism Today and Tomorrow*, 37.

16   'An Impressive Baptism', *BT* October 28, 1943, 5, reported that after baptizing four candidates, W.R. Watkins baptized a married woman who had responded to his appeal at Zion, Forge Side, Blaenavon. See also Channon, *Much Water*, 52; Winward, *New Testament Teaching on Baptism*, 33, 'Baptism should follow on conversion without undue delay', commenting on Acts 16:25-34. This practice was, however, repudiated by Bryan, 'Preparation, Administration and Visitation', 66, 'Better a man should not be baptized than that he be baptized in a hurry, with an imperfect grasp of what it means, and then should fall away.' Channon disagreed, *Much Water*, 20-21, arguing that prompt obedience to baptism would lessen the likelihood of a person falling away; Emily Venis Robinson of Bromley, Kent, 'Adequate Preparation for Baptism', *BT* July 4, 1946, 8, believed that the response to an invitation given at the end of a service should be a private talk with the minister or an experienced member and not immediate baptism. 'Let's have a world-wide day of baptism', *BT* September 6, 1990, 1 and 9, reported a service at Coombe Bissett, Salisbury, led by Pastor Ken Davies, in which three were baptized who had been through preparation classes, but a further seven were baptized following an appeal for baptism. This service was arranged to co-incide with the mass baptisms at the 16th BWC in South Korea, see 'Korean Baptismal Service', in Wendy E. Ryan (ed.), *Together in Christ: Official Report of the Sixteenth Congress* (McLean, n.d., (1990 or 1991)), 91-96, [a photograph at the front of the book claims that 8,000 were baptized]. See also 'An Unusual Baptizing Service', *BT* August 22, 1929, 636, when, after baptizing those prepared for baptism, D. Hayes invited others who 'desired publicly to confess Christ in Baptism' to come forward, and a further fourteen were baptized immediately; and 'Bonus baptism', *BT* June 10, 1999, 16.

The most contentious and still unresolved issue is who decides the fitness of a candidate for baptism.[17] Many have maintained the trend evident in the nineteenth century of separating baptism from both the church and membership.[18] They have, though, been strongly challenged by others who have maintained that the application is to be submitted to the church because, in most instances, membership is regarded as following baptism, or that the minister has desired their own judgment to be confirmed by the church.[19] Bernard Green argued from the observation that the apostles baptized as leaders of the church authorized by Christ, therefore baptism was a church ordinance,[20] and that visitors should be carefully chosen and prepared for their task.[21]

17   West, 'Baptist Church Life Today', 36-37, discussed the various procedures.

18   E.g. Williams, *Principles and Practices of the Baptists* (2nd edn, 1903), 34-35, remarked that on the whole Baptist churches did not interfere with the minister's freedom in baptizing those who asked for baptism on profession of their discipleship, adducing support from Acts 8–9. He added, 'there is nothing in the nature of baptism to make the consent and approval of the church necessary to its validity; and that evangelists may properly claim the right, which was unquestionably exercised by evangelists in the apostolic age, to baptize any individuals who may make to them a credible profession in the Lord Jesus Christ.' See also L.R. Smith, 'A Baptismal Candidates Complaint', *BT* April 8, 1948, 6, according to whom the only suitable interviewer was the minister, as this was a matter between a believer and Christ, and the Pastor was the only one deemed to have sufficient authority to examine a believer's profession of faith.

19   Payne, 'Baptism and Church Membership among the Baptists', 171. See also White, *Biblical Doctrine of Initiation*, 310 and 313, who argued that the church alone, being the recipient of the authority of Christ, should decide whether to grant baptism in individual cases, and also his *Invitation to Baptism*, 56. West, *Baptist Principles* (3rd edn, 1975), 33, noted with disapproval that some churches allowed people to be baptized at the discretion of the minister without reference to the church meeting, then, at a later date, would ask the meeting to decide the suitability of that person for church membership. 'It is doubtful, in the extreme, whether this reflects the practice of the Apostles—certainly it is against the church practice from the second and third Christian centuries.'

20   B. Green of Mansfield Road, Nottingham, 'Authority for Baptising', 19-20. According to Green the pattern to be followed ought to be: upon conversion, a person would ask for baptism and be seen by the minister who, through personal interview and/or enquirer's classes, ascertained the genuineness of the confession. The enquirer's name was then taken to the church through the deacon's and church meetings, and a visitor or visitors were appointed whose task was to obtain the person's testimony, which was then passed on to the church, and to commend the person to the church. At this stage, others and the minister could speak on the person's behalf, then the church would accept the application or not. 'This ordering ensures that everything is, as it should be, in the setting of the life of the church. Baptism thus becomes in a real way a sacrament of the church, because the minister at no point acts in his own name but in the name of the church. From the start it is the church which is involved.' Also on the necessity of the church's approval for baptismal candidates, see Middlebrook, 'Baptism and the Church',

A lesser and also unresolved issue is what is the appropriate age for baptism. Consistent with the belief in *believer's* baptism and their doctrine of the church, many have held that when someone is old enough to believe they are also old enough to be baptized, though there have always been a significant number of opponents. Proponents of the former view stress the necessity of faith not age,[22] often referring to 'the years of discretion',[23] and would have whole-heartedly agreed with R.G. Ramsey's

---

55; Pike, *Under Christ's Control*, 23. At the reception into membership, which ideally followed baptism and preceded communion, Payne and Winward, *Orders and Prayers*, 138-39, suggested the minister address the congregation: 'Beloved brethren: In the name of the Lord Jesus Christ, and in accordance with the decision of the Church Meeting, we are now to receive into membership...'

21   Green, 'Authority for Baptising', 21-22. Green noted that the office of visitor was under attack, some churches having dispensed with them altogether, others questioning their necessity. Green found biblical justification for visitors in the roles played by Ananias and Barnabas in introducing Saul to the church (Acts 9), and 'Although we cannot argue from this incident that a church visitor was appointed, it is clear that some discussion took place about Saul and his conversion before he was received into the church. The development of the office of visitor within our Baptist churches derives from such records.' 'Baptism then takes place on the authority of Christ, given to the church and expressed through the action taken on its behalf by the minister and visitors, as authorised by the church meeting.' Three valuable by-products followed: a fuller meaning to baptism; a stronger conception of church membership; and a truer understanding of the pastoral responsibilities of the church. Green also stated that he would not withold baptism from someone if they and the church were sure 'as far as is humanly possible' that the candidate was genuinely converted. With this assurance, the church would be able to give its blessing and welcome, and the candidate could proceed at once to baptism and reception into membership. Perkin, 'Interviewing of Candidates', 23, advocated the combined visitation for the purpose of baptism and membership, and criticized those churches who took a more casual approach to this matter, stressing that their appointment required careful consideration, and that interviews be thorough and meaningful and reports frank and helpful. On the responsibilities of visitors see, e.g. J.O. Barrett, *Suggestions for Visitors to Candidates for Church Membership* (1970), a copy of which has not been located [on Barrett see E.A. Payne, *A 20th Century Minister: John Oliver Barrett, 1901–1978* (privately printed, n.d.; and E.A. Payne, 'John Oliver Barrett, 1901–1978', *Frat.* 183 (March, 1978), 27-30]; and F. Bacon, *Church Administration* (1st edn, 1981), 44-45.

22   E.g. C.F. Aked, minister of Fifth Avenue Baptist Church, New York, formerly of Pembroke Chapel, Liverpool, 'The Place of Baptists in the Life of the World', *BT&F* June 12, 1908, 415; C. Williams and W.T. Whitley, *A Baptist Catechism* (n.d.), 10; Tymms, *Evolution of Infant Baptism*, 500-01; F.C. Spurr, 'A Baptist Apologetic For To-day. IV—Our Present Positive Message', *BT* November 5, 1925, 784; C. Brown, 'Dr. Whale and Infant Baptism', *BT* February 19, 1942, 88; Pike, *Under Christ's Control*, 10; Mr R. Terry, 'The proper age for baptism?', *BT* August 8, 1974, 6.

23   E.g. F.C. Bryan, 'The Sacraments', in Bryan *et al, Things Most Surely Believed*, 72. That this line of reasoning has a lower, though unfixed, limit is reflected in the anonymous writer who queried the baptism of a six year old asking whether they could

statement that, 'as soon as a response has been secured, which is an intelligent, if simple, acceptance of the Gospel, the individual has reached the stage at which the New Testament says baptism can be administered.'[24] When a youth has been baptized many have distinguished between baptism and participation in church business,[25] though George Beasley-Murray declared that, whatever the age for baptism, 'the time for joining the church is surely at baptism', because there is no theological, scriptural justification or even practical necessity for its delay, for 'To be baptized to Christ is to be baptized to his Body. And to be accepted by Christ into his church, but not by the local church in which one is baptized, would be preposterous.'[26] Others have avoided discussion of a specific age for practical and pastoral reasons, preferring instead to look at each case on its own merits.[27]

While the view that faith not age is determinative for baptism has dominated the written sources throughout the century, much practice is unwritten and many pre-teen youths have been deferred from baptism

---

have reached 'years of discretion', see 'Baptism', *BT* July 14, 1988, 11. Southern Baptists are known to baptize children at this sort of age, a practice which has not been repeated in Britain.

24   Ramsey, 'Baptism and the Great Commission', 37. Gaukroger, *Being Baptized*, 17, stressed that it was not adult baptism but 'the baptism of those who are committed to following Jesus and who want to be obedient by being baptized', and that these could be teenagers or children 'but they could not be babies, because babies are incapable of such commitment.'

25   Mountain, *My Baptism*, 121. The unresolved nature of these issues is reflected in Anon., 'Should children be church members?', *BT* January 30, 1997, 4; P.I. Taylor of Brackley, 'Should children be church members?' and R.J. Giles of Waterbeach, 'What do we mean by church membership?' both in *BT* March 13, 1997, 13; and Helen Wordsworth of Dunchurch, 'Baptism, flexibility, service, conflict and youth', *BT* March 11, 1999, 12..

26   G.R. Beasley-Murray, 'A Baptist Interpretation of the Place of the Child in the Church', *Foundations* 8 (April, 1965), 157-58. After discussing various arguments for the right age for the baptism of the young, for whom alone age was a problem, he concluded, 'There is no theological bar to a child with a faith being baptized, and in a secularized world that is loaded against a life of faith in God there is much to be said for taking the yoke of Christ in early days.' Thus, there existed no 'proper age for a declaration of faith', if by that was meant 'a standard age at which to be baptized and join the church. The age for a declaration of faith is the time when one has a faith to declare, and that varies immensely.' True faith had to be discerned, and the difficulty that this brings to ministers led Beasley-Murray to appeal to the idea of the catechumenate, pp.158-59. See also his *Baptism Today and Tomorrow*, 106-07, and for a similar position, West, 'Baptist Church Life Today', 37-38.

27   E.g. Channon, *Much Water*, 22 and 24, who, generally speaking, felt it inadvisable to baptize anyone until they were in their teens, though it would be 'folly to lay down any hard and fast rules.'

until teenage years.[28] In recent years psychological and developmental studies have been used to justify such a position. Terry Griffiths emphasized a converted and committed discipleship, therefore late adolescence was the generally normative age at which baptism was appropriate, it being 'an inappropriate response for children to make.'[29] Griffiths rejected the argument of an 'age of understanding' or 'years of discretion', usually reckoned to occur in early adolescence (12–15 years), stating that these fit better with the individualistic and atomistic spirit of western culture, which has also contributed towards the acceptance of the modern practice of divorcing baptism from membership, something he also rejected. Instead, he favoured the emphasis on reaching an 'age of responsibility' (between 15–18 years of age). The decision to baptize in adolescence involved both the individual and corporate dimensions, an owned faith being prerequisite, and for there to have been some resolution of the quest for personal identity marked by the abandonment of an affiliative faith and for cognizance to have been taken of the consequences of this once-for-all act. 'Youthful desire and enthusiasm are not enough to qualify for baptism.' While each case needed to be judged on its own merits as individuals varied greatly in their maturity, his argument indicated late rather than early adolescence.[30] In agreement, Paul Beasley-Murray declared his own view that 'it is not sufficient for a prospective baptismal candidate to love Jesus as their Saviour—rather they must be able to own him as Lord', which itself should involve some understanding of the call for discipleship to be the costly way of the

---

28   E.g. Jackie Cross (née Butler) who sought baptism at Wallingford, Oxfordshire, when she was converted aged nine but baptism was constantly put off until she was twelve. Her father, the church secretary at the time but now minister at Ferndown United Church, Bournemouth, Godfrey Butler, reported that such a delay of baptism was the norm. Details from discussion with Mrs Jackie Cross and Godfrey Butler. Though just one example this seems to be common practice which goes back many years. Fullerton, *Souls of Men*, 117, noted that Baptists stand for believer's not adult baptism and reported that he had baptized young people both at and before the age of nine.

29   T. Griffith, *The Case for Believers Baptism* (1990), 51-55, quote p.51. P.W. Martin of Watford, 'Towards a Baptist Ecclesiology Inclusive of Children' (TCDTBW; August 1999), adopted a similar approach, which included the idiosyncratic suggestion that children could share the eucharist prior to their baptism. For an older example of the study of 'child conversion', which interestingly made no reference to baptism, see C. Bonner, General Secretary of the National Sunday School Union, *The Christ, the Church and the Child* (1911), 13-32.

30   Griffith, *Case for Believers Baptism*, 54-55. In this, Griffith was making a radical departure from the majority opinion, elevating maturity of faith over simple faith, and certainly running the risk of separating conversion from baptism.

cross. Mid-adolescence, then, 'might be regarded as the earliest period when baptism might be meaningful, rather than any other earlier stage.'[31]

Such views, however, go against the normal practice which is witnessed to by the fact that many Baptists, including many leading figures, have been baptized between the ages of eight and fifteen.[32] This issue, though sometimes vigorously debated, remains an open one, with the continued practice of the different options by different ministers and churches.

The Baptismal Service

In 1927 Wheeler Robinson observed that Baptists had no prescribed form for either communion or baptism, or worship in general,[33] a point confirmed in 1979 by Ernest Payne's comment that 'Baptists have no standard, authorized procedure.'[34] Dakin reported that baptism was normally preceded by a preaching service, which would comprise a special word of exhortation to the candidates or a special presentation of the gospel or an exposition of the meaning of baptism. He also remarked that, 'Naturally, in the years, experience has fixed the details of the ceremony so that in a well-conducted church it proceeds reverently and without unseemliness', and the variations did not matter 'so long as the main symbolism...is retained.'[35] However, it would seem reasonable that the increasing number of printed orders of service and ministers' manuals and the inroads of the liturgical movement into Baptist life have influenced a growing number of ministers and churches towards a more

---

31   P. Beasley-Murray, Principal of Spurgeon's College, 'Children, Faith and the Church', *BT* March 12, 1992, 11.

32   E.g. F.T. Lord who was eleven, see R. Terry, 'The proper age for baptism?' *BT* August 8, 1974, 6; E.A. Payne was fifteen, see West, *To Be A Pilgrim*, 10; Dr Derek Tidball was eleven, see Patricia Raven, 'We have lost our bridges to the outside world. Profile of the President', *BT* May 3, 1990, 10. Several correspondents in 1970 noted the baptism of believers from the ages of eight (to over eighty), see the various contributors, 'Baptised at 8—and over', *BT* July 16, 1970, 3; 'St. Leonards-on-Sea, Sussex', *BT* November 10, 1994, 16, which reported the baptism of Rebekah and James Wilson, aged nine and ten, by their parents Richard and Anna Wilson, Richard being an elder in the church.

33   Robinson, *Life and Faith*, 118.

34   Payne, 'Baptists and Christian Initiation', 147. This view was earlier expressed by Bryan, 'Preparation, Administration and Visitation', 74, 'there is considerable variety of practice among ministers as to the nature of the service and the mode of administration'; and was independently substantiated by the study of A.E. Peaston, *The Prayer Book Tradition in the Free Churches* (1964), 122, 'Baptists...have never displayed any real liking for prayer-book worship', and this despite moves in the liturgical direction by an increasing number of Baptists, particularly 'ecumenical' Baptists.

35   Dakin, *Baptist View of Church and Ministry*, 32-33.

standardized form of service or at least put down in print what was already a fairly common order, though these statements cannot be made into generalizations.

The time of the baptismal service, as so many details, has varied greatly. Regarded as primarily a public witness,[36] it has been held on Sunday mornings or Sunday evenings,[37] sometimes even in the afternoon,[38] or at which ever service was believed would have the largest congregation.[39] While many advocated Sunday, others supported mid-

---

36   L.H. Marshall, 'Baptists and Church Membership', *BT&F* October 31, 1924, 712, described baptism as 'a public service', a declaration of the gospel, possessing evangelistic qualities and a church rite. Some, though, opposed weeknight services, e.g. Underwood, 'Conversion and Baptism', 34, who exhorted Baptists to 'make more of believer's baptism, not less. Let it not be administered, except for special reasons, at a week-night service, as though it were something that needed to be tucked away in a corner.' Others opposed week-night services because they were poorly attended, e.g. the letters by R. Anderson and J. Benoy, 'Baptismal Services', *BT&F* September 13, 1901, 622, the latter himself having been baptized on a Wednesday evening in 1859, and M. Evans, 'Our Baptist Testimony', *BT* July 25, 1935, 552. However, M.J. Sheen of Halesowen, 'Baptisms', *BT* September 20, 1990, 15, took exception to the public baptisms of the 10,000 baptized at the 1990 BWC in Seoul, South Korea, arguing that in the New Testament references to baptism as a 'public witness' were noticeable by their absence. This was a response to D. Coffey's comment on the event (which he had attended), reported in 'Moving witness', *BT* August 30, 1990, 3, 'If, amongst other things, baptism is meant to be a public witness then this was the most public witness that one could wish for.' The biblical basis for this view of a public witness, however, was supported by P. Beasley-Murray, 'Reforming baptism', *BT* February 28, 1991, 11, who remarked that, 'In many of our churches baptism is seen as first and foremost a public confession of faith. While this is certainly an element in Christian baptism (see 1 Tim 6:12), it is only part of what baptism is all about, as Rom. 6:3-4 would clearly indicate.' This understanding of baptism represents the mainline Baptist view, see also the report heading 'From *public* baptism to service overseas', *BT* September 20, 1990, 13, italics added.

37   Bryan White, details of whom are unknown, 'Let's put baptism back in its place', *BT* August 9, 1979, 6, who argued that, because baptism was often followed by reception into membership and communion, it was more convenient to hold the service in the morning, preferably at a family service so the whole church fellowship could attend.

38   As at Southwick, Wiltshire, in the historic open air baptistry, at 3pm, followed by a tea and a 5pm consecration service in the church, 'We'll be baptised in the open, they decided', *BT* July 4, 1968, 1, and 'Seven Baptised in Historic Baptistry', *BT* July 18, 1968, 1.

39   E.g. Bryan, 'Preparation, Administration and Visitation', 74. Sunday evening was also favoured for this reason by C. Black, 'If I Were Dictator of the Baptist Denomination', *BT* March 28, 1940, 201; R.W.A. Mitchell, 'The Evangelistic Use of the Baptismal Service', *BT* December 16, 1943, 6.

week baptismal services,[40] and others recognized the appropriateness of Easter Sunday morning.[41] The norm has been for baptisms to be the climax of a service, though, as with communion, some churches have held them after the close of the main service.[42]

The most important part of any baptismal service has been the candidate's profession of faith. This has taken various forms: either through a formal personal testimony,[43] or in the form of questions put to

---

40   See D. Jackman, 'An Open Letter to a Pastor from the Parent of a Baptismal Candidate', *BT* December 3, 1936, 43, who thanked a compliant minister for acceding to his wish for 'a simple weeknight service' to avoid 'the inquisitive crowd, gaping and tittering, drawn by a throw-away handbill, making a solemn and beautiful service a circus spectacle rather than..."a meeting for worship".' See the similar views aired by C. Sedgwick of Kenton, Harrow, 'Baptism doesn't have to be a public act', *BT* November 5, 1998, 7. In the 1930s under F.T. Lord, Bloomsbury Chapel held Thursday night baptismal services, information verbally from Mrs Marjorie Wilkerson (née Brown), who was baptized at Bloomsbury in 1930. See also H.C.C. McCullough of Pier Avenue, Clacton-on-Sea, 'Baptism and Evangelism', *BT* March 1, 1945, 6, who stressed baptism's role as an evangelistic witness, and also advocated open air baptismal services at least once a year; the Boston church in Lincolnshire, altered the time of its service so that other churches could attend, 'Mid-week Baptism so others could attend', *BT* February 4, 1965, 12.

41   This practice was followed by C. Thompson of Clarence Park, Weston-super-Mare, W.J. Griffiths of Rumney Cardiff, and D. Evening of London Road, Portsmouth, as noted by G.H. Davies, at the time tutor of Bristol Baptist College, 'Easter Baptisms', *BT* May 7, 1942, 224. Davies here called for all Baptist churches to open their baptistries the following Easter Sunday morning and communicate the new members in the evening.

42   Patterson, *Call to Worship*, 156, 'If the service is to take place at the end of the morning or evening worship', and he then suggested that the minister reads some scripture to start such a service. This practice was censured by the Editor of 'The Christian Advocate', 'A Liturgical Scholar on Baptism', *BT* January 14, 1943, 5.

43   P. Beasley-Murray, *Radical Believers*, 14, 'it is customary in many Baptist churches for baptismal candidates to give personal "testimonies" to God's saving power in their own lives: for, although baptism itself is a confession of faith, it is considered good to give opportunity for candidates to articulate this confession and tell what Christ means to them.' See also Channon, *Much Water*, 63; 'Boatman's Happy Day', *BT* May 17, 1990, 11; 'Testimony to the changes', *BT* August 23, 1990, 3; 'Advanced years no barrier to baptism', *BT* September 20, 1990, 13. Aubrey, *Minister's Manual*, 33, advocated a personal testimony but also noted that under the strain of the event, some 'sensitive candidates' might wish to make their verbal testimony by means of responding to a question. R.W.A. Mitchell, 'The Evangelistic Use of the Baptismal Service', *BT* December 16, 1943, 6, also suggested the use of questions for the sensitive candidate unable to give their own testimony. Gaukroger, *Being Baptized*, 41-43, set out some practical advice on preparing a testimony, and highlighted it as an effective evangelistic tool, pp.49-50.

the candidate by the presiding minister,[44] and not infrequently both.[45] This has been followed by a 'formula' spoken over the candidate immediately prior to the act of (single) immersion,[46] which incorporates reference to the Trinity, following Matthew 28:19. Typical is that suggested by Payne and Winward: 'On thy profession of repentance toward God and of faith in our Lord Jesus Christ, I baptize thee in the name of the Father and of the Son and of the Holy Spirit. Amen.'[47] It has also been the practice of some to give a promise to each candidate, often a passage of scripture[48] intended to be of encouragement and guidance to them.[49]

---

44   Such questions were first recorded in Payne and Winward, *Orders and Prayers*, 132. To those being baptized the minister says: 'Forasmuch as you now present yourselves for Baptism, it is necessary that you sincerely give answer, before God and his Church, to the questions which I now put to you.' Then to each candidate: 'Do you make profession of repentance toward God and of faith in our Lord Jesus Christ?... I do... Do you promise, in dependence on divine grace, to follow Christ and to serve him for ever in the fellowship of his Church?...I do'. See also Gilmore, Smalley and Walker, *Praise God*, 139; *Patterns and Prayers*, 100-01; Abraham-Williams and Jones, 'The Baptist Union of Great Britain', 72-73, originally published as 'The Baptist Union' in the CCLEPE document *Ministry in Local Ecumenical Projects* (1985), 34-37 (being included among unofficial statements written by officers of the main denominations on behalf of their traditions). No such questions were included in the earlier manuals which suggests that this practice either originated in the latter half of the century, or only became common in mid-century. The latter, more cautious, conclusion is to be preferred as it is well-known that just because a practice is unrecorded does not mean it was unknown, simply that sources for it have not survived/been found.

45   Gaukroger, *Being Baptized*, 43-44, commented that, 'Sometimes, in addition to giving a testimony (or instead of it) the baptism candidate may be asked to make certain promises...'

46   Whitby, *Baptists Principles*, 66, made explicit that there was only one single immersion as opposed to the triple immersion practised in the Greek Orthodox Church, which he viewed as a corruption of the ordinance.

47   Payne and Winward, *Orders and Prayers*, 133. See also Gould and Shakespeare, *Manual for Free Church Ministers*, 47; Meyer, *Free Church Service-Manual*, 26; Aubrey, *Minister's Manual*, 33; Patterson, *Call to Worship*, 158; Gilmore, Smalley and Walker, *Praise God*, 139; *Patterns and Prayers*, 101. A trinitarian form for the questions was also advocated by S.F. Winward, 'The Administration of Baptism', *Frat.* 123 (January, 1962), 11, who followed this with a vow of allegiance. Barnard, 'The Use of Symbols in the Baptist Church', 16, spoke of his use of three questions. The first concerned faith in the triune God, the second repentance and faith, the third fellowship in the church.

48   Channon, *Much Water*, 63; P. Beasley-Murray, *Faith and Festivity*, 107. This has been the regular practice of, e.g. D.K. Blades at New Road, Bromsgrove, 1978–96, though how far back it goes is unknown.

49   Several Baptists have also reintroduced the ancient practice of including the renunciation of the devil/evil in the baptismal service: S.F. Winward, *Your Baptism* (1969), 45, in the form of the question, 'Do you turn to God in Christ, repent of your sins

For over half a century ministers have dressed formally for baptism, either in waterproofs and gown or simply the gown,[50] and formal baptismal wear appears to have been the norm for candidates too.[51] But since about the 1960s,[52] and a growing casualness of dress within society,[53] particularly for men,[54] the move has been for ministers and

---

and renounce evil?' He was supported by R.F.G. Burnish, 'Baptismal Preparation—Past, Present and ...?', *Frat.* 195 (April, 1981), 13-14; also N. Wright, *The Fair Face of Evil: Putting the Power of Darkness in its Place* (1989), 125; and J. Weaver, tutor in Pastoral Studies at Regent's Park, 'Reconsidering Believers' Baptism', *BMJ* 257 (January, 1997), 6.

50   The waterproofs consisted of baptizing trousers with galoshes, waterproof vests with sleeves and a baptising gown, with the option of waterproof sleeves, see e.g. the advertisements in *BH* 1929, xi; 'Baptismal Outfits'; *BH* 1938, XXIII; and S.H. Davies of Trowbridge, 'Baptismal Outfit Wanted', *BT* June 26, 1947, 7.

51   Candidates' gowns could be either black or white, see the advertisement in *BH* 1929, xi. Joy Males, 'Whatever shall I wear?', *BT* July 25, 1985, 6, recollected white gowns for women. Others, she noted, recalled gowns of 'sombre black', of 'puritanical appearance' and not very practical. Perkin, 'The Principles and Practice of Believers' Baptism', *BT* June 11, 1959, 6, recommended that candidates wore white, with the men wearing black gowns and the women three-quarter length royal blue cloaks, decorated in silver with the Kai-Rho. Perkin cannot here be taken to be representative in these views, but was clearly influenced by liturgical developments and other traditions. However, male candidates in the early decades of the century could also wear casual clothes, so R.W. Thomson, who recalled that most churches owned heavy white cloth garments, weighted around the hems for the women, while men and boys were allowed to wear flannel trousers and a tennis shirt. It is interesting that virtually no appeal is made to the 'theological' significance of such clothing.

52   The date cannot be accurately determined, but the 1960s saw a marked shift towards the wearing of casual clothes. The charismatic movement (which originated in the early 1960s) has greatly influenced Baptist churches and has also led to less emphasis on what is worn in church, the idea of 'Sunday best' being an idea which has all but disappeared, it now being spoken of generally only by the older generations.

53   The movement towards a greater casualness could already be seen in the 1940s with Bryan's comment, 'Preparation, Administration and Visitation', 72, that 'girls' were to wear simple white dresses, while 'men' should wear a simple black gown. Later he wrote, 'The voluminous white garments of antique pattern and the rusty black clothes, almost green with age, in vogue still in some churches should surely be scrapped. It prevents young people from being at their ease if they are unbecomingly dressed, and it is a reflection on what the Church deems fitting. See Gaukroger, *Being Baptized*, 'What to wear', 45-46, 'these days people are usually baptized in their own clothes.'

54   Joy Males, 'Whatever shall I wear?', *BT* July 25, 1985, 6, lamented that men continued to wear white shirts and trousers and jeans, and remarked that in the mid–1980s women's gowns tended to be made of Italian cotton, reflecting the fact that it is still common for women to wear special baptismal dresses of thick white material and weighted at the hem, though many also dressed down. Abraham-Williams and Jones, 'The Baptist Union of Great Britain', 72, reported that women dress in a simple gown with weighted hems and the men wear white shirts and trousers.

candidates to dress down.[55] The overwhelming bulk of the discussion of baptismal wear has revolved around practical issues, with little attempt to use robes to enhance the meaning of the rite.[56]

It is clear that the minister, as the representative of the church,[57] has ordinarily been the administrant of baptism,[58] though, with a few exceptions,[59] Baptists have permitted the 'lay' administration of the rite,[60]

---

55   Ron Meloy, Secretary of Central, Stratford, London, 'Baptismal Waders', *BT* June 9, 1994, 9, reported the continued use of black waders and gown by their minister, K.D. Saunders (a non-accredited minister), appealed for help in purchasing new waders, which he had discovered were no longer made, and remarked, 'I gather these days that ministers and pastors do not wear any special attire for baptism.' This is supported from countless photographs which appear in the *BT* every year. Others, while clearly a minority, still 'dress up', e.g. C.J. Ellis who wore a white gown, see the report and photograph in 'Zairean Baptism in UK', *BT* June 20, 1996, 16.

56   An exception to this was R. Burnish, 'White robes told of new life', *B T* September 8, 1983, 4, who argued that white robes enhanced the meaning of baptism because, though purely symbolic, they speak of purity and new life.

57   'Baptist Doctrine of the Church', 444, 'It is the church which preaches the Word and celebrates the sacraments, and it is the church which, through pastoral oversight, feeds the flock and ministers to the world. It normally does these things through the person of its minister, but not solely through him. Any member of the church may be authorised by it, on occasion, to exercise the functions of the ministry, in accordance with the principle of the priesthood of all believers, to preach the Word, to administer baptism, to preside at the Lord's table...' Williams, *Principles and Practices*, 19 and 34-35, argued that the lay administration of baptism proved that baptism was not a saving ordinance and that evangelists such as Philip and Ananias could legitimately claim the right to administer baptism, which, he believed, supported his contention that baptism was not a church rite.

58   See the Minister's manuals all of which refer to the minister, e.g. Aubrey, *A Minister's Manual*, 25-33, and Payne and Winward, *Orders and Prayers*, 127-35.

59   E.g. Shakespeare, *Cross-Roads*, 158-59, who, in his desire for unity and citing the Committee on Faiths' article on the ministry (Oxford, 1916), envisioned that the 'ministration of the Sacraments' would have to be carried out by an ordained minister. It is quite possible, however, that the theory was one thing but the actual practice another; and Clark, 'The Fulness of the Church of God', 109, believed that 'only the ordained minister, called, trained, tested, and commissioned, may rightly preach the liturgical sermon and dispense the dominical sacraments.' R.W. Thomson recalled that the conducting of baptism in and around the London area, often in line with the Spurgeon tradition, was always conducted by a minister. During an interregnum a deacon was often asked to conduct the communion, yet at no time, he said, was a deacon encouraged to conduct a baptism. It is possible, then, that this procedure could have been more widespread than the number of extant sources suggest.

60   So Whitley, *Church, Ministry and Sacraments*, 72-73 and 244; Whitby, *Baptist Principles*, 54-55 and 71; Tymms, *Evolution of Infant Baptism*, 500; Meyer, *Peter*, 169; Robinson, *Life and Faith*, 124. Baptists also maintained the legitimacy of the lay administration of the Lord's Supper, see, e.g. Glover, *Free Churches and Re-Union*, 43-

particularly when there was no minister or no minister could be found to conduct the service, in which case it was possible for a deacon, elder or perhaps lay preacher, appointed by the church meeting, to conduct the baptism.[61] While offensive to their ecumenical partners who do not accept the lay administration of baptism except *in extremis*, the practice is wholly consonant with the Baptist belief in the priesthood of all believers.[62]

It would seem that for the larger part of the century ministers administered baptism unassisted, the only help being from assistants, probably deacons, who would help the candidates to and from the water,[63] though

---

44, and G. Laws, 'Baptists and Their Ministry. Reflections on Dr. T.R. Glover's Articles', *BT&F* December 21, 1923, 882.

61   Whitley, *Church, Ministry and Sacraments*, 102, stated that there was a convenience and orderliness in having baptism and communion administered as a rule by ministers but there was no reason or scriptural precedent for confining it to them, see also pp.121, 133 and 176. See also the 1938 *Reply of the Council of the Baptist Union*, 150; Bryan, 'Preparation, Administration and Visitation', 72-76, and also his 'The Sacraments', 73-74; Dakin, *Baptist View of Church and Ministry*, 41; T.M. Bamber, 'The LBA President On Baptist Belief', *BT* April 18, 1946, 6; *The Doctrine of the Ministry*, 16. 'Mediterranean Baptism', *BT* November 11, 1999, 2, reported the baptism of a 27 year-old lady by her 27 year-old friend while on holiday in Crete which received the 'blessing' by the diaconate of Lee Mount, Halifax, when they were notified.

62   E.g. W.H. Jones of Woodborough Road, Nottingham, 'The Priesthood of All Believers', *BT* May 1, 1930, 309. Advocacy and defence of the legitimacy of the lay administration of baptism also support the Baptist rejection of sacerdotalist claims which had been pressed to such effect by the Tractarians and which was one of the disagreements Baptists had with the reunion movement in general and the Lambeth Appeal of 1920 in particular. Baptists would not relinquish their position in favour of a sacerdotalist understanding of either the ministry or the sacraments, see 'The Baptist Union of Great Britain and Ireland', in Hodgson (ed.), *Convictions*, 63, 'We do not confine the administration of Sacraments to ordained ministers.' (The text continues, 'nor stipulate for the laying on of hands'.) See also the similar points made by Price, 'Laymen and Reunion', 291-92 and 294.

63   So Bryan, 'Preparation, Administration and Visitation', 73, 'The only movement in the building should be at the baptistery, and the only persons in any central or conspicuous position, the candidates and the minister.' It is unclear whether this is the meaning of Jamie Wallace's comment that the deacons' privilege included 'assisting at Baptisms', though this could mean assisting in the actual act of baptism, see S.J. Wallace, *Someone is Watching You (a way of looking at Church Membership)* (1965), 16. This is supported by photographs of baptismal services, e.g. the picture accompanying the report of the first televised baptismal service from Richmond, Liverpool, which took place on May 31, 1959, on the ABC channel. The picture has Stanley Turl of West Ham Central Mission above the baptistry in the pulpit, and Kenneth Witting, minister of the church, in the baptistry, see 'First Ever Baptism Service on Television', *BT* June 4, 1959, 1; and the widely used picture of a 1965 baptism in the open baptistry at Southwick, Wiltshire, reproduced in F. Bowers, *Who are the Baptists?* (1978), and also in Hayden, *English Baptist History and Heritage*, 100. (Details and dates

sometimes the candidates have chosen their own assistants.[64] However, over the last two decades or so it has increasingly become the practice for the minister to be assisted in the baptistry, though it is unclear precisely when this began.[65]

The commonest mode of immersion is that the candidate is 'lowered into the water so that he lies down face upward, with the water just flowing over him, as if he were being laid in a grave.'[66] However, some have baptized the candidate kneeling, the head bowing forward into the water 'as if bowing in utter surrender and submission',[67] and it was not unknown for the candidates, with the minister's hand on their head, to be gently pressed down into the water.[68] Whichever method was adopted, Bryan pleaded, 'let the movements be reverent and dignified, without

---

of all televised Baptist baptismal services up to that time were reported in 'First TV baptism', *BT* April 11, 1996, 8).

64   Gaukroger, *Being Baptized*, 48, called them the towel holders. See also J.R.C. Perkin, 'The Principles and Practice of Believers' Baptism', *BT* June 11, 1959, 6.

65   This is supported by numerous photographs accompanying the reports of baptismal services in the *BT*. E.g. 'Back to the pool seventy years on', *BT* September 14, 1989, 3; 'Tennis player baptised', *BT* July 25, 1991, 16; 'Baptised in the pool he built', *BT* June 1, 1995, 16.

66   Bryan, 'Preparation, Administration and Visitation', 75-76, who referred to this as 'The mode of baptizing common amongst us.' See also Gaukroger, *Being Baptized*, 31 and 47.

67   So E. Price of the Church of the Redeemer, Birmingham, 'The Mode of Baptism', *BT* February 11, 1943, 6, who was supported by Dr William Robinson, the Churches of Christ Principal of Overdale College, Birmingham, but opposed by F.H. King of Worthing, 'The Mode of Baptism', *BT* February 25, 1943, 4, 'As the body of Jesus was reverently laid in the garden, so the disciple commits himself absolutely to the hands of the baptiser, as he is reverently laid in the watery tomb, to be immediately followed by the resurrection to newness of life.' G.E. Page of London (details of whom are unknown: he does not appear to have been accredited or even perhaps BU), 'The Mode of Baptism', *BT* December 6, 1945, 6, noted that the prone position had been introduced by S. Blundell in 1897, and that at times ministers had placed their hands on the candidate's neck and gently lowered them forward. W. Fancutt of Andover, 'Testimonies to Baptism', *BT* December 27, 1945, 6, reported that he had been baptized by W.A. Phillips at Farnborough in 1932, in the kneeling position (in the Paulician manner) going forward, and that this had been Phillips' normal method. R. Burnish, 'Backwards or forwards?', *BT* September 1, 1983, 4, claimed that kneeling represented homage to Christ. Though the physical method did not effect baptism, he remarked that the method was probably chosen by the minister with reference to the shape of the baptistry. He also noted candidates baptizing themselves at the minister's direction. Kneeling was also shown in a photograph attributed to the 'late 1960s' which accompanied Dr A. Baines' 'The Laying on of Hands', *BT* December 9, 1993, 12; and reported in A. Correspondent, 'As three young people make their witness', *BT* May 30, 1974, 1.

68   So in a picture from Newbury, accompanying the write-up, 'Baptistery used—after 70 years', *BT* March 18, 1965, 7.

jerkiness, plunging, or any other uncouthness that would mar the suggestiveness of the symbolism—a believer being buried to a life of sin and self, and rising from the grave to a new life in Christ.'[69] On occasions, due to special circumstances (usually age, infirmity and/or illness), candidates have been baptized by affusion, water being taken from the baptistry and poured over the head.[70]

Sometimes the congregation have stood 'around the candidate at baptism'[71] but ordinarily they have remained seated.[72] Following each immersion,[73] the minister would sometimes pronounce a blessing, Payne and Winward suggested that either the choir or congregation could sing after each baptism, or, at the conclusion of the baptisms, one of the baptismal sentences from the hymnbook (*BCHR*) or the verse of a hymn or the doxology could be said.[74] The post-baptismal hymn varied, but suggestions included the Te Deum,[75] the Doxology,[76] 'Beneath the Cross

---

69   Bryan, 'Preparation, Administration and Visitation', 76. He continued, 'So administered the rite can be profoundly impressive. It has been used by God again and again as a means of grace to the candidates and a means of bringing others to decision for Christ and to incorporation into His Church.'

70   See 'Testimony to the Changes', *BT* August 23, 1990, 3, being an account of 91 year old Sophie Leal's baptism at Willesden Green. This led to the baptism of two other elderly people at Burnham-on-Crouch, 'Affusion baptism leads to two more', *BT* November 22, 1990, 3.

71   Dakin, *Baptist View of Church and Ministry*, 34. This was the usual practice at Calne, Wiltshire, when the present writer arrived there in April 1994.

72   Implicitly, Bryan, 'Preparation, Administration and Visitation', 73. The new church at New Road, Bromsgrove (built 1990) has a mounted large convex mirror over the baptistry (sited in the front left corner of the sanctuary) so that the seated congregation can see the baptisms.

73   Jackson, 'One Lord, One Faith, One Baptism', 64, recounted that for years he had taught baptismal candidates that when they had been raised from the water, to stand for a moment with their faces looking upwards.

74   Payne and Winward, *Orders and Prayers*, 133. Some editions of the *BCHR* contained no specific baptismal sentences, though Payne and Winward could have been referring to sentences from the baptismal hymns themselves, nos. 469–484. Under *BCHR* no.482, W.W. Sidey's 'Buried with Christ! Our glad hearts say', which was recommended for use during the administration of the rite, a note suggested sentences from the 'Chant Section', nos. 129 and 140–143. Not all editions of the *BCHR* included the Chants and Anthems section, and there were some editions containing only the Chants and Anthems. The later 1962 *BHB* included only one entry of relevent scriptural baptismal verses, see no.874

75   Perkin, *Divine Encounter*, 8, being *BHB* 778.

76   Payne and Winward, *Orders and Prayers*, 133. It was printed on the inside front cover of both the music and words edition of the *BCHR*.

of Jesus',[77] 'Praise to God, Almighty Maker',[78] 'Buried with Christ! Our glad hearts say',[79] and more obscurely, 'Be thou faithful unto death and I will give thee a crown of life'.[80] However, the most popular of all baptismal hymns has been 'O Jesus I have promised',[81] which could be sung before or after the act of baptism.[82] Usually an appeal has been given before the final hymn, and those responding would be asked to

---

77   *BCHR* 237, 'A Member of the Staff', 'Household Baptism at Spurgeon's Orphan Homes', *BT* October 19, 1943, 10.

78   *BHB* 299 by William Robinson, the Churches of Christ scholar, 'Anglicans and Baptists Share in Baptismal Service', *BT* December 13, 1962, 1-2, being the account of a service at New Southgate, North London, where M.J. Walker and the Rector of Friern Barnet, John Adams, shared in the baptism of one Anglican woman and eight Baptists, in which they adopted the 'customary Southgate baptismal service' with the *Book of Common Prayer*'s order for baptism for such 'as of riper years', using the baptismal preamble from Payne and Winward's *Orders and Prayers*. It was increasingly common for united baptismal services to be held, e.g. 'Anglican Vicar Baptises in BC', *BT* November 19, 1959, 12; 'Baptists and Anglicans to Unite for Baptismal Service', *BT* February 22, 1962, 8.

79   Gould and Shakespeare, *Manual for Free Church Ministers*, 59, printed hymn no.8, but *BCH* 502. The benediction 'The Lord bless thee and keep thee' was also sometimes sung, so Patterson, *Call to Worship*, 159, based on Num. 6:24-26.

80   So Dakin, *Baptist View of Church and Ministry*, 33; and R.W. Thomson. 'Be thou faithful' is in neither the *BCH* nor the *BCHR*.

81   This first appeared in the *BCH* in 1900, no.505, *BCHR* 473, *BHB* 298 and *BPW* 352. It was written by the Anglican clergyman, J.E. Bode, when his daughter and two sons were confirmed, details in R.W. Thomson (ed.), *The Baptist Hymn Book Companion* (revised, 1967), 238.

82   In the early years it preceded the baptisms, Aubrey, *Minister's Manual*, 32; confirmed by R.W. Thomson, in which he said that this 'seemed to be so in every church that I knew.' See also F.T. Lord, 'Why I Am A Baptist', *BT* June 2, 1955, 2, who noted it was used fifty years previously; J.R.C. Perkin, 'The Principles and Practice of Believers' Baptism', *BT* June 11, 1959, 6 and his *Divine Encounter*, 8 and 13; I.M. Mallard, 'The Administration of Baptism', *Frat.* 171 (September, 1974), 38, who also suggested 'At the name of Jesus'. J.B. Skemp of Durham, 'A Scottish Report on Baptism', *BT* November 3, 1955, 7, added that the following hymn, *BCHR* 474, 'Around Thy grave, Lord Jesus' was rarely chosen. He also criticized the *BCHR* and baptismal services for the way they suggested that Baptists believed baptism to be only a sign of discipleship, and therefore that it was 'No wonder that we then go on to regard it as a kind of "optional extra" for converted Christians.' 'O Jesus I have promised' was also sung at the first televised baptismal service. The whole service was criticized by the *BT* for being overly subjective, focusing on the believer's hearing of the word, his faith and obedience, there being no word about the gift of the Spirit and no prayer before the sacrament, 'First Ever Baptism Service on Television', *BT* June 4, 1959, 1. 'O Jesus, I have promised', being a subjective hymn in the sense of personal, and the most popular baptismal hymn, reflects the tendency of much Baptist theology towards a subjective and, by extension, individualistic interpretation. This tendency was also criticized by Winward, 'The Administration of Baptism', 8.

come and stand in front of the baptistry while the closing hymn was sung,[83] or to see the minister after the service or to go to a room for counselling.

While rare early in the century,[84] the laying on of hands has become more common,[85] not least through the influence of the liturgical and charismatic movements where it figures prominently, and has been understood as the recognition of the seal of the Spirit and commission for work in the priesthood of all believers.[86] Gaukroger explained, 'The leaders lay their hands on the person's head and pray, "May God bless you and fill you with His Holy Spirit as you are baptized", or something like that', linking this act and prayer with 'a definite anticipation that God will work in the life of the individual in his or her baptism.'[87]

Post-Baptism

What becomes immediately clear is that Baptists have paid little attention to post-baptismal issues, and the majority of what they have written has focused on receiving the candidates into membership. This was particularly the case in the early decades of the century.[88]

---

83   So 'An Impressive Baptism', *BT* October 28, 1943, 5, and R.W.A. Mitchell, 'The Evangelistic Use of the Baptismal Service', *BT* December 16, 1943, 6.

84   Whitley, *Church, Ministry and Sacraments*, 52, acknowledged the New Testament practice, while Robinson, *Baptist Principles* (1925), 28, remarked that some New Testament practices, such as the laying on of hands, 'Baptists in general no longer continue.' W.E. Blomfield, 'Church Reunion. Impasse', *BT* October 22, 1925, 747, acknowledged the four passages in the New Testament where the laying on of hands is mentioned and that the practice had 'not been uncommon amongst Baptists', but remarked that 'Its cessation is probably due to a revolt against what seem semi-magical conceptions.'

85   See, e.g. the photograph of the laying on of hands while in the baptistry following immersion in 'First baptism for church plant', *BT* June 29, 1995, 16.

86   This was the explanation given by the Sussex University Chaplain, G. Whitfield, see A. Correspondent, 'As three young people make their witness', *BT* May 30, 1974, 1.

87   Gaukroger, *Being Baptized*, 54.

88   This is perhaps nowhere more clearly reflected than in Bryan's 'practical' essay, whose limits are fairly reflected in the title, 'Preparation, Administration and Visitation', the visitation referring to the interview with a view to membership, pp.76-78. Bryan suggested, p.77, that the duties of the visitors included 'some responsibility for keeping in touch with the new member', though this was far from any kind of post-baptismal classes or formally arranged nurture. Perkin, 'Interviewing of Candidates for Baptism and Membership', 28-29, wrote, 'The whole business of instructing, interviewing and admitting new members through baptism is an area of church life where we must reform and systematise if we are to do our work effectively.' He suggested that those who recommend someone for membership should also be responsible for the after care. While

It has been the practice for baptismal candidates to be given a baptismal card, certifying that baptism has taken place, when and where, and which could be sent to an inquiring church on a request for transfer of membership.[89]

When baptism was to be followed by church membership, whether in an open or closed church, the reception into membership usually took place at the next communion service, when the candidate was extended the 'right hand of fellowship'.[90] This could take place up to several weeks after the baptismal service, though frequently the service of baptism took place in the morning and was followed by an evening communion at which the candidate would be welcomed into membership.[91] If the candidate was still a youth then attendance at the church meeting was often put off until they were deemed to be of a suitable age. Thomson

informal care as suggested by Bryan and Perkin might have happened in some instances, the idea has only been developed in the proposal of R. Burnish, 'Inquisitors or Befrienders?', *BT* August 25, 1983, 4, who suggested the use of sponsors at baptism who would promise to undertake special care for the baptized after baptism. The sponsors were addressed in the baptismal service: 'CB or EF do you, as A's church sponsors undertake a special relationship with him (her) expressed through prayer, interest, and encouragement to aid his (her) nurture and growth in grace?' Burnish, 'Baptismal Preparation', 16, criticized the booklet by Barrett, *Church Membership: Suggestions for Visitors to Candidates*, for omitting any hint of a continuing relationship between the visitors and the candidates until his last paragraph. He further urged, p.17, that as soon as a person expressed any form of commitment they should be linked with a mature Christian who would nurture them in the Christian faith before and beyond baptism.

89   These, along with infant dedication cards, were sold by the Kingsgate Press and now by the BU Publications' department, but there is no evidence to suggest when either were first introduced.

90   Robinson, *Life and Faith*, 98-99; Middlebrook, 'Baptism and the Church', 57; and P.R. Clifford, *The Christian Life* (1954), 38. R.W. Thomson, however, implied that this was not always the case.

91   This is supported by a criticism of churches which covered their baptistries by Winward, 'The Administration of Baptism', 10. He noted that two arguments used against the combined baptismal-membership-communion service were that it was impractical because the communion table was situated on top of the baptistry and there was insufficient space or time. He countered the former by recommending the baptismal service in the morning followed by the laying on of hands, and communion in the evening; the latter he refuted from his own experience that a baptismal–eucharist usually took about an hour and a quarter. According to West, 'Baptist Church Life Today', 39, more and more churches were following the pattern of baptizing candidates and receiving them into membership at a communion service on the same occasion. So also Payne and Winward, *Orders and Prayers*, 127, *'Since we are baptized into the Church, it is desirable that Baptism should, if possible, be followed by the Lord's Supper, at which the reception of new members should take place '*, italics theirs; and S. Voke of Walton-on-Thames, 'The Biblical Doctrine and Experience of Koinonia', *Frat.* 139 (January, 1966), 17-18.

recollected that in his own church, Dawes Road, Fulham, that age was eighteen, though in other churches youthful members were allowed to join the church but were usually unable to vote.[92] For example, on the eve of his 15th birthday in February 1917, Ernest Payne joined the Downs Chapel, Clapton. He was given the right hand of fellowship at the evening communion service, but it was not until five months later that he was baptized.[93] R.C. Ford recorded that several Yorkshire churches practised the custom of reading the church covenant to newly welcomed members, writing, 'These two may be taken as samples of many more of which', Ford admitted, 'we possess no details.'[94]

Consistent with his position on the immediacy of baptism, G.R. Beasley-Murray advanced the view that there should be teaching after baptism, and he believed it should cover 'a prolonged period and not simply a few classes'.[95] Others have concurred. Theodore Valentine attributed the loss of so many young people to the complete lack of post-baptismal care. In the process he mentioned six, eight or twelve baptismal preparation classes, and continued, 'However it is done, let as much care and prayer be given to the training of young church members as to those who have asked to be baptised.'[96] Other correspondents have also stressed the need for pre- and post-baptismal care,[97] though it must be admitted that this is a much neglected area of baptismal practice.[98]

---

92   So R.W. Thomson. Mountain, *My Baptism*, 121, wrote, 'And I see no reason why children of even tender years—if they give credible evidence of intelligent faith in Jesus—should not confess that faith in baptism, and be admitted to the Communion Table...' To which he added, quoting Spurgeon, 'although they ought not to be permitted to take part in the business of their church, until they have reached years of maturity.'

93   West, *To Be A Pilgrim*, 10. Many would assent to Bryan's position, 'Preparation, Administration and Visitation', 76, 'There should be a virtual assurance in [the minister's] mind that the candidate will be accepted [into membership], for no little damage may be done if the Church puts him back. Far better take the responsibility of keeping the candidate back a little longer than go forward with a doubtful case...', and this would have been especially so with a youth.

94   Ford, *Twenty-Five Years*, 50. He cited the 1908 history of Bethel, Shipley, which reported this as the practice under their minister, David Kentfield, but by 1937 the custom had been abandoned. In 1927, such a practice was also the norm at Hope, Hebden Bridge.

95   Beasley-Murray, 'Place of the Child', 157.

96   T. Valentine, 'Post Baptismal Care', *BT* August 5, 1954, 6. See also Dr W. Speirs of Derby, 'Post-Baptismal Care', *BT* September 2, 1954, 7; and *The Child and the Church*, 45, which argued that, whatever else it included, post-baptismal training should equip young members for their responsibilites in the business of church meetings.

97   'Ex-Church Officer', 'Post Baptismal Care', *BT* August 12, 1954, 6, argued that such should be given 'prayerful and careful consideration'; and George Neal, 'The Sacraments: more than mere symbols', *BT* July 18, 1996, 10. L.J. Wisewell of Walmer,

Baptistries

From the earliest times Baptists have baptized wherever there is water, and while the vast majority of Baptist church buildings have baptistries, several historic churches have external ones.[99] Open air baptisms have been frequently held either because of necessity[100] or intentionally to highlight baptism as a public witness and evangelistic opportunity.[101]

Kent, spoke of post-baptismal care as an after-care clinic, 'Our After-Care Clinic', *BT* September 28, 1961, 10.

98   Burnish, *Meaning of Baptism*, 223, n.4, noted that the number of meetings after baptism could range from 1–2, to over 4, while a considerable number never met after baptism, and a number had some other unspecified number of meetings. He also noted that the duration of these post-baptismal classes could vary from one to over six months.

99   E.g. Monksthorp, Lincolnshire, and Southwick, Wiltshire. For Monksthorpe, see J. Barfield, 'The little church that time forgot', *BT* November 15, 1990, 8. In 1968, the open air baptistry at Southwick, Wiltshire, was used for the first time since 1953, prior to which it had been built up and restored in 1937, see 'We'll be baptised in the open, they decided', *BT* July 4, 1968, 1.

100   The drought in 1976 proved a test to churches' ingenuity in finding alternative locations to hold baptismal services, which included the use of public and private swimming pools, rivers, the sea and even well water brought to fill a baptistry in a tanker, see 'Steady stream of baptism despite drought', *BT* September 16, 1976, 7; and 'Saving water meant a greater witness', *BT* October 14, 1976, 13. During WWI Baptist chaplains conducted open air baptismal services wherever the troops were, e.g. in a French stream, A.B. Kinsey, 'A Baptism at the Front', *BT&F* December 29, 1916, 808; A.J. White, C.F.U.B. (Baptist), Garrison Chaplain, 'Interesting Baptismal Services', *BT&F* March 28, 1919, 182, reported the baptism of three in the open sea in Alexandria; another baptism took place in a French bath house, D.O.G. (Griffith of Brecon), 'A Baptism at the Front', *BT&F* May 26, 1916, 327. During WWII baptismal services continued undaunted, even when bombing meant they took place in the ruins, see 'A Baptismal Service at Tyndale Bristol', *BT* August 21, 1941, 413. See also, e.g. 'A Blitz Baptism at Upton', *BT* June 26, 1941, 315; and 'They Built Their Own Baptistery', *BT* May 3, 1945, 3.

101   E.g. 'Witness at the Plaza', *BT* October 12, 1989, 3. Baptist evangelist, Vic Jacopson, has regularly baptized converts at the Glastonbury Pop Festival in oil drums, see 'No follow-up for travellers', *BT* June 29, 1989, 16, and L. Misselbrook, 'Church planting in Glastonbury', *BT* April 4, 1991, 6. Numerous reports underscore the frequency of open air-evangelistic baptisms: in the sea, 'A Baptism in the Sea', *BT* August 4, 1949, 5, and 'Baptism in the Sea at Ramsgate', *BT* August 31, 1950, 5; in rivers, 'River Baptism in a Suffolk Village', *BT* June 16, 1927, 434, a Whit Sunday baptismal service in the River Lark, and 'A Baptism in the River Ely', *BT* September 22, 1949, 8; in swimming pools, 'Witness at the Plaza', *BT* October 12, 1989, 3, and 'Portable swimming pool becomes baptistry', *BT* October 18, 1990, 11; and even in a cow trough, 'Nine people baptised in a cow trough', *BT* July 28, 1988, 3, at Melton Mowbray.

The major source for information on twentieth-century baptistries is the section entitled 'Architectural Descriptions and Illustrations of New Chapels, &c', which has been included in many, but by no means all, editions of the *Baptist Handbook*.[102] This shows that the position of the baptistry has varied widely and that there are two basic types of baptistry: covered and open. Covered baptistries have been situated centrally under the communion platform[103] or in the floor in front of the platform,[104] or under the choir area,[105] and one was even concealed behind a blue velvet curtain.[106] Open baptistries were variously located, centrally behind the dais or rostrum,[107] in front of the pulpit with the communion table,[108] centrally in the chancel,[109] or to one side.[110] A number of churches have a raised baptistry in order to aid visibility.[111] A number of churches have located changing rooms for the minister and candidates through a

---

102 The details included in this section have varied greatly from report to report and year to year. Many of the descriptions excluded reference to the baptistry and many omitted whether the baptistry was covered or open. The 'Architectural Supplement' became less frequent from the early 1940s onwards.

103 E.g. Union Church, Beeston (Baptist–Congregational), *BH* 1900, 364; St. Andrew's Street, Cambridge, *BH*, 1903, 375; Webster Street, Coventry, *BH* 1923, 295; Aylesham Church Hall, Kent, *BH* 1929, 327; Morden Baptist Free Church, *BH* 1935, 339; West Watford Free Church (Baptist), *BH* 1958, xi; Northolt Park, *BH* 1959, iii.

104 E.g. Romsey, Hampshire, refurbished in 1992; Calne, refurbished 1994; Ferndown Free Church (Baptist–URC), newly installed into a former URC building in 1996. This kind of placement allows great flexibility of use for the sanctuary.

105 E.g. Pier Avenue, Clacton-on-Sea, *BH* 1929, 327-28; West Worthing, *BH* 1938, 358.

106 South Oxhey church hall, Watford, either side of which were a vestry and committee room, *BH* 1958, ix.

107 E.g. Church End, Finchley, *BH* 1938, 357; Crawley, *BH* 1958, iii.

108 E.g. Brownhill Road, Catford, *BH* 1904, 374; Undercliffe Road, Felixstowe, *BH* 1927, 355; Victoria Drive, Bognor Regis, *BH* 1966, iii.

109 E.g. Abbey Road, St. John's Wood, *BH* 1936, 360; King's Langley, Hertfordshire, *BH* 1938, 365.

110 E.g. Hearsall, Coventry, *BH* 1962, v; Westbourne Park, Paddington, *BH* 1963, vii.

111 E.g. King's Langley, Hertfordshire, whose baptistry is slightly raised above the chancel floor, *BH* 1938, 365; the Metropolitan Tabernacle, Newington Butts, London, has an elevated glass-fronted baptistry situated above the pulpit in a central position, *BH* 1959, xi; and New Road Oxford, placed theirs in the front left corner, refurbished in 1982.

passage under the pulpit,[112] others to one side,[113] and some have used screens behind which the newly baptized could pass.[114]

Perusal of the details supplied in the *Baptist Handbook* suggests that more baptistries are covered than open. The reason for this appears to be more utilitarian than theological, for it is safer, allows greater flexibility in the use of the building and, as many Baptist buildings are limited for space, it uses the space available to the full. For example, the open baptistry was situated to the left of the platform at New Road, Bromsgrove, built in 1990, in order for the baptismal window, which pictures the descent of the Spirit and the cross of Christ, to be under the small, steel framed steeple on the intersection of the main road and side road, and because this location was the only one which provided backlight for the window and was nearest to the outside drainage to which water is pumped.[115] Practical considerations dominate matters in newly formed churches, often church plants, which frequently meet in temporary or rented accommodation, who usually rent portable baptistries or have even constructed their own.[116]

Some, however, have severely criticized the utilitarian approach and especially closed baptistries and have sought to use the careful placement of the pool and the open baptistry as means of either aiding worship or, perhaps more importantly, supporting the church's theology. F.C. Bryan believed it to be a great aid to worship if the baptistry was so built that the steps led straight up through the door and out of the chapel, for this would reduce unnecessary movement which would distract people. He also expressed the desirability to have the baptistry filled and the water

---

112 E.g. Ebenezer Chapel, Bury Road, Haslingden, *BH* 1902, 357; Webster Street, Coventry, *BH* 1914, 507.

113 E.g. Morecambe, *BH* 1900, 381; St. John's Free Church, Tunbridge Wells (James Mountain's church), *BH* 1902, 372.

114 E.g. Broadway Chapel, Chesham, *BH* 1902, 349.

115 Information from Mr Fred Cross, an elder of the church. The previous church building, built in 1978, had situated the open baptistry to the right of the staging platform beneath a stone cross, the reasons for its location being next to a large window and for access into the vestry-come-changing room.

116 The increase in emphasis on church planting which occurred in the late 1980s and 1990s, and the fact that many such congregations meet in hired premises, led Jaya's Company of South Brent, Devon, to manufacture a portable, self-assembly rectangular pool. The same company also offered a compact water heater which could be hired or bought. See 'Self-assembly baptistry takes a bow', *BT* March 23, 1995, 12. A similar raised, timber-frame pool was designed by a member of Padiham, Lancashire, 'Home-designed baptistry', *BT* November 29, 1990, 9. Northolt Grange, London, which usually used a local swimming pool, brought a small swimming pool into the church, 'Portable swimming pool becomes baptistry', *BT* October 18, 1990, 11. Mexborough, which first met in a public house and then moved to a portacabin, hired a portable baptistry for its first baptismal service, 'Mexborough. Baptism is a first', *BT* July 9, 1992, 16.

raised to the required temperature well before the service began, so that no-one would need to attend to it during the service.[117] After reading *Concerning Believers Baptism*, Tait Patterson suggested that the editor consider adding another chapter, with suitable illustrations, on how to build a baptistry and how to furnish robing-rooms, as 'Ofttimes the service is distorted by the inconvenience of the baptistery and the difficulty of reaching a robing-room', and he wondered why the BU Council did not insist on an ideal baptistry for every new building opened with their aid.[118]

Keith Jones identified two major influences and a third minor one on Baptist architecture, which he believed did influence worship. The first influence was the 'misterium tremendum', exemplified in the 'mock-gothic proportions of many 19th century Baptist buildings.' Second was the Greek gymnasium where the austere building is seen as 'the place of education and oratory', where the baptistry is hidden and the communion table small, dominated by the pulpit. Third, and more recently, was the 'secular "space"', being cost-effective but featureless, indistinguishable from the scout hut. He rejected each of these for the starting point of the upper room where 'our worship is based as a community around the three realities of the Word, the Table and the Baptistry.' Practically, this could be achieved by the congregation gathering around the word, table and baptistry, neither one of these dominating the others, adding a plea 'to uncover our baptistries (and light them more effectively)...if we really believe Baptism to be important.'[119]

Theological arguments, however, have been voiced more often. At their most basic, Baptists have thought little beyond the necessity of the baptistry for total immersion and its symbolism as a grave.[120] The candidate descends into the watery grave, is immersed, dying with Christ and to sin, and then emerges, rising with Christ to a new life. The candidate leaves the baptistry having literally 'passed through'[121] the

---

117 Bryan, 'Preparation, Administration and Visitation', 73.

118 D.T. Patterson, '"Concerning Believers Baptism"', *BT* April 13, 1944, 6.

119 K.G. Jones, 'Architecture and Worship', in K.G. Jones *et al, Christian Worship: Some Contemporary Issues* (Leeds, revised 1989), 11-12.

120 'A Coffin', 'Baptistery', *BT* November 29, 1934, referred to the 'coffin-shaped' baptistry at Milford-on-Sea, built in 1816, though C.F. Perry, 'Christian Baptism and the Campaign', *BT* August 31, 1933, 586, objected to the grave-like shape of the baptistry. Most baptistries are straight with steps at each end, but there were variations. Cheriton, Folkestone, J.C. Carlile's church, had a T-shaped baptistry which was situated in the chancel, *BH* 1908, 513; Yardley, Birmingham, had an elliptical one, *BH* 1967, v; New Road, Bromsgrove, built 1990, is elliptical with the steps at each end curving into the main pool; Wellingborough had an open octagonal baptistry, *BH* 1901, 371.

121 'To pass through the waters of baptism' is a standard Baptist phrase used to describe the rite. It is surprising, then, how seldom it has been recorded, though many

baptismal waters. For this reason most baptistries have steps at either end. Gilbert Laws alikened the baptistry to 'the mighty preacher..., [who] has continually spoken of the difference between nature and grace, and forbidden us to regard culture, amiability and good manners as the equivalent to a regenerate heart.'[122] The majority of twentieth-century baptistries have been situated on the communion platform in front of the pulpit and this emphasizes 'the centrality of the Word of God'.[123] W.T. Whitley, who denied any special benefit or efficacy obtaining from the administrator, similarly denied the sanctity of special places. 'Worship is acceptable not according to liturgy, celebrant, and hallowed walls, but according to the temper of the worshippers',[124] a fact which led to baptism being administered anywhere it was deemed appropriate, whether in a baptistry or the open air. However, the norm, for obvious reasons, has been in church and the specially built baptistries.

However, several have sought to address this lack of attention to the theology of the baptistry. A.J. Barnard impressed that, 'The cynosure of all eyes should be the pulpit, the baptistery and the table. They should be placed in closest juxtaposition.' For him, closed baptistries were to be deplored, arguing that in many churches 'with a little skill and design they could be rendered permanently open, a silent witness to the open confession of repentance and faith in Christ.' A number of churches had stained glass windows depicting the descending dove, while others had this on the wall behind the baptistry. 'This has more than an artistic service; it is a silent testimony to the gift of the Spirit so closely associated with baptism.'[125] His own preference was that where it was convenient candidates should enter from one side of the baptistry and come out the other 'as a sign of passing through from death to life.'[126]

T.A. Bampton similarly criticized closed baptistries when he regretted that 'usually' they were under the floorboards as though Baptists were

---

'traditional' phrases and practices are so common that few think about mentioning them or writing them down. See, e.g. C.H. Ellis, 'My Baptism', *BT* January 28, 1926, 67.

122 G. Laws, 'Denominational Self-Consciousness. The Crying Need of Baptists To-day', *BT&F* July 20, 1923, 518. An example of this is 'Here is water, what is to prevent me from being baptised?', *BT* April 16, 1998, 3, when, at a service at Guiseley, an open filled baptistry was used as a visual aid for the sermon on Rom. 6:3 and ended up being used for the unplanned baptism of six.

123 E.g. 'Emmanuel, Gravesend', *BH* 1966, v.

124 Whitley, *Church, Ministry and Sacraments*, 102, commenting on Jn 4:19-24.

125 Barnard, 'The Use of Symbols in the Baptist Church', 13. According to Winward, *Reformation of Our Worship*, 66, 'Whether near the entrance or at the centre of the building, the baptistery should always be conspicuous', a point he reiterated in almost identical words in 'Embodied Worship', in R.C.D. Jasper (ed.), *The Renewal of Worship* (1965), 49.

126 Barnard, 'The Use of Symbols in the Baptist Church', 16.

ashamed of the sacrament which distinguished them from fellow Christians. Ancient baptistries were prominent, therefore, 'an uncovered baptistery is a fine testimony to the most solemn and joyful initiatory rite known to man.'[127] Douglas McBain similarly criticized closed baptistries as though 'we [are] ashamed of the quantity [of water] we use', rather than being 'proud of our baptismal practices.'[128] Another writer criticized the continuing practice of constructing baptistries with which, he claimed, it was impossible to make the service impressive, adding, 'When planning a place of worship, one of our first considerations should be the baptistery and robing rooms, especially the necessity of having an open baptistery, which is a visible sign, not only of our practice, but of the central facts of the Gospel.'[129]

A common explanation for closed baptistries, concealed beneath the rostrum, was that there was not room for them to be given their own place. To counter this, G.W. Rusling declared that 'we have to keep before our minds the primary purpose to which the sanctuary is dedicated. Only if we have right priorities in our *thinking* is there much hope of right priorities in design.'[130] He argued that, 'To bring the baptistery into a good composite relationship with the pulpit and the table seems to present a problem in some schemes though the difficulties usually disappear when adequate space is allowed. To hide it under the platform 'is very hard to justify among us who have a distinctive witness to bear about Believers' Baptism!' He asked whether Baptist buildings should be complicit with open membership churches bringing the charge on Baptists that people could join them without being baptized at all. 'An open baptistery is preaching all the time, even when not in actual use. It is an abiding witness to the necessity of conversion and to all that wealth of truth which the New Testament associates with our new birth through the saving acts of God. It is a constant reminder to the church of its evangelistic commission. We should be eager to keep it in sight to bear its witness.'[131]

---

127 T.A. Bampton of Frome, 'Baptists and Their Baptisteries', *BT* February 6, 1947, 7. An open baptistry was clearly favoured by Channon, *Much Water*, 1; S.E.L. Larwood of Welling, Kent, 'Buried With Christ', *BT* April 11, 1963, 5. The example of the early church and the baptistries which they built, several noted, supported the mode of immersion, e.g. Flight Lt. H.W. Wheate, 'A Fifth Century Baptistery', *BT* July 5, 1945, 7, writing about, and supplying pictures of the 5th century church in Apollonia, near Cyrene; R.B. Hannen, 'A 6th Century Baptistery', *BQ* 13.2 (April, 1949), 87-89. See also Martin, 'Baptism in the Fourth Century', 370-72.

128 McBain, *Fire Over the Waters*, 178.

129 By the Editor of 'The Christian Advocate', 'A Liturgical Scholar on Baptism', *BT* January 14, 1943, 5.

130 G.W. Rusling, *Baptist Places of Worship* (1965) 9-10.

131 Rusling, *Baptist Places of Worship*, 13-14.

The newly built Baptist Church Centre in Barnoldswick, Lancashire, placed the open baptistry at the entrance of the worship room signifying the way by which people enter the church.[132] In the first of a series on worship, Henton Davies examined the importance of the sanctuary as the place of worship, dividing the sanctuary into three principal parts—the place for the Bible, namely the pulpit; then the rostrum for the communion table and baptismal pool; and then the pews/seats for the worshippers. In the second, 'Between the two "ends"', he located the communion table standing over or adjacent to the baptistry, this signalling and portraying the victory of the cross over sin and death.[133]

Closed or Open Communion

In the seventeenth century most Baptists practised strict/closed communion, that is, only baptized believers could share in communion. However, from the earliest days there were those who believed that the question should be left to the individual to decide. Controversy was the inevitable outcome, advocates of open communion arguing strongly against the strict practice,[134] and there were from the 1640s and 50s Independent churches which practised open communion.[135] In the eighteenth century the great majority of Baptist churches were closed membership and closed communion,[136] and though closed communion predominated at the beginning of the nineteenth century, as the century progressed more and more churches opened up their tables.[137] By 1877

---

132 'This plan puts baptism at the front door', *BT* March 18, 1976, 6.

133 G.H. Davies, former Principal of Regent's Park College, 'Letting Down the Ladder', *BT* October 8, 1992, 18.

134 Such as John Bunyan opposed by William Kiffin in the seventeenth century; Daniel Turner, J.C. Ryland, Robert Robinson and John Ryland were opposed by Abraham Booth and Andrew Fuller in the eighteenth; details of which see Brown, *English Baptists of the Eighteenth Century*, 130; and Robert Hall against Joseph Kinghorn in the nineteenth, on which see Walker, *Baptists at the Table*, 42-70 and 70-83; and Briggs, *English Baptists*, 61-69.

135 Though in a minority, these included Bunyan's Bedford church, and the originally Independent congregation meeting at Broadmead, Bristol, which in time became increasingly Baptist. See White, *English Baptists of the Seventeenth Century* (2nd edn, 1996), 10. On p.11, White stresses that these churches were not the norm among Particular Baptists.

136 So W.T. Whitley, reference unrecorded, cited by the 1937 *Report of the Special Committee*, 18.

137 The most infamous incident was connected with the Particular Baptist St. Mary's, Norwich, when the opening of communion in the face of trust deeds led to a protracted law suit which split the church and had to be resolved by the Master of the Rolls. See, e.g. C.B. Jewson, 'St. Mary's, Norwich', *BQ* 10.7 (July, 1941), 398-406;

John Clifford bore testimony that over the preceding fifty years all General Baptist churches had come to practise open communion[138] and that the number of open membership churches had also increased,[139] a fact which led to considerable tensions within the Connexion. By 1883 Clifford claimed that two out of every three of the leading Particular Baptist churches were open membership.[140] This movement meant that by the beginning of the twentieth century, Charles Williams could write that the majority of Baptists practised open communion.[141]

In the early years of the twentieth century, open communion was strongly advocated by some of the denomination's leaders,[142] for which they were accused of breaching the great commission.[143] But Charles Brown's comment that the Strict Baptist position had all but vanished from English life,[144] must be contested in the light of the recognition by the 1937 *Report of the Special Committee* that the advocates of closed communion and closed membership made up 'a substantial minority of the total body of Baptists in Great Britain.'[145] The 1951 BU report *The*

Payne, *The Baptist Union*, 87-89; Walker, *Baptists at the Table*, 36-41; Briggs, *English Baptists*, 44-45.

138 J. Clifford, *GBM* December 1877, 448, cited by Briggs, 'Evangelical Ecumenism: II', 166. Payne, 'Intercommunion from the Seventeenth to the Nineteenth Centuries', 99, 'During the nineteenth century...most Baptist churches adopted "open communion", in common with the other Free Churches.'

139 See Briggs, 'Evangelical Ecumenism: II', 166-67.

140 J. Clifford, *GBM* February 1883, 53-54, cited by Briggs, 'Evangelical Ecumenism: II', 167. It was these facts which led members of both traditions to question the need for continuing separation and which paved the way for the amalgamation of the two denominations in 1891. For details of the 1891 union see Briggs, *English Baptists*, 96-157, and his fuller discussion in 'Evangelical Ecumenism: I', 99-115; 'Evangelical Ecumenism: II', 160-79.

141 Williams, *Principles and Practices*, 25. This was confirmed by Whitby, *Baptist Principles*, 41-42. On this whole question in the nineteenth century, see Walker, *Baptists at the Table*. There is little to doubt that a powerful force in this movement had been the support of Charles Spurgeon, who, however, rejected the practice of open membership.

142 E.g. Williams, *Principles and Practices*, 25-26; C. Brown, 'Christian Unity', *BT&F* January 31, 1919, 56. See also Whitby, *Baptist Principles*, 42-43.

143 The divine order set down in the Great Commission was discipleship, baptism, teaching to observe all things Christ commanded and consequently observing the commandment 'This do in remembrance of Me'. This accusation was reported in both Williams, *Principles and Practices*, 26, and Whitby, *Baptist Principles*, 42-43.

144 C. Brown, 'Christian Unity', *BT&F* January 31, 1919, 56.

145 *Report of the Special Committee*, 17. This is confirmed by Ford, *Twenty-Five Years*, 41, who could only say that churches practising open communion were 'far more prevalent' than closed communion churches. Useful discussions of the open–closed communion debate are provided by the *Report of the Special Committee*, 14-23; and E.F. Clipsham, 'Should His Table be closed to the non-baptized', *BT* March 10, 1966, 8, who

Lord's Supper acknowledged the continued existence of closed membership but proceeded to ask whether maintenance of a 'closed Table' was not fundamantally incompatible with the general Baptist understanding of the Lord's Supper as set out in the report itself.[146]

So by mid-century, the overwhelming majority of Baptist churches practised open communion, and this is reflected by the comparative lack of material discussing the issues and the few writers who continued to discuss closed communion.[147] To the present, it has effectively disappeared from discussion within the BU.

Closed or Open Membership

It is not the purpose here to offer a detailed examination of the theological debate concerning closed or open membership, merely to plot the changes in practice among Baptist churches which have taken place this century.[148] As it had influenced the move to open communion, so too the recognition of the wider church led churches and individuals to advocate and practise open membership. With the growing closeness

---

asked whether it was possible that both open membership churches and open communion–closed membership churches were right in the sense that they both expressed important truths that must not be ignored.

146 R.L. Child (ed.), *The Lord's Supper: A Baptist Statement* (1951), 13-26. The report, pp.33-34, advocated the open communion position, recognizing that the Lord's table belonged to Christ alone and therefore recommended that 'we...welcome to it in His Name all who sincerely love Him, no matter to what branch of His Church they may belong?' See also p.32, after having reported the divergences of opinion on the terms of communion, 'We record [these statements on the difference among Baptists concerning open or closed communion] as expressing that liberty of conscience which we believe to be one of the most precious gifts of the Gospel, and we conclude that as no uniformity exists among Baptists in this matter, so neither should any attempt be made to impose it. They are finally answerable not to one another but to their Master.' Percy Evans used this position when he advanced that the cause of intercommunion between denominations would be most effectively furthered by the growth and practice of open communion among the Free Churches. See P.W. Evans, 'A Baptist View', in Baillie and Marsh (eds.), *Inter-Communion*, 195. The whole of this article is a helpful overview of the history and practice of open communion and intercommunion, effectively being in itself an advocacy of open communion, pp.185-195. Interestingly, the *Baptist Church Rules* (n.d., but 1950s), 3, assumed open communion, with no mention whatever of closed communion. This further supports the decline of this point of view.

147 One of the few references is to be found in Clark, *Call to Worship*, who suggested closed communion on pp.50 and 59, though he did not clearly state it.

148 While it is clear that even in 1937 there continued to be churches and ministers who both favoured and practised closed communion and membership, see *Special Report of the Committee*, 22-23, they were few indeed and no record of their continued existence within the BU beyond this point has been discovered.

between denominations reflected, for example, in the Free Church movement, it is clear that the growth of 'ecumenism' was exerting a considerable influence on Baptist theology and practice, which was reflected in the growing number of Union churches, and that, conversely, the move towards open membership was regarded as being a step towards closer co-operation or even federation with other Free Churches.[149]

However, this 'ecumenical gesture' could lead, and often has led, to the diminution of baptism among Baptists when believers have been accepted into membership who have never been baptized,[150] a practice which George Beasley-Murray described as a 'dismal feature' of Baptist life, though the motive was 'unquestionably good' seeking 'to give practical expression to the conviction that the Church of Christ is larger than the Baptist denomination.' While being 'a happy development from the ecumenical point of view', its obvious danger is allowing young people, brought up in a Baptist church, to be welcomed into membership without baptism.[151] If open membership should continue, 'let it be clearly understood that it is solely for *members of other Churches* transferring into a Baptist Church', thereby restricting open membership to what it was intended to be, 'an act of Christian charity and fellowship among the Churches, in recognition that other communions are as truly Christ's and as truly Church as Baptists are. But young people confessing their faith and converts from without should never question the need for baptism;

---

149 Bateman, *John Clifford*, 133, reported Clifford's conviction in the late 1880's early 1890s that a move towards open membership would go far towards bringing Congregationalists and Baptists closer together; and *Report of the Special Committee*, 16, 'it would be easier for Open than for Close Membership Baptists to unite with Congregationalists or Presbyterians.' In his letter to the Merseyside Baptists ministers' fraternal in which he encouraged them to make public their opposition to the union and reunion issues in 1941, R.W. Black wrote, 'The day *may* come when Baptists can join a United Church without disloyalty to truth. But that day is not yet. For the present, "open membership" is the utmost concession we can make', in Townsend, *Robert Wilson Black*, 112, italics his. In a similar way, Shakespeare, *Cross-Roads*, 135, had earlier seen open membership as a step towards Free Church federation

150 *Believing and Being Baptized*, 29, 'What had originally begun as a desire not to "unchurch" others who had previously been members of other churches, has become a lack of conviction about baptism for the "unchurched".'

151 Beasley-Murray, *Baptism Today and Tomorrow*, 86-88. He continued, 'In such circumstances it has apparently never entered the heads of leaders of the communities what a strange phenomenon it is that Christians should wish to receive the sacrament of the Church's continuing life (the Lord's Supper), but not the sacrament of initiation into the Church, and how irregular it is to permit it to happen... Nor is it realized that in these circumstances baptism has been made a purely private option for the Christian who wants it...for this is a matter of individual judgment!' Fowler, 'Baptism', 257-70, criticized those who contend that open membership is consistent with baptismal sacramentalism.

they should refrain from both Church membership and participating in the communion service until they have submitted to baptism.'[152]

The latter part of the nineteenth century and the early decades of the twentieth saw an increasing number of churches throughout the country open first their communion tables and then their memberships.[153] While the number of open membership churches were comparatively few in the early decades of the century,[154] by 1947 Underwood could comment that most of the churches in London and the South were open, though the movement in the North, and particularly Yorkshire, had made little headway.[155] The number of churches opening their membership has

---

152 Beasley-Murray, *Baptism Today and Tomorrow*, 88, his italics in the first quotation. Similarly, while recognizing the existence of 'many' open membership Baptist churches, F.C. Bryan, minister of Tyndale, Bristol, an open membership church, 'Preparation, Administration and Visitation', 65, pressed that 'it would be fatal for the ordinance to be treated in a take-it-or-leave-it-as-you-please spirit, by which the solemnity and significance attaching to it in the New Testament and in the past history of our churches would be utterly destroyed.' See also Gilmore, *Baptism and Christian Unity*, 78-80.

153 Payne, *Fellowship of Believers* (2nd edn, 1952), 82. To the open membership churches already mentioned above in John Clifford's list, can be added Union Chapel, Manchester (f.1842), Blenheim Union Chapel, Leeds, founded in 1848, and the old Accrington church when it moved to Cannon Street in 1874 under Charles Williams, on which see Underwood, *History of English Baptists*, 207-08.

154 See Williams, *Principles and Practices*, 35. This situation still pertained two decades later, see Robinson, *Life and Faith*, 120. This was confirmed by R.W. Thomson.

155 Underwood, *History of English Baptists*, 207-11. From its founding in 1865, the LBA accepted open membership churches into fellowship, while the YBA refused to admit into fellowship the church at Blenheim, Leeds. Not until 1887 was a compromise suggested by Dr Edward Parker and accepted by the Association which then recognized 'only the baptised members of the Church', and on this understanding the church was welcomed into the association, see J. Haslam, 'The Yorkshire Baptist Association', in Shipley (ed.), *Baptists of Yorkshire*, 313. This practice continued throughout the period up to 1937, when Ford, *Twenty-Five Years*, 41-42, reported that Yorkshire Baptists' reluctance to open the membership of their churches was due to their fear that their Baptist character and witness would be jeopardized. See his whole discussion of the membership issue on pp.41-45. In 1898 the YBA had responded to Shakespeare's launching of the Twentieth-Century Fund by resolving that it would 'have no hand in the formation or maintenance of Churches having what are termed "mixed memberships"', p.62. A few of the churches in the Sheffield area, Ford reported, did have open memberships, while others had a roll of 'communicant members', p.68. It would appear, however, that by 1937 even the YBA was more diversified than at the beginning of the century, so Ford could happily conclude, 'Churches that were originally General Baptist, and churches whose terms of membership permit the enrolment of unbaptized Christians now meet in hallowed fellowship with the disciples of William Gadsby', p. 70.

continued to increase,[156] as has the number of churches with closed membership and a communicant membership,[157] but many (perhaps the majority) of newly formed churches have been open membership from their opening,[158] so much so that it is now widely recognized that they comprise the majority of Baptist churches.[159]

Within the extant literature of the first half of the century it was the proponents of open membership who were most vocal because it was they

---

156 E.g. Theydon Bois was an open communion church from its founding in 1889 (previously it had been a Baptist Mission, f.1888), and it adopted open membership in 1921 after a Mr Tidball, a Congregationalist, had been elected to the diaconate, see D. Walling, *Chapel on the Green: A Short History of Theydon Bois Baptist Church* (Theydon Bois, 1994), n.p., but pp.4 and 8; Berkhamsted (a General Baptist church, f.1722) adopted open membership in 1970, though it was required that the minister had been baptized by immersion along with 75% of the diaconate, see O. Wright, *Baptists of Berkhamsted* (Berkhamsted, 1990), 53, and Miniutes of a Deacon's Meeting held on January 6, 1970, kindly supplied by the secretary, Mr O. Wright, in a detailed letter, January 19, 1991; New Malden, Surrey (f.1862), opened its communion in 1899 and its membership in 1986, see W.J. Maggs, *New Malden Baptist Church: 125 Years. A History from 1862 to 1987* (New Malden, 1987), 18-19 and 78.

157 E.g. the Baptist Tabernacle, Swindon, which in 1965, after several years' discussion, instituted associate membership, and this was the first step towards its joining Central Churches, Swindon, later known as Central Church, Swindon, see Dunscombe, *Footprints of Faith*, 48. This is also the practice of the church at Newcastle-under-Lyme, information from Prof. J.H.Y. Briggs.

158 E.g. New Milton, Weston-Super-Mare, see *Fifty Fruitful Years: A Short History of Milton Baptist Church, Weston-super-Mare, 1926–1976* (Weston-super-Mare, 1976), n.p., but p.13; Salisbury Road, Plymouth, (f.1907), see D.W. Johns, *From 1907–1987* (Plymouth, 1987), n.p.; Amesbury, near Salisbury (f.1991), see *Amesbury Baptist Church. Doctrinal Basis. Constitution. Covenant of Membership*, 5; and the Friars Congregation, an independent congregation which separated from its mother church, Shoeburyness and Thorpe Bay, in 1991, *Shoeburyness and Thorpe Bay Baptist Church. Friars Congregation Constitution and Rules* (1991), '1. MEMBERSHIP (a)'.

159 So *Believing and Being Baptized*, 28, which was written from the assumption that Baptist churches are of the 'open membership type' and called upon 'all readers of this report to ask seriously whether a membership "closed" to all except those baptized as believers takes sufficient account of the work of God's spirit among all the Christian churches.' This remark would include closed membership churches with a supplementary membership. The only firm figures have been provided by Ellis, *Baptist Worship Today*, 21, who reported that between 50.4–58.5% of churches do not make baptism a requirement of membership. He also shows that 41.4% of churches require baptism for full membership, which breaks down to (rounded up) 17% requiring baptism of all members (i.e., closed membership), and 24% requiring baptism for full but not communicant membership, pp.22-23. This study is based on a 1996 questionaire which received 1812 responses (85% of BU churches), carried out by the BU's Worship and Doctrine Committee.

who were arguing for the minority and less-established position.[160] For them it was personal faith not baptism which counted for membership[161] and it was a matter for the individual's conscience,[162] and they rejected the accusation[163] that open membership betrayed Baptist principles.[164]

---

160 See, e.g. 'United Union Meetings', *BT* September 26, 1935, 696; 'A General Baptist' from London, 'Church Membership', *BT&F* August 6, 1925, 565; H.E. Stickler, 'The Future of Denominationalism', *Frat.* 4 (October, 1931), 18; G.H. Ruffell Laslett, 'Christian Unity', *BT* October 27, 1932, 740; J.B. Skemp of Bilston, Staffs, 'Our Baptist Testimony', *BT* September 26, 1935, 696; G. and S. Morris of Ashford, Kent, 'Open or Closed Membership', *BT* May 5, 1966, 4.

161 J.E. Compton, *The Place of the Sacraments in the Baptist Church* (1910), 6-7, 'in support of the open-membership view it is pointed out that in the New Testament baptism stands related to faith in Jesus rather than membership with an organised society', a position justified by appealing to the conversion of the Ethiopian Eunuch in Acts 8. See also pp.8-9. J.H. Rushbrooke, 'The Church as a Divine Society', *BT&F* April 12, 1918, 226-27. Cook, *Why of Our Faith*, 82. Cook succeeded Dr C. Brown as minister of the open membership church at Ferme Park (1925–39), and later in his 'Must We Die Out?', *BT* April 2, 1936, 259, he wrote, 'Many of us belong to Churches that are Baptist in their witness, and yet welcome gladly to the full privileges of their membership all who love the Lord Jesus whether they are baptised by immersion or not.' R.G. Ramsey, minister at Ferme Park from 1939–43, 'Church Membership', *BT* August 30, 1928, 628, argued, 'Baptism is not Church membership. It is the symbol by which we pledge our personal discipleship to Christ. Church membership is our pledge to service.' J.P. Ede, a personal member of the BU, 'If I Were Dictator of the Baptists', *BT* July 11, 1940, 439, suggested the standardization of entry into church fellowship on the basis of profession of faith because, 'Baptism must remain a voluntary act, and on that account would not be made a condition of church membership. An "outward visible sign" must not be allowed to take the place of "inward spiritual grace". If the rite determined membership this would entail the expulsion of some of our present church members and the refusal of admission by transfer from non-Baptist Free Churches.' Such an act, he added, would also dispose with the anomaly of open and closed communions.

162 E.g. J.E. Roberts, 'Christian Unity—Our Relation to Other Churches', *Supplement to the BT&F* May 12, 1916, III; Marshall, *Conversion or the New Birth*, 373. In this they were following J. Clifford's lead and the Westbourne Park constitution which he had written, Article 2 of which stated that, 'Every applicant for membership is urged to consider the Lord's will on this subject, but the rule followed is "Let every man be fully persuaded in his own mind", and act according to his judgment of the Master's teaching. The whole question is left to the individual conscience', see Marchant, *Dr. John Clifford*, 45. Williams, *Principles and Practices*, 35, applied this same argument for the rights of individual churches to decide for themselves, a position on which Robinson, 'The Place of Baptism', 213, concurred.

163 Made by, e.g., W.T. Lea, *The Place of Baptism in the Baptist Church* (1911), 15-16, 'We are doing no man an injustice by enforcing baptism as the condition of membership... We are coercing no man's conscience. We are denying the discipleship of no man. We are keeping no man out of the Church. We cannot do that, the Baptist Churches and all other Churches are open to any man on conditions, and the man who is sincerely anxious to join our Church will accept our conditions and pay our price.' Later,

The move towards open membership has been blocked in many cases by clauses within Trust Deeds and sometimes by a refusal to change,[165]

---

he continued, 'Let our testimony be untainted by compromise and let us continue to place baptism in the Baptist Church where it has been placed from the very beginning, placed there as we believe by our Lord Himself, in the forefront of our Church life, as the authoritative condition of our membership.' See also E.W. Probert of Grantown-on-Spey, 'Our Baptist Testimony', *BT* September 12, 1935, 664; F.C. Spurr, 'Rev. F.C. Spurr's Correspondence: Baptism and Reunion', *BT* June 29, 1939, 510; E.F. Knight, 'A Reconsideration of the Sacraments', *Frat.* 82 (October, 1951), 9; Green, 'The Authority for Baptising', 20; A.S. Cooper of Thornbury, 'Open Membership', *BT* April 14, 1966; and B. Haymes, *Conversation Piece: Baptist Identity* (n.d., probably mid-1980s), 4. However, Robinson, *Life and Faith*, 120-21, conceded that the peril of open membership was lessened when the minister was a convinced Baptist, a point he reiterated in 'The Place of Baptism', 213.

164 So, e.g. Lewis, 'Baptised into Jesus Christ', 15, who declared himself to be a 'Baptist Christian' and that it was 'our' duty to uphold Baptist principles, but this did not lead him to 'plead for "close membership" churches.' In fact, four of his five pastorates had practised open membership. Robinson, in Robinson and Rushbrooke, *Baptists in Britain*, 31, described open membership as an 'anomaly', but later, 'The Place of Baptism', 214, conceded that 'If you have a convinced Baptist at the head of an open-membership Church [such as John Turland Brown at College Street, Northampton], I do not think you need fear the issue.' He then added, 'But are all Baptist ministers convinced Baptists?' noting a report he had heard of three suitable candidates being refused baptism by a Baptist minister in a Baptist church 'on the grounds that believers' baptism by immersion might offend certain paedo-baptist worshippers!'

165 E.g. Zion, Cambridge, membership of which, according to the Trust Deed of October 28, 1845, stated that 'The Chapel...and other premises hereby conveyed to be used for an assembly for a place of meeting for Religious Worship by a certain Church Society or Congregation of Evangelical Protestant Dissenters of the Particular Baptist Denomination holding the principles of open communion now assembling and meeting together therein...', there being no reference to baptism as a qualification for membership. The 'Rules of the Church of Christ of the Baptist Denomination Assembling for worship at Zion Chapel, Cambridge', agreed at the church meeting on March 7, 1859 and revised November 29, 1899, agreed that the church should practise open communion but closed membership, see section II. During the pastorate of Vellam Pitts (1931–46) the conditions of membership were queried in a letter from Mr Pitts to M.E. Aubrey, January 27, 1940. On behalf of Aubrey, the BU Solicitors, Ellis and Fairbairn, replied, stating that, in their opinion, this phrase implied closed membership, because, 'It is clearly, and always has been, a principle of the Particular Baptist Denomination that one of the qualifications for Church membership is [baptism by immersion on profession of faith], and in cases where the intention is otherwise it is usual for the Trust Deed to contain a provision that membership is open...', letter to Mr Pitts, February 1, 1940. When the issue arose again in 1990, Mr John Barfield of the BU Corporation, the church's trustees, disagreed with Ellis and Fairbairn's interpretation, noting the amalgamation of the General and Particular Baptists in 1891, writing, 'It is clear that the majority of Baptist Churches today are permitted by their Trusts to admit all Believers by Profession of Faith', a position shared by the BU's present Solicitors,

but several ways round this have been found. Some churches, like Harvey Lane (from 1845 Belvoir Street), Leicester, during Robert Hall's ministry (1808–26), developed a communicant membership,[166] where such members were barred from voting in deacon's elections[167] and usually for the appointment of a new minister. However, in May 1918 the church meeting accepted the communicant members into full membership, despite the fact that the Trust Deeds[168] of the church stipulated closed membership.[169] Little, however, has been written on this subject.[170]

Another means of joining a Baptist church is by a letter of transfer.[171] As the number of open membership churches increased, this became an increasing problem unless the closed churches were prepared to accept

---

Cameron's, adding, 'we would argue that the practice of the Denomination has changed since 1940', letter to A.R. Cross, March 28, 1990. The church meeting, however, did not open its membership. Allaway, 'Membership of a Local Church', 7, discussed a similar situation at his church in Wood Green, London.

166 Mitchell, *Not Disobedient*, 158. It is interesting that Hall's church at Harvey Lane did not practise open communion in his time as pastor and during his controversy with Kinghorn. The church did not open its table until the beginning of 1827 shortly after the arrival of the next pastor, J.P. Mursell, p.58. The origin of both the term and the practice of communicant membership, as far as Harvey Lane was concerned, was when Hall established what was known as 'the little church', a group of Paedobaptists who were worshippers but not full members of the church, to whom Hall administered the Lord's Supper separately, p.51. The origin of the term and idea of 'communicant membership' is uncertain.

167 See the discussion and statistics supplied by Ellis, *Baptist Worship Today*, 21-22.

168 On Trust Deeds, see Appendix 2 below.

169 Mitchell, *Not Disobedient*, 158, and for the relevant section of the Trust Deed, p.79. It is also called 'associate membership', e.g. *Believing and Being Baptized*, 28, which, noting this practice, encouraged these churches 'to consider how they might find creative ways to reduce the effect of this distinction [between full and associate members] between kinds of membership, as far as is possible within legal restraints.'

170 Of communicant members, J. Jones, 'Communicant Members', *BT* October 3, 1946, 9, merely noted they were those who, apart from baptism, supported the Baptist witness by their presence, service and money. It is unclear whether this is the James Jones of Tewkesbury, Cardiff or Milford Haven. Communicant members were only briefly discussed by Bacon, *Church Administration*, 45.

171 The procedure was discussed by Bacon, *Church Administration*, 45. This practice has not gone unchallenged. E.g. in 1911, Lea, *Place of Baptism*, 4-5, remarked, 'We have little to gain and perhaps much to lose by relaxing our strict rule.' He then claimed that Baptist churches only rarely received such applications for membership, and reported, 'I am enabled to say concerning the largest open Church in London, whose Pastor is one of our most popular ministers, that "the number of those who join on profession without baptism is very small indeed."'

the applicants' prior membership in an open Baptist church,[172] which many were not prepared to do.[173] This whole matter has been increasingly thrust upon churches as the population has become more mobile, and as more churches have opened their memberships.

The theological issues have been regularly debated throughout the century,[174] with little development in either of the arguments. Such dis-

---

172 Whitby, *Baptist Principles*, 90, 'We recognise membership of other Churches of our own faith and order, and a member of a Baptist Church—who has been baptised on a profession of faith—is eligible for membership in any Baptist Church the world over, on being formally transfered.' In this, however, Whitby was overly optimistic. Gilmore, 'Baptist Churches Today and Tomorrow', 144-45, believed that those baptized in infancy and in full membership with their previous church should be allowed to transfer their membership as though coming from another Baptist church, though this has not always happened. Queen's Road, Coventry, accepted new members by transfer as early as W.W.B. Emery's ministry (1906–13), if not before, see C. Binfield, *Pastors and People: The Biography of a Baptist Church, Queen's Road, Coventry* (Coventry, 1984), 145.

173 See, e.g. 'Layman', 'Baptists and Intercommunion', *BT&F* May 9, 1919, 276, whose wife, a Wesleyan Methodist, had been welcomed into membership of a large and influential Baptist church near London, but on moving to Yorkshire had found that all fourteen Baptist churches in the town practised strict membership and twelve of them strict communion. 'The demand for immersion in her case she regards—quite justifiably in my opinion—as a reflection upon the validity of her previous Christian fellowship, just as the majority of our ministers regard the demand for reordination (or as I should view a demand for "confirmation") in order to obtain recognition by the Church of England.' The options, he felt, left open to them were either to leave the Baptist denomination or to remain absentee members from the London church. He concluded, 'Let union, like charity, begin at home! How can we expect other Churches—either Free or Established—to recognize our Churchmanship when so many of our own Denomination refuse to admit theirs?' This similar situation arose in Zion, Cambridge (closed membership) in the early 1990s, when a young man, baptized as an infant and raised in the Catholic Church, and married to a Baptist, was denied membership unless he was rebaptized. This he did not do. Details from personal knowledge. Sometimes, however, the opposite situation arose, see Ruth E. Trevithick of Ealing, 'Closed or Open Membership', *BT* July 18, 1957, 6, recounted how, on moving to London from South Yorkshire, she had been unable to find a closed membership Baptist church to which she could transfer her membership. Did this mean, she asked, that she and her husband took their membership too lightly? Why should anyone wish to be identified with a Baptist church if they did not agree with Baptist principles? She then suggested that only closed membership churches should be called 'Baptist', while others should be called 'Union' churches.

174 E.g. the addresses given to the Worcestershire Association respectively in 1910 and 1911 by Compton, *Place of the Sacraments*, arguing for open membership, and Lea, *Place of the Sacraments*, arguing for closed membership. W.A. Page of Gravesend, 'The Basis of Church Membership in the Baptist Body', *Supplement to the BT&F* October 20, 1911, III (open), opposed by H. Chalmers of Redhill, Surrey, W.H. Millard of Clydebank, Mr J. Bown of Hove and Mr F. Barrett of Leeds, all in 'The Basis of Church Membership in the Baptist Body', *BT&F* November 3, 1911, 692. In 1957 the

cussions, however, have subsided in recent years not least because the majority of churches now practise either open membership or closed membership with a supplementary roll. However, the development and growth of open membership churches has led to a number of anomalies. While accepting the practice of open communion, Wheeler Robinson rejected the suggestion that the question of membership should be handled in the same way, for, if it did, 'Our dictionaries might then define a Baptist Church as the only one which did not make baptism a condition of admission!'[175] This, however, is not wholly true, as unbaptized members were known in Congregational churches,[176] and neither the Society of Friends nor the Salvation Army practise either sacrament. A number of other anomalies have also arisen in practice. In both open and closed membership churches candidates have been baptized but have not then proceeded into membership of the church,[177] and it has been common practice for candidates from other denominations to have been baptized and to have remained in membership with their own church.[178]

---

membership issue was debated in the *BT* from June to September—arguing against open membership, G. Leigh Hunt of Coulsdon in Wales, 'Closed or Open Membership', *BT* June 20, 1957, 7; Ruth E. Trevithick of Ealing, 'Closed or Open Membership', *BT* July 18, 1957, 6; N.A. Quick, 'Closed or Open Membership', *BT* July 25, 1957, 6; and, W.H. Millard of Tyronen, Montrose, 'Closed or Open Membership', *BT* August 8, 1957, 4; and for open membership, Mr W.D. Black of Edenbridge, 'Closed or Open Membership', *BT* July 11, 1957, 7; 'C.L.' of Devon, an 'Open Baptist yet Baptist!', and J.W. Ashley Smith of Wigan, both in 'Closed or Open Membership', *BT* August 8, 1957, 4; and F.J. Smart of Buckhurst Hill, 'Closed or Open Membership', *BT* September 5, 1957, 7.

175 Robinson, *Life and Faith*, 120-21. Rusling, *Baptist Places of Worship*, 13-14, also noted this and argued that baptism and church membership belonged together. *Report of the Special Committee*, 15, noted that the figures from all BUGB&I churches (excepting Bedfordshire, Buckinghamshire, Huntingdonshire and the East Midland Association) from 1903–32 showed that in almost all instances where figures were available for members joining by profession of faith without baptism 'the figures show a tendency to rise.'

176 See Dr Albert Peel, Editor of *The Congregational Quarterly*, 'Why I Worry About the Baptists', *BT* May 26, 1938, 409; F.C. Spurr, 'Rev. F.C. Spurr's Correspondence: Baptism and Reunion', *BT* June 29, 1939, 510, reviewing B.L. Manning, *Essays in Orthodox Dissent*, quoted him as saying, 'Some Congregationalists haven't been baptised...'; 'Baptists, Congregationalists and Presbyterians', *BT* May 30, 1946, 10, which reported the reissue of E.J. Price's, Principal of Yorkshire United College, *Baptists, Congregationalists and Presbyterians* ([1933], 1945 edn), 24, which recorded the fact that 'Congregationalists do not, in general, insist upon Baptism as essential for Church-membership, though many do.'

177 J.B. Middlebrook, 'Baptism and the Church', 55, though he said this was rare and not at all typical.

178 Reported by Middlebrook, 'Baptism and the Church', 55-56. Often baptismal services have been shared with an/other denomination(s), e.g. 'Not Baptists But Baptised', *BT* June 23, 1960, 16; 'Baptists and Anglicans to Unite for Baptismal

The presence of unbaptized deacons has also arisen,[179] though this has usually been compensated for by Trust Deed stipulations that the majority of deacons must be believer-baptized.[180]

The two positions on membership have not developed significantly in spite of centuries of, at times heated, debate. Advocates of closed membership appeal to the New Testament precedent of baptism as an act of initiation into the church, while open membership advocates have been able both to recognize and to take into consideration the existing divided state of the church on baptism and its rightful subjects, and at the same time clearly acknowledge the primacy of faith over the rite of baptism.[181]

Service', *BT* February 22, 1962, 8; 'Baptismal Service with local Methodists', *BT* January 12, 1967, 13; and Baptist ministers have often been willing to baptize members from other denominations who were refused baptism (seen as rebaptism) within their own Churches.

179 Payne, *Fellowship of Believers* (1st edn, 1944), 69, observed that the 'widespread opening of membership' had led to the presence of deacons and leaders who had never been baptized, pp.83-84. In his defence of open membership, Mr R. Jewson, J.P., of St. Mary's, Norwich, 'If I Were Dictator of the Baptists', *BT* May 16, 1940, 319, noted that the church's senior deacon had never been baptized and that he had worked with him on the diaconate for over twenty five years, 'and a more loyal, hard-working, and faithful colleague it would be difficult to find. If he were crossed off our membership roll to-day it would be a great loss to our church, and, further, would have far-reaching repercussions', later quoting the words of Jesus, 'for he that is not against us is for us.' Keynsham (f.1807) opened its table and membership in 1883 and opened its diaconate in 1908, see R. Leitch, *The History of Keynsham Baptist Church* (Keynsham, 1985), see pp.53 and 56, and p.63 respectively. The secretary at Calne (open mem-bership) in the mid-1990s, Mr T. Mills, was baptized as an infant in the Methodist Church, but had not been believer-baptized.

180 See Bacon, *Church Administration*, 175.

181 It needs to be noted that the reason for the existence of both traditions within Baptist life is because what was taken as read in the New Testament, that all believers were baptized on conversion (most recently argued for by Cross, '"One Baptism"', 173-93), has become separated down through the centuries, not least by Baptists. Therefore, both parties are able, with justification, to appeal to New Testament precedent for their positions. It should also be pointed out that the linking of baptism with church membership has been an oft repeated position of many Baptists. This is most obviously the rationale behind the closed membership position. But such views have failed to differentiate between the fact that in the New Testament baptism was the completion of the conversion process, nor do they differentiate between conversion-baptism into the church universal from entry into a local church fellowship. This matter has virtually never been directly raised or addressed by Baptists. One of the few who has was Champion, *Baptists and Unity*, 81, 'Membership in the church is then not dependent upon the individual's decision to join a particular local congregation; it derives from his incorporation into Christ whereby he is made to share in the whole life of the body.' It was also discussed by E.F. Clipsham of Ashford, 'Should His Table Be Closed to the Non-

Both views illustrate the point already made that the majority of Baptists have been unable to deal adequately with the fact that in the New Testament baptism is both an act of God and an act of the believer, a means of grace and a profession of faith, an ordinance and a sacrament, an individual but also a corporate act, an inward and an outward matter, initiatory yet a sign of discipleship and a pledge of allegiance, a part of conversion as well as a witness to the decision of faith, an act of obedience in the present but also an eschatological rite. Ernest Clipsham suggested that both closed and open membership churches were right in the sense that they both expressed important truths which should not be ignored. Closed membership declared the fact that as God owned the sacraments, therefore the church had no right to dispense with his ordinances, and also testified to the conviction of the church as the fellowship of believers. In contrast, open membership maintained that since God had accepted paedobaptists into his church, then Baptists had no right to unchurch them. To deny to membership those who were invited to the Lord's table was to imply that they were good enough for the Lord, but not good enough for Baptists. Both practices, he claimed, were right in what they affirmed, but wrong in what they denied, and he believed that it was not impossible to combine the positive insights from both traditions.[182]

Liturgical Developments

1900–1937

Teresa Berger has traced the antecedents of the Liturgical Movement on the European continent during the Enlightenment and particularly the nineteenth century, where, in Britain, it gained wide influence in the 1830s through the Anglo–Catholic Oxford Movement.[183] Though its very association with the Tractarians alienated the vast majority of the Free Churches, its influence eventually began to permeate, often unnoticed, into the life of the churches. Early Baptist liturgical pioneers

---

Baptised', *BT* March 10, 1966, 8, and E.A. Payne, 'The Rise and Decline of the Downs Chapel, Clapton', *BQ* 27.1 (January, 1977), 34-35.

182 E.F. Clipsham, 'Should His Table Be Closed to the Non-Baptised', *BT* March 10, 1966, 8. He cited the covenant of 1780 from the church at New Road, Oxford, which practised open membership and an open table, but it did so without regarding baptism as optional, while still recognizing a genuine difference of opinion among Christians on the subjects and mode of baptism. This is printed in Payne, *Fellowship of Believers* (2nd edn, 1952), 79-80.

183 T. Berger, 'Liturgical Movement', in Lossky *et al*, (eds), *Dictionary of the Ecumenical Movement*, 616-18. See also Davies, *Ecumenical Century* (1965), especially pp. 13-49, for its influence specifically in England see pp.38-47, and his *Worship and Theology in England: VI. Crisis and Creativity, 1965–Present* (Grand Rapids, 1996).

in this include Henry Bonner, minister of Hamstead Road, Birmingham, who introduced 'liturgical' worship to his congregation, and in 1884 issued a service book for use in the church,[184] and F.B. Meyer, who incorporated a limited measure of congregational response in the services of Christ Church, Westminster Bridge Road.[185] It must, however, be recognized that a survey of the controversies which often accompanied the introduction of such materials and the advocacy of a Baptist 'liturgy' reveals that what was usually perceived by 'liturgy' was the introduction of 'set' prayers.[186] However, it must not be overlooked that the two denominational hymnbooks of 1900 and 1933, and the various service books, introduced a wide variety of 'liturgical' material, not just new hymns and chants, to the Baptist constituency.[187] Michael Walker observed: 'That there was a more general move to order and dignity in worship is evidenced by the appearance of ministers' "manuals" that gave form to the celebration of the sacraments and introduced their users to the catholic treasury of prayer.'[188]

---

184 See the Preface to Spurr's *Come Let Us Worship*, vii-x.

185 His biographer, W.Y. Fullerton, *F.B. Meyer: A Biography* (n.d.), 76, commented on the reason for the church's non-denominational status and revised liturgy, 'that it might embrace all sections of the Church of Christ.' See also I. Randall, 'Mere Denominationalism. F.B. Meyer and Baptist Life', *BQ* 35.1 (January, 1993), 19-34, especially pp.20-21 and 26-27, where Meyer's character as an 'undenominational Baptist' is explored, particularly, though not solely, in his views on baptism. It should not be forgotten that Christ Church, Westminster Bridge was, in Randall's words, p.26, 'a Free Church which united Baptist and Congregational ingredients', and which met in the Congregational building which installed a baptistry for Meyer's pastorate. The morning and evening services, which drew the largest crowds, were more liturgical than the afternoon services in which Meyer was less austere and more informal, see Fullerton, *Meyer*, 111. See also J. Cox, *The English Churches in a Secular Society: Lambeth, 1870–1930* (Oxford, 1982), 145; Walker, 'Baptist Worship', 23.

186 E.g. see the various letters in the *BT&F* from January 5 to April 12, 1912 under the title 'A Plea for a Baptist Liturgy'.

187 See the overview by Peaston, *Prayer Book Tradition in the Free Churches*, 122-30.

188 Walker, 'Baptist Worship', 23. However, Walker is mistaken if in mentioning M.E. Aubrey's *Minister's Manual* (1927) he is implying that this was the first from a Baptist. Two prior manuals originated from Baptist pens, both intended for Free Church use, and were by that very fact 'ecumenical'—see below. Davies, *Ecumenical Century*, 44-45, linked the growing number of such manuals with the discussions of worship in the denominational journals and newspapers as the only substantial evidence of the growing influence of the Liturgical Movement on the Free Churches in the first three decades of the twentieth century. No substantial books on the subject came from the Free Churches until N. Micklem edited *Christian Worship: Studies in its History and Meaning* (1936), to which H.W. Robinson contributed an article on 'The Old Testament Background', 19-34.

The earliest two manuals were both prepared for use in the Free Churches and as such can be legitimately described as 'ecumenical'. The first appeared c.1905 and was compiled by G.P. Gould and J.H. Shakespeare[189] and suggested that the baptismal liturgy be introduced by the minister reading a prepared address, either in full or part, which began: 'We gather here to fulfill a commandment of God: not to discuss its terms.' The authors then described the need to defend the mode of immersion and to explain the rise of infant baptism as of apologetic interest only and out of place 'when we come to the baptismal pool',[190] neatly side-stepping and moving away from controversy.[191]

The second manual was arranged by F.B. Meyer.[192] Unlike the sermon supplied by Gould and Shakespeare, Meyer's addressed itself directly to the fact that believer's baptism differed 'from the ceremony which is often called Baptism in two particulars', namely, the subject and mode of baptism.[193] This was made possible by the inclusion of a section on the baptism of children by the paedobaptist Elvet Lewis.[194]

---

189 The British Library Catalogue (BLC) lists it under the title *An Order for the Solemnization of Matrimony, together with an Order for the Burial of the Dead, to which are added Hymns suitable for the Marriage and Burial Services* (n.d.), and it records it as being 32 pages long. The edition used here is G.P. Gould, President of Regent's Park College, and J.H. Shakespeare, *A Manual for Free Church Ministers containing an Order of Service for the Solemnization of Matrimony, also for the Burial of the Dead, The Dedication of Infants, and the Baptism of Believers, to which are added Suitable Hymns for each of the Services* (n.d.), which is 59 pages long, published jointly by James Clarke & Co and the Kingsgate Press. BLC lists its entry as c.1905 and the precise nature of the relationship between the two is unclear. It is possible that the latter volume is a later expanded edition, though there is no mention of this in the BLC, and if this is the case then its date of publication is unknown. This 'later' volume is the one from which all references are taken.

190 Gould and Shakespeare, *A Manual for Free Church Ministers* , 41-42, 'But when we come to the baptismal pool it is not to offer an apology for what we do there, or to engage in controversy with those from whom we dissent, but to rejoice with great joy in the fulness of meaning which the ordinance has for us'.

191 A three point message on the ordinance followed which saw baptism as a profession of discipleship, the declaration of salvation received, and an act of obedience, Gould and Shakespeare, *A Manual for Free Church Ministers*, 41-45.

192 F.B. Meyer, *Free Church Service-Manual* (n.d. [1911]), published by the NCEFC.

193 Meyer, *Free Church Service-Manual*, 23-24. Meyer described baptism as a badge of discipleship, indicative of the break with the old life and the beginning of a new and better one and as a profession of belief in the salvation won by Christ through his life, death, burial and resurrection. It ended with an epiclesis and the benediction from Jude 24-25. An interesting note is appended to the order of service as an 'N.B.', p.26: that it is 'desirable that before this ordinance is administered, the mode of its administration should be carefully explained to the candidates, so that they may not be taken unawares, but pass through it with composure and comfort'. It is unclear whether this comment

The first wholly Baptist manual was prepared by M.E. Aubrey in 1927.[195] No address was supplied, but Aubrey proposed six elements for the sermon on the meaning of baptism: it was an act of obedience to a dominical command; a distinctive act in which the believer confessed their faith in God and commitment to service; an act whereby one joined 'the company of all who, receiving God's grace in Christ, have submitted themselves to His will'; an imitation of Christ; a declaration that the believer entered into new gifts of grace, since baptism was an outward and visible sign and seal of the inward and invisible grace of baptism into Jesus; and a symbolic declaration of death to sin and resurrection to a new and regenerate life of obedience.[196]

Two further Baptist manuals were produced, both in 1930, by F.C. Spurr and D.T. Patterson. The former was a 'new and thoroughly revised' edition of Henry Bonner's service book by one of Bonner's successors at Hamstead Road, which did not contain an order for baptism or infant dedication, though it did provide a service for communion.[197] Patterson's manual provided a brief order for baptism, incorporating mainly scripture readings, and, in contrast to previous services, invited the congregation to stand throughout the baptism(s) 'in reverent and prayerful silence.'[198] Both books, and the 1937 volume *Readings for Worship* by J. Isaiah Jones of Christ Church, Aston,[199] exemplify the contention that at this time the 'Baptist liturgical movement' was primarily concerned with participatory corporate prayer.

The publication of these manuals is clear evidence of a movement within the denomination towards a greater degree of standardization within worship,[200] though this can in no way be claimed for the whole of

---

suggests the general absence of baptismal preparation classes or not, for it would be reasonable to suppose that were such classes held such matters as the actual act of baptism itself would be both described and explained.

194 Meyer, *Free Church Service-Manual*, 40-45.

195 M.E. Aubrey, *A Minister's Manual* (n.d. [1927]), 25-33. The edn used here is the revised version of 1940.

196 Aubrey, *A Minister's Manual*, 29-30.

197 F.C. Spurr, *Come Let Us Worship: A Book of Common Worship for Use in Free Churches* (1930), 'Preface', vii.

198 Patterson, *Call to Worship*, 156-59. The 4th edn of 1947 is used here.

199 See Peaston, *The Prayer Book Tradition*, 130.

200 There were few dissimilarities in the orders of service presented in the four manuals. See, e.g. Aubrey, *A Minister's Manual*, 25-33: Scripture, Address, Prayer, Immersion (sung/organ verse), Benediction. The only variations were that Gould and Shakespeare, *A Manual for Free Church Ministers*, 45, added a hymn between the address and prayer; Meyer, *Free-Church Service Manual*, 21-26, had the choir sing the verse of a hymn during the immersion; while Patterson, *Call to Worship*, 158-59, added a hymn and scripture sentences between the prayer and immersion, and an optional verse between the sung verse or the blessing from Num. 6:24-26 and the benediction.

the denomination. There can be little doubt that a great many ministers used only parts of such orders for services, supplementing them with their own material, as was accommodated by the rubrics in the manuals at specific places. What these manuals do provide evidence of is a more deliberate structuring of worship services. Equally, it cannot be doubted that many continued to use familiar forms not directly reflected in the published manuals, especially as Meyer, Shakespeare and Spurr were known advocates of both reunion and the introduction of 'liturgy' into Baptist worship and were held in suspicion by many more conservative Baptists who were still antagonistic towards anything approximating to ritualism, sacerdotalism or Catholicism.[201] These manuals also introduced material from other Christian traditions, often not explicitly, but paving the way for later developments in the liturgical movement's influence within Baptist circles.

The major sources introducing non-Baptist material into Baptist worship and which gained widespread popularity and use were the two new Baptist hymn books of 1900 and 1933. Eighteenth-century Baptists had pioneered the incorporation of hymns from other traditions into their hymn books[202] and this practice continued when *The Baptist Church Hymnal*[203] included metrical litanies, chants and anthems. Many of the older Baptist hymns disappeared and surprisingly few hymns by Baptists were retained.[204] The section on baptism totalled seventeen hymns, only five of which were by Baptists.[205] *The Baptist Church Hymnal (Revised)*

---

201 And this despite the fact that Meyer clearly came from the theologically conservative wing of the denomination, as did Spurr, who had been the BU Missioner from 1890–1904, see *BH* 1935, 250.

202 J.O. Barrett 'Hymns Among the Baptists', in H. Martin (ed.), *A Companion to the Baptist Church Hymnal (Revised)* (1953), xxiv.

203 The chairman of the Editorial Committee for the *BCH* was Dr S.G. Green, Principal Emeritus of Rawdon College and first Book Editor, then Secretary of the Religious Tract Society, see J.O. Barrett, *Rawdon College (Northern Education Society), 1804–1954: A Short History* (1954), 27-28. He was ably assisted by John Clifford, George Hawker, Edward Medley and J.R. Wood.

204 E.A. Payne, 'Baptists and Their Hymns', in R.W. Thomson (ed.), *The Baptist Hymn Book Companion* (revised edn, 1967), 20-21.

205 *BCH* 490—'In all my Lord's appointed ways', J. Ryland (1753–1825); *BCH* 494—'Hast Thou said, exalted Jesus', J.E. Giles (1805-1875). Originally with six verses, the full text can be found in the 1879 *Baptist Hymnal*, see Martin (ed.), *Companion to the Baptist Church Hymnal (Revised)*, 124; *BCH* 498—'Glory to God, whose Spirit draws', B.W. Noel of John Street Baptist Church (1799–1873); *BCH* 500—'Dear Master, in Thy Way', John Thomas (1859–1944) minister in Huddersfield, Myrtle Street, Liverpool and Sutton; *BCH* 502—'Buried with Christ! Our glad hearts say', W.W. Sidey of Tottenham (1856–1909), written in 1900. Of the remaining hymns, four were by Congregationalists, five by Anglicans, one by an Anglican who later became a Catholic, one Brethren and one Presbyterian.

contained sixteen baptismal hymns, only five by Baptists, a sixth having been altered by a Baptist.[206] Of these only two were new additions, including the one altered.[207] Ian Randall has also contended that a number of ministers, including R.H. Coats of Handsworth, Wheeler Robinson, F.T. Lord, M. Glover and F.C. Spurr, wrote critically of Baptist worship and spirituality and planted the 'seeds of future liturgical developments...in the inter-war years.'[208]

Two *Companions* were produced to accompany the *BCHR*, the first in 1935, the second eighteen years later, edited by the ecumenist Hugh Martin.[209] The former provided introductory essays, which were not solely historical sketches, and helps to the use of the hymn book, and included several pages under the heading, 'Through the Year in Church Life',[210] reflecting and encouraging the growing use of 'liturgy' in the churches.

In 1927 Wheeler Robinson commented that Baptists needed 'an "Oxford Movement" of their own order' and that such would recapture a nobler church-consciousness and that this would doubtless bring some changes not only in polity but also in worship.[211] The radical nature of such a statement can only be fully realized when the strength of the Baptist reaction against Tractarianism is remembered,[212] and is evidence of how far Baptist thinking had progressed in nearly a century. This was further reflected nine years later when J.O. Barrett took up Robinson's

---

206   *BCHR* 472—'Hast Thou said'; *BCHR* 475—'Jesus, and shall it ever be', by the Presbyterian J. Grigg, altd. by Benjamin Francis (1734–1799), minister at Sodbury then Horsley. His alterations were generally considerable; *BCHR* 476—'Glory to God'; *BCHR* 480—'Dear Master, in Thy Way'; *BCHR* 428—'Buried with Christ!; *BCHR* 484— 'Master, we Thy footsteps follow', F.A. Jackson (1867-1942), written in 1932 while at Campden.

207   John Ryland's hymn was omitted. The remaining hymns were made up of six by Anglicans, two by Congregationalists, and one each by an Anglican come Catholic and Brethren.

208   Randall, *Evangelical Experiences*, 190-91.

209   C. Bonner and W.T. Whitley (eds.), *A Handbook to the Baptist Hymnal Revised* (1935); Martin (ed.), *Companion to the Baptist Church Hymnal (Revised)*.

210   Bonner and Whitley, *Handbook to the Baptist Hymnal Revised* , 124-25.

211   Robinson, *Life and Faith*, 174.

212   So N. Clark, 'In the Study', reviewing S.F. Winward's *Teach Yourself to Pray*, (1961), *BQ* 19.7 (July, 1962), 320, 'in one sense the story of Nonconformist worship at the middle of the nineteenth century is the story of reaction to the Oxford Movement... This influence of the worship of the Church of England upon that of the Free Churches whether *positively or negatively is one of the continuing factors in the historical scene*', italics added.

challenge,[213] providing further evidence within the denomination of how seriously Baptist worship was being reassessed.

Liturgical developments in mid-century were reflected in several areas: a growing consciousness on the part, chiefly it must be said, of ministers who began to think more liturgically about the actual conduct of worship, the numbers of articles and books which dealt either directly with Baptist liturgy or the subject of worship, the revision of several service manuals, a number of catechetical booklets, and the participation by a number of Baptist leaders in liturgical groups.

The 1948 statement on 'The Baptist Doctrine of the Church' described the general pattern of Baptist worship as 'in the Reformed tradition and....not generally regulated by liturgical forms. Our tradition is one of spontaneity and freedom, but we hold that there should be disciplined preparation of every part of the service.'[214] Ernest Payne confessed, 'Not many Baptists...have a reasoned theory or theology of worship',[215] and this fact was itself illustrated by Baptist hesitation and even disdain of the word 'liturgy' itself,[216] and by the outspoken disapproval of the liturgical movement by the BRF, who saw it as a betrayal of the denomination's evangelicalism. Both the ecumenical and liturgical movements, it was asserted, were evidence of increasing liberal trends within the denomination which over-emphasized the sacraments. This had led to dialogue with other traditions and a resulting shift in Baptist thinking on baptism, where it was now being suggested that there existed a direct link between the rite of baptism and the gift of the Spirit.[217]

Two figures stand out in particular in their commitment to the liturgical renewal of Baptist worship. The first is Neville Clark, whose writings incorporated not just abstract theorizing but the fruits of the regular leading of worship. He wrote, 'as a Baptist to Baptists',[218] remarking that of all the major denominations it was probably the Baptists who had been least affected by the liturgical movement. 'Our worship is

---

213   J.O. Barrett of Newcastle-on-Tyne, then, from 1949, General Superintendent of the North Eastern Area, 'An "Oxford Movement" Amongst Baptists', *Frat.* 22 (April, 1936), 9.

214   'Baptist Doctrine of the Church', 442.

215   Payne, *Fellowship of Believers* (2nd edn, 1952), 100. Payne also provided an important study on 'The Free Church Tradition and Worship', *BQ* 21.2 (April, 1965), 51-63, which dealt with recent Baptist developments on pp.60-61, reprinted in Payne's *Free Churchmen, Unrepentant and Repentant and other papers*, 15-29.

216   West, *Baptist Principles*, 21.

217   *Liberty in the Lord*, 34-36.

218   Clark, *Call to Worship*, Preface.

the result of the interplay of many curious historical factors; our tradition is strangely tangled; our cherished emphases are sometimes more fortuitous and often more recent than we imagine.'[219] The two sacraments, he insisted, belonged together, baptism, laying on of hands and first communion being the pattern of Christian initiation. The liturgy, he pressed, provided the ground plan for pre-baptismal instruction and church membership, and in countless ways would also be the governing and determinative factors for the whole life of the church and the whole existence of the baptized.[220] The goal, then, towards which the catechumenate moved 'in any church practising only believers' baptism' was the baptismal eucharist.[221]

The second figure is Stephen Winward, who produced two books of responsive prayers and readings[222] and presented the Whitley lectures in 1963, arguing that worship should be understood as a dialogue which did not consist in words alone. This was exemplified by the sacraments where 'The Lord acts through that which is done by his people with water, and with bread and wine, in obedience to his ordinances.' In language reminiscent of Brunner, Winward held that only when they were understood in terms of personal encounter and dialogue, could the nature of sacramental grace be rightly understood. In both, God met the believer through Christ in the Spirit, calling for the response of repentance, faith and allegiance. 'Both alike are intended to be encounter, word and answer.' Baptism is the sacrament of the word of God which had already been spoken to the catechumen through the preaching and teaching of the gospel in the power of the Spirit. Having been born anew the catechumen responded in repentance, faith and promise to God's initiative. The baptismal rite itself was both spoken and enacted word.[223]

In 1963, both Clark and Winward contributed to the controversial *The Pattern of the Church*, in which the four authors critically examined Baptist worship in the light of liturgical developments, Morris West noting that 'there is today a developing movement within the denomination towards a fuller and richer understanding of worship.'[224] Clark declared

---

219 Clark, *Call to Worship*, 9 and 31.

220 Clark, *Call to Worship*, 54.

221 Clark included an order for this service which he had used, Clark, *Call to Worship*, 58-59.

222 Neither of which dealt with baptism: S.F. Winward, *Responsive Praises and Prayers for Minister and Congregation* (1958), and *Responsive Service Book* (1965). Winward was minister at Highams Park, Walthamstow (1938–1966), after which he moved to Selly Oak Colleges, Birmingham, where he was to make perhaps the most valuable contributions of any Baptist in the area of liturgy.

223 Winward, *Reformation of Our Worship*, 27-28.

224 West, 'Baptist Church Life Today', 28, but see the whole discussion on pp.27-30.

that 'In the end, all roads lead at last to liturgy. It is at this point that the heart of the Church is unveiled; it is here that reform is most urgent and crucial.'[225] Gilmore encouraged a new approach to worship and this included a new understanding of baptism and the Lord's Supper. On baptism he wrote, 'From being simply a personal matter connected with decision or the experience of conversion, baptism must come to be regarded as the great act of initiation whereby a man is made a member of the Church of God.'[226]

Alongside a number of other books and articles which dealt with the overall subject of worship and in varying degrees baptism,[227] several older service books were revised and reprinted in the late 1930s to early 1950s,[228] while Stephen Winward collaborated with Ernest Payne in the preparation of what was to become the standard minister's manual for over thirty years, *Orders and Prayers for Church Worship*.[229] It also marked a radical departure from previous manuals in that it presented services for 'Christian initiation'—baptism–membership–communion with the option of the laying on of hands, as well as a service for the dedication of children.[230] The importance of *The Baptist Hymn Book*

---

225 Clark, 'The Fulness of the Church of God', 108

226 Gilmore, 'Baptist Churches Today and Tomorrow', in Gilmore (ed.), *Pattern of the Church*, 118-19. He also argued that baptism should also always take place before communion, p.125.

227 E.g. R.P. Martin's 'The Composition of 1 Peter in Recent Study', *Vox Evangelica* I (1962), 29-42, 'Aspects of Worship in the New Testament Church', *Vox Evangelica* II (1963), 6-32, and *Worship in the Early Church* (1964).

228 Patterson, *Call to Worship* (3rd edn, 1938 and 4th edn, 1947); Aubrey, *Minister's Manual* (reissued in 1946 and 1952, one of these reissues was also revised, though it is unclear which). Patterson was positively though briefly reviewed in *BQ* 9.4 (October, 1938), 256, and Aubrey even more briefly in *BQ* 10.4 (October, 1940), 240.

229 Its significance was recognized from the first. W.M.S. West, 'Editorial', *BQ* 19.1 (January, 1961), 1-3, compared it with it predecessors: 'Discerning readers will notice significant changes within the orders [of dedication and the two sacraments] as set out in the new manual. It is obviously at this point that the theology of the Church and its sacraments impinged upon the liturgy', p.2. Further, p.3, he viewed the order for baptism (baptism–communion–membership) as 'the most significant order' in the book.

230 Payne and Winward, *Orders and Prayers*, 123-27, 127-35 and 135-38 respectively. Payne and Winward's order of service suggested the following pattern: Baptismal hymn, Selection of scripture readings, Sentences explaining and setting out the meaning of baptism, Questions to the candidate(s), Prayer, Immersion followed by the Blessing or Hymn sung by the choir and/or congregation and/or one of the baptismal sentences from the *BHB*, Prayers, Hymn and Blessing (unless the normal order of worship be continued), pp.128-35. This order was more complex than the ones provided in the earlier manuals, and paved the way for the more complex and liturgically detailed orders of service to be found in *Praise God* and *Patterns and Prayers* (see below). *Orders and Prayers* also contained an important introductory essay on the subject of worship, ix-xxii, which explained, 'In the order for Believers' Baptism...it is not sufficient to set

(1962) is also difficult to overestimate, providing not just hymns for many and various occasions, including four for the presentation of infants,[231] seventeen for baptism[232] and three baptismal sentences,[233] but also a section for private use, and one containing canticles, psalms and selected scriptures for congregational chanting or alternate reading. Catechetical materials began to be published in the early 1950s,[234] coinciding with a growing emphasis on the need for a Baptist catechumenate,[235] but while this idea has never taken off,[236] it continues to be advocated.[237]

---

forth the response required of the candidates; a whole, balanced service must also declare the divine action and promises', xix. It was positively reviewed by W.W. Bottoms, 'New Manual for Ministers', *BT* December 29, 1960, 7, and N. Clark, 'Radio Review of New Manual for Ministers', *BT* January 19, 1961, 4, 8. This has been without doubt the most widely used and influential of all Baptist service manuals. Its wide use is referred to, e.g. by K.W. Clements, 'Editorial', *BQ* 28.7 (July, 1980), 291.

231 Including Hugh Martin's hymn 'Christ who welcomed little children', *BHB* 284.

232 Hymns by Baptists included the American F.W. Boreham, 'Eternal Father, whose great love—', *BHB* 288; B.W. Noel's 'Glory to God, whose Spirit draws', *BHB* 290; J.P Giles, 'Here, in this water, I do vow to Thee', *BHB* 291; J. Griggs, 'Jesus, and shall it ever be', *BHB* 293, altd by B. Francis; H. Martin's 'Lord Jesus, in Thy footsteps', *BHB* 295; F.A. Jackson, 'Master, we Thy footsteps follow', *BHB* 296; and B. Beddome, 'Witness, ye men and angels, now', *BHB* 304.

233 These (*BHB* 305), it was recommended, were suitable for singing by the choir or by the congregation as a whole, as the candidate emerged from the water, and were taken from Num. 6:24-26, Rev. 2:10 and 5:13, see Thomson (ed.), *Baptist Hymn Book Companion*, 241-42.

234 Other important catechetical material was produced by S.F. Winward, *The New Testament Teaching on Baptism, in the form of daily Bible readings for the instruction of Candidates for baptism* (1952), 11th impression 1982; P.R. Clifford, *The Christian Life: A Book about Baptism and Church Membership* (1954); R.E.O. White, *Invitation to Baptism: A Manual for Inquirers* (1962), which was still being reprinted in the 1980s; it is possible to include here R.L. Child, *A Conversation About Baptism* (1963); J.R.C. Perkin, *Divine Encounter: An Outline for Discussion of Believer's Baptism* (1965); Wallace, *Someone is Watching You*; P.J. Goodland, P.J. Hetherington, J.L. Pretlove and D.J. Warner, *Faith and Life: Practical Lessons in Christian Living* (1966), a church membership preparation course prepared by the Radlett Fellowship.

235 Though not unknown before 1960, the idea of the catechumenate came to prominence in an article by G.W. Rusling, Vice-Principal of Spurgeon's College, 'The Status of Children', *BQ* 18.6 (April, 1960), 250-51, and was advocated by *The Child and the Church*, 9-10, 14, 22-25, which, p.34, understood infant dedication to be the moment when the child was added to the church's catechumenate. D.F. Tennant, Head of the Church Education Department, Westhill College, Birmingham, 'The Child in Communion—An Enquiry', *Frat.* 173 (May, 1975), 18 and 26, stated that 'Baptism signifies the transfer from catechumenate to membership of the Body.' The number of those who advocated it rapidly increased. See also Beasley-Murray, *Baptism in the New Testament*, 373, 394; the contributors in Gilmore (ed.), *Pattern of the Church*, e.g. West, 'Baptist Church Life Today', p.18, and Winward, 'The Church in the New Testament',

Baptists were also officially represented in the newly formed Joint Liturgical Group (JLG)[238] in 1963 by Stephen Winward and Neville Clark.[239] The unofficial conference on worship and liturgy held at Swanwick in November 1962 also showed that the liturgical movement had gained significant ground within Baptist circles,[240] so much so that, in 1966, Alec Gilmore could confidently write, 'The growth of the liturgical movement everywhere is an indication of the way things are going', and this was reflected in the increasing appreciation of the sacraments.[241]

---

p.60; Gilmore, *Baptism and Christian Unity*, 101. The idea was, however, opposed by the conservative evangelical Radlett Fellowship, *The Gospel, the Child and the Church* (1967), 18-19.

236 D.F. Tennant, 'A Critical Look at Present Baptist Practice Regarding Children and Worship in the Light of Recent Thinking on Christian Nurture', *Frat.* 189 (October, 1979), 4, 'Some have tried to resurrect the "catechumenate" but without success.' He made the same point in his 'Anabaptist Theologies of Childhood and Education. (1) The Repudiation of Infant Baptism', *BQ* 29.7 (July, 1982), 299.

237 It has most recently been advocated by West, 'Child and the Church', 110.

238 The JLG is a joint venture between the Church of England, the Episcopal Church of Scotland, BU, Presbyterian Church of England, Methodist Church, CU and Church of Scotland. It has played an important part in helping British churches find common forms of worship and has provided a body through which they have participated in the search for internationally and ecumenically agreed English liturgical texts, so D. Gray, Anglican chairman of the JLG, 'Foreword', *Confirmation and the Re-affirmation of Baptismal Faith* (1992), 7. This and other books mistakenly record the establishment of the JLG as 1965, when its first meeting was actually October 10-11, 1963, see its founding 'Statement', R.C.D. Jasper (ed.), *The Renewal of Worship* (Oxford, 1965), n.p..

239 'Churches to Talk of Liturgy. Joint Group Formed', *BT* December 19, 1963, 1. Winward contributed an article to the JLG's first publication, see S.F. Winward, 'Embodied Worship', in Jasper (ed.), *Renewal of Worship*, 42-57, in which he sought to draw together the inward and outward components of worship.

240 'Churches to Talk on Liturgy', *BT* December 19, 1963, 1. Eric Sharpe of Oxford chaired the meetings, and though considerable interest was aroused, some eighty ministers attending and a booklist was published, it was decided not to form a separate liturgical group within the denomination. This meeting was negatively linked together with the publication of *The Pattern of the Church* as evidence of the existence within the BU of a 'liturgical movement and sacramental fellowship', see *Liberty in the Lord*, 45. Sharpe's interests were later shown in his contribution to the BU's Living Issues booklets, *Treasures of Christian Worship* (1964).

241 Gilmore, *Baptism and Christian Unity*, 48.

Comparison of three orders for baptism, by Jim Perkin,[242] Stephen Winward[243] and Alec Gilmore,[244] published between 1959 and 1966, show that the influence of the liturgical movement had led to a greater complexity in the baptismal service which included a larger number of components than ever before and reflected the broader interest in Christian initiation.[245] While at this time such complex services would have formed only a minority practice of baptism, membership and eucharist, their influence within the local churches depended almost entirely upon the inclinations and interests of the minister of the church.[246]

1967–1999

From the mid-1960s to the end of the century[247] Baptists, if anything, increased their interest in worship, an interest which has operated at various levels. This has in part been forced upon churches by the many changes within society which have accelerated in practically every area of life. This has caused churches many problems as change has become one of the most contentious issues within contemporary church life.[248]

---

242 J.R.C. Perkin, 'The Principles and Practice of Believers' Baptism', *BT* June 11, 1959, 6. The order of service he had adopted for the past three years at Altrincham lasted 90 minutes for four candidates. In *Divine Encounter*, 15, he provided another outline service, containing still more components.

243 Winward, 'The Administration of Baptism', 11.

244 Gilmore, *Baptism and Christian Unity*, 73-74.

245 Perkin's baptism–reception into membership–communion service contained twenty four distinct parts. Winwards baptism–reception into membership–communion service also contained twenty four distinct parts, while Gilmore's baptismal eucharist contained five main sections totalling twenty four parts.

246 'Baptism and Membership', *BT* November 1, 1962, 2, being the account of a service of baptism, communion and admission to membership in one service, led by Ian Mallard at Broad Clyst, Exeter, following a pattern similar to that outlined by Payne and Winward noted above.

247 A useful overview is provided by Davies, *Crisis and Creativity*, 127-36.

248 The whole issue of change has been with the churches since the 1960s, when the rate of change in both the church and society accelerated. Writing specifically on the issues involved peaked in the 1980s and early 90s. Baptist studies on the issue of change include D. McBain, minister of Lewin Road, Streatham, *No Gentle Breeze: Baptist Churchmanship and the Winds of Change* (Mainstream, 1981); N. Wright, tutor at Spurgeon's College, *The Radical Kingdom* and *Challenge to Change: A radical agenda for Baptists* (Eastbourne, 1991). The latter was highly recommended by D. Tidball in 'An Extended Review of Nigel Wright's Challenge to Change', *Mainstream Newsletter* 39 (April, 1991), 2-3, and a study guide was provided for it by S. Hembery of Crawley and R. Searle of Enon, Sunderland, 'Challenge to Change. A Study Guide', *Mainstream Newsletter* 42 (October, 1991), 8-14. See also S. Gaukroger of Stopsley, Luton, with D.

Change has affected most areas of Baptist worship, though, it must be noted, there is little to no evidence that such factors have significantly affected the practice of baptism.

THE LITURGICAL MOVEMENT

While many Baptists have continued to be resistant to 'liturgy' *per se*, a growing number of Baptist ministers and churches have welcomed liturgical developments,[249] many of them fuelled by personal ecumenical involvement and/or simply the growing openness among the denominations to influence from one another. Over the last three decades the number of opportunities for inter-denominational contact have increased, with a flourishing array of Christian conferences, retreats and holidays, chief among the latter being Spring Harvest.[250] Further, with increased population mobility, people tend to join churches like their previous one, whether or not it is of the same denomination,[251] and this has increased the cross-fertilization of ideas.

Since the 1960s Baptists have continued to develop liturgically, though not as uniformly as those of the previous period had imagined and hoped. In 1972 Stephen Winward wrote specifically of baptism, though it applies more generally to other forms of Baptist worship: 'Baptists have no prescribed liturgy, but administer the rite in the threefold context of the fellowship, the word, and the prayers. Baptism is not regarded as a private or domestic occasion, but is administered in the setting of the

---

Cohen, General Director of Scripture Union in England and Wales, *How to Close Your Church in a Decade* (1992); N. Mercer, Assistant Principal of London Bible College, who some years later entered the Anglican ministry, 'Coping with Change', *Frat.* 234 (April, 1991), 3-7. Clearly the matter of change was high on the agenda of evangelical and evangelical–charismatic Baptists, a fact supported by the many essays printed in the *Mainstream Newsletter*, e.g. D. Tidball, at the time of Mutley, Plymouth, 'Questions for the Present Time', no.20 (September, 1985), 2-4; R. Warner of Herne Hill, 'Worship and Culture (Part 1)', no.36 (April, 1990), 6-11 and 'Part 2', no. 37 (July, 1990), 6-10, and also Warner's *21st Century Church: Why Radical Change Cannot Wait* (n.d., [1993]).

249 E.g. see the whole volume of *Frat.* 165 (September, 1972), which was entirely given over to Christian worship, especially S.F. Winward's, 'Recent Trends and Developments in the Liturgical Movement', 5-11, but there was not a single reference to baptism in the whole issue. Baptism/initiation has never received the attention which communion/eucharist has received by Baptist writers on worship.

250 The importance of Spring Harvest is discussed by McBain, *Fire Over The Waters*, 134-40.

251 This point was clearly made by the report *Signs of Hope: An examination of the numerical and spiritual state of churches in membership with the Baptist Union of Great Britain and Ireland* (1979), 33, which, discussing geographical and social mobility, noted that 'many of our churches include members who have come from other traditions, often in sizeable numbers... It remains...that very many of those who have been baptised in our churches settle with their families in churches of other orders.'

congregation at worship, and of the reading and preaching of the word.'[252]

Baptists continue to prize highly their freedom of worship, freedom, that is, from prescribed liturgical forms,[253] so that there continues to be 'a wide variety of practice, from liturgical formality to charismatic exuberance, from reformed traditionalism to ecumenical experiment.'[254]

Three major factors can be identified which have influenced Baptist worship: the liturgical movement, the charismatic movement and the Baptist (reformed) tradition.[255] Because of its conservative nature the latter of these has not introduced anything new into Baptist worship and so attention will be focused on the first two.[256]

Liturgical developments have themselves taken place at two levels: through the various formal expressions of the liturgical movement such as the JLG and specifically liturgical texts, and through a growing general interest in worship which certainly has been fed by the former but which is separate from it.

The JLG has played an important role within British church life and a number of Baptists have been key figures within it.[257] Since 1965 the

---

252 S.F. Winward, "Baptism: 5. Baptist', in J.G. Davies (ed.), *A Dictionary of Liturgy and Worship* (1972), 50.

253 So *Patterns and Prayers*, 'Preface', v, 'Baptists have their roots deep within the Free Church tradition. Therefore the freedom of the Holy Spirit is a significant factor in their worship, and they do not have a fixed liturgy or approved prayer–book. This does not mean that worship has no shape or basic content, or that preparation and forms are despised.'

254 *Patterns and Prayers*, 'Preface', v. In fact, *Patterns and Prayers*, the most recent service manual, discusses 'Flexible Patterns', 'Rich Variety' and 'Different Influences' at the beginning of its opening essay on 'Christian Worship', pp.1-4.

255 Ruth Gouldbourne, Associate Minister at Bunyan Meeting, Bedford, and from 1995 tutor in Church History at Bristol Baptist College, 'Praise and Prayer', *BQ* 35.2 (April, 1993), 91-92, identified four categories of change: the ecumenical movement, the rise of charismatic renewal, changes in attitude towards liturgy and the general differences in society. Ellis, *Baptist Worship Today* 41, discussed the charismatic and liturgical influences. As such both are in general agreement with the influences identified here.

256 It should be recognized that any divisions for the sake of convenience or clarity can give the false impression that the two are separate things, whereas the actual situation is far more complicated and the various influences frequently overlap.

257 Chiefly N. Clark, S.F. Winward, C.J. Ellis and P. Sheppy. The latter two were involved in the JLG's *Confirmation and Re-affirmation of Baptismal Faith* (Norwich, 1992). This provided for those coming to confirmation, those needing to reaffirm their baptismal faith and those being recognized as members by the several participating churches, the third provision being useful for those coming from denominational churches to membership in an LEP. This document was itself stimulated by an earlier collection by Hugh Cross, at the time the BCC's ecumenical officer, for use in churches with joint Anglican–Free Church membership, see the letter to J.M. Cassidy from Michael Vasey, a member of the JLG and the Anglican Liturgical Commission, cited by

JLG has published a number of books which have dealt with initiation. For example, *Initiation and Eucharist* asked whether sufficient theological agreement existed to make possible the increasing adoption of recognizably common structures for the two sacraments.[258] It claimed that a wide measure of mutual recognition of baptism already existed across denominational frontiers, specifically in terms of the use of water and the trinitarian formula, and it sought to build on this minimal base. It also identified the total rite of Christian initiation as baptism, confirmation and first communion.[259] The JLG also keenly advocated use of the liturgical calendar and lectionary. For example, Neville Clark asserted that baptism 'should be tied closely to the Epiphany Festival' and that at Pentecost the 'baptized move forward from their baptism', the subject for year one being the life of the baptized.[260]

There have been a considerable number of books and booklets seeking to further the impact of the liturgical movement among Baptists, but

---

Cassidy, 'Membership of the Church', 'Part 1: The L.E.P.s', chapter 2, 'Denominational Membership', under the heading 'Joint Confirmation' see p.55, n.155.

258 N. Clark and R.C.D. Jasper (eds.), *Initiation and Eucharist. Essays on their Structure by the Joint Liturgical Group* (1972), 'General Introduction', 8. This had developed from the BCC's report *Areas of Ecumenical Experiment* (1968), recommendation 9: 'That the [JLG] be asked to draw up an agreed form of service for Baptism as a basis for further discussion', see *Initiation and Eucharist*, 9.

259 *Initiation and Eucharist*, 11 and 13 respectively. The language of the initiation section is strongly suggestive of N. Clark's style, though this cannot be proved. Liturgically, a recommended pattern of Christian initiation would include, pp.14-20: 1. The Scriptural warrant. 2. The act of renunciation. 3. Prayer at the font or baptistry. 4. The act of baptism, which would include use of questions to elicit a profession of faith and commitment. 5. The laying on of hands/anointing with chrism.

260 N. Clark, 'The Lectionary', in R.C.D. Jasper (ed.), *The Calendar and Lectionary* (Oxford, 1967), 21-22 and 24 respectively. The appropriateness of certain times of the Christian calendar was also acknowledged by P. Beasley-Murray, who noted that baptism was particularly fitting at Advent, that Lent was a period of preparation for baptism, that Easter was appropriate for the renewal of baptismal vows and Easter Sunday as a day for baptism, Epiphany as an opportunity for expounding the meaning of baptism in the ongoing context of the Church's mission in the world, while Mothering Sunday was a day when those baptized as believers could be invited back to the church. See P. Beasley-Murray, *Faith and Festivity*, 127, 151-52 and 161, 163, 148, 149, 152 respectively. Epiphany was similarly identified as an occasion for baptism by S.F. Winward, *Celebration and Order: A Guide to Worship and the Lectionary* (1981), 31. Gilmore, Smalley and Walker (eds.), *Praise God*, outlined the Christian year, and noted the appropriateness of the first Sunday in Advent as a baptismal service, 'the baptized being brought into the community of hope that awaits the coming of Christ'; of Epiphany as an opportunity for expounding the meaning of baptism, including fitting prayers; and Easter day for a baptismal communion, while Holy Saturday (an Easter eve vigil) was a fitting occasion for the renewal of baptismal vows, see pp.3; 14 and 16; 21, and 27-28 respectively.

those that did mention it generally contained only cursory references to baptism.[261] The seemingly peripheral place which baptism/initiation has played in this subject is further reflected by the *Worship File*, first published in the autumn of 1992, which provides resource material for worship leaders, produced by Baptist Publications.[262] The *File*, while largely dependent upon the contributions of the readership and reflecting the growing interest in and importance attached to worship and the adequate provision of worship materials, nevertheless has provided material on baptism on only seven occasions.[263] But by far the most important

---

261 E.g. M. Taylor, Principal of Northern Baptist College, *Variations on a Theme: Some guidelines for everyday Christians who want to reform the Liturgy* (1973), who made only a few historical references to the baptized, e.g. 29, 51 and 80-81; J. Wallace of College Street, Northampton, *What Happens in Worship* (1982), which contains one reference to baptism, p.12, and one to infant dedication, p.41; Winward, *Celebration and Order*, 31; and W.E. Whalley (ed.), *Christian Worship—Some Contemporary Issues* (Leeds, 1984, revised 1989), which included references to baptism in only three of the seven essays, e.g. p.2 'the sacraments', p.9 the closed—open communion debate, and pp.11-13 on the place of the baptistry in Baptist architecture (page references are the same in both editions).

262 The original editorial committee comprised C.J. Ellis, B. Green, former BU General Secretary, S. Jenkins of Cheadle Hulme, K.G. Jones, Deputy General Secretary of the BU, M. Nicholls of Bromley, and Tony Turner, tutor at Bristol Baptist College. It should be noted that the editorial committee has considerably changed over the years.

263 One of these occurred in a hymn by C. Ellis on Mt. 28:16-20, v.3 'This is news you can share,/ teaching all how to care./ Baptize those who will dare./ Here is your vocation:/ telling every nation', *Worship File* 1 (Autumn, 1992), M8; a baptismal hymn by Miss Stella Read, Librarian at Bristol Baptist College and a member at Horfield, Bristol, set to the tune 'Mit Freunden Zart', vs 2 and 4 declare: 'To show himself as one with us,/ Christ came for John's baptizing,/ And I would be as one with him,/ In dying and in rising./ This water shows my death to sin,/ My coming forth, life to begin,/ The new birth symbolising.' (v4) 'Christ joins me to his body now,/ That bonds be broken never:/ His earthly family be mine,/ Their strength my strength for ever./ Christ's life to live, his light to shed,/ His Kingdom in this world to spread,/ This be our great endeavour', *Worship File* 4 (Autumn, 1993), O17; another occurred in a report that some churches use a covenant service 'as a significant date for the act of Believers' Baptism', *Worship File* 9 (Winter, 1995), S85; B. Green, 'Preaching from Passiontide to Pentecost', believed this season to be a good one for preaching on baptism, while J. Tattersall of Burton Latimer advocated an Easter Sunday evening baptismal service, which included reference to baptism in the prayer of confession, *Worship File*, second series 1 (February, 1996), 4 and 19-20 respectively; an opening prayer at a baptismal service by I. Green of Walsworth Road, Hitchin, *Worship File* second services 2 (May, 1996), 37; and a baptismal meditation by David Pountain of Brighton, *Worship File* second series 12 (September, 1999), 32-33.

contributions to Baptist worship in this period have come from the two service manuals and the new hymn book.[264]

Praise God[265] identified five essential elements to the whole process of Christian initiation: the reading of scripture and the reasons for engaging in Christian initiation; profession of faith and commitment; prayers, including an invocation of the Spirit; baptism in the name of the Trinity, possibly with the laying on of hands; reception into membership and admission to communion.[266] The accompanying 'Statement'[267] set out the benefits promised by the Lord,[268] attributing them to those receiving believers' baptism *and* becoming members of his church.

Patterns and Prayers for Christian Worship is notable for its attempt to reflect the varied patterns and styles represented within BU churches,[269]

---

264 In 1974, the Psalms and Hymns Trust published *Praise for Today* as a supplement of modern hymns to the 1962 *BHB*. It was edited by E.P. Sharpe and R.W. Thomson. While recommending ten hymns for Holy Communion, it included none on baptism.

265 A. Gilmore, General Secretary of the United Society for Christian Literature, E. Smalley, Eastern Area General Superintendent, and M.J. Walker of Beckenham, (eds.), *Praise God*. M.J. Walker, 'Praise God: A New Service Book', *BQ* 28.7 (July, 1980), 314-16, noted the many changes in worship which had taken place since 1960: a greater variety of gifts and methods in public worship; the charismatic movement; the liturgical movement; new Bible translations; and changes of worship patterns in other churches and the resulting mutual influence of denominations upon each other.

266 *Praise God*, 137. Surprisingly for Baptists, *Praise God*, 121-66, recognized five sacraments and ordinances: Sunday worship, infant dedication and thanksgiving, Christian initiation, Christian marriage, and Christian burial.

267 Walker, 'Praise God: A New Service Book', 320, referred to the 'Service of Baptism', not 'Christian Initiation', and that the norm is baptism, reception into membership and communion. He noted that the order in no way varied from that in Payne and Winward's *Orders and Prayers*, though it was shorter and simpler. This perhaps explains why exactly twice the number of pages were given over to infant dedication and thanksgiving, the newer/less established rite, than Christian initiation, see 'Infant Dedication and Thanksgiving', pp.129-36, 'Christian Initiation', pp.137-40. G.H. Taylor, 'Michael Taylor *Guidelines: Variations on a Theme*', *BQ* 25.8 (October, 1974), 386, spoke of the 'shared beauty and power of the Baptismal–Communion service.'

268 These were in baptism the believer becomes one with Christ through faith, sharing his death and resurrection, the washing of the body with water being a sign of the cleansing of the whole of life and personality. It marks the reception of the Spirit and is an act of obedience, making a personal confession of faith and becoming part of 'the one holy, catholic and apostolic church.' The rubric, *Praise God*, 139, noted that some ministers might prefer to conduct the baptism at the beginning of the service, using the sermon as an opportunity to charge the newly-baptized, and that an appeal for those thinking of baptism should either come forward or to the vestry afterwards, adding that this was 'not necessarily with a view to being baptised at that moment.'

269 P. Tongeman, 'A book whose value far exceeds it's price', *BT* April 25, 1991, 10. Much of the work for *Patterns and Prayers* was done by the Baptist Ministers'

seeking to accommodate these variations by offering two patterns for the whole process of initiation,[270] followed by material for each of the constituent elements.[271] Like its immediate predecessors, the pattern of believers' baptism and reception into membership at the Lord's Supper was advocated,[272] as was 'the laying on of hands', whether in the baptistry or before or after reception into membership, because they 'all relate to our one initiation into the Body of Christ.'[273]

In line with the new emphasis on initiation rather than just baptism, the section dealing with it in *Baptist Praise and Worship* was headed 'Baptism and Membership' and contains sixteen hymns,[274] only nine of which are about baptsim.[275] The greatest potential contribution of this

---

Fellowship, with the consultative help at various times from the Federation of Lay Ministries, the BMS, College Principals, General Superintendents and various individuals informed about worship developments in churches experiencing spiritual renewal. For details and those involved see the 'Preface', *Patterns and Prayers*, v-vii.

270 The first pattern is for a single service of baptism, reception into membership and communion, the second a baptismal service on its own, which would be followed by a subsequent service at which the newly baptized would be received into membership, *Patterns and Prayers*, 93-95. The first pattern comprises twenty one parts, the second pattern is made up of twenty individual parts. Both these services reflect the greater complexity which has been incorporated into baptismal services due to the influence of liturgical developments.

271 The two patterns are followed by 'The Laying on of Hands', *Patterns and Prayers*, 102-04, and 'Reception into Membership', pp.104-07.

272 That this is becoming the normal pattern is shown by Ellis, *Baptist Worship*, 21-22: 15% of candidates are usually received into membership at the same service as their baptism; 47.8% are usually received at the same or next convenient communion service; while 7% are received into membership sometime later; and only 23.7% of churches do not necessarily link church membership to baptism. This pattern was described by M.J. Walker, 'Baptism: Doctrine and Practice among Baptists in the United Kingdom', *Foundations* 22.1 (1979), 78-80.

273 *Patterns and Prayers*, 93. These elements might take place in a single act of worship or may be divided between morning and evening services or between consecutive Sundays. Reception into membership, it was recognized, is not always linked directly with baptism but could follow a profession of faith or membership transfer.

274 The most notable fact about this section is its inclusion of ten new, twentieth-century hymns, only 2 of which are identifiable as being by Baptists (the denominations of the remaining 20th century hymn-writers are uncertain): *BPW* 416 by B. Beddome, 'Witness, both earth and heaven now', an altered version of *BHB* 304 'Witness, ye men and angels, now'; and P. Tongeman, General Superintendent for the South Eastern Area and, in 1995-96, President of the BU, *BPW* 410 'For me to live is Christ'. Based on Phil. 1:21-22, Tongeman's hymn is not specifically baptismal. A third hymn, *BPW* 415, 'May we learn to love each other', has a second verse added by Dr M. Ball of Sutton, but this is a hymn on membership.

275 *BPW* 402-405, 407, 408, 412, 414 and 416.

section to Baptist worship lies in its provision of ten readings, of which four relate to baptism.[276]

In 1972 Stephen Winward recognized the impact of the new perspective on Christian initiation: 'In some churches, the laying on of hands after baptism...has been restored. The practice of baptizing at the Lord's Supper is also on the increase. The desire to enrol the candidates as members of the church at the baptismal service itself is one outcome of the new emphasis upon baptism as initiation into the body of Christ.'[277] This still applies over twenty five years later, as services of baptism, reception into membership and communion have become more common,[278] though many churches still remain unaffected by this liturgical development.[279]

BIBLICAL WORSHIP

Since the 1960s there has been a growing interest in worship from the biblical perspective. A leader in this field has been Professor Ralph P. Martin.[280] A leading evangelical biblical scholar, Martin has written num-

---

276 *BPW* 417-420. The first three of these are responsive readings.

277 Winward, 'Baptism 5. Baptist', 50.

278 Walker, 'Praise God: A New Service Book', 315, 'Conversion, baptism and admission to church membership are more clearly seen as a unity and, even where baptism, reception into membership and communion are not celebrated in the one service there is at least the recognition of a sequence and the fact that the events, though separated by time, nevertheless hold together.' Similarly P. Beasley-Murray, *Faith and Festivity*, 59, noted that this practice is one of several possibilities, there being no *one* way in which new members are welcomed into the fellowship; and Hayden, 'Believers Baptized: An Anthology', 19, commented, 'This single liturgical act is now current practice for many Baptist congregations.' See also the services set out in *Orders and Prayers*, 127-61 (this material could be used for separate services or for one service of baptism–membership–communion); *Praise God*, 138; and *Patterns and Prayers*, 93-94.

279 Gilmore, Smalley and Walker (eds.), *Praise God*, 137, noted that 'Among Baptists of late there has been a growing tendency to bring closer together the act of baptism, reception into membership and admission to communion', but later added that this was 'by no means universal, many ministers and churches preferring to separate baptism and reception into membership either by several hours on the same day or perhaps even by several weeks.' Also Walker, 'Baptist Worship', 25, 'the uniting of baptism, communion and reception into membership into one liturgical act is practised in a number of our churches.' He continued: 'But there would still be many who see it as nothing more than an example of liturgical exotica and happily continue to sunder conversion, baptism, communion, church membership and, more recently, the gift of the Spirit one from the other.'

280 Martin, who left his position as lecturer in New Testament at Manchester University in 1969 to become Professor of New Testament at Fuller Theological Seminary in California, had served churches in Gloucester and Dunstable from 1949–1959, becoming a tutor at LBC until 1965 before taking up his appointment at Manchester. In 1988 he returned to Britain, becoming Professor in the Department of

erous books and articles on worship and other New Testament subjects, many of which have included discussion of baptism.[281] These scholarly works, while known, do not appear to have altered Baptist baptismal practice, though they have clearly provided an academically respectable biblical basis for believer's baptism.[282]

Biblical Studies at Sheffield University, during which time he served the church at Norwood Avenue, Stockport from 1988–93, and then as Associate Minister at Scarisbrook New Road, Southport, from 1993–95, shortly after which he returned to the USA.

281 R.P. Martin, *Worship in the Early Church* (1964, revised 1974); *The Worship of God: Some Theological, Pastoral, and Practical Reflections* (Grand Rapids, 1982). His articles on worship include: 'Patterns of Worship in New Testament Churches', *JSNT* 37 (1989), 59-85; 'New Testament Worship: Some Puzzling Practices', *AUSS* 2 (Summer, 1993), 119-26; 'Worship', in Hawthorne, Martin and Reid (eds.), *Dictionary of Paul*, 982-91; and 'Worship and Liturgy', in R.P. Martin and P.H. Davids (eds.), *Dictionary of the Later New Testament and Its Developments* (Leicester, 1997), 1224-38. Discussion of baptism also figures in a number of his other books and commentaries not already discussed: *Colossians: The Church's Lord and the Christian's Liberty. An Expository Commentary with a Present-Day Application* (Exeter, 1972), *passim*; *Colossians and Philemon* (NCBC; 1973), *passim*; *New Testament Foundations: A Guide for Christian Students. Vol.1: The Four Gospels* (Exeter, 1975), 179-80; *Vol.2: Acts–Revelation* (Exeter, 1978); *The Family and the Fellowship: New Testament Images of the Church* (Exeter, 1979), 76-81, 127-28; *Reconciliation: A Study in Paul's Theology* (1981), *passim*; *2 Corinthians* (WBC, 40; Dallas, 1986), 28, 131-32; *1, 2 Corinthians* (WBT; Dallas, 1988), *passim*; *Ephesians, Colossians, and Philemon: Interpretation: A Bible Commentary for Teaching and Preaching* (Atlanta, 1991). It should be noted that Martin's Festschrift was entitled, *Worship, Theology and Ministry in the Early Church: Essays in Honour of Ralph P. Martin*, M.J. Wilkins and T. Paige (eds.), (Sheffield, 1992), and contains a brief biographical outline by L.A. Losie, 'Ralph Philip Martin: Curriculum Vitae', pp. 21-32, and L.C. Allen, 'Personal Reminiscences', pp.33-36.

282 This interest in biblical worship is also evinced in H.H. Rowley, *Worship in Ancient Israel: Its Forms and Meaning* (1967); B.R. White, Principal of Regent's Park College, 'Worship among the English Baptists Today', *Mainstream Newsletter* 33 (July, 1989), 3-6; P. Beasley-Murray, 'Worship and Wineskins', *Third Way* (May, 1991), 20-22. Only the latter of these mentioned baptism at all, and that briefly. Such brief references to baptism, or none at all, is typical of much of the material from Baptists on worship at this time. However, see G.R. Beasley-Murray, 'Worship and the Sacraments', in *The Second Holdsworth–Grigg Memorial Lecture, Whitley College: The Baptist College of Victoria* (Melbourne, 1970), n.p.. Discussion of baptism is also to be found in the following which have not been previously mentioned: R. Brown, *Christ Above All: The Message of Hebrews* (BST; Leicester, 1982); P.S. Fiddes, *Past Event and Present Salvation: The Christian Idea of Atonement* (1989), *passim*; G.R. Beasely-Murray, *Jesus and the Kingdom of God* (Exeter, 1986), 247-52, discussing the metaphorical use of 'baptism' for Jesus' suffering; D. Guthrie, *The Pastoral Epistles* (TNTC; Leicester, 1957, 2nd edn, 1990), *A Shorter Life of Christ* (1970), *Jesus the Messiah* (1972), *Galatians* (NCBC; 1973), *The Apostles* (1975) and *Hebrews* (TNTC; Leicester, 1983). Dr Guthrie was lecturer in New Testament at LBC from 1970 to his retirement. His origins were

A figure who spans the academic and the popular is Dr Paul Beasley-Murray. In his *Faith and Festivity* he noted two purposes of baptismal services: the evangelistic which understands baptism as a proclamation of the gospel, and that which directed the preaching at the candidates themselves, emphasizing discipleship. He believed that the second, which is increasingly popular not least because it is represented in many books of orders of service, no longer sees baptism as the climax of the service, but rather as leading to the celebration of the Lord's Supper where the candidates are received into membership. Its emphasis on the corporate dimension, baptism being the rite of initiation, means that baptism leads to communion. But the first model also has much to commend it, for it emphasizes baptism as the moment for confessing faith, and enabling baptismal services to be occasions for the proclamation of the gospel. For this reason, Beasley-Murray favours this tradition.[283]

THE INFLUENCE OF CHARISMATIC RENEWAL ON WORSHIP

The charismatic-renewal movement has also had a major influence on Baptist worship.[284] A central emphasis within the charismatic tradition is

---

among the Strict Baptists in Suffolk, though he later joined the BU. For many years he was a deacon at Stanmore Road, and in his retirement he was moderator at Rayners Lane, North Harrow. Details from a conversation with Dr D.J. Tidball, Principal of LBC. For a tribute to Guthrie, see P. Cotterell, 'Dr. Donald Guthrie, 1916–1992', *LBC Review* (Autumn, 1992), 2, and also H.H. Rowden, 'Donald Guthrie: An Appreciation', in H.H. Rowden, *Christ the Lord: Studies in Christology presented to Donald Guthrie* (Leicester, 1982), ix-xi. The most recent 'academic' discussions of baptism can be found in Porter and Cross (eds.), *Baptism*, including—E.W. Burrows, 'Baptism in Mark and Luke', 99-115; J.E. Morgan-Wynne, 'References to Baptism in the Fourth Gospel', 116-35; L.J. Kreitzer, 'On Board the Eschatological Ark of God: Noah–Deucalion and the "Phygian Connection" in 1 Peter 3:19-22', 228-72; A. Campbell, 'Dying with Christ: The Origin of a Metaphor', 273-93 (see also Campbell's earlier 'Jesus and His Baptism', *TynBul* 47.2 (1996), 191-214).

283   P. Beasley-Murray, *Faith and Festivity*, 103-05. His suggested order of service reflected the clear influence of liturgical developments, including seven (possibly eight) sections, made up of twenty three parts, see pp.106-07. He then discussed each major section of the service, pp.107-16.

284   See McBain, *No Gentle Breeze*, 14-16. McBain believed that the effect of the charismatic movement on patterns of worship was actually anticipated in Payne and Winward's introductory essay in *Orders and Prayers*, in which they wrote, 'This element of congregational participation needs to be restored to our churches today, which, apart from the singing of hymns, is often the monopoly of the Minister. The scriptural doctrine of the priesthood of all believers has implications for worship which for too long have been ignored. As the fellowship of the Holy Spirit the local church should endeavour to develop a truly congregational worship, utilising the spiritual gifts of all its members', pp.XII-XIII. A less than positive assessment of the movement was presented by Walker, 'Baptist Worship', 27-29.

the immediacy of the inspiration of the Spirit,[285] and this makes somewhat paradoxical the observation that the movement has also led to a greater appreciation of liturgy.[286] A further benefit of this movement is its ecumenical dimension, for it transcends denominational boundaries and has indirectly contributed to the ecumenical life of the British churches, though charismatic churches have often not become involved in official ecumenical bodies.[287] However, there is no evidence that as a movement it has contributed in any significant way to the conduct of baptismal services, except in the practice of the laying on of hands which is widely practised in charismatic circles.

THE LAYING ON OF HANDS

The place of the laying on of hands within the baptismal rite was reintroduced into Baptist worship, largely by the advocacy of Payne and Winward,[288] and it has been further developed by both the liturgical and charismatic movements,[289] though it is not confined to either grouping.[290] In the former category, it is often the ecumenically-minded ministers and churches that reflect the influence of the liturgical movement in their practice,[291] and both *Praise God* and *Patterns and Prayers*

---

285 So 'The Report', in Fiddes, *Charismatic Renewal*, 4, 'the most characteristic feature of charismatic renewal is spontaniety of praise.'

286 So N. Wright, 'Introducing Believers' Church Anglicanism', *BT* April 25, 1991, 8, 'not a few Baptists of charismatic inclination are coming to appreciate the whole notion of liturgy and the value of freedom within a structure of worship that provides rhythm, balance, theological depth and dignity to their praise.'

287 See 'Ecumenical Dimension', in the 'Report' in Fiddes, *Charismatic Renewal*, 7, which stated that 'there has been a very marked growth in toleration of those Christians of other communions who are involved in charismatic renewal. During charismatic meetings there has been much sharing and participation with other Christians and traditional hostility, for example to Roman Catholics, has disappeared. A common experience has accomplished rapidly what many years of patient discussion and explanation has failed to do.' It continues: 'But this ecumenical experience has not at the same time increased the support of charismatic Baptist churches for such ecumenical bodies as the [BCC] and [WCC].'

288 This indebtedness to Payne and Winward, *Orders and Prayers*, 135-36, was expressed by Dr A. Baines of Chesham, 'The Laying on of Hands', *BT* December 9, 1993, 12.

289 The charismatic movement has been an influential advocate of the use of the laying on of hands in water-baptism, in prayer for the 'baptism of the Spirit', healing, commissioning and 'deliverance'.

290 E.g. some pray over baptismal candidates with the laying on of hands while still in the baptistry immediately after immersion, finding adequate justification for the practice in scripture alone.

291 E.g. the Church of Christ the Cornerstone, Milton Keynes, has adopted a form of service which unites baptism with the laying on of hands, reported by A. Baines, 'The

have provided material for a service of the laying on of hands.[292] When the Old Baptist Union joined the BU in 1993, Arnold Baines wrote of the laying on of hands, a practice still continued by the Old General Baptists, 'No one supposes that the grace promised in this ordinance differs from the grace of baptism...'[293]

Paul Beasley-Murray has provided perhaps the fullest (though still brief) discussion of this. From acknowledging its biblical basis and the variations in its practice among Baptist churches, he argued that its purpose is 'to invoke the Spirit to come and fill the candidates with fresh power for service. As the candidates have been baptised in water, so fresh baptism of the Spirit is requested. Clearly the candidates have already received the Spirit, but now they desire yet more of Him.' Theologically, the ceremony, following *Praise God*, is a form of 'lay ordination', the candidates being set apart for service.[294] Beasley-Murray linked the laying on of hands with the formal welcoming of candidates into church membership, arguing that it provided a fitting climax by means of its 'loving solemnity', whereas extending 'the right hand of fellowship' was 'something of an anti-climax.'[295]

The laying on of hands, then, has become a common part of Baptist sacramental worship, though it must be added that there is still no unanimity on its significance and no standardized place for it within the sacramental act.[296]

Laying on of Hands', *BT* December 9, 1993, 12. A second example is the Church of Christ the King, Milton Keynes, where the laying on of hands in confirmation takes place immediately after baptism by immersion, see 'Milton Keynes', *BT* July 27, 1995, 15.

292 See *Praise God*, 137, and *Patterns and Prayers*, 102-04. In both instances the act followed baptism once the candidate(s) and minister had changed, and was a part of their reception into membership, *Praise God*, 140, *Patterns and Prayers*, 94, though the latter included the laying on of hands following baptism if the service did not include reception into membership, p.95. In neither manual were hands laid on the candidate in the water, either before or after the act of immersion.

293 A. Baines, 'The Laying on of Hands', *BT* December 9, 1993, 12. See also his letter, 'Laying on of Hands', *BT* February 3, 1994, 6.

294 See *Praise God*, 140.

295 P. Beasley-Murray, *Faith and Festivity*, 114-16, citing Acts 8:17; 19:6; Heb. 6:2.

296 P. Beasley-Murray, *Faith and Festivity*, 106-07, 'Customs vary as to when this rite is carried out. It can take place in the waters of baptism, immediately after baptism itself. This gives a sense of immediacy. The disadvantage is that the candidate is still recovering from having been dipped under the water. It is probably better to give the candidates time to get changed.' For its administration before baptism, see 'Hands together, eyes open', *BT* December 15, 1988, 1, reporting the baptism of Mike Kozak at Didcot, having his eyes open during the prayer preceding baptism with the laying on of hands administered while he knelt. The laying on of hands immediately after the act of

CONCLUSION

Christopher Ellis described one of the benefits of the liturgical movement as bringing 'the sacraments into the centre of the church's life. For those practising infant baptism this has meant infants being presented in the main services, and for Baptists there has been an increased emphasis on the link between baptism and church membership. There are three parties in the sacramental partnership: God, the person being baptized, and the people of God. This recognition encourages an acknowledgement of the function of the sacraments within the life of the church.'[297] Only a qualified agreement can be given to this assessment. In certain contexts it has much to commend it, for within the ecumenical and liturgical scene it is unquestionably true, but, as many Baptists continue to remain outside (though admittedly not uninfluenced by) these movements, it is not wholly true. Baptism continues to be regarded with ambivalence by many Baptists, an observation suggested by the general decline in baptisms from 1985 to 1999, with increases only in 1989 and 1996–99.[298]

While a considerable number of liturgists and service manuals have paid great attention to the baptismal liturgy, there continues to be a wide difference between these and much of the baptismal practice within local churches. Agreement can, therefore, be given to Michael Walker's observation concerning Baptist baptismal practices, that 'We have a theology in search of an adequate liturgy.'[299] Assent can also be given to the summary offered by the American, John E. Skoglund:

> Baptists have not been at the centre of the movement for liturgical renewal. Individuals have participated in liturgical conferences and have written on the issues of worship, but for the most part church life has not been greatly influenced. The freedom allowed in worship in Baptist congregations has afforded opportunities for a number of experiments. Baptist worship can be readily adapted to

---

immersion was my practice at Calne. For its use after leaving the pool or at communion when the candidate is received into membership, see 'Service was a show case for Baptist rites', *BT* October 4, 1990, 7, reporting a service at Westbury-on-Trym, including infant dedication followed by believers' baptism, the latter being 'followed by the laying-on of hands to commission the candidates for service and reception into membership.'

297 Ellis, 'Baptism and the Sacramental Freedom of God', 26.

298 See D. Jackson, Evangelism Adviser to the BU, 'Baptist membership: Has the tide turned?', *BT* November 19, 1998, 5; 'Baptisms up 15 per cent', *BT* January 1, 1998, 1; and the comparison of figures for 1998 and 1999 in the table 'Baptism', *BT* December 16/23, 1999, 13.

299 M.J. Walker, 'Another Perpsective on Baptist Identity' (unpublished, Cardiff, c.1988–89), 14.

such informal gatherings as house-churches, to services with high lay participation, and to other experimental forms.[300]

Pioneers in the Baptism of the Handicapped

A group of Baptists, under the inspiration of Faith Bowers, have pioneered ministry to the handicapped, a work that has crossed denominational boundaries.[301] In September 1983 the BU Working Group on Mental Handicap and the Church was set up,[302] bringing together people such as Faith Bowers and her husband, Brian, who have a handicapped son, with professionals including health workers, educationalists, chaplains and ministers. The work, which began in 1984, became known as BUild, 'the Baptist Union initiative with people with learning disabilities', in 1991.[303]

The work of BUild has covered many areas of handicap,[304] not least baptism.[305] Faith Bowers implicitly accepted the necessity of preparation classes for baptism and church membership, and, through anecdotal evidence, their value, especially but not solely when pitched at an ap-

---

300 J.E. Skoglund, 'Baptist Worship', in Davies (ed.), *Dictionary of Liturgy and Worship*, 67. Skoglund's final remark, however, does not seem to be likely in the foreseeable future at least: 'In this Baptists may make in the future a significant contribution to liturgical renewal.' It should be noted that Skoglund's comments are on behalf of Baptists world-wide, though they are certainly applicable to British Baptist practice.

301 So B. Green, 'Foreword' to F. Bowers (ed), *Let Love Be Genuine: Mental Handicap and the Church* (1985). F. Bowers, 'The Story of BUild', *Frat.* 242 (April, 1993), 8, 'The numbers needing such groups are not great, so they lend themselves to inter-church activity, whether denominationally or ecumenically.'

302 So B. George, Education Advisor for the BU, 'Introduction' to Bowers (ed.), *Let Love Be Genuine*, 1.

303 See 'New name as group grows in influence', *BT* January 17, 1991, 5. A slightly fuller, though still brief, history of the group is supplied by F. Bowers, 'The Story of BUild', 7-9.

304 This is clear by the wide variety of subjects discussed in *Let Love Be Genuine*.

305 The following essays by Baptists in *Let Love Be Genuine*, all refer to baptism: 'The Hospital Chaplain', by Judy Martin, a member of Carshalton Beeches Baptist Free Church, 35-36; 'Include Them Out?', by Michael Taylor, Director of Christian Aid, 46-50; 'Should She Be Allowed?', by Tom Rogers, Secretary for Evangelism for the BU, 51-53; 'With Understanding', by George Neal of Acocks Green, Birmingham, 53-54; 'Where Ministers Fear to Tread. Some Lay Thoughts', by Faith Bowers, 55-64; 'What doth hinder...?' and 'Alan's Baptism', by Jim Clarke of West Watford Free Church, pp.83-86; 'Stephen's Baptism', by Barbara Crowe MBE, a member of Avenue, Westcliff on Sea, pp.86-88; and 'Exploring Together', by Barbara Stanford, Assistant Minister of Bloomsbury Central, London, pp.88-91. Also see F. Bowers, *Who's This Sitting in My Pew?* (1988), 72-95.

propriate level for candidates with a mental handicap.[306] BUild has also sought to provide such materials for use in churches,[307] and has raised awareness of the issues facing the handicapped within Baptist and other churches which have often precluded them from such things as baptism and church membership. That BUild has already made an impact[308] is shown by the number of reported baptisms of handicapped people within Baptist churches,[309] discussion of the isues by Baptist authors,[310] and notes on the practicalities of baptizing handicapped people in *Patterns and Prayers*.[311]

---

306 Bowers, *Who's Sitting*, 78, 91. She noted at least one instance where Stephen, a Downs Syndrome eighteen year old, benefited from 'the normal baptismal class...and this was clearly right for him, even if he could not understand every word', pp.92-93.

307 See the booklets F. Bowers, *Knowing Jesus*; F. Bowers, Ena Robertson, a head teacher in north London and member of Winchmore Hill, and Susan Wright, a special needs teacher and member of Tonbridge, Kent, *The Church*; E. Robertson, *Following Jesus*; and S. Wright, *Joining the Church*; all published by BUild in 1991. The fourth booklet introduced baptism and communion within the context of joining the church. See also the accompanying leaflet 'Guide to Using the Discipleship Booklets with People with Learning Disabilities' (1991). The booklets were linked with the BU's *AIM 3* programme.

308 At the time of its change of name to BUild, the Group's Secretary, David Clark of Hall Green, Birmingham, 'New name as group grows in influence', *BT* January 17, 1991, 5, was reported as saying, 'I sometimes wonder if Baptists find particular difficulty in understanding this field because we are very wordy people. If people are not very good at "confessing with their mouths" we have problems. However, in BUild, we do see a considerable change in the attitudes of churches all over the country over the last few years. We are finding that churches are starting clubs for people with learning difficulties.'

309 See, e.g. 'Spelling it out in baptism', *BT* May 31, 1990, 6; 'Paraplegic baptismal challenge overcome', *BT* May 16, 1991, 16; 'Baptism: "a very special occasion"', *BT* March 26, 1992, 20; 'Baptism evokes Bible incident', *BT* March 18, 1993, 16; 'Determination of MS baptismal candidate', *BT* October 14, 1993, 15; 'Electric hoist for baptismal service', *BT* September 1, 1994, 16.

310 E.g. Griffith, *Case for Believers Baptism*, 59; P. Beasley-Murray, *Radical Believers*, 22; and *Believing and Being Baptized* (1996), 45, in section XI entitled 'Different ways of belonging', which concluded, 'We do not think...that baptism should be the *only* way that those who are severely disabled can be received and accepted within the Body, be affirmed as being in Christ, and be there for others to learn from', italics original.

311 *Patterns and Prayers*, 97. This focused primarily on the mode suitable for a person with an illness or disability, stating, 'The most appropriate means for the person concerned should be used, and informed medical advice should be sought and followed where necessary', be it the pouring of water over the head of the candidate while they are in the water or even being lowered into the water in a chair. 'In cases of mental handicap, care must be taken to find a means by which the candidate can appropriately make a declaration of faith.'

Conclusion

The adequacy of much baptismal preparation has been called into question from time to time. In his 1939 BWA Commission Report based on responses received to a questionaire distributed among Alliance members before the Sixth Congress, Wheeler Robinson suggested that the BWA could render useful service by compiling an adequate syllabus for baptismal candidates, and failing agreement on this, alternative booklets could be produced for use.[312] Other writers have similarly observed that Baptist baptismal practice was not what it should be.[313] It was also claimed that there had been a decline in the preaching on baptism, and this had in part contributed towards the situation.[314] By mid-century, the results of Baptist theological reflection and discussion had begun to filter down into the churches and baptismal practice and examination of both the theory and practice of baptism reflect the attempts of many to apply the lessons of the theologians and liturgists, but also the resistance of others to any change either from within or without Baptist circles. However, in 1996 the registered decline in the number of baptisms since 1990, prompted David Coffey and Darrell Jackson to raise serious questions concerning both the state of the denomination and the place of baptism within Baptist life. These included what these statistics said about the traditional views of believing and belonging in the local Baptist church. Does this situation reflect a changing demographic, that people are now coming to faith at a later age? While Baptists have usually seen baptism as 'a defining event in the life of the believer', are Baptist churches now attracting people into their churches who do not share this understanding of baptism? Do Baptists still consider the call to baptism to be an essential part of conversion and are people now coming to faith without expressing their conversion in baptism? And how can people be

---

312 Robinson, 'The Baptist Contribution to Christian Unity', 116. The questions used are recorded on pp.115-16.

313 White, *Biblical Doctrine of Initiation*, 280; Winward, 'The Administration of Baptism', 8-11; W.E. Moore, a tutor at Northern Baptist College, '*Baptism Today and Tomorrow* and *Baptism and Christian Unity* ', *BQ* 21.8 (October, 1966), 383, who believed that the two books by Beasley-Murray and Gilmore would 'serve as a vital check on the "maladministration of baptism" in our own denomination as well as in others.'

314 R.W.A. Mitchell, 'The Evangelistic Use of the Baptismal Service', *BT* December 16, 1943, 6, 'It is painfully evident from our statistics that many Baptists have grown neglectful of the scriptural ordinance of baptism.' The appeal to the evangelistic use of baptism like that by Mitchell who stated that 'the baptismal service has been the greatest agency in his ministry in precipitating decision for Jesus', was criticized by Winward, 'The Administration of Baptism', 8, 'there is very little, if any, direct teaching in the New Testament about baptism as witness—unless we start off with the assumption that confession and witness are synonymous terms.' This is not to suggest that Winward would not have agreed with Mitchell's point about the lack of preaching on baptism.

encouraged to move from congregational attendance to committed discipleship expressed through baptism and membership?[315] These questions reflect contemporary changes in attitude towards both faith and commitment,[316] the decrease in denominational loyalty whereby people moving from one district to another tend to go to a church of similar type to their previous one rather than to one of the same denomination, and present Baptists with a challenge as they enter the twenty first century.[317]

---

315 D. Coffey and D. Jackson, 'An Open Letter from the Evangelism Office', *BT* October 31, 1996, 5.

316 See, e.g., G. Davie, *Religion in Britain since 1945* (Oxford, 1994), which is significantly subtitled *Believing Without Belonging*.

317 D. Coffey and D. Jackson, 'An Open Letter from the Evangelism Office', *BT* October 31, 1996, 5, wrote: 'Decreasing numbers of reported baptisms may not beckon us into the future as did the dreams and visions of the Denominational Consultation but God may be speaking as clearly through the former as he is through the latter. How do we hold our dreams and visions alongside damning statistics?' For baptismal statistics from 1946 to 1998, see 'How baptismal figures rise and fall', *BT* October 29, 1998, 2, which attributes the two peaks in that period, 1956 and 1984, to the effects of the Billy Graham crusades of 1954–55 and 1984. Another suggested reason for the rise is the use of Alpha courses, 'Baptisms and Alpha', *BT* November 27, 1997, 6. Such statistics, however, are never complete because an unknown number of baptisms occur which are never reported to the *BT* for various reasons.

Conclusion[1]

The purpose of this study has been to examine the breadth, depth and variety of the theology and practice of baptism as practised by twentieth-century Baptists. The result of dividing the period into three has been justified as each has exhibited distinct emphases. From 1900–1937 the focus of attention, as in the nineteenth century, was on the mode and subjects of baptism, though there were those, most prominently H. Wheeler Robinson and A.C. Underwood, who were beginning to recognize the importance of the theology of baptism. Between 1938–1966 this emphasis was developed, principally by the contributors to *Christian Baptism*, chief among whom, as far as their influence on the denomination, were George Beasley-Murray and R.E.O. White. However, from 1967–1999 attention moved away from baptism to the wider discussion of the ecumenical developments taking place, in which baptism occupied an important but by no means predominant role. A simple comparison of the titles of the books, articles and essays written in each of the three periods shows that baptism now no longer occupies the prominent place it once did. Whereas in both earlier periods it was very much in the forefront of Baptist thought and was discussed as an important subject in its own right, it is so no longer. This gives added credence to the suggestion that Baptists view baptism pragmatically, a point supported by the fact that discussion of baptism is now often found within discussions of other related subjects which are apparently regarded as more important.

A survey of the discussion of baptism over the last three decades reveals the fact that the overwhelming majority of Baptists writing on baptism have done so within the ecumenical context, which suggests that Baptists hold an ambivalent attitude towards baptism. On the one hand, when debating the issue with paedobaptists, they have defended, sometimes vehemently, the confining of baptism to believers by immersion and denied the validity of infant baptism. On the other hand, when not involved in such discussion they have, like the Baptists of the nineteenth century, made little of the rite.[2] In fact, it has been an oft

---

1   An expanded version of this conclusion is A.R. Cross, 'Baptism and the Baptists: A Baptist Perspective', *BHH* 35.1 (Winter, 2000), 104-21.

2   This has been challenged by Pain, 'Dying and Rising with Christ', 19, who criticized what he believed is sole assumption here that 'authorship' is the sole criterion for this statement. However, while the statement is based on the written evidence (as no other sources are available which would be representative of enough Baptists throughout both the century and across the country), but also on the many Baptists (discussed

repeated criticism by Baptist scholars and leaders that baptism has not held the place in Baptist life or thought that it should.[3] Further, Baptists are essentially pragmatists, emphasizing not so much what is true but what works and what feels good.[4] Their theology of baptism is subordinated to their evangelistic enthusiasms, for they emphasize the importance of conversion but not the act of initiation into the church.

The present study has shown conclusively that there is no single Baptist theology or practice of baptism, only theologies and practices, and this diversity accords with Baptist ecclesiology which continues to tend towards independency, each local church and individual minister exercising their liberty in the administration and interpretation of Christ's laws. These theologies and practices vary widely in their theological sophistication, in their complexity and expression, though there are fewer variations in the practices of baptism than there are in the theologies, although in the last thirty years LEPs have introduced a greater variety of baptismal practice. It is significant that these variations in theology and practice have been able to coexist within one denominational body in a creative tension,[5] and this fact needs to be recognized by Baptists and could enable the continued and deeper and more widespread development of Baptist involvement within the ecumenical movement.

It has also been seen that Baptists have now generally accepted the word 'sacrament', whereas, for over half the century, the word was re-

---

throughout this work) who have criticized the inadequacies of Baptist theologies and practices of baptism. While I do not doubt that there are those, like Pain, who have been and are interested in baptism within non-ecumenical settings, it is simply that there is little evidence of this for it to be anything less than supposition as to the nature and extent of it.

3   This was one of the criticisms levelled against Baptists in 1953 by Ross, 'Theology of Baptism in Baptist History', 100, who remarked on the difficulty facing paedobaptists who tried to discover the Baptist position on many issues related to baptism and to the rite itself: 'The task has not been altogether easy, because the doctrine of baptism does not occupy a central place in Baptist theology.' This remains true of contemporary Baptist theology.

4   See, e.g., Haymes, *A Question of Identity*, 4, who drew attention to 'the rise in the last fifteen years of what I call "non-rational conservatism". By this frail phrase I mean an attitude to Christian truth and life that places great store by "feeling right"...', noting that it becomes 'easy prey to the rising contemporary dogmatic neo-biblicism.' In these comments, Haymes sums up so well the Baptist tendency towards anti-intellectualism and what is here described as pragmatism.

5   This is not to deny that there is not friction within the BU over either the theology of baptism or its practice, as this study has shown it to be a constant feature of Baptist thought the twentieth century. Those churches and ministers who could not accept this diversity have left the BU, most recently following the Assembly decisions of 1989 and 1995, though it should be noted that those who left the BU did so over the primary issue of ecumenical involvement, of which the issue of baptism was but a part.

garded with suspicion and frequently rejected. However, by mid-century Baptist sacramentalists had claimed back the word for use by Baptists, even if this has not always led to an accompanying sacramental theology. Among many Baptists the word 'sacrament' is used but the theology attached to it continues to be largely symbolic,[6] though a sacramental theology is increasingly common, chiefly among the theologically literate, ecumenically committed and liturgically oriented. This is nowhere more clearly evinced than in the growing practice of services of baptism–membership–communion, often including the laying on of hands. Further, it should be noted that over the last thirty to forty years anti-sacramentalist writings have all but disappeared.

It is also significant that Baptist attitudes towards infant baptism have changed drastically. While many continue to repudiate it outright, others have become more accepting, as reflected in the mutual recognition of it for the sake of preserving the right of conscience of individual believers. But the biggest surprise has been the apparent *volte face* of their leading scholar, George Beasley-Murray, whose attitude softened to one of recognizing in certain circumstances the 'possibility' of acknowledging the legitimacy of infant baptism.

The main purpose of this book has been to see whether or not Baptist baptismal theology and practice has developed and to identify what these influences have been and in what directions they have taken Baptist thought and practice, not forgetting that these developments have varied from church to church and writer to writer.

Changes in society have clearly, though indirectly, affected baptism and related issues, particularly communion and membership, forcing many churches to reconsider and even alter their constitutions, if not their Trust Deeds when possible. As people have become more mobile, the composition of churches has changed and there is greater fluidity in membership. Denominational loyalty has also decreased as people now look for churches to their liking rather than those of the same

---

6   In this regard see Beasley-Murray, *Baptism Today and Tomorrow*, 14, who quoted the American Baptist, R.E. Neighbour, 'The Moral Significance of Baptism', *RevExp* 6 (1911), 420, 'An intelligent Baptist, if he ever permits himself to speak of "the sacrament of baptism" does so thoughtlessly. In the Baptist estimate of the value of the ordinance we deny its efficacy as a means for the transmission of grace; on the other hand we insist on its utility simply as a beautiful and expressive symbol of certain basal facts in the redemptive mission of our Lord Jesus Christ, together with certain correlated and dependent issues.' Beasley-Murray then commented, 'It is my impression that most Baptists...would still subscribe to that statement, but that a majority of their theologians would repudiate it. The theologians, however, appear to exercise little influence on the preaching and administration of baptism in the churches.' A decade later, this assessment was affirmed by Matthews, *Baptism*, 18, and this study contends that it is still applicable to the present position of Baptists on baptism.

denomination.[7] Those loyal to one tradition tend to be among the older generations, and it is evident that the younger generations are impatient with and intolerant of the exclusivity of the past, and have worked for the breaking down of old denominational barriers and have displayed a greater willingness to experiment both theologically and practically. This is also seen in LEPs. Attitudes in society are now generally pragmatic, and this pragmatism has also influenced attitudes among Christians, not least towards doctrines and practices, including baptism, which is increasingly treated less dogmatically.[8]

Second, the individualism, so characteristic of Baptists in the nineteenth century, has, if anything, become more ingrained in both British society and church life.[9] The emphasis placed on baptism continues to centre on the candidate, their decision to be baptized and their personal testimony to what God has done in their lives, and is reflected in the most popular baptismal hymn being 'O Jesus, *I* have promised'. This individualism has meant Baptists have continued to find difficulty in expressing the prevenience of God's grace and the corporate dimension of the rite. While Baptists whole-heartedly believe that salvation is by grace through faith (Eph. 2:8), this is rarely emphasized in the baptismal rite. The corporate dimension continues to revolve around the congregation as predominantly spectators of that which the candidate is doing. The fact that the overwhelming majority of Baptist churches practise either open membership, or closed membership with the offer of associate membership to those not baptized as believers, has further increased the tendency to focus on the candidate's decision to be baptized. Baptism separated from entry into church membership has further reduced the corporate aspect, and this despite the protestations of the denomination's scholars who have criticized both the practice of permitting into membership

---

7   This practice has been most recently criticized by McBain, *Fire Over The Waters*, 186-87, under the heading 'Church Commitment'.

8   In his survey of the articles published in the *BMJ* during three periods, 1947–51, 1967–71 and 1987–91, P. Shepherd, 'The Baptist Ministers' Journal, 1946–1992', *BQ* 35.5 (January, 1994), 253-54, observed a growing pragmatism in approach to subjects, with fewer doctrinal subjects being covered and theological reflection being more practical and less dogmatic, concluding, 'Christian doctrine would appear to be a less central concern for Baptist ministers today, and theology is primarily of interest when it sheds light on a particular aspect of ministerial activity or serves some practical purpose.'

9   This confirms the legitimacy of the line of approach adopted from comparison with Bebbington's work on Evangelicalism noted in the Introduction. N. Wright, '"Koinonia" and Baptist Ecclesiology. Self-Critical Reflections from Historical and Systematic Perspectives', *BQ* 35.8 (October, 1994), 367, referred with approval to Walton, *Gathered Community*, 110, who argued that individualism had invaded the church in the eighteenth century in the wake of the Enlightenment. See the whole of the discussion of other Baptist writers on individualism by Wright, pp.366-70.

those never baptized by any means and the perpetuation of separating baptism from intitiation into church membership. It is also enigmatic that while open membership, which is a recognition of the status of Christians from paedobaptist traditions, has become the norm, this has not led to the acceptance of infant baptism as a valid form of baptism, as is reflected in the Baptist refusal to recognize a 'common baptism'. This has led to a position which is effectively inimical to ecumenical accommodation while practising something akin to it, a pattern which can also be seen in the position of Baptist congregations involved in LEPs which make accommodations to infant baptism while still maintaining an exclusive validity for the practice of believer's baptism.

The single most important ecclesiastical development in the British churches has already been mentioned, and is the rise and growth of the ecumenical movement. This has taken place at formal and informal levels. Formally, Baptist involvement has been through national bodies such as the Free Church movement, BCC and CTE and CCBI, and through international organizations such as F&O and the WCC, but also locally in Union churches, LEPs and councils of churches. Despite vigorous opposition from within, the BU has remained at the centre of national ecumenical schemes since their origins in the 1890s' Free Church movement, and internationally since the early 1930s. Informally, Baptists have benefited from the increase in the amount of contact which Christians have one with another through parachurch organizations, Christian conferences such as Spring Harvest, and through the growth of a Christian sub-culture which includes conferences, holidays, newspapers, magazines and a whole book industry all of which aid the cross-fertilization of ideas. As a result, Baptists have opened first communion then their membership (or added a supplementary roll), re-introduced a rite for their children,[10] and have rediscovered the sacramental and liturgical aspects of not just baptism but Christian initiation. This inter-action has not been one-way, for example, there is an Anglican 'Movement for the Reform of Infant Baptism' (MORIB, f.1986),[11] and there are a growing number of Anglican clergy advocating the practice of discriminate infant baptism.[12]

---

10   T.L. Underwood, 'Child Dedication Services among British Baptists in the Seventeenth Century', *BQ* 23.4 (October, 1969), 164-69, argued that seventeenth-century Baptists practised a rite of infant dedication. See also, but more cautiously, M.J. Walker, 'Baptist Theology of Infancy in the 17th Century', *BQ* 21.6 (April, 1966), 250, and also his 'Early Baptist Thought on the Child in the Church' (King's College, University of London MTh, 1963). The most recent discussion is West, 'The Chld and the Church', 75-110, on the seventeenth century see pp. 75-80.

11   On which see C. Owen (ed.), *Reforming Infant Baptism* (1990).

12   See J. Capon, 'Chester C of E clergy reject indiscriminate baptism', *BT* June 20, 1991, 2.

More than at any time before, the BU is open to the development of ecumenical relationships, and this has been assisted by a considerable amount of baptismal pragmatism. Whereas in previous generations, for example, the 1930s, movement towards a United Church in England foundered principally on the twin rocks of baptism and episcopacy, since the mid-1960s both matters have become marginalized in ecumenical discussions which now focus primarily, not on questions of theology, but on structures and agreements, how to implement these and on how further unity can be achieved. This pragmatism is most evident in the baptismal policies of LEPs where the onus is on finding ways in which it is possible to practise both forms of baptism rather than solving the many theological and practical difficulties concerning the rite. In this the BU is only in a position to advise as it has no powers to make multilateral decisions, though a move in this direction is evident in the concordats with the Methodists and URC .

This research has led me to conclude that the *Baptist Times* has been an accurate barometer reflecting ecumenical developments, Baptist ecumenical interest and involvement and also the place that baptism has held within this process and Baptist life more generally. Periods of intense ecumenical activity have, up until late 1960s, always been accompanied by a considerable and often heated debate of the baptismal issue. However, since the early 1960s the issue of baptism has moved from both the centre of the ecumenical debate, with the exception of *BEM* which, notwithstanding the response it provoked from the BU, made very little impact on domestic Baptist theology or practice. This movement towards the margins of the Baptist agenda is shown by the observation that the majority of references to baptism now occur in reports of baptismal services, there being relatively little debate about its meaning.

The practice of baptism has witnessed a number of significant developments, chiefly through the influence of liturgical scholars, not all of whom can be placed within the liturgical movement itself, as a number of them owe more to biblical studies than the liturgical movement *per se*, though hard and fast distinctions cannot be made. This is reflected in the development of services reflecting the whole process of Christian initiation (baptism–membership–communion) emphasizing the greater use of the laying on of hands, though much of the practice in local churches continues to be essentially conservative in form and content.

The discipline of biblical studies, which traverses denominational barriers and therefore has an 'ecumenical' dimension to it,[13] has also influenced Baptists, though to a lesser extent than perhaps it should. The

---

13   At the Theological Consultation on Doing Theology in a Baptist Way, Regent's Park College, Oxford, August 16, 1999, Brian Haymes referred to this as the 'naturally assumed ecumenism' of twentieth-century biblical scholarship.

leading British scholar on initiation in the present generation is the Professor James D.G. Dunn of Durham University. While Baptists have had their own New Testament scholars, G.R. Beasley-Murray, R.E.O. White, R.P. Martin and Donald Guthrie, it has been Dunn's three volumes which have made the most impact in theological circles.[14] Baptists have continued to separate baptism from conversion, often by years, in spite of the arguments of these and other scholars that New Testament baptism is conversion-baptism. This can be attributed as much to Baptist belief in the individual's right to decide when and whether they will be baptized, as to a lack among Baptists of emphasis on baptism in preaching and discipleship training. Theological studies, then, have made relatively little impact on the beliefs of 'grass-roots Baptists' and have only influenced the baptismal practice of theologically literate ministers and those liturgically informed.

Further, since 1967, there have been proportionally fewer Baptist works specifically on baptism than at any other time this century. This fact is quickly established by even a cursory survey of the bibliography, which also shows that discussion of baptism now largely takes place within the study of other subjects, the majority of which are broadly ecumenical. The reasons for this are unclear. It could be that some Baptists feel confident that all that could be said has been said: perhaps this is true for some. It could reflect a fear of controversy and the possibility of schism, not least because of the christological controversy sparked off by Michael Taylor in the early 1970s, which was reminiscent of the downgrade controversy of the 1880s.[15] It could reflect a lack of interest in baptism: this is possible because other matters have come to be regarded as more pressing or important, such as the ecumenical and charismatic movements in their various expressions, issues of worship, the place of the child in the church, matters concerning change within the church and questions of the survival of the local church in the midst of the decline of church attendance across all denominations.[16] Or it could

---

14   J.D.G. Dunn, *Baptism in the Holy Spirit*; *Jesus and the Spirit: A Study of the Religious and Charismatic Experience of Jesus and the First Christians as Reflected in the New Testament* (1975); and *Unity and Diversity in the New Testament* ([1977], 2nd edn 1990).

15   See G.R. Beasely-Murray, *The Christological Controversy in the Baptist Union* (n.d., c.1971-72); and McBeth, *Sourcebook*, 386-90. On downgrade see Briggs, *English Baptists*, 158-98; Payne, *The Baptist Union*, 127-43.

16   Shepherd, 'The Baptist Ministers' Journal', 254, noted that 'Recently there seems to have been an increase in articles dealing with problems and questions in contemporary church life, such as restorationaism, church management and congregational church government, probably reflecting the increasing variety and change in church practice', whereas in his first period he examined, 1947–51, 'the sacraments were a recurring theme.'

be that baptism has slipped from the denominational and ecumenical agendas to a minor position when compared with the place it once held because of its capacity to be divisive. In all probability it is a mixture of all these elements.

The charismatic movement has also proved to be an important factor in breaking down denominationalism, and though baptism/initiation has been important in the second and fourth waves of the movement, it has not significantly affected the theology of baptism other than its positive reinforcement of the role of the Spirit in conversion and in heightening the candidate's expectation of a definite experience at the time of their baptism. Negatively, it has intensified the individualism associated with baptism.

The key issues on the ecumenical agenda now appear to be predominantly organizational, whereas for the larger part of the century they were theological. Here again, Baptist pragmatism is evident. While they believe that baptism is the immersion of believers in the name of the Trinity, as stipulated in the second Declaration of Principle, nevertheless there are a growing number of Baptists, leading figures among them, who are no longer prepared to interpret this in exclusive terms. The goal of LEPs is unity, and the means to achieving it is baptismal accommodation, allowing two different patterns of initiation to co-exist. The advantages of such accommodation is that it respects the convictions of others and shows the value placed on unity. The disadvantage is that it has alienated other Baptists who have often not seen that there is a problem with denying the initiation patterns of paedobaptist churches. The theology behind baptismal accommodation has been carefully thought through and honed over many years of theological and practical discussion which first began in the seventeenth century and the mixed communion and membership churches and the Bunyan tradition, through Union churches, into the twentieth-century discussions at local, national and international levels. Despite the assertions of its opponents, baptismal accommodation makes a serious attempt to grapple with issues of ecclesiology and initiation, but in a way that its opponents are unwilling to accept. The anti-ecumenists tend not to recognize the ecumenical context of all modern-day theology and practice. What both the ecumenists and non-ecumenists are struggling with is a dialectic, both striving to affirm seemingly contradictory beliefs, and what sets them apart is the weight they give to these beliefs and the balance they strike between them. These beliefs include ecclesiology and the nature of the unity of the church, the grace of God and the response of the believer, the individual and the corporate dimensions of faith, the place of the child in the church, and the right of conscience for all believers in regard to faith and practice. Neither the ecumenists nor the anti-ecumenists see infant baptism as valid in itself, but the former accept infant baptism's potential as validated when completed by confirmation.

Denominationally and ecumenically it appears that there is a certain frustration that theological issues have held back real progress for too long and so ecumenical debate tends now to shy away from those areas where it is known that progress will not be made easily, among these are baptism, episcopacy and the church-state relationship,[17] each of which used to be major stumbling blocks as far as Baptists were concerned to the emerging ecumenical movement, and none of which have been satisfactorily answered. Once it became evident that the believer's baptism–infant baptism debate was not going to attain a consensus, the ecumenical movement adopted the search for convergence in which there is a certain amount of pressure exerted on participants to agree. This was seen in *BEM* which has an element of 'the majority wins the day' about it. In Britain, ecumenism seems to have abandoned the detailed study of the biblical and theological study of baptism in favour of a *modus vivendi*, common baptism. However, Baptists have rejected this as a possibility. To date, the BU maintains that the mutual recognition of different patterns of baptism as a concession to the liberty of conscience which they defend for all believers is, at present, the only tenable way forward for Baptists in the ecumenical movement.

It is also clear that much depends on the convictions of the ministers within the churches, many of whom have taken upon themselves the prerogative of determining the church's baptismal policy, manifested in the task of deciding the fitness of candidates, interviewing, preparing and administering the rite. In the early years it was individuals such as J.H. Shakespeare and Hugh Martin who pioneered ecumenical involvement and without their stubborn advocacy it is unlikely that there would be today the number of Baptists involved at all levels of the ecumenical developments both internationally, nationally and locally. It is an irony that while many Baptists have been opponents of ecumenism or just sceptical towards Baptist involvement in it, nevertheless Baptists have been some of the pioneers of the movement and have held leading positions within it.[18] Individual Baptists have also led the way in the liturgical

---

17   On the church-state relationship in the Anabaptist and Baptist traditions, see N.G. Wright, *Disavowing Constantine: Mission, Church and the Social Order in the Theologies of John Howard Yoder and Jürgen Moltmann* (PBTM; Carlisle, 2000), and his Whitley Lecture (1996–97) *Power and Discipleship: Towards a Baptist Theology of the State* (Oxford, 1996).

18   The degree of Baptist involvement within the ecumenical movement at all levels has been frequently underestimated, often misrepresented or simply unknown, see Cross, 'Service to the Ecumenical Movement', which catalogues many Baptists, ministers and lay men and women, and their positions within various local, national and international ecumenical bodies.

movement, chiefly Neville Clark and Stephen Winward, and also in the charismatic and renewal movements, such as David Pawson.

As far as Baptists are concerned, a century of baptismal debate and controversy, both internal and external, discussion and developments, seems to have created a schizophrenic denomination in which the only ones apparently interested in the theology and practice of baptism appear to be those involved within the ecumenical movement. Further, Baptists are themselves no nearer consensus in answering the most important theological question than they were at the beginning of the century—is baptism a mere symbol however important a one, or an effective rite? This second position now commands more respect than in earlier years, but no one side has convinced the other and Baptists are left with competing theologies and practices of baptism/initiation. One of the consequences of all these observations for the future of Baptist ecumenical involvement was spelled out by George Beasley-Murray when he wrote, 'In reality there is no such thing as a Baptist theology of baptism, accepted by all Baptists; *what they do not themselves possess they should not demand of others.*'[19]

Writing in 1989 Dr David Russell concluded:

> The past 50 years, then, have witnessed a greater involvement of some Baptists in the ecumenical movement, but a continuing reticence and even opposition on the part of others. The principles for which Baptists stand, not least that of believers' baptism, have become matters of increasing theological debate in ecumenical circles and are recognised as of no small importance in the search for that convergence of belief and practice leading to consensus and to that visible unity of Christ's Church which, in all its diversity, is a sign and instrument of God's mission in today's world.[20]

---

19   Beasley-Murray, 'The Problem of Infant Baptism', 7, italics added.
20   Russell, 'The Ecumenical Role of Baptists', 130-31.

APPENDIX 1

Sources

It is always important for any historical research to be conscious of the types, extent and limitations of the sources that are available to it. The aim of this present study is to examine as broadly as possible the understanding of baptism among British Baptists in the twentieth century.

The sources that have been available have been many and varied. Much has been written by Baptist scholars on baptism and associated themes, including the church, conversion, evangelism, the ecumenical movement, the Lord's Supper, Baptist principles and contemporary issues. These have taken the form of academic books and papers, including scholarly articles and commentaries. Official BU documents of the consensus and creative kind contain much that is important and informative on the position of the BU and churches within its membership. Many of these sources have provided a wealth of material; however, 'theological' and 'official' works are not always representative of the grass-roots, popular understanding of baptism. In fact, they are often written in order to challenge popular views. So, for example, George Beasley-Murray's *Baptism in the New Testament*, which continues to be printed over thirty years after its first appearance, is undoubtedly the single most important and detailed study of baptism by any Baptist this century. However, despite Beasley-Murray's breadth of church involvement in Britain and America, as a local church minister, Baptist College Principal, leader within the BU and participant in the national and international ecumenical scene, and scholar, his book has tragically made less lasting impact within local churches than it deserved. However, this book contains so much information that it cannot be overlooked or dismissed. Perhaps it is true that the influence of such works take years (decades?) to filter down into the mainstream of denominational life?

The same observations apply to books and articles written by ministers which themselves vary from the academic to the popular. Greater weight, though, has been placed on the works by those who have wide knowledge and experience of Baptist life and whose writings have reflected this. Lay people, too, have written several books and a number of articles and these need to be weighed carefully as to their representative character.

The present study, however, has put great store on the *Baptist Times* and its predecessor the *Baptist Times and Freeman*, for there is no other extant source which contains so much information on baptism and related issues from so many varied sources, from minister to lay, from scholar to ordinary church member. The material includes detailed articles specifically on baptism by 'professional' scholars and ministers and laity alike, reactions to those articles, reports of contemporary beliefs and practices, and many letters on matters regarded as important by correspondents. While it cannot be taken for granted that such views are always representative of the breadth of contemporary opinion within the BU, for some are undoubtedly idiosyncratic and even extreme, nevertheless the denominational newspaper is the only major source which provides such a broad base of Baptist thought, reflection and opinion. Further justification for the weight put on the *Baptist Times* comes from the recognition, borne out throughout the study, that it has generally been an accurate barometer of the place baptism has occupied in Baptist thought.

The importance, then, of the *Baptist Times* has meant that use has been made of even brief letters precisely because they could reflect popular and potentially widespread opinion, for during the course of the research for this study it has become clear that many Baptists at grass-roots level have a very simple, even minimalist, understanding of baptism, which focuses on baptism as an act of obedience and a profession of the candidate's personal faith.

Local church histories, constitutions, baptismal policy agreements, personal correspondence, baptismal class material, College course notes, church magazines and the like, though sketchy, have been used where available. Sadly, some material, though sought after, was not forthcoming or was simply untraceable. It will also be clear that brief statements in tracts, pamphlets, Bible study aids, publicity matter and dictionary articles have also found a place. It could be argued that such material is too brief to provide any useful information on baptism, but, as has already been noted, experience and the course of research has shown that all too often this is the level of many Baptists' information on and understanding of baptism. Therefore, this kind of material has been included.

Some use has been made of oral tradition. However, such has been sparingly used for a number of reasons. First, recollections are often difficult to verify, so their representativeness cannot be assessed. Second, recollections tend to be vague on details, characters and, not least, dating.

Finally, it must be recognized that popular views of baptism are often so widespread that they are frequently assumed rather than recorded. 'Popular' views of baptism have not been defended by any major treatises, but are to be found in apologetic tracts, sermons at baptismal services, material for ministers preparing baptismal candidates, hence the importance of these sources. This fact makes a study like this difficult. At times the present study has remarked on what the popular view has been or is and this has been done recognizing that there is a substantial element of subjectivity involved, though with the rider that such comments have never been made lightly and have arisen from the course of the present research which has sought to read as much as is available on the subject by twentieth-century Baptists. Conjecture, though, has been kept to a minimum and generally the rule has been to record and assess *only* what has been uncovered during the course of the study.

APPENDIX 2

Trust Deeds

The whole of the debate concerning the terms of communion and membership could not take place in isolation from individual church's Trust Deeds.[1] From 1837 to 1840 an attempt was made by the Southern Association to get the BU to draw up a Model Trust Deed, but this ended in failure. It was not until May 1850 that such a Model Deed was adopted by the Baptist Building Fund, and it quickly became the standard form of Deed in Particular Baptist churches for three or four decades. In 1855 the General Baptist New Connexion published its own Model Deed. This was followed in Yorkshire in 1888 when the Association adopted its own Model Deed which ignored the doctrinal issues which distinguished the Particular from the General Baptists and left open the question of membership, baptism and communion.[2] In 1892, when the General and Particular Baptists of Lancashire and Yorkshire united, the Model Trust Deed was altered, allowing the individual churches the right to decide the communion question for themselves, but setting down that 'always the Church should consist only of baptised believers.'[3] It was this view which predominated in the North well into the twentieth century. This Trust Deed was itself shortened and simplified in 1907.[4] It also sought to reintroduce closed membership and to assume closed communion

---

1   The importance of the place of Trust Deeds in Baptist life was discussed by S.J. Price, 'Baptist Trust Deeds', *BQ* 5.3 (July, 1930), 102-10; *BQ* 5.4 (October, 1930), 172-76; *BQ* 5.5 (January, 1931), 209-19.

2   K.G. Jones, 'The Authority of the Trust Deed: A Yorkshire Perspective', *BQ* 33.3 (July, 1989), 113. Other details on the 1888 Deed are to be found on pp.111-12, and Jones also contests S.J. Price on several dates, specifically 1855 not 1854 for the New Connexion Deed, and 1888 not 1889 for the YBA Model Deed.

3   J. Haslam, 'The Yorkshire Baptist Association', in Shipley (ed.), *The Baptists of Yorkshire*, 313-14. On the YBA and Trust Deeds see Jones, 'The Authority of the Trust Deed', 103-18.

4   This paragraph is based largely on the account by Price, 'Trust Deeds', 172-76. For the background to the 1850 Model Trust Deed and the role played in Parliament by Sir Morton Peto in passing the Act which made possible the simplification of the duties of trustees to Nonconformist chapels making easier the appointment of new trustees, see Payne, *The Baptist Union*, 77.

though it did provide for church members to allow open communion should they wish so to do.[5]

As a direct result of the fusion in 1891 of the Particular and General Baptists, the BU Council and specially appointed committees met throughout the 1890s to consider the issue of a Model Trust Deed which would be suitable for the whole denomination. In 1902 the Council reported to the Assembly that there were two Model Trust Deeds, one for when the BU Corporation were to be the trustees, the other for when other persons were nominated as trustees.[6] The Model Trust made provision for churches to be either open or closed in communion and/or membership, the appropriate clauses to be included or excluded as required, though it was not possible for a change in practice if the issue was stipulated in the original Trust Deed. Whether practising open or closed membership, in both cases baptism was understood to be believer's immersion and nothing else.[7] This Model Trust Deed, Seymour Price reported in 1931, was widely used and he expressed his opinion that 'matters of domestic concern, such as "open" or "close" communion and membership, are advisedly left to the judgment of the individual church.'[8] Clauses were included or excluded, as appropriate, governing the eligibility for elders or deacons, but the minister had to have been immersed on a confession of faith and also be an advocate of the doctrine and practice of believer's baptism.[9] The model form was gradually evolved by varying and adding to earlier versions until 1936 when the *Forward Movement Model Deed for Churches and Halls* was prepared, and which remained in use until 1951.[10]

In the 1940s and 50s a series of *Baptist Church Rules* were published on behalf of the BU, in which provision was made for either open or closed membership, and that in the case of the former members were 'usually received after baptism by immersion, but the Church welcomes

5   For details of the *1907 Model Deed of the Building and Extension Fund of the Yorkshire Baptist Association*, see Jones, 'The Authority of the Trust Deed', 112-13.

6   See Price, 'Trust Deeds', 209-15. The Model Trust was printed as an appendix in Williams, *Principles and Practices* (2nd edn, 1903), 127-33.

7   The relevant section reads, 'and having been immersed on a confession of faith in the Lord Jesus Christ and maintaining and practising the doctrine and rite of the Immersion of Believers and no other Baptism', Williams, *Principles and Practices*, 128. C. Fry of Liverpool, '"Union of Baptists and Congregationalists" and "Baptist Principles"', *BT* October 9, 1930, 706, lamented the BU Trust Deed's clause which left open the membership of churches rather than laying down that all of them should be closed.

8   Price, 'Trust Deeds', 210 and 217.

9   Williams, *Principles and Practices*, 128.

10   See Mr R. Fairbairn, 'Baptist Model Trusts', *BT* September 7, 1961, 10. The development of the 1936 Model Deed was a result of the impetus of establishing new churches stimulated and encouraged by the Forward Movement and was intended to aid this process, see Payne, *The Baptist Union*, 203-04.

to full membership all who conscientiously follow our Lord Jesus Christ.'[11] When closed membership occurred in the context of open communion, the *Rules* recommended a communicant roll be kept containing the names of all those wishing to be affiliated to the church but who had not been baptized by immersion, and that the church should decide what powers, if any, should be given to them.[12] The ordinance of believer's baptism was to be administered as required, all believers being admitted whether or not they desired church membership.[13]

A second set of *Baptist Church Rules* were published in the 1950s, probably following the *Fuller Trusts*, though this is not clear.[14] Again, both open and closed membership rules were catered for, and in the case of the former members were 'usually received after baptism by immersion', all applicants being asked to consider the New Testament teaching on baptism. In the case of closed membership, again a communicant roll was recommended, the church having to decide what powers be extended to communicants, though these could not extend to matters covered by the Trust Deed.[15] As with the earlier *Rules*, baptism was to be administered irrespective of whether the candidate was applying for membership. However, in open membership churches, it was now only 'usual' that the majority of deacons would be baptized members.[16]

During these developments the YBA had continued to be active over the matter of Trust Deeds. The 1907 Deed remained in use until 1941, when it adapted the 1936 BU Model Trusts. Earlier YBA trusts had referred to baptism by immersion, but now 'and no other Baptism' was added, and any appointed minister was required to be an immersed believer and one who maintained and practised the rite of believer's immersion and no other.[17] But now, the Deed allowed for the adoption of either open or closed membership, but, if open, two thirds of the diaconate had to be baptized believers.[18]

---

11   *Baptist Church Rules* (1944), 1, 'II Membership a)'.
12   *Baptist Church Rules* (1944), 2, 'II Membership b)'.
13   *Baptist Church Rules* (1944), 3 'III Ordinaces b)'.
14   *Baptist Church Rules* (n.d., [1950s]), 'Notes', which refer to the *Fuller Trusts* and the forthcoming *Fairbairn Trust* of 1962.
15   *Baptist Church Rules* (1950s), 2-3.
16   *Baptist Church Rules* (1950s), 3-4.
17   1941 Model Deed, clauses 4 (e) and 6 respectively, cited by Jones, 'The Authority of the Trust Deed', 114 nn.41-42.
18   Jones, 'The Authority of the Trust Deed', 114. Jones noted that the 1941 Deed was the last in the line of Association deeds, succeeding years either adapting the 1941 Deed or using the BU's Model Trust Deed.

Up until the mid-1920s the only way to change Trust Deeds had been by a Private Act of Parliament, which a number of churches did.[19] From the mid-1920s to 1951 Trust Deeds could only be changed by a Charity Commission Scheme, which was also required if the original Trusts were missing or if the church had no Trustees, the Commission preparing various Model Baptist Trusts to ease their own tasks.[20] But in 1951 Parliament passed the Baptist and Congregational Trusts Act, which for the first time allowed the Trust Corporations of the two denominations to act as Sole Trustee, whatever number had been stipulated in the Foundation Deed, and also permitted the two denominations to produce Model Trusts which could be deposited with the Charity Commission. For the first time the Baptist and Congregational Unions were officially recognized by Parliament, receiving power to approve their own trust corporations for certain purposes, to set up model forms of trust deeds and to vary them from time to time and even to accede to individual churches' requests to adopt the model form in place of an existing one, thereby enabling churches to modernize out-of-date or inadequate trusts. In order to preserve the Baptist character of the Trusts, the Act provided that the Model Trust could override the old trusts except when dealing with the qualifications of members, elders, deacons and ministers, doctrinal matters and the identity of the ultimate beneficiaries in the event of the total dissolution of the church.[21] The *Forward Movement Trusts* were, therefore, revised in 1951 and became known as the *Fuller Trusts*.

The *Fuller Trusts* of 1951[22] were similar to the 1941 YBA Deed, though they eased the doctrinal requirement for membership,[23] upholding Foundation Deeds which stipulated closed membership, but the requirement for the diaconate was reduced from two thirds to a simple majority.[24]

This was the position until 1960 when the Charities Act of that year was passed. At this time, it was felt that the *Fuller Trust Deed* was not adequate

---

19   See, e.g. the discussion of this matter in the section on 'Union Churches' in ch. 3, which records the Private Act of Parliament which enabled Wells Baptist and Congregational churches to unite to form Wells United Church in 1919.

20   Information from a letter from Mr John Barfield of the BU Corporation, July 19, 1991. These Model Trusts were variously named after the churches for which they were first devised, e.g. Wolverhampton, Boscombe and Trealaw.

21   Payne, *The Baptist Union*, 253-54. See also the discussion of the impact of the Act by R. Fairbairn, 'Baptist Model Trusts', *BT* September 7, 1961, 10.

22   Here Jones, 'The Authority of the Trust Deed', 115, needs to be corrected when he wrongly dates the *Fuller Trusts* as 1956.

23   So Jones, 'The Authority of the Trust Deed', 115.

24   *Baptist Model Trusts for Chapels and Halls* (*Fuller Trusts*) (1951), clauses 16 (a) and (b) and 16 (e) respectively.

for the new situation,[25] and so the opportunity was taken by the BU to alter the Model Trust. The *Fairbairn Trusts*, as they became known, had to go before the Baptist Assembly in both 1961 and 1962 before they could be adopted.[26] Here it was stipulated that the premises could only be used 'for maintaining and practising the doctrine and rite of the Baptism of Believers and no other Baptism', and that all ministers must have been 'immersed on a confession of faith in the Lord Jesus Christ and maintaining and practising the doctrine and rite of the Immersion of Believers and no other Baptism.'[27] The Trusts could not be altered on 'the doctrines to be held and proclaimed', and this meant that if a Foundation Deed required closed membership then that could not be changed. Further, if the membership was not closed then 'all or at least a majority' of the deacons and elders 'shall nevertheless at all times consist of persons who have been baptised that is to say immersed upon a confession of faith in the Lord Jesus Christ', and should the church need a moderator, he should have been baptized 'as aforesaid.'[28]

In all of this, it was never the case that where a Trust Deed stipulated one term of membership, whether open or closed, the adoption of the Model Trust Deed could change this, which is why both the *Fuller* and *Fairbairn* Model Trusts had either/or clauses. However, the 1969 Sharing of Church Buildings Act made it possible for Paedobaptists and Baptists to share the same building for worship provided that the managing trustees of the building(s) concerned were persuaded that the church in question was fully desirous of proceeding with the agreement. Under the Act, then, it became possible for two or more local congregations to come together into one worshipping community, legally retaining their separate identities, which left it open for them to revert back to those identities should they wish to do so, but in fact and experience they would become one body.[29] The Act granted permission for the observance of the rites and practices of all participating denominations, thereby allowing a Baptist church's premises to be used for infant baptism, provided that a shared buildings agreement had been signed and one or more of the

---

25   Details of these inadequacies, none of which had a bearing on baptism or membership, were set out by R. Fairbairn, 'Baptist Model Trusts', *BT* September 7, 1961, 10.

26   See *Baptist Model Trust for Chapels and Halls (Fairbairn Trusts)* (n.d., but 1962), n.p., but front cover.

27   *Fairbairn Trusts*, 3, 3-4 respectively.

28   *Fairbairn Trusts*, 8 and 10 respectively.

29   E.B. Hardy of Great Bookham, Surrey, 'Trust Deeds Need Not Be A Hindrance', *BT* August 6, 1970, 3. See also S.G. Jackson, of Castleton near Cardiff, 'How Act Works for sharing buildings', *BT* June 25, 1970, 6.

signatories represented a paedobaptist tradition.[30] Without this Act the developments which have taken place in LEPs could not have happened.

APPENDIX 3

Recent Studies

A number of recent books have come to hand too late to be included in the notes of this book, but which, though none of them deal primarily with baptism, provide valuable background to some of the people and issues discussed in this book and thereby deserve mention, even if briefly.

Ian Randall's history of London Bible College provides a wealth of background information about the many Baptists who have taught and studied at LBC and who have also contributed to the Baptist understanding of the theology and practice of baptism. The most important of these are Ralph P. Martin, G.R. Beasley-Murray, Donald Guthrie, Derek Tidball, Douglas McBain, E.F. Kevan, Max Turner, John Balchin and T.M. Bamber, though there are many other Baptists who come into the LBC story.[1] Similarly, Bernard Green's history of the European Baptist Federation provides further background details about the work of key figures discussed in this book.[2]

Finally, Faith Bowers' history of Bloomsbury Central Baptist Church, London, is a source of a great deal of valuable information, not just on a number of important individuals,[3] but also on a number of key issues linked to baptism. Among the latter are discussions of the terms of membership, for, while its trust deeds identified baptism as the immersion of believers, the church has practised open membership from its beginning and has allowed believers to transfer their membership from other evangelical denominations without further initiation;[4] brief discussion of baptismal practice and the procedure followed for entry into membership;[5] and William Brock's pastorate at St. Mary's Norwich and his support of C.H. Spurgeon during the baptismal regeneration con-

---

1   I. Randall, *Educating Evangelicalism: The Origins, Development and Impact of London Bible College* (Carlisle, 2000), *passim*.

2   B. Green, *Crossing the Boundaries: A History of the European Baptist Federation* (Didcot, 1999), e.g. J.H. Rushbrooke, F.T. Lord, H. Cook, E.A. Payne, A. Gilmore, D.S. Russell, K.G. Jones and D. Coffey, *passim*.

3   F. Bowers, *A Bold Experiment: The Story of Bloomsbury Chapel and Bloomsbury Central Baptist Church 1848–1999* (1999), such as the church's ministers Drs William Brock, F.T. Lord and H.H. Williams, *passim*.

4   Bowers, *Bold Experiment*, 42-43, 45, 77, cf. p. 346.

5   Bowers, *Bold Experiment*, 77-78, 80-81, 206.

troversy of 1864, though he was by no means uncritical of the latter's tone.[6]

---

6   Bowers, *Bold Experiment*, 35-39 and 50-51.

BIBLIOGRAPHY[1]

Festschriften

Beasley-Murray, P. (ed.). *Mission to the World: Essays to celebrate the 50th anniversary of the ordination of George Raymond Beasley-Murray to the Christian Ministry* (*BQSup*, 1991).

Briggs, J.H.Y. (ed.). *Bible, Church and World: A Supplement to the Baptist Quarterly Published in Honour of Dr. D.S. Russell* (*BQSup*, 1989).

Briggs, J.H.Y. (ed.). *Faith, Heritage and Witness: A Supplement to the Baptist Quaterly Published in Honour of Dr. W.M.S. West* (*BQSup*, 1987).

Champion, L.G. (ed.). *The Communication of the Christian Faith: Presented to The Rev. Dr. A. Dakin Principal Emeritus of Bristol Baptist College on the occasion of his 80th birthday 21st November, 1964* (Bristol, 1964).

Durham, J.I. and Porter, J.R. (eds.). *Proclamation and Presence: Old Testament Essays in Honour of Gwynne Henton Davies* (1970).

Gloer, W.H. (ed.), *Eschatology and the New Testament: Essays in Honour of George Raymond Beasley-Murray* (Peabody, 1988).

Hayden, R. and Haymes, B. (eds.). *Bible, History and Ministry: Essays for L.G. Champion on his Ninetieth Birthday* (Bristol, 1997).

Porter, S.E. and Cross, A.R. (eds.). *Baptism, the New Testament and the Church: Historical and Contemporary Studies in Honour of R.E.O. White* (JSNTSup, 171; Sheffield, 1999).

Rowden, H.H. *Christ the Lord: Studies in Christology presented to Donald Guthrie* (Leicester, 1982).

Wilkins, M.J. and Paige, T. (eds.). *Worship, Theology and Ministry in the Early Church: Essays in Honour of Ralph P. Martin* (JSNTSup, 87; Sheffield, 1992).

— 'In Honour of Ernest A. Payne: Christian Scholar, Administrator and Statesman', *BQ* 22.3 (July, 1967).

— 'The Rev. Ernest A. Payne', *Frat.* 145 (July, 1967).

— 'Celebration of the Centenary of the birth of Henry Wheeler Robinson, Ninth Principal of Regent's Park College, 7th February, 1872', *BQ* 24.6 (April, 1972).

---

1   Unless otherwise stated all books were published in London. The primary source bibliographies are set out chronologically and books are listed first and alphabetically, followed by articles which are set out chronologically. The bibliographies of secondary material are set out alphabetically. In the chronological bibliographies any anonymous books or articles are marked by a hyphen in the name column before the title. In the alphabetical bibliographies, all subsequent works by an author occur underneath the first reference.

Theses

Cassidy, J.M. 'Membership of the Church with special reference to Local Ecumenical Projects in England' (draft copy of a Birmingham University PhD).

Cross, A.R. 'The Theology and Practice of Baptism amongst British Baptists, 1900–1996' (Keele University PhD, 1997).

Fowler, S.K. 'Baptism as a Sacrament in 20th-Century British Baptist Theology' (Wycliffe College and University of Toronto DTh, 1998).

Pain, A. 'Dying and Rising with Christ: A Study of the Baptismal Practice of Sutton Coldfield Baptist Church, 1978–1998' (Westminster College, Oxford, MTh, 1998).

Perkin, J.R.C. 'Baptism in Non-Conformist Theology, 1820-1920, with special refernce to the Baptists' (Oxford University DPhil, 1955).

Shepherd, P. 'John Howard Shakespeare and the English Baptists, 1898–1924' (Durham University PhD, 1999).

Walker, M.J. 'Early Baptist Thought on the Child and the Church' (King's College, University of London MTh, 1963).

Willmer, H. 'Sealing and Enlightenments: Aspects of the Early Christian Doctrine of Baptism' (Cambridge University PhD, 1970).

Unpublished Papers

Allaway, R. 'Membership of a Local Church—A Gospel Basis' (TCDTBW; August, 1999).

Bowers, F. 'Baptism: A Baptist Perspective' (unpublished paper presented to the Society for Ecumenical Studies; April, 1996).

BUGB FUE Committee 'Response of the Council of the Union to the Report *Called to be One* of Churches Together in England prepared for the Forum of CTE in July 1997' (final draft copy, March, 1997).

Burnish, R.F.G. 'Baptism in Ecumenical Theology' (a paper read to the Biblical Theology and Christian Doctrine Study Group, Tyndale House, Cambridge, July, 1988).

Clements, K.W. 'Baptism, Eucharist and Ministry' (student study document, Bristol Baptist College, 1983).

Fiddes, P.S. 'The British Church Scene: Issues of Identity for Baptists in Discussion with Others' (presented to the Commission on Baptist Doctrine and Inter-Church Relations: BWA, Montreal; July, 1991).

Haymes, B. 'Further Reflections on the Baptismal Waters' (CTS–NABPR; June, 1999).

Jones, K.G. 'Baptist Evangelistic Patterns and Inter-Church Relations. A perspective from the United Kingdom' (presented to the BWA Commission on Baptist Doctrine and Inter-Church Cooperation; July, 1994).

Martin, P.W. 'Towards a Baptist Ecclesiology Inclusive of Children' (TCDTBW; August, 1999).

Misselbrook, L. *Food for Faith: A course for converts and others who want to grow in faith and in the knowledge of Jesus Christ* (n.d., probably 1980s).

Quicke, M.J. 'Developing the Debate on "Baptist Identity"' (a paper for the BWA Commissionon Doctrine and Interchurch Cooperation; July, 1992).

Russell, D.S. 'Roots and Branches: Unprofound reflections on a full life' (privately published, n.d.).

— 'The sacraments' (lecture notes from Rawdon College, 1950s).

— 'The Sacrament of Baptism in the Light of Recent Statements' (lecture notes from Rawdon College, 1950s).

Sheppy, P.J. 'Life-Cycle Liturgies' (presented to the JLG Sarum Conference, September, 1996).

Taylor, D. 'The Baptism of Believers and Church Membership' (TCDTBW; August, 1999).

Thompson, D.M. 'Baptism, Church and Society in Britain Since 1800' (unpublished Hulsean Lectures for 1983–1984).

Thompson, P.E. 'Practicing the Freedom of God: Formation in Early Baptist Life', (CTS–NABPR; June, 1999).

West, W.M.S. 'Churches Together in England: Called to be One. Christian Initiation and Church Membership. A Report' (1995).

Walker, M.J. 'Another Perspective on Baptist Identity' (Cardiff, c.1988-1989).

Minutes

WORGLEP minutes from the late 1980s–early 1990s.

Minutes from the CTE 'Working Party on Baptism and Church Membership' (1995–1996)—confidential, used as background information.

Church Constitutions and Procedures

Amesbury Baptist Church. Doctrinal Basis. Constitution. Covenant of Membership (n.d.).

Bunyan Meeting, Bedford—Rules (amended 1993).

Central Church, Swindon—Interim Statement—Living with two forms of Baptism (1976).

Central Church, Swindon, Constitution (1995).

Central Church, Swindon—Local Ecumenical Project Standing Orders (1995).

Constitution of the Ferndown United Church, Wimborne Road, Ferndown, Dorset (n.d., but probably 1985).

Girlington Methodist/Baptist Church (1984).

Grove Hill Church (Anglican/Free Church), Hemel Hempstead—'Grovehill/ Woodhall Farm LEP-Policy to be followed when a person baptised as an infant requests baptism by immersion' (1995).

North Bletchley LEP (Anglican/Baptist). Interim policy on baptism (1982).

St. Thomas Church, Crookes, Sheffield— 'Initiation—the golden thread?' (1991).

The Church in Binley Woods—Statement of Baptism Policy (1997).
The Whaddon Way Ecumenical (Anglican/Baptist) Church. Constitution (1994).
Wendover—Our God Reigns (1993).
Wendover Free Church Constitution (n.d., c.1983).
Zion Baptist Church, Cambridge—'Rules of the Church of Christ of the Baptist Denomination Assembling for worship at Zion Chapel, Cambridge' (1859, revised, 1899).

Videos

Baptist Basics (1993).
Called to be One (1996).

Undated   Tracts/Publications

Aubrey, M.E. *The Baptist Union and Its Work.*
Branch, W.G. *The Baptist A.B.C..*
BUGB *Baptists and LEPs* (n.d. [1990]).
BUGB *BASIX* (n.d. [1996]).
BUGB 'What Baptists Believe' (n.d., pre-1992, probably 1970s–80s).
BUGB *5 Core Values for a Gospel People* (n.d., [1998]).
Carlile, J.C. *Why Should I Be Baptized?* (n.d., [pre-August 1933]).
Clark, A.S. *Should a Fellow be Baptized?*
Clark, A.S. *Should a Fellow Follow Christ?*
Floyd, L.R. *Baptism in the New Testament.*
Fullerton, W.Y. *Baptism.*
Laws, G. *What Is Baptism?*
Lloyd, F.C. *Eighteen Axioms Concerning New Testament Baptism.*
Lord, F.T. and Thomson, P.T. *A Baptist Catechism. Questions and Answers for Young People.*
MacBeath, A.G.W. *Why Are We Baptists?* (n.d., [between February 1922–August 1933]).
Middlebrook, J.B. *Baptist Principles and Believer's Baptism.*
Powell, W. *Christian Baptism as Understood by the Baptists.*
Rudman, E.G. *'The Reason Why!'*
Rushbrooke, J.H. *Christian Ordinances and Christian Experience.*
Shakespeare, J.H. *Christian Baptism* (n.d., [pre-1928]).
Thomson, P.T. *What is a Christian? A Minister's Talks with Young People.*
Willmot, A.E. *After Baptism.*

Bibliography of Sources on the Nineteenth Century[2]

Anonymous 'Sacramental Meditations', *BM* 49 (January, 1857), 22-24.

Bebbington, D.W. 'The Life of Baptist Noel: Its Setting and Significance', *BQ* 24.8 (October, 1972), 389-411.

Breed, G.R. *The Baptist Evangelical Society—an early Victorian Episode* (Dunstable, 1987).

Briggs, J.H.Y. *The English Baptists of the Nineteenth Century* (Didcot, 1994).

Carson, A. *Baptism Its Mode and Subjects* ([1844] Grand Rapids, 1977).

Hall, R. *On Terms of Communion*, in O. Gregory (ed.), *The Entire Works of the Rev. Robert Hall, A.M., with A brief Memoir of his Life, and a Critical Estimate of his Character and Writings* (Vol. II; 1831).

Heasman, K. *Evangelicals in Action: An Appraisal of their Social Work in the Victorian Era* (1962).

Hinton, J.H. *The Theological Works of the Rev. John Howard Hinton, M.A.. Volume 5. Lectures* (1865).

Short, K.R. 'Baptist Wriothesley Noel. Anglican—Evangelical—Baptist', *BQ* 20.2 (April, 1963), 51-61.

Toon, P. *Evangelical Theology 1833–1856: A Response to Tractarianism* (1979).

Ward, W.R. 'The Baptists and the Transformation of the Church', *BQ* 25.4 (October, 1973), 167-84.

Whitley, W.T. *The Witness of History to Baptist Principles* (1897).

Whitley, W.T. 'Witness of History to Baptist Principles', *BM* 88 (1896), 270-76, 311-17, 377-81.

Williams, C. *The Principles and Practices of the Baptists* (1879).

Wolffe, J. *The Protestant Crusade in Great Britain, 1829–1860* (Oxford, 1991).

Wolffe, J. (ed.) *Evangelical Faith and Public Zeal: Evangelicals and Society in Britain 1780-1980* (1995).

— *Psalms and Hymns* (1858).

— *Psalms and Hymns* (1891).

Chronological Bibliography of Primary Sources—1900–1937

1900   — *The Baptist Church Hymnal* (1900).

Meyer, F.B. *John the Baptist* (n.d., [1900]).

Slater, F. 'The Influence of Baptist Belief on Character', *BM* 92 ns 11 (March, 1900), 136-42.

Cooke, J.H. 'Jewish Rabbis on the Baptism of Proselytes', *BM* 92 ns 11 (September, 1900), 423-29.

1901   Pike, E.C. *Some Unique Aspects of the Baptist Position* (n.d., [1901]).

---

2   Included here are primary and secondary sources which are not mentioned elsewhere in the thesis or bibliography.

An Old Baptist 'Concerning Article XXVII: Of Baptism', *BM* 93 ns 12 (July, 1901), 318-23.

Slater, F. 'On Sin After Baptism: A Study of John XIII.10', *BM* 93 ns 12, Part 1 (August, 1901), pp.359-64, Part 2 (September, 1901), 426-30.

Black, J. 'Why Did Christ Institute Baptism? A Baptist Reply to the "Disciples of Christ"', *BM* 93 ns 12 (October, 1901), 480-86.

1902   Black, J. 'Why Did Christ Institute Baptism? An Open Letter to Christian Endeavourers of All Denominations', *BM* 94 ns 13 (February, 1902), Part 1 pp.58-61, Part 2 pp.105-09.

Kirby, F.J. '"Baptism" in the New Bible Dictionary", *BM* 94 ns 13 (September, 1902), 374-76.

1903   Phillips, A. *What Baptists Stand For; and Gleanings in the Field of Baptist History* (1903).

Whitley, W.T. *Church, Ministry and Sacraments in the New Testament* (1903).

Williams, C. *The Principles and Practices of the Baptists* (2nd edn, 1903).

Ennals, J.E. 'Our Ordinances and Their Mode of Observance', *BM* 95 ns 14 (June, 1903), 225-31.

1904   Mountain, J. *My Baptism and What Led to It* (n.d., [1904]).

Cooke, J.H. 'The Latest Manifesto on Baptism', *BM* 96 ns 15 (July, 1904), 252-53.

1905   Brown, J. *Baptism, True and False* (1905).

Ewing, J.W. *Talks on Free Church Principles: Addressed to the Young People of Nonconformity* (1905).

Roberts, J.E. *Christian Baptism, Its Significance and its Subjects* (n.d., [1905]).

— *The Baptist World Congress: London, July 11-19, 1905* (1905).

Gould, G.P. and Shakespeare, J.H. *A Manual for Free Church Ministers containing an Order for the Solemnization of Matrimony also for the Burial of the Dead, the Dedication of Infants, and the Baptism of Believers, to which are added Suitable Hymns for each of the Services* (n.d., [c.1905]).

1906   Shakespeare, J.H. *Baptist and Congregational Pioneers* (1906).

1908   Stockwell, A.H. *Baptism: Who? How? Why?* (n.d., [1908]).

Whitby, F.F. *Baptist Principles from a Layman's point of view* (n.d., [1908]).

Whitley, W.T. *Missionary Achievement* (1908).

1909   Glover, T.R. *The Conflict of Religions in the Early Roman Empire* (1909).

Marshall, N.H. *Conversion or the New Birth* (1909).

Wood, H.G. '"BAPTISM" (Later Christian)', in J. Hastings (ed.), *Encyclopaedia of Religion and Ethics II* (Edinburgh, 1909), 390-406.

1910 Compton, J.E. *The Place of the Sacraments in the Baptist Church* (1910).

Wood, J.R. and Chick, S. *A Manual of the Order and Administration of a Baptist Church* (1910, 2nd edn n.d.).

Marshall, N.H. 'Baptists', in *The Encyclopaedia Britannica III* (Cambridge, 11th edn 1910), 370-74.

Whitley, W.T. 'The Baptist History We Need (Continued)', *Frat.* os 4.3 (September, 1910), 72-77.

1911 Bonner, C. *The Christ, the Church, and the Child* (1911).

Lea, W.T. *The Place of Baptism in the Baptist Church* (1911).

Robinson, H.W. *The Christian Doctrine of Man* (Edinburgh, 1911).

Gould, G.P. 'The Origins of the Modern Baptist Denomination', *TBHS* II.3 (1911), 193-212.

Clifford, J. 'The Baptist World Alliance: Its Origin and Character, Meaning and Work', *The Baptist World Alliance, Second Congress, Philadelphia, June 19–25, 1911* (Philadelphia, 1911), 53-70.

Rushbrooke, J.H. 'Form of Service for the Dedication of Infants', *Frat.* os 5.2 (June, 1911), 42-47.

Meyer, F.B. *Free Church Service-Manual* (n.d., [c.1911]).

1912 Shipley, C.E. (ed.). *The Baptists of Yorkshire: Being the Centenary Memorial Volume of the Yorkshire Baptist Association* (1912).

Tymms, T.V. *The Evolution of Infant Baptism and Related Ideas* (n.d., [1912]).

1913 Robinson, H.W. *The Christian Doctrine of Man* (Edinburgh, 2nd edn, 1913).

1914 Whitley, W.T. *The Witness of History to Baptist Principles* (2nd edn, 1914).

1915 Collins, B.G. 'The Sacrament of Baptism in the New Testament', *ExpTim* 27.1 (October, 1915), 36-39; 27.2 (November, 1915), 70-73; 27.3 (December, 1915), 120-23.

1917 Forsyth, P.T. *Lectures on the Sacraments* (1917).

Roberts, J.E. '"Thoughts on Infant Baptism"', *The Expositor*, 8th series, Vol. 13 (1917), 432-46.

1918 Shakespeare, J.H. *The Churches at the Cross-Roads: A Study in Church Unity* (1918).

1919   Meyer, F.B. *Peter: Fisherman, Disciple, Apostle* (n.d., [1919]).
Morris, I. *Thoughts on Church Memebership* (1919).

1920   Clifford, J. *The Gospel of World Brotherhood According to Jesus* (1920).
Greenwood, B.I. *Two Letters on Infant Baptism* (1920).

1921   Glover, T.R. *Jesus in the Experience of Man* (1921).
Glover, T.R. *The Free Churches and Re-Union* (Cambridge, 1921).
Robinson, H.W. 'The Sacrament of Baptism', *Frat.* os 13.2 (April, 1921), 3-6.

1922   Robinson, T.H. *St. Mark's Life of Jesus* (1922).
Clifford, J. 'Dr. Clifford on the Baptist Outlook', *BQ* 1.1 (January, 1922), 27-30.
Freeman, J.D. 'The Lambeth Appeal', *Frat.* os 13.5 (March, 1922), 3-10.
Lord, F.T. 'The Value of Baptist Witness To-Day', *BQ* 1.2 (April, 1922), 50-57.

1923   Glover, T.R. *The Jesus of History* (1923).
Rowley, H.H. *Aspects of Reunion* (1923).
Whitley, W.T. (ed.) *Third Baptist World Congress, Stockholm, July 21–27, 1923* (1923).
Carlile, J.C. 'Realities of To-day', in J. Marchant (ed.), *The Coming Renaissance* (1923), 54-68.
Shakespeare, J.H. 'The Great Need', in J. Marchant (ed.), *The Coming Renaissance* (1923), 79-92.
Robinson, H.W. 'The Place of Baptism in Baptist Churches of To-day', *BQ* 1.5 (January, 1923), 209-18.
Roberts, J.E. 'World Conference on Faith and Order', *Frat.* os 14.2, (April, 1923), 4-6.
Fullerton, W.Y. 'The Stockholm Congress and Exhibition', *BQ* 1.7 (July, 1923), 289-93.
Dakin, A. 'Review: *A History of British Baptists*, By W.T. Whitley', *BQ* 1.8 (October, 1923), 388-390.

1924   Cook, H. *The Why of Our Faith* (1924).

1925   Robinson, H.W. *Baptist Principles* (1925).
Underwood, A.C. *Conversion: Christian and Non-Christian: A Comparative and Psychological Study* (1925).
Farrer, A.J.D. 'The Present Position of Church and Dissent', *BQ* 2.5 (January, 1925), 193-206.
Lord, F.T. '"Conversion" (Review of A.C. Underwood's *Conversion, Christian and Non-Christian*)', *BQ* 2.6 (April, 1925), 284-87.
Robinson, H.W. 'The Psychology of Religion', *BQ* 2.6 (April, 1925), 283-84.
Robinson, H.W. 'Faith and Creed', *BQ* 2.8 (October, 1925), 348-57.

1926 Robinson, H.W. *Baptist Principles* (2nd edn, 1926).

Rushbrooke, J.H. (ed.). *The Faith of the Baptists* (n.d., [1926]).

Whitley, W.T. 'Baptists', in *Encyclopaedia Britannica I* (Cambridge, 13th edn, 1926), 330.

Flowers, H.J. 'The Holy Spirit', *BQ* 3.4 (October, 1926), 156-65.

1927 Aubrey, M.E. *A Minister's Manual* (n.d., [1927]).

Fullerton, W.Y. *Souls of Men: Studies in the Problems of the Church To-day* (1927).

Glover, T.R. *Paul of Tarsus* (1927).

Robinson, H.W. *The Life and Faith of the Baptists* (1927).

Robinson, H.W. 'Prophetic Symbolism', in D.C. Simpson (ed.), *Old Testament Essays* (1927), 1-17.

Whitley, W.T. 'Review: "The Life and Faith of the Baptists"', *BQ* 3.7 (July, 1927), 333-34.

Robinson, H.W. 'The Faith of the Baptists', *ExpTim* 28 (1927), 451-55.

Flowers, H.J. 'The Unity of the Church', *BQ* 3.8 (October, 1927), 340-55.

Whitley, W.T. 'Lausanne and Stockholm', *BQ* 3.8 (October, 1927), 337-39.

Lewis, J. 'Baptised into Jesus Christ', *Frat.* os 19.3 (December, 1927), 15-24.

1928 Robinson, H.W. *The Christian Experience of the Holy Spirit* (1928).

Robinson, T.H. *The Gospel of Matthew* (1928).

Whitley, W.T. (ed.), *Fourth Baptist World Congress, Toronto, Canada, June 23-29, 1928* (n.d., [1928]).

Lord, F.T. 'A Modern Estimate of Calvinism', *BQ* 4.2 (April, 1928), 82-89.

Farrer, A.J.D. 'Dr. H. Wheeler Robinson's "Christian Experience of the Holy Spirit"', *BQ* 4.4 (September, 1928), 188-92.

1930 Cook, H. *The Call of the Church* (n.d., [1930]).

Cook, H. *The Epistle to the Romans* (1930).

Lord, F.T. *The Acts of the Apostles* (n.d., [1930]).

Patterson, D.T. *The Call to Worship: A Book of Services for the help and guidance of those who minister in the house of God* (1930).

Spurr, F.C. *Come Let Us Worship* (1930).

Wicks, H.J. 'Baptismal Regeneration', *BQ* 5.1 (January, 1930), 20-22.

Price, S.J. 'Baptist Trust Deeds', *BQ* 5.3 (July, 1930), 102-10; *BQ* 5.4 (October, 1930), 172-76; *BQ* 5.5 (January, 1931), 209-19.

Whitley, W.T. 'Lambeth and Mürren', *BQ* 5.4 (October, 1930), 145-50.

1931 Langley, A.S. *The Faith and Heritage and Mission of the Baptists* (1931).

Patterson, D.T. *The Call to Worship: A Book of Services for the help and guidance of those who minister in the house of God* (2nd edn, 1931).

Wilson, C.E. *The Baptist Missionary Society: How It Works and Why* (n.d., [1931]).

— 'Church Union by Federation', *BQ* 5.6 (April, 1931), 241-48.

Price, S.J. 'Laymen and Reunion', *BQ* 5.7 (July, 1931), 289-300.

Stickler, H.E. 'The Future of Denominationalism', *Frat.* n.s. 4[3] (Oct, 1931), 16-19.

Whitley, W.T. 'Faith and Order', *BQ* 5.8 (October, 1931), 358-61.

1932 Martin, H. *The Unity of the Free Churches: Being An Address delivered to the Federal Council of the Evangelical Free Churches of England on September 13th, 1932* (n.d., [1932]).

Whitley, W.T. (ed.), *The Doctrine of Grace: Papers of a Theological Committee of the Faith and Order Movement* (1932).

Payne, E.A. '*Baptische Grundsätze*. By H. Wheeler Robinson. Deutsch von E.K. Gemeinde und Gegenwart, Heft 3, Oncken Verlag, Kassel 1931', *BQ* 6.2 (April, 1932), 95.

Underwood, A.C. 'The Place of Conversion in Christian Experience', *BQ* 6.4 (October, 1932), 157-63.

1933 Cook, H. *The Why of Our Faith* (2nd edn, 1933).

Robinson, T.H. *The Epistle to the Hebrews* (1933).

Tymms, T.V. 'Independents or Congregationalists', in C.S. Carter and G.E.A. Weeks (eds.), *The Protestant Dictionary, Containing Articles on the History, Doctrines, and Practices of the Christian Church* (2nd edn, 1933), 312-17.

Whitley, W.T. 'Our Attitude to Young People', *Frat.* 11 (July, 1933), 1-7.

1934 Martin, H. (ed.) *Towards Reunion: What the Churches Stand For* (1934).

Rushbrooke, J.H. (ed.). *Fifth Baptist World Congress, Berlin, August 4-10, 1934* (1934).

— 'Baptist Union of Great Britain and Ireland', in L. Hodgson (ed.), *Convictions: A Selection from the Responses of the Churches to the Report of the World Conference on Faith and Order, Held at Lausanne in 1927* (n.d., [1934]), 61-64.

Torrance, W.U. 'The Sacraments and Authority', *Frat.* 13 (January, 1934), 10-15.

1935 Le Quesne, C.T. 'The Significance of the Berlin Congress', *Frat.* 17 (January, 1935), 2-6.

1936 Lord, F.T. *The Great Decision: An Outline of Christian Discipleship* (1936).

Martin, H. *Are We Uniting? The Prospects for Reunion in England* (1936).

— *The Baptist Forward Movement. Handbook for Speakers* (n.d., [1936]).

---

3   All editions of *The Fraternal* from this point onwards are from the new series, therefore, n.s. will not appear in reference to this fact.

Robinson, H.W. 'The Old Testament Background', in N. Micklem (ed.), *Christian Worship: Studies in Its History and Meaning by Members of Mansfield College* (Oxford, 1936), 19-34.

Barrett, J.O. 'An "Oxford Movement" Amongst Baptists', *Frat.* 22 (April, 1936), 9-12.

Child, R.L. 'The Baptist Contribution to the One Church', *BQ* 8.2 (April, 1936), 81-86.

1937   Ford, R.C. *Twenty-Five Years of Baptist Life in Yorkshire, 1912–1937* (1937).

Martin, H. *Edinburgh 1937: The Story of the Second World Conference on Faith and Order* (1937).

Martin, H. (ed.). *Towards Reunion: What the Churches Stand For* (2nd edn, 1937).

Robinson, H.W. and Rushbrooke, J.H. *Baptists in Britain* (1937).

— *A Plan for Unity between Baptists, Congregationalists and Presbyterians in England* (n.d., [1937]).

— *Report of the Special Committee Appointed by the Council on the Question of Union between Baptists, Congregationalists and Presbyterians* (n.d., [1937]).

Underwood, A.C. 'Views of Modern Churches (g) Baptists (2)', in R. Dunkerley (ed.), *The Ministry and the Sacraments* (1937), 223-29.

Whitley, W.T. 'Baptists and the Bible', *BQ* 8.6 (April, 1937), 298-301; *BQ* 8.7 (July, 1937), 366-69; *BQ* 8.8 (October, 1937), 417-20.

Chronological Bibliography of Primary Sources—1938-1966

1938   Martin, H. *Can We Unite? An Examination of the Outline of a Reunion Scheme issued by the Lambeth Joint Conference* (1938).

Patterson, D.T. *The Call to Worship: A Book of Services for the help and guidance of those who minister in the house of God* (3rd edn, 1938).

Robinson, H.W. *Baptist Principles* (3rd edn, 1938).

Bowie, W.T. 'Edinburgh 1937', review of Hugh Martin's *The Story of the Second World Conference on Faith and Order, BQ* 9.1 (January, 1938), 62-63.

Laws, G. 'The Edinburgh Conference: What Was the Good of it?', *BQ* 9.1 (January, 1938), 21-29.

Rushbrooke, J.H. 'The Baptist World Alliance: Origin: Constitution: Achievements: Objects', *BQ* 9.2 (April, 1938), 67-79.

Child, R.L. 'The Ministry and the Sacraments: A Free Church Point of View', *BQ* 9.3 (July, 1938), 132-38.

Dakin, A. 'Calvin's Doctrine of Baptism', *BQ* 9.3 (July, 1938), 160-64.

Jewson, C.B. 'The Baptistery of St. John at Poictiers', *BQ* 9.3 (July, 1938), 158-59.

Ramsey, R.G. 'The Means of Grace: A Personal Confession', *BQ* 9.4 (October, 1938), 212-18.

1939   Carey, S.P. *Jesus* (1939).

Rushbrooke, J.H. (ed.), *Sixth Baptist World Congress: Atlanta, Georgia, USA, July 22–28, 1939* (Atlanta, 1939).

Robinson, H.W. 'Believers' Baptism and the Holy Spirit', *BQ* 9.7 (July, 1939), 387-97.

1940   Aubrey, M.E. *A Minister's Manual* (revised, 1940).

Dakin, A. *Calvinism* (1940).

Dunning, T.G. 'Baptist Ecumenicity', *BQ* 10.2 (April, 1940), 85-88.

Rowley, H.H. 'Jewish Proselyte Baptism and the Baptism of John', *HUCA* XV (1940), 313-34.

1941   Martin, H. *Christian Reunion: A Plea for Action* (1941).

1942   Robinson, H.W *Redemption and Revelation in the Actuality of History* (1942).

Robinson, H.W. 'Hebrew Sacrifice and Prophetic Symbolism', *JTS* 43 (January-April, 1942), 129-39.

Robinson, H.W. 'The Five Points of a Baptists Faith', *BQ* 11.1 and 2 (January/April, 1942), 4-14.

1943   Bryan, F.C. (ed.). *Concerning Believers Baptism* (1943).

Whitley, W.T. 'Baptists and Their Allied Groups', in A.S. Peake and R.G. Parsons (eds.), *An Outline of Christianity: The Story of Our Civilization. Volume III. The Rise of the Modern Churches* (n.d.), 248-69.

Evans, P.W. 'Can Infant Baptism Be Justified?', *EvQ* 15 (1943), 292-97.

Rowley, H.H. Review—'*The Origin and Significance of the New Testament Baptism*, by H.G. Marsh', *JTS* 44 (1943), 79-81.

Whitley, W.T. 'Baptized—Dipped for Dead', *BQ* 11.4-7 (January/December, 1943), 175-77.

Beasley-Murray, G.R. 'The Church and the Child', *Frat.* 50 (April, 1943), 9-13.

Dakin, A. 'Original Sin', *Frat.* 50 (April, 1943), 6-9.

Marshall, L.H. 'The Church', *Frat.* 51 (July, 1943), 13-16.

1944   Brunner, E. *The Divine–Human Encounter* (1944) (*Wahrheit als Begegnung* (Zürich, 1938)).

Bryan, F.C. (*et al*). *Things Most Surely Believed* (1944).

Dakin, A. *The Baptist View of the Church and Ministry* (1944).

Payne, E.A. *The Fellowship of Believers: Baptist Thought and Practice Yesterday and Today* (1944).

— 'Baptist Church Rules'. Suggested by the Baptist Union of Great Britain and Ireland (1944).

Champion, L.G. '*The Baptist View of the Church and Ministry*, by A. Dakin', *BQ* 11.8-9 (January–July, 1944), 241-45.

Dakin, A. 'Towards a Doctrine of the Church', *Frat.* 55 (September, 1944), 2-3.

Middlebrook, J.B. 'Towards a Doctrine of the Church. III', *Frat.* 55 (September, 1944), 8-10.

Winward, S.F. 'Towards a Doctrine of the Church. II', *Frat.* 55 (September, 1944), 2-5.

Bampton, T.A. 'The Sacramental Significance of Christian Baptism', *BQ* 11.10-11 (October–December, 1944), 270-76.

Underwood, A.C. '*The Free Church Tradition in the Life of England*, by Ernest A. Payne', *BQ* 11.10-11 (October–December, 1944), 302-04.

1945 Rowley, H.H. 'The Origin and Meaning of Baptism', *BQ* 11.12-13 (January–April, 1945), 308-20.

Dunning, T.G. 'A Baptist Oxford Movement', *BQ* 11.14-15 (July–October, 1945), 411-16.

Townsend, H. 'The Free Churches and Ourselves', *Frat.* 58 (September, 1945), 1-5.

Shildrick, B.C. 'Baptist Witness and the Ecumenical Movement', *Frat.* 58 (September, 1945), 5-8.

1946 Child, R.L. *The Blessing of Infants and the Dedication of Parents* (1946).

Cook, H. *Speak—That They Go Forward: A Report on Spiritual Welfare in Churches of the Baptist Denomination* (1946).

Robinson, H.W. *The Life and Faith of the Baptists* (2nd edn, 1946).

Walton, R.C. *The Gathered Community* (1946).

1947 Bottoms, W.W. *Meet the Family: A Handbook for Baptist Young People* (1947).

Cook, H. *The Why of Our Faith* (3rd edn, 1947).

Cook, H. *What Baptists Stand For* (1947).

Evans, P.W. *Sacraments in the New Testament with Special Reference to Baptism* (1947).

Patterson, D. T. *The Call to Worship: A Book of Services for the help and guidance of those who minister in the house of God* (4th edn, 1947).

Barnard, A.J. 'The Use of Symbols in the Baptist Church', *Frat.* 64 (April, 1947), 11-16.

Champion, L.G. Review '*The Gathered Community*, by R.C. Walton', *BQ* 12.6-7 (April–July, 1947), 223-25.

Hughes, G.W. Review '*The Life and Faith of the Baptists*, by H. Wheeler Robinson, *The Great Succession*, by Ernest A. Payne', *BQ* 12.6-7 (April–July, 1947), 228-29.

Worstead, E.H. 'Essentials to Salvation', *Frat.* 64 (April, 1947), 7-11.

Marshall, L.H. Review '*Henry Wheeler Robinson*, a memoir, by Ernest A. Payne', *BQ* 12.6-7 (April–July, 1947), 225-28.

Payne, E.A. Review '*What Baptists Stand For*, by Henry Cook', *BQ* 12.8 (October, 1947), 295-97.

1948   Barth, K. *The Teaching of the Church Regarding Baptism* (1948).

Child, R.L. *Baptists and Christian Unity* (1948).

Evans, P.W., Townsend, H., Robinson, W. *Infant Baptism To-day* (1948).

Cook, H. 'Baptists and the World Council of Churches', in W.O. Lewis (ed.), *Seventh Baptist World Congress. Copenhagen, Denmark, July 29–August 3, 1947* (1948), 56-59.

Read, L.A. 'The Ordinances', *Frat.* 67 (January, 1948), 8-10.

Beasley-Murray, G.R. 'The Sacraments', *Frat.* 70 (Oct, 1948), 3-7.

Child, R.L. '*The Teaching of the Church Regarding Baptism*, by Karl Barth', *BQ* 12.12 (October, 1948), 449-52.

— 'The Baptist Doctrine of the Church. *A Statement approved by the Council of the Baptist Union of Great Britain and Ireland, March, 1948*', *BQ* 12.12 (October, 1948), 440-48.

1949   Martin, H. 'Judson on Baptism', *BQ* 13.1 (January, 1949), 25-28.

Hannen, R.B. 'A 6th Century Baptistery', *BQ* 13.2 (April, 1949), 87-89.

1950   Channon, W.G. *Much Water and Believers Only* (1950).

Flew, R.N. and Davies, R.E. (eds.). *The Catholicity of Protestantism, being a report presented to His Grace the Archbishop of Canterbury by a group of Free Churchmen* (1950).

Ohrn, A.T. (ed.), *Eighth Baptist World Congress, Cleveland, Ohio, U.S.A., July 22–27, 1950* (Philadelphia, 1950).

Pike, C.J. *Under Christ's Control: Studies in Discipleship and Church Membership* (1950).

— *Church Relations in England: Being the Report of Conversations between Representatives of the Archbishop of Canterbury and Representatives of the Evangelical Free Churches, together with the Sermon Preached by the Archbishop of Canterbury on November 3rd, 1946, Entitled A Step Forward in Church Relations* (1950).

White, R.E.O. 'Some Important Issues for Baptismal Theology', *ExpTim* 61.4 (January, 1950), 108-11.

Argyle, A.W. 'The New Testament Doctrine of the Resurrection of Our Lord Jesus Christ', *ExpTim* 61.1 (March, 1950), 187-88.

Payne, E.A. 'Professor T.W. Manson on Baptism', *SJT* 3 (March, 1950), 50-56.

Dykes, K.C. 'The Biblical Doctrine of Church and Covenant', *Frat.* 76 (April, 1950), 16-18.

Martin, H. 'Baptism and Circumcision', *Theology* 53, no.362 (August, 1950), 301-03, and no.365 (November, 1950), 423-24.

Bottoms, W.W. 'Christian Baptism', *Frat.* 78 (October, 1950), 40-43.

Martin, H. 'Baptism in the Fourth Century', *BQ* 13.8 (October, 1950), 370-72.

White, R.E.O. 'Advance and Reunion', *BQ* 13.8 (October, 1950), 341-49.

1951   Champion, L.G. *The Church of the New Testament* (1951).

Child, R.L. (ed.). *The Lord's Supper: A Baptist Statement* (1951).

Cook, H. *The Theology of Evangelism: The Gospel in the World of Today* (1951).

Payne, E.A. *The Doctrine of Baptism. An Address, A Report, A Questionnaire, A Bibliography* (1951).

Roberts-Thomson, E. *Baptists and Disciples of Christ* (n.d., [1951]).

—*Baptist Model Trust Deed for Chapels and Halls (Fuller Trusts)* (1951).

— *Fuller Trust* (1951).

— 'Baptist Church Rules'. Suggested by the Baptist Union of Great Britain and Ireland (between 1951 and 1962).

Payne, E.A. 'The Reverend Dr. E.A. Payne', in R.D. Whitehorn (ed.), *The Approach to Christian Unity: Sermons Preached before the University of Cambridge 1951* (Cambridge, 1951), 21-27.

White, R.E.O. 'Theological Issues Involved in Baptism', *ExpTim* 62 .4 (January, 1951), 124.

Payne, E.A. 'Professor Oscar Cullmann on Baptism', *BQ* 14.2 (April, 1951), 56-60.

White, R.E.O. 'Church Relations in England', *Frat.* 80 (April, 1951), 7-10.

Child, R.L. 'Baptists and Disciples of Christ', *BQ* 14.4 (October, 1951), 188-90.

Clarkson, H. 'The Doctrine of the Church in Contemporary Theology', *Frat.* 82 (October, 1951), 1-5.

James, H.I. 'Church Relations in England', *Frat.* 82 (October, 1951), 29-32.

Knight, E.F. 'A Reconsideration of the Sacraments', *Frat.* 82 (October, 1951), 5-9.

— '*The Lord's Supper: A Baptist Statement*', *BQ* 14.4 (October, 1951), 193-94.

1952   Bottoms, W.W. *Who Are The Baptists?* (Advance Series of Pamphlets no.2; 1952).

Cook, H. *Why Baptize Believers Only?* (Advance Series of Pamphlets no.3; 1952).

Floyd, L.R. *What is a Baptist Church?* (Advance Series of Pamphlets no. 4; 1952).

Payne, E.A. *The Fellowship of Believers: Baptist Thought and Practice Yesterday and Today* (2nd edn, 1952).

Winward, S.F. *The New Testament Teaching on Baptism: In the form of Daily Bible Readings for the Instruction of Candidates for Baptism* (1952).

Evans, P.W. 'A Baptist View. (b) P.W. Evans (Great Britain)', in D. Baillie and J. Marsh (edd.), *Inter-Communion: The Report of the Theological Commission Appointed by the Continuation Committee of the World Conference on Faith and Order together with a selection from the material presented to the Commission* (1952), 185-95.

Payne, E.A. 'Intercommunion from the Seventeenth to the Nineteenth Centuries', in D. Baillie and J. Marsh (edd.), *Inter-Communion: The Report of the Theological Commission Appointed by the Continuation Committee of the World Conference on Faith and Order together with a selection from the material presented to the Commission* (1952), 84-104.

Martin, H. 'Baptism and Circumcision', *BQ* 14.5 (January, 1952), 213-21.

Griffths, D.R. 'An Approach to the Theology of Baptism', *ExpTim* 63.5 (February, 1952), 157-59.

Clarkson, H. 'The Holy Spirit and the Sacraments', *BQ* 14.6 (April, 1952), 265-70.

Payne, E.A. 'Baptism and Church Membership among the Baptists', *Theology* 55, no.383 (May, 1952), 170-73.

Clarkson, H. 'The Holy Spirit and Personal Experience', *BQ* 14.7 (July, 1952), 320-24.

Martin, H. 'Baptists and the Great Church: or Independency and Catholicity', *BQ* 14.7 (July, 1952), 310-19.

Peacock, H.F. 'Baptism and the Holy Spirit. An Exegetical Study of Titus iii,5', *Frat.* 85 (July, 1952), 17-20.

1953   Clifford, P.R. *The Mission of the Local Church* (1953).

Cook, H. *What Baptists Stand For* (2nd edn, 1953).

Rowley, H.H. *The Unity of the Bible* (1953).

—— *The Response of the Baptist Union of Great Britain and Ireland to the Report of the Third World Conference on Faith and Order* (1953).

Evans, P.W. 'The Baptismal Commission in Matthew xxviii.19', *BQ* 15.1 (January, 1953), 19-28.

Gilmore, A. 'Leenhardt on Baptism', *BQ* 15.1 (January, 1953), 35-40.

Argyle, A.W. 'Church Relations in England', *Frat.* 89 (July, 1953), 6-8.

Bamber, T.M. 'The Baptist Revival Fellowship', *Frat.* 89 (July, 1953), 29-31.

Rowley, H.H. 'Marcel on Infant Baptism', *ExpTim* 64.12 (September, 1953), 361-63.

Griffiths, D.R. 'Baptism in the New Testament', *Frat.* 90 (October, 1953), 21-26.

Hastings, B.G. 'An Outline of the History of Baptism', *Frat.* 90 (October, 1953), 28-32.

Hudson, W.D. 'Some Insights of Personalism', *Frat.* 90 (October, 1953), 32-35.

Mason, R.A. 'The Theology of Baptism', *Frat.* 90 (October, 1953), 6-11.

Whilding, W.E. 'Conversion, Baptism and Church Membership', *Frat.* 90 (October, 1953), 111-14.

1954   Clifford, P.R. *The Christian Life: A Book about Baptism and Church Membership* (1954).

Payne, E.A. 'Baptists and the Laying on of Hands', *BQ* 15.5 (January, 1954), 203-15.

Rowley, H.H. 'Infant Baptism', *ExpTim* 65.5 (February, 1954), 158.

Champion, L.G. 'Doctrine of the Church', *Frat.* 92 (April, 1954), 26-29.

Dakin, A. '*Calvin's Doctrine of the Word and Sacrament*, by Ronald S. Wallace', *BQ* 15.6 (April, 1954), 282-83.

Davies, G.H. 'What Baptists Stand For', *BQ* 15.6 (April, 1954), 277-80.

Davies, W.S. '*The Unity of the Bible*, by H.H. Rowley', *BQ* 15.6 (April, 1954), 281.

Gilmore, A. 'Some Recent Trends in the Theology of Baptism', *BQ* 15.7 (July, 1954), 311-18; *BQ* 15.8 (October, 1954), 338-45; *BQ* 16.1 (January, 1955), 2-9.

Jones, N.B. 'Infant Dedication', *Frat.* 93 (July, 1954), 24-28.

1955 Ohrn, A.T. (ed.), *Baptist World Alliance Golden Jubilee Congress (Ninth World Congress), London, England, 16th–22nd July, 1955* (1955), 58-70.

Aldwinckle, R.F. 'Believer's Baptism and Confirmation', *BQ* 16.3 (July, 1955), 123-27.

Argyle, A.W. 'O. Cullmann's Theory Concerning κωλύειν', *ExpTim* 67.1 (October, 1955), 17.

Evans, P.W. 'Sealing as a term for Baptism', *BQ* 16.4 (October, 1955), 171-75.

1956 Clark, N. *An Approach to the Theology of the Sacraments* (SBT, 17; 1956).

Buse, S.I. 'The Markan Account of the Baptism of Jesus and Isaiah LXIII', *JTS* 7 (1956), 74-75.

Beasley-Murray, G.R. 'The Church of Scotland and Baptism', *Frat.* 99 (January, 1956), 7-10.

Child, R.L. 'The Church of Scotland on Baptism', *BQ* 16.6 (April, 1956), 244-51.

Gilmore, A. 'The Scottish Report on Baptism', *Frat.* 102 (October, 1956), 16-19.

White, R.E.O. 'Theology and Logic: A Logical Analysis of the Exegetical Method of the Church of Scotland's Interim Report on Baptism', *BQ* 16.8 (October, 1956), 356-64.

1957 Guthrie, D. *The Pastoral Epistles: An Introduction and Commentary* (TNTC; Leicester, 1957).

Schneider, J. *Baptism and Church in the New Testament* (1957).

White, R.E.O. *Into the Same Image: Expository Studies of the Christian Ideal* (1957).

Trent, H.W. 'Ourselves and the Ordinances', *BQ* 17.1 (January, 1957), 10-22.

Argyle, A.W. '"Outward" and "Inward" in Biblical Thought', *ExpTim* 68.7 (April, 1957), 196-99.

Russell, D.S. 'The Ministry and the Sacraments', *BQ* 17.2 (April, 1957), 67-73.

— '*Baptism and Church in the New Testament*, by Johannes Schneider', *BQ* 17.3 (July, 1957), 129-30.

1958 Winward, S.F. *Responsive Praises and Prayers for Minister and Congregation* (1958).

Gilmore, A. 'Some Baptismal Problems', *Frat.* 109 (July, 1958), 12-15.

West, W.M.S. 'Editorial', *BQ* 17.8 (October, 1958), 337-40.

1959 Gilmore, A. (ed.). *Christian Baptism: A Fresh Attempt to Understand the Rite in terms of Scripture, History, and Theology* (1959).

Rowley, H.H. 'The Baptism of John and the Qumran Sect', in A.J.B. Higgins (ed.), *New Testament Essays in Memory of Thomas Walter Manson, 1893–1953* (Manchester, 1959), 218-29.

Champion, L.G. 'The Baptist Doctrine of the Church in Relation to Scripture, Tradition and the Holy Spirit', *Foundations* 2.1 (January, 1959), 27-39.

Champion, L.G. '*Christian Baptism*, edited by A. Gilmore', *BQ* 18.3 (July, 1959), 135-40.

Russell, D.S. 'Christian Baptism I', *Frat.* 113 (July, 1959), 5-8.

Kevan, E.F. 'Christian Baptism II', *Frat.* 113 (July, 1959), 8-12.

Rowley, H.H. '*Christian Baptism*', *ExpTim* 70.10 (July, 1959), 301-02.

Rowley, H.H. 'Recent Foreign Theology' (review of J. Jeremias' *Infant Baptism in the First Four Centuries*), *ExpTim* 70.10 (July, 1959), 310.

Clark, N. 'Christian Baptism Under Fire', *Frat.* 114 (October, 1959), 16-18.

West, W.M.S. 'Editorial', *BQ* 18.4 (October, 1959), 145-47.

Scroggie, W.G. *The Baptism of the Spirit and Speaking with Tongues* (n.d., c.1950s).

1960   Barrett, J.O. *Your Child and the Church* (1960).

Barth, K. *Church Dogmatics IV.4. The Doctrine of Reconciliation (Fragment)* (Edinburgh, 1960).

Clark, N. *Call to Worship* (1960).

Payne, E.A. and Winward, S.F. *Orders and Prayers for Church Worship: A Manual for Ministers* (1960).

West, W.M.S. *Baptist Principles* (1960).

White, R.E.O. *The Biblical Doctrine of Initiation* (1960).

Winward, S.F. *The Dedication of Your Child* (1960).

Beasley-Murray, G.R. 'Baptism in the New Testament', *Foundations* 3 (January, 1960), 15-31.

Jones, N.B. 'Christian Baptism III', *Frat.* 115 (January, 1960), 18-23.

Payne, E.A. 'Believers' Baptism in Ecumenical Discussion', *Foundations* 3 (January, 1960), 32-39.

West, W.M.S. 'Editorial', *BQ* 18.5 (January, 1960), 193-95.

Rusling, G.W. 'The Status of Children', *BQ* 18.6 (April, 1960), 245-57.

Payne, E.A. 'Implications of Baptism for Christian Unity', *Encounter* 21.3 (Summer, 1960), 311-16.

Child, R.L. 'The Biblical Doctrine of Initiation', *Frat.* 118 (October, 1960), 18-23.

White, R.E.O. 'Baptism: The Domestic Debate', *Frat.* 118 (October, 1960), 14-17.

1961   Champion, L.G., Barrett, J.O. and West, W.M.S. *The Doctrine of the Ministry* (1961).

Child, R.L. *The Lord's Supper: A Baptist Statement* (revised, 1961).

Cook, H. *What Baptists Stand For* (4th edn, 1961).

Jackson, W.D. 'One Lord, One Faith, One Baptism', in A.T. Ohrn (ed), *Tenth Baptist World Congress. Rio de Janeiro, Brazil, June 26–July 3, 1960* (Nashville, 1961), 60-65.

Green, B. 'Authority for Baptising', *Frat.* 119 (January, 1961), 19-22.

Reid, J.K.S. '*The Biblical Doctrine of Initiation*, by R.E.O. White', *BQ* 19.1 (January, 1961), 45-47.

West, W.M.S. 'Editorial', *BQ* 19.1 (January, 1961), 1-3.

West, W.M.S. 'The Child and the Church', *Frat.* 119 (January, 1961), 15-19.

Clark, N. 'In the Study', *BQ* 19.2 (April, 1961), 86-87.

Cowlan, W.T. 'The Child and the Church', *Frat.* 121 (July, 1961), 25-28.

West, W.M.S. 'Editorial', *BQ* 19.7 (July, 1961), 289-91.

Argyle, A.W. 'Joachim Jeremias: *Infant Baptism in the First Four Centuries* ', *BQ* 19.4 (October, 1961), 190-91.

Bryan, A.K. 'Young People and the Church', *Frat.* 122 (October, 1961), 20-24.

1962 Beasley-Murray, G.R. *Baptism in the New Testament* (1962).

Champion, L.G. *Baptists and Unity* (1962).

Jackson, W.D. *Alive to Our Heritage and Opportunity* (1962).

White, R.E.O. *Invitation to Baptism: A Manual for Inquirers* (1962).

—— *Baptist Model Trust for Chapels and Halls (Fairbairn Trusts)* (1962).

Martin, R.P. 'The Composition of 1 Peter in Recent Study', *Vox Evangelica* 1 (1962), 29-42.

Williams, M.F. '*One Lord, One Baptism*—Reports of the Faith and Order Commission of the World Council of Churches, with a Preface by Oliver Tomkins', *BQ* 19.5 (January, 1962), 237-38.

Winward, S F. 'The Administration of Baptism', *Frat.* 123 (January, 1962), 8-11.

Clark, N. 'In the Study', *BQ* 19.7 (July, 1962), 318-21.

1963 Beasley-Murray, G.R. 'Introduction. The Baptismal Controversy in the British Scene', in K. Aland, *Did the Early Church Baptize Infants?*, trans. by G.R. Beasley-Murray (1963), 17-27.

Child, R.L. *A Conversation About Baptism* (1963).

Crabtree, A.B. *The Restored Relationship: A Study in Justification and Reconciliation* (1963).

Gilmore, A. (ed.). *The Pattern of the Church: A Baptist View* (1963).

Payne, E.A. 'The Baptists', in R.J.W. Bevan (ed.), *The Churches and Christian Unity* (1963), 131-46.

Rowley, H.H. 'Jewish Proselyte Baptism and the Baptism of John' and 'The Qumran Sect and Christian Origins', in H.H. Rowley, *From Moses to Qumran: Studies in the Old Testament* (1963), 211-35 and 239-79.

Martin, R.P. 'Aspects of Worship in the New Testament Church', *Vox Evangelica* 2 (1963), 6-32.

Every, G. 'G.R. Beasley-Murray: *Baptism in the New Testament*', *BQ* 20.1 (January, 1963), 42-43.

Clark, N. 'In the Study (Review of G.R. Beasley-Murray's *Baptism in the New Testament*)', *BQ* 20.2 (April, 1963), 82-84.

Clark, N. 'In the Study (Review of K. Aland's *Did the Early Church Baptize Infants?*)', *BQ* 20.3 (July, 1963), 133-35.

Ennals, J.E. 'Our Baptist Witness: Baptism in Practice', *BQ* 20.4 (October, 1963), 183-86.

Sparkes, D.H. 'R.L. Child: *A Conversation About Baptism*', *BQ* 20.4 (October, 1963), 190.

Williams, M.F. 'A. Gilmore (ed.), *The Pattern of the Church: A Baptist View*', *BQ* 20.4 (October, 1963), 188-90.

1964   BRF, *Liberty in the Lord: Comment on Trends in Baptist Thought* (1964).

Cook, H. *What Baptists Stand For* (5th edn, 1964).

Gilmore, A. *The Family of God* (1964).

Martin, R.P. *Worship in the Early Church* (1964).

Payne, E.A. *Baptists and Church Relations* (1964).

Sharpe, E.P. *Treasures of Christian Worship* (1964).

Skemp, J.B. *The Greeks and the Gospel* (1964).

White, R.E.O. *An Open Letter to Evangelicals: A Devotional and Homiletic Commentary on the First Epistle of John* (1964).

Winward, S.F. *The Reformation of our Worship* (1964).

— *Baptist Trust Corporations. Information and Procedure* (1964).

— *Registration of Baptist Trusts Under the Charities Act, 1960* (1964).

Moon, L.J. 'Partnership', *Frat.* 132 (April, 1964), 19-23.

Clark, N. 'In the Study' (review of *Liberty in the Lord* by the Baptist Revival Fellowship), *BQ* 20.7 (July, 1964), 326-28.

Kennedy, W.H. 'Incorporate in Christ', *Frat.* 133 (July, 1964), 22-27.

Williams, H.H. 'Unity in Christ' [sermon on Eph. 4.5], *ExpTim* 75.11 (August, 1964), 348-49.

Beasley-Murray, G.R. '*Greek Baptismal Terminology: Its Origins and Early Development*, by J. Ysebaert', *JTS* n.s. 15 (October, 1964), 381-84.

Beasley-Murray, G.R. 'The Case Against Infant Baptism', *Christianity Today* October 9, 1964, 11-14.

1965   Argyle, A.W. *God in the New Testament* (1965).

Beasley-Murray, G.R. *Reflections on the Ecumenical Movement* (1965).

Payne, E.A. *Free Churchmen, Unrepentant and Repentant and other papers* (1965).

Perkin, J.R.C. *Divine Encounter: An Outline for Discussion of Believer's Baptism* (1965).

Rusling, G.W. *Baptist Places of Worship* (1965).

Wallace, S.J. *Someone is Watching You (a way of looking at Church Membership)* (1965).

Winward, S.F. *Responsive Service Book* (1965).

Clark, N. 'Baptism and Redemption', in B.S. Moss (ed.), *Crisis for Baptism: The Report of the 1965 Ecumenical Conference sponsored by the Parish and People Movement* (1965), 71-75.

Gilmore, A. 'Baptism and Creation: Comment', in B.S. Moss (ed.), *Crisis for Baptism: The Report of the 1965 Ecumenical Conference sponsored by the Parish and People Movement* (1965), 62-64.

Winward, S.F. 'Baptism, Confirmation and the Eucharist: Comment', in B.S. Moss (ed.), *Crisis for Baptism: The Report of the 1965 Ecumenical Conference sponsored by the Parish and People Movement* (1965), 123-27.

Winward, S.F. 'Embodied Worship', in R.C.D. Jasper (ed.), *The Renewal of Worship: Essays by Members of the Joint Liturgical Group* (1965), 42-57.

Elwyn, T.S.H. Review 'John Baillie: *Baptism and Conversion*', *BQ* 21.1 (January, 1965), 46-47.

Hudson, W.D. '1980: Must They Include Us Out?', *Frat.* 135 (January, 1965), 12-14.

Perkin, J.R.C. 'The Interviewing of Candidates for Baptism and Membership', *Frat.* 135 (January, 1965), 23-29.

Beasley-Murray, G.R. 'A Baptist Interpretation of the Place of the Child in the Church', *Foundations* 8 (April, 1965), 146-60 [reprinted as 'Church and Child in the New Testament' in *BQ* 21.5 (January, 1966), 206-218].

Clark, N. 'In the Study', reviewing R. Schnackenburg's *Baptism in the New Testament* (1964), *BQ* 21.2 (April, 1965), 82-83.

Payne, E.A. 'The Free Church Tradition and Worship', *BQ* 21.2 (April, 1965), 51-63.

Pawson, J.D. '1980: Must They Include Us In?', *Frat.* 136 (April, 1965), 9-13.

Black, D.D. Reviews '*Worship in the Early Church*, by Ralph P. Martin, *The Reformation of Our Worship*, by Stephen F. Winward', *BQ* 21.3 (July, 1965), 138-39.

Scott, W. 'The Spiritual and the Sacramental in the Theology of Baptism', *Frat.* 135 (July, 1965), 22-28.

Clark, N. 'Christian Initiation. A Baptist Point of View', *SL* IV.3 (Autumn, 1965), 156-65.

Matthews, J.F. 'The Contemporary Ecumenical Situation: A Comment on Recent Articles', *Frat.* 138 (October, 1965), 29-32.

1966   Beasley-Murray, G.R. *Baptism Today and Tomorrow* (1966).

Gilmore, A. *Baptism and Christian Unity* (1966).

Goodland, P.J., Hetherington, P.J., Pretlove, J.L. and Warner, D.J. *Faith and Life: Practical Lessons in Christian Living* (1966).

— *The Child and the Church: A Baptist Discussion* (1966).

Beasley-Murray, G.R. 'Baptists and the Baptism of Other Churches', in J. Nordenhaug (ed.), *The Truth That Makes Men Free: Official Report of the Eleventh Congress Baptist World Alliance, Miami Beach, Florida, U.S. A., June 25–30, 1965* (Nashville, 1966), 261-73.

Beasley-Murray, G.R. 'The Holy Spirit, Baptism, and the Body of Christ', *RevExp* 63 (1966), 177-85.

Clements, R.E. 'The Relation of Children to the People of God in the Old Testament', *BQ* 21.5 (January, 1966), 195-205.

Walker, M.J. 'Baptist Theology of Infancy in the 17th Century', *BQ* 21.6 (April, 1966), 242-62.

Moore, W.E. Review '*Baptism Today and Tomorrow*, by G.R. Beasley-Murray, *Baptism and Christian Unity*, by A. Gilmore', *BQ* 21.8 (October, 1966), 382-83.

Chronological Bibliography of Primary Sources—1967–1999

1967   Bottoms, W.W. *Meet the Family* (1967).

Goodland, P.J., Hetherington, P.J., Pretlove, J.L. and Warner, D.J. *The Gospel, the Child and the Church* (1967).

— *Baptists and Unity* (1967).

Clark, N. 'The Lectionary', in R.C.D. Jasper, *The Calendar and the Lectionary: A Reconsideration by the Joint Liturgical Group* (Oxford, 1967), 15-29.

Hayward, V.E.W. 'Can Our Controversy with the Paedobaptists be Resolved?', *BQ* 22.2 (April, 1967), 50-64.

Perkin, J.R.C. 'New Testament Theology: The Search for Essentials', *BQ* 22.3 (July, 1967), 114-25.

West, W.M.S. 'Baptists and the Future', *BQ* 22.3 (July, 1967), 176-85.

Beasley-Murray, G.R. 'I Still Find Infant Baptism Difficult', *BQ* 22.4 (October, 1967), 225-36.

Elwyn, T.S.H., Hayden, R., and Voke, S.J. 'Baptists and Unity', *Frat.* 146 (October, 1967), 23-28.

Hobbs, J.G. 'Introducing Dr. David S. Russell', *Frat.* 146 (October, 1967), 5-9.

1968   — *Baptists For Unity* (1968).

Westlake, A.J. 'Let Baptists Beware', *Frat.* 147 (January, 1968), 5-11.

Dunning, T.G. 'Instant Unity', *Frat.* 148 (April, 1968), 5-10.

Hayward, V.E.W. 'Infant Baptism: A Further Comment', *BQ* 32.6 (April, 1968), 313-15.

Roberts-Thomson, E. 'Baptism and Church Union', *Frat.* 149 (July, 1968), 10-16.

West, W.M.S. 'Membership and Mobility', *Frat.* 149 (July, 1968), 7-10.

1969   ACCR '*Baptists and Unity*' *Reviewed* (1969).

Winward, S.F. *Your Baptism: A booklet for the instruction of candidates for baptism and church membership* (1969).

Mowvley, H. 'The Child and the Church', *Frat.* 151 (January, 1969), 16-24.

Brown, J.J. 'Baptists and Some Contemporary Issues. I', *Frat.* 153 (July, 1969), 6-10.

Wragg, W.H. 'Baptists and Some Contemporary Issues. II', *Frat.* 153 (July, 1969), 10-15.

1970 Barrett, J.O. *Church Membership: Suggestions for Visitors to Candidates* (1970).

Beasley-Murray, G.R. 'Worship and the Sacraments', *The Second Holdsworth-Grigg Memorial Lecture: Whitley College: The Baptist College of Victoria* (Melbourne, 1970), n.p..

Beasley-Murray, G.R. 'The Child and the Church', in C. Ingle, *Children and Conversion* (Nashville, 1970), 127-41.

— 'The Baptist Rites 1960', in Jagger, P.J. (ed.), *Rites of Baptism and Confirmation Since the Reformation Period* (Alcuin Club Collections, 52; 1970), 205-10.

Payne, E.A. 'Dr. Dakin', *BQ* 23.5 (January, 1970), 193-94.

1971 Beasley-Murray, G.R. '2 Corinthians', in *The Broadman Bible Commentary: Vol. 11. 2 Corinthians–Philemon* (Nashville, 1971 [London, 1972]), 1-76.

White, R.E.O. 'Colossians', in *The Broadman Bible Commentary: Vol. 11. 2 Corinthians–Philemon* (Nashville, 1971 [London, 1972]), 217-56.

White, R.E.O. '*Baptism in the Holy Spirit*. James D.G. Dunn', *BQ* 24.2 (April, 1971), 93-94.

Morgan-Wynne, J.E. 'The Holy Spirit in the New Testament', *Frat.* 161 (July, 1971), 9-16.

1972 Beasley-Murray, G.R. *The Christological Controversy in the Baptist Union* (n.d., c.1971–72).

Clark, N. and Jasper, R.C.D. (eds.). *Initiation and Eucharist: Essays on their Structure* (JLG, 1972).

EMBA, *Church Membership* (Nottingham, 1972).

Martin, R.P. *Colossians: The Church's Lord and the Christians Liberty. An Expository Commentary with a Present-Day Application* (Exeter, 1972).

Winward, S.F. 'Baptism. 5. Baptist', in J.G. Davies (ed.), *A Dictionary of Liturgy and Worship* (1972), 50-51.

Nunn, R. 'Upheaval in Christian Initiation', *Voyage* (January/February, 1972), 13-14.

Winward, S.F. 'Recent Trends and Developments in the Liturgical Movement', *Frat.* 165 (September, 1972), 5-11.

Ballard, P.H. 'Baptists and Covenanting', *BQ* 24.8 (October, 1972), 372-84.

1973 Bridge, D. and Phypers, D. *Spiritual Gifts and the Church* (Leicester, 1973).

Guthrie, D. *Galatians* (NCBC; 1973).

Martin, R.P. *Colossians and Philemon* (NCBC; 1973).

Neil, D.F. *The Way of Christ: A study booklet for new Church Members* (1973).

Taylor, M. *Variations on a Theme: Some guidelines for everyday Christians who want to reform the Liturgy* (1973).

Beasley-Murray, G.R. 'The Second Chapter of Colossians', *RevExp* 70 (1973), 469-79.

1974   Martin, R.P. *Worship in the Early Church* (Grand Rapids, 2nd edn, 1974).

Pawson, D. and Buchanan, C. *Infant Baptism Under Cross-Examination* (GBMW, 24; Bramcote, 1974).

Mallard, I.M. 'The Administration of Baptism', *Frat.* 171 (September, 1974), 37-40.

Barnard, A.J. '*Children of Abraham.* David Kingdon', *BQ* 25.8 (October, 1974), 384-85.

Cherry, J.F. 'Baptismal Rights in an Early Christian Basilica', *BQ* 25.8 (October, 1974), 350-53.

Taylor, G.H. 'Michael Taylor *Guidelines: Variations on a Theme*', *BQ* 25.8 (October, 1974), 385-86.

1975   Martin, R.P. *New Testament Foundations: A Guide for Christian Students. Volume 1. The Four Gospels* (Exeter, 1975).

West, W.M.S. *Baptist Principles* (3rd edn, 1975).

Beasley-Murray, G.R. 'Baptism, Wash', in C. Brown (ed.), *The New International Dictionary of New Testament Theology. Volume 1:A–F* (Exeter, 1975), 143-54.

Winward, S. 'A Baptist Point of View', in R.C.D. Jasper (ed.), *Worship and the Child: Essays by the Joint Liturgical Group* (1975), 47-50.

Payne, E.A. 'Baptists and Initiation', *BQ* 26.4 (October, 1975), 147-57.

1976   ACCR *A Statement to the Churches in membership of the Baptist Union of Great Britain and Ireland* (1976).

Martin, G.W. *The Church: A Baptist View* (1976).

Matthews, J.F. *Baptism: A Baptist View* (1976).

Pawson, D. and Buchanan, C. *Infant Baptism Under Cross-Examination* (GBMW, 24; Bramcote, 2nd edn, 1976).

Russell, D.S. 'An Ecumenical Bird's Eye View', *Frat.* 175 (February, 1976), 5-11.

Willmer, H. 'Twice-Baptized Christians—A Way Forward for Church Reform and Unity', *Frat.* 175 (February, 1976), 12-16.

1977   Bridge, D. and Phypers, D. *The Water That Divides: The Baptism Debate* (Leicester, 1977).

Pawson, D. *Truth to Tell* (1977).

White, R.E.O. *Christian Baptism: A Dialogue* (1977).

Wood, J. *The Baptists* (Christian Denominations Series; Exeter, 1977).

— 'Rite of Renewal (Authorised by the General Assembly of the Presbyterian Church of New Zealand, November 1977, for use in congregations)', (BCC, 1977).

— *Visible Unity in Life and Mission: Reply by the Council of the Baptist Union of Great Britain and Ireland to the Ten Propositions of the Churches' Unity Commission* (1977).

Smart, R.S. 'Authority; Baptism; Church; Ministry', review, *Frat.* 178 (January, 1977), 25-26.

Burrows, E.W. 'Understanding of Baptism in Baptist Traditions, with special reference to Modern Trends', *IJT* 26 (1977), 12-28.

1978   Martin, R.P. *New Testament Foundations: A Guide for Christian Students. Volume 2. Acts-Revelation* (Exeter, 1978).

Tennant, D.F. *Children in the Church: A Baptist View* (1978).

1979   Balchin, J.F. *I Want to Know What the Bible Says About the Church* (Eastbourne, 1979).

Martin, R.P. *The Family and the Fellowship: New Testament Images of the Church* (Exeter, 1979).

Peck, J. *I Want to Know What the Bible Says About the Holy Spirit* (Eastbourne, 1979).

White, R.E.O. *The Answer is the Spirit* (Edinburgh, 1979).

White, R.E.O. *The Changing Continuity of Christian Ethics. Volume 1: Biblical Ethics* (Exeter, 1979).

— *Signs of Hope: An examination of the numerical and spiritual state of the churches in membership with the Baptist Union of Great Britain and Ireland* (1979).

Walker, M.J. 'Baptism: Doctrine and Practice among Baptists in the United Kingdom', *Foundations* 22 (1979), 72-80.

Tennant, D.F. 'Children and Worship', *Frat.* 189 (October, 1979), 3-7.

1980   Crix, F. *Tap Roots No.15: Anglican–Baptist LEP in Milton Keynes* (n.d., [1980]).

Fiddes, P.S. *Charismatic Renewal: A Baptist View* (1980).

Gilmore, A., Smalley, E. and Walker, M J. (eds.), *Praise God: A Collection of Resource Material fo Christian Worship* (1980).

Hayden, R. *Baptist Union Documents: 1948–1977* (1980).

Russell, D.S. *A Call to Commitment: Baptist Christians through the 80s* (1980).

Beasley-Murray, G.R. 'The Authority and Justification for Believers' Baptism', *RevExp* 77.1 (Winter, 1980), 63-70.

Clements, K.W. 'Editorial', *BQ* 28.5 (January, 1980), 194-95.

West, W.M.S. 'Towards A Consensus on Baptism? Louisville 1979', *BQ* 28.5 (January, 1980), 225-32.

West, W.M.S. 'Towards a Possible Agenda', *RevExp* 77.1 (Winter, 1980), 13-20.

— 'Baptism: Report of the Faith and Order Consultation, Louisville 1979', *BQ* 28.5 (January, 1980), 232-39.

Nicholson, J.F.V. 'Baptism in Context: Further Reflections on Louisville 1979', *BQ* 28.6 (April, 1980), 275-79.

West, W.M.S. 'Foundation Documents of the Faith. VIII. Baptists and Statements of Faith', *ExpTim* 91 (May, 1980), 228-33.

Walker, M.J. 'Praise God: A New Service Book', *BQ* 28.7 (July, 1980), 314-21.

1981   Beasley-Murray, P. and Wilkinson, A. *Turning the Tide: An assessment of Baptist Church Growth in England* (1981).

Clements, K.W., *et al. A Call to Mind: Baptist Essays Towards a Theology of Commitment* (1981).

EMBA *To Be A Christian* (1981).

Guthrie, D. *New Testament Theology* (Leicester, 1981).

McBain, D. *No Gentle Breeze: Baptist Churchmanship and the Winds of Change* (1981).

Martin, R.P. *Reconciliation: A study of Paul's theology* (1981).

Walker, M.J. *Infant Dedication* (1981).

West, W.M.S. and Quicke, M.J. *Church, Ministry and Baptism: Two Essays on Current Questions* (1981).

White, R.E O. *The Changing Continuity of Christian Ethics. Volume 2: The Insights of History* (Exeter, 1981).

Winward, S.F. *Celebration and Order: A Guide to Worship and the Lectionary* (1981).

Wenger, E.L. 'Indian Baptists' "Covenant"', *ExpTim* 92 (February, 1981), 149.

Burnish, R.F.G. 'Baptismal Preparation—Past, Present, and...?', *Frat.* 195 (April, 1981), 12-18.

Ellis, C.J. 'Relativity, Ecumenism and the Liberation of the Church', *BQ* 29.2 (April, 1981), 81-91.

West, W.M.S. 'Relationships—in the Church', *Free Church Chronicle* 36.2 (Summer, 1981), 8-16.

Quicke, M.J. 'Baptists and the Current Debate on Baptism', *BQ* 29.4 (October, 1981), 153-68.

1982   Beasley-Murray, P. *6. Why Baptism and Church Membership?* (Baptist Basics series; 1982).

Brown, R. *Christ Above All: The Message of Hebrews* (BST; Leicester, 1982).

Martin, R.P. *The Worship of God: Some Theological, Pastoral and Practical Reflections* (Grand Rapids, 1982).

Mills, R. *5. For those Visiting Applicants for Church Membership* (Baptist Basics series; 1982).

Milne, B. *Know the Truth: A Handbook of Christian Belief* (Leicester, 1982).

Quicke, M.J. *2. Baptist Beliefs* (Baptist Heritage series; c.1982 or after).

Wallace, J. *What Happens in Worship* (1982).

Wortley, P. *3. What is a Baptist Church?* (Baptist Basics series; 1982).

— *Baptism, Eucharist and Ministry* (F&O Paper 111; Geneva, 1982).

Ellis, R. 'How Relative Should Theology Be?', *BQ* 29.5 (January, 1982), 220-24.

Tennant, D.F. 'Anabaptist Theologies of Childhood and Education: (1) The Repudiation of Infant Baptism', *BQ* 29.7 (July, 1982), 293-307; 'Anabaptist Theologies of Childhood and Education: (1) The Repudiation of Infant Baptism (Continued)', *BQ* 29.8 (October, 1982), 356-73; 'Anabaptist Theologies of Childhood and Education: (2) Child Rearing', *BQ* 30.7 (July, 1984), 301-18.

Beasley-Murray, G.R. 'Faith in the New Testament: A Baptist Perspective', *ABQ* 1.2 (December, 1982), 137-43.

Beasley-Murray, G.R. 'The Theology of the Child', *ABQ* 1.2 (December, 1982), 197-204.

1983 Clements, K.W. 'Baptist Theology', in A. Richardson and J. Bowden (eds.), *A New Dictionary of Christian Theology* (1983), 61-62.

EMBA *Growing Together: A Study Guide to Baptism, Eucharist and Ministry. I— Baptism* (Nottingham, n.d., early–mid 1980s).

Guthrie, D. *The Letter to the Hebrews: An Introduction and Commentary* (TNTC; Leicester, 1983).

Jones, K.G. *Baptismal Policy in LEPs: A Discussion Document* (Leeds, 1983).

Winward, S.F. 'Baptist Spirituality', in G.S. Wakefield (ed.), *A Dictionary of Christian Spirituality* (1983), 36-38.

YBA *Baptismal Policy in LEPs: A Discussion Document* (1983).

Martin, G.W. 'Congregationalism', *SBET* I (1983), 21-24.

1984 Jones, K.G. *et al. Christian Worship: Some Contemporary Issues* (Leeds, 1984).

Martin, R.P. *The Spirit and the Congregation: Studies in 1 Corinthians 12–15* (Exeter, 1984).

Matthews, J. *Baptism, Eucharist and Ministry. Seven Studies* (BCC, n.d., between 1982–1985).

Simpson, R. *How We Grew A Local Ecumenical Project* (Grove Pastoral Series 17; Bramcote, 1984).

Winward, S. F. *The Dedication Service* (5th edn, 1984).

WORGLEP *With Charity and With Conviction* (1984).

Wright, N. *The Church* (1984).

Fiddes, P.S. 'The Theology of the Charismatic Movement', in D. Martin and P. Mullen (eds.), *Strange Gifts? A Guide to Charismatic Renewal* (Oxford, 1984), 19-40.

White, R.E.O. 'Baptism of the Spirit', in W.A. Elwell (ed.), *Evangelical Dictionary of Theology* (Grand Rapids, 1984), 121-22.

Nunn, R. 'Eight "C"s on the Unity Road', *Frat.* 206 (January, 1984), 10-16.

Price, J. 'Grass-roots Ecumenism (I)', *Frat.* 206 (January, 1984), 18-20.

Rowland, D. 'Grass-roots Ecumenism (II)', *Frat.* 206 (January, 1984), 22-24.

West, W.M.S. 'Baptism, Eucharist and Ministry: A Baptist Comment', in *One in Christ* 20.1 (1984), 24-30.

— 'London Baptist Association Response to "Baptism, Eucharist and Ministry"', *Free Church Chronicle* 39.1 (Spring, 1984), 13-18.

Campbell, A. 'Believers Baptism for Children of the Church', *Mainstream Newsletter* 17 (September, 1984), 12-13.

1985   Bowers, F. (ed.), *Let Love Be Genuine: Mental Handicap and the Church* (1985).

BUGB *Baptism, Eucharist and Ministry: The response of the Council of the Baptist Union of Great Britain to the Faith and Order Paper No.111 of the World Council of Churches, 1982* (1982).

Burnish, R.F.G. *The Meaning of Baptism: A Comparison of the Teaching and Practice of the Fourth Century with the Present Day* (Alcuin Club Collections, 67; 1985).

CCLEPE *Local Church Unity: Guidelines for Local Ecumenical Projects and Sponsoring Bodies* (1985).

CCLEPE *Ministry in Local Ecumenical Projects* (1985).

Fiddes, P.S., *et al. Bound to Love: The Covenant Basis of Baptist Life and Mission* (1985).

Rinaldi, F. *Stepping Out: Preparing for Believer's Baptism* (Beginnings Bible study booklets; Swindon, 1985).

Briggs, J.H.Y. 'Make Disciples—Baptizing Them', in R. Keeley *et al* (eds.), *The Quiet Revolution* (Oxford, 1985), 66-71.

Beasley-Murray, P. 'When is a Baptist Church not a Baptist Church?', *Mainstream Newsletter* 20 (September, 1985), 7-10.

Beasley-Murray, G.R. *The Holy Spirit* (CTP C.7; n.d., possibly mid-1980s).

— 'What Baptists Believe' (n.d., [c.1980s])

1986   Beasley-Murray, G.R. *Jesus and the Kingdom of God* (Exeter, 1986).

Coffey, D. *Build That Bridge: Conflict and Reconciliation in the Church* (Eastbourne, 1986).

Haymes, B. *A Question of Identity: Reflections on Baptist Principles and Practice* (Leeds, 1986).

Matthews, J. *The Unity Scene* (n.d., [1986]).

Wright, N. *The Radical Kingdom: Restoration in Theory and Practice* (Eastbourne, 1986).

BUGB 'Baptist Union of Great Britain', in M. Thurian (ed.), *Churches Respond to BEM: Official Responses to the 'Baptism, Eucharist and Ministry' text. Volume 1* (F&O Paper 129; Geneva, 1986), 70-77.

Beasley-Murray, G.R. 'John 3:3, 5: Baptism, Spirit and the Kingdom', *ExpTim* 97 (March, 1986), 167-70.

West, P. 'A Question of Identity, by Brian Haymes', *Frat.* 216 (October, 1986), 24-25.

Haymes, B. *Conversation Piece: Baptist Identity* (n.d., probably mid-1980s).

1987   Beasley-Murray, G.R. *John* (WBC, 36; Waco, 1987).

Slater, D. (ed.). *A Perspective on Baptist Identity* (Mainstream, 1987).

— *Not Strangers But Pilgrims* (1987).

Clements, K.W. 'A New Baptist Hymn Book', *Frat.* 218 (April, 1987), 4-9.

Sparkes, D.C. '"Not Strangers but Pilgrims"', *Frat.* 218 (April, 1987), 20-25.

1988   Amess, R. *One in the Truth: Fighting the Cancer of Division in the Evangelical Church* (Eastbourne, 1988).

Bowers, F. *Who's This Sitting in My Pew? Mentally handicapped people in the church* (1988).

Martin, R.P. *1, 2 Corinthians* (WBT; 1988).

Beasley-Murray, G.R. 'Baptism. 1. Biblical Theology', in D.F. Wright and J.I. Packer (eds.), *New Dictionary of Theology* (Leicester, 1988), 69-71.

Brown, R. 'Baptist Theology', in D.F. Wright and J.I. Packer (eds.), *New Dictionary of Theology* (Leicester, 1988), 75-76.

Burnish, R.F.G. 'Baptism. 2. Historical and Systematic Theology', in D.F. Wright and J.I. Packer (eds.), *New Dictionary of Theology* (Leicester, 1988), 71-73.

Clements, K.W. 'Baptism', in C. Davey (ed.), *British and Irish Churches respond to BEM: Analysis and Implications of The British and Irish Churches' Responses to the Lima Report* (1988), 9-21.

Griffith, T. 'Look, Here Is Water', *Mainstream Newsletter* 27 (January, 1988), 1-3.

Thacker, A. '"Re-baptism" and Ecumenicity', *Mainstream Newsletter* 28 (April, 1988), 7-9.

Beasley-Murray, P. 'The Big Decision', *Leadership Today* October 1988, 24-25.

1989   Fiddes, P.S. *Past Event and Present Salvation: The Christian Idea of Atonement* (1989).

Jones, K.G. *Baptismal Policy in LEPs: A Discussion Document* (Leeds, 2nd edn, 1989).

Jones, K.G. *et al. Christian Worship: Some Contemporary Issues* (Leeds, 2nd edn, 1989).

Jones, K.G. (ed.), *Fellowship in the Gospel: A series of six studies on Baptist principles and practice in belonging to the Church* (Leeds, 1989).

Pawson, J.D. *The Normal Christian Birth: How to give new believers a proper start in life* (1989).

White, R.E.O. *Meet St. Paul* (Cambridge, 1989).

Wright, N. *The Fair Face of Evil: Putting the Power of darkness in its Place* (1989).

YBA *Baptismal Policy in LEPs: A Discussion Document* (2nd edn, 1989).

YBA 'Position Paper of the Yorkshire Baptist Association Council on Baptist Church Planting in an Ecumenical Context within the County' (Leeds, 1989).

— *The Next Steps for Churches Together in Pilgrimage: Including definitive proposals for ecumenical instruments* (1989).

Russell, D.S. 'The Ecumenical Role of Baptists', in F.H. Littel (ed.), *The Growth of Interreligious Dialogue 1939–1989* (Lewiston, NY, 1989), 112-31.

Martin, R.P. 'Patterns of Worship in New Testament Churches', *JSNT* 37 (1989), 59-85.

Clements, K.W. 'Towards the Common Expression of the Apostolic Faith Today: Baptist Reflections on this Faith and Order Project', *BQ* 33.2 (April, 1989), 63-71.

Green, B. 'Churches Together in Pilgrimage', *Frat.* 226 (April, 1989), 26-27.

Jones, K.G. 'The Authority of the Trust Deed: A Yorkshire Perspective', *BQ* 33.3 (July, 1989), 103-18.

Slater, D. 'Being a review article of *The Normal Christian Birth*, David Pawson', *Mainstream Newsletter* 33 (July, 1989), 12-13.

White, B.R. 'Worship among the English Baptists Today', *Mainstream Newsletter* 33 (July, 1989), 3-6.

Hooton, M. 'The Normal Christian Birth by David Pawson', *Frat.* 228 (October, 1989), 26.

1990 CCLEPE *Constitutional Guidelines for a Local Ecumenical Project* (1990).

Ellis, C.J. *Together on the Way: A Theology of Ecumenism* (1990).

Griffith, T. *The Case for Believers Baptism* (Eastbourne, 1990).

Guthrie, D. *The Pastoral Epistles: An Introduction and Commentary* (TNTC; Leicester, 2nd edn, 1990).

Pendrich, S. *Advances in Ecumenism in 1990 or The End of Protestantism?* (n.d., [1990]).

Rushworth-Smith, D. *Baptists have a special role* (Crich, n.d., post 1989).

Russell, D.S. *Poles Apart: The Gospel in Creative Tension* (Edinburgh, 1990).

Wright, N. *Lord and Giver of Life: An Introduction to the Person and Work of the Holy Spirit* (CTP, C7; 1990).

Wright, N. and Slater, D. *A Theology of Mission* (AIM 2; Didcot, 1990).

Clements, K.W. 'A Response to the Faith and Order Commission Document No.140', in W.H. Brackney and R.J. Burke (eds.), *Faith, Life and Witness: The Papers of the Study and Research Division of the Baptist World Alliance—1986–1990* (Birmingham, Alabama, 1990), 48-53.

— 'Baptist Heritage Commission in Zagreb, Yugoslavia July, 1989', in W.H. Brackney and R.J. Burke (eds.), *Faith, Life and Witness: The Papers of the Study and Research Division of the Baptist World Alliance—1986–1990* (Birmingham, Alabama, 1990), 146-49 [prepared by J.H.Y. Briggs, also in W.B. Shurden, *The Baptist Identity: Four Fragile Freedoms* (Macon, GA, 1993), 63-66].

— 'The Responses to the Baptism Section', in *Baptism, Eucharist and Ministry 1982–1990: Report on the Process and Responses* (F&O Paper No. 149; Geneva, 1990), 39-55 (uncredited, but by W.M.S. West and M. Tanner).

Weller, P. 'Freedom and Witness in a Multi-Religious Society: A Baptist Perspective: Part I', *BQ* 33.6 (April, 1990), 252-64.

Briggs, J.H.Y. 'Evangel, Evangelicals and Evangelicalism' (editorial) *BQ* 33.7 (July, 1990), 297-301.

Weller, P. 'Freedom and Witness in a Multi-Religious Society: A Baptist Perspective: Part II', *BQ* 33.7 (July, 1990), 302-15.

Gilmore, A. 'New Baptist Hymnbook', *Frat.* 232 (October, 1990), 15.

Jenkins, S.P. 'New Baptist Service Book', *Frat.* 232 (October, 1990), 15-16.

1991 Beasley-Murray, G.R. *Gospel of Life: Theology in the Fourth Gospel* (Peabody, 1991).

Beasley-Murray, P. *Faith and Festivity: A guide for today's worship leaders* (Eastbourne, 1991).

Bowers, F. *Knowing Jesus* (BUild, 1991).

Bowers, F., Robertson, E. and Wright, S. *The Church* (BUild, 1991).

Martin, R.P. *Ephesians, Colossians, and Philemon* (Atlanta, 1991).

Robertson, E. *Following Jesus* (BUild, 1991).

Wright, N. *Challenge to Change: A radical agenda for Baptists* (1991).

Wright, S. *Joining the Church* (BUild, 1991).

— *Baptist/Methodist Agreement on Baptismal Policy within Local Ecumenical Projects* (1991).

— *Patterns and Prayers for Christian Worship: A guidebook for worship leaders* (Oxford, 1991).

West, W.M.S. 'Lund Principle', in N. Lossky *et al.*, *Dictionary of the Ecumenical Movement* (Geneva, 1991), 633-34.

Walker, M.J. 'Praying Our Baptism', *Frat.* 233 (January, 1991), 12-18.

Kreitzer, L. 'Baptism and the Pauline Epistles: with special reference to the Corinthian Letters', *BQ* 34.2 (April, 1991), 67-78.

Beasley-Murray, P. 'Worship and Wineskins', *Third Way* May 1991, 20-22.

1992 Beasley-Murray, P. *Radical Believers: The Baptist way of being the church* (Didcot, 1992).

Blakeborough, E. *Permission to Be* (1992).

Cohen, D. and Gaukroger, S. *How to Close Your Church in a Decade* (1992).

Gray, D. (ed.). *Confirmation and Re-affirmation of Baptismal Faith* (Norwich, 1992).

Monkcom, D. *John's Portrait of Jesus* (CTP; 1992).

Pawson, J.D. *Explaining Water Baptism* (Explaining series; Tonbridge, 1992).

Tidball, D.J. *AIM 3: AIM Discipleship* (Didcot, 1992).

— *A Five Year Plan Towards 2000*. The Listening Day Process (Didcot, 1992).

Beasley-Murray, P. 'Baptism' in R. Keeley *et al* (eds.), *An Introduction to the Christian Faith* (Oxford, 2nd edn, 1992), 237-40.

Clements, K.W. 'A Baptist View', in R.E. Davies (ed.), *The Truth in Tradition: A Free Church Symposium* (1992), 6-32.

Turner, M.M.B. 'Holy Spirit', in J.B. Green, S. McKnight and I.H. Marshall (eds.), *Dictionary of Jesus and the Gospels* (Leicester, 1992), 341-51.

Staple, D. 'Pilgrims Together: Has Dissent Become Consent? The Free Churches and the Inter Church Process', *BQ* 34.6 (April, 1992), 252-62.

Slater, D. 'Church Membership', *Mainstream Newsletter* 44 (May, 1992), 4-8.

Bottoms, R.A. 'Patterns and Prayers for Christian Worship: A Reflection', *BMJ* 240 (October, 1992), 25-26.

1993   Beasley-Murray, P. *Believers' Baptism* (Baptist Basics series; 1993).

Bochenski, M.I. (ed.) *Evangelicals and Ecumenism: When Baptists Disagree* (Didcot, 1993).

Coffey, D. *Church Membership* (Baptist Basics series; 1993).

Gaukroger , S. *Being Baptized* (1993).

Haymes, B. *Why Be A Baptist?* (Baptist Basics series; 1993).

Jones, K.G. *The Lord's Supper* (Baptist Basics series; 1993).

Milne, B. *The Message of John: Here is your King!* (BST; Leicester, 1993).

Pawson, J.D. *Fourth Wave: Charismatics and evangelicals, are we ready to come together?* (1993).

Quicke, M.J. *Visiting New Church Members* (Baptist Basics series, 1993).

Warner, R. *21st Century Church: Why Radical Change Cannot Wait* (n.d., [1993]).

— *A Ten Year Plan Towards 2000 incorporating the National Mission Strategy* (Didcot, 1993).

Beasley-Murray, G.R. 'Baptism', 'Dying and Rising with Christ', in G.F. Hawthorne, R.P. Martin and D.G. Reid (eds.), *Dictionary of Paul and His Letters* (Leicester, 1993), 60-65, 218-22.

Kreitzer, L.J. 'Resurrection', in G.F. Hawthorne, R.P. Martin and D.G. Reid (eds.), *Dictionary of Paul and His Letters* (Leicester, 1993), 805-12.

Martin, R.P. 'Worship', in G.F. Hawthorne, R.P. Martin and D.G. Reid (eds.), *Dictionary of Paul and His Letters* (Leicester, 1993), 982-91.

Tidball, D.J. 'Social Setting of Mission Churches', in G.F. Hawthorne, R.P. Martin and D.G. Reid (eds.), *Dictionary of Paul and His Letters* (Leicester, 1993), 883-92.

Clark, N. 'Baptist Praise and Worship', *BQ* 35.2 (April, 1993), 95-100.

Gouldbourne, R. 'Praise and Prayer', *BQ* 35.2 (April, 1993), 90-94.

Smith, M. '*Baptists at the Table* by Michael Walker', review, *Frat.* 242 (April, 1993), 24-25.

Martin, R.P. 'New Testament Worship: Some Puzzling Practices', *AUSS* 2 (Summer 1993), 119-26.

Campbell, R.A. 'Romans Through New Eyes: Part 2: The Real Issue', *BMJ* 243 (July, 1993), 11-14.

Wilson, B.E. 'The Fellowship of Believers and the Status of Children', *BMJ* 243 (July, 1993), 20-22.

Beasley-Murray, P. 'Celebrating the Faith in Baptism', *BMJ* 244 (October, 1993), 11-14.

1994   — *The Nature of the Assembly and the Council of the Baptist Union of Great Britain* (Didcot, 1994).

Beasley-Murray, G.R. 'The Problem of Infant Baptism: An Exercise in Possibilities', in *Festschrift Günther Wagner*, ed. by the Faculty of the Baptist Theological Seminary, Rüschlikon (Berne, 1994), 1-14.

Shepherd, P. 'The Baptist Ministers' Journal 1946–1992', *BQ* 35.5 (January, 1994), 251-55.

Abernethy, M. 'Reflections on A Word and Spirit Network', *Mainstream Newsletter* 50 (June, 1994), 12-15.

Bochenski, M.I. 'A Word and Spirit Network—the story so far', *Mainstream Newsletter* 50 (June, 1994), 9.

Mainstream Executive, 'A Word and Spirit Network', *Mainstream Newsletter* 50 (June, 1994), 10-11.

Wright, N.G. '"Koinonia" and Baptist Ecclesiology: Self-Critical Reflections from Historical and Systematic Perspectives', *BQ* 35.8 (October, 1994), 363-75.

1995   Clark, N. *Invitation to a Conversation 2. Baptism and Church Membership* (Cardiff, 1995).

Nunn, R. *This Growing Unity: A handbook on ecumenical developments in the counties, and large cities and new towns of England* (1995).

Winward, S.F. and Quicke, M.J. (ed.). *Countdown to Baptism: The New Testament teaching on baptism in daily readings* (Didcot, 1995).

— *Who'd be a Baptist?* (Didcot, 1995).

Green, J. 'A Baptist Dilemma: Children, Baptism and the Lord's Supper', *BMJ* 251 (July, 1995), 21-25.

1996   Beasley-Murray, P. *Radical Disciples: A course for new Christians* (Didcot, n.d., 1996).

Fiddes, P.S. *Reflections on the Water: Understanding God and the World through the Baptism of Believers* (Regent's Study Guides, 4; Oxford, 1996).

Jones, K.G. *From Conflict to Communion* (Didcot, 1996).

Kidd, R.L. (ed.), *Something to Declare: A study of the Declaration of Principle* (Oxford, 1996).

Lidgett, H. *Called to be One: The Workbook* (1996).

Sparkes, D.C. *The Constitutions of the Baptist Union of Great Britain* (Didcot, 1996).

Turner, M.M.B. *Power from on High: The Spirit in Israel's Restoration and Witness in Luke–Acts* (JPTSup, 9; Sheffield, 1996).

Turner, M.M.B. *The Holy Spirit and Spiritual Gifts Then and Now* (Carlisle, 1996).

Wright, N.G. *Power and Discipleship: Towards a Baptist Theology of the State* (Oxford, 1996).

— *Basix* (Didcot, 1996).

— *Believing and Being Baptized: Baptism, so-called re-baptism, and children in the church* (Didcot, 1996).

— *Called to be One* (1996).

— *The Baptist Union of Great Britain/United Reformed Church Agreed Policy for Baptismal Policy in Local Ecumenical Partnerships* (Didcot, 1996).

White, R.E.O. 'Baptism for the Dead' and 'Baptize, Baptism', in W.A. Elwell (ed.), *Evangelical Dictionary of Biblical Theology* (Grand Rapids, 1996), 49 and 50-53.

Bowers, F. 'Baptism: A Baptist Perspective', *Society for Ecumenical Studies* (1996).

Campbell, R. A. 'Jesus and His Baptism', *TynBul* 47.2 (1996), 191-214.

West, W.M.S. 'Churches Together in England: "Called to be One". Christian Initiation and Church Membership: a Report', *One In Christ* 32.3 (1996), 263-81.

1997   Clark, N. *Invitation to a Conversation 9. Life in the Spirit* (Cardiff, 1997).

Clark, N. *Invitation to a Conversation 10. Belonging and Believing* (Cardiff, 1997).

Kreitzer, L.J. *The Epistle to the Ephesians* (Peterborough, 1997).

Pawson, J.D. *Jesus Baptises in One Holy Spirit: Who? How? When? Why?* (1997).

Martin, R.P. 'Worship and Liturgy', in R.P. Martin and P.H. Davids (eds.), *Dictionary of the Later New Testament and Its Developments* (Leicester, 1997), 1224-38.

— *Baptism and Church Membership with particular reference to Local Ecumenical Partnerships* (1997).

Weaver, J.D. 'Reconsidering Believers' Baptism', *BMJ* 257 (January, 1997), 3-7.

Clifford, P.R. 'Barth's Theology of Baptism', *BMJ* 259 (July, 1997), 11-13.

Ballard, P.H. 'Baptists and Baptism: A Socio-Ecumenical Issue', *BMJ* 260 (October, 1997), 18-23.

1998   Bridge, D. and Phypers, D. *The Water That Divides: A survey of the doctrine of baptism* (Fearn, Ross-shire, 2nd edn, 1998).

Clark, N. *Invitation to a Conversation 11. Baptist Churchmanship* (Cardiff, 1998).

Clark, N. *Invitation to a Conversation 12. Ecumenical Dilemma* (Cardiff, 1998).

Milne, B. *Know the Truth: A Handbook of Christian Belief* (Leicester, 2nd edn, 1998).

— *5 Core Values for a Gospel People* (Didcot, 1998).

Mason, R. 'H. Wheeler Robinson Revisited', *BQ* 37.5 (January, 1998), 213-26.

White, R.E.O. 'Baptists and Baptism', *BMJ* 262 (April, 1998), 17.

— 'What makes a Baptist?:', http://www.baptist.org.uk/baptism.htm, February 28, 1999.

— 'What makes a Baptist?: Believers Baptism', http://www.baptist.org.uk/baptism.htm, February 28, 1999.

1999   Ellis, C.J. *Baptist Worship Today* (Didcot, 1999).

West, W.M.S. 'The Child and the Church: A Baptist Perspective', in W.H. Brackney, P.S. Fiddes and J.H.Y. Briggs (eds.), *Pilgrim Pathways: Essays in Baptist History in Honour of B.R. White* (Macon, GA, 1999), 75-110.

Cross, A.R. 'Kevin Roy, *Baptism, Reconciliation and Unity*', review, *BQ* 38.4 (October, 1999), 202-03.

2000 Briggs, J.H.Y. and Bowers, F. (eds.), *Baptists Together* (Didcot, 2000) (being the memorial volume for W.M.S. West).

Wright, N.G. *Disavowing Constantine: Mission, Church and the Social Order in the Theologies of John Howard Yoder and Jürgen Moltmann* (PBTM; Carlisle, 2000).

Bibliography of Secondary Sources

Alten, D. 'Baptism in Recent German Theology', *ResQ* 7.3 (1963), 124-31.

Aubrey, M.E. 'J.H. Rushbrooke', *BQ* 15.8 (October, 1954), 369-77.

— 'John Howard Shakespeare, 1857–1928', *BQ* 17.3 (July, 1957), 99-108.

— 'T.R. Glover. Review and Reminiscence', *BQ* 15.4 (October, 1953), 175-82.

Bacon, F. *Church Administration: A Guide for Baptist Ministers and Church Officers* (1981, 2nd edn 1992).

Barrett, J.O. *Rawdon College (Northern Baptist Education Society), 1804–1954: A Short History* (1954).

Bateman, C.T. *John Clifford: Free Church Leader and Preacher* (1902).

Bebbington, D.W. 'Baptists and Fundamentalism in Inter-War Britain', in K. Robbins (ed.), *Protestant Evangelicalism: Britain, Ireland, Germany and America, c1750–c1950*, Essays in Honour of W.R. Ward (Studies in Church History 7; Oxford, 1990), 297-326.

— *Evangelicalism in Modern Britain: A History from the 1730s to the 1980s* (1989).

— *The Nonconformist Conscience: Chapel and Politics, 1870–1914* (1982).

— *Victorian Nonconformity* (Headstart History Papers; Bangor, 1992).

Bell, G.K.A. (ed.). *Documents on Christian Unity, 1920–4* (1924).

— *Documents on Christian Unity: A Selection from the First and Second Series, 1920–30* (1955).

— *Documents on Christian Unity: Third Series 1930–48* (1948).

— *Documents on Christian Unity: Fourth Series 1948–57* (1958).

Bell, G.K.A. *Randall Davidson: Archbishop of Canterbury* (2 Vols; Oxford, 1935).

Berger, T. 'Baptism and the Church. Baptist Faith and Practice in a Biblical and Ecumenical Light', *BQ* 18.3 (July, 1959), 125-31; 'Baptism and the Church (continued)', *BQ* 18.4 (October, 1959), 159-71.

Binfield, C. *Pastor's and People: The Biography of a Baptist Church, Queen's Road, Coventry* (Coventry, 1984).

Bonner, C. and Whitley, W.T. *A Handbook to the Baptist Church Hymnal Revised* (1935).

Bonsall, H.E. and Robertson, E.H. *The Dream of an Ideal City: Westbourne Park 1877–1977* (1978).

Bowers, F. *A Bold Experiment: The Story of Bloomsbury Chapel and Bloomsbury Central Baptist Church 1848–1999* (1999).

— *Called to the City: Three Ministers of Bloomsbury* (1989).

— H. Howard Williams: Preacher, Pastor—Prophet without honour?' *BQ* 37.7 (July, 1998), 316-35 (also published separately, London, 1998).

— 'The Story of BUild', *Frat.* 242 (April, 1993), 7-9.

— *Who are the Baptists?* (1978).

Bradshaw, P. *Early Christian Worship: A basic introduction to ideas and practice* (1996).

Brierley, P. (ed.), *Christian England: What the English Church Census Reveals* (1991).

Briggs, J.H.Y. 'Baptists and Higher Education in England', in W.H. Brackney and R.J. Burke (eds.), *Faith, Life and Witness: The Papers of the Study and Research Division of the Baptist World Alliance—1986–1990* (Birmingham, Alabama, 1990), 92-111.

— 'Evangelical Ecumenism: The Amalgamation of General and Particular Baptists in 1891', Part I *BQ* 34.3 (July, 1991), 99-115; Part II *BQ* 34.4 (October, 1991), 160-79.

— 'The Revd Dr W.M.S. West', *BQ* 38.5 (January, 2000), 211.

Brown, J. *Centenary Celebration of the Bedfordshire Union of Christians: The Story of a Hundred Years* (1896).

Brown, J. and Prothero D. *The History of the Bedfordshire Union of Christians* (1946).

Brown, R. *The English Baptists of the Eighteenth Century* (1986).

Bruce, F.F. 'Obituary. Harold Henry Rowley', *PEQ* 101 (1969), 134.

Buchanan, C., Owen, C. and Wright, A. *Reforming Infant Baptism* (1990).

Butler, D. *Dying to be One: English Ecumenism: History, Theology and the Future* (1996).

Byrt, G.W. *John Clifford: A Fighting Free Churchman* (1947).

Cawley, F. 'Percy William Evans', *BQ* 14.4 (October, 1951), 148-52.

Carlile, J.C. *My Life's Little Day* (1935).

Champion, L.G. 'Arthur Dakin (1884–1969)', *Frat.* 155 (January, 1970), 5-8.

Clements, K.W. *Lovers of Discord: Twentieth-Century Theological Controversies in England* (1988).

Clements, R.E. 'The Biblical Scholarship of H.H. Rowley (1890–1969)', *BQ* 38.2 (April, 1999), 70-82.

Clifford, P.R. *An Ecumenical Pilgrimage* (1994).

Colwell, J. 'Alternative Approaches to Believer's Baptism (From the Anabaptists to Barth)', *SBET* 7 (Spring, 1989), 3-20.

Cook, H. *Charles Brown* (1939).

Cotterell, P. 'Dr. Donald Guthrie, 1916–1992', *LBC Review* (Autumn, 1992), 2.

Cowell, H.J. *These Forty Years: 1900–1940, Pages from a Journalist's Note-book* (1940).

Cox, J. *The English Churches in a Secular Society: Lambeth, 1870–1930* (Oxford, 1982).

Cross, A.R. 'Baptists and Baptism: A British Perspective', *BHH* 35.1 (Winter, 2000), 104-21.

— 'Dispelling the Myth of English Baptist Baptismal Sacramentalism' (TCDTBW; August, 1999, forthcoming in *BQ*).
— 'Revd. Dr. Hugh Martin. Publisher and Writer. Part 1', *BQ* 37.1 (January, 1997), 33-49; 'Revd. Dr. Hugh Martin: Ecumenist. Part 2', *BQ* 37.2 (April, 1997), 71-86; 'Revd. Dr. Hugh Martin: Ecumenical Controversialist and Writer', *BQ* 37.3 (July, 1997), 131-46.
— 'Service to the Ecumenical Movement: The Contribution of British Baptists', *BQ* 38.3 (July, 1999), 107-22.

Davie, G. *Religion in Britain since 1945: Believing Without Belonging* (1994).

Davies, H. *Worship and Theology in England: V. The Ecumenical Century, 1900–1965* (Oxford, 1965).

Davies, H. *Worship and Theology in England: VI. Crisis and Creativity, 1965–Present* (Grand Rapids, 1996).

Davies, R.E. *Methodism* (1963).

Dekar, P. 'Twentieth Century British Baptist Conscientious Objectors', *BQ* 35.1 (January, 1993), 35-44.

Dunn, J.D.G. *Baptism in the Holy Spirit: A Re-examination of the New Testament Teaching on the Gift of the Spirit in relation to Pentecostalism today* (SBT, 15; 1970).

—*Jesus and the Spirit: A Study of the Religious and Charismatic Experience of Jesus and the First Christians as Reflected in the New Testament* (1975).

— *Unity and Diversity in the New Testament: An Inquiry into the Character of Earliest Christianity* (1977, 2nd edn 1990).

Dunscombe, H. *Footprints of Faith: A History of Central Church, Swindon* (Swindon, 2nd edn, 1990).

Edwards, D.L. *Christian England* (revised and combined edn, 1989).

Finney, J. *Finding Faith Today: How does it happen?* (Swindon, 1992).

Foreman, H. *Old Dissent in Wellington, Shropshire 1700–1920: The Story of Union Free Church* (Wellington, 1986).

Fullerton, W.Y. *At the Sixtieth Milestone: Incidents of the Journey* (n.d.).

— *F. B. Meyer: A Biography* (n.d.).

Gassmann, G. (ed.), *Documentary History of Faith and Order: 1963–1993* (F&O Paper 159; Geneva, 1993).

Garrett, D.A. 'H. Wheeler Robinson', in T. George and D.S. Dockery (eds.), *Baptist Theologians* (Nashville, 1990), 400-18.

Glover, W.B. *Evangelical Nonconformists and Higher Criticism in the Nineteenth Century* (1954).

Goodall, N. *The Ecumenical Movement: What it is and what it does* (1961).

Grant, J.W. *Free Churchmanship in England, 1870–1940* (n.d.).

Green, B. *Crossing the Boundaries: A History of the European Baptist Federation* (Didcot, 1999).

— *Tomorrow's Man: A Biography of James Henry Rushbrooke* (Didcot, 1997).

Griffiths, R. and Lemon, C. *Fifty Fruitful Years: The Story of Milton Baptist Church 1926–1976* (1976).

Hall, C.S. and Mowvley, H. *Tradition and Challenge: The Story of Broadmead Baptist Church, Bristol from 1685–1991* (Bristol, 1991).

Hart, G.S. *The Story of Pill Union Church* (Bristol, 1987).

Hastings, A. *A History of English Christianity, 1920–1990* (3rd edn, 1991).

Hayden, R. *English Baptist History and Heritage* (CTP, G3; 1990).

— 'Leornard George Champion 1907–1997), *BQ* 37.5 (January, 1998), 211-12.

—'Still at the Crossroads? Revd. J.H. Shakespeare and Ecumenism', in K.W. Clements (ed.), *Baptists in the Twentieth Century* (1983), 31-54.

— *The Records of a Church of Christ in Bristol, 1640–1687* (Bristol, 1974).

Himbury, D. M. *The South Wales Baptist College (1807–1957)* (Landysul, 1957).

Hipper, K. *Rev. J.H. Shakespeare MA, 1857–1928* (Norwich, n.d.).

Huxtable, J. *A New Hope for Christian Unity* (Glasgow, 1977).

Jeremy, D.J. *Capitalists and Christians: Business Leaders and the Churches in Britain 1900–1960* (Oxford, 1990).

Jewson, C.B. *The Baptists of Norfolk* (1957).

— 'St. Mary's, Norwich', Part I *BQ* 10.2 (April, 1940), 108-17; Part II *BQ* 10.3 (July, 1940), 168-77; Part III *BQ* 10.4 (October, 1940), 227-36; Part IV *BQ* 10.5 (January, 1941), 282-88; Part V *BQ* 10.6 (April, 1941), 340-46; Part VI *BQ* 10.7 (July, 1941), 398-406.

Johnson, W.C. *Encounter in London: The Story of the London Baptist Association 1865–1965* (1965).

Jones, R.T. *Congregationalism in England, 1662–1962* (1962).

Jordan, E.K.H. *Free Church Unity: History of the Free Church Council Movement, 1896–1941* (1956).

Kaye, E. *Mansfield College Oxford: Its Origin, History, and Significance* (Oxford, 1996).

Kingsley, H. *Crusader: The Life and Times of Sir Cyril Black* (privately published, 1996).

Koss, S. *Nonconformity in Modern British Politics* (1975).

Lampe, G.W.H. *The Seal of the Spirit: A Study in the Doctrine of Baptism and Confirmation in the New Testament and the Fathers* (1951).

Lawrence, J. *Churches Working Together in Loughton 1944 to 1994* (Loughton, n.d., c.1994).

Lea, J.H. 'Charles Williams of Accrington, 1827–1907', *BQ* 23.4 (October, 1969), 177-91.

Leitch, R. *The History of Keynsham Baptist Church* (Keynsham, 1985).

Lewis, V. *Come With Us. Loughton Union Church, 1813–1973* (Loughton, 1974).

Lossky, N. *et al* (eds.). *Dictionary of the Ecumenical Movement* (Geneva, 1991).

Lumpkin, W.L. *Baptist Confessions of Faith* (Chicago, 2nd edn, 1969).

McBain, D. *Fire Over the Waters: Renewal among Baptists and Others from the 1960s to the 1990s* (1997).

McBeth, H.L. *A Sourcebook for Baptist Heritage* (Nashville, 1990).

— *The Baptist Heritage: Four Centuries of Baptist Witness* (Nashville, 1987).

McGlothin, W.J. *Baptist Confessions of Faith* (1910).

McGrath, A.E. *Reformation Thought: An Introduction* (Oxford, 2nd edn, 1993).

Maggs, W.J. *New Malden Baptist Church. 125 Years. A History from 1862 to 1987* (New Malden, 1987).

Mason, R.A. 'H. Wheeler Robinson Revisited', *BQ* 37.5 (January, 1998), 213-26.

Marchant, J. *Dr. John Clifford, C.H., Life, Letters and Reminiscences* (1924).

Martin, H. (ed.). *A Companion to the Baptist Church Hymnal (Revised)* (1953).

— *The Baptist Hymn Book Companion* (1962).

Matheney, M.P. 'Teaching Prophet: The Life and Continuing Influence of Theodore Henry Robinson', *BQ* 29.5 (January, 1982), 199-216.

Matthews, W.R. 'H. Wheeler Robinson', *BQ* 12.1-2 (January–April, 1946), 5-8.

Middlemiss, D. *Interpreting Charismatic Experience* (1996).

Mitchell, S. *Not Disobedient... A History of United Baptist Church, Leicester, including Harvey Lane 1760–1845, Belvoir Street 1845–1940 and Charles Street 1831–1940*, incorporating G. Lee, *United Baptist Church, 1940–1983* (Leicester, 1984).

Murray, D.B. *Scottish Baptist College Centenary History, 1894–1994* (Glasgow, 1994).

Neill, S. 'Towards Christian Unity' in S. Neill (ed.), *Twentieth Century Christianity: A survey of modern religious trends by leading churchmen* (1961), 340-75.

Nicholls, M. *Lights to the World: A History of Spurgeon's College, 1856–1992* (Harpenden, 1994).

— *C.H. Spurgeon. The Pastor Evangelist* (1992).

Nicholson, J.F.V. 'H.H. Rowley on "Aspects of Reunion"', *BQ* 38.4 (October, 1999), 196-99.

Otzen, R. *Whitley: The Baptist College of Victoria 1891–1991* (South Yarra, Victoria, 1991).

Payne, E. A. *A 20th Century Minister: John Oliver Barrett, 1901–78* (n.d.).

— *Baptists Speak to the World: A Description and Interpretation of the Sixth Baptist World Congress, Atlanta, 1939* (1939).

— *Free Churchmen, Unrepentant and Repentant and Other Papers* (1965).

— *Henry Wheeler Robinson: Scholar, Teacher, Principal: A Memoir* (1946).

— 'John Oliver Barrett, 1901–1978', *Frat.* 183 (March, 1978), 27-30.

— 'H.H. Rowley (1890–1969)', *Frat.* 155 (January, 1970), 9-12.

— *James Henry Rushbrooke: A Baptist Greatheart* (1954).

— 'John Howard Shakespeare (1857–1928)', in A.S. Clement (ed.), *Baptists Who Made History: A Book about Great Baptists written by Baptists* (1955), 126-36.

— *The Baptist Union and Its Headquarters* (1953).

— *The Baptist Union: A Short History* (1959).

— *The Free Church Tradition in the Life of England* (1st edn, 1944, 4th edn, 1965).

— 'The Rise and Decline of the Downs Chapel, Clapton', *BQ* 27.1 (January, 1977), 34-44.

— *The World Council of Churches, 1948–1969* (1970).

— *Thirty Years of the British Council of Churches, 1942–1972* (1972).

Peaston, A.E. *The Prayer Book Tradition in the Free Churches* (1964).

Poolman, R. and Barfield, J. *Church Administration* (CTP, D4; n.d.).

Price, E.J. *Baptists, Congregationalists and Presbyterians* (1933).

Price, S. J. 'William Thomas Whitley', *BQ* 12.10-11 (April–July, 1948), 357-63.

Randall, I. *Educating Evangelicalism: The Origins, Development and Impact of London Bible College* (Carlisle, 2000).

— *Evangelical Experiences: A Study in the Spirituality of English Evangelicalism 1918–1939* (PBTM; Carlisle, 1999).

— 'Mere Denominationalism. F.B. Meyer and Baptist Life', *BQ* 35.1 (January, 1993), 19-34.

Roberts-Thomson, E. *With Hands Outstretched: Baptists and the Ecumenical Movement* (1962).

Root, M. and Saarinen, R. (eds.). *Baptism and The Unity of the Church* (Grand Rapids, 1998).

Ross, J.M. 'The Theology of Baptism in Baptist History', *BQ* 15.3 (July, 1953), 100-12.

Rouse, R. and Neill, S. (eds.). *A History of the Ecumenical Movement, 1517–1948* (3rd edn, 1986).

Roy, K. *Baptism, Reconciliation and Unity* (Carlisle, 1997).

Runia, K. 'Recent Developments in Baptist Theology', *RTR* 20.1 (February, 1961), Part 1 pp.12-23, Part 2, pp.47-49.

Russell, D.S. *In Journeyings Often* (1981).

Ryan. W.E. (ed.), *Together in Christ: Official Report of the Sixteenth Congress, Baptist World Congress, Seoul, Korea, August 14–19, 1990* (McLean, n.d., (1990 or 1991)).

Sellars, I. (ed.). *Our Heritage: The Baptists of Yorkshire, Lancashire and Cheshire, 1647–1987* (Leeds, 1987).

— 'W.T. Whitley: A Commemorative Essay', *BQ* 37.4 (October, 1997), 159-73.

Shakespare, G. *Let Candles Be Brought In: The Memoirs of the Rt. Hon. Sir Geoffrey Shakespeare Bt* (1949).

— 'John Howard Shakespeare', *BQ* 17.2 (April, 1957), 51-52.

Shakespeare, J.H. *The Story of the Baptist Union Twentieth Century Fund, with the Financial Report* (1904).

Shepherd, P. 'Denominational Renewal: A Study in English Baptist Church Life and Growth 1901–1906', *BQ* 37.7 (July, 1998), 336-50.

Skoglund, J.E. 'Baptist Worship', in J.G. Davies (ed.), *A Dictionary of Liturgy and Worship* (1972), 64-68.

Smith, R.G. (ed.) *The Enduring Gospel* (1950).

Stanley, B. *The History of the Baptist Missionary Society 1792–1992* (Edinburgh, 1992).

Street, J.S. *F.B. Meyer: His Life and Work* (1902).

Tatlow, T. *The Story of the Student Christian Movement of Great Britain and Ireland* (1933).

Thompson, D.M. *Let Sects and Parties Fall: A Short History of the Association of Churches of Christ in Great Britain and Ireland* (Birmingham, 1980).
— 'The Older Free Churches', in R. Davies (ed.), *The Testing of the Churches, 1932–1982: A Symposium* (1982), 87-115.
— 'The Theology of Adult Initiation in the Nineteenth and Twentieth Centuries', in D.A. Withey (ed.), *Adult Initiation* (Alcuin/GROW Liturgical Study 10 (Grove Liturgical Study 58; Bramcote, 1989), 6-23.
Thompson, P.E. 'A New Question in Baptist History: Seeking a Catholic Spirit among Early Baptists', *Pro Ecclesia* 8.1 (Winter, 1999), 51-72.
Thomson, R.W. *Heroes of the Baptist Church* (1937).
— *The Psalms and Hymns Trust: A Short History of the Trust and the Work of Publishing Baptist Hymn Books* (1960).
Thomson, R.W. (ed.). *The Baptist Hymn Book Companion* (revised 1967).
Thurian, M. and Wainwright, G. *Baptism and Eucharist: Ecumenical Convergence in Celebration* (F&O Paper 117; Geneva, 1983).
Tidball, D. *Who Are The Evangelicals? Tracing the Roots of Today's Movements* (1994).
Till, B. *The Churches Search for Unity* (Harmondsworth, 1972).
Townsend, H. *Robert Wilson Black* (1954).
— *The Claims of the Free Churches* (1949).
Townsend, M. 'John Howard Shakespeare: Prophet of Ecumenism', *BQ* 37.6 (April, 1998), 298-312.
Underwood, A.C. *A History of the English Baptists* (1947).
Underwood, T.L. 'Child Dedication Services in the 17th Century', *BQ* 23.4 (October, 1969), 164-69.
Wagner, G. 'Baptism from Accra to Lima', in M. Thurian (ed.), *Ecumenical Perpsectives on Baptism, Eucharist and Ministry* (F&O Paper 116; Geneva, 1983), 12-32.
Walker, A. *Restoring the Kingdom: The Radical Christianity of the House Church Movement* (3rd edn, 1989).
Walker, M.J. *Baptists at the Table: The Theology of the Lord's Supper amongst English Baptists in the Nineteenth Century* (Didcot, 1992).
— 'Baptist Theology of Infancy in the 17th Century', *BQ* 21.6 (April, 1966), 242-62.
— 'Baptist Worship in the Twentieth Century', in K.W. Clements (ed.), *Baptists in the Twentieth Century* (1983), 21-30.
Walling, D. *Chapel on the Green: A short history of Theydon Bois Baptist Church* (Theydon Bois, 1994).
Warren, R. *In the Crucible: The Testing and Growth of a Local Church* (Crowborough, 1989).
Welch, E. and Winfield, F. *Travelling Together: A Handbook on Local Ecumenical Partnerships* (n.d., [1995]).
Weller, J. *One Church, One Faith, One Lord: A Short History of Union Church, Heathfield* (Heathfield, 1979).

West, W.M.S. 'Baptists in Faith and Order: A Study in Baptismal Convergence', in K.W. Clements (ed.), *Baptists in the Twentieth Century* (1983), 55-75.

— *To Be A Pilgrim: A Memoir of Ernest A. Payne* (Guildford, 1983).

— 'The Young Mr. Aubrey', *BQ* 33.8 (October, 1990), 351-63; 'The Reverend Secretary Aubrey', Part I *BQ* 34.5 (January, 1992), 199-223; Part II *BQ* 34.6 (April, 1992), 263-81; Part III *BQ* 34.7 (July, 1992), 320-36.

White, B.R. 'Open and Closed Membership Among English and Welsh Baptists', *BQ* 24.7 (July, 1972), 330-34.

— *The English Baptists of the Seventeenth Century* (1983, Didcot, 2nd edn, 1996).

Whitley, W.T. *A History of British Baptists* (1923, 2nd edn, 1932).

Wood, H.G. *Terrot Reaveley Glover: A Biography* (Cambridge, 1953).

Wright, D.F. 'Scripture and Evangelical Diversity with Special Reference to the Baptismal Divide', in P.E. Satterthwaite and D.F. Wright (eds.), *A Pathway into the Holy Scripture* (Grand Rapids, 1994), 257-75.

Wright, O. *Baptists of Berkhamsted* (Berkhamsted, 1990).

— *Baptism, Eucharist and Ministry, 1982–1990: Report on the Process and Responses* (F&O Paper 149; Geneva, 1990).

Author Index

Paternoster Biblical and Theological Monographs

(Uniform with this Volume)

Eve: Accused or Acquitted?

*An Analysis of Feminist Readings of the
Creation Narrative Texts in Genesis 1–3*

Joseph Abraham

Two contrary views dominate contemporary feminist biblical scholarship. One finds in the Bible an unequivocal equality between the sexes from the very creation of humanity, whilst the other sees the biblical text as irredeemably patriarchal and androcentric. Dr. Abraham enters into dialogue with both camps as well as introducing his own method of approach. An invaluable tool for anyone who is interested in this contemporary debate.

2000 / 0-85364-971-5

Deification in Eastern Orthodox Theology

An Evaluation and Critique of the Theology of Dumitru Staniloae

Emil Bartos

Bartos studies a fundamental yet neglected aspect of Orthodox theology: deification. By examining the doctrines of anthropology, Christology, soteriology and ecclesiology as they relate to deification, he provides an important contribution to contemporary dialogue between Eastern and Western theologians.

1999 / 0-85364-956-1 / 386pp

The Weakness of the Law

Jonathan F. Bayes

A study of the four New Testament books which refer to the law as weak (Acts, Romans, Galatians, Hebrews) leads to a defence of the third use in the Reformed debate about the law in the life of the believer.

2000 / 0-85364-957-X

The Priesthood of Some Believers

Developments in the Christian Literature of the First Three Centuries

Colin J. Bulley

The first in-depth treatment of early Christian texts on the priesthood of all believers shows that the developing priesthood of the ordained related closely to the division between laity and clergy and had deleterious effects on the practice of the general priesthood.

2000 / 0-85364-958-8

Paul as Apostle to the Gentiles
His Apostolic Self-awareness and its Influence
on the Soteriological Argument in Romans
Daniel J-S Chae

Opposing 'the post-Holocaust interpretation of Romans', Daniel Chae competently demonstrates that Paul argues for the equality of Jew and Gentile in Romans. Chae's fresh exegetical interpretation is academically outstanding and spiritually encouraging.

1997 / 0-85364-829-8 / 392pp

Parallel Lives
The Relation of Paul to the Apostles in the Lucan Perspective
Andrew C. Clark

This study of the Peter-Paul parallels in Acts argues that their purpose was to emphasize the themes of continuity in salvation history and the unity of the Jewish and Gentile missions. New light is shed on Luke's literary techniques, partly through a comparison with Plutarch.

2000 / 085364-979-0

Baptism and the Baptists
Theology and Practice in Twentieth-Century Britain
Anthony R. Cross

At a time of renewed interest in baptism, *Baptism and the Baptists* is a detailed study of twentieth-century baptismal theology and practice and the factors which have influenced its development.

2000 / 0-85364-959-6 / 530pp

The Crisis and the Quest
A Kierkegaardian Reading of Charles Williams
Stephen M. Dunning

Employing Kierkegaardian categories and analysis, this study investigates both the central crisis in Charles Williams's authorship between hermeticism and Christianity (Kierkegaard's Religions A and B), and the quest to resolve this crisis, a quest that ultimately presses the bounds of orthodoxy.

1999 / 0-85364-985-5 / 278pp

The Triumph of Christ in African Perspective
A Study of Demonology and Redemption in the African Context
Keith Ferdinando

This book explores the implications for the gospel of traditional African fears of occult aggression. It analyses such traditional approaches to suffering and biblical responses to fears of demonic evil, concluding with an evaluation of African beliefs from the perspective of the gospel.

1999 / 0-85364-830-1 / 439pp

Suffering and Ministry in the Spirit
Paul's Defence of His Ministry in 2 Corinthians 2:14 – 3:3
Scott J. Hafemann
Shedding new light on the way Paul defended his apostleship, the author offers a careful, detailed study of 2 Corinthians 2:14 – 3:3 linked with other key passages throughout 1 and 2 Corinthians. Demonstrating the unity and coherence of Paul's argument in this passage, the author shows that Paul's suffering served as the vehicle for revealing God's power and glory through the Spirit.

1999 / 0-85364-967-7 / 276pp

The Words of our Lips
Language-Use in Free Church Worship
David Hilborn
Studies of liturgical language have tended to focus on the written canons of Roman Catholic and Anglican communities. By contrast, David Hilborn analyses the more extemporary approach of English Nonconformity. Drawing on recent developments in linguistic pragmatics, he explores similarities and differences between 'fixed' and 'free' worship, and argues for the interdependence of each.

2001 / 0-85364-977-4

One God, One People
*The Differentiated Unity of the People of God
in the Theology of Jürgen Moltmann*
John G. Kelly
The author expounds and critiques Moltmann's doctrine of God and highlights the systematic connections between it and Moltmann's influential discussion of Israel. He then proposes a fresh approach to Jewish–Christian relations, building on Moltmann's work and using insights from Habermas and Rawls.

2000 / 0-85346-969-3

Calvin and English Calvinism to 1649
R.T. Kendall
The author's thesis is that those who formed the Westminster Confession of Faith, which is regarded as Calvinism, in fact departed from John Calvin on two points: (1) the extent of the Atonement and (2) the ground of assurance of salvation. 'No student of the period can ignore this work' – *J.I. Packer*.

1997 / 0-85364-827-1 / 224pp

Karl Barth and the Strange New World within the Bible
Neil B. MacDonald
Barth's discovery of the strange new world within the Bible is examined in the context of Kant, Hume, Overbeck, and, most importantly, Wittgenstein. Covers some fundamental issues in theology today: epistemology, the final form of the text and biblical truth-claims.

2000 / 0-85364-970-7

Attributes and Atonement
The Holy Love of God in the Theology of P.T. Forsyth
Leslie McCurdy
Attributes and Atonement is an intriguing full-length study of P.T. Forsyth's doctrine of the cross as it relates particularly to God's holy love. It includes an unparalleled bibliography of both primary and secondary material relating to Forsyth.

1999 / 0-85364-833-6 / 323pp

Towards a Theology of the Concord of God
A Japanese Perspective on the Trinity
Nozomu Miyahira
This book introduces a new Japanese theology and a unique Trinitarian formula based on the Japanese intellectual climate: three betweennesses and one concord. It also presents a new interpretation of the Trinity, a co-subordinationism, which is in line with orthodox Trinitarianism; each single person of the Trinity is eternally and equally subordinate (or serviceable) to the other persons, so that they retain the mutual dynamic equality.

1999 / 0-85364-863-8

Your Father the Devil?
A New Approach to John and 'The Jews'
Stephen Motyer
Who are 'the Jews' in John's Gospel? Defending John against the charge of anti-Semitism, Motyer argues that, far from demonising the Jews, the Gospel seeks to present Jesus as 'Good News for Jews' in a late first century setting.

1997 / 0-85364-832-8 / 274pp

**Origins and Early Development of Liberation Theology
in Latin America**
With Particular Reference to Gustavo Gutierrez
Eddy José Muskus
This work challenges the fundamental premise of Liberation Theology: 'opting
for the poor', and its claim that Christ is found in them. It also argues that
Liberation Theology emerged as a direct result of the failure of the Roman
Catholic Church in Latin America.
2000 / 0-85364-974-X

'Hell': A Hard Look at a Hard Question
The Fate of the Unrighteous in New Testament Thought
David Powys
This comprehensive treatment seeks to unlock the original meaning of terms
and phrases long thought to support the traditional doctrine of hell. It concludes
that there is an alternative – one which is more biblical, and which can
positively revive the rationale for Christian mission.
1999 / 0-85364-831-X / 500pp

Evangelical Experiences
A Study in the Spirituality of English Evangelicalism 1918–1939
Ian M Randall
This book makes a detailed historical examination of evangelical spirituality
between the First and Second World Wars. It shows how patterns of devotion
led to tensions and divisions. In a wide-ranging study, Anglican, Wesleyan,
Reformed and Pentecostal-charismatic spiritualities are analysed.
1999 / 0-85364-919-7 / 320pp

Is World View Neutral Education Possible and Desirable?
A Christian Response to Liberal Arguments
(Published jointly with The Stapleford Centre)
Signe Sandsmark
This thesis discusses reasons for belief in world view neutrality, and argues that
'neutral' education will have a hidden, but strong world view influence. It
discusses the place for Christian education in the common school.
1999 / 0-85364-973-1 / 205pp

The Extent of the Atonement
A Dilemma for Reformed Theology from Calvin to the Consensus
G. Michael Thomas

A study of the way Reformed theology addressed the question, 'Did Christ die for all, or for the elect only?', commencing with John Calvin, and including debates with Lutheranism, the Synod of Dort and the teaching of Moïse Amyraut.

1997 / 0-85364-828-X / 237pp

The Power of the Cross
Theology and the Death of Christ in Paul, Luther and Pascal
Graham Tomlin

This book explores the theology of the cross in St Paul, Luther and Pascal. It offers new perspectives on the theology of each, and some implications for the nature of power, apologetics, theology and church life in a postmodern context.

1999 / 0-85364-984-7 / 368pp

Constrained by Zeal
Female Spirituality amongst Nonconformists 1825–1875
Linda Wilson

Constrained by Zeal investigates the neglected area of Nonconformist female spirituality. Against the background of separate spheres, it analyses the experience of women from four denominations, and argues that the churches provided a 'third sphere' in which they could find opportunities for participation.

1999 / 0-85364-972-3

Disavowing Constantine
*Mission, Church and the Social Order in the Theologies of
John Howard Yoder and Jürgen Moltmann*
Nigel G. Wright

This book is a timely restatement of a radical theology of church and state in the Anabaptist and Baptist tradition. Dr. Wright constructs his argument in dialogue and debate with Yoder and Moltmann, major contributors to a free church perspective.

2000 / 0-85364-978-2 / 247pp

The Voice of Jesus
Studies in the Interpretation of Six Gospel Parables
Stephen Wright
This literary study considers how the 'voice' of Jesus has been heard in different periods of parable interpretation, and how the categories of figure and trope may help us towards a sensitive reading of the parables today.
2000 / 0-85364-975-8

The Paternoster Press
P O Box 300
Carlisle Cumbria
CA3 0QS UK

Web: www.paternoster-publishing.com